Praise for

Programming Micros C# 2005: The Langua (Microsoft Press)

"How deep do you want to go? Most books only skim the surface of many topics, but Donis Marshall's book will take you as deep as you want to go in every topic. I'm excited to see that Donis is sharing his vast knowledge and I hope to see future books from him."

—Glenn Johnson; Author of *Microsoft ASP.NET Step by Step* (Microsoft Press)

"Donis Marshall is easily the best C# and C++ trainer in the business. His deep practical knowledge combined with a talent for knowledgeable transfer is legendary. Given that, this book is a crucial resource for any developer serious about going deeper into C#."

—John Alexander; Director, Visionspace, Microsoft Regional Director, Kansas City

"Donis Marshall's book does not just give the reader a roadmap to C#; it delivers the keys to being a better .NET developer. Donis' expert knowledge of the many topics gets the reader to think about programming C# from multiple levels. If you develop in C#, this book should be the cornerstone of your collection."

—John Bruno; Systems Consultant, NCCI Holdings, Inc.

"This book covers C#, the internal workings of the .NET Framework, much better than any other book on the market because Donis has such a vast amount of knowledge on this subject. I'm excited to see that Donis is sharing this knowledge and I hope to see more books from him in the future."

—Amy Vargo; Technical Account Manager, Microsoft Corporation

"Donis Marshall really has written the 'core reference' book. His practical experience and deep understanding of .NET are revealed on every page."

—Richard Hundhausen; Microsoft Regional Director, MVP for Visual Developer— Visual Studio Team System

i

Programming Microsoft Visual C# 2008: The Language

Donis Marshall

PUBLISHED BY
Microsoft Press
A Division of Microsoft Corporation
One Microsoft Way
Redmond, Washington 98052-6399

Library of Congress Control Number: 2008920576

Printed and bound in the United States of America.

1 2 3 4 5 6 7 8 9   QWT   3 2 1 0 9 8

Distributed in Canada by H.B. Fenn and Company Ltd.

A CIP catalogue record for this book is available from the British Library.

Microsoft Press books are available through booksellers and distributors worldwide. For further information about international editions, contact your local Microsoft Corporation office or contact Microsoft Press International directly at fax (425) 936-7329. Visit our Web site at www.microsoft.com/mspress. Send comments to mspinput@microsoft.com.

Acquisitions Editor: Ben Ryan
Developmental Editor: Devon Musgrave
Project Editor: Rosemary Caperton and Carol Vu
Editorial Production: ICC Macmillan, Inc.
Technical Reviewer: Kurt Meyer; Technical Review services provided by Content Master, a member of CM Group, Ltd.
Cover: Tom Draper Design

Body Part No. X14-60362

This book is dedicated to my children: Jason, Kristen, and Adam.
Jason is a young man finding his way in the world.
Kristen is about to graduate from high school to embark on her own journeys.
Adam, who is in middle school, is an accomplished violinist,
soccer player, and chess player. I am proud of them.

Contents at a Glance

Table of Contents

Part I   Core Language

What do you think of this book? We want to hear from you!

Microsoft is interested in hearing your feedback so we can continually improve our books and learning resources for you. To participate in a brief online survey, please visit:

www.microsoft.com/learning/booksurvey

Part II Core Skills

Part IV Debugging

15   Debugging with Visual Studio 2008 527

Part V **Advanced Features**

What do you think of this book? We want to hear from you!

Microsoft is interested in hearing your feedback so we can continually improve our books and learning resources for you. To participate in a brief online survey, please visit:

www.microsoft.com/learning/booksurvey

Acknowledgments

Programming Microsoft Visual C# 2008: The Language is more than simply a revision of *Programming Microsoft Visual C# 2005: The Language*—it is a new project. The result is a greatly enhanced book. This could not have been accomplished without the time and patience provided by everyone at Microsoft. I want to especially acknowledge the contributions of Ben Ryan, Rosemary Caperton, and Kurt Meyer. Ben, the program manager at Microsoft Learning, provided the support and not-so-gentle push when necessary. Rosemary is the project manager and made invaluable contributions and guidance. Finally, Kurt was the technical editor. His detailed review and helpful comments made this a better book.

Writing a book is an all-consuming project. This affects friends and loved ones. I want to acknowledge some of them: Rose, Herb, Jr., John B., Paul, and Patty. As for all my other friends that were treated shabbily during this project, thanks for your understanding.

I have been fortunate to have excellent opportunities, such as writing this book. I want to acknowledge everyone that has a dream but not yet an opportunity. Follow your dreams until they become an opportunity.

Introduction

Microsoft Visual C# 2008 is the latest product release in the evolution of C#. It is a worthy successor to earlier versions and includes new features such as Language Integrated Query (LINQ), multi-targeting of environments, and better integration of Windows Communication Foundation (WCF) and Windows Presentation Foundation (WPF). This is the short list of updated information. The complete list includes new features for everyone, regardless of their role in the software life cycle. If you want to learn Visual C# 2008, including its exciting new features, *Programming Microsoft Visual C# 2008: The Language* provides a comprehensive exploration of the language.

LINQ is the most important addition to Visual C# 2008. Under the LINQ umbrella, you can find many enhancements. Lambda expressions, extension methods, expression trees, anonymous objects, and other features are introduced because of LINQ. These features are often applicable beyond LINQ. Two chapters are dedicated to LINQ (Chapter 6, "Introduction to LINQ," and Chapter 11, "LINQ Programming"), which underscores the importance of LINQ to Visual C# 2008.

This book encompasses the software life cycle: design, implementation, maintenance, and debugging. This book covers all these topics, which are of interest to every C# developer.

Who Is This Book For?

Programming Microsoft Visual C# 2008: The Language is for developers seeking a comprehensive explanation of Visual C# 2008 or who want to explore a specific aspect of the language. The chapters are sequenced to provide a rational and complete review of the language. Each chapter also is reviewable as an independent unit that encapsulates a specific topic.

This book targets both professional and casual developers. Readers should have a basic understanding of programming concepts and object oriented programming. There is no other expectation. Practical and in-depth explanations are provided. Where beneficial, sample code is provided to complement explanations. Sample code often provides the clearest explanation of in-depth concepts. For this reason, this book contains a large number of code examples.

Organization of This Book

Programming Microsoft Visual C# 2008: The Language is organized into five parts.

Part I, "Core Language," introduces the basic concepts of the language. Chapter 1, "Introduction to Microsoft Visual C# Programming," is a general overview of the language. Chapter 2, "Types," introduces the subject of types, which includes classes and value types.

Chapter 3, "Inheritance," explains inheritance and related keywords, such as *virtual*, *override*, *sealed*, and *abstract*.

Part II, "Core Skills," covers the core skills required to create a C# application. Chapter 4, "Introduction to Visual Studio 2008," reviews Visual Studio 2008, which is the central tool in developing a managed application. Chapter 5, "Arrays and Collections," explains arrays and collections. It is hard to imagine a competent C# application that does not employ an array. Chapter 6, "Introduction to LINQ," discusses LINQ using LINQ to Objects, which is the implicit LINQ provider. Chapter 7, "Generics," is about generics, which are parameterized types. Chapter 8, "Enumerators," pertains to the enumeration of collection-related classes and iterators.

Part III, "More C# Language," focuses on additional language features. Chapter 9, "Operator Overloading," reviews operator overloading and how to expand the behavior of user-defined types to include operators. Chapter 10, "Delegates and Events," details managed function references, which are represented by delegates and events in managed code. Chapter 11, "LINQ Programming," is a further exploration of LINQ programming using LINQ to XML and LINQ to SQL providers. Chapter 12, "Exception Handling," explains structured exception handling, which is provided by the Common Language Runtime (CLR).

Part IV, "Debugging," is an all-inclusive exploration of debugging managed code. The first two chapters in this section provide an internal view of an assembly, which is critical for anyone debugging a managed application: Chapter 13, "Metadata and Reflection," introduces metadata and reflection; Chapter 14, "MSIL Programming," is an overview of Microsoft Intermediate Language (MSIL) programming. Chapter 15, "Debugging with Visual Studio 2008," discusses debugging with Visual Studio, which is the preferred debugging environment for most developers. Finally, Chapter 16, "Advanced Debugging," discusses advanced debugging using the MDbg, WinDbg, and SOS debugger extensions.

The final part of this book, Part V, is "Advanced Concepts." Chapter 17, "Memory Management," covers managed memory and garbage collection in the managed environment. Chapter 18, "Unsafe Code," explains unsafe code, direct pointer manipulation, and calling native functions.

System Requirements

You'll need the following hardware and software (at a minimum) to build and run the code samples for this book in a 32-bit Windows environment:

- Windows Vista, Windows Server 2003 with Service Pack 1, Windows Server 2008, or Windows XP with Service Pack 2

- Visual Studio 2008 Express Edition or greater

- 1 gigahertz (GHz) CPU; and 2 GHz CPU is recommended
- 512 megabytes (MB) of RAM; and 1 gigabyte (GB) is recommended
- 8 GB of available space on the installation drive
- CD-ROM or DVD-ROM drive
- Microsoft mouse or compatible pointing device

Technology Updates

As content related to this book is updated, links to additional information will be added to the Microsoft Press Technology Updates Web page. Visit this page periodically for updates about Visual Studio 2008 and other technologies:

http://www.microsoft.com/mspress/updates/

Find Additional Content Online

As new or updated material becomes available that complements this book, it will be posted online on the Microsoft Press Online Developer Tools Web site. The type of material you might find includes updates to book content, articles, links to companion content, errata, sample chapters, and more. This Web site will be available soon at *http://www.microsoft.com/ learning/books/online/developer* and it will be updated periodically.

The Companion Web Site

This book features a companion Web site that makes available to you all the code used in the book. This code is organized by chapter, and you can download it from the companion site at this address: *http://www.microsoft.com/mspress/companion/9780735625402/*

Support for This Book

Every effort has been made to ensure the accuracy of this book and the companion content. As corrections or changes are collected, they will be added to a Microsoft Knowledge Base article.

Microsoft Press provides support for books and companion content at the following Web site:

http://www.microsoft.com/learning/support/books/

Part I
Core Language

Chapter 1

Introduction to Microsoft Visual C# Programming

Microsoft Visual Studio 2008, known during development as Orcas, is the successor to Microsoft Visual Studio 2005. The launch of the latest version of Visual Studio coincides with the release of Visual C# 2008, .NET Framework 3.5, and ASP.NET 3.5. Microsoft continues to shift Visual Studio from simply a comprehensive developer tool to a solution for the software lifecycle. This includes an Integrated Development Environment (IDE), components (testing tools, code analysis, and more), and tools for software design, development, testing, quality assurance, and debugging.

Anders Hejlsberg, technical fellow and chief architect of the C# language at Microsoft, has discussed Visual C# 2008 on numerous occasions. He highlights Language Integrated Query (LINQ) and related enhancements as the primary new features in Visual C# 2008. LINQ is a unified query model that is object-oriented and integrated into the C# language. New features, such as lambda expressions, extension methods, expression trees, implicitly typed local variables and objects, and other new features are useful in isolation, but they also extend the language to support LINQ. These and other changes are sure to secure the stature of C# as the preeminent development language for .NET.

With LINQ, Visual C# 2008 changes the relationship between developers and data. LINQ is an elegant solution for accessing specific data using a query language that is independent of the data source. LINQ is also object-oriented and extensible. LINQ moves C# a measure closer to functional programming, it refocuses developers from managing the nuts and bolts of data (state) to behavior of information (objects), and it provides a unified model for querying data that no longer depends on the vagaries of a specific language or technology. With LINQ, you can access with the same unified query model a Structured Query Language (SQL) database, an Extensible Markup Language (XML) file, or even an array.

LINQ removes the distinction between data and objects. Traditional queries are strings that are not entirely type-safe and return a vector of information, which defines the disconnect between data and objects (objects being type-safe, supporting IntelliSense, and not necessarily rectangular). LINQ forms an abstraction layer that allows developers to treat data as objects and focus on solutions in a unified manner without sacrificing specificity.

Visual Studio 2008 epitomizes the term *unified*. For example, Visual Studio 2008 provides a unified environment for developing to different .NET targets. In addition, the Visual Studio Designer provides a unified canvas where Microsoft Windows Forms, Extensible Application Markup Language (XAML), and Windows XP and Windows Vista visually themed applications can be designed and implemented. Visual Studio C# 2008 has additional capabilities for creating enterprise, distributed, or Web-based applications—most notably with Microsoft Silverlight. Silverlight is a plug-in that provides a unified environment for building Web applications with cross-browser support and that promotes enhanced rich interactive applications (RIA).

Visual Studio 2008, with ASP.NET 3.5, further separates design and implementation responsibilities, allowing for clearer separation of designer and developer roles.

The trend towards collaborative and team development continues. No developer can be completely self-reliant, and Visual Studio 2008 has additional features that benefit a wide variety of teams ranging from small to large in size. Visual Studio 2008 also recognizes the important role of everyone—not just developers but others on the software team. For example, the new database project separates language developer and database developer/ architect roles.

As mentioned, Visual Studio 2008 encompasses the entire life cycle of a software application. The product boasts new revisions of tools for testing and quality assurance. Many of these tools were introduced in Visual Studio 2005. Furthermore, testing tools have been extended to the Professional revision of the product, making them available to more developers and not reserved for Microsoft Visual Studio Team editions. Both developers and non-developers, such as quality assurance staff, can use the testing tools that have been incorporated into Visual Studio 2008. The testing tools are easy to use but comprehensive, and performance also has been improved. Finally, the testing tools are integrated better, including seamless access to unit testing in the IDE. Chapter 17, "Testing," reviews Visual Studio 2008 testing tools.

.NET Framework 3.5 and the Common Language Runtime (CLR) platform continues to provide important services for managed applications, such as memory management, security services, type-safety, and structured exception handling. The .NET Framework now supports LINQ and other new features. Some favorite new elements of the .NET Framework include (but are not limited to) Active Directory APIs (System.DirectoryServices. AccountManagement.dll), ASP.NET AJAX (System.Web.Extensions), Peer-To-Peer (P2P) support (System.NET.dll), STL to CLR for Managed C++ developers (System.VisualC.STLCLR.dll), Window Presentation Foundation (WPF; System.Windows.Presentation.dll), and Windows Communication Foundation (System.WorkflowServices.dll). .NET Framework 3.5 offers numerous other enhancements, including improved network layers and better performing sockets.

Visual C# 2008 is a modern, object-oriented, and type-safe programming language. C# has its roots in the C family of languages and will be immediately comfortable to C, C++, and Java programmers. The ECMA-334 standard and ISO/IEC 23270 standard apply to the C# language. Microsoft's C# compiler for the .NET Framework is a conforming implementation of both of these standards.

A Demonstration of Visual C# 2008

To introduce programming in Visual C# 2008, the following code examples are presented with explanations. Some of the programming concepts given in this section are explained in depth throughout the remainder of the book.

Sample C# Program

In deference to Martin Richards, the creator of the Basic Combined Programming Language (BCPL) and author of the first "Hello, World!" program, I present a "Hello, World!" program. Actually, I offer an enhanced version that displays "Hello, World!" in English, Italian, or Spanish. The program is a console application.

Here is my version of the "Hello, World!" program, which is stored in a file named hello.cs:

```
using System;

namespace HelloNamespace {

    class Greetings{
        public static void DisplayEnglish() {
            Console.WriteLine("Hello, world!");
        }
        public static void DisplayItalian() {
            Console.WriteLine("Ciao, mondo!");
        }
        public static void DisplaySpanish() {
            Console.WriteLine("Hola, imundo!");
        }
    }

    delegate void delGreeting();

    class HelloWorld {
        static void Main(string [] args) {
            try {
                int iChoice = int.Parse(args[0]);
                delGreeting [] arrayofGreetings={
                    new delGreeting(Greetings.DisplayEnglish),
                    new delGreeting(Greetings.DisplayItalian),
                    new delGreeting(Greetings.DisplaySpanish)};

                arrayofGreetings[iChoice - 1]();
            }
            catch(Exception ex) {
                Console.WriteLine(ex.Message);
            }
        }
    }
}
```

Csc.exe is the C# compiler. Enter the following **csc** command at the Visual Studio command prompt to compile the hello.cs source file and create the executable hello.exe:

```
csc hello.cs
```

The hello.exe file is a .NET single-file assembly. The assembly contains metadata and Microsoft Intermediate Language (MSIL) code but not native binary. Mixed assemblies (both native and managed) may contain binary.

Run the Hello application from the command line. Enter the program name and the language (**1** for English, **2** for Italian, or **3** for Spanish). For example, the following command line displays "Ciao, mondo!" ("Hello, world!" in Italian).

```
Hello 2
```

The source code of the Hello application highlights the common elements of most .NET applications: using statement directive, a namespace, types, access modifiers, methods, exception handling, and data.

> **Note** C# is case-sensitive.

The *HelloNamespace* namespace contains the *Greetings* and *HelloWorld* types. The *Greetings* class has three static methods, and each method displays "Hello, World!" in a different natural language. Static methods are invoked on the type (*classname.member*), not an instance of that type. The static methods of the *Greetings* type are also public and therefore visible inside and outside the class.

Delegates define a type of function pointer. The *delGreeting* delegate is a container for function pointers. A *delGreeting* delegate points to functions that return *void* and have no parameters. This is (not so coincidentally) the function signature of the methods in the *Greetings* type.

The entry point of this and any other C# executable is a *Main* method. Command-line parameters are passed as the *args* parameter, which is a string array. In the HelloWorld program, the first element of the *args* array is used as a number indicating the language of choice, as input by the user. The Hello application converts that element to an integer. Next, the program defines an array of function pointers, which is initialized to point to each of the methods of the *Greetings* class. The following statement invokes a function pointer to display the selected HelloWorld message:

```
arrayofGreetings[iChoice - 1]();
```

The value *iChoice - 1* is an index into the delegate array. Since arrays are zero-based in C#, *iChoice* is offset by -1.

Most of the code in the *Main* method is contained in a *try* block. The code in the *try* block is a guarded body. A guarded body is protected against exceptions defined in the corresponding catch filter. When an exception is raised that meets the criteria of the *catch* filter, execution is transferred to the *catch* block, which displays the exception message. If no exception is raised, the *catch* block is not executed. In our HelloWorld application, omitting the choice or entering a non-numeric command-line parameter when running the program will cause an exception, which is caught, and the *catch* block displays the appropriate message.

There are several statement blocks in the sample code. A statement block contains zero or more statements bracketed with curly braces {}. A single statement can be used separately or within a statement block. The following two code examples are equivalent:

```
// Example 1
if (bValue)
    Console.WriteLine ("information");

// Example 2
if (bValue)
{
    Console.WriteLine ("information");
}
```

Sample LINQ Program

Because LINQ plays such an important role in Visual C# 2008, here are two sample applications to demonstrate LINQ. Actually, the LINQ example comprises two examples: a traditional version and a LINQ version. Both examples list the names of people that are 30 years old or older. The traditional example filters the names with an *if* statement. The LINQ example uses a LINQ query to ascertain the correct names. The result of both applications is identical.

Here is the traditional example, stored in a file named people.cs:

```
using System;

namespace Example {

    class Person {
        public Person(string _name, int _age) {
            name = _name;
            age = _age;
        }
        public string name = "";
        public int age = 0;
    }
```

```
class Startup {
    static void Main() {
        Person [] people = {new Person("John", 35),
                            new Person("Jill", 37),
                            new Person("Jack", 25),
                            new Person("Mary", 28)};
        foreach (Person p in people) {
            if (p.age >= 30) {
                Console.WriteLine(p.name);
            }
        }
    }
}
```

The code has a single namespace, which is *Example*. *Example* contains the *Person* and *Startup* types. The *Person* class has a public two-argument constructor. A constructor is a method with the same name as its class. This constructor is used to initialize instances of the *Person* class. The *Person* type contains two fields—name and age.

Main, the entry point function, is in the *Startup* class. In *Main,* an array of four employees is defined. The *foreach* statement iterates through the elements in the *people* array. Next, the *if* statement filters the employees and displays the names of people 30 years old or older in the console window.

The program is compiled with the C# compiler as follows:

```
csc people.cs
```

Here is the LINQ version of this example:

```
using System;
using System.Linq;

namespace Example {

    class Person {
        public Person(string _name, int _age) {
            name = _name;
            age = _age;
        }
        public string name = "";
        public int age = 0;
    }

    class Startup {
        static void Main() {
            Person [] people={new Person("John", 35),
                              new Person("Jill", 37),
                              new Person("Jack", 25),
                              new Person("Mary", 28)};
```

```
var ageQuery = from p in people
        where p.age >= 30
        select p;
foreach (var p in ageQuery) {
    Console.WriteLine(p.name);
}


        }
    }
}
```

The LINQ version filters people using a LINQ query instead of an *if* statement. This highlights the seminal difference between a traditional query and LINQ. The *if* statement in the traditional version filters data, whereas the LINQ query in the LINQ example filters *Person* objects. In this way, LINQ removes the disconnect between objects and data.

The *var* keyword in the *ageQuery* variable declaration is for type inference. Type inference is not typeless. A specific type is inferred at compile time from the result of the LINQ query expression. This keeps the code type-safe, which is an important tenet of .NET. In our example, the query expression evaluates to an array of *Person* types. Therefore, at compile time, *"var query"* implies *"Person [] query"*.

Common Elements in Visual C# 2008

The remainder of the chapter discusses the common elements of Visual C# 2008 programs.

Namespaces

Namespaces provide hierarchical clarity of classes within and across related assemblies. The .NET Framework Class Library (FCL) is an example of the effective use of namespaces. The FCL would sacrifice clarity if it were designed as a single namespace with a flat hierarchy. Instead, the FCL is organized using a main namespace (*System*) and several nested namespaces. *System*, which is the root namespace of the FCL, contains the classes ubiquitous to .NET, such as *Console*. Types related to LINQ are grouped in the *System.Linq* namespace. Other .NET services are similarly nested in .NET namespaces. For example, data services are found in the *System.Data* namespace and are further delineated in the *System.Data.SqlClient* namespace, which contains classes specific to Microsoft SQL.

A nested namespace is considered a member of the containing namespace. Use the dot punctuator (.) to access members of the namespace, including nested namespaces.

A namespace at file scope, not nested within another namespace, is considered part of the compilation unit and included in the global declaration space. (A compilation unit is a source code file. A program partitioned into several source files has multiple compilation units—one compilation unit for each source file.) Any namespace can span multiple compilation units.

For example, all namespaces defined at file scope are included in a single global declaration space that also spans separate source files.

The following code has two compilation units and three namespaces. *ClassB* is defined in the global declaration space of both compilation units, which is a conflict. *ClassC* is defined twice in *NamespaceZ*, which is another conflict. For these reasons, the following program will not compile.

The global declaration space has four members. *NamespaceY* and *NamespaceZ* are members. The classes *ClassA* and *ClassB* are also members of the global namespaces. The members span the File1.cs and File2.cs compilation units, which both contribute to the global namespace:

```
// file1.cs

public class ClassA {
}

public class ClassB {
}

namespace NamespaceZ {
    public class ClassC {
    }
}

// file2.cs

public class ClassB {
}

namespace NamespaceY {
    public class ClassA {
    }
}

namespace NamespaceZ {

    public class ClassC {
    }

    public class ClassD {
    }
}
```

Attempt to compile the above code into a library from the command line with this statement. You will receive compile errors because of the conflicts:

```
csc /t:library file1.cs file2.cs
```

The relationship between compilation units, the global namespace, and nonglobal namespaces are illustrated in Figure 1-1.

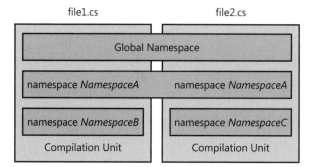

FIGURE 1-1 Global declaration space vs. namespaces

The *using* directive makes a namespace implicit. You then can access members of the named namespace directly without their fully qualified names. Do you refer to members of your family by their "fully qualified names" or just their first names? Unless your wife is the queen of England, you probably refer to her directly, simply using her first name. The *using* directive means that you can treat members of a namespace like family members.

The *using* directive must precede the first member within a namespace in a compilation unit. The following code defines the namespace member *ClassA*. The fully qualified name is *NamespaceZ.NamespaceY.ClassA*. Imagine having to type that several times in a program!

```
using System;

namespace NamespaceZ {
    namespace NamespaceY {
        class ClassA {
            public static void FunctionM() {
                Console.WriteLine("FunctionM");
            }
        }
    }
}

namespace Application {
    class Starter {
        public static void Main() {
            NamespaceZ.NamespaceY.ClassA.FunctionM();
        }
    }
}
```

The *using* directive in the following code makes *NamespaceZ.NamespaceY* implicit. Now you can directly access *ClassA* without further qualification:

```
namespace Application {
    using NamespaceZ.NamespaceY;
    class Starter {
        public static void Main() {
            ClassA.FunctionM();
        }
    }
}
```

Ambiguities can occur when separate namespaces with identically named members are made implicit. When this occurs, the affected members can be assessed only with their fully qualified names.

The *using* directive also can define an alias for a namespace or type. Aliases are typically created to resolve ambiguity or simply as a convenience. The scope of the alias is the space where it is declared. The alias must be unique within that space. In this source code, an alias is created for the fully qualified name of *ClassA*:

```
namespace Application {
    using A=NamespaceZ.NamespaceY.ClassA;
    class Starter {
        public static void Main() {
            A.FunctionM();
        }
    }
}
```

In this code, *A* is the alias and a nickname for *NamespaceZ.NamespaceY.ClassA* and can be used synonymously.

Using directive statements are not cumulative and are evaluated independently. Take the following example:

```
using System.Text;
```

The previous statement makes *System.Text* implicit but not the *System* namespace. The following code makes both namespaces implicit:

```
using System;
```

```
using System.Text;
```

The *extern alias* directive is an alias to another assembly. The resulting alias can be combined with a namespace to make an explicit reference to a namespace in a different assembly. Separate the alias and referenced assembly with two colons as follows:

```
extern alias::namespace
```

Here is sample code for a library that contains two namespaces, stored in a file named mylib.cs:

```
using System;

namespace ANamespace{
    namespace BNamespace {
        public class XClass {
            public static void MethodA() {
                Console.WriteLine("MyLib::XClass.MethodA");
            }
        }
    }
}
```

The following command will compile the source file into a Dynamic Link Library (DLL) assembly:

```
csc /t:library mylib.cs
```

Here is sample code, stored in a file named program.cs, for an executable that uses the DLL assembly. The *extern alias* statement resolves the ambiguity between the library and the executable:

```
extern alias MyLib;
using System;

namespace ANamespace{
    namespace BNamespace {
        class XClass {
            public static void MethodA() {
                Console.WriteLine("Program::XClass.MethodA");
            }
        }
    }
}

class Startup{
    public static void Main() {
        MyLib::ANamespace.BNamespace.XClass.MethodA();
    }
}
```

The following command will compile the program and define *MyLib* as an alias for mylib.dll:

```
csc program.cs /r:MyLib=mylib.dll
```

In the preceding code, the call to *XClass.MethodA* is not ambiguous because of the *extern* alias. Because of the alias, the call to *XClass.MethodA* executes the version in the library rather than the version in the current compilation unit.

Main Entry Point

Main is the entry point method for a C# application and a member function of a class or struct (the entry point method is where the C# application starts executing). There are four valid signatures for *Main* when being used as the entry point method:

```
static void Main() {
    // main block
}

static int Main() {
    // main block
}

static void Main(string [] args) {
    // main block
}

static int Main(string [] args) {
    //
}
```

A class or struct can contain only one entry point method. *Main* must be static and should be private, although that is not required. Naturally, a public *Main* method is accessible as an entry point method.

Application arguments are passed into the program as a string array parameter of the *Main* function. Arrays in .NET are instances of the *System.Array* class. You can use the properties and methods of *System.Array* to examine the application arguments, including the *Length* field to determine the number of arguments passed into *Main*. The command arguments start at element zero of the string array. When no arguments are passed, the *arg* parameter is non-null but the array length is zero.

The return value of an entry point method is cached internally for interprocess communication. If the application is part of a system of applications and spawned to complete a specific task, the return value could represent a status code or the result of that task. The default exit code of an application is zero. The exit code of a process is stored in the Process Environment Block (PEB) and is accessible through the *GetExitCodeProcess* application programming interface (API).

What if the entry point is ambiguous? Look at this code, stored in main.cs:

```
using System;

namespace Application{
    class StarterA{
        static void Main() {
```

```
        }
    }
    class StarterB{
        static void Main() {

        }
    }
}
```

This code has two valid entry points, which is inherently ambiguous. The compiler option *main* is available to designate the class name where the desired entry point method is found. The following command successfully compiles the previous program:

```
csc /main:Application.StarterB main.cs.
```

Local Variables

Local variables are local to a statement block. Local variables can be declared anywhere in the block, but they must be defined before use. Local variables can refer to either value or reference types. A value type is allocated storage on the stack, whereas reference types have memory allocated on the managed heap. Actually, the reference itself is on the stack, while the object being referenced is on the managed heap. Value types are types such as primitives, structures, and enumerations. The memory storage for value types is released deterministically when the variable is no longer in scope. Reference types are types such as user defined types, interfaces, strings, arrays, and pointers. They are always initialized with the new keyword and removed nondeterministically by the Garbage Collector, which is a component of the CLR. Value types can be initialized with a simple assignment and declared in an individual declaration or in a daisy-chain:

```
int variablea = 5, variableb, variablec = 10;
```

The scope and visibility of a local variable is the statement block, where it is declared, and any subsequent nested code blocks in the current statement block. This is called the *variable declaration space,* in which local variables must be uniquely declared.

In the following code, several local variables are defined. The storage for *variablea, variableb, variablec,* and *variabled* is released at the end of the function block when the variables are no longer within scope. However, the lifetime of *variablee,* a local variable and reference type, is managed by the Garbage Collector. It is generally good policy to set reference types to *null* when they are no longer needed:

```
void Function() {
    int variablea = 0;
    int variableb = 1,variablec, variabled = 4;
    const double PI = 3.1415;
    UserDefined variablee = new UserDefined();
```

```
    // function code

    variablee = null;
}
```

Nullable Types

In the previous code, a reference type is set to *null*. Assigning *null* to an object indicates that it is unused. This is consistent for all reference types. Can you similarly flag an integer as unused? How can you stipulate that a value type contains nothing? Nulls are not assignable to primitive value types like an integer or *char* (a compilation error would occur).

```
int variablea = null;   // compiler error
```

Setting an integer to −1 is a possible solution, assuming that this value is outside the range of expected values. However, this solution is non-portable, requires explicit documentation, and is not very extensible. Nullable types provide a consistent solution for setting a value type to *null*. This is especially important when manipulating data between C# and a database source, where primitives often contain *null* values.

Declare a nullable type by adding the *?* type modifier in the value type declaration. Here is an example:

```
double? variable1 = null;
```

The object *variable1* is a nullable type and the underlying type is double. A nullable type extends the interface of the underlying type. The *HasValue* and *Value* properties are added. Both properties are public and read-only. *HasValue* is a Boolean property, whereas the type of *Value* is the same as the underlying type. If the nullable type is assigned a non-null value, *HasValue* is true and the *Value* property is accessible. Otherwise, *HasValue* is false, and an exception is raised if the *Value* property is accessed. The acceptable range of values for a nullable type includes the *null* value and the limits of the underlying type.

The *null* coalescing operator (??) evaluates the value of a nullable type. The syntax is as follows:

```
variable ?? r_value
```

If the nullable type contains a value, the expression evaluates to that value. If the nullable type is empty (that is, it contains *null*), the expression evaluates to the *r_value* of the *null* coalescing operator. The stated *r-value* of the *null* coalescing operator must be the same type as the underlying type. The following code sets *variable2* to the value of *variable1* if *variable1* is not null and to zero otherwise:

```
double variable2 = variable1 ?? 0;
```

Here is another example of nullable types:

```
static void Main() {
    int? variablea = null;
    Console.WriteLine(variablea.HasValue); // false
    int variableb = variablea ?? 5;
    Console.WriteLine(variableb);  // 5
}
```

Expressions

Expressions resolve to a value. An expression commonly contains one or more operators. However, an expression also can be a single value or constant. Operators are unary, binary, or ternary.

With the exception of the assignment and ternary operators, expressions are evaluated from left to right. Expressions can contain multiple operators; operators are evaluated in order of precedence. Use parentheses to change the precedence or to clarify the desired precedence.

Table 1-1 lists the order of precedence.

TABLE 1-1 Order of precedence for expressions

Precedence	Operator
1	array '[ ]', *checked*, function '( )', member operator '.', *new*, postfix decrement, postfix increment, *typeof*, *default*, anonymous method, *delegate*, and *unchecked* operators
2	unary addition '+', casting '( )', one's complement '~', logical not '!', prefix decrement, prefix increment, and negation '-' operators
3	division '/', modulus '%', and multiplication '*' operators
4	binary addition '+' and binary subtraction '–' operators
5	left-shift '<<' and right-shift '>>' operators
6	*as*, *is*, less than '<', less than or equal to '<=', greater than '>', and greater than or equal to '>=' operators
7	equals '==' and not equal '!=' operators
8	Logical And '&' operator
9	Logical XOR '^' operator
10	Logical Or '|' operator
11	Conditional And '&&' operator
12	Conditional Or '||' operator
13	Null coalescing '??'operator
14	Conditional '?:' operator
15	Assignment '=', compound '*=, /=, %=, +=, –=, <<=, >>=, &=, ^=, and |=', and lambda operator '=>'

Selection Statements

A selection statement evaluates an expression to determine what code branch is executed next. Selection statements include *if* statements, *while* loops, *for* loops, and *goto* and *switch* statements.

An *if* statement evaluates a Boolean expression. If the expression is *true,* control is transferred to the next *true_statement.* If the expression is *false,* execution is transferred to the first statement after the *true_statement.*

Here is the syntax of the *if* statement:

```
if (Boolean_expression) true_statement
```

In the preceding code, the *true_statement* is executed when *Boolean_expression* is *true.* When combined with an *else* condition, the *if* statement has *true_statement* and *false_statement.* The *false_statement* immediately follows the *else* statement. When the *Boolean_expression* is true, you are transferred to the *true_statement.* If it is false, control is transferred to the *false_statement.* If nested, the *else* statement belongs to the nearest *if* statement.

Here is the syntax:

```
if (Boolean_expression)
     true_statement;
else
     false_statement;
```

An alternative to nested *if* and *else* statements is the *else if* clause, which is particularly useful in evaluating choices. The *else if* statement can be used along with an *else* statement.

The syntax appears here:

```
if (Boolean_expression_1)
     true_statement_1;
else if (Boolean_expression_2)
     true_statement_2;

...

else if (Boolean_expression_n)
     true_statement_n;
else
     false_statement;
```

This is an example of various *if* statements:

```
static void Main() {
    Console.WriteLine("Enter command:");
    string menuChoice=(Console.ReadLine()).ToLower();
```

```
if (menuChoice == "a")
    Console.WriteLine("Doing Task A");
else if (menuChoice == "b")
    Console.WriteLine("Doing Task B");
else if (menuChoice == "c")
    Console.WriteLine("Doing Task C");
else
    Console.WriteLine("Bad choice");
}
```

A *switch* statement is sometimes a better solution then an *if* statement. Within a *switch* statement, execution jumps to the case label that matches the *switch* expression. The *switch* expression must resolve to an integral, *char, enum,* or *string* type. The case label is a constant or literal and must have the same underlying type as the *switch* expression.

Here is the syntax for the *switch* statement:

```
switch (switch_expression)
{
    case label1:
        switch_statement1;
    case  label2:
        switch_statement2;
    default:
        default_statement;
}
```

A *switch* statement contains a *switch* expression and is followed by a *switch* block, which contains one or more *case* statements. Within the *switch* block, each *case* statement must evaluate to a unique label. After the *switch* expression is evaluated, control is transferred to the matching case label. The matching case has the same value as the *switch* expression. If no case label matches the *switch* expression, control is transferred to the *default* case statement or (if the *default* case statement is not present) to the next statement after the *switch* statement.

Unlike C and C++, cascading between *case* statements is not allowed—that is, you cannot "crash the party" of another *case* statement. Each case block must conclude with a transfer of control, such as *break, goto, return,* or *throw.* The exception is cases that have no statements, where *fallthrough* is allowed.

This is sample code for a *switch* statement:

```
static void Main() {
    Console.WriteLine("Enter command:");
    string resp = (Console.ReadLine()).ToLower();
    switch (resp) {
        case "a":
            Console.WriteLine("Doing Task A");
            break;
```

```
        case "b":
            Console.WriteLine("Doing Task B");
            break;
        case "c":
            Console.WriteLine("Doing Task C");
            break;
        default:
            Console.WriteLine("Bad choice");
            break;
    }
}
```

Any object, value, or reference type that is convertible to an integral, *char*, *enum*, or *string* type is acceptable as the *switch_expression*, which is demonstrated in the following code. You are allowed a one-step conversion to one of the acceptable types.

```
class Employee {
    public Employee(string f_Emplid) {
        m_Emplid = f_Emplid;
    }

    static public implicit operator string(Employee f_this) {
        return f_this.m_Emplid;
    }

    private string m_Emplid;
}

class Starter {
    static void Main() {
        Employee newempl = new Employee("1234");
        switch (newempl) {
            case "1234":
                Console.WriteLine("Employee 1234");
                return;
            case "5678":
                Console.WriteLine("Employee 5678");
                return;
            default:
                Console.WriteLine("Invalid employee");
                return;
        }
    }
}
```

Iterative Statements

C# has the full repertoire of C-style iterative statements. C# also has a *foreach* statement. Iterative statements repeat a statement until a condition has been satisfied.

The *for* statement is designed for structured iteration. The *while* and *do* statement iterations are more flexible. The *for* statement contains three clauses. First is the *initializer_clause*, where the loop iterators are declared. The scope of an iterator is the *for* statement and *for_statement*. Second is the *Boolean_expression,* which must evaluate to a Boolean type. The expression normally compares the iterator to a *stop* value. Third, the *iterator_expression* is executed at each iteration, which is usually responsible for updating the iterator. Each clause is optional and delimited with a semicolon. The *for_statement* is repeated until the *Boolean_expression* is false.

The *for_statement* is repeated zero or more times. If the *Boolean_expression* is initially false, the *for_statement* is executed zero times. The syntax of the *for* statement is as follows:

```
for (initializer_clause; Boolean_expression; iterator_expression) for_statement
```

The following is a rather mundane *for* loop:

```
static void Main() {
    for (int iCounter = 0; iCounter < 10; ++iCounter) {
        Console.Write(iCounter);
    }
}
```

Both the *initializer_clause* and *iterator_expression* can contain multiple statements delimited by commas, not semicolons. This allows additional flexibility and complexity. Here is an example:

```
static void Main() {
    for (int iBottom = 1, iTop = 10; iBottom < iTop; ++iBottom, --iTop) {
        Console.WriteLine("{0}x{1} {2}", iBottom, iTop, iBottom * iTop);
    }
}
```

The *while* statement, which is an iterative statement, is more free-form than the *for* statement. The body of the *while* statement is executed zero or more times; it is executed when the *Boolean_expression* is true. If the *Boolean_expression* is initially false, the body is executed zero times.

Typically, the *while* statement or expression is responsible for altering an iterator or other factors, eventually causing the *Boolean_expression* to evaluate to *false,* which ends the loop. Care should be taken to avoid unintended infinite loops.

The syntax for the *while* statement is as follows:

```
while (Boolean_expression) body_statement
```

This is source code for selecting a choice rewritten with a *while* statement:

```
static void Main() {
    string resp;
    Console.WriteLine("Enter command ('x' to end):");
    while ((resp=(Console.ReadLine()).ToLower()) != "x") {
        switch (resp) {
```

```
            case "a":
                Console.WriteLine("Doing Task A");
                break;
            case "b":
                Console.WriteLine("Doing Task B");
                break;
            default:
                Console.WriteLine("Bad choice");
                break;
        }
    }
}
```

A *do* statement is a loop that evaluates the *Boolean_expression* at the end. This is the reverse of the *while* statement. The impact is that the body of the *do* statement is repeated one or more times. The niche for the *do* statement is when the body must be executed at least once. The iteration of the body continues while the *Boolean_expression* is true.

Here is the syntax of the *do* statement:

```
do body_statement  while (Boolean_expression)
```

Here is sample code of the *do* statement:

```
static void Main() {
    string resp;
    do {
        Console.WriteLine("Menu\n\n1 - Task A");
        Console.WriteLine("2 - Task B");
        Console.WriteLine("E - E(xit)");
        resp = (Console.ReadLine()).ToLower();
    }
    while(resp!="e");
}
```

The *foreach* statement is a convenient mechanism for automatically iterating elements of a collection. The alternative is manually iterating a collection with an enumerator object obtained with the *IEnumerable.GetEnumerator* method. All collections implement the *IEnumerable* interface. The *foreach* statement is unquestionably simpler.

This is the syntax of the *foreach* statement:

```
foreach (type variable in collection) body_statement
```

The *foreach* statement iterates the elements of the *collection*. As each element is enumerated, the *variable* is assigned the current element, and the body of the *foreach* statement is executed. The scope of the *variable* is the *foreach* statement. When the *collection* is fully iterated, the iteration stops.

The *variable* type should be related to the type of objects contained in the *collection*. In addition, the *variable* is read-only. Even using the *variable* in a context that implies change, such as passing the *variable* as a *ref* function parameter, is an error.

This code iterates an array of numbers:

```
static void Main() {
    string [] numbers={ "uno", "dos", "tres",
        "quatro", "cinco"};
    foreach (string number in numbers) {
        Console.WriteLine(number);
    }
}
```

The *break* statement forces a premature exit of a loop or switch. Control is transferred to the statement after the loop or switch. In a *switch* block, the break prevents fallthrough between *switch_labels*. For an iterative statement, a break stops the iteration unconditionally and exits the loop. If the switch or iterative statement is nested, only the nearest loop is exited.

The *continue* statement transfers control to the end of a loop where execution of the loop is allowed to continue. The *Boolean_expression* of the iterative statement then determines whether the iteration continues.

This is sample code of the *break* statement:

```
static void Main() {
    string resp;
    while(true) {
        Console.WriteLine("Menu\n\n1 - Task A");
        Console.WriteLine("2 - Task B");
        Console.WriteLine("E - E(xit)");
        resp = (Console.ReadLine()).ToLower();
        if (resp == "e") {
            break;
        }
    }
}
```

C# Core Language Features

Now that some basic examples and the framework of Visual C# 2008 code have been presented, we can discuss the fundamental building blocks of any C# application. This section starts by discussing symbols and tokens, the most elemental components of a Visual C# 2008 application.

Symbols and Tokens

Symbols and tokens are the basic constituents of the C# language. C# statements consist of symbols and tokens—indeed, they cannot be assembled without them. Table 1-2 provides a list of the C# symbols and tokens. Each entry in Table 1-2 is explained in the text that follows.

TABLE 1-2 C# Symbols and tokens

Description	Symbols or tokens
White space	Space, Form Feed
Tab	Horizontal_tab, Vertical_tab
Punctuator	. , : ;
Line terminator	Carriage return, line feed, next line character, line separator, paragraph separator, carriage return and line feed together
Comment	// /* */ /// /** */
Preprocessor directive	#
Block	{}
Lambda expression	=>
Generics	< >
Nullable type	?
Character	Unicode_character
Escape character	\code
Integer suffix (case-insensitive)	u l ul lu
Real suffix (case-insensitive)	f d m
Operator	+ - * % / > < ? ?? ( ) [ ] | || ^ ! ~ ++ -- = is as & && -> :: << >>
Compound operator	== != <= >= += -= *= /= %= &= |= ^= <<= >>= =>

White Space

White space is defined as a *space, horizontal tab, vertical tab,* or *form feed* character. White space characters can be combined; where one whitespace character is required, two or more contiguous characters of white space can be substituted.

Tabs

Tabs—horizontal and vertical—are white-space characters, as discussed just previously.

Punctuators

Punctuators separate and delimit elements of the C# language. Punctuators include the semicolon (;), dot (.), colon (:), and comma (,).

Semicolon punctuator   In Visual C#, statements are terminated with a semicolon (;). C# is a free-form language in which a statement can span multiple lines of source code and can start in any position. Conversely, multiple statements can be combined on a single source code line. Here are some variations:

```
int variablea =
        variableb +
            variablec;

variableb = variableb + 3; variablec = variablec + 1;

++variableb;
```

Dot punctuator   Dot syntax connotes membership. The dot character (.) binds a target to a member, in which the target can be a namespace, type, structure, enumeration, interface, or object. This assumes the member is accessible. Membership is sometimes nested and described with additional dots.

Here is the syntax for the dot punctuator:

```
Target.Member
```

This is an example of the dot punctuator:

```
System.Windows.Forms.MessageBox.Show("A nice day!");
```

System, Windows, and *Forms* are namespaces. *MessageBox* is a class. *Show,* the most nested member, is a static method.

Colon punctuator   The colon punctuator primarily delimits a label, indicates inheritance, indicates interface implementation, sets a generic constraint, or is part of a conditional operator.

Labels are tags for locations to which program execution can be transferred. A label is terminated with a colon punctuator (:). The scope of a label is limited to the containing block and any nested block. There are various methods for transferring to a label. For example, you can jump to a label with the *goto* statement. Within a *switch* block, you also can use the *goto* statement to jump to a *case* or *default* statement.

Here is the syntax for the label punctuator:

label_identifier: *statement*

A statement must follow a label, even if it's an empty statement.

Here is an example of a *goto* statement:

```
public static void Main() {
    goto one;
    // do stuff
one:    Console.WriteLine("one");
    }
```

Comma punctuator   The comma punctuator delimits array indexes, function parameters, types in an inheritance list, statement clauses, and other language elements. The comma punctuator separates clauses of a *for* statement in the following code:

```
for (int iBottom = 1, iTop = 10; iBottom < iTop; ++iBottom, --iTop) {
    Console.WriteLine("{0}x{1} {2}", iBottom, iTop, iBottom*iTop);
}
```

A statement clause is a substatement in which multiple statement clauses can be combined into a single statement. Statement clauses are not always available—check documentation related to the language artifact to be sure.

Line Terminators

Line terminators separate lines of source code. Where one line terminator is available, two or more are allowed. Except in string literals, line terminators can be inserted anywhere white space is allowed. The following code is syntactically incorrect:

```
int variableb, variablec;

int variablea = var
            iableb+variablec; // wrong!
```

The *variableb* identifier cannot contain spaces. Therefore, it also cannot contain a line terminator.

Comments

C# supports four styles of comments: single-line, delimited, single-line documentation, and multi-line documentation comments. Although comments are not required, the liberal use of comments is considered good programming style. Be kind to those maintaining your program (present and future) —comment! I highly recommend reading *Code Complete, Second Edition* (Microsoft Press, 2004), by Steve McConnell; this book provides valuable best practices on programming, including how to document source code properly.

Single-line comments: //   Single-line comments start at the comment symbol and conclude at the line terminator, as follows:

```
Console.WriteLine(objGreeting.French);  // Display Hello (French)
```

Delimited comments: /* and */   Delimited comments, also called *multi-line* or *block* comments, are bracketed by the /* and */ symbols. Delimited comments can span multiple lines of source code:

```
/*
        Class Program: Programmer Donis Marshall
*/
class Program {
    static int Main(string[] args) {
        Greeting objGreeting = new Greeting();
        Console.WriteLine(objGreeting.French);  // Display Hello (French)
        return 0;
    }
}
```

Single-line documentation comments: ///   Documentation comments apply a consistent format to source code comments and use XML tags to classify comments. With the documentation generator, documentation comments are exportable to an XML file. The resulting file is called the *documentation file,* which is identified in the Visual Studio project options. IntelliSense and the Object Browser use information in this file.

Single-line documentation comments are partially automated in the Visual Studio IDE. The Visual Studio IDE has Smart Comment Editing, which automatically continues or creates a skeleton for a document comment after initially entering the /// symbol. For example, the following code snippet shows sample code with single-line documentation comments. After entering an initial ///, Smart Comment Editing completed the remainder of the comment framework, including adding comments and XML tags for the type, methods, method parameter, and return value. You only need to update the comment framework with specific comments and additional comment tags that might be helpful:

```
/// <summary>
///
/// </summary>
class Program {
    /// <summary>
    ///
    /// </summary>
    /// <param name="args"></param>
    /// <returns></returns>
    static int Main(string[] args) {
        Greeting objGreeting = new Greeting();
        Console.WriteLine(objGreeting.French); // Display Hello (French)
        return 0;
    }
}
```

Here are the documentation comments with added details:

```
/// <summary>
/// Starter class for Simple HelloWorld
/// </summary>
class Program {
    /// <summary>
    /// Program Entry Point
    /// </summary>
    /// <param name="args">Command Line Parameters</param>
    /// <returns>zero</returns>
    static int Main(string[] args) {
        Greeting objGreeting = new Greeting();
        Console.WriteLine(objGreeting.French);    // Display Hello (French)
        return 0;
    }
}
```

The C# compiler is a documentation generator. The */doc* compiler option instructs the compiler to generate the documentation file. This can be done using the Visual Studio IDE. Select *Project* Properties from the Project menu. In the Properties window, select the Build tab. Toward the bottom of the Build pane (shown in Figure 1-2), you can specify the name of the XML documentation file.

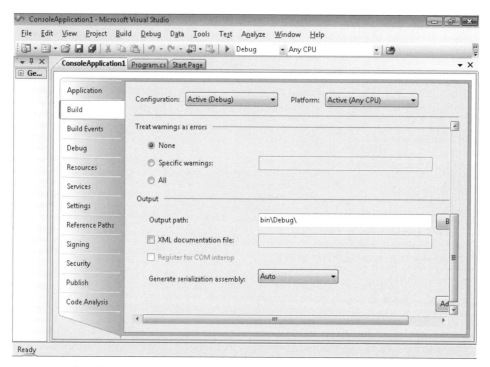

FIGURE 1-2 The Build pane of the Project Settings window

For the preceding source file, this is the documentation file generated by the C# compiler:

```xml
<?xml version="1.0"?>
<doc>
    <assembly>
        <name>ConsoleApplication1</name>
    </assembly>
    <members>
        <member name="T:ConsoleApplication1.Program">
            <summary>
            Starter class for Simple HelloWorld
            </summary>
        </member>
        <member name="M:ConsoleApplication1.Program.Main(System.String[])">
            <summary>
            Program Entry Point
            </summary>
            <param name="args">Command Line Parameters</param>
            <returns>zero</returns>
        </member>
    </members>
</doc>
```

The documentation generator prefixes IDs to element names of the *member* name tag. In the preceding documentation file, *T* is the prefix for a type, whereas *M* is a prefix for a method. Here's a listing of IDs:

E	Event
F	Field
M	Method
N	Namespace
P	Property
T	Type
!	Error

Multi-line documentation tags   Multi-line documentation tags are an alternative to single-line documentation tags. Smart Comment Editing is not available with multi-line documentation tags. You must enter the documentation tags explicitly. However, Intellisense is available. Multi-line documentation comments must adhere to a degree of consistency, which is explained in the article titled "Delimiters for Documentation Tags (C# Programming Guide)," in Visual Studio Help *(ms-help://MS.VSCC.v90/MS.MSDNQTR.v90.en/dv_csref/html/9b2bdd18-4f5c-4c0b-988e-fb992e0d233e.htm).*

Here is an example of delimited documentation tags:

```
/**
 *<summary>this is an example.</summary>
 */
```

Preprocessor Directives

Preprocessor directives define symbols, undefine symbols, include source code, exclude source code, name sections of source code, and set warning and error conditions. The variety of preprocessor directives is limited compared with C++, and many of the C++ preprocessor directives are not available in C#. There is not a separate preprocessor or compilation stage for preprocessor statements. Preprocessor statements are processed by the normal C# compiler. The term *preprocessor* is used because the preprocessor directives are semantically similar to related commands in C++.

Here is the syntax for a preprocessor directive:

```
#command expression
```

This is a list of preprocessor directives available in C#:

#define	*#undef*	*#if*
#else	*#elif*	*#endif*
#line	*#error*	*#warning*
#region	*#endregion*	*#pragma*

The preprocessor symbol (#) and subsequent directive are optionally separated with white space but must be on the same line. A preprocessor directive can be followed with a single-line comment but not a multi-line comment.

Declarative preprocessor directives The declarative preprocessor directives are *#define* and *#undef*, which define and undefine a preprocessor symbol, respectively. Defined symbols are implicitly true, whereas undefined symbols are false. Declarative symbols must be defined in each compilation unit where the symbol is referenced. Undeclared symbols default to *undefined* and *false*. The *#define* and *#undef* directives must precede any source code. Redundant *#define* and *#undef* directives have no effect.

Preprocessor symbols can also be set as a compiler option. In the Build pane of the *Project* Properties dialog box, you can define one or more symbols in the Conditional Compilation Symbols text box. This is shown in Figure 1-3. Other preprocessor symbols, such as *DEBUG* and *TRACE*, are commonly set implicitly as a compiler option.

Here is the syntax for declarative preprocessor directives:

```
#define identifier
#undef identifier
```

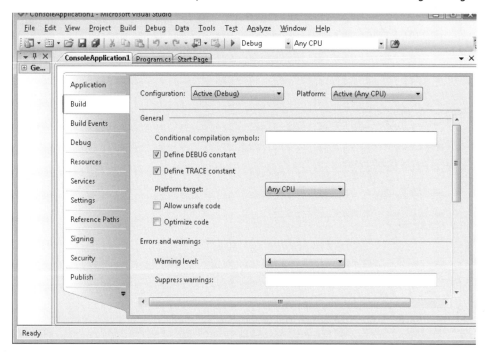

FIGURE 1-3 The Conditional Compilation Symbols text box

Conditional preprocessor directives   Conditional preprocessor directives are the *#if*, *#else*, *#elif*, and *#endif* directives, which exclude or include source code. A conditional preprocessor directive begins with *#if* and ends with *#endif*. The intervening conditional preprocessing directives, *#else* and *#elif*, are optional.

Here is the syntax for conditional preprocessor directives:

```
#if Boolean_expression
#elif Boolean_expression
#else
#endif
```

The *Boolean_expression* of the *#if* and *#elif* directive is a combination of preprocessor symbols and Boolean operators (*! == != && ||*). If the *Boolean_expression* is true, the source code immediately after the *#if* or *#elif* directive and before the next conditional preprocessor directive is included in the compilation. If the *Boolean_expression* is false, the source code is excluded from source compilation. The *#else* directive can be added to a *#if* or *#elif* combination. If the *Boolean_expression* of *#if* and *#elif* is false, the code following the *#else* is included in the compilation. When true, the source code after the #*else* is not included. Here's sample code with preprocessor symbols and related directives:

```
#define DEBUGGING

using System;

namespace Donis.CSharpBook {
    class Starter{
#if DEBUGGING
        static void OutputLocals() {
            Console.WriteLine("debugging...");
        }
#endif
        static void Main() {
#if DEBUGGING
            OutputLocals();
#endif
        }
    }
}
```

Finally, the #*elif* directive is a combination of an *else* and *if* conditional preprocessor directive. It is matched with the nearest #*if* directive:

```
#if expression
    source_code
#elif expression
    source_code
#else
    source_code
#endif
```

Diagnostic directives   Diagnostic directives include the #*error*, #*warning*, and #*pragma* directives. The #*error* and #*warning* directives display error and warning messages, respectively. The diagnostic messages are displayed in the Error List window of the Visual Studio IDE. Similar to standard compilation errors, an #*error* directive prevents the program from compiling successfully; a #*warning* directive does not prevent the program from successfully compiling unless Treat Warnings As Error is set as a compiler option. You can use conditional directives to conditionally apply diagnostic directives.

Here is the syntax for diagnostic directives:

```
#error error_message
#warning error_message
```

The *error_message* is of string type and is optional.

Pragma directives   The *#pragma* directive disables or enables compilation warnings. When disabled, the warning or error is suppressed and will not appear in the Error List window. This is useful for suppressing an unwanted warning or error temporarily or permanently.

Here is the syntax for pragma directives:

```
#pragma warning disable warning_list
#pragma warning restore warning_list
```

The *warning_list* contains one or more warnings delimited with commas. A disabled warning remains disabled until it is restored or the compilation unit ends.

The following code demonstrates the *pragma* warning directive. In this example, the *219* warning (Variable Is Assigned But Its Value Is Never Used) is initially disabled and then restored. Therefore a warning is received about *variableb* but not *variablea*.

```
class Starter
{
#pragma warning disable 219
    static void Main()
    {
        int variablea = 10;
    }
#pragma warning restore 219

    static void FuncA()
    {
        int variableb = 20;
    }
}
```

Region directives   Region directives mark sections of source code. The *#region* directive starts a region, whereas the *#endregion* directive ends the region. Region directives can be nested. The Visual Studio IDE outlines the source code based on region directives. In Visual Studio, you can collapse or expand regions of source code.

Here is the syntax for region directives:

```
#region identifier
source_code
#endregion
```

Line directives   Line directives modify the line number reported in subsequent compiler errors and warnings. There are three versions of the line directive.

Here is the syntax for line directives:

```
#line line_number source_filename
#line default
#line hidden
```

The first *#line* directive renumbers the source code from the location of the directive until the end of the compilation unit is reached or overridden by another *#line* directive. In the following code, the *#line* directive resets the current reporting line to *25*:

```
#line 25
static void Main() {
    Console.WriteLine("#line application");
    int variablea=10;   // 219 warning
}
```

The *#line default* directive undoes any previous *#line* directives. The line number is then reset to the natural line number.

The *#line hidden* directive is only tangentially related to the line number. This directive does not affect the line number; it hides source code from the debugger when stepping. The source code is skipped until the next *#line* directive is encountered. This is helpful in stepping through source code. Hidden code is essentially stepped over. For example, when stepping in the following source, the *for* loop is stepped over. The *#line default* directive then returns normal stepping.

```
    static void Main()
    {
        int variablea = 10;
        variablea++;
#line hidden
        for (int i = 0; i < 5; ++i)
        {
            variablea++;
        }
#line default
        Console.WriteLine(variablea);
    }
```

Blocks

A type, which can be a class, struct, interface, or enum, is defined within a block. Members of the type are contained inside the block.

Here is the syntax for a type block:

```
type typename {  // block
}
```

A block can also be a statement block. Statement blocks contain one or more statements. Each statement of the statement block is delimited by a semicolon. Typically, where a single statement is allowed, a statement block can be substituted. Statement blocks are commonly used as function bodies, conditional statements, and iterative statements. For function bodies, a statement block is required.

The *if* path in the following code consists of a single statement. Therefore, a statement block is not required. The *Console.WriteLine* is the only statement within the context of the *if* statement:

```
static void Main() {
    int variablea = 5, variableb = 10;
    if (((variablea + variableb) % 2) == 0)
        Console.WriteLine("the sum is even");
}
```

In the modified code, the *if* path contains multiple statements and a statement block is needed. Some would suggest, and I agree, that always using statement blocks with conditional or iterative statements is a good practice. This prevents an inadvertent future error when a single statement is expanded to multiple statements as shown below, but the block is forgotten:

```
static void Main() {
    int variablea = 5, variableb = 10;
    if (((variablea + variableb) % 2) == 0) {
        Console.WriteLine("{0} {1}", variablea,
            variableb);
        Console.WriteLine("the sum is even");
    }
}
```

Generic types

A generic is an abstraction of a type, which itself is an abstraction of a noun, place, or thing.

The *NodeInt* class is an abstraction of a node within a linked list of integers. The following is a partial implementation of the code (the full implementation is presented later in this book):

```
class NodeInt {
    public NodeInt(int f_Value, NodeInt f_Previous) {
        m_Value = f_Value;
        m_Previous = f_Previous;
    }

    // Remaining methods

    private int m_Value;
    private NodeInt m_Previous;
}
```

The *Node* generic type further abstracts a linked list. Unlike *NodeInt, Node* is not integer-specific but a linked list of any type. In the generic type, integer specifics of the *NodeInt* class have been removed and substituted with placeholders.

```
class Node<T> {
    public Node(T f_Value, Node<T> f_Previous) {
        m_Value = f_Value;
        m_Previous = f_Previous;
    }
```

```
    // Remaining methods

    private T m_Value;
    private Node<T> m_Previous;
}
```

In the preceding example, *T* is the generic type parameter, which is then used as a placeholder throughout the class for future type substitution.

There is much more about generics later in Chapter 7, "Generics."

Characters

C# source files contain Unicode characters, which are the most innate of symbols. Every element, keyword, operator, or identifier in the source file is a composite of Unicode characters.

Numeric Suffixes

Numeric suffixes cast a literal value to the underlying or a related type. Literal integer values can have the *l, u, ul,* and *lu* suffixes appended to them; literal real values can have the *f, d,* and *m* suffixes added. The suffixes are case-insensitive. Table 1-3 describes each suffix.

TABLE 1-3 Description of suffixes

Description	Type	Suffix
Unsigned integer or unsigned long	*uint* or *ulong*	U
Long or unsigned long	*long* or *ulong*	L
Unsigned long	*ulong*	ul or lu
Float	*float*	F
Double	*double*	D
Money	*decimal*	M

When casting a real type using the *m* suffix (for monetary or currency calculations), rounding might be required. If so, banker's rounding is used.

Here is an example of a numeric suffix:

```
uint variable = 10u;
```

Escape Characters

The escape character provides an alternate means of encoding Unicode characters, which is particularly useful for special characters that are not available on a standard keyboard. Escape sequences can be embedded in identifiers and string literals. Unicode escape sequences must have four hexadecimal digits and are limited to a single character.

A Unicode escape sequence looks like this:

```
\u hexdigit1 hexdigit2 hexdigit3 hexdigit4
```

Hexadecimal escape sequences contain one or more digits as defined by the location of a Unicode character.

A hexadecimal escape sequence looks like this:

```
\x hexdigit1 hexdigit2 ... hexdigitn
```

Table 1-4 shows a list of the predefined escape sequences in C#.

TABLE 1-4 Predefined escape sequences

Simple escape	Sequence
Single quote	\'
Double quote	\"
Backslash	\\
Null	\0
Alert	\a
Backspace	\b
Form feed	\f
New line	\n
Carriage return	\r
Horizontal tab	\t
Unicode character	\u
Vertical tab	\v
Hexadecimal character(s)	\x

This is an unconventional version of the traditional "Hello World!" program:

```
using System;

class HelloWorld {
    static void Main() {
        Console.Write("\u0048\u0065\u006C\u006C\u006F\n");
        Console.Write("\x77\x6F\x72\x6C\x64\x21\b");
    }
}
```

Verbatim Characters

The verbatim character (@) prevents the translation of a string or identifier, where it is treated "as-is." To create a verbatim string or identifier, prefix it with the verbatim character. This is helpful, for example, when storing directory paths in a string literal.

A verbatim string is a string literal prefixed with the verbatim character. The characters of the verbatim string, including escape sequences, are not translated. The exception is the escape character for quotes, which is translated even in a verbatim string. Unlike a normal string, verbatim strings can even contain physical line feeds.

Here is a sample verbatim string:

```
using System;

class Verbatim{
    static void Main() {
        string fileLocation = @"c:\datafile.txt";
        Console.WriteLine("File is located at {0}",
                          fileLocation);
    }
}
```

A verbatim identifier is an identifier prefixed with the verbatim character that prevents the identifier from being parsed as a keyword. When porting source code from another programming language where allowable keywords and identifiers may be different, this feature could be useful. Otherwise, it is a best practice not to use this technique because verbatim identifiers almost always make your code less readable and harder to maintain.

The following source code is technically correct:

```
public class ExampleClass {
    public static void Function() {
        int @for = 12;
        MessageBox.Show(@for.ToString());
    }
}
```

In the preceding code, the *for* keyword is being used as a variable name. This is confusing at best. The *for* keyword is common in C# and many other programming languages, and therefore most developers would find this code confusing.

Operators

Operators are used in expressions and always return a value. There are three categories of operators: unary, binary, and ternary. Some operators, such as *is, as,* and *default,* also are considered keywords. The following sections describe all the operators in C#.

Unary operators   Unary operators have a single operand. Table 1-5 lists the unary operators.

TABLE 1-5 Unary operators

Operator	Symbol	Sample	Result
unary plus	+	*variable = +5;*	5
unary minus	–	*variable = –(–10);*	10
Boolean negation	*!*	*variable = !true;*	false
bitwise 1's complement	~	*variable = ~((uint)1);*	4294967294
prefix increment	++	*++variable;*	11
prefix decrement	– –	*– –variable;*	10
postfix increment	++	*variable++;*	11
postfix decrement	– –	*variable – –;*	10
cast	*( )*	*variable = (int)123.45;*	123
function	*( )*	FunctionCall(parameter);	return value
array index	*[ ]*	arrayname[index];	nth element
dot	.	container.member	member
global namespace qualifier	::	*global*::globalmember	Globalmember

Here are some more details on unary parameters:

- Prefix operators are evaluated before the encompassing expression.
- Postfix operators are evaluated after the encompassing expression.

Binary operators   Binary operators have a left and right operand. Table 1-6 details the binary operators.

TABLE 1-6 Binary operators

Operator	Symbol	Sample	Result
assignment	=	*variable =10;*	10
binary plus	+	*variable = variable + 5;*	15
binary minus	–	*variable = variable – 10;*	5
multiplication	*	*variable = variable * 5;*	25
division	/	*variable = variable / 5;*	5
modulus	%	*variable = variable % 3;*	2
bitwise AND	&	*variable = 5 & 3;*	1
bitwise OR	|	*variable = 5 | 3;*	7
bitwise XOR	^	*variable = 5 ^ 3;*	6
bitwise shift left	<<	*variable = 5 << 3;*	40
bitwise shift right	>>	*variable = 5 >> 1;*	2
null coalescing	??	*variableb = variable??5*	2

Here's more information on binary operators:

- Integer division truncates the floating point portion of the result.

- The operands in a bitwise shift left are *value << bitcount*.

- The operands in a bitwise shift right are *value >> bitcount*.

Compound operators   Compound operators combine an assignment and another operator. If the expanded expression is *variable = variable operator value*, the compound operator is *variable operator= value*. For example, assume that we want to code the following:

```
variable = variable + 5;
```

The preceding statement is equivalent to this:

```
variable += 5;
```

Compound operations are a shortcut and are never required in lieu of the expanded statement. Table 1-7 lists the compound operators.

TABLE 1-7 Compound operators

Operator	Symbol	Sample
addition assignment	+=	*variable += 5;*
subtraction assignment	−=	*variable −= 10;*
multiplication assignment	*=	*variable *= 5;*
division assignment	/=	*variable /= 5;*
modulus assignment	%=	*variable %= 3;*
AND assignment	&=	*variable &= 3;*
OR assignment	|=	*variable |= 3;*
XOR assignment	^=	*variable ^= 3;*
left-shift assignment	<<=	*variable <<= 3;*
right-shift assignment	>>=	*variable >>= 1;*

Boolean operators   Boolean expressions evaluate to *true* or *false*. Unlike C++, the integer values of nonzero and zero are not equivalent to a Boolean *true* or *false*.

There are two versions of the logical *and* and *or* operators. The && and || operators support short-circuiting, whereas & and | do not. What is short-circuiting? If the result of the expression can be determined with the left side, the right side is not evaluated. Without disciplined coding practices, short-circuiting might cause unexpected side effects.

Next is an example of possible short-circuiting. If *FunctionA* evaluates to *false,* the entire Boolean expression is false. Therefore the right-hand expression (*FunctionB*) is not evaluated. If calling *FunctionB* has a required side effect, short-circuiting in this circumstance could cause a bug.

```
if (FunctionA() && FunctionB()) {

}
```

Table 1-8 shows the Boolean operators.

TABLE 1-8 Boolean operators

Operator	Symbol
equals	==
not equal	!=
less than	<
greater than	>
logical AND (allows short-circuiting)	&&
logical OR (allows short-circuiting)	||
logical AND	&
logical OR	|
less than or equal	<=
greater than or equal	>=
logical XOR	^

Ternary operators   The conditional operator is the sole ternary operator in C# and is an abbreviated *if else* statement.

Here is the syntax of the conditional operator:

```
Boolean_expression ? true_statement : false_statement
```

This is the conditional operator in source code:

```
char e = (x > 0) ? '>' : '<'
```

Type operators   Type operators act on a type. The *as* and *is* operators are binary operators, while the *typeof* operator is unary. Table 1-9 lists the type operators.

TABLE 1-9 Type operators

Operator	Syntax	Description
as	*object* as *type*	Casts object to type if possible. If not, returns null.
is	*object* is *type*	Expression evaluates to true if object is related to type; otherwise, evaluates to false.
typeof	*typeof*(object)	Returns the type of the object.

Pointer operators   Pointer operators are available in unsafe mode. This allows C# developers to use C++ style pointers. The *unsafe* compiler option sets unsafe mode. From the Visual Studio IDE, you can choose the Allow Unsafe Mode option in the *Project* Properties dialog box on the Build pane. Table 1-10 lists the pointer operators.

TABLE 1-10 Pointer operators

Operator	Symbol	Description
asterisk operator (postfix)	*	Declare a pointer
asterisk operator (prefix)	*	Dereference a pointer
ampersand operator	&	Obtain an address
arrow operator	->	Dereference a pointer and member access

Here is some sample code using pointers:

```
static void Main(string[] args)
{
    unsafe {
        int variable = 10;
        int* pVariable = &variable;
        Console.WriteLine("Value at address is {0}.",
            *pVariable);
    }
}
```

A more extensive review of pointers is presented later in the book in Chapter 19, "Unsafe Code."

Miscellaneous operators   The miscellaneous operators are unary but do not otherwise fit into a clear category. Table 1-11 lists the miscellaneous operators.

TABLE 1-11 Miscellaneous operators

Operator	Syntax	Description
New	*new* type(parameters)	Calls a matching constructor of the type. For a reference type, creates an instance of the object on the managed heap. For a value type, creates an instance of an initialized object on the stack.
checked	*checked*(expression)	Exception is raised if *expression* overflows.
delegate	*delegate* return_type method	Defines a type that holds type-safe function references.
lambda	=>	Separates the input and expression body of a *lambda* expression.
unchecked	*unchecked*(expression)	Overflows are ignored in *expression*.

Identifiers

An identifier is the name of a C# entity, which includes type, method, property, field, and other names. Identifiers can contain Unicode characters, escape character sequences, and underscores. A verbatim identifier is prefixed with the verbatim character (as discussed in the section "Verbatim Characters" earlier in this chapter).

Keywords

One of the strengths of C# is that the language has relatively few keywords. Table 1-12 provides an overview of the C# keywords. Extended explanations of each keyword are provided in context at the appropriate location in this book.

TABLE 1-12 Overview of C# keywords with explanations

Keyword	Syntax	Explanation
abstract	*abstract* class identifier	The class cannot be instantiated.
	abstract method	The method is implemented in a descendant class. This includes properties, indexers, and events.
base	*base*.member	Accesses a member of the base class.
break	*break*	Exits current loop or switch statement.
case	*case* label	Target of a switch expression.
catch	*catch*(filter){ handler }	The *catch* clause is where an exception is handled. The exception filter determines if the exception is handled in the handler.
checked	*checked* { statement }	If an expression within the *statement_block* overflows, throws an exception.
class	*class* identifier	Defines a new class.
const	*const* type identifier	Declares a constant local variable or field. Constants cannot be modified.
continue	*continue*	Continues to the next iteration of the loop, if any.
do	*do* { statement } *while* (expression)	The *do* loop is iterated until the expression is false.
else	*else* { statement }	The *else* statement is matched to the nearest *if* statement and provides the *false* path.
enum	*enum* identifier	Defines an enumeration type.
event	*event* delegatename identifier	Defines an event of the *delegatename* type.
explicit	*explicit* operator conversiontype	This user-defined conversion requires an explicit cast.
extern	*extern* return_type method	A method implemented externally—outside the current assembly.

TABLE 1-12 Overview of C# keywords with explanations

Keyword	Syntax	Explanation
false	*false*	A Boolean value.
finally	*finally { statement }*	Associated with the nearest *try* block. The *finally* block has cleanup code for resources defined in the *try* block.
fixed	*fixed (declaration)*	Fixes a pointer variable in memory and prevents relocation of that variable by the Garbage Collector.
for	*for (initializers; Boolean_expression; iterators) statement*	The *for* loop iterates the statement until the *Boolean_expression* is false.
foreach	*foreach (element in enumerable_collection)*	Iterates elements in a enumerable_collection.
get	*get*	Accessor method of a property member.
goto	*goto identifier*	Transfers control to a label.
	goto case identifier	Transfers control to a label inside a *switch* statement.
	goto default	Transfers control to a default label inside a *switch* statement.
if	*if (Boolean_expression) statement*	The statement is executed if the *Boolean_expression* resolves to *true*.
implicit	*implicit operator conversiontype*	This user-defined conversion requires only an implicit cast.
in	*foreach (element in enumerable_collection)*	Iterate elements in an *enumerable_collection*.
interface	*interface identifier*	Defines an interface.
internal	*internal identifier*	Type or member accessible only within the current assembly.
lock	*lock(object) { statement }*	Statement blocks locked on the same object are protected by a shared critical section, and access to those blocks is synchronized.
namespace	*namespace identifier*	Defines a namespace.
new	*new return_type method*	The *new* method hides the matching method of the base class.
	new type	The *new* operator declares a new structure or class. The *new* operator is not required for structures.
null	*null*	*null* can be assigned to references and nullable value types.

TABLE 1-12 Overview of C# keywords with explanations

Keyword	Syntax	Explanation
object	*object*	The *object* keyword is an alias for *System.Object*, which is the base class to all .NET objects (value or reference type).
operator	*operator* operator	Define a user-defined operator as a class or struct member.
out	*out* type parameter	The actual parameter is passed by reference into the method and can be modified directly. The parameter can be uninitialized prior to the function call.
override	*override* method	Override a virtual method in a base class. Method includes a member function, property, indexer, or an event.
params	*params* type [] identifier	Variable-length parameter list. The *params* parameter must be the last parameter in a parameter list.
private	*private* member	The member is visible only within the containing class or struct.
protected	*protected* member	Protected members are visible to the parent and any descendant classes.
public	*public* member	Public members are visible to everyone. This includes inside and outside the class.
readonly	*readonly* type identifier	Read-only fields can be initialized at declaration or in a constructor but nowhere else.
ref	*ref* type parameter	The parameter is passed by reference into the method and can be modified directly in the called function. The parameter must be initialized prior to the function call. The ref keyword is also required at the call site.
return	*return* expression	Returns the result of an expression from a method. Functions with a void return can have a return statement without a value (i.e., *return;*).
sealed	*sealed* identifier	Class is not inheritable.
set	*set*	Mutator method of property member.
sizeof	*sizeof(*valuename*)*	*Sizeof* returns the size of a value type. *Sizeof* of non-primitive types requires unsafe mode.
stackalloc	*stackalloc* type [expression]	Allocates an array of a value type on the stack; available only in unsafe mode. Expression determines the size of the array.

TABLE 1-12 Overview of C# keywords with explanations

Keyword	Syntax	Explanation
static	*static* method	Method is class-bound and not associated with a specific object instance.
struct	*struct* identifier	Defines a new structure.
switch	*switch(*expression*) { statement }*	Control is transferred to either a matching case label or the default label, if present.
this	*this*	The *this* object is a reference to the current object instance.
throw	*throw* object	Throws a user-defined exception. Exception objects should be derived from *System. Exception.*
true	*true*	A Boolean value.
try	*try { statement }*	Code in *statement_block* of *try* is guarded. If an exception is raised, control is transferred to the nearest *catch* statement.
unchecked	*unchecked { statement }*	Overflows in unchecked statements are ignored.
unsafe	*unsafe* type	Type can contain unsafe code, such as pointers. Also requires the *unsafe code* compiler option.
	unsafe return_type method	The method can contain unsafe code such as pointers. Also requires the *unsafe code* compiler option.
using	*using* identifier	The *using* keyword makes the specified namespace implicit.
	*using (*identifier_constructor_statement*) statement*	*IDisposable.Dispose,* which is the explicit destructor, is called on the named object after the statement is executed.
virtual	*virtual* method	Makes the method overridable in a derived class.
void	*void* method	A void return means that the method does not return a value. The method can omit a return statement or have an empty return.
	*void *identifier	*Identifier* is a pointer name. A void pointer is a typeless pointer; supported only in unsafe mode.
volatile	*volatile* fieldname	Access to volatile fields is serialized. This is especially useful in a multi-threaded environment. In addition, volatile fields also are not optimized.
while	*while (*expression*) statement*	The statement is repeated while the expression is true.

Primitives

Primitives are the predefined data types that are intrinsic to C#. Primitives are also keywords. Primitives historically found in C-base languages, including *int, long,* and many others, are included in C#. The intrinsic types are declared as C# keywords but are aliases for types in the .NET FCL. Except for the string type, the primitives are value types and allocated on the stack as structures. The string type is a class and allocated on the managed heap.

The primitives are listed in Table 1-13. Primitives have a published interface. For numeric types, the *min* property, *max* property, and *Parse* methods of the interface are particularly useful. The *min* and *max* property are invaluable for bounds checking, whereas the *Parse* method converts a string to the target primitive.

TABLE 1-13 Primitives in C#

Type	Primitive	Description	Range
bool	System.Boolean	Boolean	*true* or *false*.
byte	System.Byte	8-bit integer	0 to 255.
char	System.Char	16-bit Unicode character	/u0000 to /uFFFF.
decimal	System.Decimal	128-bit decimal	0 and $\pm 1.0 \times 10^{-28}$ to $\pm 7.9 \times 10^{28}$, with 28 digits of precision.
double	System.Double	64-bit floating point	0 and $\pm 5.0 \times 10^{-324}$ to $\pm 1.7 \times 10^{308}$, with 15 digits of precision.
float	System.Single	32-bit floating point	0 and $\pm 1.5 \times 10^{-45}$ to $\pm 3.4 \times 10^{38}$, with 7 digits of precision.
int	System.Int32	32-bit unsigned integer	−2,147,483,648 to 2,147,483,647.
long	System.Int64	64-bit integer	−9,223,372,036,854,775,808 to 9,223,372,036,854,775,807.
sbyte	System.SByte	8-bit integer	−128 to 127.
short	System.Int16	16-bit integer	−32,768 to 32,767.
string	System.String	not applicable	String is an immutable variable length string.
uint	System.UInt32	32-bit unsigned integer	0 to 4,294,967,295.
ulong	System.UInt64	64-bit unsigned integer	0 to 18,446,744,073,709,551,615.
ushort	System.UInt16	16-bit unsigned integer	0 to 65,535.

Types

This chapter is an introduction of Microsoft Visual C# 2008, including LINQ, which is the most important new feature in C#. The remaining chapters of this book provide the underlying details of LINQ and other topics introduced in this chapter, beginning with the next chapter, which pertains to types.

The core ingredient of most programming languages is the type. The term *type* encompasses classes, structures, interfaces, and enumerations. Classes are reference types and are placed on the managed heap, structures are value types and appear on the stack, and an enumeration is a set of flags.

Even a nontrivial C# program has at least one type. Literarily, except for namespaces, every entity in C# is a type or a member of a type. This includes the common primitives, such as *int*, *float*, and *double*. Classes are the nouns of the C# language, and it is certainly difficult to write a great story without any nouns. It is impossible to write a C# program without classes.

Chapter 2
Types

Types are the places, persons, and things found in an application. Object-oriented programs model real-world problems, in which types represent identities from your problem domain. An employee in a personnel program, a general ledger entry in an accounting package, and geometric shapes in a paint application are examples of types. Types include reference types, value types, and unsafe pointers. Reference types and value types will be discussed in this chapter; unsafe pointers are covered in Chapter 19, "Unsafe Code."

A *reference type* refers to an object created on the managed heap, and the lifetime of the resulting object is controlled by the Garbage Collector, which is a component of the Common Language Runtime (CLR). The local or member reference holds the location of an object created on the managed heap. Reference types are derived from *System.Object* implicitly and created with the *new* keyword. The most common reference type is a *class*. Other reference types are *interfaces, arrays,* and *delegates.*

Value types are lightweight components that are placed on the stack. Value types directly contain their value. Value types are usually created statically. For custom initialization, a value type can be constituted using the *new* statement, which will call the appropriate constructor. Unlike with a reference type, doing this with a value type does not create an object on the managed heap. It still resides on the stack. Value types derive from *System.ValueType*, which is derived from *System.Object. System.ValueType* defines a value type by rewriting some of the semantics of *System.Object*. Primitives such as *int, float, char,* and *bool* are archetypal value types. As a primitive, a string is a hybrid. Strictly speaking, strings are reference types, but they have some of the characteristics of value types.

Classes and structures are the primary focus of this chapter. A class or structure is a template for creating components of similar behavior and state. A class instance is called an object, whereas a structure instance is called a value. An *Employee* class would describe the common state and behavior of any employee. Each instance of the Employee class is an object. A *Fraction* structure would be a template for calculating fractions. Each instance of the Fraction structure is a value. The *Employee* and *Fraction* instances share common behavior with their siblings but have distinct identities. Within a classification of objects, the *GetHashCode* method returns a unique identity that distinguishes a specific component from any other sibling—even when the state is identical.

You should view classes and structures as independent contractors. They should be self-sufficient. Types collaborate with others through a published interface and hide extraneous details. In this way, classes and structures should be fully abstracted. This avoids dependencies between components, which leads to software that is error-prone and hard to maintain.

Classes

In C#, types have an important role. First, all code must be contained in a type. Global functions and variables are not permitted, preventing dependencies that can plague an otherwise robust application. Second, classes published in the .NET Framework Class Library provide essential services that are integral to any .NET application.

A class is described in a class declaration. A class declaration consists of a class header and body. The class header includes attributes, modifiers, the *class* keyword, an identifier, and the base class list. The class body encapsulates the members of the class, which are the data members and member functions. Here is the syntax of a class declaration:

attributes accessibility modifiers class *identifier*: *baselist* { *class_body* };

Attributes provide additional context to a class. If you think of a class as a noun, attributes are the adjectives. For example, the *Serializable* attribute identifies a class that can be serialized to storage. There is an assortment of predefined attributes. You can also define custom attributes. Attributes are optional and classes have no default attributes. Further details on attributes are in Chapter 13, "Metadata and Reflection."

Accessibility is the visibility of the class. Public classes are visible in the current assembly and in assemblies referencing that assembly. Internal classes are visible solely in the containing assembly. The default accessibility of a class is internal. Nested classes have additional accessibility options, which are described later in this chapter.

Modifiers refine the declaration of a class. For example, the *abstract* modifier prevents instances of the class from being created. Modifiers are optional, and there is no default. Table 2-1 lists the modifiers.

TABLE 2-1 Class modifiers

Modifier	Description
abstract	Class is abstract; instances of the class cannot be created.
sealed	Class cannot be inherited by a derived class.
static	Class contains only static members.
unsafe	Class can contain unsafe constructs, such as a pointer; also requires the unsafe compiler option.

A class can inherit the members of a single base class. Multiple inheritance is not supported in the Common Language Specification of .NET. However, a class can inherit and implement multiple interfaces. The *baselist* lists the inherited class, if any, and interfaces to be implemented. By default, classes inherit from the *System.Object* type. Inheritance and *System.Object* are discussed in more detail in Chapter 3, "Inheritance."

The class body contains the members of the class, which define the behavior and state of that class. The member functions are the behavior, whereas data members are the state. As a design goal, classes should expose an interface composed of the public functions of the class. Only those functions necessary to collaborate with the class should be exposed. Other functions should remain private or protected—internal functionality should remain private. The state of the class should be abstracted and described through the behavior of the class, which means the class is fully abstracted. You then manage the state of an object entirely through its public interface.

Classes do not require members. Most members can be inherited by a child class.

Unlike C++, classes are not terminated with a semicolon, which was commonly omitted by C++ programmers.

XInt is a class and a thin wrapper for an integer:

```
internal sealed class XInt {
    public int iField = 0;
}
```

The *XInt* class has internal accessibility and visibility in the current assembly, but is not visible to a referencing assembly. The sealed modifier means that the class cannot be refined through inheritance.

The following code uses the *new* statement to create an instance of the *XInt* class:

```
public void Func() {
    XInt obj = new XInt();
    obj.iField = 5;
}
```

Class Members

Classes are composed of members: member functions and fields. Use the member operator (.) to access members. The dot binds an instance member to an object or a static member to a class. In the following code, *jim.name* accesses the *name* field of the *jim* object:

```
using System;

namespace Donis.CSharpBook {
    public class Employee {
        public string name;
    }
    public class Personnel {
        static void Main() {
            Employee jim = new Employee();
            jim.name = "Wilson, Jim";
        }
    }
}
```

Table 2-2 describes the list of possible class members.

TABLE 2-2 **Type members**

Member	Description
Class	Nested class
Constant	Invariable data member
Constructor	Specialized method that initializes a component or class
Delegate	Container of one or more type-safe function references
Destructor	Specialized method that performs cleanup of object resources upon garbage collection
Event	Callbacks to method provided by a subscriber
Field	Data member
Indexer	Specialized property that indexes the current object
Interface	Nested interface
Method	Instance or static function
Operator	Operator member function that overrides implicit operator behavior
Properties	Get and set functions presented as a data member
Structure	Nested structure within a class

When a member is declared, attributes can be applied and accessibility defined. Members are further described with attributes. Accessibility sets the visibility of a class member.

Member Accessibility

Members defined in a class are scoped to that class. However, the visibility of the member is defined by accessibility keywords. The most common accessibility keywords are *public* and *private*. Public members are visible inside and outside the class. The visibility of private members is restricted to the containing class. Private is the default accessibility of a class member. Table 2-3 details the accessibility keywords.

TABLE 2-3 **Accessibility keywords**

Keyword	Description
internal	Visible in containing assembly
internal protected	Visible in containing assembly or descendants of the current class
private	Visible inside current class
protected	Visible inside current class and any descendants
public	Visible in containing assembly and assemblies referencing that assembly

Member Attributes

Attributes are usually the first element of the member declaration and further describe a member by extending the metadata of that element. The *Obsolete* attribute is an example of an attribute and marks a function as deprecated. Attributes are optional. By default, a member has no attributes.

Member Modifiers

Modifiers refine the definition of the applicable member. Modifiers are optional, and there are no defaults. Some modifiers are reserved depending on the classification of members. For example, the *override* modifier is applicable to member functions but not data members. Table 2-4 lists the available member modifiers.

TABLE 2-4 **Member modifiers**

Modifier	Description
abstract	A member function has no implementation and is described through inheritance.
extern	Implemented in an external dynamic-link library (DLL).
new	Hides a matching member in the base class.
override	Indicates that a member function in a derived class overrides a virtual method in the base class.
readonly	Fields declared as *readonly* are initialized at declaration or in a constructor.
sealed	The member function cannot be further refined through inheritance.
static	Member belongs to the class and not an instance.
virtual	Virtual member functions are overridable in a derived class.
volatile	Volatile fields are assumed to be accessible from multiple threads, which limits the applicable optimizations. This keeps the most current value in the field.

Instance and Static Members

Members belong either to an instance of a class or to the class itself. Static members are bound to a class. Except for constants, class members default to instance members and are bound to an object via the *this* reference. Constant members are implicitly static. Static members are classwise and have no implied *this* context. Certain types of members cannot be static and others cannot be instance members; destructors and operator member functions are an example. Destructors cannot be static, whereas operator member functions cannot be instance members.

Instance members when used are qualified by the object name. Here is the syntax of an instance member:

objectname.instancemember

Static members are prefixed with the class name:

classname.staticmember

The lifetime of static members is closely linked to the lifetime of the application. The lifetime of instance members is linked to an instance and is accessible from the point of instantiation. Access to instance members of a local reference cease when the instance variable is no longer in scope. Therefore, the lifetime of an instance member is a subset of the lifetime of an application. Static members are essentially always available, whereas instance members are not. Static members are similar to global functions and variables but have the benefit of encapsulation. Static members can be private to limit their visibility.

Your design analysis should determine which members are instance members and which are static members. For example, in a personnel application for small businesses, there is an *Employee* class. The employee number is an instance member of the class. In the problem domain, each employee is assigned a unique identifier. However, the company name member is static because all employees work for the same company. The company name does not belong to a single employee, but to the classification.

Static class   A static class contains static members but no instance members. Because static classes have no instance data, a static class cannot be instantiated. The following is a static class:

```
public static class ZClass {
    public static void MethodA() {}
    public static void MethodB() {}
}
```

this Object

The *this* reference is a *readonly* reference to the current object. Instance member functions are passed a *this* reference as a hidden parameter of the function. In an instance function, the *this* reference is automatically applied to any instance members. This assures that within an instance member function, you can implicitly refer to members of the same object. In the following code, *GetEmployeeInfo* is an instance member function referring to other instance members (the *this* reference is implied):

```
public void GetEmployeeInfo() {
    PrintEmployeeName();
    PrintEmployeeAddress();
    PrintEmployeeId();
}
```

Here is the same code, except that the *this* pointer is explicit (the behavior of the function remains the same):

```
public void GetEmployeeInfo() {
    this.PrintEmployeeName();
    this.PrintEmployeeAddress();
    this.PrintEmployeeId();
}
```

In the preceding code, the *this* reference was not required. The *this* reference is sometimes useful as a function return value or as a parameter. In addition, the *this* reference can improve code readability and provide IntelliSense for class members when editing the code in Microsoft Visual Studio.

Static member functions are not passed a *this* reference as a hidden parameter. For this reason, a static function member cannot directly access nonstatic members of the class. Therefore, you cannot refer to an instance member from a static member. Static members are essentially limited to accessing other static members. Instance members have access to both instance and static members of the class.

Data and Function Members

Members are broadly grouped into data and function members. As mentioned, types consist of states and behaviors. Data members are states, whereas function members define behavior. Data members include constants, fields, and nested types. As previously mentioned, data members are typically private to enforce encapsulation and to adhere to the principle of data hiding and abstraction. The class developer gains implementation independence and the freedom to modify the type so long as the public interface is not changed. Once published, the interface should be immutable.

Constants

Constants are data members. They are initialized at compile time using a constant expression and cannot be modified at run time. Constants are assigned a type and must be used within the context of that type. This makes constants type-safe. Constants are usually value types, such as *integer* or *double*. A constant can be a reference type, but with limitations. Reference types are typically initialized at run time, which is prohibited with a constant. Therefore, reference types as constants must be set to null at declaration. The sole exception are strings, which are reference types but can be assigned a non-null value at declaration.

The following is the syntax of a constant member:

accessibility modifier const *identifier* = *initialization*;

With constants, the only allowable modifier is *new*, which hides an inherited constant of the same name in the base type. Constants are implicitly static. The initialization is performed at compile time. You can declare and initialize several constants simultaneously.

The following class has several constant data members:

```
public class ZClass {
    public const int fielda = 5, fieldb = 15;
    public const int fieldc = fieldd + 10;  // Error

    public static int fieldd = 15;
}
```

The assignment to *fieldc* causes a compile error. The *fieldd* member is a nonconstant member variable and is evaluated at run time. Thus, *fieldd* cannot be used in an assignment to a constant variable.

Fields

Instance fields hold state information bound to a specific object. The state information is stored in managed memory created for the object. Static fields are data owned by the class. A single instance of static data is created for the class. It is not replicated for each instance. Fields can be reference or value types. Here is the syntax for declaring a field:

accessibility modifier type fieldname = initialization;

Fields support the full assortment of accessibility. Valid modifiers for a field include *new*, *static*, *readonly*, and *volatile*.

Initialization is optional but recommended. Uninitialized fields are assigned a default value of zero or null. Fields can be initialized individually or in an initialization list.

Initialization is performed in the textual order in which the fields appear in the class, which is top-down. The textual order is demonstrated in the following code:

```
using System;

namespace Donis.CSharpBook{
    internal class ZClass {
        public int iField1 = FuncA(), iField2 = FuncC();
        public int iField3 = FuncB();

        public static int FuncA() {
            Console.WriteLine("ZClass.FuncA");
            return 0;
        }
```

```
        public static int FuncB() {
            Console.WriteLine("ZClass.FuncB");
            return 1;
        }

        public static int FuncC() {
            Console.WriteLine("ZClass.FuncC");
            return 2;
        }
    }

    public class Starter {
        public static void Main() {
            ZClass obj = new ZClass();
        }
    }
}
```

Running this code confirms that *FuncA*, *FuncC*, and *FuncB* are called in sequence based on the textual order of field initialization.

Constants must be initialized at compile time. This limits some of the flexibility of a constant. For example, if the constant value is not known until run time, a constant variable cannot be used. This is where a *readonly* field is helpful. A *readonly* field is similar to a constant except that it also can be initialized in a constructor at run time. In addition, the initialization expression of a *readonly* field can refer to other static fields. However, you cannot refer to a instance field. Unlike constant fields, *readonly* fields can be instance or static members.

The following code contains an example of a *readonly* field:

```
public class ZClass {
    public ZClass() { // constructor
        fieldc = 10;
    }

    public static int fielda = 5;
    public readonly int fieldb = fielda + 10;
    public int fieldc;
};
```

Member Functions

Member functions contain the behavior of the class. Methods, properties, and indexers are the member functions. Methods are straightforward functions that accept parameters as input and return the result of an operation. A property functions as a data member, but it is implemented as a pair of accessor methods: the *get* and *set* method pair. An indexer is a specialized property. Indexers apply *get* and *set* methods to the *this* reference, which refers to the current object. The discussion of indexers is deferred to Chapter 5, "Arrays and Collections."

Functions

Methods contain the code of the class. A method can contain one or more *return* statements, which provide an orderly exit to a function. Void functions do not require a *return* statement and can simply fall through the end of the function. The C# compiler extrapolates all possible paths within the function. One reason for this is to make sure that all possible code paths have an appropriate *return* statement. Another is that the compiler is looking for unreachable code. The following code, stored in unreachable.cs, includes both unreachable code and a code path without a proper *return* statement:

```
public static int Main() {
    if (true) {
        Console.WriteLine("true");
    }
    else {
        Console.WriteLine("false");
    }
}
```

The *if* statement is always true. Therefore, the *else* code is unreachable. *Main* returns *int*. However, the method has no *return* statement. For these reasons, the application generates the following errors when compiled:

```
unreachable.cs(10,17): warning CS0162: Unreachable code detected
unreachable.cs(5,27): error CS0161: 'Donis.CSharpBook.Starter.Main()': not all code
paths return a value
```

Keep functions relatively short. Longer functions are harder to debug and test. A class comprised of a number of short functions, which is the class interface, is preferable to a class that contains only a few convoluted long functions. Remoted components are the exception: A narrower interface is preferred because it minimizes client calls and optimizes network traffic. Comparatively, local invocations are quick and efficient.

In addition to code, functions own local variables and parameters. The local variables and parameters represent the private state of the function.

Function Return   The result of a function is reported with a *return* statement. A value type or reference type can be returned from a function. Returning a value type returns a copy of the value, while returning a reference type returns a reference to an object. Functions can have multiple *return* statements, each on a separate code path. More than one *return* statement along a single code path results in unreachable code, which will cause a compiler warning.

Functions can return an actual value or a *void* return type. Functions that return a value must have an explicit *return* statement, while functions that return *void* can be exited explicitly or implicitly.

To explicitly exit a function with a *void* return, use an empty *return* statement. For an implicit exit, allow the execution to exit the function naturally and without a *return* statement. At the end of the statement block, the function simply exits. A function can have multiple explicit *return* statements but only one implicit return. In the following code, *Main* has both an explicit and implicit exit:

```
static void Main(string [] arg) {
    if (arg.Length > 0) {
        // do something
          return;
    }

    // implicit return
}
```

A function evaluates to its return value. A method that returns *void* cannot be used in an expression. This type of method evaluates to nothing and is therefore not assignable. In other words, a function that returns *void* cannot be used either as a left-value or right-value of an assignment. Functions that return a value can be used in expressions. If the function returns a reference, it also can be used as the left-value in an assignment. The following code demonstrates the use of functions in expressions:

```
public class ZClass {
    public int MethodA() {
        return 5;
    }

    public void MethodB() {
        return;
    }

    public int MethodC() {
        int value1 = 10;
        value1 = 5 + MethodA() + value1;   // Valid
        MethodB();                         // Valid
        value1 = MethodB();                // Invalid
        return value1;
    }
}
```

At the call site, the return value of a function is temporarily copied to the stack. The return value is discarded after the calling statement or expression is evaluated. To preserve the return value, assign the function's return value to something. Returns are always *copied by value*. When returning a value type, a copy of the result is returned. For reference types, a copy of the reference is returned. This creates an alias to an object in the calling function. Look at the following code:

```
using System;

namespace Donis.CSharpBook {
```

```
public class XInt {
    public int iField = 0;
}

public class Starter {

    public static XInt MethodA() {
        XInt inner = new XInt();
        inner.iField = 5;
        return inner;
    }

    public static void Main() {
        XInt outer = MethodA();
        Console.WriteLine(outer.iField);
    }
}
}
```

In the preceding code, *MethodA* creates an instance of *XInt* called *inner*. This variable is then returned from the function. After the return, *outer* is an alias to the *inner* object, which prevents the object from becoming a candidate for garbage collection. The alias *outer* then can be used to access members of the *inner* object, as shown in the sample code.

Function parameters   Functions have zero or more parameters. Pass zero parameters with an empty call operator. Parameter lists can be of fixed or variable length. Use the *param* keyword to declare a variable length parameter list. This is discussed in Chapter 5. Parameters default to being passed by value and are copied to the stack. Changes to a parameter in the called function are discarded when the method is exited and the value is removed from the stack. In the following code, changes made in the function are lost when the function returns:

```
using System;

namespace Donis.CSharpBook {
    public class Starter {

        public static void MethodA(int parameter) {
            parameter = parameter + 5;
        }    // change discarded

        public static void Main() {
            int local = 2;
            MethodA(local);
            Console.WriteLine(local); // Writes 2
        }
    }
}
```

Parameters that are reference types are also passed by value, in that a copy of the reference itself is placed on the stack. The called function receives an alias to an object that resides on the managed heap. Using the alias, you can change the referenced object directly from the called function.

The previous example passes a parameter by value. The next example also passes a parameter by value, but the parameter is a reference type (*XInt*). Changes made to the object in *MethodA* are not discarded at the end of the called function:

```
using System;

namespace Donis.CSharpBook {

    public class XInt {
        public int iField = 2;
    }

    public class Starter {

        public static void MethodA(XInt alias) {
            alias.iField += 5;
        }

        public static void Main() {
            XInt obj = new XInt();
            MethodA(obj);
            Console.WriteLine(obj.iField);  // Writes 7
        }
    }
}
```

Pass a parameter *by reference* using the *ref* modifier. When passed by reference, a reference to the object is passed and not a copy of the value. Because a reference to the object is passed, changes to the parameter in the called function affect the actual object and not a copy. Therefore, changes to the parameter persist beyond the called function. The *ref* attribute must precede the parameter in the function signature and at the call site. The function signature consists of the function name and parameter types but not the return type. The following sample code passes an integer parameter by reference. Unlike the first version of this code, which implicitly passed an integer parameter by value, changes made in *MethodA* are not lost.

```
using System;

namespace Donis.CSharpBook {
    public class Starter {

        public static void MethodA(ref int parameter) {
            parameter = parameter + 5;
        }

        public static void Main() {
            int var = 2;
            MethodA(ref var);
            Console.WriteLine(var); // Writes 7
        }
    }
}
```

What happens when a reference type is passed *by reference*? The function receives the local reference and not an alias. First, look at the following code, in which a reference is passed by value. Inside the called function, the parameter is assigned a new instance. However, because the reference is passed by value, the change is lost when the function exits. Therefore, the original reference (*obj*) is unchanged:

```
using System;

namespace Donis.CSharpBook {

    public class XInt {
        public int iField = 2;
    }

    public class Starter {

        public static void MethodA(XInt alias) {
            XInt inner = new XInt();
            inner.iField = 5;
            alias = inner;
        }  // reference change lost

        public static void Main() {
            XInt obj = new XInt();
            MethodA(obj);
            Console.WriteLine(obj.iField);  // Writes 2
        }
    }
}
```

The next code is updated to pass the parameter by reference. The reference is passed into *MethodA* and updated. When the function exits, the original reference (obj) has been changed to point to the new instance:

```
using System;

namespace Donis.CSharpBook {

    public class XInt {
        public int iField = 2;
    }

    public class Starter {

        public static void MethodA(ref XInt alias) {
            XInt inner = new XInt();
            inner.iField = 5;
            alias = inner;
        }
```

```
        public static void Main() {
            XInt obj=new XInt();
            MethodA(ref obj);
            Console.WriteLine(obj.iField);   // Writes 5
        }
    }
}
```

Parameters must be initialized before being passed by reference. The following code presents an error. In *Main*, the *obj* reference is unassigned before the method call. Notice that even though the parameter is initialized in the called function, the following code causes a compile error:

```
using System;

namespace Donis.CSharpBook {

    public class XInt {
        public int iField = 5;
    }

    public class Starter {

        public static void MethodA(ref XInt alias) {
            XInt inner = new XInt();
            alias = inner;
        }

        public static void Main() {
            XInt obj;
            MethodA(ref obj); // Error
            Console.WriteLine(obj.iField);   // Won't compile
        }
    }
}
```

Like the *ref* modifier, the *out* modifier passes a parameter by reference, but there is one significant difference. The *out* parameter does not have to be initialized prior to the function call. However, the parameter must be initialized before the called function exits. The following code is identical to the previous code except the parameter is declared and passed with the *out* modifier (shown in bold type) and not the *ref* modifier. For this reason, the code now compiles successfully:

```
using System;

namespace Donis.CSharpBook {

    class XInt {
        public int iField = 5;
    }

    class Starter {
```

```
        public static void MethodA(out XInt alias) {
            XInt inner = new XInt();
            alias = inner;
        }

        public static void Main() {
            XInt obj;
            MethodA(out obj);
            Console.WriteLine(obj.iField);   // Writes 5
        }
    }
}
```

Function Overloading

Function overloading allows multiple implementations of the same function in a class, which promotes a consistent interface for related behavior. Overloaded methods share the same name but have unique signatures. Parameter attributes, such as *out*, are distinctive and considered part of the signature (the function header minus the return type). Because the return type is excluded from the signature, functions cannot be overloaded on the basis of a different return type alone. The number of parameters, the type of parameters, or both must be different. With the exception of constructors, a function cannot be overloaded based on whether it is a static or instance member.

The process of selecting a function from a set of overloaded methods, which occurs during compile time, is called *function resolution*. The compiler calls the function that matches the number and types of parameters in the function invocation. Sometimes a call site matches more than one function in the overloaded set. When function resolution matches two or more methods, the call is considered ambiguous and a compile error occurs. A compiler error also results if no overloaded function matches the call site.

This sample code overloads the *SetName* method:

```
using System;

namespace Donis.CSharpBook {

    public class Employee {

        public string name;

        public void SetName(string last) {
            name = last;
        }

        public void SetName(string first, string last) {
            name = first + " " + last;
        }

        public void SetName(string saluation, string first, string last) {
            name = saluation + " " + first + " " + last;
        }
```

```
        }

    public class Personnel {
        public static void Main() {
            Employee obj = new Employee();
            obj.SetName("Bob", "Kelly");


        }
    }
}
```

Functions with variable-length parameter lists can be included in the set of overloaded functions. The function first is evaluated with a fixed-length parameter list. If function resolution does not yield a match, the function is evaluated with variable-length parameters.

Local Variables

Local variables can be either reference or value types. You can declare a local variable anywhere in a method, but there is one caveat. The local variable must be defined before use. There are competing philosophies as to when to declare local variables. Some developers prefer to declare local variables at the beginning of a method or block, where they are readily identifiable; others like to declare local variables near where they are used because they think that local variables are more maintainable when located near the affected code. Local variables are not assigned a default value prior to initialization. They can be initialized at declaration or later. At declaration, local variables can be initialized separately or in an initialization list. It is good practice to initialize local variables to something at declaration. That way, the local variable always has a known state. Referring to an unassigned local variable in an expression causes a compiler error.

This is the syntax for declaring a local variable:

modifier type variablename = initialization;

The only modifier available to local variables is *const*. Variables that are *const* must be initialized at compile time and cannot be changed thereafter.

The scope of a local variable is the entire function—regardless of where the local variable is declared. The scope of a parameter is also the entire function. Basically, local variables cannot have the same name as a parameter.

Visibility   Local variables are declared at the top level or in a child block within the method. The visibility of a local variable starts where the local variable is declared. Visibility ends when the block where the local variable is declared ends. Local variables are visible in child blocks, but not in parent blocks. Because local variables maintain scope throughout the block in which they are declared, names of local variables cannot be reused in a child block. Figure 2-1 illustrates the relationship between scope and visibility of local variables.

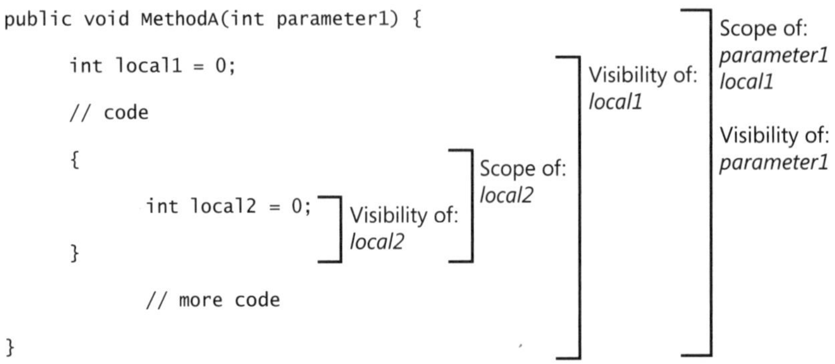

```
public void MethodA(int parameter1) {

    int local1 = 0;

    // code

    {
        int local2 = 0;
    }

        // more code

}
```

Scope of:
parameter1
local1

Visibility of:
local1

Visibility of:
parameter1

Scope of:
local2

Visibility of:
local2

FIGURE 2-1 Diagram of the scope and visibility of a local variable

Local variables of a value type are removed from the stack when the function is exited. Local references are also removed from the stack at that time, but the reference object may or may not become a candidate for garbage collection. Assuming that no other references exist at function exit, the object will become a candidate for garbage collection. It is a good idea to assign *null* to a reference when the reference is no longer needed. Local variables are private to the current function and are not accessible from another function. Identically named local variables in different functions are distinct and separate entities, which are stored at different memory addresses. To share data between functions, declare a field.

Methods

Methods are the most common function member. Methods accept parameters as input, perform an operation, and return the result of the operation. Both parameters and a return result are optional. Methods are described through the method header, and implemented in the method body. Here is the syntax of a method:

attributes accessibility modifiers return_type identifier(parameter_list) { statement };

Various attributes apply to methods, such as *Obsolete, StrongNameIdentityPermission,* and *InternalsVisibleTo.* Methods can be *private, public, protected,* or *internal.* Methods can be assigned the *sealed, abstract, new,* and other modifiers, as explained in Chapter 3. The *return_type* is the result of the method. Methods that return nothing must have a void *return_type.* The parameter list, which consists of zero or more parameters, is the input of the method. The method body contains zero or more statements.

Constructors

A constructor is a specialized function for initializing the state. An instance constructor initializes an instance of a class, while a static constructor initializes the classwise state. This guarantees that the class or object is always in a known state. Constructors have the same name as the class. Instance constructors are invoked with the *new* operator and cannot be called in the same manner as other member functions. Here is the syntax of a constructor:

accessibility modifier typename(parameterlist)

The accessibility of a constructor determines where new instances of the reference type can be created. For example, a public constructor allows an object to be created in the current assembly or a referencing assembly. A private or protected constructor prevents an instance from being created outside the class or a descendant of the class. The *extern* modifier is the only modifier applicable to constructors. Constructors can have zero or more parameters. Finally, note that constructors return *void* but do not have an explicitly declared return type.

This code shows one constructor for an *Employee* class:

```
using System;

namespace Donis.CSharpBook {

    public class Employee {

        public Employee(params string []_name) {
            switch(_name.Length) {
                case 1:
                    name = _name[0];
                    break;
                case 2:
                    name = _name[0] + " " + _name[1];
                    break;
                default:
                    // Error handler
                    break;
            }

        }

        public void GetName() {
            Console.WriteLine(name);
        }

        private string name = "";
    }

    public class Personnel {

        public static void Main() {
            Employee jim = new Employee("Jim", "Wilson");
            jim.GetName();
        }
    }
}
```

Classes with no constructors have an implicit constructor—the default constructor, which is a parameterless constructor. Default constructors assign default values to fields. A *new* statement with no parameters invokes the default constructor. You can replace a default constructor with a custom parameterless constructor. The following *new* statement calls the default constructor of a class:

```
Employee empl = new Employee();
```

Constructors can be overloaded. The function resolution of overloaded constructors is determined by the parameters of the new statement. The following *Employee* class has overloaded constructors:

```
using System;

namespace Donis.CSharpBook {

    public class Employee {

        public Employee(string _name) {
            name = _name;
        }

        public Employee(string _first, string _last) {
            name = _first + " " + _last;
        }

        private string name = "";
    }

    public class Personnel {
        public static void Main() {
            Employee jim = new Employee("Jim", "Wilson");  // 2 argument constructor
        }
    }
}
```

In the preceding code, an instance of the *Employee* class (*jim*) is created using the two-argument constructor. Creating an instance using the default constructor would cause a compile error:

```
Employee jim = new Employee();
```

This is the error message:

```
Donis.CSharpBook.Employee' does not contain a constructor that takes '0' arguments
```

Why does this error occur? Although the statement is syntactically correct, the *Employee* class does not have a default constructor. Adding any custom constructor to a class removes the default constructor. A custom one-argument and two-argument constructor were added to the *Employee* class, which removed the default constructor. In this circumstance, you could explicitly add a default (parameterless) constructor to the class if needed.

A constructor can call another constructor using the *this* reference, which is useful for reducing redundant code. A constructor cannot call another constructor in the method body. Instead, constructors call other constructors using the colon syntax after the constructor header. This syntax is available with constructors but not with other member functions. In the following code, all the constructors of the *Employee* class delegate to the one-argument constructor:

```
class Employee {

    public Employee()
        : this("") {
    }

    public Employee(string _name) {
        name = _name;
    }

    public Employee(string _first, string _last)
        : this(_first + " " + _last) {
    }

    public void GetName() {
        Console.WriteLine(name);
    }

    private string name = "";
}
```

Constructors also can be static. You create a static constructor to initialize static fields. The static constructor is called when the class is first referenced. These are the limitations to static constructors:

- The accessibility of a static constructor cannot be set.

- Static constructors are parameterless.

- Static constructors cannot be overloaded.

Static constructors are not called explicitly with the *new* statement. As mentioned, static constructors are called when the class is first referenced. In the following code, *ZClass* has a static constructor. The static constructor is stubbed to output the time. In *Main*, the time is also displayed, execution is paused for about five seconds, and then *ZClass* is accessed. *ZClass. GetField* is called and that triggers the invocation of the static constructor. This will display the time, which should be about five seconds later:

```
using System;
using System.Threading;

namespace Donis.CSharpBook {

    public class ZClass {

        static private int fielda;
        static ZClass() {
            Console.WriteLine(DateTime.Now.ToLongTimeString());
            fielda = 42;
        }
```

```
            static public void GetField() {
                Console.WriteLine(fielda);
            }
        }
    }

    public class Starter {
        public static void Main() {
            Console.WriteLine(DateTime.Now.ToLongTimeString());
            Thread.Sleep(5000);
            ZClass.GetField();
        }
    }
}
```

Singleton   A *singleton* is an object that appears once in the problem domain. Singletons provide an excellent example of private and static constructors. Singletons are limited to one instance, but that instance is required. This requirement is enforced in the implementation of the singleton. A complete explanation of the singleton pattern is found at *http://www.microsoft.com/patterns*.

The singleton presented in this chapter has two constructors. The private constructor initializes an instance of the class. Because this is a private constructor, the instance cannot be created outside the class. The single instance of the class is created in the static constructor. Because the static constructor is called automatically and only once, one instance—the singleton—always exists. The instance members of the class are accessible through the static instance of the class made available in the public interface.

A chess game is played with a single board—no more, no less. This is the singleton for a chess board:

```
using System;

namespace Donis.CSharpBook {

    public class Chessboard {
        private Chessboard() {
        }

        static Chessboard() {
            board = new Chessboard();
            board.start = DateTime.Now.ToShortTimeString();
        }

        public static Chessboard board=null;
        public string player1;
        public string player2;
        public string start;
    }

    public class Game {
        public static void Main() {
            Chessboard game = Chessboard.board;
```

```
            game.player1 = "Sally";
            game.player2 = "Bob";
            Console.WriteLine("{0} played {1} at {2}",
                game.player1, game.player2,
        game.start);
        }
    }
}
```

In *Main*, *game* is an alias for the *ChessBoard.board* singleton. The local reference is not another instance of *Chessboard*. It is an alias and simply a convenience.

Object initializers   Object initializers are a convenient method for initializing public fields and properties. When creating an instance of a new type, provide an initialization list, which includes field or property names and assignments. You do not have to assign a value to every field. Because the fields are named, they can appear in any order in the initialization list. This is new to Visual C# 2008.

The following code provides an example of an object initializer:

```
public class Name
{
    public string GetName()
    {
        return first + " " + middle +
            " " + last;
    }

    public string first = "";
    public string last = "";
    public string middle = "";
}

class Names
{
    public static void Main()
    {
        Name donis = new Name { first = "Donis",
            last = "Marshall" };
        Name lisa = new Name { first = "Lisa",
            last = "Miller" };
        Console.WriteLine(donis.GetName());
        Console.WriteLine(lisa.GetName());
    }
}
```

Destructors

It is good practice to remove unused objects from resources. That is the purpose of the *destructor* method. Destructors are not called directly in source code but during garbage collection. This provides an opportunity for an object to clean itself before it is removed from memory. Garbage collection is nondeterministic. A destructor is invoked at an undetermined moment in the future. Like a constructor, the destructor has the same name as the class, except a destructor is prefixed with a tilde (~). The destructor is called by the *Finalize* method, which is inherited from *System.Object*. In C#, you cannot override the *Finalize* method. For deterministic garbage collection, inherit the *IDisposable* interface and implement *IDisposable. Dispose* based on the disposable pattern. The disposable pattern is discussed in Chapter 18, "Memory Management."

Destructors differ from other member functions in the following ways:

- Destructors cannot be overloaded.

- Destructors are parameterless.

- Destructors are not inherited.

- Accessibility cannot be applied to destructors.

- Extern is the sole available modifier.

- The return type cannot be set explicitly. Destructors implicitly return void.

Here is the syntax of a destructor:

modifier ~typename()

Destructors have usage patterns. They also have performance and efficiency implications. Understand the ramifications of destructors before adding a destructor in a class. These topics are also reviewed in Chapter 18.

The following code implements a *destructor* and a *Dispose* method. The *WriteToFile* class is a wrapper for a *StreamWriter* object. The constructor initializes the internal object, and the *Dispose* method closes the file resource. The destructor delegates to this *Dispose* method. You can call the *Dispose* method explicitly or have the destructor called implicitly at garbage collection. The *Main* method tests the class:

```
using System;
using System.IO;

namespace Donis.CSharpBook {

    public class WriteToFile: IDisposable {

        public WriteToFile(string _file, string _text) {
            file = new StreamWriter(_file, true);
            text = _text;
        }

        public void WriteText() {
            file.WriteLine(text);
        }

        public void Dispose() {
```

```
            if (null != file)
            {
                file.Close();
                file = null;
            }
        }

        ~WriteToFile() {
            if (null != file)
            {
                Dispose();
            }
        }

        private StreamWriter file;
        private string text;
    }

    public class Writer {
        public static void Main() {
            WriteToFile sample = new WriteToFile("sample.txt", "My text file");
            sample.WriteText();
            sample.Dispose();
        }
    }
}
```

Properties

A property provides the convenience of a field but the safety of a function. Properties are visible like a field but are actually a *get* and *set* method. The *get* method is called when a value is returned from the property. Conversely, the *set* method is used when a value is assigned to the property. Fields are typically private, which protects the state of the object or class. You access the private fields through the public interface. Properties combine a private field and a public interface in a single entity. There are several benefits of using properties instead of public fields:

- Properties are safer than public or protected fields. The *set* method can be used to validate any input for a property.

- Properties can be computed, which adds some flexibility.

- Lazy initialization can be used with properties. This is particularly useful when the target data is expensive to initialize or obtain. Datasets are an ideal example. The cost of loading a dataset can be delayed until the property is actually accessed. This is more difficult to accomplish with fields.

- Write-only and read-only properties are supported. Fields support only read-only accessibility.

- Properties can be included as a member in an interface type. Fields are not allowed in interfaces.

A property is a *get* and *set* method. Neither method is called directly. Depending on how the property is being used, the correct method is called implicitly. As a left-value of an assignment, the *set* method of the property is called. When used as a right-value, the *get* method of the property is called. The *get* method also is called if a property is used within an expression.

Here is the syntax of a property declaration:

accessibility modifier type identifier { accessibility get *{statement} accessibility* set *{statement} }*

The *accessibility* and *modifier* apply to both the *get* and *set* method. However, either the *set* or *get* method can override the accessibility when necessary. In this way, for example, the *get* method could be public, while the *set* method is private. *Type* is the underlying type of the property. Neither the *get* nor *set* method has an explicit return type or parameter list. Both are inferred. The *get* method returns the property type and has no parameters. The *set* method returns void and has a single parameter, which is the same type as the property. In the *set* method, the *value* keyword represents the implied parameter.

In this code, the *Person* class has an age property:

```
using System;

namespace Donis.CSharpBook {

    public class Person {
        private int prop_age;
        public int age {
            set {
                // perform validation
                prop_age = value;
            }
            get {
                return prop_age;
            }
        }
    }

    class People{

        public static void Main() {
            Person bob = new Person();
            bob.age = 30; // Calls set method
            Console.WriteLine(bob.age);  // Call gets method
        }
    }
}
```

Properties have no inherent data storage, which can be efficient because data storage is not always required. For example, computed properties might not require data storage. If desired, a corresponding data store can be declared in the class. The data store of a property can be a single field. This one-to-one relationship between the property and the data store is not required. A composite property can consist of multiple fields. Conversely, multiple properties can rely on the same field. The latter case is demonstrated in the following code, where the *name*, *first*, and *last* properties rely on the *prop_name* field:

```csharp
using System;

namespace Donis.CSharpBook {

    public class Employee {

        private string prop_name;
        public string name {
            get {
                return prop_name;
            }
            set {
                prop_name = value;
            }
        }

        public string first {
            get {
                return (prop_name.Split(' '))[0];
            }
            set {
                string lastname = name.Split(' ')[1];
                prop_name = value + " " + lastname;
            }
        }
        public string last {
            get {
                return (prop_name.Split(' '))[1];
            }
            set {
                string firstname = name.Split(' ')[0];
                prop_name = firstname + " " + value;
            }
        }

    }

    public class Personnel{
        public static void Main() {
            Employee jim=new Employee();
            jim.name="Jim Wilson";
            jim.first="Dan";
            Console.WriteLine(jim.name);  // Dan Wilson
            Console.WriteLine(jim.last);  // Wilson
        }
    }
}
```

Read-only and write-only properties   Read-only properties implement the *get* method but not the *set* method. Birth date is an ideal read-only property. Conversely, write-only properties have a *set* method alone, which is common with a password property:

```
public class SensitiveForm{
    private string prop_password;
    public string password {
        set {
            prop_password = value;
        }
    }
}
```

Automatically implemented properties   Automatically implemented properties are one of the new features of Visual C# 2008. In the previous sample code, a backing variable of the property was created for storage. Automatically implemented properties automatically have storage for the property. This is a convenience because the developer does not have to implement the storage explicitly. Both the *get* and *set* methods of the automatically implemented property must be provided—the property cannot be either read-only or write-only.

This is the syntax for creating an automatically implemented property:

accessibility modifier type identifier { modifier get {;} modifier set {;} }

The following is sample code of an automatically implemented property:

```
using System;
namespace Donis.CSharpBook {
    public class Person {
        public int age {
            get;
            set;
        }
    }

    class People {
        public static void Main() {
            Person bob = new Person();
            bob.age = 30; // Calls set method
            Console.WriteLine(bob.age);  // Call gets method
        }
    }
}
```

Error handling   Validating the state of an object is important to avoid the "garbage-in/garbage-out" syndrome. An object or class is only as useful as the quality of the data it contains. Validation can be performed in the *set* method of a property. What is the appropriate action if the validation fails? You cannot return an error code from a *set* method. There are two options. The first (and preferable) option is to throw an exception. The second option, if the property type is a reference or nullable type, is to set the storage to *null*.

The estimated maximum age of a person is 120 years. This check can be added to our age property. In this example, an exception is thrown for an invalid age:

```
public class Person {

    private int prop_age;
    public int age {
        set {
            if (value < 0 || value > 120) {
                throw new ApplicationException("Invalid age!");
            }
            prop_age = value;
        }
        get {
            return prop_age;
        }
    }
}
```

In the next example, when the input value is invalid, the property is set to *null*:

```
public class Person {
    private int? prop_age;
    public int? age {
        set {
            if (value < 0 || value > 120) {
                prop_age = null;
                return;
            }
            prop_age = value;
        }
        get {
            return prop_age;
        }
    }
}
```

Nested Types

Nested types are created inside a class or structure. This is an example of a nested class:

```
public class Outer {

    public void FuncA() {
    }

    public class Inner {

        static public void FuncB() {
            Console.WriteLine("Outer.Inner.FuncB()");
        }
    }
}
```

Nested types can be public or private or have other accessibility. The full complement of modifiers is available. Use the dot syntax to access members of the nested class. The following code calls a static method of the *Inner* class:

```
Outer.Inner.FuncB();
```

You can create an instance of the nested class. If the nested class is public, references to the nested class can be created inside or outside the outer class depending on the visibility. A nested class that is private can be instantiated only inside the outer class. This is one reason for using nested classes. Invoking the *this* object within the nested class refers to members of the nested class alone. Instance members of the outer class are not accessible from the *this* object within the nested class. You can provide access to the outer object through the constructor of the nested class. Pass a reference of the outer object as a parameter. The back reference is then available to access the instance members of the outer object from within the nested class. The static members of the outer class, regardless of accessibility, are available to the nested class.

The *Automobile* class models a car engine, which is a system. An automobile system contains an alternator, ignition, steering, and other subsystems. This is an abbreviated version of an *Automobile* class:

```
using System;

namespace Donis.CSharpBook {

    public class Automobile {

        public Automobile() {
            starter = new StarterMotor(this);
        }

        public void Start() {
            starter.Ignition();
        }

        private bool prop_started = false;
        public bool started {
            get {
                return prop_started;
            }
        }

        private class StarterMotor {
            public StarterMotor(Automobile _auto) {
                auto = _auto;
            }

            public void Ignition() {
                auto.prop_started = true;
            }
            Automobile auto;
        }
```

```
        private StarterMotor starter;
    }

    public class Starter {
        public static void Main() {
            Automobile car = new Automobile();
            car.Start();
            if (car.started) {
                Console.WriteLine("Car started");
            }
        }
    }
}
```

Partial Type

A *partial* type can span multiple source files. When compiled, the elements of the *partial* type are combined into a single type in the assembly. With partial types, each source file has a complete type declaration and body. The type declaration is preceded with the *partial* keyword. The type body in each source file includes only the members that the *partial* type is contributing to the overall type. Code generators benefit from *partial* types. You can rely on the Integrated Development Environment (IDE) or wizard to generate the core code. The developer can then extend the code in a separate source file without disturbing the core code. Teams of developers collaborating on an application also benefit from *partial* types. The type can be parceled based on responsibility. Each developer works in a separate source file, which isolates changes and allows each developer to focus only on code for which he or she is directly responsible.

 Consistency is the key to partial types, with the rules as follows:

- Each partial type is preceded with the *partial* keyword.

- The partial types must have the same accessibility.

- If any partial type is sealed, the entire class is sealed.

- If any partial type is abstract, the entire class is abstract.

- Inheritance of any partial type applies to the entire class.

Here is an example of a class separated into partial types:

```
// partial1.cs

using System;

namespace Donis.CSharpBook {

    public partial class ZClass {
```

```
        public void CoreMethodA() {
            Console.WriteLine("ZClass.CoreMethodA");
        }
    }

    public class Starter {
        public static void Main() {
            ZClass obj = new ZClass();
            obj.CoreMethodA();
            obj.ExtendedMethodA();
        }
    }
}

// partial2.cs

using System;

namespace Donis.CSharpBook {


    public partial class ZClass {

        public void ExtendedMethodA() {
            Console.WriteLine("ZClass.ExtendedMethodA");
        }
    }
}
```

Figure 2-2 shows the *ZClass* in the Intermediate Language Disassembler (ILDASM) tool. It confirms that the partial types are merged into a single class.

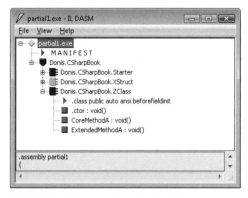

FIGURE 2-2 ZClass depicted in ILDASM

Partial Method

A *partial* method is a method that is declared in one partial class but implemented in another. There can be only one declaration and only one implementation of the partial method across the related partial classes. Partial methods have many of the same benefits of a partial class. The declaration can be provided by the code generator but implementation is completed by the developer. Partial methods must return *void* and default to private accessibility. In addition, partial methods cannot have *out* parameters. If the partial method is not implemented, the declaration and any calls to the method are removed at compile time by the compiler. This is another new feature of Visual C# 2008.

This is sample code of a partial method:

```
// corecode.cs

public partial class XClass{
    partial void ToBeImplemented();
}

// source2.cs

public partial class XClass{
    partial void ToBeImplemented() {
        Console.WriteLine("XClass.ToBeImplemented");
    }
}
```

Structures

Structures are lightweight classes. Just like classes, structures have behaviors and attributes. As a value type, structures directly contain their value and are stored on the stack. Because structures reside on the stack, keep them small. The implementation of structures in C# enforces the policy of using a structure as a lightweight class. The following list details the differences between structures and classes:

- Structures are sealed and cannot be inherited.
- Structures cannot inherit from classes or other structures.
- A structure implicitly inherits from *System.ValueType*.
- The default constructor of a structure cannot be replaced.
- Custom constructors of a structure must initialize every field of that structure.
- Structures cannot have destructors.
- Fields cannot be initialized in the declaration of the structure. However, *const* members of a structure can be initialized.

Here is the syntax of a structure:

attributes accessibility struct *identifier: interfacelist { body };*

Structures support attributes. Actually, some attributes apply to structures explicitly—check the documentation of the attribute. Structures have the same accessibility options that a class does. Structures can implement interfaces. The structure body encompasses the member functions and fields of the structure.

The default constructor of a structure initializes each field to a default value. You cannot replace the default constructor of a structure. Unlike a class, adding constructors with parameters to a structure does not remove the default constructor. Invoke a custom constructor with the *new* operator. It allows you to call a constructor other than the default constructor. The *new* operator will not place the structure on the managed heap. It is just another alternative to initializing the structure. Structures are commonly declared without the *new* operator. In that circumstance, the default constructor is called.

In the following code, *Fraction* is a structure that models a fraction. *Fraction* has two members—both doubles. The structure is small, which is ideal. The following code is an example:

```
using System;

namespace Donis.CSharpBook {

    public struct Fraction {

        public Fraction(double _divisor, double _dividend) {
            divisor = _divisor;
            dividend = _dividend;
        }

        public double quotient {
            get {
                return divisor / dividend;
            }
        }

        private double divisor;
        private double dividend;

    }

    public class Calculate {
        public static void Main() {
            Fraction number = new Fraction(4,5);
            Console.WriteLine("{0}", number.quotient);
        }
    }
}
```

Enumeration

An *enumeration* is a set of discrete and related values. You would use an enumeration if you wanted to create a variable that is limited to a set of values, such as one that represents months or one that includes a list of flags. Enumerations expand into a type where the members of the enumeration are defined as constants. The default underlying type of an enumeration is *integer*. An enumeration is never required; an integer variable can be used directly instead. However, enumerations are safer and more extensible than integer variables, and they enhance readability. In the following sample code, the *Months.GetMonth* method outputs the name of a month. The method relies on integer values:

```
public class Months {
    static public void GetMonth(int iMonth) {
        switch(iMonth) {
            case 1:
                Console.WriteLine("January");
                break;
            case 2:
                Console.WriteLine("Febuary");
                break;
            case 3:
                Console.WriteLine("March");
                break;
            // and so on...
            default:
                Console.WriteLine("Invalid Month");
                break;
        }
    }
}
```

Here is the *Months* class rewritten using enumeration. The code is simpler and more readable:

```
public enum Month {
    January = 1,
    February,
    March
}
public class Months{
    public static void GetMonth(Month m) {
        Console.WriteLine(m.ToString());
    }
}
```

Here is the syntax of an enumeration:

accessibility modifiers enum *identifier*: *basetype* { *memberlist* };

Enumerations support all accessibility. As previously mentioned, the default underlying type is *integer*. The *basetype* element changes the underlying type. The base type can be any integral type. For the *Month* enumeration, changing the underlying type from *integer* to *byte* is more efficient. The *memberlist* includes all the constants of the enumeration. By default, the constant members are numbered in textual order from zero to (*number of elements* - 1). Each member can be assigned a specific value. Successive members are incremented by 1 from that value. Here is another enumeration for *months*:

```
public enum Month: byte {
    January = 1,
    February,
    March
}
```

When assigning values to enumeration members, sequential ordering is not required. In addition, duplicate values are allowed. Some members can be set without initializing others. *ZEnum* is a mixture of explicitly and implicitly initialized members. Implicit values are listed in the comments:

```
public enum ZEnum {
    item1 = 6,
    item2 = 3,
    item3,     // 4
    item4,     // 5
    item5 = 8,
    item6      // 9
}
```

Enumerations are instances of the *System.Enum* class, which offers important services for enumeration types. Table 2-5 lists some of the more important methods.

TABLE 2-5 Important *System.Enum* methods

Method name	Description
static string GetName(Type enumtype, object value)	Returns the string representation of a specific element in the enumeration. The *ToString* method also returns the string representation of the value.
static string[ ] GetNames(Type enumtype)	Returns a string array containing the string representation of every item of the specified enumeration.
static Array GetValues(Type enumtype)	Returns an array of the underlying type. The array contains the numerical representation of each value of the enumeration.
static Type GetUnderlyingType(TypeenumType)	Returns the underlying type of the enumeration.

Bitwise Enumeration

Bitwise enumeration is for mutually inclusive flags. Each member of the enumeration is assigned a unique bitwise value. Apply the *flags* attribute to an enumeration to specify bitwise enumeration.

Combine bitwise flags using the *OR* operator (|). Confirm the existence of a flag with the bitwise *AND* operator (&).

The following code demonstrates the *[Flags]* attribute and enumeration:

```
using System;

namespace Donis.CSharpBook {

    [Flags] public enum Contribution {
        Pension = 0x01,
        ProfitSharing = 0x02,
        CreditBureau = 0x04,
        SavingsPlan = 0x08,
        All=Pension|ProfitSharing|CreditBureau|SavingsPlan
    }

    public class Employee {
        private Contribution prop_contributions;
        public Contribution contributions {
            get {
                return prop_contributions;
            }
            set {
                prop_contributions = value;
            }
        }
    }

    public class Starter {
        public static void Main() {
            Employee bob = new Employee();
            bob.contributions = Contribution.ProfitSharing|
                Contribution.CreditBureau;
            if ((bob.contributions & Contribution.ProfitSharing)
                == Contribution.ProfitSharing) {
                Console.WriteLine("Bob enrolled in profit sharing");
            }
        }
    }
}
```

Equivalence versus Identity

Equivalence depends on the value or state of an instance. Related objects that have the same value are equivalent. *Identity* is the location of an object. Objects can be equivalent but have different identities.

In the following code, integer variables *locala* and *localc* are equivalent—they contain the same value. However, the variables are not identical because they are stored at different locations on the stack. The variables *locala* and *localb* are neither equivalent nor identical. They have different values and are stored at different locations on the stack:

```
int locala = 5;
int localb = 10;
int localc = 5;
```

Assigning a value type copies the value. The target and source are equivalent after the following assignment, but they are not identical:

```
locala = localb;  // locala and localb are equivalent.
```

For reference types, there is synchronicity of equivalence and identity. Related references containing the same value are equivalent and identical because they refer to the same object. Assigning a reference to another reference creates an alias, which can create unplanned side effects. For this reason, be careful when assigning references. The following code has some unplanned side effects:

```
using System;

namespace Donis.CSharpBook {

    public class XInt {
        public int iField = 0;
    }

    public class Starter {
        public static void Main() {
            XInt obj1 = new XInt();
            obj1.iField = 5;
            XInt obj2 = new XInt();
            obj2.iField = 10;

            // Alias created and second instance lost
            obj2 = obj1;
            obj1.iField = 15; // side affect
            Console.WriteLine("{0}", obj2.iField); // Writes 15
        }
    }
}
```

The object *obj2* is assigned *obj1*. They are now both identical and equivalent. Essentially, *obj2* has become an alias for *obj1*, which means that changes to either object will affect the other.

Class Refinement

For a group of related classes, you can refactor the common code into a base class. The base class can then be inherited into one or more specific (derived) classes where the code is reused. Derived classes also are called *descendants* or *child classes*. Inheritance implies code reuse. The child classes then can extend (refine) the base class. A personnel application might have *SalariedEmployee*, *HourlyEmployee*, and *CommissionedEmployee* classes that inherit from the *Employee* class. The *Employee* class contains the common members of the *Employee* related classes. Each derived class adds methods or fields to extend and refine the base class. Inheritance and polymorphism are closely related. Polymorphism calls the correct method at run time from a base reference to a derived object. Delaying method binding to run time can provide needed flexibility. This can also add efficiencies and code clarity to an application.

Inheritance and polymorphism are discussed in the next chapter.

Chapter 3
Inheritance

Inheritance is a "is a kind of" relationship and the cornerstone of object-oriented programming. For example, a rectangle, an ellipse, and a triangle are "a kind of" shape. Without inheritance, you would have to fully and independently implement the *rectangle, ellipse, and triangle* classes. It is better to extrapolate the common elements of any shape and place those elements into a general class. That general class then can be inherited into the specific shape classes. This avoids having to implement the same code in every shape class. Code reuse is one of the primary benefits of inheritance. The general class is called a *base class*. The specific classes, such as *rectangle, ellipse,* and *triangle,* are considered *derived classes*. The base class contains the common members of the related types, which are inherited by a derived class.

A base type represents a generalization, whereas a derived type represents a specialty. Specialties are derivatives of generalizations. A personnel program, for instance, might contain different types of employees, such as hourly, salaried, commissioned, temporary, and retired. Each type is distinct from every other employee specialization. *Employee* is a generalization of all employees and is therefore the base class. Conversely, *HourlyEmployee, SalariedEmployee, CommissionedEmployee, TemporaryEmployee,* and *RetiredEmployee* are specializations and are therefore derived classes. The derived class inherits the members of the base class and adds new members specific to the derived class. The new members of the derived class extend the base class and create a specialty, which can be further specialized through inheritance.

For example, all employees must have a name and an employee identifier. Every employee also should be able to report his or her name and employee identifier. Because this is common to all employees, the name, employee identifier, and related behavior should be placed in a base class (e.g., *Employee*). *SalariedEmployee,* a derived class, would inherit from the *Employee* base class and add members for salary, number of pay periods, and related behavior. The *HourlyEmployee* class would inherit from the *Employee* class and add members for hourly rate, number of hours worked, and related behavior.

Inheritance provides hierarchical clarity. The *Employee* class and the derived types form a hierarchy. A real-world example is the .NET Framework Class Library (FCL), which contains hundreds of classes. The FCL is organized along namespaces and inheritance. Without inheritance, it would be harder to navigate the FCL. A great example is the *SocketException* class. Figure 3-1 shows the hierarchy of the *SocketException* class. It is helpful to know that all exception classes start with *System.Exception*.

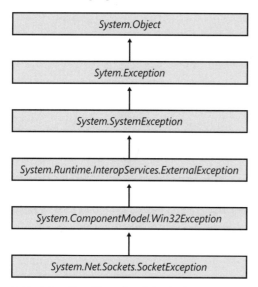

FIGURE 3-1 Class hierarchy of the *SocketException* class

Classes can inherit from a single class and one or more interfaces. When inheriting from a class, the derived class inherits the members—including the code—of the base class. Destructors and constructors are not inherited from the base class. Inheriting an interface is a contract. The derived class contracts to implement every member of the interface, and the interface commits to being immutable. This is important because any change to the interface would break the derived type. Value types and primitives are sealed and cannot be inherited by new classes. For example, you cannot create a class that inherits from an integer type (*int*).

Terminology is important. Accurate terminology enhances a conversation, whereas incorrect or unclear terminology muddles the discussion. Object-oriented analysis and design introduced a plethora of new terms, some of which are identical or similar. Some terms are intended for design, whereas others are for the implementation phase. However, this distinction is often lost. Table 3-1 shows a list of terms similar to base and derived types. In this chapter, the *base/derived* and *parent/child* terms are used interchangeably.

TABLE 3-1 Inheritance terminology

Inheritable class	Inheriting class
superclass	subclass
parent	child
ascendant	descendant
base	derived

Inheritance is not a mechanism to simply drop members into a class. From a design perspective, those members should belong in that class. For example, a timestamp has the properties of time and a stamp. A timestamp is a kind of stamp and has a time element. However, a timestamp is not a kind of time. A *TimeStamp* class should inherit from the *Stamp* class but not from the *Time* class. The "is a" relationship between a timestamp and a stamp implies inheritance. The "has a" relationship between the timestamp and time implies containment. Deriving a *TimeStamp* class from a *Stemp* class and embedding a *Time* class in the *TimeStamp* class is the preferable implementation.

Inheritance Example

Before reviewing the specifics of inheritance, an example might be helpful. In the following code, *XParent* is the base class. *XChild* is the derived class and inherits from the *XParent* class. The inheritance operator (:) is used to indicate inheritance. *XChild* inherits a method, property, and field from the base class. *XChild* extends *XParent* by adding a method and field. For this reason, *XChild* has five members: three from the base and two from itself. In *Main*, instances of the *XParent* and *XChild* classes are created. Base methods are called on the *XParent* instance. An instance of a child class combines members of both the base and derived classes. Therefore, the base and added methods are available on the *XChild* instance. Look at the following code example:

```
using System;

namespace Donis.CSharpBook {
    public class Starter {
        public static void Main() {

            XParent parent = new XParent();
            parent.MethodA();
            XChild child = new XChild();
            child.MethodA();
            child.MethodB();
            child.FieldA = 10;
            Console.WriteLine(child.FieldA);
            Console.WriteLine(child.fieldB);
        }

        public class XParent {
            public void MethodA() {
                Console.WriteLine("XParent.MethodA called from {0}.",
                    this.GetType().ToString());
            }

            private int propFieldA;

            public int FieldA {
                get {
                    return propFieldA;
                }
                set {
```

```
                        propFieldA = value;
                }
            }

        }

        public class XChild : XParent {
            public int MethodB() {
                Console.WriteLine("XChild.MethodB called from {0}.",
                    this.GetType().ToString());
                return fieldB;
            }

            public int fieldB = 5;
        }
    }
}
```

Cross-Language Inheritance

Inheritance in .NET is language-agnostic. Prior to .NET, there was no cross-language inheritance. You cannot create a class in C++ and then inherit that class in Microsoft Visual Basic. In .NET, classes written in one managed language can inherit a class of another managed language. Cross-language inheritance offers many benefits. Team members collaborating on a product can develop in the language of their choice. The entire team is not forced to adopt the same source language. You can use a third-party class library even if written in a different managed language.

All .NET or managed languages compile to Microsoft Intermediate Language (MSIL) code. This means ultimately, regardless of the language, .NET code compiles to a unified language. The Common Language Runtime (CLR) does not perceive a Visual Basic .NET class inheriting from a C# class. It interprets one MSIL class inheriting from another MSIL class.

Cross-language inheritance assumes that both the base and derived classes adhere to the Common Language Specification (CLS). If not, there is no guarantee that cross-language inheritance will work. For example, the following class, although perfectly okay in C#, is incompatible with Visual Basic .NET. Visual Basic .NET is case-insensitive, making *MethodA* in the following code ambiguous:

```
public class XBase {
    public void MethodA() {
    }
    public void methoda() {
    }
}
```

The following code is an example of successful cross-language inheritance. The base class is written in C#, whereas the derived class is written in Visual Basic .NET:

```csharp
// C# Code: which includes base class

using System;

namespace Donis.CSharpBook {
    public class XParent {
        public void MethodA() {
            Console.WriteLine("XParent.MethodA called from {0}.",
                this.GetType().ToString());
        }

        private int propFieldA;

        public int FieldA {
            get {
                    return propFieldA;
            }
            set {
                    propFieldA = value;
            }
        }
    }
}
```

```vbnet
' VB Code: which includes derived class.

Imports System
Imports Donis.CSharpBook

Namespace Donis.CSharpBook
    Public Class Starter
        Public Shared Sub Main
            Dim child as New XChild
            child.MethodA()
            child.MethodB()
        End Sub
    End Class

    Public Class XChild
        Inherits XParent

        Public Sub MethodB
            Console.WriteLine("XChild.MethodB called from {0}.", _
                Me.GetType().ToString())
        End Sub
    End Class
End Namespace
```

Compile the code from the command line with these compiler commands:

```
csc /target:library librarycs.cs
```

```
vbc /reference:librarycs.dll applicationvb.vb
```

System.Object

System.Object is the ubiquitous base type. All classes and structures inherit from *System. Object*, either directly or indirectly. *System.Object* encompasses the baseline behavior of all managed types. Reference types without an explicit base class inherit from *System.Object* implicitly. Reference types that explicitly inherit from another type still inherit from *System. Object*, but indirectly. You can inherit from *System.Object* explicitly. However, that is somewhat redundant and therefore is not often seen. Value types inherit from *System.ValueType*, which in turn inherits from *System.Object*. *System.ValueType* overrides *System.Object* members to implement the semantics of a value type.

The members of the *System.Object* class are explained in Table 3-2.

TABLE 3-2 *System.Object* **methods**

Method	Description
Constructor	*public Object( )*
	This is the default constructor of the *System.Object* class. It is called whenever an instance of any object is created. The *object* keyword is an alias for the *System.Object* type.
Equals	*public virtual bool Equals(object obj)*
	public static bool Equals(object obj1, object obj2)
	Equals returns true if the value of two objects is equal (in the case of the single-argument form, the value of *obj* is compared to the instance on which the method is called). For reference types, identities are compared. For value types, the values are compared, which is an equivalency test. This method can be overridden to implement a custom comparison.
Finalize	*protected virtual void Finalize()*
	In the *Finalize* method, cleanup for unmanaged resources takes place. *Finalize* is called during garbage collection. In C#, the destructor is equivalent to the *Finalize* method. Destructors and the finalization process are discussed in Chapter 18, "Memory Management."
GetHashCode	*public virtual int GetHashCode()*
	This method returns the hash code of an instance. The default hash code is not guaranteed to be unique or to have even distribution. You can override this method to return a meaningful hash code for a derived type or provide better distribution. For example, the *Employee* class could override *GetHashCode* to return the employee ID as the hash code.

TABLE 3-2 *System.Object* **methods**

Method	Description
GetType	*public Type GetType()* *GetType* returns a *Type* reference, which is useful for examining a type at runtime. This is called *reflection*. Reflection is discussed in Chapter 13, "Metadata and Reflection."
MemberwiseClone	*protected object MemberwiseClone()* This method returns a cloned instance of the current object. It performs a shallow copy. Members that are reference types in the original object will point to the same objects as members in the cloned object, which can lead to side effects.
ReferenceEquals	*public static bool ReferenceEquals(object obj1, object obj2)* This method returns true if the identity of two objects is the same.
ToString	*public virtual string ToString()* This method returns a string representation of the current instance. The default result is the type name of the current instance. *ToString* is frequently overridden to return useful information about an instance. For the *Employee* class, *ToString* could be overridden to return the employee name.

Object.Equals Method

For reference types, the *Object.Equals* method compares identity. In the default implementation of this method, references are equal when pointing to the same object; references that point to different objects are not equal even if they have the same state. You can override the *Equals* method to perform a value comparison. For value types, the *Equals* method is already overridden to compare values.

In *Applied Microsoft .NET Framework Programming* (Microsoft Press, 2001), author Jeffrey Richter mentions four tenets of the *Equals* method: reflexivity, symmetry, transitivity, and consistency. These rules are important when overriding the Equals method. Breaking one of these rules can cause unexpected results.

- **Reflexivity**   An object is always equal to itself. The *obj1.Equal(obj1)* call always must return *true*.

- **Symmetry**   If *obj1.Equals(obj2)* is *true*, then *obj2.Equals(obj1)* also must be *true*.

- **Transitivity**   If *obj1.Equals(obj2)* and *obj2.Equals(obj3)* are both *true*, then *obj3. Equals(obj1)* also must be *true*.

- **Consistency**   If *obj1.Equals(obj2)* is *true*, then *obj1.Equals(obj2)* must always be *true* as long as the state of neither object has changed.

This code shows the override of the *Equals* method in the *Employee* class:

```
public static bool operator==(Employee obj1, Employee obj2) {
    return obj1.Equals(obj2);
}

public static bool operator!=(Employee obj1, Employee obj2) {
    return !obj1.Equals(obj2);
}

public override bool Equals(object obj) {
    Employee _obj = obj as Employee;

    if (obj == null) {
        return false;
    }
    return this.GetHashCode()==_obj.GetHashCode();
}
```

The preceding code overrides the *Equals, operator==*, and *operator!=* methods. The default implementation of these operators will not call the overridden *Equals* method. This can cause inconsistencies, where the comparison operators behave differently from the explicit *Equals* method. For this reason, both operators have been overridden.

When overriding the *Equals* method, you also should override the *GetHashCode* method. If you do not, a compiler warning occurs. Objects that are equal should have the same hash code, so that equality can be based on comparing hash codes. In the *Equals* method, call *GetHashCode* to retrieve and compare hash codes.

Object.GetHashCode Method

GetHashCode returns a hash code as an integer. Override this method to return a unique identifier for an instance. As indicated in the previous section, the *Equals* and *GetHashCode* methods should be implemented in tandem.

The data used to calculate a hash code should be constant. If not, when the data changes, the hash code also changes. This could cause problems, particularly if the hash code is used as a key in a collection. If the key dynamically changes, the original key is stale. Stale keys can cause conflicts in a collection. For this reason, data related to the hash code should not change.

The following code overrides the *GetHashCode* method for the *Employee* class. The *EmplID* field used for the hash is read-only. After the *Employee* instance is created, *EmplID* cannot be modified. This adheres to the requirement that the hash code be constant. There are a variety of algorithms for creating efficient and distributed hash codes—some quite complex. For simplicity, in the following example, *GetHashCode* simply returns the *EmplID* property:

```
public override int GetHashCode() {
    return EmplID;
}
```

Object.GetType Method

The *GetType* method returns a *Type* object. This *Type* instance can be used to perform reflection on the related object. Members of the *Type* class, such as *GetMethods*, *GetFields*, and other similar methods, return information on the object.

The following code demonstrates reflection. In the code, the public methods of *System. Object* are enumerated and displayed. As expected, the methods of Table 3-2 are displayed. The exception is the *Object.MemberwiseClone* method, which is not a public method:

```
using System;
using System.Collections;
using System.Reflection;

namespace Donis.CSharpBook {

    public class Starter {
        public static void Main() {
            Object obj = new Object();
            Type t = obj.GetType();
            foreach (MethodInfo m in t.GetMethods()) {
                Console.WriteLine(m.Name);
            }
        }
    }
}
```

Object.ToString Method

The *ToString* method returns a string representation of an instance. The default return value is the fully qualified name of the type. The *ToString* method of a primitive value type is already overridden to display a string representation of the value. The following code displays the default string representation of a value type and of a reference type:

```
int locala = 10;
Console.WriteLine(locala.ToString());  // Writes 10
Object obj = new Object();
Console.WriteLine(obj.ToString());     // Writes System.Object
```

For the *Employee* class, *ToString* could be overridden to return the name of the employee:

```
public override string ToString() {
  return FullName;
}
```

Object.MemberwiseClone Method

MemberwiseClone returns a new instance of an object. A shallow copy is performed. An object is cloned by performing a bitwise copy of each member. If a member is a value type, the values are copied and there is no side effect. For a member that is a reference type, the member reference—not the member object—is copied. The result is that the reference members of the new instance are aliases for the corresponding members in the original object, as shown in Figure 3-2. Changes in the objects referenced by these members will affect the same objects for both the original and cloned object.

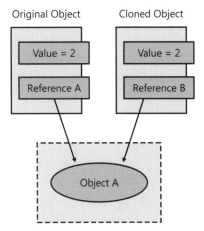

FIGURE 3-2 The result of *MemberwiseClone*

MemberwiseClone is protected and cannot be overridden. The method is called from a derived class when implementing the *ICloneable* interface. The *ICloneable* interface defines an interface for cloning objects. The only member is the *ICloneable.Clone* method.

The following code shows the implementation of the *ICloneable.Clone* method in the *Employee* class. To clone an object, the *MemberwiseClone* method is called in *ICloneable. Clone*. In the *Employee* class (shown in full in the section titled "*Employee* Class," later in this chapter), *propFirst* and *propLast* are a member and a reference type. Cloning the object would copy the references of *propFirst* and *propLast* but not their values. In *Main*, *obj2* is cloned from *obj1*. The hash of both objects confirms different identities. Nonetheless, changes to the employee name of one object affects both, which is a nasty side effect of *MemberwiseClone*. Both objects reference the same name in memory:

```
using System;
public class Starter {
    public static void Main() {
        Employee obj1 = new Employee(5678);
        Employee obj2 = (Employee) obj1.Clone();
        obj1.Last = "Marshall";
        obj2.First = "Donis";
         Console.WriteLine("Obj1 HC " +
            obj1.GetHashCode().ToString());
        Console.WriteLine(obj1.EmplID + ": " + obj1.FullName); // 5678: Donis Marshall
        Console.WriteLine("Obj2 HC " +
            obj2.GetHashCode().ToString());
```

```
        Console.WriteLine(obj2.EmpID + ": " + obj2.FullName); // 5678: Donis Marshall
    }
}

class Employee : ICloneable {

    public Employee(int id) {
        if ((id < 1000) || (id > 9999)) {
            throw new Exception(
                "Invalid Employee ID");
        }

        propID = id;
    }

    public object Clone() {
        return MemberwiseClone();
    }
// end of partial listing...
```

Object.ReferenceEquals Method

The *ReferenceEquals* method compares identity. If the objects are the same, *ReferenceEquals* returns *true*. Otherwise, *false* is returned. *ReferenceEquals* is not virtual and cannot be overridden in the derived class. The following code compares an original object and a cloned object, as detailed in the section titled *"Object.MemberwiseClone* Method," later in this chapter. The objects have the same state but different identities. Because the identities are distinct, the *ReferenceEquals* method returns *false:*

```
Employee obj1 = new Employee(5678);
Employee obj2 = (Employee) obj1.Clone();
if (Employee.ReferenceEquals(obj1, obj2)) {
    Console.WriteLine("objects identical");
}
else {
    Console.WriteLine("objects not identical");
}
```

Employee Class

The following code includes the complete listing of the *Employee* class, including the overridden methods of the *System.Object* class. This reviews many of the topics already mentioned in this chapter:

```
using System;
using System.Collections;

namespace Donis.CSharpBook {
```

```csharp
public class Starter {
    public static void Main() {
        Employee obj1 = new Employee(5678);
        Employee obj2 = new Employee(5678);
        if (obj1 == obj2) {
            Console.WriteLine("equals");
        }
        else {
            Console.WriteLine("not equals");
        }
    }
}

class Employee {

    public Employee(int id) {
        if ((id < 1000) || (id > 9999)) {
            throw new Exception(
                "Invalid Employee ID");
        }

        propID = id;
    }

    public static bool operator==(Employee obj1, Employee obj2) {
        return obj1.Equals(obj2);
    }

    public static bool operator!=(Employee obj1, Employee obj2) {
        return !obj1.Equals(obj2);
    }

    public override bool Equals(object obj) {
        Employee _obj = obj as Employee;

        if (obj == null) {
            return false;
        }
        return this.GetHashCode() == _obj.GetHashCode();
    }

    public override int GetHashCode() {
        return EmplID;
    }

    public string FullName {
        get {
            return propFirst + " " +
                propLast;
        }
    }

    private string propFirst;
    public string First {
        get {
```

```
                return propFirst;
            }
            set {
                propFirst = value;
            }
        }

        private string propLast;
        public string Last {
            get {
                return propLast;
            }
            set {
                propLast = value;
            }
        }

        private readonly int propID;
        public int EmplID {
            get {
                return propID;
            }
        }

        public override string ToString() {
            return FullName;
        }
    }
}
```

Implementing Inheritance

Inheritance involves a base class and a derived class. The derived class inherits from the base class. With few exceptions, members of the base class are inherited into the derived type. Derived classes can override inherited members and add new members to extend the base class.

Here is the inheritance syntax:

```
class derivedclass: baseclass, interface1, interface2, …,  interfacen {
    body
}
```

In the class header, the inheritance operator (:) indicates inheritance and is followed by the inheritance list. The inheritance list is a comma-delimited list that includes a maximum of one base class and any number of interfaces. Classes are limited to inheriting a single class. However, a class can implement multiple interfaces. C++ developers are familiar with multiple base-class inheritance. Omitting this feature from C# was an important design decision. First, multiple inheritance was never that popular. Second, multiple inheritance often causes more problems than it resolves. Third, multiple inheritance introduces the potential for member ambiguity.

A base type must have the same or greater accessibility as the derived type. A compiler error occurs in the following code because the accessibility of the base class is narrower than the derived class, which is an error:

```
internal class ZClass {
}
public class YClass : ZClass { // Error
}
```

.NET supports only public inheritance. C++ supports public, protected, and private inheritance. Despite this flexibility in C++, practically all inheritance is public inheritance. Most C++ developers were not familiar with or ever used any other kind of inheritance. Thus, protected and private inheritance probably will not be missed.

Accessibility

Accessibility sets the visibility of members to the outside world and to derived types. Members are always visible in the current or containing type. Table 3-3 describes member accessibility.

TABLE 3-3 Member accessibility

Member access modifier	Outside world	Derived class
public	Yes	Yes
private	No	No
protected	No	Yes
internal	Yes (this assembly)	Yes (this assembly)
internal protected	Yes (this assembly)	Yes

Are private members of the base class inherited? Private members indeed are inherited, but they are not visible or directly accessible in the derived class. These members are accessible through the public and protected functions also inherited from the base class. Therefore, a derived type has two realms of private members. One realm includes private members that are defined in a derived class. These members are visible in the derived type. The other realm includes inherited private members, which are not visible to the derived type.

Overriding Inherited Behavior

A derived class can override behavior inherited from the base class, which allows a derived type to apply more specific behavior. The *Pay* method of the *Employee* class is overridden in *CommissionedEmployee* to consider commissions when calculating a paycheck. In the *SalariedEmployee* class, the *Pay* method is overridden to calculate pay by prorating annual income. Methods, properties, indexers, and events can be overridden. Fields and static members cannot be overridden. However, they can be hidden in the derived class.

Can a child override a member of the parent at any time? With human beings, most parents hope that their children inherit and observe their recommended behavior. However, the behavior of the parent is merely a suggestion to the children. Children often are inclined to override the behavior of the parent, and the parent is helpless to prevent this. In many object-oriented languages, that is essentially the model. Child or derived classes can, without restriction, override the behavior of the parent or the base class. This openness means a derived class can inappropriately override a behavior and break the code inherited from the base class. This is called the *fragile base class problem:* a problem that is acute with class libraries, where a child class is more likely to unknowingly or incorrectly override a base member. The model is different in C#. By default, methods cannot be overridden. Parent classes identify members that are available for overriding. In addition, the child class must acknowledge its intent to override the method. This prevents the child from inadvertently overriding a member of the base class.

Virtual and *Override* Keywords

The *virtual* keyword indicates that a member is a candidate for being overridden in a derived class. *Virtual* can be applied to methods, properties, indexers, and events. In the derived class, the *override* keyword indicates an intention to override a virtual member of the base class. The *virtual* and *override* keywords complement each other. The *virtual* keyword propagates to all descendants. This means that the *virtual* method is overridable in not just the most immediate derived class, but in all descendants.

Overriding is not an all-or-nothing condition. Using the *base* keyword, the *public* and *protected* members of the base class are accessible in the derived type. The syntax is as follows:

`base.member`

You cannot skip levels of class hierarchy with the *base* keyword. For example, you cannot access a member in a grandfather class. Syntax such as *base.base.member* is illegal. With the *base* keyword, you can have both the derived and base behavior. In the overridden method, simply call the base behavior using the *base* keyword. This is demonstrated in the following code. With the *base* keyword, the *SalariedEmployee.Pay* method calls the *Employee.Pay* method to display an employee name on a paycheck:

```
public class Employee : ICloneable {

    public Employee() {
    }

    public Employee(int id) {
        if ((id < 1000) || (id > 9999)) {
            throw new Exception(
                "Invalid Employee ID");
```

```
        }

        propID = id;
    }

    public virtual void Pay() {
        Console.WriteLine("Employee: " + FullName);
    }

    // partial listing
}

public class SalariedEmployee: Employee {

    public override void Pay() {
        base.Pay();
        Console.WriteLine("Pay is: {0,6:c}",
            propSalary / (decimal) propPeriods);
    }

    // partial listing

}
```

Overload versus Override

Override and overload are different concepts. When a member of a base class is overridden, the signature of the base and the signature of the derived member are identical. Overloading requires different signatures. In a derived class, a function can be overloaded, overridden, or both. When a member is overridden with a different signature, a compiler error occurs in the derived type. This prevents an accidental overload, when method overriding was intended. This is shown in the following code, where *MethodA* is overloaded in the *YClass* class but not overridden. In *Main*, both the base and the derived implementation are called:

```
using System;

namespace Donis.CSharpBook {

    public class Starter {
        public static void Main() {
            YClass obj = new YClass();
            obj.MethodA();
            obj.MethodA(10);
        }
    }


    public class ZClass {
        public virtual void MethodA() {
            Console.WriteLine("ZClass.MethodA");
        }
    }
}
```

```
public class YClass : ZClass
{
    public override void MethodA(int a) {
        Console.WriteLine("YClass.MethodA");
    }

}
}
```

Overriding Events

Events are implemented using an *add* and *remove* method pair. The following is sample code for overriding an event. Events are discussed in detail in Chapter 10, "Delegates and Events."

```
public class ZClass {

    public virtual void MethodA() {
    }

    public delegate void MyDel();
    public virtual event MyDel MyEvent {
        add {
        }
        remove {
        }
    }
}

public class YClass : ZClass {

    public override event MyDel MyEvent {
        add {
            // different implementation
        }
        remove {
            // different implementation
        }
    }
}
```

Extension Method

Microsoft Visual C# 2008 provides integers as a primitive type. What if the integer type (or any type, for that matter) is inadequate for your purposes? You might want to extend the interface of that type to include additional behavior. That is the purpose of extension methods. An extension method extends the interface of an object, which allows you to extend the otherwise closed interface of a type.

Extension methods are defined as static methods in a static class. The first parameter of the extension method must be the *this* keyword followed by the type of the target object. The type defines where the extension method can be applied. You can call the extension method on an object of that type, just as you would call a normal method.

Here is sample code of an extension method. In the sample code, extension methods are created for an integer type. The extension methods return *true* or *false* depending on whether the integer is an odd or even number:

```
static class IntegerExtensions {
    public static bool IsOdd(this int number) {
        return (number % 2) == 0 ? false : true;
    }

    public static bool IsEven(this int number) {
        return (number % 2) == 0 ? true : false;
    }
}
class Startup {
    public static void Main() {
        bool result = 6.IsOdd();
        if (result) {
            Console.WriteLine("odd");
        }
        else{
            Console.WriteLine("even");
        }
    }
}
```

Extension methods also can be applied to interfaces. Then you can use the extension method on any object that implements that interface. In the following code, two extension methods are defined for the *IDisposable* interface. The methods are fairly straightforward as to their purpose. In Main, the *DisposeAndTrace* extension method is called on the instance of a *ZClass*, which implements the *IDisposable* interface. The *IDisposable* extensions can be called on any object that implements the *IDisposable* interface:

```
static class DisposableExtensions {
    public static void DisposeAndCollect(this IDisposable obj) {
        obj.Dispose();
        GC.Collect();
    }

    public static void DisposeAndTrace(this IDisposable obj) {
        obj.Dispose();
        System.Diagnostics.Debug.WriteLine("Disposed " + obj.ToString());
    }
}

class ZClass : IDisposable {
    public void Dispose() {
        // cleanup resources
    }
}
```

```
class Startup {
    public static void Main() {
        ZClass obj = new ZClass();
        obj.DisposeAndTrace();
    }
}
```

The following additional rules pertain to extension methods:

■ If an instance method and extension method have identical signatures, the instance method is called.

■ If two extension methods have identical signatures, either extension method must be called as a normal static method.

■ The static class of the extension method must be within scope. If it is not, the extension method cannot be called.

The *new* Modifier

The *new* modifier hides the specified member of the base class. The *new* modifier is the default modifier when a member is repeated (with the same signature) in the derived type. However, unless the *new* keyword is enunciated, a compiler warning is presented to prevent the accidental hiding of a member of the base class. Explicit use of the *new* keyword avoids the warning. A *virtual* member and *override* member are related, which is important to polymorphism. The derived member with the *new* modifier and the base member are unrelated.

.NET supports hide-by-signature and hide-by-name techniques. C# supports only hide-by-signature, where a single member is hidden using the *new* modifier. Hide-by-name hides the entire interface of a member, which may entail several functions. This feature is available in Visual Basic .NET.

In the following code, *ZClass* is the base class and contains *MethodA* and *MethodB* members. Both are virtual methods, where *MethodB* calls *MethodA*:

```
public virtual void MethodB() {
    MethodA();
}
```

YClass is a derived class and inherits from *ZClass*. *MethodA* is overridden in the derived type, but *MethodB* is not overridden. Therefore, two versions of *MethodA* exist: a base version and a derived version. When *YClass.MethodB* is called, which version of *MethodA* is invoked in the method? Because *MethodA* is virtual, the most derived method is called. *YClass.MethodA* is invoked. With a virtual method, the compiler prefers the most derived method.

Here is the code:

```
using System;
```

```
namespace Donis.CSharpBook {

    public class Starter {
        public static void Main() {
            YClass obj = new YClass();
            obj.MethodB();  // Writes YClass.MethodA
        }
    }


    public class ZClass {
        public virtual void MethodA() {
            Console.WriteLine("ZClass.MethodA");
        }

        public virtual void MethodB() {
            MethodA();
        }
    }

    public class YClass : ZClass
    {
        public override void MethodA() {
            Console.WriteLine("YClass.MethodA");
        }
    }
}
```

The following code is almost identical to the previous code. However, *ZClass.MethodA* is not overridden in the derived class. The *new* modifier defines a new *MethodA* in the derived class that is unrelated to *MethodA* of the base class. Because *ZClass.MethodA* and *YClass. MethodA* now are unrelated, methods inherited from a base class cannot call the derived *MethodA* implicitly. Instead, the nearest related method in an ascendant class is called. In the example, the nearest related *MethodA* is in the base class. Therefore, the compiler will not delegate to *YClass.MethodA*. For this reason, *YClass.MethodB* calls *ZClass.MethodA*. This prevents functions inherited by the derived class from calling unrelated functions, which could cause the fragile base class problem:

```
using System;

namespace Donis.CSharpBook {

    public class Starter {
        public static void Main() {
            YClass obj = new YClass();
            obj.MethodB();  // Writes ZClass.MethodA
        }
    }

    class ZClass {
        public virtual void MethodA() {
```

```
                Console.WriteLine("ZClass.MethodA");
        }

        public virtual void MethodB() {
            MethodA();
        }
    }

    class YClass : ZClass {
        public new void MethodA() {
            Console.WriteLine("YClass.MethodA");
        }
    }
}
```

Interestingly, although the *new* modifier hides the base class member, you still can access the base class implementation with the *base* keyword (shown in bold type in the following code). This is demonstrated here:

```
public class ZClass {
    public virtual void MethodA() {
        Console.WriteLine("ZClass.MethodA");
    }
}

public class YClass : ZClass
{
    public new void MethodA() {
        base.MethodA();
        Console.WriteLine("YClass.MethodA");
    }
}
```

Virtual methods are overridable in all descendants. However, the *new* modifier stops the method from being virtual at that point in the hierarchy. The *new* modifier means the derived member replaces the base member in its entirety—this includes any modifiers. A method can be declared with both *new* and *virtual* modifiers. In that circumstance, the method hides the base method and the replacement method is also virtual.

The following code demonstrates that a member with the *new* modifier, but without the *virtual* modifier, cannot be overridden. The *virtual* modifier of the base class does not extend to the same method with the *new* modifier.

```
public class ZClass {
    public virtual void MethodA() {
    }

    public virtual void MethodB() {
    }
}
```

```
public class YClass : ZClass {
    public new virtual void MethodA() {
    }

    public new void MethodB() {
    }

}

public class XClass : YClass {
    public override void MethodA() {
    }

    /*   ERROR

    public override void MethodB() {
    }
    */
}
```

In the preceding code, *XClass.MethodB* causes a compiler error. *XClass* inherits from *YClass*. In *YClass*, *MethodB* is replaced but not tagged with the *virtual* modifier. Therefore, *XClass. MethodB* cannot override *YClass.MethodB*. *XClass.MethodA* can override *YClass.MethodA* because *YClass.MethodA* has both the *new* and *virtual* modifiers.

Data members or static members in a base class cannot be overridden in a derived class. However, both can be hidden with the *new* modifier. Hiding data members and static members can cause confusion. When you use this feature, thoroughly document your code.

In the following code, *ZClass* has a static method and a static field. Their purpose is to count *ZClass* instances. *YClass* inherits *ZClass* and hides the two static members of the base type. The new members count the instances of *YClass*. Therefore, there are simultaneous counts— the base class and derived class counters. In *Main*, multiple instances of *ZClass* and *YClass* are created. Both counters are then displayed:

```
using System;

namespace Donis.CSharpBook {

    public class Starter {
        public static void Main() {
            ZClass obj1 = new ZClass();
            YClass obj2 = new YClass();
            YClass obj3 = new YClass();
            ZClass.DisplayCounter();
            YClass.DisplayCounter();
        }
    }


    public class ZClass {
        public ZClass() {
```

```
            ++count;
        }

        public static int count = 0;
        public static void DisplayCounter() {
            Console.WriteLine("ZClass.Count:");
            Console.WriteLine(count);
        }

    }

    public class YClass : ZClass
    {
        public YClass() {
            ++count;
        }

        private new static int count = 0;

        public new static void DisplayCounter() {
            Console.WriteLine("YClass count:");
            Console.WriteLine(count);
        }
    }
}
```

Abstract Classes

Abstract classes represent intangible entities. Object-oriented applications should model the real world, which is full of intangible concepts. For example, a geometric shape is a concept. Have you even seen a geometric shape? No. Rather, you have seen specific shapes, such as triangles, ellipses, rectangles, and lines. *Geometric shape* is a description of an intangible concept —a kind of shape. Conversely, a rectangle is tangible: a television, a box, and this book are actual rectangles.

The *Employee* class presented in this section is an abstract class. Why? *Employee* is not tangible. You do not hire a generic employee. Instead, you hire a specific kind of employee: an hourly, salaried, or commissioned employee. The *Employee* class represents the generic employee, while *HourlyEmployee, SalariedEmployee,* and *CommissionedEmployee* classes represent specific, tangible employees. Abstract classes also are typically incomplete. Because an abstract class is incomplete, you cannot create an instance of that type. For example, the *Employee* class has no method for paying an employee. It is incomplete and correctly marked as abstract.

The *abstract* keyword makes a class abstract. Abstract classes exist primarily for inheritance. You cannot create an instance of an abstract class. Nonabstract classes are concrete classes. You can create an instance of a concrete class. Static classes, value types, and interfaces do not support the abstract modifier.

In the next example, *Employee* is the base class and is abstract. *HourlyEmployee* is the derived class and is concrete. Since *Employee* is abstract, you cannot create a new instance. A compiler error will occur if you attempt to create an instance of the *Employee* class:

```
public class Starter {
    public static void Main() {
        Employee obj1 = new Employee();              // Not valid
        HourlyEmployee obj2 = new HourlyEmployee();  // Valid
    }
}

public abstract class Employee { // abstract
}

public class HourlyEmployee : Employee {  // concrete
}
```

Member functions also can be abstract. Methods, properties, indexers, and events can be abstract. A class with one or more abstract members must be abstract as well. An abstract member has a signature but no function body. The *virtual* keyword is implied with abstract functions because an abstract function member must be overridden and implemented in the derived type. Finally, static members cannot be abstract.

In the real world, a parent can ask a child to do something with or without instructions. The parent can provide instruction to the child to complete the task. Alternatively, the child must complete the task without help—the parent does not provide any directions. In this case, the parent does not care about the details of the implementation. An abstract function is an example of the latter. Abstract methods are a means of assuring that derived types (children) implement required methods. The derived type inherits no implementation (instructions) from the base type (parent). If the derived type is concrete, it must implement all inherited abstract functions. If not, the derived type is incomplete and in error.

In the following code, the *Employee* class mandates that derived types implement the *CalculatePay* method. Because the class contains an abstract method, the *Employee* class also must be abstract:

```
public abstract class Employee {
    public virtual void Pay() {
    }

    public abstract void CalculatePay();
}

public class HourlyEmployee : Employee {
    public override void Pay() {
        CalculatePay();
    }

    public override void CalculatePay() {
    }
}
```

Here is an example of an abstract property:

```
public abstract class ZClass {
    public abstract int PropA {
        get;
        set;
    }
}

public class YClass : ZClass {
    public override int PropA {
        get {
            return 0;
        }
        set {
        }
    }
}
```

Sealed Classes

Sealed classes are the reverse of abstract classes. While abstract classes are inherited and re-fined in the derived type, sealed classes cannot be inherited. A sealed class cannot be refined any further. An abstract class is "abstract" (which perhaps goes without saying), while a sealed class is concrete. You can create instances of a sealed class. Sealed classes are terminating nodes in a class hierarchy, while an abstract class is typically near the top of a class hierarchy. A sealed class is used to prevent further refinement through inheritance. For example, I am a developer of a class library. Some of the classes in the class library are extensible. However, other classes are intended to be used "as is." Those classes are marked as sealed.

The *sealed* modifier also can be used with instance methods, properties, events, and indexers. Static members do not support the *sealed* modifier. A *sealed* member can override a *virtual* member, such as a *virtual* or *abstract* member. However, a *sealed* member itself cannot be overridden, but a *sealed* member can be hidden in a derived type with the *new* modifier.

The following code demonstrates a *sealed* member. In this example, the *HourlyEmployee.Pay* method cannot be overridden:

```
public abstract class Employee {
    public virtual void Pay() {
    }

    public abstract void CalculatePay();
}
```

```
public class HourlyEmployee : Employee {
    public sealed override void Pay() {
        CalculatePay();
    }

    public override void CalculatePay() {
    }
}
```

Constructors and Destructors

Constructors and destructors in a base class are not inherited in the derived class. A derived class has a base portion and a derived portion. The base constructor initializes the base portion, and the constructor of the derived class initializes the derived portion. For the derived object, the default constructor of the base class is called by default to initialize the state of the base class. If the base class does not have a default constructor, a compiler error occurs unless the derived class calls a constructor in the base class that has parameters. In the following code, *ZClass* does not have a default constructor. A compiler error will occur:

```
public class ZClass {
    public ZClass(int param) {
    }
}

public class YClass : ZClass {
}
```

You might want to use something other then the default constructor for the base portion of a derived class. In the derived class, you can call a constructor other than the default constructor in the base class. These constructors can be called from the derived class using a constructor initializer list. The initializer list applies only to instance constructors of a derived type.

Here is the constructor initializer syntax:

accessibility modifier typename(parameterlist1) : base(*parameterlist2*)

   {body}

The constructor initializer list follows the constructor name and colon operator. The *base* keyword refers to the base class constructor, while *parameterlist2* determines which over-loaded base class constructor is called. Parameters of the derived constructor can be used in the parameter list of the base class constructor to pass parameters up the hierarchy to the base class constructor.

In the following example, the *YClass* constructor explicitly calls the one-argument constructor of the base class:

```
public class ZClass {
    public ZClass(int param) {
    }
}

public class YClass : ZClass {
    public YClass(int param) : base(param) {
    }
}
```

Instances of a derived type are created inside-out. The base element is created and initialized first, and then the derived elements. In support of this model, the constructors are walked bottom-up. This facilitates passing parameters from derived constructors to base constructors. After the parameters are passed up the class hierarchy, the constructors are executed top-down, beginning with the constructor in the root class.

The following code confirms that constructor initializers are called bottom-up, but the constructors are invoked top-down, starting with the constructor in the base class:

```
using System;

namespace Donis.CSharpBook {

    public class Starter {
        public static void Main() {
            XClass obj = new XClass();
        }
    }


    public class ZClass {
        public ZClass(int param) {
            Console.WriteLine("ZClass constructor");
        }
    }

    public class YClass : ZClass {
        public YClass(int param) : base(YClass.MethodA()) {
            Console.WriteLine("YClass constructor");
        }

        public static int MethodA() {
            Console.WriteLine("YClass constructor initializer");
            return 0;
        }
    }

    public class XClass : YClass {
        public XClass() : base(XClass.MethodA()) {
            Console.WriteLine("XClass constructor");
        }
```

```
        public static new int MethodA() {
            Console.WriteLine("XClass constructor initializer");
            return 0;
        }
    }
}
```

The following is the output from the preceding code, which confirms the order of constructor initializer lists and the actual invocation of constructors:

```
XClass constructor initializer
YClass constructor initializer
ZClass constructor
YClass constructor
XClass constructor
```

Objects are not fully created until the constructor has finished completely. Therefore, the *this* reference of the derived type cannot be used as a parameter in the base class constructor initializer list:

```
public class ZClass {
    public ZClass(YClass obj) {
    }
}

public class YClass : ZClass {
    public YClass() : base(this) {  // Illegal
    }
}
```

Destructors are called in reverse order of constructors. Derived objects are destroyed outside-in, where the most-derived component is destroyed first. Correspondingly, destructors are called bottom-up. Because destructors are parameterless, there is no information to pass from derived to base class destructors. The derived class destructor automatically calls the base class destructor.

The following code has three classes—each with a destructor—that form a class hierarchy. At the end of the program, the destructors are invoked bottom-up, which confirms the sequencing of destructors:

```
using System;

namespace Donis.CSharpBook {

    public class Starter {
        public static void Main() {
            XClass obj = new XClass();
        }
    }
```

```
public class ZClass {
    ~ZClass() {
        Console.WriteLine("ZClass destructor");
    }
}

public class YClass : ZClass {
    ~YClass() {
        Console.WriteLine("YClass destructor");
    }
}

public class XClass : YClass {
    ~XClass() {
        Console.WriteLine("XClass destructor");
    }
}
}
```

This is the output from the program:

```
XClass destructor
YClass destructor
ZClass destructor
```

Interfaces

An *interface* is a contract with the type that inherits and implements the interface. As part of that contract, interfaces are immutable. If the interface changes, it could break the type that inherited the interface. Conversely, the type promises to implement the interface fully.

For example, all vehicles have the same basic behavior: ignition on, ignition off, turn left, turn right, accelerate, and decelerate. A car, truck, bus, and motorcycle are all considered vehicles. As such, they must implement the basic functions of any vehicle. The *vehicle* interface defines that baseline. The different vehicle types inherit the *vehicle* interface and implement the behavior specific to that type. A car accelerates differently from a motorcycle. A motorcycle turns differently than a bus does. An interface mandates a set of behaviors, but not the implementation. The derived type is free to implement the interface in an appropriate manner. In this way, interface members are similar to abstract members of a class.

You cannot create an instance of an interface. Interfaces must be implemented.

Any class or structure that inherits from an interface commits to implementing the members of that interface. An interface is a set of related functions that must be implemented in a derived type. Members of an interface are implicitly both public and abstract.

Interfaces are similar to abstract classes. First, both types must be inherited. Second, you cannot create an instance of either. Finally, both have members that must be implemented in the derived type. Although abstract classes and interfaces are similar, there are several differences:

- An abstract class can contain some implementation. Interfaces have no implementation.

- Abstract classes can inherit from other classes and interfaces. Interfaces can inherit only other interfaces.

- Abstract classes can contain fields. Interfaces do not have states.

- Abstract classes have constructors and destructors. Interfaces have neither.

- Interfaces can be inherited by structures. Abstract classes are not inheritable by structures.

When choosing between defining an interface and defining an abstract class with all abstract members, select the interface. With an interface, the derived type still can inherit from other types. Furthermore, the interface is more straightforward. The *ZClass* in the following code is simply not as clear as a comparable interface:

```
public abstract class ZClass {
    abstract public void MethodA (int a);
    abstract public void MethodB (int a);
    abstract public void MethodC (int a);
    abstract public void MethodD (int a);
}

public interface IZ {
    void MethodA (int a);
    void MethodB (int a);
    void MethodC (int a);
    void MethodD (int a);
}
```

This is the syntax of an interface:

attributes accessibility modifiers interface *identifier:baselist*
  { *body* }

An interface can begin with an attribute. Use attributes to describe an interface further, such as the *Obsolete* attribute. For *accessibility,* non-nested interfaces can be public or internal. Nested interfaces have all the accessibility options. Interfaces can be nested in classes and structs, but not in other interfaces. For nested interfaces, the *new* modifier is also applicable. In this syntax, *baselist* is a list of zero or more interfaces from which the derived interface inherits. The interface body contains the members of the interface, which consists of methods, properties, indexers, and events. As mentioned previously, interface members are implicitly both public and abstract.

When interfaces inherit from other interfaces, the inherited members are added to the derived interface. The inherited interface essentially extends the current interface. A type inheriting from the derived interface must implement the aggregate interface, which includes the current interface and members that were inherited from other interfaces. If a member appears in both the derived interface and base interfaces, there is no ambiguity. However, a compiler warning is generated. Add the *new* modifier to the duplicated member in the derived interface to avoid the warning.

In the following code, *IZ* and *IY* are interfaces. The *IY* interface inherits from *IZ*. *MethodB* is a member of both interfaces. For that reason, *IY.MethodB* hides *IZ.MethodB* with the *new* modifier. Types implementing the *IY* interface must implement the *MethodA*, *MethodB*, and *MethodC* methods, which are the combined members of both interfaces:

```
public interface IZ {
    void MethodB();
    void MethodC();
}

public interface IY : IZ {
    void MethodA();
    new void MethodB();
}
```

A type can inherit multiple interfaces. The type must implement the members of each interface that is inherited. Those interfaces may have identical members. A single implementation in the derived type satisfies the requirement from all interfaces providing the ambiguous member. Therefore, the same method inherited from multiple interfaces is not ambiguous. In the following code, the *ZClass* inherits both the *IX* and *IY* interfaces. *MethodA* appears in both interfaces. However, it is necessary to implement the method only once in the derived type. The *ZClass* type implements *MethodA* and *MethodB* functions, which are the combined members from both interfaces:

```
interface IX {
    void MethodA();
}

interface IY{
    void MethodA();
    void MethodB();
}

public class ZClass : IX, IY{
    public void MethodA() {
    }

    public void MethodB() {
    }
}
```

Implementing Interfaces

Classes or structs that inherit from an interface should define each member of the interface in the type. The function signature in the type must match the function header in the interface. Members of an interface are implicitly public. The implementation in the type also must be public.

In the following code, the *Car* class inherits the *IVehicle* interface. As required, the members of the *IVehicle* interface are implemented in the *Car* class:

```
public interface IVehicle {
    void IgnitionOn();
    void IgnitionOff();
    void TurnLeft();
    void TurnRight();
}

public class Car : IVehicle{

    public void IgnitionOn() {
    }

    public void IgnitionOff() {
    }

    public virtual void TurnLeft() {
    }

    public virtual void TurnRight() {
    }
}
```

A class that inherits multiple interfaces has multiple specialties. An amphibious vehicle is a combination of a vehicle and a boat. In the following code, the *Amphibious* class inherits both the *IVehicle* and *IBoat* interfaces. The members of both interfaces are implemented in the *Amphibious* class. As discussed, duplicate interface members are implemented only once:

```
using System;

namespace Donis.CSharpBook {

    public interface IVehicle {
        void IgnitionOn();
        void IgnitionOff();
        void TurnLeft();
        void TurnRight();
    }

    public interface IBoat {
        void IgnitionOn();
        void IgnitionOff();
        void TurnLeft();
```

```
        void TurnRight();
        void FishFinder();
        void Rudder();
    }


    public class Amphibious : IVehicle, IBoat {
        public void IgnitionOn() {
        }
        public void IgnitionOff() {
        }
        public void TurnLeft() {
        }
        public void TurnRight() {
        }
        public void FishFinder() {
        }
        public void Rudder() {
        }
    }
}
```

Explicit Interface Member Implementation

You can implement and bind a member to a specific interface. This is called *explicit inter-face member implementation*. In the type, prefix the member name with the interface name. Members implemented in this manner are not accessible through the derived type. For this reason, the *accessibility* modifier is omitted from explicitly implemented interface members. When used, explicitly interface members are available only via an interface cast.

In the following code, the *ZClass* implements the *IA* interface. *IA.MethodA* is implemented explicitly, whereas *IA.MethodB* is implemented in a normal manner. In *ZClass*, *MethodA* is prefixed with the interface name (*IA.MethodA*). This binds *MethodA* specifically to interface *IA*. *MethodB* is visible from the *ZClass* interface but *MethodA* is hidden. You must cast an instance of *ZClass* to the *IA* interface to call *MethodA*. This is shown in the code:

```
using System;

public class Starter {
    public static void Main() {
        ZClass obj = new ZClass();
        obj.MethodA(); // Error
        obj.MethodB();
        IA i = obj;
        i.MethodA();
    }
}

public interface IA {
    void MethodA();
    void MethodB();
```

```
    }

public class ZClass : IA {

    void IA.MethodA() {
        Console.WriteLine("IA.MethodA");
    }

    public void MethodB() {
        Console.WriteLine("IA.MethodB");
    }
}
```

Explicit interface implementation is useful when needing to implement ambiguous members inherited from more than one interface separately. Normally, they are consolidated into a single implementation. This is also helpful when the interface and the derived type share the same member. The interface member is implemented explicitly to preserve the separate implementation in the derived type. Explicit interface implementation provides separate implementation without ambiguity. To call the interface implementation, cast to the appropriate interface first.

The following code is an updated version of the amphibious vehicle. Steering a boat is different from steering a car. Therefore, *TurnLeft* and *TurnRight* are explicitly implemented for the *IBoat* interface. *TurnLeft* and *TurnRight* also are implemented explicitly for the *IVehicle* interface. The *TurnLeft* and *TurnRight* functions of the *Amphibious* type (the derived type) delegate to *IVehicle.TurnLeft* and *IVehicle.TurnRight,* making them the default behaviors:

```
using System;

namespace Donis.CSharpBook {

    public class Starter {
        public static void Main() {

            Amphibious marinevehicle = new
                    Amphibious();
            marinevehicle.IgnitionOn();
            marinevehicle.TurnLeft();
            IBoat boatmaneuvers = marinevehicle;
            boatmaneuvers.TurnLeft();
            marinevehicle.IgnitionOff();
        }
    }

    public interface IVehicle {
        void IgnitionOn();
        void IgnitionOff();
        void TurnLeft();
        void TurnRight();
    }

    public interface IBoat {
```

```csharp
        void IgnitionOn();
        void IgnitionOff();
        void TurnLeft();
        void TurnRight();
        void FishFinder();
        void Rudder();
    }


    public class Amphibious : IVehicle, IBoat {

        public void IgnitionOn() {
            Console.WriteLine("Ignition on.");
        }

        public void IgnitionOff() {
            Console.WriteLine("Ignition off.");
        }

        public void TurnLeft() {
            IVehicle vehicle = this;
            vehicle.TurnLeft();
        }

        public void TurnRight() {
            IVehicle vehicle = this;
            vehicle.TurnRight();
        }

        void IVehicle.TurnLeft() {
            Console.WriteLine("Turn vehicle left.");
        }

        void IVehicle.TurnRight() {
            Console.WriteLine("Turn vehicle right.");
        }

        void IBoat.TurnLeft() {
            Console.WriteLine("Turn boat left.");
        }

        void IBoat.TurnRight() {
            Console.WriteLine("Turn boat right.");
        }

        public void FishFinder() {
            Console.WriteLine("Fish finder in use.");
        }

        public void Rudder() {
            Console.WriteLine("Adjust rudder.");        }
    }
}
```

Another reason to use explicit interface implementation is to hide some portion of a class or struct from specific clients. You can use an interface cast to expose as much or as little of the component as desired. In a class library, a developer can expose different aspects of an internal component by returning an interface or using an interface parameter in a callback.

In the following code, the *Car* class inherits and implements the *IVehicle* and *IEngine* interfaces. The two interfaces have no overlapping members. A driver doesn't usually interface directly with the engine. That is usually left to the mechanic. Therefore, the *IEngine* interface is hidden in the *Car* class:

```csharp
using System;

namespace Donis.CSharpBook {

    public class Starter {
        public static void Main() {
            Car auto = new Car();
            auto.IgnitionOn();
            auto.IgnitionOff();

            // Access engine.

            IEngine e = auto.AccessEngine();

            // Inspect engine.
        }
    }

    public interface IVehicle {
        void IgnitionOn();
        void IgnitionOff();
        void TurnLeft();
        void TurnRight();
    }

    public interface IEngine {
        void Alternator();
        void Ignition();
        void Transmission();
    }

    public class Car : IVehicle, IEngine {

        public void IgnitionOn() {
            Console.WriteLine("Ignition on.");
            AccessEngine().Ignition();
        }

        public void IgnitionOff() {
            Console.WriteLine("Ignition off.");
        }

        public void TurnLeft() {
```

```
        Console.WriteLine("Turn left.");
    }

    public void TurnRight() {
        Console.WriteLine("Turn right.");
    }

    public IEngine AccessEngine() {
        return this;
    }

    void IEngine.Alternator() {
        Console.WriteLine("Alternator.");
    }

    void IEngine.Ignition() {
        Console.WriteLine("Ignition");
    }

    void IEngine.Transmission() {
        Console.WriteLine("Transmission");
    }
    }
}
```

Reimplementation of Interfaces

When a class inherits from an interface, it must implement the members of the interface. In the derived class, the implemented functions can be virtual. Descendants of the derived class will inherit the implemented functions. However, descendants of the derived class where the interface is implemented cannot be cast to the interface. Only types that directly implement an interface can be cast to that interface. However, descendants of that class can cast back to the interface through the parent type. This is demonstrated in the following code:

```
interface IY {
    void MethodA();
    void MethodB();
}

public class ZClass : IY {
    void IY.MethodA() {
        Console.WriteLine("IY.MethodA");
    }

    public virtual void MethodA() {
    }

    public virtual void MethodB() {
    }
}

public class WClass : ZClass {
```

```
        public override void MethodA() {
            Console.WriteLine("WClass.MethodA");
        }

        public override void MethodB() {
            Console.WriteLine("WClass.MethodB");
        }
    }

    class Startup {
        public static void Main() {
            IY obj = (IY)((ZClass)new WClass());
            obj.MethodA();  // Writes IY.MethodA
            obj.MethodB();  // Writes WClass.MethodB
        }
    }
```

Explicitly implemented interface members cannot be overridden in descendants. If you want to replace the behavior of an inherited explicitly implemented member, reimplement the explicit interface member in the descendant. Inherit the interface in the descendant of the derived type, where the interface is originally inherited, and explicitly reimplement only the interface members that are being hidden. This is demonstrated in the following code:

```
    interface IY {
        void MethodA();
        void MethodB();
    }

    public class ZClass : IY {
        void IY.MethodA() {
            Console.WriteLine("test");
        }

        public virtual void MethodA() {
        }

        public virtual void MethodB() {
        }
    }

    public class WClass : ZClass, IY {
        void IY.MethodA() {
            Console.WriteLine("IY.MethodA in WClass");
        }

        public override void MethodB() {
            Console.WriteLine("WClass.MethodB");
        }
    }

    class Startup {
        public static void Main() {
            IY obj = (IY)((ZClass) new WClass());
```

```
        obj.MethodA();   // Writes IY.MethodA in WClass
        obj.MethodB();   // Writes WClass.MethodB
    }
}
```

This statement appears in the preceding code: *IY obj = (IY)((ZClass) new WClass())*. This statement casts the derived instance to a base type, where the *IY* interface is implemented explicitly. The result is then successfully cast to the *IY* interface.

Polymorphism

Polymorphism is one of the major benefits of inheritance. With polymorphism, the correct function call is decided at run time based on the derived type of a base reference. This is called *late binding* and is accomplished by casting instances of related types back to a common base class reference. The common base class makes the derived classes related. A graphics program provides a good example. In the graphics program, instead of having separate routines for rectangle, ellipse, and triangle shapes, you write a generic algorithm that uses the base type. This is more extensible and maintainable than handling each type of geometric shape differently. At run time, process a specific instance, such as a rectangle, ellipse, or triangle shape, in the generic routine. Then the appropriate behavior will be chosen from the derived type.

The following program draws rectangles, ellipses, and triangles. This program uses inheritance but not polymorphism:

```
using System;

namespace Donis.CSharpBook {

    public class Starter {
        public static void Main() {
            Rectangle shape1 = new Rectangle();
            Rectangle shape2 = new Rectangle();
            Ellipse shape3 = new Ellipse();

            shape1.Draw();
            shape2.Draw();
            shape3.Draw();
        }
    }

    public abstract class Geoshape {
        public Geoshape() {
            ++count;
            ID = count;
        }
```

```
            private static int count = 0;
            protected int ID = 0;

            public virtual void Draw() {
            }
        }

        public class Rectangle : Geoshape {
            public override void Draw() {
                Console.WriteLine("Drawing Shape {0} : rectangle",
                    ID.ToString());
            }
        }

        public class Triangle : Geoshape {
            public override void Draw() {
                Console.WriteLine("Drawing Shape {0} : triangle",
                    ID.ToString());
            }
        }

        public class Ellipse : Geoshape {
            public override void Draw() {
                Console.WriteLine("Drawing Shape {0} : ellipse",
                    ID.ToString());
            }
        }
    }
}
```

The two primary advantages to polymorphism are late binding and extensibility:

- Late binding in the context of polymorphism is binding a specific object to a function call at run time. Early binding binds a function to a specific object at compile time, which is not always possible. For example, in an interactive graphics program, users decide the objects to draw at run time. The previous program does not use polymorphism and decides the shapes to draw at compile time. The same objects are drawn every time.

- Extensible code adapts easily to future changes. In the preceding code, the *Draw* method is called separately for each kind of geometric type. A rectangle is drawn differently from an ellipse. An ellipse is drawn differently from a triangle. As the program evolves in the future, more geometric shapes are likely to be added. It eventually could support dozens of shapes. An extensible process for drawing a variety of shapes is needed. Do you want to change the global draw routine every time a new shape is added to the application?

Polymorphism starts with related classes, such as specific geometric shapes. In the base class, define abstract function members that each derived type must override and implement. To use polymorphism, create a base class reference to instances of a derived type. When a virtual function is called on the base class reference, the correct function is chosen from the derived type. The method in the derived type is either inherited or overridden. *BaseReference.VirtualMethod* calls different implementations at run time depending on the type of derived object to which the base class reference points. This is the key behavior of polymorphism.

The sample code that follows illustrates these concepts. In the following code, *Geoshape* is the base class reference, and *Draw* is the abstract (and virtual) method. The *Draw* method is overridden in the *Rectangle, Ellipse,* and *Triangle* child classes. In the example, two derived instances are created in an array of base class objects. *Geoshape* references *shape[0]* and *shape[1]*, which hold *Ellipse* and *Rectangle* objects, respectively. The *Draw* method then is invoked on the *Geoshape* base class references. At that time, the correct *Draw* method of the derived type is called. Therefore, the base method call has different behavior depending on the kind of object assigned to the reference:

```
Geoshape [] shapes = { new Ellipse(),
                       new Rectangle() };

shapes[0].Draw();    // Geoshape.Draw()->Ellipse.Draw()
shapes[1].Draw();    // Geoshape.Draw()->Rectangle.Draw()
```

In the next code, the *DrawShape* method draws a geometric shape. Can you predict which *type.Draw* is called? The method has one parameter, which is the *Geoshape* base class. On the first call to *DrawShape* method, the base reference is assigned an *Ellipse* instance, which means *Ellipse.Draw* is called. On the second call, a *Rectangle* instance is passed, and then *Rectangle.Draw* is called. Therefore, one statement, *shape.Draw*, calls different implementations. The *shape.Draw* statement is both polymorphic and extensible:

```
public static void Main() {
    DrawShape(new Ellipse());
    DrawShape(new Rectangle());
}

public static void DrawShape(Geoshape shape) {
    shape.Draw();  // which Draw is called?
}
```

Polymorphism has three ingredients:

- Related classes
- Common method
- Different behavior

The following code is a better example of the benefits of polymorphism. The program has the three elements of polymorphism. There are related types: *Triangle, Ellipse,* and *Rectangle*. The common method is *Draw*. Each *Draw* method is implemented differently in the derived class. At run time, command-line arguments indicate which shapes to draw. The following command draws a rectangle, ellipse, triangle, and another rectangle, which highlights the benefits of polymorphism and late binding:

```
shapes r e t r
```

At compile time, we know that clients will draw shapes. But we don't know which shapes or how many. Therefore, a collection of *Geoshape* base class references, which are a generalization of all shape types, is defined at compile time. Polymorphism always begins with base references to derived instances. In the first loop, derived instances are created and added to the collection of base class references. In the second loop, the array of *Geoshape* base class references is iterated and *Geoshape.Draw* is called. At run time, *Rectangle.Draw*, *Ellipse.Draw*, or *Triangle.Draw* actually is called for each element of the *Geoshape* collection. This is the polymorphic behavior:

```
using System;
using System.Collections.Generic;

namespace Donis.CSharpBook {

    public class Starter {
        public static void Main(string [] shapeArray) {
            List<Geoshape> shapes = new List<Geoshape>();
            Geoshape obj=null;
            foreach (string shape in shapeArray) {
                if (shape.ToUpper() == "R") {
                    obj = new Rectangle();
                }
                else if (shape.ToUpper() == "E") {
                    obj = new Ellipse();
                }
                else if (shape.ToUpper() == "T") {
                    obj = new Triangle();
                }
                else {
                    continue;
                }
                shapes.Add(obj);
            }

            foreach (Geoshape shape in shapes) {
                shape.Draw();   // polymorphic behavior
            }
        }
    }

    public abstract class Geoshape {
        public Geoshape() {
            ++count;
            ID = count;
        }

        private static int count = 0;
        protected int ID = 0;

        public abstract void Draw();   }

    public class Rectangle : Geoshape {
        public override void Draw() {
```

```
            Console.WriteLine("Drawing Shape {0} : rectangle",
                ID.ToString());
        }
    }

    public class Triangle : Geoshape {
        public override void Draw() {
            Console.WriteLine("Drawing Shape {0} : triangle",
                ID.ToString());
        }
    }

    public class Ellipse : Geoshape {
        public override void Draw() {
            Console.WriteLine("Drawing Shape {0} : ellipse",
                ID.ToString());
        }
    }
}
```

Geoshape is an abstract class, not a concrete one. A generic geometric shape is intangible. In addition, the *Geoshape.Draw* method is abstract, which means the containing class must be abstract as well. There is an added benefit of an abstract *Draw*. Derived types are forced to implement their own *Draw* method.

Interface Polymorphism

Interface polymorphism is the same as regular polymorphism except that interfaces are used instead of abstract classes and methods. The result is also the same. Because the *Geoshape* class has some implementation, and interfaces cannot have implementation, the *Geoshape* class cannot be converted to an interface. Instead, the *Draw* abstract method can be lifted from the class and placed in a separate *IDraw* interface. That interface then can be used for polymorphism, as shown in the following code:

```
using System;
using System.Collections.Generic;

namespace Donis.CSharpBook {

    public class Starter {
        public static void Main(string [] shapeArray) {
            List<Geoshape> shapes = new List<Geoshape>();

            // partial listing
            foreach (IDraw shape in shapes) {
                shape.Draw();
            }
        }
    }
}
```

```
    public interface IDraw {
        void Draw();
    }

    public abstract class Geoshape : IDraw {
        public Geoshape() {
            ++count;
            ID = count;
        }

        private static int count = 0;
        protected int ID = 0;

        public abstract void Draw();
    }
// partial listing
```

The *new* Modifier and Polymorphism

The *new* modifier affects polymorphism and can cause unexpected results. Unlike an overridden member, the *new* method is not considered related to the *virtual* member of the same function in the base class. As mentioned, the *virtual* modifier propagates to all descendants. A virtual method in a base class remains virtual when overridden in the derived class, even if the *virtual* modifier is not present. Polymorphism calls the function either inherited or overridden in the derived class. The exception is a method with the *new* modifier, which is not considered related to a *virtual* method of the base class. In that case, an overridden or inherited method closest to the derived type is called.

The following code is typical polymorphism. *ZClass* is abstract with a single abstract method—*MethodA*. *YClass* inherits *ZClass* and overrides *MethodA*. Finally, *XClass* inherits *YClass* and also overrides *MethodA* again. In *Main*, an instance of *XClass* is cast to *ZClass*, which is a reference to a base type. *MethodA* is called on the base type and predictably, *XClass.MethodA* is invoked:

```
    using System;

    public abstract class ZClass {
        public abstract void MethodA();
    }

    public class YClass : ZClass {
        public override void MethodA()
        {
            Console.WriteLine("YClass.MethodA");
        }
    }

    public class XClass : YClass {
        public override void MethodA() {
```

```
            Console.WriteLine("XClass.MethodA");
        }
    }
    class Startup {
        public static void Main() {
            ZClass obj = new XClass();
            obj.MethodA();   // Writes XClass.MethodA
        }
    }
```

The following code is identical to the preceding code, except for the *MethodA* header in *XClass*. Instead of overriding *MethodA*, *XClass.MethodA* uses the *new* modifier, shown in bold type, to replace the inherited function. In *Main,* the *XClass* instance is cast to *ZClass,* which is the base type as before. The call to *ZClass.MethodA* now invokes *YClass.MethodA*, not *XClass.MethodA*. The *new* modifier indicated that *XClass.MethodA* was unrelated to *ZClass. MethodA*. If not planned or expected, this could be a problem.

```
    using System;

    public abstract class ZClass {
        public abstract void MethodA();
    }

    public class YClass : ZClass {
        public override void MethodA()
        {
            Console.WriteLine("YClass.MethodA");
        }
    }

    public class XClass : YClass {
        public new void MethodA()
        {
            Console.WriteLine("XClass.MethodA");
        }
    }
    class Startup {
        public static void Main() {
            ZClass obj = new XClass();
            obj.MethodA();   // Writes YClass.MethodA
        }
    }
```

Casting

Casting an instance of a derived class to a base type is always safe. As shown in the previous section, this is the cast for polymorphism and is legitimate in all circumstances. Derived types extend base types. Because derived types encompass everything about the base type, a cast that is derived to the base type is guaranteed to be safe. You can even cast a derived instance to an abstract base class. This has already been demonstrated more than once in this chapter. Casting from a derived object to a base reference provides a base view of the instance. You are limited to members of the base type. The extensions of the derived type are not visible through a base reference to a derived instance. After the cast to the base type, the base reference is an alias to the base portion of the derived object.

Casting a value type to a base interface has different semantics. When casting a value type to an interface, a separate entity is created. Interfaces are reference types. Boxing occurs any time a value type is cast to a reference type, including casting a value type to an interface. Boxing allocates memory and copies the value type to the managed heap. The original and the copy are unrelated. Changes to one will not affect the other.

In the following code, the *ZStruct* structure, which is a value type, implements the *IAdd* interface. The implementation of the *Increment* method increments an internal counter. In *Main*, a *ZStruct* local variable is cast to an *IAdd* interface, which is legitimate. Boxing happens, and a copy of the *ZStruct* is placed on the managed heap. The *val* variable is the instance on the stack, while *obj* references the copy placed on the managed heap. Changes to one will not affect the other. When the counts are displayed for the variables *val* and *obj*, they are different. This confirms their separate identities:

```
using System;

namespace Donis.CSharpBook {

    public class Starter {
        public static void Main() {
            XStruct val = new XStruct();
            val.Increment();
            IAdd obj = val;
            val.Increment();
            Console.WriteLine("Val: {0}",
                val.Count);
            Console.WriteLine("Obj: {0}",
                obj.Count);

        }
    }

    public interface IAdd {
    void Increment();
        int Count {
            get;
        }
    }

    public struct XStruct : IAdd {

        public void Increment() {
            ++propCount;
        }
```

```
        private int propCount;
        public int Count {
            get {
                return propCount;
            }
        }
    }
}
```

In the preceding code, *XStruct.propCount* is initialized implicitly. As mentioned in Chapter 2, "Types," fields in a *struct* are initialized to default values automatically.

A base class or interface can be used as a function parameter or return value. Then you can provide an instance of a derived type as the parameter or return value. This will provide polymorphic behavior in the called function or calling function, respectively. These are some reasons to use a base class or interface as a parameter or return value:

■ It generalizes a function call or return. The function parameter or return can be used with different but related types.

■ A specific parameter or return type might not be known at compile time. A base reference supports late binding, where the type is selected at run time (polymorphism).

■ Returning a base class or interface restricts access to an object. This is especially useful for class libraries that want to hide some portion of a public interface.

The following code is an example of a class library—albeit a rather small library. The library contains a single class, *ZClass*. It is marked as internal and is visible solely within the class library. *IExposed* defines the public face of the *ZClass* type to clients of the library. *LibraryClass.GetSomething* returns a *ZClass* instance through the *IExposed* public interface, which includes *MethodA* and *MethodB*. This prevents clients from accessing the other methods of *ZClass*. Those methods are internal and reserved for use in the class library:

```
using System;
namespace Donis.CSharpBook {

    public class LibraryClass {
        public IExposed GetSomething() {
            ZClass obj = new ZClass();
            // do something
            obj.InternalA();
            obj.InternalB();
            obj.MethodA();
            return obj;
        }
    }

    public interface IExposed {
        void MethodA();
        void MethodB();
    }
```

```
    internal class ZClass : IExposed {
        public void MethodA() {
        }

        public void MethodB() {
        }

        public void InternalA() {
        }

        public void InternalB() {
        }
    }
}
```

As shown several times already in this chapter, casting a derived object to a base reference is safe. However, you cannot cast a base object implicitly to a derived reference. The derived type might have members that are not defined in the base type. Therefore, the derived reference could access members that are not available to the base object. For this reason, the cast is not type-safe. An explicit cast can force the compiler to accept the improper cast of a base object to a derived reference. Because this remains invalid, an exception is raised at run time at the cast. You have simply deferred the problem from compile time to run time.

This code raises an exception at run time because of an invalid cast:

```
using System;

namespace Donis.CSharpBook {

    public class Starter {
        public static void Main() {
            ZClass obj = new ZClass();

            // Fails at compile time
            // YClass alias = obj;

            // Fails at run time
            YClass alias = (YClass) obj;

            obj.MethodA();
            obj.MethodB();
        }
    }

    public class ZClass {
        public virtual void MethodA() {
        }
        public virtual void MethodB() {
        }
    }
```

```
    public class YClass : ZClass {
        public override void MethodA() {
        }
    }
}
```

Type Operators

The *is* and *as* type operators are convenient tools for testing the pedigree of an instance. These operators confirm the presence of a class or interface somewhere in the hierarchy of an instance. This provides run-time type information where decisions can be made at run time based on the type of an instance. For example, you might display extra menu items for employees who are managers.

Here is the syntax of the *is* operator, which is an expression that evaluates to a Boolean result:

instance is *type*;

The *is* operator returns *true* if the *instance* is related to the *type*. (*Related* means it is the same type or is derived from the type.) If the *instance* and *type* are unrelated, *false* is returned.

The following code displays a menu. If the employee is a manager, additional menu items are displayed. The *is* operator confirms that the employee is a manager:

```
using System;

namespace Donis.CSharpBook {

    public class Starter {
        public static void Main() {
            Manager person = new Manager("Accounting");
            Console.WriteLine("[Menu]\n");
            Console.WriteLine("Task 1");
            Console.WriteLine("Task 2");
            if (person is IManager) {
                IManager mgr = person;
                Console.WriteLine("\n[{0} Menu]\n",
                    mgr.Department);
                Console.WriteLine("Task 3");
            }
        }
    }

    public interface IManager {
        string Department {
            get;
        }
    }
```

```
public class Employee {
}

public class SalariedEmployee : Employee {
}

public class Manager : SalariedEmployee, IManager {

    public Manager(string dept) {
        propDepartment = dept;
    }

    private string propDepartment;
    public string Department {
        get {
            return propDepartment;
        }
    }
}
}
```

Here is the syntax of the *as* operator:

instance1 = *instance2* as *type*

The *as* operator casts *instance2* to the related *type*. The result of the cast is placed in *instance1*. If *instance2* is unrelated to *type*, *instance1* is set to *null*.

Here is the previous code rewritten with the *as* operator (this is a partial listing):

```
using System;

namespace Donis.CSharpBook {

    public class Starter {
        public static void Main() {
            Manager person = new Manager("Accounting");
            Console.WriteLine("[Menu]\n");
            Console.WriteLine("Task 1");
            Console.WriteLine("Task 2");
            IManager mgr = person as IManager;
            if (mgr != null) {
                Console.WriteLine("\n[{0} Menu]\n",
                    mgr.Department);
                Console.WriteLine("Task 3");
            }
        }
    }
}

// Partial listing
```

Attribute Inheritance

By default, custom attributes are not inherited. However, the *AttributeUsage* attribute can make an attribute inheritable. For the *AttributeUsage* attribute, set the *Inherited* option to *true* to enable inheritance.

Inheriting classes with attributes sometimes can cause interesting behavior. In the following code, *ZClass* is the base class and *YClass* is the derived class. Both classes have the *PrincipalPermission* attribute, which identifies the users or roles that can call functions of a particular class. The *PrincipalPermission* attribute is inheritable. In the example, *ZClass* functions are available to managers; *YClass* function calls are available to accountants. The *YClass* inherits and does not override *MethodA* from *ZClass*. Who can call *YClass.MethodA*? Because *MethodA* is not overridden in the derived class, *YClass* is relying on the implementation of *MethodA* in the base class, which includes any applicable attributes. Therefore, only managers can call the *YClass.MethodA*, which contradicts the *PrincipalPermission* attribute of *YClass*. *YClass.MethodB* remains available to accountants and not managers, as demonstrated in the following code:

```
using System;
using System.Security;
using System.Security.Permissions;
using System.Security.Principal;
using System.Threading;

namespace Donis.CSharpBook {
    public class Starter {
        public static void Main() {
            GenericIdentity g = new GenericIdentity("Person1");
            GenericPrincipal p = new GenericPrincipal(g,
                new string [] {"Manager"});
            Thread.CurrentPrincipal = p;
            ZClass.MethodA();
            YClass.MethodA();
//          YClass.MethodB();     // Security exception.
        }
    }

    [PrincipalPermission(SecurityAction.Demand,
        Role="Manager")]
    public class ZClass {
        static public void MethodA() {
            Console.WriteLine("ZClass.MethodA");
        }
    }
```

```
[PrincipalPermission(SecurityAction.Demand,
    Role="Accountant")]
public class YClass : ZClass {
    static public void MethodB() {
        Console.WriteLine("ZClass.MethodB");
    }
}
}
```

Visual Studio 2008

The next chapter introduces Visual Studio 2008, including an overview and walkthrough. In the integrated development environment of Visual Studio, you can develop managed code in a variety of languages. It is an environment for creating secure, robust, enterprise, tested, and scalable applications. In addition, Visual Studio hosts a variety of rapid application development tools that facilitate the quick and painless development of managed applications.

Visual Studio 2008 includes several enhancements. Improved testing capabilities have been added. A suite of testing tools is available now in the Professional edition of the product. Multi-targeting of .NET environments has been added. It is now simple to compile an application to different versions of the .NET environment. There are new refactoring features as well. These and many more enhancements make Visual Studio 2008 the preferred tool for developing managed applications.

Part II
Core Skills

Chapter 4
Introduction to Visual Studio 2008

Microsoft Visual Studio 2008, the latest evolution of Visual Studio, is the centerpiece of a suite of products used to develop, debug, and deploy Microsoft Windows applications, including managed applications. Visual Studio 2008 includes several enhancements: improved testing tools, the ability to create applications with the Windows Vista persona, flexibility to target specific versions of the .NET Framework, JavaScript debugging, the new Test menu and (in Visual Studio Team System) the new Analyze menu, introduction of Language Integrated Query (LINQ), AJAX-enabled Web applications, Report projects, and more. Microsoft Visual Studio Team System 2008 continues to be improved and expanded, with new features that better integrate database managers and designers. Visual Studio Team System 2008 provides a team of professionals (developers, architects, designers, etc.) with tools for collaboration and Application Lifetime Management (ALM). Visual Studio 2008 is a worthy successor to the previous strong versions of Visual Studio products.

Visual Studio 2008 is Web-enabled. Developers can easily participate in the developer community, submit questions to Microsoft, and visit a variety of online resources from the Integrated Development Environment (IDE). Help is also Web-enabled, including access to MSDN and the Microsoft Knowledge Base.

This chapter will highlight various features, including the code editor, IDE Navigator, code snippets, refactoring, building and deployment, targeting multiple platforms, MSBuild, and Click Once Deployment. This chapter is only an overview; for more detail, consult other reference materials.

Migrating to Visual Studio 2008

When installing a new version of Visual Studio, why spend time configuring the basic settings from the previous version? Depending on the extent to which you have customized your environment, this setup could be time-consuming. You can export and import certain Visual Studio settings, including many from the Options settings of the Tools menu, to simplify this process. Settings related to the code editor, project options, and debugging can be saved and later imported into the same version or a later version of Visual Studio.

These are the primary reasons to persist Visual Studio options:

- It allows you to back up Visual Studio options, so they can be restored if needed in the future.

- If you are working on a team, you can share settings with and import settings from other team members.

- Finally, this is a convenient way to migrate settings between different versions of Visual Studio, making it simpler to set up a new environment.

To export Visual Studio options, choose Import And Export Settings from the Tools menu. The Imports and Setting Wizard will appear, as shown in Figure 4-1.

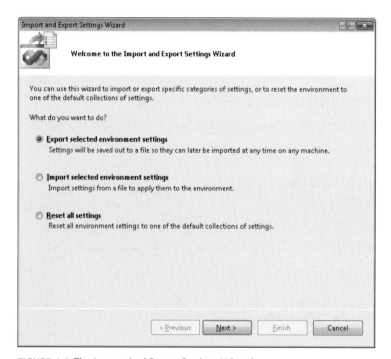

FIGURE 4-1 The Import And Export Settings Wizard

The second page of the wizard (shown in Figure 4-2) is where you choose which settings to export to a file. You can choose to export specific settings or all of them. The selected settings are persisted to a file with the .vssettings extension. You specify the filename in the final page of the wizard.

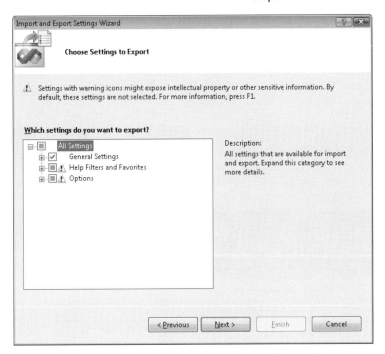

FIGURE 4-2 The second page of the Import And Export Settings Wizard

To import, choose the Import Selected Environment Settings option from the first page of the wizard. On the second page, specify the vssettings file to import. Specify which settings to import on the final page of the wizard.

The Reset All Settings option allows you to restore the default settings.

Integrated Development Environment

Visual Studio 2008 is an IDE for developing and maintaining managed, native, and mixed-mode applications. Many project templates are available to create a diverse assortment of projects and applications. There are templates for Microsoft Windows Forms, Console, ASP. NET Web Site, ASP.NET Web Service, Windows Presentation Foundation (WPF), Windows Communication Foundation (WCF), Microsoft Office, and many more application types. You also can create Microsoft SQL Server, Testing, Setup And Deployment, and other projects. There are templates that target specific devices, including mobile devices.

In addition, developers can choose the language of their choice, including C#, Microsoft Visual Basic .NET, and Managed C++. Some templates, such as the Windows Forms application, are language-specific.

The Visual Studio 2008 IDE has many rapid application development (RAD) tools. The Visual Studio Code Editor, Microsoft IntelliSense, Solution Explorer, Class View, Object Browser, and the class diagram are essential elements of the user interface and contribute to improved developer productivity, accuracy, and efficiency. Many of the mature tools, such as IntelliSense, have been enhanced further in Visual Studio 2008.

Start Page

The Start Page, shown in Figure 4-3, is the gateway screen into Visual Studio. For developers, the Start Page is the first window presented in Visual Studio after installation. Visual Studio often presents the Start Page upon startup as well. If the page is not visible, you can open the Start Page from the View menu by selecting Other Windows and then selecting Start Page.

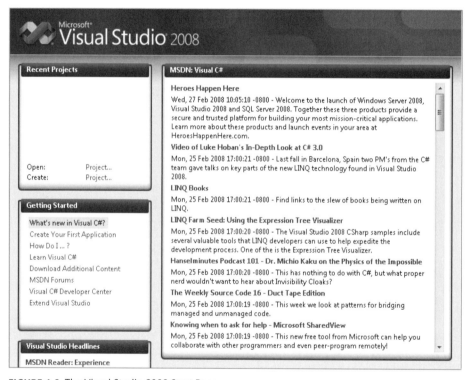

FIGURE 4-3 The Visual Studio 2008 Start Page

The Start Page has four panes:

- **Recent Projects**   This pane lists the recently opened projects. Select an item in the project list to open that project. The Open and Create buttons at the bottom of this pane open and create a new project, respectively.

- **MSDN: Visual C#**   This pane contains links to recent news articles pertaining to Visual Studio or related topics. Each topic has preview text to help the user. Click the related link to view the complete article.

- **Getting Started** This pane contains helpful links for new Visual Studio developers.
- **Visual Studio Headlines**   This pane is where Microsoft posts links on topics of interest for Visual Studio developers, including new product releases.

Creating Projects

Developing an application in Visual Studio typically starts with the creation of a project. Projects are the basic organization component of Visual Studio, in which files, resources, reference, and other constituents of an application are grouped. Related projects are sometimes grouped into solutions, which can contain projects from different templates and languages. For example, it is common to group applications, related libraries, and test projects in the same solution.

Create a new project by selecting File, New, and then Project. Figure 4-4 shows the New Project dialog box. Toward the bottom of the dialog box is a drop-down list box containing the Create New Solution and Add To Solution options. (Note that the Add To Solution option is not available unless a solution is currently open.) To add the new project to the current solution, choose Add To Solution. If no solution is opened, the only choice is to create a new solution. Select the Create Directory For Solution check box to create a dedicated directory for the new solution.

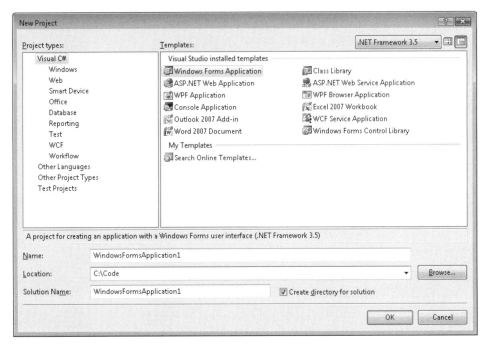

FIGURE 4-4 The New Project dialog box

Multiple-Targeting

Multiple-targeting of the .NET Framework version is a feature introduced in Visual Studio 2008. This feature allows you to set the build context of an application to a specific version of the .NET Framework. For example, imagine that you maintain an application that was created initially in .NET Framework 2.0. Compiling the application with a new version of the .NET Framework might introduce dependencies or other unforeseen problems, and is not necessary simply to maintain the product. With Visual Studio 2008, this can be avoided by targeting the .NET Framework 2.0 version.

Select the target .NET Framework in the upper right corner of the New Project dialog box. Click .NET Framework and a list of available .NET Framework versions is presented. The choices are .NET Framework 2.0, 3.0, and 3.5.

Here are some of the reasons to use multiple-targeting:

- You can build applications toward specific platforms based on customer expectations.

- You maintain applications created in an earlier version of the .NET Framework, while developing new applications to the newest platform in Visual Studio 2008.

- You can develop what-if scenarios based on different .NET platforms, which is important for testing.

- Most important, you now can create and deploy to the .NET platform of your choice.

In Visual Studio 2008, the default platform is .NET Framework 3.5. Visual Studio will enable and remove specific features based on the target platform. For example, if targeting .NET Framework 2.0, LINQ is not available. (LINQ had not been introduced in .NET Framework 2.0, so references to LINQ are not allowed.) In addition, references and user interface elements that are not supported in a specific version of the .NET Framework are not available and typically are not shown in Visual Studio.

Solution Explorer

Solution Explorer provides a view into a solution, including projects contained in that solution. You can configure both solutions and projects from the Solution Explorer window (shown in Figure 4-5). If it is not visible, display the Solution Explorer window by selecting Solution Explorer from the View menu. In the example shown in the figure, the solution is named Airline Seats and has two projects: Airline Seats and Person.

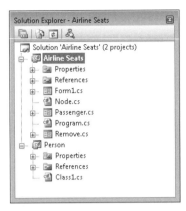

FIGURE 4-5 The Solution Explorer window

To change solution or project settings, right-click the solution or project icon in Solution Explorer to open a context menu. Select the Properties command from the context menu. The Properties command for a project opens the Project Designer window, as shown in Figure 4-6. In the Project Designer window, you can configure application settings, the build environment, debug settings, and resources. You also can define default application settings, sign assemblies, or create ClickOnce manifests (explained later in this chapter). You also can open the Project properties by choosing *<project name>* Properties from the Project menu.

The location of the Solution Explorer window and other Visual Studio windows default to a docking window. Figure 4-7 shows Solution Explorer in a tabbed window. You can select the correct window orientation from a context menu. Open the context menu by right-clicking the title bar of the window.

Where is AssemblyInfo.cs? The AssemblyInfo.cs file contains assembly attributes that define assembly level metadata, such as the version number and culture. (Metadata is discussed in Chapter 13, "Metadata and Reflection.") Source code files and related files are displayed in the Solution Explorer window. Users of previous versions of Visual Studio might be accustomed to seeing AssemblyInfo.cs at the root of the project, with other source files. However, the AssemblyInfo.cs file now has been moved to the Properties folder. Open the Properties folder to view the file.

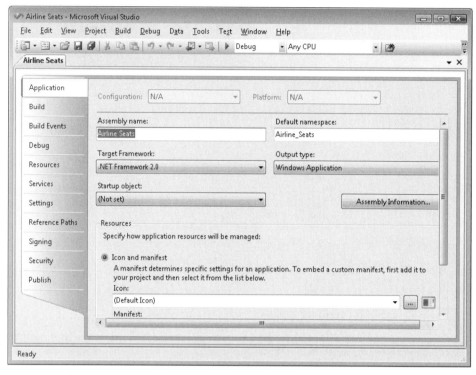

FIGURE 4-6 The Project Designer window

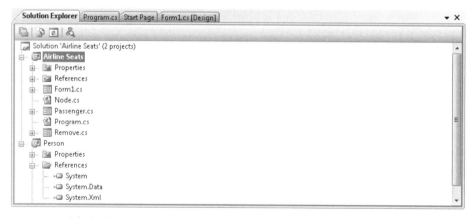

FIGURE 4-7 Solution Explorer as a tabbed window

Project Types

Several project types are available in Visual Studio 2008, the most commonly used of which are Windows Application and Class Library. Project templates are grouped in categories. The Windows Application and Class Library templates are included in the Visual C# templates and are part of the Windows category. Table 4-1 lists all the templates found in the Windows category.

TABLE 4-1 Project templates in the Windows category

Template name	Description
Windows Forms Application	Creates a Windows Forms desktop application.
Class Library	Creates a managed dynamic-link library (DLL).
WPF Application	Creates a WPF client application.
WPF Browser Application	Creates a WPF browser application.
Console Application	Creates a console application.
Empty Project	Creates an empty project, which has no files, You are responsible for building the project essentially from scratch, including adding the necessary files.
Windows Service	Creates a Windows Service application, which is a daemon process that can run across logon sessions.
WPF Custom Control Library	Creates a library that hosts WPF custom controls, which is likely a composite of standard controls with some customization.
WPF User Control Library	Creates a library that hosts WPF user controls. User controls extend a standard control with custom properties and behavior.
Windows Forms Control Library	Creates custom controls for Windows Forms Applications.

Adding References

A project can access external code, managed or unmanaged, by adding a reference. You can add a normal reference or you can add a Web reference to a Web service. From the Project menu, select Add Reference to add a normal reference and select Add Web Reference to add a reference to a Web service. References also can be added from the Solution Explorer window by right-clicking the References folder and choosing Add Reference or Add Web Reference from the context menu.

The Add Reference dialog box, shown in Figure 4-8, has five tabbed windows. References can be added from any of these windows:

- The .NET window displays libraries from the Common Language Runtime (CLR) and .NET Framework Class Library (FCL).

- The COM window displays registered COM servers, which contain unmanaged code.

- The Projects window displays other projects of the current solution. You can create references to those projects.

- The Browse window allows you to look for a reference.

- The Recent window displays recent references. The reference may not still be valid; in that case, you can add a reference to that item again.

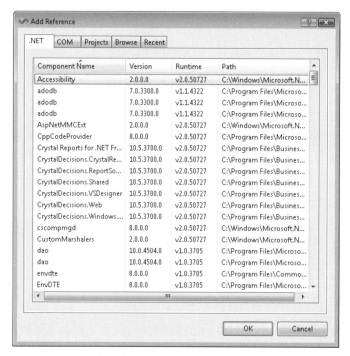

FIGURE 4-8 The Add Reference dialog box

Managing Windows in Visual Studio

Visual Studio offers an assortment of windows that serve a variety of purposes. This includes the code editor, debugging windows, the Server Explorer, Solution Explorer, and Properties windows, and a variety of toolboxes. The positioning of these windows is flexible. Most of them can float or be tabbed, docked, hidden, or auto-hidden. In the past, it has been relatively easy to hide, overlap, or otherwise muddle the Visual Studio IDE. Visual Studio 2008 provides visual clues to aid in moving and docking windows, including a guide diamond with docking arrows to help you position windows appropriately.

The Visual Studio IDE can become crowded with various windows and files. The IDE Navigator (shown in Figure 4-9) provides easy switching to help you scroll through windows and files. Pressing Ctrl+Tab opens the IDE Navigator. Once there, you can navigate between open files and windows. When the window is open, use Ctrl+arrow keys or press Ctrl+Tab or Ctrl+Shift+Tab repeatedly to navigate the items.

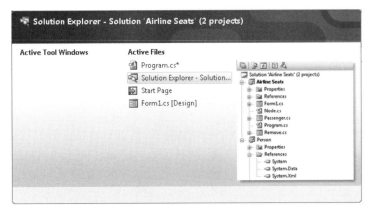

FIGURE 4-9 The IDE Navigator

AutoRecover

AutoRecover is another excellent feature of Visual Studio 2008. This option periodically saves a project and prevents the loss of data when Visual Studio is not closed properly. Figure 4-10 shows the AutoRecover window of the Options dialog box. Open this window by selecting Options from the Tools menu, then expanding the Environment node in the left-hand pane. In the AutoRecover window, set the frequency of auto saves and the length of time that backups are retained.

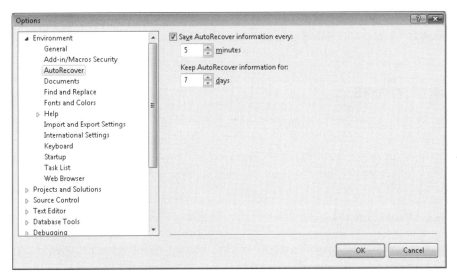

FIGURE 4-10 The AutoRecover window

When re-entering Visual Studio after an abnormal termination, the Microsoft Visual Studio Recovered Files dialog box (shown in Figure 4-11) automatically displays. In the dialog box, confirm the files that you want to recover. The AutoRecover option controls how often changes are saved and recovery files created.

FIGURE 4-11 The Microsoft Visual Studio Recovered Files dialog box

Class Hierarchies

Visual Studio 2008 offers several windows that document class hierarchies and show relationships between classes, including inheritance. The Class View, Object Browser, and Class Diagram windows are examples. The Class View and Object Browser windows have been available for some time, but the Class Diagram window was introduced in Visual Studio 2005.

Class View Window

The Class View window provides a visual representation of the types included in the projects of the current solution. Expand the project and then expand class nodes to display the class hierarchy. Each item in the class hierarchy has a context menu with helpful commands. For example, use the context menu to render classes in a class diagram. The Class View window even shows external classes from referenced applications. Open the Project References folder to find external classes. For example, many of the FCL classes will be found in this folder. Figure 4-12 shows the Class View window, including the Project References folder. If the Class View window is closed, you can open it by selecting Class View from the View menu.

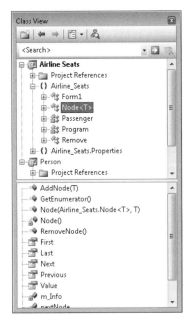

FIGURE 4-12 The Class View window

The Class View window has two panes. The top pane contains the hierarchy, whereas the bottom pane displays the details of whatever type is selected. The bottom pane presents information about a type, such as its members. Across the top of the Class View window are five icons: Class View New Folder, Back, Forward, Class View Settings, and View Class Diagram. Beneath these icons is the Search combo box, which is used to search the hierarchy for a symbol. This is especially helpful with extensive class hierarchies. Type the search text and press Enter to initiate a search. All symbols—such as classes, methods, fields, and properties—that contain some part of the search text are returned in the Class View window.

Object Browser

The Object Browser window (shown in Figure 4-13) offers similar information as the Class View window. The Object Browser displays the class hierarchy of the current project and referenced applications, such as the system libraries. If the Object Browser is not visible, open it by selecting Object Browser from the View menu.

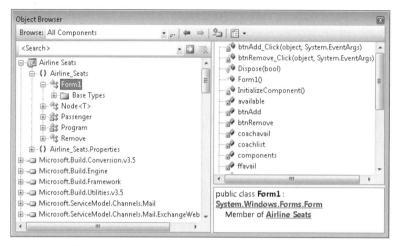

FIGURE 4-13 The Object Browser window

The Object Browser contains three panes. The left pane has the class hierarchy. The remaining two panes are vertically aligned on the right of the window. The top pane on the right lists the members of the item selected in the class hierarchy. (Members are not listed for namespaces.) A description of the selected item is found in the bottom pane. The Object Browser toolbar has the Choose Object Browsing Scope, Edit Custom Component Set, Back, Forward, Add To References, and Object Browser Settings buttons. The Browser Scope button filters the class hierarchy. You can display classes from the current solution, custom component set, .NET Framework, or all classes. Load another application into the Object Browser using the Edit Custom Component Set button. The imported information is found in the Custom Component Set scope of the Object Browser window. The Add To References button adds a reference to an application to this project. For example, you can add references from items listed at the Edit Custom Component Set scope. Use the Search box below the toolbar to enter and find specific information in the class hierarchy.

Class Diagram

Class diagrams were introduced in Visual Studio 2005. Developers can model object-oriented applications using class diagrams. Class diagrams present a visual representation of a type and type hierarchy. It's important to note that class diagrams are not static. Developers can add new types, create new relationships, insert members, delete members, and much more. In addition, the class diagram is synchronized with the source code of the application. Changes to types modeled in the class diagram are immediately updated in the affected code. Conversely, changes in the source code immediately appear in a relevant class diagram. Therefore, the code base and diagram dynamically remain in sync. Updated design documents are one of the seminal benefits of the class diagram. Where do design documents disappear to after the project has started? This problem frequently plagues developers of object-oriented applications. For many applications in the past, original design documents were not available or were not updated as the project progressed. Stale design documents sometimes are worse than nothing. They are definitely more misleading. Class diagrams help keep design documents current. With the class design, the design and implementation phase is truly iterative, which translates into better-developed applications. You also can preserve diagrams at important milestones, which then can be examined in source control for posterity. Class diagrams are preserved as snapshots. From the Class Diagram menu, choose the Export Diagram As Image command.

Class diagrams provide a high-level perspective of an application, which is beneficial throughout the life cycle of the application. This is particularly useful in complex systems, where there can be hundreds of classes and relationships. In projects of this size, it is easy to get lost in the details. Class diagrams provide visual clarity that windows such as the Class View window cannot present. Class diagrams start as an abstracted view, where introspection is available as needed.

You control how much or little information is presented in the class diagram. You can view one class, a dozen types, or everything in the class diagram. Relationships between types, such as inheritance and association, also can be shown. In addition, separate class diagrams can be created to group-related types or simply to reduce the amount of information presented in a single diagram.

In Visual Studio 2008, there are several ways to create a class diagram. One way is to select the Add New Item command from the Project menu. In the Add New Item dialog box, choose Class Diagram. In the Name text box, name the class diagram. (Class diagram files are given the .cd file extension automatically.) You also can open a new class diagram from the Solution Explorer or Class View window. In Solution Explorer, right-click the project or source file and then choose View Class Diagram. This creates a new class diagram that contains all the classes found in the project or source file. In Class View, right-click a namespace or class and choose View Class Diagram from the context menu.

Class diagrams have a surface. There are several ways to add existing or new types to this surface:

- Drag a type from the Class View window or the Object Browser to the class diagram surface.

- Drag a file from Solution Explorer to the class diagram surface. All classes in the file will be added to the class diagram.

- Add a new type from the Class Designer toolbox.

Figure 4-14 shows a class diagram with a single class on the surface. The class is contained in a shape that has a header across the top and a details pane below that. Click once on the label in the header to change the name of the class. Double-click the header to view the source code related to that shape (type). There is also an expand button or collapse button. The expand button is the double-down arrow and shows the details of the type, such as the members. The collapse button is the double-up arrow and hides the details of the type. The expand and collapse buttons toggle, depending on whether the details are visible or not.

FIGURE 4-14 A class diagram that contains a single class

In addition to adding shapes, you can remove types from a class diagram. To do this, select the shape for the target type, right-click the header, and select Remove From Diagram. The type is removed from the diagram, but it remains in the program. An easier method of removing a class from the diagram is simply to select the type and then press the Delete key. Doing this is similar to using the Remove From Diagram command. The Delete Code option is different in that it not only removes the class from the class diagram, but it also deletes it from the project.

You also can view, change, delete, add, hide, or unhide members of the type. The Hide command hides a member. Right-click the item and choose Hide. Hidden members can be shown with the Show All Members command, found on the context menu when you right-click the shape header.

Class Details

The Class Details window shows the members of the class. Members are grouped by category (fields, methods, properties, and other member types). Each group can be collapsed or expanded. Members also can be viewed and managed in the Class Details window, as shown in Figure 4-15. If the Class Details window is not visible, display it by right-clicking anywhere on the shape and choosing Class Details.

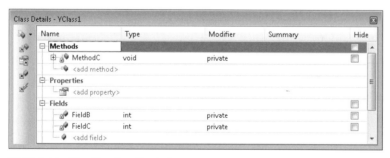

FIGURE 4-15 The Class Details window

In the Class Details window, you can change the name, type, or accessibility of a member. The Class Details toolbox has five buttons. The New *<member>* button adds a Method, Property, Field, Event, Constructor, Destructor, or Constant to a class. The Navigate To Methods button navigates to the Methods section in the Class Details window. This is helpful for large classes that have dozens of members, or even more. The final three buttons are Navigate to Properties, Navigate to Fields, and Navigate to Events.

Class Diagram Toolbox

Class diagrams have a toolbox, as shown in Figure 4-16. The topmost buttons of the toolbox add new types to the class diagram and application. You can add a new class, enumeration, interface, abstract class, structure, or delegate. Double-clicking one of these "new type" buttons adds the new type to the application, and the new type then is displayed in the class diagram. Alternatively, you can drag the button from the toolbox onto the class diagram surface to add the new type. The New Class dialog box is displayed when a new type is added. (See Figure 4-17.) The type name, accessibility, and file name can be entered in the dialog box.

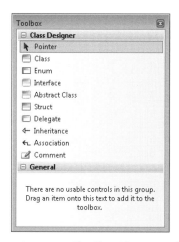

FIGURE 4-16 The Class Diagram toolbox

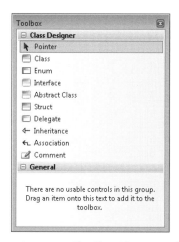

FIGURE 4-17 The New Class dialog box

The Inheritance and Association buttons appear below the New Type button on the toolbox. The Inheritance button creates an inheritance line, which links a base class and a derived class. You draw the inheritance line from the derived type to the parent type to define inheritance. The Association button creates an association line that defines the relationship between an embedded class and an outer class. Drag the association line from the outer class to the embedded class. The Comment button is the last item in the toolbox and adds comments to the class diagram.

Inheritance

Inheritance is shown in the class diagram. Inheritance lines depict the base-to-derived-type relationship. Implicit inheritance of *System.Object* and *System.ValueType* is not shown in the class diagram. Figure 4-18 shows how class inheritance is depicted in a class diagram. In the figure, *YClass* inherits from the *ZClass* class. The inheritance line has a triangular arrowhead pointing to the base class. The other end of the arrow originates at the derived class. Select and then delete the inheritance line to remove the inheritance relationship. Alternatively, you can remove the inheritance line by right-clicking the inheritance line and selecting Delete Code.

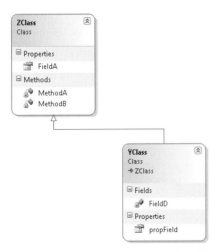

FIGURE 4-18 Class inheritance in a class diagram

You can create new base-to-derived-class relationships in the class diagram. Select the Inheritance button in the toolbox. Click anywhere in the derived class and drag the inheritance line from the derived to the base class. (In the initial release of Visual Studio 2008, you might have to switch to a different application and back after clicking the Inheritance button to use the Inheritance tool.) This assumes that both the base and derived classes are already on the class diagram.

Interface and class inheritance are manipulated similarly in the class diagram. Add interface inheritance to a type using the Inheritance button in the toolbox. Visual Studio automatically stubs the interface members in the derived type. In the Code Editor, developers can replace the stubs with the appropriate implementation. Interface inheritance is not depicted as an inheritance line. Instead, interface inheritance is displayed as a lollipop atop the derived type. This is shown in Figure 4-19, in which *ZClass* inherits the *IA* interface.

FIGURE 4-19 Interface inheritance in a class diagram

Relationship lines, which are both inheritance and association lines, can be rerouted within a diagram simply by selecting and dragging the lines. Rerouting lines can fix poorly drawn class diagrams. Lines can be rerouted multiple times and additional nodes (segments) added. Figure 4-20 shows a rerouted inheritance line. Dragging either endpoint of a line repositions the relationship line on the target shape. The mouse cursor looks like a cross when positioned correctly over the end point of a relationship line. The context menu of a relationship line has a Reroute command, which reroutes the relationship line automatically for you. This assumes that there is a better path to which the line can be routed.

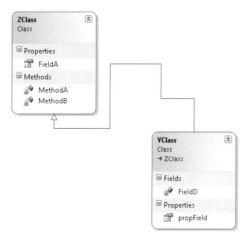

FIGURE 4-20 A rerouted inheritance line

The class diagram can locate the base or derived class of a type. Right-click a shape header to open the context menu. The Show Base Class command selects the base class in the class diagram. Conversely, choose Show Derived Classes to highlight derived classes. If the base or derived class is not already in the class diagram, the class is added automatically.

Association

Association lines define a "has-a" relationship, where one type has a member that is another type. The inner type is embedded as a property. Figure 4-21 shows an association relationship in a class diagram. In the figure, the *YClass* class has a member of the *ZClass* type embedded as a property. The association line looks slightly different from the inheritance line. Association lines have an open arrowhead pointing to the embedded type.

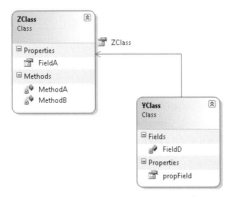

FIGURE 4-21 An association relationship in a class diagram

To create a new relationship in a class diagram, select the Association button in the toolbox. Click the outer type and drag the association line from the outer type to the inner (embedded) type. (In the initial release of Visual Studio 2008, you might have to switch to a different application and back after selecting the Association button to use the Association tool.) In the outer type, a property of the inner type is added. You then can switch to the Code Editor and implement the property, which should return an instance of the inner type. For example, if you drag the association line from *ZClass* to *XClass*, *XClass* will be the inner type. A property will be added to *ZClass*. That property should return an instance of *XClass*.

When the association line is visible, the related property is not shown in the details of the shape belonging to the outer type. Alternatively, you can show the association as a property and remove the association line. Right-click the association line and select the Show As Property command. To reverse this behavior, right-click the property and select Show As Association. (If the embedded type is not displayed, Visual Studio will add it to the diagram.)

A Class Diagram Example

The following example demonstrates the use of the class diagram—particularly in creating new types and relationships:

1. Create a new class library. In Visual Studio 2008, choose New from the File menu, then choose Project to create a new project. You also can accomplish this by clicking New Project on the Standard toolbar. Select the Visual C# node in the Project Types pane and then select the Class Library template. Name the project Personnel.

2. Add a class diagram to the project. Open the Project menu and select Add New Item. In the Add New Item dialog box, add a class diagram. Name the class diagram Employee.

3. Add a new interface using the class diagram toolbox. Name the interface *IEmployee*. Accept the remaining defaults for the interface.

4. Add a new abstract class using the class diagram toolbox. Name the class *Employee*. Accept the remaining defaults for the class.

5. Add another class using the class diagram toolbox. Name this class *HourlyEmployee*. Accept the remaining defaults for the class.

6. Add a new struct using the class diagram toolbox. Name the struct *Name*. Accept the defaults. Structs are depicted in the class diagram as rectangles with square corners.

7. From the Class Details window, add three members to the *IEmployee* interface: the *EmployeeInfo* method, the *Age* property, and the *Fullname* property. (See Figure 4-22.) The *EmployeeInfo* method returns a string. The *Age* property is an integer and gets and sets the age of an employee. Finally, the *Fullname* property is of the *Name* type and returns the employee name.

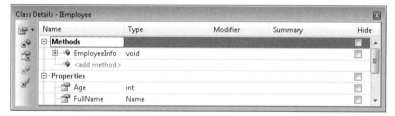

FIGURE 4-22 *IEmployee* interface details

8. The *Employee* class should inherit and implement the *IEmployee* interface. Select the Inheritance button in the class diagram toolbox. Click the *Employee* class and drag the inheritance line from the *Employee* class to the *IEmployee* interface. The interface members now appear in the class details of the *Employee* class. In addition, *Employee* is given the stubbed implementations of the interface members:

```
public abstract class Employee : IEmployee
{
    #region IEmployee Members

    public int Age
    {
        get
        {
            throw new Exception(
                "The method or operation is not implemented.");
        }
        set
        {
```

```
        throw new Exception(
            "The method or operation is not implemented.");
    }
}

// Partial listing
}
```

9. Derived types of the *Employee* class must have a calculate pay operation. Add an abstract *CalculatePay* method to the *Employee* class. (The method returns a decimal.) To do so, right-click the header of the *Employee* class. From the context menu, select Add and then select Method . Name the new method *CalculatePay*. In the Class Details window, set *decimal* as the return type. The method should be abstract, so double-click the header to view the source code for the method, then replace the body with a semi-colon (;) and change the method to abstract.

10. The *HourlyEmployee* class should inherit the *Employee* class. This relationship is created with the Inheritance button in the toolbox. Click the *HourlyEmployee* class and drag the inheritance line from the *HourlyEmployee* class to the *Employee* class.

11. Finally, add a *Pay* method to the *HourlyEmployee* class. (The *Pay* method has a single parameter, which is the hours worked.) In the Class Details window, expand the row for the *Pay* method to expose the Add Parameter item. Select the Add Parameter row and enter **Hours** as the parameter name. Change the parameter's type to *decimal*. To complete the class, add an *HourlyRate* property to the class as a decimal type.

The *Name* struct has two string properties: *FirstName* and *LastName*. Both properties can be added in the Class Details window.

The final class diagram for the Personnel application is shown in Figure 4-23.

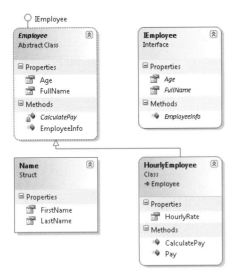

FIGURE 4-23 The class diagram of the Personnel application

The following code is generated for the class diagram. The functions are stubbed. Implementing the stubbed methods is the only remaining step. You might have to add the keyword *override* to the *CalculatePay* method.

```csharp
public interface IEmployee
{
    int Age
    {
        get;
        set;
    }

    Name Fullname
    {
        get;
        set;
    }

    string EmployeeInfo();
}

public struct Name
{
    public string FirstName
    {
        get
        {
            throw new System.NotImplementedException();
        }
        set
        {
        }
    }

    public string LastName
    {
        get
        {
            throw new System.NotImplementedException();
        }
        set
        {
        }
    }
}

public abstract class Employee : IEmployee
{
    #region IEmployee Members

    public int Age
    {
        get
        {
```

```csharp
            throw new NotImplementedException();
        }
        set
        {
            throw new NotImplementedException();
        }
    }

    public Name Fullname
    {
        get
        {
            throw new NotImplementedException();
        }
        set
        {
            throw new NotImplementedException();
        }
    }

    public string EmployeeInfo()
    {
        throw new NotImplementedException();
    }

    #endregion

    public abstract decimal CalculatePay();
}

public class HourlyEmployee : Employee
{
    public decimal HourlyRate
    {
        get
        {
            throw new System.NotImplementedException();
        }
        set
        {
        }
    }

    public override decimal CalculatePay()
    {
        throw new System.NotImplementedException();
    }

    public void Pay(decimal Hours)
    {
        throw new System.NotImplementedException();
    }
}
```

Error List Window

The Error List window (shown in Figure 4-24) displays errors and warnings as you type in the Code Editor window, from the compiler, and from the linker. Each type of message has a unique icon. For example, an error message is decorated with a red circle that contains an "x". If the window is not open, you can display it by selecting Error List from the View menu.

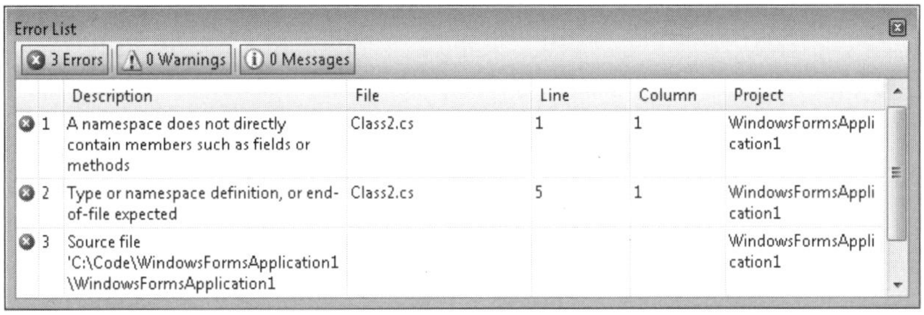

FIGURE 4-24 The Error List window

In the Error List window, the Errors, Warnings, and Messages buttons hide or show categories of messages. These buttons indicate the number of messages for each category. Click the buttons to filter messages of that category. In addition, you can use the column headers to sort the error list. Column headers can be dragged horizontally to change column order. For each error, the error number, description, and location are shown in the window. Double-clicking a specific error or warning message in the error list opens the Code Editor window and shows the pertinent source code.

Code Editor

Developers can enter, delete, format, and edit code from the Code Editor window. The Code Editor includes features such as IntelliSense, code snippets, smart tags, and formatting options.

IntelliSense

IntelliSense suggests valid options for completing keystrokes for code snippets, types, members, and other information. It helps you enter information correctly and efficiently. It minimizes the keystrokes required to enter code while improving developer accuracy. IntelliSense is available in the Code Editor and other windows.

IntelliSense provides a dynamic drop-down list called the *completion list*. It appears as developers type new commands or identifiers. The completion list automatically appears when useful, such as after entering a dot (.) for a member. You also can prompt the completion list by pressing Ctrl+spacebar. The completion list might contain namespaces, types, type members, language keywords, and code snippets. The content depends on the context where the completion list is displayed. As text is entered, the nearest matching item in the list is selected. As more text is entered, the match is refined in the completion list. When the desired item is selected, press Tab to insert it. You also can select an item with the mouse. Assuming that the IntelliSense For Most Recently Used Members option is enabled, recently used items that match the input text are selected first. This option is set in the Options command on the Tool menu. It is enabled by default. Function overloads are not shown in the completion list. For example, there are several overloads of the *Console.WriteLine* method. However, *WriteLine* appears in the member list just once. The overload versions of a function, if any, are displayed by IntelliSense as you enter parameters.

IntelliSense displays the parameters of a function, including any overloaded versions, which have different signatures. Use the up and down arrows (shown in Figure 4-25) to cycle through the available overloads. Parameter information is presented after entering the open parentheses for a function. The Ctrl+Shift+spacebar combination of keystrokes displays parameter information on demand.

FIGURE 4-25 Parameter information for *Console.WriteLine*

IntelliSense in Visual Studio 2008 automatically detects generics, types, and arguments. In the example shown in Figure 4-26, a generic dictionary is defined where entries have an integer key and a string value.

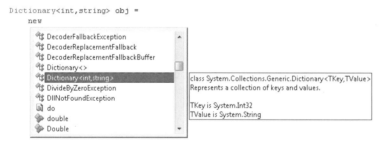

FIGURE 4-26 IntelliSense for a generic type

Have you ever attempted to use a type without the proper *using* statement? It requires stop-ping, researching the correct namespace, and then adding the *using* statement or explicitly specifying the namespace. The Add Using feature of IntelliSense automates this process—yet another way IntelliSense improves developer productivity.

When an unbound type is entered, a smart tag appears beneath the last character as a narrow red box. The smart tag is shown when the cursor is within the unbound text or immediately thereafter. From the Add Using smart tag menu (shown in Figure 4-27), you have two choices: Either insert the *using* statement or prefix the unbound type with the required namespace. Alternatively, right-click the unbound type, choose Resolve from the context menu, and then choose from the two submenu choices.

FIGURE 4-27 The Add Using smart tag menu

Surround With

You can surround code with an item from the completion list. For example, a block of statements can be surrounded with a *for* loop. The Surround With feature surrounds selected text with the selected item from the completion list. First select the text to be surrounded. Right-click the selected text and choose the Surround With command. The Surround With command displays the completion list. Select the item that should surround the text.

Font and Color Formatting

Visual Studio allows you to customize the font and color settings. Customize them in the Options dialog box, which is opened from the Tools menu. In the dialog box, expand the Environment node in the left-hand pane, and then select the Fonts And Colors node. Figure 4-28 shows the Fonts And Colors settings in the Options dialog box.

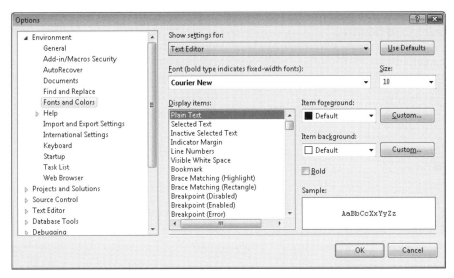

FIGURE 4-28 Fonts And Colors settings in the Options dialog box

Source Code Formatting

Visual Studio 2008 provides excellent control of code formatting. You can control code indentation, line spacing, code spacing, and the wrapping of blocks. This is done in the Options dialog box on the Tools menu. Expand the Text Editor node in the left-hand pane, and then select the C# node. (See Figure 4-29.) The Tabs, Advanced, Formatting, and IntelliSense nodes provide additional options.

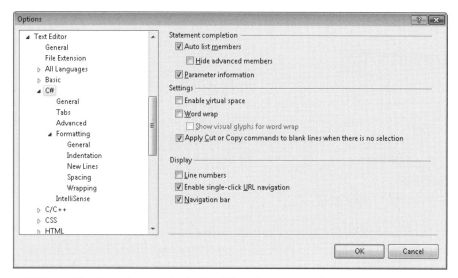

FIGURE 4-29 The General settings in the Text Editor, C# category of the Options window

Change Tracking

Change tracking distinguishes saved from unsaved code. Visual Studio 2008 displays a colored bar on the left of the Code Editor window to indicate the code status. Saved code has a green bar, while unsaved code has a yellow bar. Original code, which is code that is unchanged since the source file was opened, has no colored bar at all.

Code Snippets

Developers are connoisseurs of code and tend to collect useful code in a variety of places. While other people collect coins, books, or PEZ dispensers, developers collect code snippets. Why? Developers do not like typing. There is some irony in that, considering how much typing is involved in programming. Still, the principle is unshakable: If you want to improve developers' productivity, reduce the amount they have to type. Code snippets provide an organized method of managing fragments of code, which then can be reinserted when needed. Developers traditionally cut and paste code to prevent typing the same code over and over. However, this has some limitations, including limited persistence of the Clipboard.

Code snippets reduce the number of typos and resulting compiler errors. Code reuse is another reason why developers collect code. Even applications perceived as unique are largely composed of small and modular code snippets. Some of these code fragments, such as loops, classes, and exception handling, are common to every program.

Code snippets are capsules of reusable source code: essentially, aliases for pieces of code. Use a code snippet to insert the aliased code into the source file as needed.

There are multiple sources for snippets. Visual Studio 2008 has a set of default snippets for common tasks, such as the *for*, *try*, and *while* snippets. Snippets also are available online and can be downloaded. Finally, developers can create custom snippets.

There are three kinds of snippets, described as follows:

- **Expansion**   Inserts code at the cursor
- **Surround With**   Envelops selected code
- **Refactoring**   Used with refactoring

A single snippet might fit into more than one category. For example, *while* is both an Expansion snippet and a Surround With snippet.

Insert a Code Snippet

Use the following techniques to select and insert code snippets:

- Insert a code snippet using IntelliSense. This is the most convenient way to add a snippet. Code snippets appear in the completion list as a torn page. To insert a code snippet, either enter the complete name at the prompt (IntelliSense automatically completes the name of the category and the snippet as you begin to type it) or double-click the snippet in the completion list.

- Insert a code snippet from a context menu in the Code Editor window. Choose the Insert Snippet menu command. This is called the *code snippet picker*. You are presented folders that group related snippets together. Open the proper category and then select the correct snippet or enter the name of the snippet at the prompt. (IntelliSense automatically completes the name of the category and the snippet as you begin to type it.)

- Hitting Ctrl+K and then Ctrl+X is the keyboard shortcut for the Insert Snippet menu command. At the prompt, enter the name of the snippet. (IntelliSense automatically completes the name of the category and the snippet as you begin to type it.)

- Insert a code snippet using Auto IntelliSense. Position the cursor where the snippet should be inserted, type the name of the snippet, and then press Tab twice. For example, type **for** and then press Tab twice. The *for* snippet will be inserted. Of course, you should do this where a *for* loop is appropriate

Some code snippets are templates and contain editable fields. After inserting the code snippet, a developer customizes the template by assigning values to each field. The first field is selected automatically when the code snippet is inserted. Other fields in the code template are highlighted in color. There can be multiple instances of a field in the same code snippet. For example, there are several instances of the *i* field in the *for* snippet. The first instance of a field is highlighted in color and editable. Remaining instances are notated with a dotted border. When entering data, pressing Tab moves you to the next field, whereas pressing Shift-Tab moves you to the previous file. You can select a field by double-clicking it. Fields with tool tips display the tip when the field is selected. Figure 4-30 shows the *for* snippet. It has the *'i'* and *length* fields. Figure 4-31 shows the snippet with the fields populated with values.

```
for (int i = 0; i < length; i++)
{

}
```

FIGURE 4-30 The *for* snippet

```
for (int count = 0; count < 9; count++)
{

}
```

FIGURE 4-31 A customized code snippet

When using a Surround With template, select the target code first and then add the snippet. The snippet will surround the code. For example, the following code increments a counter:

```
int count = 0;
Console.WriteLine(++count);
if (count == 10)
{
    break;
}
```

The following code is the result of selecting the previous code and adding the code snippet for the *while* keyword:

```
while (true)
{
    int count = 0;
    Console.WriteLine(++count);
    if (count == 10)
    {
        break;
    }
}
```

Default Snippets

Visual Studio 2008 has default snippets for routine tasks. The default snippets include a mixture of Expansion and Surround With code snippets. Default snippets appear in the IntelliSense completion list and the code snippet picker. Table 4-2 lists some of the default code snippets.

TABLE 4-2 Default code snippets

Code snippet	Description
#if	Surrounds code with the #if and #endif directives
#region	Surrounds code with the #region and #endregion directives
~	Inserts a destructor
attribute	Inserts a class definition for a custom attribute, which is derived from System.Attribute
checked	Surrounds code with a checked block
class	Inserts a class definition
ctor	Inserts a constructor
cw	Inserts a Console.WriteLine statement
do	Surrounds code with a do while block
else	Inserts an else block
enum	Inserts an enum type
equals	Overrides the Equals method inherited from the System.Object type
exception	Inserts a class definition for an application exception, which is derived from System.Exception
for	Surrounds code with a for loop
foreach	Surrounds code with a foreach loop
forr	Surrounds code with a for loop that automatically decrements the loop variable
if	Surrounds code with an if block
indexer	Inserts an indexer function
interface	Inserts an interface definition
iterator	Inserts an iterator
interindex	Inserts a named iterator and indexer
invoke	Inserts an event followed by an invocation of the event
lock	Surrounds code with a lock block
mbox	Inserts the MessageBox.Show statement
namespace	Surrounds code with a namespace
prop	Inserts a property and backing field
propg	Inserts a read-only property. Read-only properties have only a get method
sim	Inserts an entry point (Main) method that is static and returns an integer
struct	Inserts the definition of a struct
svm	Inserts an entry point (Main) method that is static and returns void
switch	Inserts a switch statement

TABLE 4-2 Default code snippets

Code snippet	Description
try	Surrounds code with a *try-catch* block
tryf	Surrounds code with a *try-finally* block
unchecked	Surrounds code with an *unchecked* block
unsafe	Surrounds code with an *unsafe* block
using	Surrounds code with a *using* block
while	Surrounds code with a *while* loop

Code Snippets Manager

Use the Code Snippets Manager (shown in Figure 4-32) to manage snippets, including adding, removing, importing, and searching for snippets.

The Code Snippets Manager can be opened from the Tools menu. The folders shown in the Code Snippets Manager are snippet directories. Each directory contains a group of related snippets. Open a directory and possible subdirectories to view individual snippets. For each snippet, the following information is provided:

- Description of the code snippet
- The alias or shortcut of the code snippet
- The snippet type
- The author of the snippet

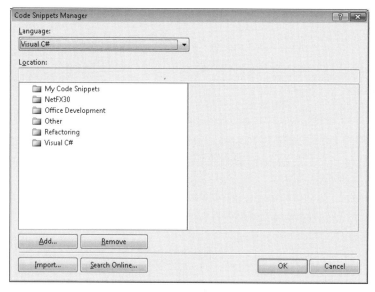

FIGURE 4-32 The Code Snippets Manager

The Add button in the Code Snippets Manager adds a directory to the list of code snippet directories. A code snippets directory contains code snippet files, which are Extensible Markup Language (XML) files with the .snippet suffix. The Remove button removes a snippet directory from the list. The Import button imports a code snippet file. Use the Search Online button to browse for code snippets online. This button opens a general search window, in which developers can search for code snippets. When you find the code snippet you're searching for, you can download the file.

Be aware, however, that downloading snippets you find online is a security risk. The XML of the snippet poses a potential security problem. The snippet might hide malicious scripts. Also, code snippets can silently add references, which then makes it possible for malicious calls to be made to functions in the reference. Be careful when downloading code snippets with database access, code-access security, role-base security, or validation code. As a best practice, carefully review the source code of code snippets that you download before using them in an application.

Creating Snippets

You can create custom code snippets to encapsulate reusable code not found online or in a default snippet, which allows you to maintain private libraries of reusable code. Different industries already may have specialized code snippets. For example, a developer of medical software could use code snippets designed for medical applications, and a developer of legal software could benefit from code snippets designed specifically for legal applications. The availability of snippet libraries will expand in the future.

Custom code snippets are defined with XML files that have the .snippet extension. Microsoft publishes an XML schema for code snippets. Once the schema is declared, Visual Studio 2008 offers IntelliSense on the XML elements and attributes, which helps considerably in creating properly formed code snippet files. You can group custom snippets in directories. Add these directories to the Code Snippets Manager to make using customized snippets more convenient.

The XML schema for code snippets defines the structure of a code snippet file. For a complete explanation of the schema, visit the Code Snippet Schema Reference at *http:// msdn2.microsoft.com/en-us/library/ms171418(en-us,vs.80).aspx*. Some parts of the schema are discussed next.

CodeSnippets and CodeSnippet Elements

The *CodeSnippets* element is the root element of the code snippet file. The *xlmns* attribute names the code snippet schema, as follows:

```
<CodeSnippets xmlns="http://schemas.microsoft.com/VisualStudio/2005/CodeSnippet">
  <CodeSnippet Format="1.0.0">
```

A code snippet is described inside the *CodeSnippet* elements, as follows:

```
<CodeSnippet>
  <!-- Insert code snippet here. -->
</CodeSnippet>
```

Header Element

The *Header* element has child elements, which provide the basic information about the code snippet. The title, author, description, shortcut, and snippet type are some of the details that can be provided. The title is the name of the code snippet as it appears in the code snippet picker, while the shortcut name appears in the IntelliSense completion list. The description of the snippet found in the Code Snippets Manager is read from this element.

Here is the *Header* element for an example snippet for the *StringBuilder* type:

```
<Header>
  <Title>StringBuilder</Title>
  <Shortcut>sb</Shortcut>
  <Description>Creates a new String Builder</Description>
  <Author>Donis Marshall</Author>
</Header>
```

Snippet, References, and *Imports* Elements

The *Snippet* element encapsulates the actual code of the code snippet. *References* and *Imports* are child elements of the *Snippet* element. The *References* element identifies references required for the code snippet. Within the *References* element, there are *Reference* child elements for each individual reference. The *Imports* element names implicit namespaces. Within the *Imports* element, there are *Import* child elements that identify each namespace to import. Each namespace is identified within *Namespace* elements. Importing a namespace allows implicit access of members in a namespace without explicitly naming the namespace. An *Import* element generates a *using <namespace>* statement.

Here is an example of the *References* and *Import* elements. The *System.Text* namespace contains the *StringBuilder* type:

```
<Snippet>
  <References>
    <Reference>
      <Assembly>System.Text.Dll</Assembly>
    </Reference>
  </References>
  <Imports>
    <Import>
      <Namespace>System.Text</Namespace>
    </Import>
  </Imports>
```

Declarations, Literal, and *Object* **Elements**

The *Declarations* element describes the fields used in the code snippet. It is a child element of the *Snippet* element and has *Literal* and *Object* child elements. The *Literal* element declares a literal field, which is a field that is fully contained in the code snippet. This would include string and numeric literals. The *Object* element also declares a field, but the field is defined outside the snippet. This element usually describes a type.

The *Literal* and *Object* elements can contain *ID*, *Default*, *Tooltip*, *Type*, and *Function* child elements, which are as follows:

- The *ID* element is the name of the field.

- The *Default* element is the default value of the field.

- The *Tooltip* element is the tool tip of the field.

- The *Type* element sets the type of the field.

- The *Function* element is a function name. This is a function to call whenever the field receives the focus in Visual Studio.

Here is the *Declarations* element of the *StringBuilder* code snippet:

```
<Declarations>
  <Literal>
    <ID>Name</ID>
    <Default>mytext</Default>
    <ToolTip>Name of new StringBuilder</ToolTip>
  </Literal>
  <Literal>
    <ID>Size</ID>
    <ToolTip>Capacity of String</ToolTip>
  </Literal>
</Declarations>
```

Code and *<![CDATA]>* **Elements**

The *Code* element contains individual lines of code. It also selects the language of the code snippet. *Code* is a child element of the *Snippet* element. The target language is set in the *Language* attribute. Valid languages are *CSharp*, *VB*, *VJSHARP*, and *XML*.

Each line of code is placed in a *<![CDATA]>* element. The code must be written in the syntax of the chosen language.

Here is the *CDATA* syntax:

```
<![CDATA[snippetcode]]>
```

In snippet code, fields are bounded with dollar signs ($*<field>*$). This is the snippet code for the *StringBuilder* snippet:

```
<Code Language="CSharp">
  <![CDATA[StringBuilder $Name$=]]>
  <![CDATA[    new StringBuilder($Size$);]]>
</Code>
```

String Builder Code Snippet

The following code is the complete listing of the sample code snippet, which creates a new *StringBuilder* type. The *StringBuilder* type is found in the *System.Text.Dll* library and the *System.Text* namespace. Fields are defined for the name and size of the *StringBuilder* type.

```
<?xml version="1.0" encoding="utf-8"?>
<CodeSnippets xmlns="http://schemas.microsoft.com/VisualStudio/2005/CodeSnippet">
  <CodeSnippet Format="1.0.0">
    <Header>
      <Title>StringBuilder</Title>
      <Shortcut>sb</Shortcut>
      <Description>Creates a new String Builder</Description>
      <Author>Donis Marshall</Author>
    </Header>
    <Snippet>
      <References>
        <Reference>
          <Assembly>System.Text.Dll</Assembly>
        </Reference>
      </References>
      <Imports>
        <Import>
          <Namespace>System.Text</Namespace>
        </Import>
      </Imports>
      <Declarations>
        <Literal>
          <ID>Name</ID>
          <Default>mytext</Default>
          <ToolTip>Name of new StringBuilder</ToolTip>
        </Literal>
        <Literal>
          <ID>Size</ID>
          <ToolTip>Capacity of String</ToolTip>
        </Literal>
      </Declarations>
      <Code Language="CSharp">
        <![CDATA[StringBuilder $Name$=]]>
        <![CDATA[new StringBuilder($Size$);]]>
      </Code>
    </Snippet>
  </CodeSnippet>
</CodeSnippets>
```

Code Snippet Creation Example

This section provides an example of creating a code snippet. Before creating a snippet, it is best to write and test any snippet code in a conventional application. Convert the code into a code snippet only after a successful test has been performed. You should place custom snippets in a dedicated directory. Make sure the directory is identified as a directory with code snippets by adding the directory in the Code Snippets Manager. For this example, name the custom directory "snippets."

The example in this section creates a code snippet that reflects the methods of a type. The following code tests the proposed snippet:

```
// Snippet starts
Type t = typeof(Object);
string typename = t.Name;
string typenamespace = t.Namespace;
MethodInfo[] methods = t.GetMethods();
// Snippet ends
Console.WriteLine("Type Name:" + typename);
Console.WriteLine("Namespace Name:" + typenamespace);
foreach (MethodInfo method in methods)
{
    Console.WriteLine(method.Name);
}
```

Create a snippet from the preceding code using the following procedure:

1. Create an XML file in Visual Studio. The filename of the code snippet is *reflectmethod. snippet.*

2. All snippet files begin with the *CodeSnippets*, *CodeSnippet*, and *Header* elements, which name the file schema and describe the basic attributes of the code snippet. This is the basic element for our snippet:

```
<?xml version="1.0" encoding="utf-8"?>
<CodeSnippets xmlns="http://schemas.microsoft.com/VisualStudio/2005/CodeSnippet">
  <CodeSnippet Format="1.0.0">
    <Header>
      <Title>ReflectMethod</Title>
      <Shortcut>rm</Shortcut>
      <Description>Reflects methods of a type.</Description>
      <Author>Donis Marshall</Author>
    </Header>
  </CodeSnippet>
</CodeSnippets>
```

3. Performing reflection naturally requires the *Reflection* namespace. Import the *System. Reflection* namespace with an *Import* element, which is contained within the *Imports* element. The *System.Reflection* namespace is declared in System.dll. System.dll is implicitly available to managed code, so a *Reference* element is not needed for this snippet:

```
<Snippet>
  <Imports>
    <Import>
      <Namespace>System.Reflection</Namespace>
    </Import>
  </Imports>
</Snippet>
```

4. The code snippet has five fields, which are the type, type instance, namespace, and a *MethodInfo* array. The type instance is an object field. The other fields are literals and contained within the code snippet. Defaults for the fields are gleaned from the code used to test the code snippet. Fields are defined within the *Declarations* element with *Literal* and *Object* elements:

```
<Declarations>
  <Literal>
    <ID>Instance</ID>
    <Default>t</Default>
    <ToolTip>Name of instance.</ToolTip>
  </Literal>
  <Literal>
    <ID>TypeName</ID>
    <Default>typename</Default>
    <ToolTip>Name of type.</ToolTip>
  </Literal>
  <Literal>
    <ID>TypeNamespace</ID>
    <Default>typenamespace</Default>
    <ToolTip>Namespace of type.</ToolTip>
  </Literal>
  <Literal>
    <ID>Methods</ID>
    <Default>Methods</Default>
    <ToolTip>Type methods</ToolTip>
  </Literal>
  <Object>
    <ID>Type</ID>
    <Default>Object</Default>
    <ToolTip>object type</ToolTip>
    <Type>System.Object</Type>
  </Object>
</Declarations>
```

5. Paste the tested code for the snippet into separate *<![CDATA]>* elements. Then place the *<![CDATA]>* elements within the *Code* element. Add extra line feeds to separate lines of source code. After entering the code, substitute the field names into the code:

```
<Code Language="CSharp">
  <![CDATA[Type $Instance$ = typeof($Type$);
  ]]>
  <![CDATA[string $TypeName$ = $Instance$.Name;
  ]]>
  <![CDATA[string $TypeNamespace$ = $Instance$.Namespace;
  ]]>
  <![CDATA[MethodInfo [] $Methods$ = $Instance$.GetMethods();
  ]]>
</Code>
```

6. Save the file for the code snippet in the directory reserved for custom code snippets.

7. Test the snippet in Visual Studio 2008. To do so, open a source file and insert the code snippet using the code snippet picker. Figure 4-33 shows both the snippet in the code snippet picker and the snippet after it has been inserted.

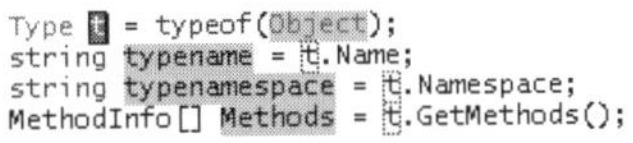

```
Type t = typeof(Object);
string typename = t.Name;
string typenamespace = t.Namespace;
MethodInfo[] Methods = t.GetMethods();
```

FIGURE 4-33 The *Reflect Method* snippet

Copy and Paste

Of course, copying and pasting code remains available as an alternative to using snippets. One of the main disadvantages of this approach, however, is that the Clipboard is a shared resource in Windows. A second problem is that Clipboard data is not retained across logon sessions. Visual Studio resolves these shortcomings by allowing you to copy source code directly to the toolbox, which then preserves the code on the toolbox for future placement. Code placed in the toolbox is preserved between Visual Studio sessions as well as between logon sessions. This technique is not as elegant as using a snippet, but sometimes it is quicker and more convenient, especially when a custom snippet is required. Unlike the Clipboard, the toolbox is not a shared resource and is available only to Visual Studio.

There are two methods of placing code on the toolbox. The first is to select the code, copy it to the Clipboard, click on the toolbox, and paste the code. The second way is simply to drag the selected code onto the toolbox. A button is then created on the toolbox for the code. Multiple items can be added to the toolbox. After code is placed on the Clipboard, moving the mouse over a code button in the toolbox displays the saved code. Click the code button to insert the code at the cursor. As a best practice, create a separate tab on the toolbox to group code buttons together, as intermingling code with nonrelated buttons can be distracting. To add a tab, right-click the toolbox, choose Add Tab from the context menu, and then enter a name for the new tab. A toolbox populated with code buttons is shown in Figure 4-34. A tab called Code was added to the toolbox for grouping these buttons.

FIGURE 4-34 A toolbox with code buttons

Refactoring

Most, if not all, applications evolve. They sometimes require local or even global changes. During the lifetime of an application, considerable time is spent re-engineering, usually with the objective of improving the code. This sometimes starts as early as the development phase and accelerates as the application matures. This includes—but is not limited to—renaming variables, moving code into methods, changing method signatures, and redesigning classes. Finding and changing a variable in a software system that spans dozens of source files can be challenging. Another task that can be difficult is changing the signature of a commonly used method. When you do this, you must locate and change method calls throughout the application. However, if you make a mistake, these changes might not achieve the desired effects. Worst-case scenario: these changes might introduce bugs into otherwise pristine applications. Refactoring helps developers re-engineer code and removes much of the tedium of maintaining an application. Visual Studio 2008 provides refactoring as a viable, multifaceted tool to help developers. Refactoring assists in renaming variables, changing method signatures, extrapolating interfaces, converting fields to properties, and much more.

The Visual Studio 2008 user interface has a Refactoring menu that provides the operations listed in Table 4-3. The Refactoring menu is also available in the Code Editor using a context menu.

TABLE 4-3 Refactoring operations

Operations	Description
Rename	Renames a symbol, such as a variable or method name, throughout an application.
Extract Method	Creates a new method that encapsulates the selected code.
Encapsulate Field	Creates a property that abstracts the selected field.
Extract Interface	Extracts an interface from a type.

TABLE 4-3 **Refactoring operations**

Operations	Description
Promote Local Variable To Parameters	Promotes a local variable to a parameter of the current method.
Remove Parameters	Removes a parameter from the parameter list of a function. Call sites for the function are updated to reflect the removed parameter.
Reorder Parameters	Reorders the parameters of a function. Call sites for the function are updated for the new sequence of parameters.

The Preview Changes dialog box, such as the one shown in Figure 4-35, is invaluable because it provides you with an opportunity to preview refactoring changes before applying them.

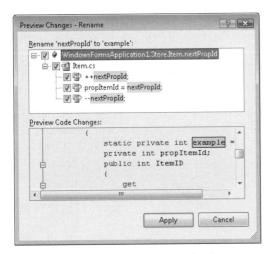

FIGURE 4-35 The Preview Changes dialog box

Refactoring can span multiple projects of the same solution, which occurs with project-to-project references. A project-to-project reference is a reference where the projects for both the referencing and referenced assemblies are in the current solution. The Projects tab of the Add Reference dialog box inserts a project-to-project reference. This was shown in the "Adding References" section, earlier in this chapter.

Refactoring Example

This example demonstrates some of the features of refactoring, including renaming variables and extracting interfaces. On the Web site, this code is in the Refactoring project for Chapter 4. The scenario refactors the Airline Seats application. This application manages the first class and coach standby lists of an airline flight. Figure 4-36 shows the screen presented to the ticket clerk at an airline check-in counter.

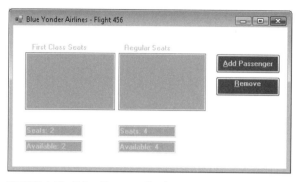

FIGURE 4-36 Airline Seats application

The following steps outline this example procedure:

1. The application defines a *Node* class, which is a generic collection class in the *node.cs* file. The value of a node is returned from the *Info* property. The property should be renamed *Value*, which is more intuitive. Right-click the *Info* name in the source file. From the context menu, choose Refactor and then choose the Rename command.

2. The Rename dialog box appears, as shown in Figure 4-37. The selected text is displayed with its location. Three check boxes are presented. The Preview Reference Changes option provides a preview dialog box before the changes are applied. This option is selected by default. The Search In Comments option searches comments, in addition to code, for the renamed text. The Search In Strings option extends the search to literals, such as string literals. Enter Value in the New Name text box and proceed with the renaming operation by clicking OK.

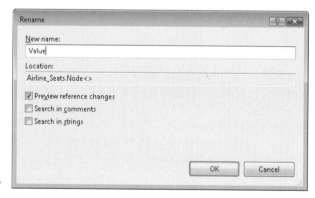

FIGURE 4-37 The Rename dialog box

3. The Preview Changes dialog box appears, as shown in Figure 4-38. You can review the pending changes in this window. Specific changes can be selected or unselected. When acceptable, click Apply, and the specified changes are applied. If necessary, you can undo refactoring changes using the Undo (Ctrl+Z) feature of Visual Studio.

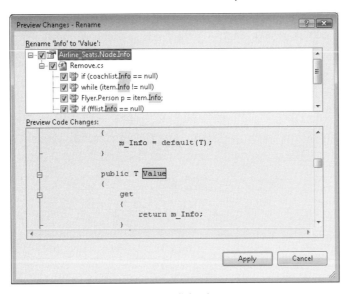

FIGURE 4-38 The Preview Changes dialog box

4. The ability to extrapolate interfaces from classes is another great feature of refactoring. Manually extracting interfaces from types is a time-consuming process for developers, so refactoring can be a great way to speed this task. The Airline Seats application has a *Person* class that represents the flyer. In the future, other types of people may be added to the application, such as flight attendants. For that reason, you want to extrapolate the *Person* interface for future use. To do so, right-click anywhere within the class and choose Refactor, then choose the Extract Interface command. The Extract Interface dialog box appears, as shown in Figure 4-39. Enter the new interface name and a new file name. A list of potential members is presented. You can select the members to include in the interface. As a convenience, Select All and Deselect All buttons are provided. Click Select All, and then click OK.

FIGURE 4-39 The Extract Interface dialog box

5. The *Passenger* class has two public fields. A tenet of object-oriented programming is that fields should be private. Exposing the fields as public properties is more secure. Look at the following code:

```
public Node<Flyer.Person> coachlist = null;
public Node<Flyer.Person> fflist = null;
```

6. Right-click the first field. From the context menu, select Refactor, and then choose the Encapsulate Field command. The Encapsulate Field dialog box appears, as shown in Figure 4-40. Enter the property name and click OK.

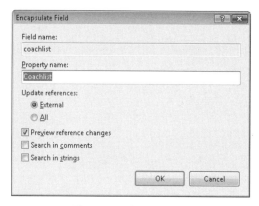

FIGURE 4-40 The Encapsulate Field dialog box

7. The Preview Reference Changes dialog box appears, showing the potential changes. You can accept or reject individual changes.

8. Repeat Steps 6 and 7 to convert the second field to a property.

This is the interface created from the Extract Interface refactoring operation. It is saved to a separate file. In the file, change the namespace containing the interface appropriately. For the sample application, change the namespace to *Flyer*. Despite the numerous changes in various parts of the application, you now can compile and run the program successfully.

```
interface IPerson
{
    string FirstName { get; set; }
    bool FrequentFlyer { get; set; }
    string ID { get; set; }
    string LastName { get; set; }
}
```

Refactoring also updated the *Person* class to inherit the *IPerson* interface (and the namespace has been updated to *Flyer*):

```
public class Person : Flyer.IPerson
{
    // partial listing
}
```

This is one of the properties created from refactoring a field in the *Passenger* class:

```
private Node<Flyer.Person> coachlist = null;

public Node<Flyer.Person> Coachlist
{
    get { return coachlist; }
    set { coachlist = value; }
}
```

Building and Deployment

The Microsoft Build Engine (MSBuild) is the build environment for Visual Studio. The build process is described in an XML-based project file. MSBuild replaces traditional .mak files. The project file describes the build process, build configuration, and input and output.

For deployment, Visual Studio 2008 supports traditional deployment based on Windows Installer technology. With Windows Installer technology, an application is packaged in a Setup.exe file, which is then deployed to the local machine or a public share. The Setup.exe program installs the application on the local machine. ClickOnce deployment is available in Visual Studio 2008 as an alternate deployment strategy. ClickOnce deploys an application from a central location and combines the functionality and "look and feel" of a desktop application with a Web-based delivery system.

MSBuild

MSBuild does not require Visual Studio. This program is ideal to use in lab environments in which Visual Studio is not installed. Individual builds are organized in project files. Build project files are XML files and have a .proj extension. As an XML file, the build project is platform-independent and extensible. For a complete explanation of MSBuild, consult the MSBuild Reference MSDN at *http://msdn2.microsoft.com/en-us/library/0k6kkbsd.aspx*.

Build projects consist of items, properties, and tasks, as described in the following sections.

Items

Items are the input of the build process. Items are created as child elements of the *ItemGroup* element. Items that share the same name are considered a collection. Item collections are addressable in the build project as @(*ItemCollectionName*). Item collections are primarily used as parameters in build tasks.

For example, the *Compile* element is a standard item. It defines the source files that are included or excluded from the build. The *Include* attribute specifies a file to be included in the build. The *Exclude* attribute, naturally, excludes files. The following code defines a *Compile* collection, which includes two items and excludes a third item:

```
<ItemGroup>
  <Compile Include="source1.cs"/>
  <Compile Include="source3.cs" Exclude="source2.cs"/>
</ItemGroup>
```

Properties

Properties are configuration data for the build process that represent individual values and cannot be grouped into collections. They are defined as child elements of the *PropertyGroup* element. Refer to properties in the project using the $(*property*) syntax.

```
<PropertyGroup>
  <ApplicationVersion>1.2.3.4</ApplicationVersion>
</PropertyGroup>
```

There are several reserved properties in the MSBuild environment. Table 4-4 lists the reserved properties.

TABLE 4-4 **Reserved properties**

Property	Description
MSBuildProjectDirectory	The absolute path to the MSBuild project file.
MSBuildProjectFile	The name and extension of the MSBuild project file.
MSBuildProjectExtension	The file extension of the MSBuild project file. It should be prefixed with a dot (.).
MSBuildProjectFullPath	The fully qualified name of the MSBuild project file.
MSBuildProjectName	The name of the MSBuild project file without the extension.
MSBuildBinPath	The path to the MSBuild binaries.
MSBuildProjectDefaultTargets	The list of targets available to the *DefaultTargets* attribute of the *Project* element in the MSBuild project file. Refer to documentation of the *DefaultTargets* attribute for more information.
MSBuildExtensionsPath	The supplemental directory for custom target files. This is a subdirectory of the Program Files directory.

Tasks

Tasks are the build operations of an MSBuild project. Each task is a child element of the *Target* element. Tasks can accept parameters, which are attributes of a *Task* element. Item collections and properties, as described previously, are valid parameters to tasks. Create multiple targets to batch groups of build operations. The MSBuild tool can invoke different targets. For example, you can create targets for release versus debug builds.

Tasks are written in a managed language and are available to any MSBuild project. You can create custom tasks for MSBuild projects. All tasks must implement the *ITask* interface.

Table 4-5 lists the default tasks available in the MSBuild environment.

TABLE 4-5 Default tasks

Task	Description
AL	Invokes the Assembly Linker (AL) tool.
AspNetCompiler	Invokes aspnet_compiler.exe, which precompiles ASP.NET applications.
AssignCulture	Creates culture metadata for files that have a culture identifier.
CallTarget	Invokes the specified target.
CombinePath	Combines paths into a single path.
ConvertToAbsolutePath	Converts a relative path to an absolute path.
Copy	Copies files to a specified directory.
CreateCSharpManifestResourceName	Creates a C# manifest name for a resource or resource file.
CreateItem	Copies task items between collections.
CreateProperty	Copies task properties.
CreateVisualBasicManifestResourceName	Creates a Visual Basic manifest name for a resource or resource file.
Csc	Invokes csc.exe, which is the C# compiler.
Delete	Deletes files.
Error	Stops a build and logs an error.
Exec	Executes an application or command.
FindUnderPath	Determines which files are found within a specified directory and its subdirectories.
GenerateApplicationManifest	Creates an application or native manifest for a ClickOnce application.
GenerateBootstrapper	Locates, downloads, and installs an application.
GenerateDeploymentManifest	Creates a deployment manifest for a ClickOnce application.
GenerateResource	Creates .resources files from .txt and .resx files.
GetAssemblyIdentity	Returns assembly metadata and stores the results in an item collection.
GetFrameworkPath	Obtains the path of the .NET Framework assemblies.
GetFrameworkSDKPath	Obtains the path of the .NET Framework software development kit (SDK).
LC	Converts a .licx file to a .license file.
Makedir	Makes a directory.
MSBuild	Builds an MSBuild project from another build project.

TABLE 4-5 Default tasks

Task	Description
ReadLinesFromFile	Reads MSBuild items from a file.
RegisterAssembly	Reads the metadata of an assembly and registers the assembly as a COM server, which allows COM clients to access the assembly.
RemoveDir	Deletes a directory.
RemoveDuplicates	Removes duplicates from an item collection.
ResGen	Uses the GenerateResource task to convert between .resources files.
ResolveAssemblyReference	Determines which assemblies depend on another assembly.
ResolveComReference	Resolves the location of type library (TLB) files.
ResolveKeySource	Determines the strong name of a key source.
ResolveNativeReference	Resolves native references.
Sgen	Wraps the XML Serialization Generator Tool (sgen.exe).
SignFile	Signs a file with a certificate.
Touch	Sets the access and modification timestamp of a file.
UnregisterAssembly	Unregisters an assembly from the registry. Afterward, the assembly is no longer available to COM clients.
Vbc	Invokes vbc.exe, which is the Visual Basic .NET compiler.
VcBuild	Acts as a proxy to vcbuild.exe, which builds a Visual C++ project.
WriteLinesToFiles	Writes the paths of the specified items to a file.

Project File

MSBuild elements and attributes are assembled in a project file. An MSBuild project can have any number of tasks, item collections, and properties. This is a general skeleton of an MSBuild project:

```
<?xml version="1.0" encoding="utf-8"?>
<!-- MSBuild Schema -->
<Project xmlns="http://schemas.microsoft.com/developer/msbuild/2003">
  <ItemGroup>
    <!-- Item Collection -->
  </ItemGroup>
  <Target Name="Task1">
    <!-- Task(s) -->
  </Target>
  <PropertyGroup>
    <!-- Properties -->
  </PropertyGroup>
```

```
<ItemGroup>
  <!-- Item Collection -->
</ItemGroup>
<Target Name="Task2">
  <!-- Task(s) -->
</Target>
</Project>
```

Here is the syntax to execute the project from an MSBuild command line:

```
Msbuild switches projectfile
```

MSBuild command-line switches are listed in Table 4-6.

TABLE 4-6 MSBuild command-line switches

Task	Description
/help	Displays help information on the MSBuild command; */?* and */h* are also help switches.
/noconsolelogger	Disables the default console logger. Events will not be logged to the console window.
/nologo	Suppresses the startup banner and copyright information.
/version	Displays the version of the MSBuild tool.
@file	Reads command-line instructions from a batch file, which allows scripting of the build process.
/noautoresponse	Disables the automatic include of the MSBuild.rsp file.
/target:targetnames	Identifies the targets to execute, such as release or debug. The targets are delimited by commas or semicolons.
/property:name=value	Sets the value of a property. Multiple properties are delimited by commas or semicolons.
/logger:logger	Logs MSBuild events to a logger.
/consoleloggerparameters: parameters	Sets the parameters of the console logger.
*/verbosity:*level	Sets the amount of information written to the event log. The levels filter what is written to the event log as follows: *q*—quiet *m*—minimal *n*—normal *d*—detailed *diag*—diagnostic
/validate:schema	Validates the project file. If no schema is provided, the default schema is used to perform the validation.

MSBuild Example

This section provides an example of a normal MSBuild project. The project contains two tasks: The first task compiles an assembly from the available source files, and the second task creates a DLL from a source file. The project then compiles the remaining source files, which need a reference to the just-built DLL. The sample MSBuild project is documented with steps. Here is the project, followed by a description of each step:

```xml
<?xml version="1.0" encoding="utf-8"?>
<!-- Step One-->
<Project xmlns="http://schemas.microsoft.com/developer/msbuild/2003">
  <!-- Step Two -->
  <ItemGroup>
    <Compile Include="source1.cs"/>
    <Compile Include="source2.cs"/>
  </ItemGroup>
  <!-- Step Three -->
  <PropertyGroup>
    <DebugType>none</DebugType>
  </PropertyGroup>
  <PropertyGroup>
    <AssemblyName>sample.exe</AssemblyName>
  </PropertyGroup>
  <!-- Step Four -->
  <Target Name="Application1">
    <Csc Sources="*.cs" OutputAssembly="$(AssemblyName)"
         DebugType="$(DebugType)"/>
  </Target>
  <!-- Step Five-->
  <Target Name="Application2">
    <Csc Sources="source3.cs" TargetType="library"/>
    <Csc Sources="@(compile)" References="source3.dll"
         OutputAssembly="$(AssemblyName)" DebugType="$(DebugType)"/>
  </Target>
</Project>
```

Step One sets the schema for the MSBuild schema.

Step Two creates an item collection for the *Compile* element. The source files *source1.cs* and *source2.cs* are named in the collection.

Step Three sets the defaults for the *DebugType* and *AssemblyName* properties.

Step Four defines target *Application1*, which has a single task. The task compiles the source files in the current directory. It uses both the *AssemblyName* and *DebugType* properties.

Step Five defines target *Application2*, which contains two tasks. The first task compiles *source3.cs* and places the results in a library assembly; the second task compiles the item collection and references the library assembly.

The following MSBuild command reads the *sample.proj* project file. The output is the *donis. exe* assembly. The *DebugType* property is assigned *full* and the *AssemblyName* property is assigned *donis.exe*. This overwrites the default values of those properties. Finally, MSBuild invokes the *Application1* target:

```
C:\>msbuild /p:debugtype=full,assemblyname=donis.exe sample.proj /target:application1
```

The following MSBuild command executes the tasks of the *Application2* target:

```
C:\ >msbuild /p:debugtype=full,assemblyname=donis.exe sample.proj /target:application2
```

ClickOnce Deployment

With ClickOnce deployment, users can browse and install Windows applications published on an ASP.NET Web server. Setup and deployment of desktop and non-Web applications have become increasingly complex. For desktop applications, installation must be repeated for updates and future versions of the product. There is also the productivity problem of having to install the product physically on multiple, individual machines. Conversely, deployment of Web applications is hands-free. You simply browse to the application using the proper Uniform Resource Locator (URL). No installation is required. Web applications are also self-updating. Users automatically obtain the latest version of the Web application whenever an updated Web site application is browsed. Productivity is improved because per-machine updates are automatic. The benefits of Web distribution extend to ClickOnce deployment.

ClickOnce deployment is nonintrusive. Conversely, Windows Installer technology is intrusive because the application is installed to the local machine. ClickOnce deployment downloads an application into the download cache, in which there is only a limited impact on the local machine. There are security considerations because these applications execute in the download cache with potentially limited security privileges. These security considerations must be addressed in the application or on the local machine. Because the deployment is hands-free, the user experience improves.

ClickOnce applications are self-updating, which is particularly useful for applications that require frequent updates. Deploying applications that require frequent updates within the Windows Installer technology model is a time-consuming process. ClickOnce applications are deployed once and updated online automatically. Updates simply require online connectivity.

Another benefit includes the security privileges required to perform an installation. Windows Installer technology sometimes requires administrative permissions, but ClickOnce deployment does not require administrative permissions to deploy the application.

ClickOnce deployment publishes an application at a Web site on an ASP.NET server. The client machine must support the .NET Framework. This is more likely in an intranet deployment, where the client desktops are more controlled. It is also feasible in an extranet environment, in which requirements can be published and a reasonable level of compliance can be expected. ClickOnce applications can be initially deployed in a traditional manner, but require online connectivity for self-updating.

ClickOnce deployment has two modes of deployment. The online-only mode executes the application from the Web (in the download cache), which requires the client to be connected to the server whenever the application is executed. The full installation mode performs the installation on the client computer. This is similar to a traditional installation from an .msi or .cab file. Updates still require online connectivity.

ClickOnce deployment uses an application manifest (which is an XML file) to define dependent assemblies, files, and security permissions required for the application. ClickOnce deployment also uses a deployment manifest. This manifest contains deployment configuration information, such as the current version, the location of required files, deployment mode, and update policies.

Create application and deployment manifests with the Manifest Generation And Editing Tool (Mage), which is distributed with the Windows SDK Update for Windows Vista. To create a new application manifest, choose the File menu and then choose the New submenu. From the submenu, select Application Manifest. The application manifest appears with the Name entry selected in the left-hand pane. The Name window contains the general information on the deployment. The Airline Seats application, referred to earlier in this chapter, is published as a ClickOnce application. (The section "Publish a ClickOnce Application," later in this chapter, explains how to create a manifest.exe file.) You can open an existing manifest file (which will have a .manifest extension) by choosing Open from the File menu and browsing to the appropriate location. Figure 4-41 shows a view of the Name window in the Mage tool for the Airline Seats application.

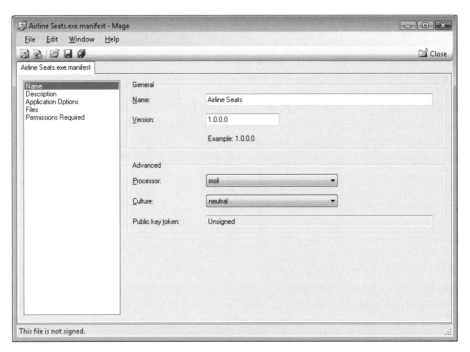

FIGURE 4-41 Application manifest—the Name window

The Files window, shown in Figure 4-42, lists the files included in the deployment.

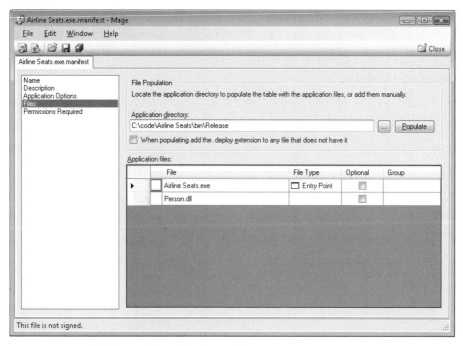

FIGURE 4-42 Application manifest—the Files window

The Permissions Required window (shown in Figure 4-43) sets the security required to execute the deployed application.

You also can open the deployment manifest (which will have a .application extension) using the Mage tool. The Name window is the same for both the deployment and application manifests. For the deployment manifest, the two most important windows are the Deployment Options window and the Update Options windows.

The Deployment Options window (shown in Figure 4-44) sets the ClickOnce deployment mode and the URL of the published application.

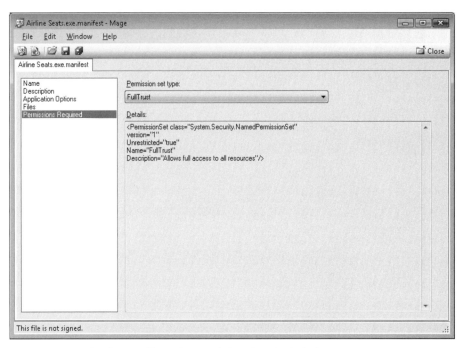

FIGURE 4-43 Application manifest—the Permissions Required window

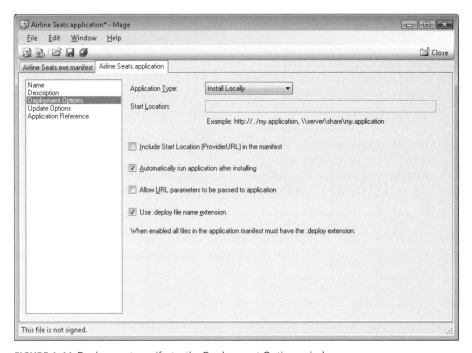

FIGURE 4-44 Deployment manifest—the Deployment Options window

The Update Options window (shown in Figure 4-45) configures how updates are managed for an application deployed with ClickOnce technology.

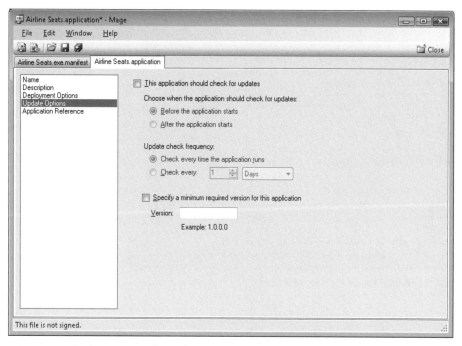

FIGURE 4-45 Deployment manifest—the Update Options window

Publish a ClickOnce Application

Fortunately, ClickOnce deployment is automated in Visual Studio 2008, including the creation of manifest files and configuration of Web servers. In Visual Studio 2008, developers use the Publish Wizard to set up an application for ClickOnce deployment. Right-click the project and choose Publish to start the Publish Wizard.

The Publish Wizard has several steps. The first step identifies the URL to which the application is to be published. Figure 4-46 shows the first window of the Publish Wizard.

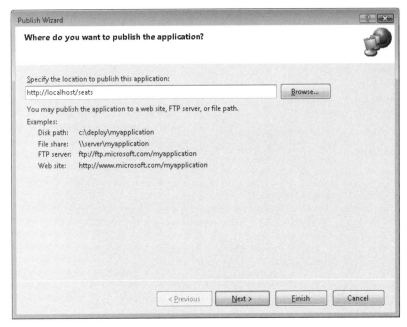

FIGURE 4-46 Step 1 of the Publish Wizard

Step 2 of the Publish Wizard, shown in Figure 4-47, sets how the application is deployed.

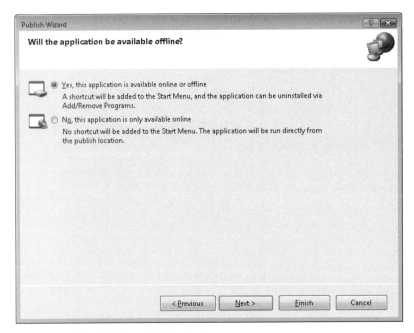

FIGURE 4-47 Step 2 of the Publish Wizard

Step 3 of the wizard, shown in Figure 4-48, is the confirmation window, in which a developer can review the ClickOnce settings and confirm the deployment.

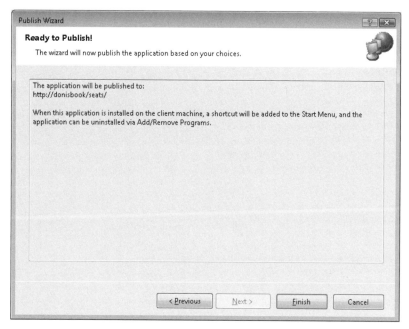

FIGURE 4-48 Step 3 of the Publish Wizard

Arrays and Collections

Chapter 5, "Arrays and Collections," discusses *arrays,* which are collections of related types. C# supports one-dimensional and multidimensional arrays. Jagged arrays, which are arrays of arrays, also are supported. *System.Array* is the underlying type of all arrays and defines the baseline behavior of all arrays. You can learn a lot about arrays by examining the *System.Array* class. For example, the *Array.SyncRoot* property is used to synchronize access to an array. Arrays implement a myriad of interfaces, such as *ICloneable, ICollection,* and *IEnumerable.* The next chapter discusses the members and purpose of each of these interfaces.

More sophisticated collections are sometimes needed. The .NET Framework offers *ArrayList, Queue, Stack, HashTable,* and other useful collections. Specialty collections also are available, including *BitVector32, HybridDictionary,* and *NameValueCollection.* These collections are reviewed in the next chapter.

Chapter 5
Arrays and Collections

An *array* is a collection of related items, either value or reference types. Arrays are immutable, such that the number of dimensions and size of the array are fixed at instantiation. C# supports single-dimensional, multidimensional, and jagged arrays. Single-dimensional arrays, sometimes called *vectors*, consist of a single row. Multidimensional arrays are rectangular and consist of rows, columns, and so on. A jagged array also consists of rows and columns but is irregular in shape.

Arrays are available in most programming languages, and therefore, most developers have some familiarity with this concept. Arrays are employed in a variety of ways. A personnel program, for example, might have an array of employees. A graphics program might have one array for each type of geometric object, such as ellipses, rectangles, or triangles. An accounting and scheduling application for automobile repair likely would have an array of automobile repair tickets. An application for NASA's space shuttle program might have an array of astronauts.

Arrays are intrinsic to the language. Other collections, such as *Stack*, *Queue*, and *Hashtable*, are not native to the language. As such, ease of use is one of the benefits of arrays compared to other collections. Another benefit is familiarity. Arrays are available and are functionally similar to arrays in other programming languages.

As a collection, an array contains zero or more items, which are called *elements*. Elements of an array are always related, such as an array of apples or an array of oranges. An array might consist of *SalariedEmployee*, *HourlyEmployee*, and *CommissionedEmployee* instances. However, an array consisting of both apples and employees is nonsensical because apples and employees are unrelated.

Arrays are reference types and are instances of *System.Array*. As such, memory for an array is allocated from the managed heap. Even an array of value types is allocated on the managed heap and not on the stack. The elements of an array reside in contiguous memory. An array of 30 integer values would have 32 four-byte elements allocated in contiguous memory. With arrays of reference types, the references are allocated in contiguous memory. The objects themselves are stored in noncontiguous memory, which is pointed to by the references. Figure 5-1 shows the difference in memory allocation between arrays of reference versus value types.

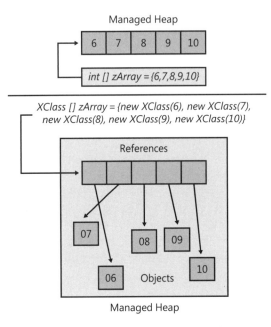

FIGURE 5-1 Array of reference types versus value types

Elements are identified with indexes that are relative to the beginning of the array. Indexes are either integer types or long types. Indexes also are commonly called *indices* or *subscripts*, and are placed inside the indexing operator (*[ ]*). Arrays are zero-based so that the index is actually an offset. Array indexes are offsets from the beginning of the array to a particular element. Therefore, the first element is at the start of the array, which is an offset of zero. For an array of five elements, a proper index is from zero to four. Therefore, the last element of the array of *n* elements is at index *n-1*. This is a common cause of fencepost errors. Fencepost errors are references to indexes that lie outside the bounds of an array. If an array has five elements, using an index of six would cause a fencepost error.

As mentioned, arrays are immutable. This means that an array is statically sized, and the dimensions cannot be changed at run time. The *System.Array.Resize* method, which is a generic method, seemingly resizes an array. However, appearances can be deceiving. *Array.Resize* creates an entirely new array of the stipulated size. The elements of the original array are then copied to the elements of the new array. Afterwards, the array reference is updated to point to the new array. Look at the following code:

```
int[] obj = new int[] { 4, 5, 6 };
Console.WriteLine(obj.GetHashCode().ToString());
Array.Resize(ref obj, 10);
Console.WriteLine(obj.GetHashCode().ToString());
```

The hash code returns the identity of an object. The preceding code displays a different identity for the *obj* reference after *Array.Resize* is called.

Single-dimensional arrays are indigenous to the Common Language Runtime (CLR). There are specific Microsoft Intermediate Language (MSIL) instructions for vectors, including *newarr*, *ldelem*, *ldlen*, and *stelem*. There are no built-in instructions for multidimensional arrays. This direct manipulation of single-dimensional arrays makes them more efficient. In addition, some of the members of the *System.Array* type cannot be applied to multidimensional arrays. Conversely, all the methods and properties of the *System.Array* type are applicable to single-dimensional arrays.

The *System.Array* type is the underlying type of all arrays. Instances of arrays are always instances of the *System.Array* type. Thus, all arrays are implicitly reference types. Arrays can directly access the public interface and properties of the *System.Array* type. *System.Array* implements a series of interfaces. Table 5-1 lists those interfaces.

TABLE 5-1 Interfaces implemented by *System.Array*

Interface	Description
ICloneable	This interface defines the ability to clone an array.
ICollection	This interface defines methods to add, count, and iterate the elements of an array.
IEnumerable	This interface defines a method that returns an enumerator, which can be used to enumerate the array elements.
IList	This interface defines methods to safely access an index-based collection, which includes an array.

Arrays also can be used as fields, local variables, method parameters, and return values. Because an array is a reference type, it is passed by reference when used as a parameter or a return value. This allows you to change the array values in the called method.

Arrays

The following is the syntax for declaring a one-dimensional array. A vector has a single index. When declaring an array, the empty square brackets define an array, while the indexing operator on the right-hand side of the assignment sets the size of the array:

> *typea*[] *arrayname1*;

> *typea*[] *arrayname2* = new *typeb*[*n*];

> *typea*[] *arrayname3* = new *typeb*[*n*] { *ilist* };

> *typea*[] *arrayname4* = new *typeb*[] { *ilist* };

> *typea*[] *arrayname5* = { *ilist* };

The first syntax declares a reference to an array that is not initialized. You can initialize the reference to an instance of an array later. The following is sample code of the first syntax for declaring an array. It declares an integer array named *zArray*. The array is then assigned a new array of 10 integers, which initializes the reference. The array elements of 10 integers also are initialized. Array elements default to zero or null: zero for value type elements and null for reference type elements. Because integers are value types, the array elements of the following array are set to zero:

```
int[] zArray;
zArray = new int[10];
```

The second syntax declares and initializes a reference to an array. The array reference is immediately assigned a reference to the new instance of an array. An array must be initialized to an array of the same or related type as the declaration. The array declaration and the array instantiation must be related. For example, bytes are not related to integers. You can cast a byte to an integer, but this does not mean that the types are related. Because bytes and integers are not related types, a byte array cannot be assigned to an integer array declaration.

Here is sample code of the second syntax:

```
byte aValue = 10;
int bValue = aValue;         // valid
int[] zArray = new byte[5];  // invalid
int[] yArray = new int[5];   // valid
```

In the following example, *XBase* and *XDerived* classes are related. Therefore, you can assign an array of the derived type to an array of the base type:

```
public class Starter {
    public static void Main() {
        XBase[] obj = new XDerived[5];  // base     <- derived
        XDerived[] obj2 = new XBase[5]; // derived <- base [invalid]
    }
}

public class XDerived : XBase {
}

public class XBase {
}
```

The third syntax declares an array, initializes the reference, and assigns values to the array elements. The initialization list (*ilist*) contains the initial values for the elements of the array, where the values are comma-delimited. The number of values in the list must match the number of elements in the array exactly—no more and no less.

This code shows an example of the third syntax for declaring an array:

```
int[] zArray = new int[3] {1,2,3};  // valid
int[] yArray = new int[3] {1,2};    // invalid
ZClass[] xArray = new ZClass[3] {   // valid
    new ZClass(5), new ZClass(10),
    new ZClass(15) };
```

The fourth and third syntax are identical except that the initialization list sets the number of elements. The array size is not set explicitly in the assignment. The compiler counts the number of items in the initialization list to set the length of the array.

This is an example of the fourth syntax:

```
int[] zArray = new int[] {1,2,3,4,5};  // 5 elements
```

The fifth syntax is an abbreviation of the fourth syntax, where the array type and number of elements are inferred from the initialization list.

This is an example of the fifth syntax:

```
int[] yArray = {1,2,3,4,5};
```

Local variable and field definitions can be defined simultaneously. Multiple declarations of arrays can also be combined, as shown here:

```
public class ZClass{
    private int[] first = {1,2,3},
                  second = {4,5,6},
                  third = {7,8,9};

    // Remainder of class...
}
```

Array Elements

Array indexing operators refer to elements of an array. With an index, the indexing operator returns a specific element of the array. When an indexing operator is used on the left-hand side, you can assign a value to the array element. On the right-hand side, the indexing operator returns the value of the element.

The following *for* loop lists the elements of an array. The indexing operator is used to return the element value. The program calculates the total value of elements in the array. It is also used on the right-hand side to assign a value of the array element to a local variable:

```
int[] zArray = {1,2,3,4,5};
int total = 0;
for (int count = 0; count < zArray.Length; ++count) {
    total += zArray[count];              // r-value
    int number = zArray[count];          // r-value
    Console.WriteLine(number);
}
Console.WriteLine("\nThe total is {0}.",
    total);
```

Multidimensional Arrays

You are not limited to one-dimensional arrays. Multidimensional arrays are rectangular arrays and have multiple dimensions and indices. Two-dimensional arrays, which consist of rows and columns, are the most common kind of multidimensional array. Each row contains the same number of columns, thus making the array rectangular. From a memory perspective, the *x*-axis is the rows and the *y*-axis defines the columns. Multidimensional arrays are stored and retrieved in row-major order.

The total number of elements in a multidimensional array is the product of the indices. For example, an array of 5 rows and 6 columns has 30 elements. The *Array.Length* property returns the total number of elements in the array. The *Array.GetLength* method returns the number of elements per indice. The indices are numbered from zero. For a two-dimensional array, the row is the zero dimension, whereas the column is the one dimension. *GetLength(0)* would then return the number of rows in the multidimensional array.

The following is the syntax to declare a two-dimensional array. Notice the indexing operator. Row (*r*) and column (*c*) indexes in the indexing operator are delimited with a comma. In the declaration, there is a comma in the array operator (*[,]*). In general when declaring an array there are *n-1* commas for *n* number of indices. For a two-dimensional array, then, there would be one comma:

> *typea[,] arrayname1;*

> *typea[,] arrayname2* = new *typeb[r,c];*

> *typea[,] arrayname3* = new *typeb[r,c] { ilist };*

> *typea[,] arrayname4* = new *typeb[,] { ilist };*

> *typea[,] arrayname5* = { *ilist* };

The initialization list of a multidimensional array includes nested initialization lists for each row. If an array has two rows, the initialization list includes two nested initialization lists. This is the syntax of a nested initialization list:

{ { *ilist* }, { *ilist* }, { *ilist* } ...}

The following sample code demonstrates the various declaration syntaxes, including nested initialization lists:

```
int[,] array1;                  // syntax 1
array1 = new int[2,2];
int[,] array2 = new int[2,3]; // syntax 2
int[,] array3 = new int[2,3]   // syntax 3
    { {1,2,3}, {4,5,6} };
int[,] array4 = new int[,]     // syntax 4
    { {1,2,3}, {4,5,6} };
```

```
int[,] array5 =              // syntax 5
    { {1,2,3}, {4,5,6} };
```

To access an element of a multidimensional array, specify a row and column index in the indexing operator. It can be used on the left-hand side or right-hand side to set or get the value of an element, respectively. The following code calculates the total of the elements. This requires enumerating all the elements of a multidimensional array:

```
int[,] zArray = new int[2,3]
    { {1,2,3}, {4,5,6} };
int total = 0;
for (int row = 0; row < zArray.GetLength(0); ++row) {
    for (int col = 0; col < zArray.GetLength(1); ++col) {
        total += zArray[row, col];              // r-value
        int number = zArray[row, col];          // r-value
        Console.WriteLine(number);
    }
}
Console.WriteLine("\nThe total is {0}.",
    total);
```

We have been focusing thus far on two-dimensional arrays. However, arrays can have more than two dimensions. In fact, there is no limit to the number of dimensions an array can have. Three-dimensional and four-dimensional arrays are less common than two-dimensional arrays, but are seen nonetheless. Arrays with more than four dimensions are rarely seen. Most developers find multidimensional arrays beyond two indices mind-numbing to manage and manipulate. Additional dimensions require added comma-delimited indexes when the array is declared, defined, and used.

This is an example of a four-dimensional array:

```
int [,,,] array = new int[1,2,3,2]
    { { { {1,2}, {1,2}, {1,2} }, { {1,2},{1,2},{1,2} } } };
```

How is the preceding code interpreted? A multidimensional array can be viewed as a hierarchical array that consists of layers. Each layer represents a different level of array nesting. The previous example defines a single-dimensional array with only one element, which is itself a single-dimension array that contains two nested arrays. The two nested arrays each contain three arrays. Each of these arrays contains two elements.

This is a diagram of the array hierarchy, where the numbers indicate the index into that node in the hierarchy:

```
{                               1                                       };   layer 1
{ {              1                  }, {                 2              } };   layer 2
{ {   { 1   }, { 2   }, { 3   } }, { { 1   }, { 2   }, { 3   } } };   layer 3
{ { { { 1, 2 }, { 1, 2 }, { 1, 2 } }, { { 1, 2 }, { 1, 2 }, { 1, 2 } } } };   layer 4
```

The following code demonstrates a practical use of a multidimensional array. The program maintains the grades of students. Each student attends two classes, where each class has a name and grade. This is an array of object types, which means each element can contain anything. Strings, integers, reference types, or anything else can be placed in an array of objects. Everything in the .NET Framework Class Library (FCL) is derived (related) to *System.Object.* The downside is boxing and unboxing of value types placed in the array. In the example, grades are value types:

```
using System;

namespace Donis.CSharpBook {
    public class Starter {
        public static void Main() {

            string[] names = {"Bob", "Ted", "Alice"};
            object[,,] grades = new object[3,2,2]
                { { {"Algebra", 85},  { "English", 75} },
                  { {"Algebra", 95},  { "History", 70} },
                  { {"Biology", 100}, { "English", 92} } };

            for (int iName = 0; iName < names.Length; ++iName) {
                Console.WriteLine("\n{0}\n", names[iName]);
                for (int iCourse = 0; iCourse < 2; ++iCourse) {
                    Console.WriteLine("{0} {1}",
                        grades[iName, iCourse, 0],
                        grades[iName, iCourse, 1]);
                }
            }
        }
    }
}
```

Jagged Arrays

The most frequent way of explaining a jagged array is to say that it is an array of arrays. More specifically, a jagged array is an array of vectors. Although other two-dimensional arrays are rectangular, a jagged array, as the name implies, is jagged. Each vector of the jagged array can be of a different length. With jagged arrays, first define the number of rows or vectors in the jagged array. Second, declare the number of elements in each row.

The syntax for declaring a jagged array is similar to a two-dimensional array. Instead of a single bracket (*[,]*), jagged arrays have two brackets (*[][]*).You initialize the jagged array by specifying the number of rows but omitting the number of columns (*[r][]*). Later, each row of the jagged array is individually initialized to a vector, each of which can be of varying sizes. This is the syntax of a jagged array:

> *typea[][] arrayname1;*

> *typea[][] arrayname2 = new typeb[r][];*

typea[][] *arrayname3* = new *typeb*[*r*][] { *ilist* };

typea[][] *arrayname4* = new *typeb*[][] { *ilist* };

typea[][] *arrayname5* = { *ilist* };

Here is sample code for declaring or initializing jagged arrays:

```
int[][] zArray;                        // syntax 1
int[][] yArray = new int[3][];         // syntax 2
int[][] xArray = new int[3][]          // syntax 3
    {new int[] {1,2,3},
     new int[] {1,2},
     new int[] {1,2,3,4}};
int[][] wArray = new int[][]{          // syntax 4
     new int[] {1,2,3},
     new int[] {1,2},
     new int[] {1,2,3,4}};
int[][] wArray = {                     // syntax 5
     new int[] {1,2,3},
     new int[] {1,2},
     new int[] {1,2,3,4}};
```

After initialization, each row of the jagged array is set to a one-dimensional array. Because each row is a distinct array, the length of each row can vary—hence, the array is jagged:

```
jarray[row] = new type[elements];
```

Here is sample code that employs a jagged array. In the example, each successive row has one more element in its vector. The first nested loop creates the vector for each row and initializes the new values. The final loop totals the values of each row and displays the result:

```
using System;

namespace Donis.CSharpBook {
    public class Starter {
        public static void Main() {
            int[][] jagged = new int[7][];
            int count = 0;
            for (int row = 0; row < jagged.GetLength(0); ++row) {
                Console.Write("\nRow {0}:", row);
                jagged[row] = new int[row + 1];
                for (int index = 0; index < row + 1; ++index) {
                    ++count;
                    jagged[row][index] = count;
                    Console.Write(" {0}", count);
                }
            }
            Console.WriteLine("\n\nTotals");
            for (int row = 0; row < jagged.GetLength(0); ++row) {
                int total = 0;
```

```
            for (int index = 0; index < jagged[row].GetLength(0);
                    ++index) {
                total += jagged[row][index];
            }
            Console.Write("\nRow {0}: {1}",
                row, total);
        }
    }
    }
}
```

System.Array

The *System.Array* type implements the fundamental methods and properties that are essential to an array. This includes sorting, reversing, element count, synchronization, and much more. Table 5-2 lists the methods of the *System.Array* type. Many of the methods are static, which is noted in the syntax. In addition, some methods are for single-dimensional arrays and are not usable with multidimensional arrays. This fact is noted in the description of the method in Table 5-2. Some of these methods are covered in more detail later in this chapter.

TABLE 5-2 System.Array members

Description	Syntax

AsReadOnly
 	
This is a generic method that returns a read-only wrapper for an array.
	`static ReadOnlyCollection<T>`
	`    AsReadOnly<T>(`
	`    T[] sourceArray)`

BinarySearch
 	
This method conducts a binary search for a specific value in a sorted one-dimensional array and returns an index. If the value is not found, a negative value is returned.
 	
There are several overloads for this method. The two most common overloads are shown.
	`static int BinarySearch(`
	`    Array sourceArray,`
	`    object searchValue)`
	
	`static int BinarySearch<T>(`
	`    T[] sourceArray,`
	`    T value)`

Clear This method sets a range of elements to a default value: zero, null, or false.	`static void Clear(Array sourceArray,` `    int index, int length)`
Clone This method clones the current array.	`object Clone()`

ConstrainedCopy
 	
This method copies a range of elements from the source array into a destination array. You set the source index and destination index, indicating where the copy is started in both arrays. Changes are guaranteed to be undone if the copy does not complete successfully.
	`static void ConstrainedCopy{`
	`    Array sourceArray,`
	`    int sourceIndex`
	`    Array destinationArray,`
	`    int destinationIndex,`
	`    int length)`

TABLE 5-2 System.Array members

Description	Syntax
ConvertAll This is a generic method that converts the type of an array. The results are returned in an array of the destination type.	```static <destinationType> ConvertAll<sourceType, destinationType>(sourceType sourceArray, Converter<sourceType, destinationType> converter)```

Copy
 	
This method copies elements from the source array to the destination array. The specified number of elements is copied. This method does not make the same guarantees as *ConstrainedCopy*.
 	
There are four overloads to this method. The two most common overloads are listed in this table.
	```static void Copy(Array sourceArray, Array destinationArray, int length)```
	
	```static void Copy(Array sourceArray, int sourceIndex, Array destinationArray, int destinationIndex, int length)```

CopyTo
 	
This method copies the current one-dimensional array to the destination array starting at the specified index.
	```void CopyTo(Array destinationArray, int index)```
	
	```void CopyTo(Array destinationArray, long index)```

CreateInstance
 	
This method creates an instance of an array at run time.
 	
This method has several overloads. One-dimensional and two-dimensional versions of the method are listed in this table.
	```static Array CreateInstance(Type arrayType, int length)```
	
	```static Array CreateInstance(Type arrayType, int rows, int cols)```

Exists This is a generic method that confirms that at least one element matches the conditions set in the predicate function.	```static bool Exist<T> { T [] sourceArray, Predicate<T> match)```
Find This is a generic method that finds the first element that matches the conditions set in the predicate function. If not found, the default value of the *T* type is returned.	```static T Find<T>(T[] sourceArray, Predicate<T> match)```
FindAll This is a generic method that returns all the elements that match the conditions set in the predicate function.	```static T[] FindAll<T>(T[] sourceArray, Predicate<T> match)```

TABLE 5-2 System.Array members

Description	Syntax

FindIndex
 	
This is a generic method that returns the index to the first element that matches the conditions set in the predicate function. If no match is found, -1 is returned.
	```static int FindIndex<T>(`   `T[] sourceArray,`   `Predicate<T> match)`
	
	```static int FindIndex<T>(`   `T[] sourceArray,`   `int startingIndex,`   `Predicate<T> match)`
	
	```static int FindIndex(`   `T[] sourceArray,`   `int startingIndex,`   `int count,`   `Predicate<T> match)`

FindLast This is a generic method that returns the last element that matches the conditions set in the predicate function. If no match is found, the default value of the *T* type is returned.	```static T FindLast<T>(`   `T[] sourceArray,`   `Predicate<T> match)`

FindLastIndex
 	
This is a generic method that returns the index to the last element that matches the conditions set in the predicate function. If no match is found, -1 is returned.
	```static int FindLastIndex(`   `T[] sourceArray,`   `Predicate<T> match)`
	
	```static int FindLastIndex(`   `T[] sourceArray,`   `int startingIndex,`   `Predicate<T> match)`
	
	```static int FindLastIndex(`   `T[] sourceArray,`   `int startingIndex,`   `int count,`   `Predicate<T> match)`

ForEach This is a generic method that performs an action on each element of the array, where the action refers to a function.	```public static void ForEach<T>(`   `T[] array,`   `Action<T> action)`
GetEnumerator This method returns an enumerator that implements the enumerator pattern for collections. You can enumerate the elements of the array with the enumerator object.	```sealed IEnumerator GetEnumerator()`
GetLength This method returns the number of elements for any dimension of an array.	```int GetLength(int dimension)`

TABLE 5-2 System.Array members

Description	Syntax
GetLongLength This method returns the number of elements, as a 64-bit integer, for any dimension of an array.	`long GetLongLength(int dimension)`
GetLowerBound This method returns the lower bound of a dimension. In C#, the lower bound of an array is zero.	`int GetLowerBound(int dimension)`
GetUpperBound This method returns the upper bound of a dimension.	`int GetUpperBound(int dimension)`

GetValue
 	
This method returns the value of an element at the specified index.
 	
This method has several overloads. A one-dimensional version and a multidimensional version of the method are shown in this table.
	`object GetValue(int index)`
	
	`object GetValue(params int[] indices)`

IndexOf
 	
This method returns the index of the first element in a one-dimensional array that matches the specified value.
 	
This method has several overloads. A generic and a non-generic version of the method are listed in this table.
	`static int IndexOf(Array sourceArray,`
	`    object find)`
	
	`static int IndexOf<T>(T[] sourceArray,`
	`    T value)`

Initialize This method initializes every element of the array. The default constructor, if any, of each element is called.	`void Initialize()`

LastIndexOf
 	
This method returns the index of the last element that matches the specified value in a one-dimensional array.
 	
This method has several overloads. A generic version and a non-generic version are listed in this table.
	`static int LastIndexOf(Array sourceArray,`
	`    object value)`
	
	`static int LastIndexOf<T>(T[] sourceArray,`
	`    T value)`

Resize
 	
This is a generic method that changes the size of a one-dimensional array.
	`static void Resize<T>(`
	`    ref T[] sourceArray,`
	`    int newSize)`

Reverse
 	
This method reverses the order of elements in a one-dimensional array.
	`static void Reverse(Array sourceArray)`
	
	`static void Reverse(Array sourceArray,`
	`    int index, int length)`

TABLE 5-2 System.Array members

Description	Syntax

SetValue
 	
This method sets the value of a specific element of the current one-dimensional array.
 	
This method has several overloads. Two of the more common overloads are listed in this table.
	`void SetValue(object value, int index)`
	
	`void SetValue(object value,`
	`    params int[] indices)`

Sort
 	
This method sorts the elements of a one-dimensional array using the *IComparable* interface of the element type.
 	
This method has several overloads. A non-generic version and a generic version of the method are listed in this table.
	`static void Sort(Array sourceArray)`
	
	`static void Sort<T>(`
	`    T[] sourceArray)`

TrueForAll
 	
This is a generic method that returns *true* if all elements of an array match the conditions set in the predicate function.
	`static bool TrueForAll<T>(`
	`    T[] array,`
	`    Predicate<T> match)`

The following sections offer further descriptions and sample code for some of the *System.Array* methods.

Array.AsReadOnly Method

The following code creates an integer array and initializes the values. The second element of the array is then modified, which confirms the read-write capability of the array. *Array.AsReadOnly* is then called to wrap the array in a read-only collection. The *ReadOnlyCollection* type is found in the *System.Collections.ObjectModel* namespace. After displaying the elements of the read-only collection, the program attempts to modify an element of the collection. Because the collection is read-only, a compiler error occurs:

```
using System;
using System.Collections.Generic;
using System.Collections.ObjectModel;

namespace Donis.CSharpBook {
    public class Starter {
        public static void Main() {
            int[] zArray = {1,2,3,4};
            zArray[1] = 10;
            ReadOnlyCollection<int> roArray = Array.AsReadOnly(zArray);
            foreach (int number in roArray) {
                Console.WriteLine(number);
            }
            roArray[1] = 2;   // compiler error
        }
    }
}
```

Array.Clone Method

In the following code, the *CommissionedEmployee* class inherits from the *Employee* class. An array of commissioned employees is defined and then cloned with the *Clone* method. The result is cast to an array of *Employees*. Because *Clone* returns an object array, which is unspecific, you should cast to a specific array type. The cast from *System.Object[]* is not type-safe, and an incorrect cast could cause an exception later in the application. Polymorphism is employed in the subsequent *foreach* loop to call the correct *Pay* method on the derived instance:

```
using System;
using System.Collections.Generic;

namespace Donis.CSharpBook {
    public class Starter {
        public static void Main() {
            CommissionedEmployee[] salespeople =
                { new CommissionedEmployee("Bob"),
                  new CommissionedEmployee("Ted"),
                  new CommissionedEmployee("Sally") };

            Employee[] employees =
                (Employee[])salespeople.Clone();

            foreach(Employee person in
                    employees) {
                person.Pay();
            }
        }
    }

    public class Employee {
        public Employee(string name) {
            m_Name = name;
        }

        public virtual void Pay() {
            Console.WriteLine("Paying {0}", m_Name);
        }

        private string m_Name;
    }

    public class CommissionedEmployee : Employee {
        public CommissionedEmployee(string name) :
            base(name) {
        }

        public override void Pay() {
            base.Pay();
            Console.WriteLine("Paying commissions");
        }
    }
}
```

Array.CreateInstance Method

The following code demonstrates both the *CreateInstance* and *SetValue* methods.
CreateInstance creates a new array at run time. This requires a degree of reflection, which
is discussed in Chapter 13, "Metadata and Reflection." This code first creates an array at run
time using *Activator.CreateInstance.* The type of array is input from the command line. In the
for loop, values are assigned to each element of the array. The values also are input from
the command line. *Activator.CreateInstance* creates the values, which are then assigned to
elements of the array. In the subsequent *foreach* loop, the elements of the array are enumerated. A member function is then invoked on the element. The name of the method is read
from the command line:

```csharp
using System;
using System.Reflection;

namespace Donis.CSharpBook {
    public class Starter {
        public static void Main(string[] argv) {
            Assembly executing=Assembly.GetExecutingAssembly();
            Type t = executing.GetType(argv[0]);
            Array zArray = Array.CreateInstance(
                t, argv.Length - 2);
            for (int count = 2; count < argv.Length; ++count) {
                System.Object obj = Activator.CreateInstance(t, new object[] {
                    argv[count]});
                zArray.SetValue(obj, count - 2);
            }
            foreach (object item in zArray) {
                MethodInfo m = t.GetMethod(argv[1]);
                m.Invoke(item, null);
            }
        }
    }

    public class ZClass {
        public ZClass(string info) {
            m_Info = "ZClass " + info;
        }

        public void ShowInfo() {
            Console.WriteLine(m_Info);
        }

        private string m_Info;
    }

    public class YClass {
        public YClass(string info) {
            m_Info = "YClass " + info;
```

```
        }

        public void ShowInfo() {
            Console.WriteLine(m_Info);
        }

        private string m_Info;
    }

    public class XClass {
        public XClass(string info) {
            m_Info = "XClass " + info;
        }

        public void ShowInfo() {
            Console.WriteLine(m_Info);
        }

        private string m_Info;
    }
}
```

A typical command line and results of the application are shown in Figure 5-2.

FIGURE 5-2 A command line and the results from running the application

System.Array and Predicates

Several *System.Array* methods use predicates, including the *Exists*, *Find*, *FindAll*, and *FindLastIndex* methods. Predicates are essentially delegates. The predicate function is called for each element of the array. An array predicate performs a test on some condition. If the condition is met, *true* is returned. If not, *false* is returned.

This section makes references to generics, which is discussed in Chapter 7, "Generics." Refer to Chapter 7 for a complete explanation on generics and related topics.

This is the syntax of the *Predicate* delegate:

```
delegate bool Predicate<T>(T obj)
```

Predicate methods are generic methods. The type parameter indicates the element type. The return value is the result of the test.

The following code finds all elements equal to 3. *MethodA* is the predicate method, which compares each value to 3. The Boolean value *true (result == 0)* is returned in *MethodA* if the element equals 3:

```
public static void Main() {
    int[] zArray = {1,2,3,1,2,3,1,2,3};
    Predicate<int> match = new Predicate<int>(MethodA<int>);
    int[] answers = Array.FindAll(zArray, match);
    foreach (int answer in answers) {
        Console.WriteLine(answer);
    }
}

public static bool MethodA<T>(T number) where T : IComparable {
    int result = number.CompareTo(3);
    return result == 0;
}
```

Array.Resize Method

The *Resize* method resizes a one-dimensional array.

Here is sample code for resizing an array. The elements added, if any, to the array are initialized to a default value:

```
using System;

namespace Donis.CSharpBook {
    public class Starter {
        public static void Main() {
            int[] zArray = {1,2,3,4};
            Array.Resize<int>(ref zArray, 8);
            foreach (int number in zArray) {
                Console.WriteLine(number);
            }
        }
    }
}
```

System.Array Properties

System.Array has several properties that are useful when working with arrays. Table 5-3 lists the various properties.

TABLE 5-3 *System.Array* **properties**

Description	Syntax
IsFixedSize This property returns *true* if the array is a fixed size. Otherwise, it returns *false*. This is always true for arrays.	`virtual bool IsFixedSize {` `    get; }`
IsReadOnly This property returns *true* if the array is read-only. Otherwise, it returns *false*. This is always false for arrays.	`virtual bool IsReadOnly {` `    get; }`
IsSynchronized This property returns *true* if the array is thread-safe. Otherwise, it returns *false*. This is always false for arrays.	`virtual bool IsSynchronized{` `    get; }`
Length This property returns the number of elements in the array.	`int Length {` `    get; }`
LongLength As a 64-bit value, this property returns the number of elements in the array.	`long LongLength {` `    get; }`
Rank This property returns the rank of the array, which is the number of dimensions. For example, a two-dimensional array has a rank of two.	`int Rank {` `    get; }`
SyncRoot This property returns a synchronization object for the current array. Arrays are not inherently thread-safe. You can synchronize access to the array with this synchronization object.	`virtual object SyncRoot {` `    get; }`

Many of the array properties are used in the sample code previously shown in this chapter. The *SyncRoot* property is not included in a previous example and is particularly important.

Array.SyncRoot Property

The purpose of the *SyncRoot* object is to synchronize access to an array. Arrays are not thread-safe. As documented in Table 5-3, the *IsSynchronized* property always returns *false* for an array. When accessed from multiple threads, arrays are easily synchronized with the *lock* statement, where the *SyncRoot* object is the parameter.

In the following code, the array is a field in the *Starter* class. The *DisplayForward* and *DisplayReverse* methods list array elements in forward and reverse order, respectively. The functions are invoked in separate threads, where *DisplayForward* and *DisplayReverse* might be called at the same time. This overlapping execution and access to the array could cause incorrect output. The *SyncLock* property of the array field is used to prevent simultaneous access by the concurrent threads:

```
using System;
using System.Threading;

namespace Donis.CSharpBook {
    public class Starter {

        public static void Main() {
            Array.Sort(zArray);
            Thread t1 = new Thread(
                new ThreadStart(DisplayForward));
            Thread t2 = new Thread(
                new ThreadStart(DisplayReverse));
            t1.Start();
            t2.Start();
        }

        private static int[] zArray = {1,5,4,2,4,2,9,8};

        public static void DisplayForward() {
            lock(zArray.SyncRoot) {
                Console.Write("\nForward: ");
                foreach (int number in zArray) {
                    Console.Write(number);
                }
            }
        }

        public static void DisplayReverse() {
            lock(zArray.SyncRoot) {
                Array.Reverse(zArray);
                Console.Write("\nReverse: ");
                foreach (int number in zArray) {
                    Console.Write(number);
                }
                Array.Reverse(zArray);
            }
        }
    }
}
```

Comparable Elements

The following *System.Array* methods compare elements to a value or another element:

- Array.IndexOf

- Array.LastIndexOf

- Array.Sort

- Array.Reverse

- Array.BinarySearch

As such, the elements must be instances of comparable types. Comparable types implement the *IComparable* interface, which requires the implementation of the *CompareTo* method.

The *IComparable.CompareTo* method returns zero when the current and target instances are equal. If the current instance is less than the target, a negative value is returned, and if the current instance is greater than the target, a positive value is returned. The previously listed *System.Array* methods call *IComparable.CompareTo* to perform the necessary comparisons for sorting, retrieving elements on value, or otherwise accessing the array in an ordered manner.

A run-time error occurs in the following code when *Array.Sort* is called. Why? The *XClass instances, which are the array elements,* do not implement the *IComparable* interface:

```
using System;

namespace Donis.CSharpBook {
    public class Starter {
        public static void Main() {
            XClass[] objs = {new XClass(5), new XClass(10),
                new XClass(1)};
            Array.Sort(objs);
        }
    }

    public class XClass {
        public XClass(int data) {
            propNumber = data;
        }

        private int propNumber;
        public int Number {
            get {
                return propNumber;
            }
        }
    }
}
```

Here is the proper code, where the *XClass* implements the *IComparable* interface. This program runs successfully:

```
using System;

namespace Donis.CSharpBook {
    public class Starter {
        public static void Main() {
            XClass[] objs = { new XClass(5), new XClass(10),
                new XClass(1) };
```

```
                Array.Sort(objs);
                foreach (XClass obj in objs) {
                    Console.WriteLine(obj.Number);
                }
            }
        }
    }

    public class XClass : IComparable {
        public XClass(int data) {
            propNumber = data;
        }

        private int propNumber;
        public int Number {
            get {
                return propNumber;
            }
        }

        public int CompareTo(object obj) {
            XClass comp = (XClass) obj;
            if (this.Number == comp.Number) {
                return 0;
            }
            if (this.Number < comp.Number) {
                return -1;
            }
            return 1;
        }
    }
}
```

Many of the methods and properties of *System.Array* are required from interfaces that *System.Array* inherits. The following section lists those interfaces and methods.

ICollection Interface

The *ICollection* interface defines behavior to return the count of elements, copy a collection, and provide synchronization support for collections. The members of the *ICollection* interface are as follows:

- CopyTo method
- Count property
- IsSynchronized property
- SyncRoot property

ICloneable Interface

System.Array also implements the *ICloneable* interface. This is the interface for duplicating an object, including an array. The only member of this interface is the *Clone* method.

IEnumerable

System.Array implements the *IEnumerable* interface to support enumeration. *IEnumerable. GetEnumerator* is the sole member of this interface. *GetEnumerator* returns an enumerator object that implements the *IEnumerator* interface. The enumerator provides a consistent interface for enumerating any collection. Enumerable objects are also convenient. For example, the *foreach* statement can enumerate the elements of an array easier than the more generic *for* statement can. Incorrectly iterating an array is a common error in programs. The *foreach* statement makes array iteration trivial.

Chapter 8, "Enumerators," will focus more on enumerators.

Here is sample code that enumerates an array using an enumerator object:

```
using System;
using System.Collections;

namespace Donis.CSharpBook {
    public class Starter {
        public static void Main() {
            int[] numbers = { 1, 2, 3, 4, 5 };
            IEnumerator e = numbers.GetEnumerator();

            // first iteration
            while (e.MoveNext()) {
                Console.WriteLine(e.Current);
            }

            // second iteration
            foreach (int number in numbers) {
                Console.WriteLine(number);
            }
        }
    }
}
```

IList Interface

System.Array type implements the *IList* interface. However, only part of this implementation is publicly available. Some members of the *IList* interface are contrary to the array paradigm, such as the *RemoveAt* method. Arrays are immutable. You cannot remove elements from the middle of an array. For this reason, *RemoveAt* is implemented privately. Other methods of the *IList* interface are implemented privately for similar reasons.

Table 5-4 lists the *IList* interface and whether the implementation in *System.Array* is public or private.

TABLE 5-4 List members

Member	Public or private?
Add	Private
Clear	Public
Contains	Private
IndexOf	Public
Insert	Private
Remove	Private
RemoveAt	Private

Indexers

Indexers are properties with the outward appearance of an array. They allow you to access an object as an array. For types that contain a collection as a member, indexers are helpful because they allow you to provide safe and convenient access to the internal collection. The backing data of an indexer is typically an array or a collection. The indexer defines a *set* and *get* method, which is common for all properties. However, the *get* and *set* method of an indexer are for the *this* reference. Indexers are considered a default property because the indexer is a nameless property. Internally, the compiler uses the *get_Item* and *set_Item* method to support indexers.

Here are some of the similarities and differences between indexers and standard properties:

- Indexers can be overloaded.

- Indexers can be overridden.

- Indexers can be members of interfaces.

- Indexers support the standard access modifiers.

- Indexers cannot be static.

- Indexers are nameless and associated with the *this* reference.

- Indexers' parameters are indices, while properties do not have indices.

- Indexers are accessed using indices.

- Indexers in a *base* class are accessed as *base*[indices], while a property in a *base* class is accessed as *base.Property.*

- Indexers support numeric and non-numeric indices, while arrays support only integral indices.

Using an indexer is functionally similar to using an array. However, there are a couple of important differences:

- Indexers typically have a data store, whereas an array is the data store.

- Indexers can perform automatic data validation, and an array cannot.

Here is the syntax of an indexer:

accessibility modifier type this[*parameters*]

{ *attributes* get {*getbody*} *attributes* set {*setbody*} }

Except for static accessibility, indexers have the same accessibility and modifiers as a normal property. Indexers cannot be static. At declaration, the parameters of an indexer are a comma-delimited list of indexes. The list includes the type and name of each parameter. Indexer indices can be nonintegral types, such as a string type or any reference type.

The following is example code for indexers. The *Names* type is a wrapper of an array of names and ages. The indexer for the *Names* type will provide access to this array. In this example, the indexer is read-only providing only read access to the internal array. The indexer in the example has a single parameter, which is an integer index. Flexibility is one of the benefits of indexers versus standard arrays. With a single indice, the indexer returns both the name and age of the employee. This task would be harder to accomplish with an array:

```
using System;

namespace Donis.CSharpBook {
    public class Starter {
        public static void Main() {
            Names obj = new Names();
            Console.WriteLine(obj[1]);
        }
    }

    public class Names {
        object[,] _names = {
            { "Valerie", 27 },
            { "Ben", 35 },
            { "Donis", 29 } };

        public object this[int index] {
            get {
                return _names[index,0] + " " + _names[index,1];
            }
        }
    }
}
```

Indexers can be overloaded based on the parameter list. Overloaded indexers should have a varying number of parameters, varying parameter types, or both. The following code overloads an indexer twice. The first indexer is read-only and returns the name and age information. The second indexer is a read-write property that sets and gets the age of a person. This indexer, which has a string parameter, demonstrates a non-numerical index:

```
using System;

namespace Donis.CSharpBook {
    public class Starter {
        public static void Main() {
            Names obj = new Names();
            obj["Donis"] = 42;
            Console.WriteLine(obj["Donis"]);
        }
    }

    public class Names {
        object [,] _names = {
                { "Valerie", 27 },
                { "Ben", 35 },
                { "Donis", 29 } };

        public object this[int index] {
            get {
                return _names[index,0] + " " + _names[index,1];
            }
        }

        public object this[string sIndex] {

            get {
                int index = FindName(sIndex);
                return _names[index, 1];
            }
            set {
                int index = FindName(sIndex);
                _names[index, 1] = value;
            }
        }

        private int FindName(string sIndex) {
            for (int index = 0; index < _names.GetLength(0);
                    ++index) {
                if ((string)(_names[index,0]) == sIndex) {
                    return index;
                }
            }
            throw new Exception("Name not found");
        }
    }
}
```

params Keyword

The *params* keyword is a parameter modifier. It indicates that the target parameter is a one-dimensional array of variable length. By extension, the keyword defines a variable-length parameter list. The *params* modifier can be applied only to the last parameter of a parameter list. Unlike standard parameters, the *ref* and *out* modifiers cannot be used with a *params* parameter.

Initialize the *params* argument with an implicit or explicit array. This is done at the call site. For implicit initialization, the C# compiler consumes for the array the optional parameters that follow the fixed parameter list. The fixed parameters are the parameters that precede the *params*-modified parameter in the function signature. The optional arguments are rolled into an array. If there are six optional arguments after the fixed arguments, an array of six elements is created and initialized. Alternatively, an explicit array can be given as the *params* argument. Finally, the *params* argument can be omitted in the method call. When omitted, the *params* argument is treated as an empty array. An empty array is different from a null array. Empty arrays have no elements but are valid instances.

In the following code, *Names* is a static method, which has a *params* parameter. The *employees* parameter is a single-dimensional string array. Consequently, the *Names* method has a variable-length parameter list:

```
public static void Names(string company,
    params string[] employees) {
    Console.WriteLine("{0} employees: ",
        company);
    foreach (string employee in employees) {
        Console.WriteLine("  {0}", employee);
    }
}
```

For a variable-length parameter list, the number of parameters is set at the call site. The following code shows the *Names* method being called with varying numbers of arguments. In both calls, the first parameter is consumed by the *company* parameter. The remaining arguments are used to create an array, which is assigned to the last parameter. A three-argument array is created for the first method call, whereas the second method has a six-argument array as the *param* argument:

```
Names("Fabrikam", "Fred", "Bob", "Alice");
Names("Contoso", "Sally", "Al", "Julia",
    "Will", "Sarah", "Terri");
```

The following code calls the *Names* method with an explicit array. This is identical to calling the method with four arguments:

```
Names("Fabrikam", new string[] {"Fred", "Bob",
        "Alice"});
```

In the following statement, the *Names* method is called without a *params* argument. For the omitted parameter, the compiler creates an array with no elements, which is subsequently passed to the method as the last parameter:

```
Names("Fabrikam");
```

Like any method, variable-length methods can be overloaded. You even can overload a method having a fixed number of parameters with a method having a variable number of parameters. Where there is ambiguity, the method with the fixed number of parameters is preferred and will be called.

In the following code, the *Names* method is overloaded with three methods. The first two overloads have a variable-length parameter list, whereas the final method has a fixed-length parameter list. In *Main*, the first two calls of the *Names* method are not ambiguous. The final call is ambiguous and can resolve to either the first or third overloaded method. The first overload of the method has a variable-length parameter list. Because the third overload has a fixed-length parameter list, it is preferred and will be called:

```
using System;

namespace Donis.CSharpBook {
    public class Starter {
        public static void Main() {
            Names("Fabrikam", "Fred", "Bob", "Alice");
            Names("Fabrikam", 1234, 5678, 9876, 4561);
            Names("Fabrikam", "Carter", "Deborah");
        }

        public static void Names(string company,
            params string[] employees) {
            Console.WriteLine("{0} employees: ",
                company);
            foreach(string employee in employees) {
                Console.WriteLine("  {0}", employee);
            }
        }

        public static void Names(string company,
            params int[] emplid) {
            Console.WriteLine("{0} employees: ",
                company);
            foreach (int employee in emplid) {
                Console.WriteLine("  {0}", employee);
            }
        }

        public static void Names(string company,
            string empl1, string empl2) {
            Console.WriteLine("{0} employees: ",
                company);
```

```
                Console.WriteLine("  {0}", empl1);
                Console.WriteLine("  {0}", empl2);
        }
    }
}
```

Array Conversion

You can cast between arrays. Arrays are implicit *System.Array* types, and therefore, regard-less of type or the number of dimensions, any array can be cast to *System.Array*. All arrays are compatible with their underlying type.

When casting or converting between arrays, the source and destination array are required to have the same dimensions. In addition, an array of value types is convertible only to arrays of the same dimension and type. Arrays of reference types are somewhat more flexible. Arrays of reference types can be cast to arrays of the same or ascendant type. This is called *array covariance*. Array reference types are covariant, whereas arrays of value types are not.

Arrays can be used as function parameters and returns. In these circumstances, implicit cast-ing may occur. Array covariance may also occur at this time.

Arrays as Function Returns and Parameters

Arrays used as a function argument are passed by reference. This is more efficient than plac-ing a potentially large number of elements on the stack. As a reference type, the array state can be changed in the called method. Arrays used as parameters are normal parameters and support the regular assortment of modifiers. Of course, the array instance must be convert-ible to the type of array parameter.

In the following code, *ZClass* has two static methods, which both have an array parameter. The *ListArray* method has a *System.Array* parameter, which accepts any array as an argument. This allows the *ListArray* method to be called in *Main* with different types of array arguments. The *Total* method also has an array argument, which is an integer array. This means the argument must be an integer array:

```
using System;

namespace Donis.CSharpBook {
    public class Starter {
        public static void Main() {
            int[] zArray = { 10,9,8,7,6,5,4,3,2,1 };
            string[] xArray = { "a", "b", "c", "d" };
            Console.WriteLine("List Numbers");
            ZClass.ListArray(zArray);
            Console.WriteLine("List Letters");
            ZClass.ListArray(xArray);
```

```
            Console.WriteLine("Total Numbers");
            ZClass.Total(zArray);
        }
    }


    public class ZClass {

        public static void ListArray(Array a) {
            foreach( object element in a) {
                Console.WriteLine(element);
            }
        }

        public static void Total(int[] iArray) {
            int total = 0;
            foreach (int number in iArray) {
                total += number;
            }
            Console.WriteLine(total);
        }
    }
}
```

Arrays also can be returned from functions, which is one way to return more than a single item from a function. You can return multiple items as elements of an array. Arrays are not returned on the stack. Returning an array gives the calling function a reference to the array, which provides direct access to the array values.

Collections

Arrays are the most popular kind of collection. However, the .NET FCL offers a variety of other collections with different semantics. Collections are abstractions of data algorithms. *ArrayList* abstracts a dynamic array; the *Stack* collection abstracts a stack data structure; the *Queue* collection abstracts queues; the *Hashtable* collection abstracts a lookup table; and so on. Each collection exposes both unique and standard interfaces. The unique interface is specific to the collection type. For example, the *Stack* type has *pop* and *push* methods, whereas the *Queue* type has *Dequeue* and *Enqueue* methods. In addition, collections implement the *ICollection*, *IEnumerable*, and *ICloneable* interfaces. (These interfaces were described earlier in this chapter in separate sections specific to each interface.) The non-generic collection classes are implemented in the *System.Collections* namespace. For similar solutions to arrays, lists, and dictionaries, generic collections are preferred to non-generic and are implemented in *System.Collections.Generic*. Generics are detailed in Chapter 7.

Table 5-5 lists the non-generic collections in the .NET FCL.

TABLE 5-5 Collection types

Class	Description
ArrayList	Dynamic array
BitArray	Bit array
Hashtable	Lookup table of keys and values
Queue	First-in/first-out (FIFO) collection of elements
SortedList	Sorted list of elements
Stack	Last-in/first-out (LIFO) collection of elements

What follows is a detailed explanation of each collection found in the *Collections* namespace. The explanations are complemented with sample code that highlights the uniqueness and strength of each collection. In addition to the listed member functions, many of the collections also support these extension methods: *Queryable.AsQueryable, Enumerable.Cast,* and *Enumerable.OfType.* These extension methods are explained in Chapter 7.

ArrayList Collection

An array list is a dynamic array. While a conventional array has a fixed number of elements, elements can be added or deleted at run time with a dynamic array. *ArrayList* elements are accessible using the indexing operator and indices.

In addition to the standard collection interfaces, *ArrayList* also implements the *IList* interface.

Table 5-6 lists the *ArrayList*-specific methods and properties. The static members of *ArrayList* are thread-safe, whereas instance members are not.

TABLE 5-6 ArrayList members

Member	Syntax

Constructor
The *ArrayList* constructor is overloaded. These are the overloaded constructors.
	`ArrayList()`
	
	`ArrayList(`
	`    ICollection sourceCollection)`
	
	`ArrayList(int capacity)`

Adapter This method creates a wrapper *ArrayList* from an *IList* collection.	`static ArrayList Adapter(` `    IList list)`
Add This method adds an element to the end of the *ArrayList* collection.	`virtual int Add(object value)`
AddRange This method adds a range of elements to the *ArrayList* collection. The additional elements are received from any type that implements the *ICollection* interface.	`virtual void AddRange(` `    ICollection elements)`

TABLE 5-6 ArrayList members

Member	Syntax

BinarySearch
 	
This method performs a binary search for a specific value in a sorted *ArrayList* collection. The sort is controlled by the *IComparable* interface.
	`virtual int BinarySearch(`
	`    object value)`
	
	`virtual int BinarySearch(`
	`    object value,`
	`    IComparer comparer)`
	
	`virtual int BinarySearch(`
	`    int index,`
	`    int count,`
	`    object value,`
	`    IComparer comparer)`

Capacity This property gets or sets the number of elements allowed in the collection. Capacity is different from the actual number of elements. The capacity is the number of elements the *ArrayList* can store. The capacity is increased automatically as elements are added. When the number of elements exceeds the current capacity, the capacity doubles. You can use the capacity to improve the memory management of elements in a collection.	`virtual int Capacity {` `    get; set; }`
Clear This method removes all the elements of the collection.	`virtual void Clear()`
Contains This method returns *true* if the specified element is found in a collection. If the element is not found, it returns *false*.	`virtual bool Contains(object item)`
Count This property returns the number of elements in the collection.	`virtual int Count {` `    get; }`

FixedSize
 	
This method returns a fixed-sized version of the collection parameter.
	`static ArrayList FixedSize(`
	`    ArrayList sourceArray)`
	
	`static IList FixedSize(`
	`    IList sourceList)`

GetRange This method returns a span of elements from the current array list. The result is returned as an *ArrayList*.	`virtual ArrayList GetRange(` `    int index, int count)`

TABLE 5-6 ArrayList members

Member	Syntax

IndexOf
This method returns the index of the first matching element in the collection.
	`virtual int IndexOf(`
	`    object value)`
	
	`virtual int IndexOf(object value,`
	`    int startIndex)`
	
	`virtual int IndexOf(object value,`
	`    int startIndex,`
	`    int count)`

Insert This method inserts an element into the collection at the specified index.	`virtual void Insert(int index,` `    object value)`

InsertRange
This method inserts multiple elements into the collection at the specified index.
	`virtual void InsertRange(`
	`    int index,`
	`    ICollection sourceCollection)`

IsFixedSize This property returns *true* if the collection is of fixed length. Otherwise, the property returns *false*.	`virtual bool IsFixedSize {` `    get; }`
IsReadOnly This property returns *true* if the collection is read-only. Otherwise, the property returns *false*.	`virtual bool IsReadOnly {` `    get; }`
Item This property gets or sets the value of the element at the index.	`virtual object this[int index] {` `    get; set; }`

LastIndexOf
This method returns the index of the last matching element in the collection.
	`virtual int LastIndex(`
	`    object value)`
	
	`virtual int LastIndexOf(object value,`
	`    int startIndex)`
	
	`virtual int LastIndexOf(object value,`
	`    int startIndex,`
	`    int count)`

ReadOnly
This method creates a read-only wrapper for an *IList* object.
	`static ArrayList ReadOnly(`
	`    ArrayList sourceArray)`
	
	`static IList ReadOnly(`
	`    IList sourceList)`

Remove This method removes the first element in the collection that matches the value.	`virtual void Remove(` `    object value)`

TABLE 5-6 ArrayList members

Member	Syntax
RemoveAt At the specified index, this method removes the element from the collection.	```virtual void RemoveAt(int index)```
RemoveRange This method removes a range of elements from a collection.	```virtual void RemoveRange(int index, int count)```
Repeat This method returns an *ArrayList* with each element initialized to the specified value. Count is the number of elements in the returned *ArrayList*.	```static ArrayList Repeat(object value, int count)```

Reverse
 	
This method reverses the order of elements in the collection.
	```virtual void Reverse()```
	
	```virtual void Reverse(int beginIndex, int endingIndex)```

SetRange This method copies elements from the source collection over the same elements in the current collection. The copy starts at the index.	```virtual void SetRange(int index, ICollection sourceCollection)```

Sort
 	
This method sorts an *ArrayList*. The sort is controlled by the *IComparable* interface of the element types.
	```virtual void Sort()```
	
	```virtual void Sort(IComparer comparer)```
	
	```virtual void Sort(int index, int count, IComparer comparer)```

Synchronized
 	
This method returns a thread-safe wrapper of an *ArrayList* or *IList* object.
	```static ArrayList Synchronized(ArrayList sourceArray)```
	
	```static IList Synchronized(IList sourceList)```

ToArray
 	
This method copies the current array. The *Type* parameter specifies the target type of the array.
	```virtual object [] ToArray()```
	
	```virtual Array ToArray(Type type)```

TrimToSize This method sets the capacity to the number of elements in the collection.	```virtual void TrimToSize()```
IEnumerable members	*GetEnumerator*
ICloneable members	*Clone*
ICollection members	*CopyTo, Count, IsSynchronized*, and *SyncRoot*

The following code uses some *ArrayList* methods and properties. It creates a new *ArrayList*. Elements then are added from command-line arguments. The command-line arguments should be integer values. Then the values of the elements in the cloned *ArrayList* are doubled. Afterward, the cloned *ArrayList* is enumerated and every element is displayed:

```
using System;
using System.Collections;

namespace Donis.CSharpBook {
    public class Starter {
        public static void Main(string [] argv) {

            ArrayList al1 = new ArrayList();
            foreach(string arg in argv) {
                al1.Add(int.Parse(arg));
            }
            al1.Sort();
            ArrayList al2 = (ArrayList)al1.Clone();
            for (int count = 0; count < al2.Count; ++count) {
                al2[count] = ((int)al2[count]) * 2;
            }
            foreach (int number in al2) {
                Console.WriteLine(number);
            }
        }
    }
}
```

BitArray Collection

The *BitArray* collection is a composite of bit values. Bit values are 1 and 0, where 1 is *true* and 0 is *false*. This collection provides an efficient means of storing and retrieving bit values.

Table 5-7 lists the methods and properties specific to a *BitArray* collection. The static members of the *BitArray* are thread-safe, whereas instance members are not.

TABLE 5- 7 BitArray members

Member	Syntax

Constructor
The *BitArray* constructor is overloaded. These are some of the overloaded constructors.
	`BitArray(bool [] bits)`
	
	`BitArray(int [] bits)`
	
	`BitArray(int count,`
	`    bool default)`

And This method performs a bitwise *AND* on the current instance and the *BitArray* parameter. The result is the returned *BitArray*.	`BitArray And(BitArray value)`

TABLE 5-7 **BitArray members**

Member	Syntax
Get This method returns a specific bit in the *BitArray* collection.	`bool Get(int index)`
IsReadOnly This property returns *true* if the collection is read-only. Otherwise, the property returns *false*.	`virtual bool IsReadOnly {` `  get; }`
Item This property gets or sets the bit at the index.	`virtual object this[int index] {` `  get; set; }`
Length This property gets or sets the number of bits in the collection.	`public int Length {` `  get; set; }`
Not This method negates the bits of the *BitArray* collection. The result is the returned *BitArray*.	`BitArray Not()`
Or This method performs a bitwise *OR* on two *BitArray* collections, the current instance and the parameter. The result is in the returned *BitArray*.	`BitArray Or(BitArray value)`
Set This method sets a specific bit in the collection.	`void Set(int index, bool value)`
SetAll This method sets all the bits of the collection to *true* or *false*.	`void SetAll(bool value)`
Xor This method performs an exclusive *OR* on the current instance and the *BitArray* parameter.	`BitArray Xor(` `  BitArray value)`
IEnumerable member	*GetEnumerator*
ICloneable members	*Clone*
ICollection members	*CopyTo, Count, IsSynchronized, and SyncRoot*

The following code demonstrates the *BitArray* collection. The *Employee* class contains a *BitArray* collection that tracks employee enrollment in various programs, such as the health plan and the credit union. This is convenient because program enrollment is always either *true* or *false*. In the *Employee* class, properties are provided to *set* and *get* enrollment in various programs:

```
using System;
using System.Collections;

namespace Donis.CSharpBook {
    public class Starter {
        public static void Main() {
```

```
            Employee ben = new Employee();
            ben.InProfitSharing = false;
            ben.InHealthPlan = false;
            Employee valerie = new Employee();
            valerie.InProfitSharing = false;
            Participation("Ben", ben);
            Participation("Valerie", valerie);
        }

    public static void Participation(string name, Employee person) {
        Console.WriteLine(name + ":");
        if (person.InProfitSharing) {
            Console.WriteLine("   Participating in" +
                " Profit Sharing");
        }
        if (person.InHealthPlan) {
            Console.WriteLine("   Participating in" +
                " Health Plan");
        }
        if (person.InCreditUnion) {
            Console.WriteLine("   Participating in" +
                " Credit Union");
        }
    }
}

public class Employee {
    public Employee() {
        eflags.SetAll(true);
    }

    private BitArray eflags = new BitArray(3);

    public bool InProfitSharing {
        set {
            eflags.Set(0, value);
        }
        get {
            return eflags.Get(0);
        }
    }

    public bool InHealthPlan {
        set {
            eflags.Set(1, value);
        }
        get {
            return eflags.Get(1);
        }
    }

    public bool InCreditUnion {
        set {
            eflags.Set(2, value);
        }
        get {
```

```
                return eflags.Get(2);
            }
        }
    }
}
```

Hashtable Collection

The *Hashtable* collection is a collection of key/value pairs. Entries in this collection are in-stances of the *DictionaryEntry* type. *DictionaryEntry* types have a *Key* and *Value* property to get and set keys and values.

In addition to the standard collection interfaces, the *Hashtable* collection implements the *IDictionary*, *ISerializable*, and *IDeserializationCallback* interfaces.

The entries are stored and retrieved in order based on the hash code contained in the key.

Table 5-8 lists the members of the *Hashtable* collection.

TABLE 5-8 Hashtable members

Member	Syntax

Constructor
 	
 The *Hashtable* constructor is overloaded. This is the syntax of some of the overloaded constructors.
	`Hashtable()`
	
	 `Hashtable(int capacity)`
	
	 `Hashtable(int capacity,`
	 `    float loadFactor)`

Add This method adds an element to the collection.	`virtual void Add(object key,` `    object value)`
Clear This method deletes all elements in the collection.	`virtual void Clear()`
Contains This method returns *true* if the key is found in the collection. If the key is not present, the method returns *false*.	`virtual bool Contains(` `    object key)`
ContainsKey This method returns *true* if the key is found in the collection. If the key is not present, it returns *false*. Identical to the *Contains* method.	`virtual bool ContainsKey(` `    object key)`
ContainsValue This method returns *true* if the value is found in the collection. If the value is not present, the method returns *false*.	`virtual bool ContainsValue(` `    object value)`

TABLE 5-8 Hashtable members

Member	Syntax
GetEnumerator This method returns an *IDictionaryEnumerator* object, which can be used to enumerate the elements of the hashtable.	```virtual IDictionaryEnumerator
GetEnumerator()```
GetHash This method returns the hash code for the specified key.	```virtual int GetHash(
object key)```
GetObjectData This method serializes the hashtable collection.	```virtual void GetObjectData(
SerializationInfo info,
StreamingContext context)```
IsFixedSize This property returns *true* if the collection is of fixed size. Otherwise, it returns *false*.	```virtual bool IsFixedSize {
get; }```
IsReadOnly This property returns *true* if the collection is read-only. Otherwise, it returns *false*.	```virtual bool IsReadOnly {
get; }```
IsSynchronized This property returns *true* if the collection is synchronized.	```virtual bool IsSynchronized {
get; }```
Item This property gets or sets a value pertaining to a key.	```virtual object this[object key] {
get; set; }```
KeyEquals This method compares a key to a value. If they are equal, *true* is returned; if not, *false* is returned. This method is used primarily to compare two keys.	```virtual bool KeyEquals(
object item,
object key)```
Keys This method returns a collection that contains the keys of the hashtable.	```virtual ICollection Keys {
get; }```
OnDeserialization This method is called when deserialization is completed.	```virtual void OnDeserialization(
object sender)```
Remove This method removes an element of the specified key from the collection.	```virtual void Remove(
object key)```
Synchronized This method returns a thread-safe wrapper of the collection.	```static Hashtable Synchronized(
Hashtable sourceTable)```
Values This property returns a collection that has the values of the hashtable.	```virtual ICollection Values {
get; }```

TABLE 5-8 Hashtable members

Member	Syntax
IEnumerable members	*GetEnumerator*
ICloneable members	*Clone*
ICollection members	*CopyTo, Count, IsSynchronized,* and *SyncRoot*

Hashtable.GetEnumerator implements *IDictionary.GetEnumerator*, which returns an *IDictionaryEnumerator*. *IDictionaryEnumerator* implements the *IEnumerator* interface, while also adding three properties: *Entry*, *Key*, and *Value*.

The following code extends the previous sample code for the *BitArray* collection. The program creates a *Hashtable*, where each element is an employee. The key is the employee ID, and the value is an instance of an *Employee* type:

```
using System;
using System.Collections;

namespace Donis.CSharpBook {
    public class Starter {
        public static void Main() {
            Hashtable employees = new Hashtable();
            employees.Add("A100", new Employee(
                "Ben", true, false, true));
            employees.Add("V100", new Employee(
                "Valerie", false, false, true));
            Participation((Employee) employees["A100"]);
            Participation((Employee) employees["V100"]);
        }

        public static void Participation(Employee person) {
            Console.WriteLine(person.Name + ":");
            if (person.InProfitSharing) {
                Console.WriteLine("   Participating in" +
                    " Profit Sharing");
            }
            if (person.InHealthPlan) {
                Console.WriteLine("   Participating in" +
                    " Health Plan");
            }
            if (person.InCreditUnion) {
                Console.WriteLine("   Participating in" +
                    " Credit Union");
            }
        }
    }

    public class Employee {

        public Employee(string emplName) {
            propName = emplName;
            eflags.SetAll(true);
        }
```

```
        public Employee(string emplName,
                        bool profitSharing,
                        bool healthPlan,
                        bool creditUnion) {
            propName = emplName;
            InProfitSharing = profitSharing;
            InHealthPlan = healthPlan;
            InCreditUnion = creditUnion;
        }

        private BitArray eflags = new BitArray(3);

        public bool InProfitSharing {
            set {
                eflags.Set(0, value);
            }
            get {
                return eflags.Get(0);
            }
        }

        public bool InHealthPlan {
            set {
                eflags.Set(1, value);
            }
            get {
                return eflags.Get(1);
            }
        }

        public bool InCreditUnion {
            set {
                eflags.Set(2, value);
            }
            get {
                return eflags.Get(2);
            }
        }

        private string propName;
        public string Name {
            get {
                return propName;
            }
        }
    }
}
```

This is sample code that shows the use of an *IDictionaryEnumerator* enumerator:

```
using System;
using System.Collections;

namespace Donis.CSharpBook {
    public class Starter {
        public static void Main() {
            Hashtable zHash = new Hashtable();
```

```
            zHash.Add("one", 1);
            zHash.Add("two", 2);
            zHash.Add("three", 3);
            zHash.Add("four", 4);
            IDictionaryEnumerator e =
                zHash.GetEnumerator();
            while (e.MoveNext()) {
                Console.WriteLine(
                    "{0} {1}",
                    e.Key, e.Value);
            }
        }
    }
}
```

Queue Collection

A *Queue* collection abstracts a FIFO data structure. *Queue* collections are ideal for implementing messaging components.

Table 5-9 lists the members of the *Queue* collection.

TABLE 5-9 Queue members

Member	Syntax

Constructor
The Queue constructor is overloaded. This is the syntax of the overloaded constructors.
	`public Queue()`
	
	`public Queue(`
	`    ICollection sourceCollection)`
	
	`public Queue(int capacity)`
	
	`public Queue(int capacity,`
	`    float factor)`

Clear This method removes all the elements of the collection.	`virtual void Clear()`
Contains This method returns *true* if the specified value is found in the collection. If the value is not found, the method returns *false*.	`virtual bool Contains(object value)`
Dequeue This method removes and returns the first element on the queue.	`virtual object Dequeue()`
Enqueue This method adds an element to the queue.	`virtual void Enqueue(` `    object element)`
Peek This method returns the first element of the queue without removing it.	`virtual object Peek()`

TABLE 5-9 Queue members

Member	Syntax
Synchronized This method returns a thread-safe wrapper for a queue object.	`static Queue Synchronized(` `    Queue sourceQueue)`
ToArray This method creates a new array from the elements of the queue.	`virtual object[] ToArray()`
TrimToSize This method sets the capacity to the number of elements in the collection.	`virtual void TrimToSize()`
IEnumerable members	*GetEnumerator*
ICloneable members	*Clone*
ICollection members	*CopyTo*, *Count*, *IsSynchronized*, and *SyncRoot*

This is sample code of the *Queue* collection. Customers are added to the queue and then displayed:

```csharp
using System;
using System.Collections;

namespace Donis.CSharpBook {
    public class Starter {
        public static void Main() {
            Queue waiting = new Queue();
            waiting.Enqueue(new Customer("Bob"));
            waiting.Enqueue(new Customer("Ted"));
            waiting.Enqueue(new Customer("Kim"));
            waiting.Enqueue(new Customer("Sam"));

            while (waiting.Count != 0) {
                Customer cust =
                    (Customer) waiting.Dequeue();
                Console.WriteLine(cust.Name);
            }
        }

        public class Customer {
            public Customer(string cName) {
                propName = cName;
            }

            private string propName;
            public string Name {
                get {
                    return propName;
                }
            }
        }
    }
}
```

SortedList

The *SortedList* collection is a combination of key/value entries and an *ArrayList* collection, where the collection is sorted by the key. Elements of the collection are accessible either through the key or through an index.

Table 5-10 includes the members of the *SortedList* collection.

TABLE 5-10 SortedList members

Member	Syntax

Constructor
 The SortedList constructor is overloaded. These are some of the overloaded constructors.
	`SortedList()`
	
	 `SortedList(IComparer comparer)`
	
	 `SortedList(`
	 `    IDictionary sourceCollection)`

Add This method adds an element to the collection.	`virtual void Add(object key,` `    object value)`
Capacity This property gets or sets the capacity of the collection.	`virtual int Capacity {` `    get; set; }`
Clear This method removes all the elements of the collection.	`virtual void Clear()`
Contains This method returns *true* if the specified value is found in the collection. If the value is not found, the method returns *false*.	`virtual bool Contains(object value)`
ContainsKey This method returns *true* if the key is found in the collection. If the key is not present, it returns *false*. Identical to the *Contains* method.	`virtual bool ContainsKey(` `    object key)`
ContainsValue This method returns *true* if the value is found in the collection. If the value is not present, it returns *false*.	`virtual bool ContainsValue(` `    object value)`
GetByIndex This method returns the value at the specified index.	`virtual object GetByIndex(` `    int index)`
GetKey This method returns the key at the specified index.	`virtual object GetKey(` `    int index)`
GetKeyList This method returns all the keys of the collection in a list.	`virtual IList GetKeyList()`
GetValueList This method returns all the values of the *SortedList* in a new list.	`virtual IList GetValueList()`

TABLE 5-10 SortedList members

Member	Syntax
IndexOfKey This method returns the index of a key found in the collection. If not found, -1 is returned.	`virtual int IndexOfKey(` `    object key)`
IndexOfValue This method returns the index to the first instance of this value in the collection.	`virtual int IndexOfValue(` `    object value)`
IsFixedSize This property returns *true* if the collection is of fixed size. Otherwise, it returns *false*.	`virtual bool IsFixedSize {` `    get; }`
IsReadOnly This property returns *true* if the collection is read-only. Otherwise, it returns *false*.	`virtual bool IsReadOnly {` `    get; }`
Item This property gets or sets the value of this key.	`virtual object this[object key] {` `    get; set; }`
Keys This property returns the keys of the *SortedList* in a collection.	`public virtual ICollection Keys {` `    get; }`
Remove This method removes the element identified by the key from the collection.	`virtual void Remove(` `    object key)`
RemoveAt This method removes the element at the specified index.	`virtual void RemoveAt(` `    int index)`
SetByIndex This method sets the value of the element at the specified index.	`virtual void SetByIndex(` `    int index, object value)`
Synchronized This method returns a thread-safe wrapper for a *SortedList* object.	`static SortedList Synchronized(` `    SortedList sourceList)`
TrimToSize This method trims the capacity to the actual number of elements in the collection.	`virtual void TrimToSize()`
Values This property returns the values in a collection.	`virtual ICollection Values {` `    get; }`
IEnumerable members	GetEnumerator
ICloneable members	Clone
ICollection members	CopyTo, Count, IsSynchronized, and SyncRoot

The following program is an application that tracks auto repair tickets. Each ticket, which is an instance of the *AutoRepairTicket* class, is added to a sorted list. The key is the customer name. The value is the actual ticket. After populating the *SortedList* type, the *CustomerReport* method lists the open tickets:

```csharp
using System;
using System.Collections;

namespace Donis.CSharpBook {
    public class Starter {
        public static void Main() {
            SortedList tickets = new SortedList();
            AutoRepairTicket ticket = NewTicket("Ben");
            tickets.Add(ticket.Name, ticket);
            ticket = NewTicket("Donis");
            tickets.Add(ticket.Name, ticket);
            ticket = NewTicket("Adam");
            tickets.Add(ticket.Name, ticket);
            CustomerReport(tickets);
        }

        public static AutoRepairTicket NewTicket(
                string customerName) {
            return new AutoRepairTicket(customerName,
                DateTime.Now);
        }

        public static void CustomerReport(SortedList list) {
            foreach (DictionaryEntry entry in list) {
                int nextTag = ((AutoRepairTicket) entry.Value).Tag;
                string nextTime = ((AutoRepairTicket)
                    entry.Value).Time.ToShortTimeString();
                Console.WriteLine("Customer: {0} Ticket: {1} Time: {2}",
                    entry.Key, nextTag, nextTime);
            }
        }
    }

    public class AutoRepairTicket{
        public AutoRepairTicket(string customerName,
                DateTime ticketTime) {
            propName = customerName;
            propTime = ticketTime;
            propTag = ++count;
        }

        private string propName;
        public string Name {
            get {
                return propName;
            }
        }

        private DateTime propTime;
        public DateTime Time {
            get {
                return propTime;
```

```
            }
        }

        private int propTag;
        public int Tag {
            get {
                return propTag;
            }
        }

        private static int count = 1000;
    }
}
```

Stack Collection

A *Stack* collection abstracts a LIFO data structure.

Table 5-11 lists the members of the *Stack* collection.

TABLE 5-11 *Stack* **members**

Member	Syntax
Clear This method removes all the elements of the collection.	`virtual void Clear()`
Contains This method returns *true* if the specified value is found in the collection. If the value is not found, the method returns *false*.	`virtual bool Contains(object value)`
Peek This method previews the most recent element on the stack. The element is returned without removing it from the stack.	`virtual object Peek()`
Pop This method returns and removes the top element of the stack.	`virtual object Pop()`
Push This method pushes an element onto the stack.	`virtual void Push(object obj)`
Synchronized This method returns a thread-safe wrapper for the *Stack* collection.	`static Stack Synchronized(` `    Stack sourceStack)`
ToArray This method returns the elements of the *Stack* collection as a regular array.	`virtual object[] ToArray()`

The following code adds numbers to a *Stack* collection. The values of the elements in the collection are removed from the stack and then displayed to the Console window:

```
using System;
using System.Collections;

namespace Donis.CSharpBook {
    public class Starter {
        public static void Main() {
            Stack numbers = new Stack(
                new int[] {1,2,3,4,5,6});
            int total = numbers.Count;
            for (int count = 0; count < total; ++count) {
                Console.WriteLine(numbers.Pop());
            }
        }
    }
}
```

Specialized Collections

In addition to the common collections that most developers use, the .NET FCL offers specialized collections. These collections are found in the *System.Collections.Specialized* namespace. Although these collections are used infrequently, they are valuable in certain circumstances.

Table 5-12 lists the specialized collections.

TABLE 5-12 Specialized collections in the .NET FCL

Member	Description
BitVector32	This is an array of 32 bits. It is similar to a *BitArray,* but it is limited to 32 bits. Because of this array's refined use, *BitVector32* structures are more efficient than a *BitArray* collection.
HybridDictionary	This collection is a combination of a *ListDictionary* and a *Hashtable*. It operates as a *ListDictionary* when it contains a small number of elements. For optimum performance, the collection switches to a *Hashtable* as the number of elements increases.
NameValueCollection	This is a collection of keys and values, in which both the keys and values are strings. The collection is accessible via an index or key. A key can refer to multiple values.
OrderedDictionary	This is a collection of key and value pairs, where each entry is accessible by either the key or the value.
StringCollection	This is a collection of strings.
StringDictionary	This is a combination of the *Hashtable* and *StringCollection* collections, in which both the keys and values are strings.

LINQ

Language Integrated Query (LINQ) is the most important addition to Microsoft Visual Studio C# 2008. Previously, there had been competing models for information access: arrays, object properties, data readers, data sets, and much more. In addition, different query syntax sometimes existed in these disparate models. This approach made effective and extensible managing of data a challenge for even the most experienced developer. LINQ provides a single model for information access. However, LINQ is much more. It offers the following features:

- LINQ provides object-oriented access to data.

- LINQ merges the hierarchical and relational data models.

- LINQ has full support for Extensible Markup Language (XML), including navigation capabilities.

- LINQ query syntax is promoted to the language level of Visual C# 2008.

LINQ is presented in more detail in Chapter 6, "Introduction to LINQ."

Chapter 6
Introduction to LINQ

Language Integrated Query (LINQ), which was discussed briefly in Chapter 1, "Introduction to Microsoft Visual C# Programming," is a unified model for accessing data in a declarative and object-oriented manner. This chapter covers LINQ more fully. Why the additional attention? The reason is that LINQ is the distinguishing new feature of Microsoft Visual Studio C# 2008. C# 3.0 has been extended in several ways to accommodate LINQ. Language extensions such as extension methods, lambda expressions, expression trees, anonymous types, and object initializers provide support for LINQ. Of course, many of these extensions are useful as stand-alone features. For example, extension methods now are employed in several places in the .NET Framework Class Library (FCL) apart from LINQ, and extension methods have been added to the string class. Some of these extension methods, such as the *Reverse* extension method, are useful beyond LINQ.

LINQ is a data abstraction layer. Programming is largely about data. The first commercial computer was delivered in 1951 to the U.S. government. The Census Bureau used UNIVAC 1 to complete the census, which was an enormous challenge. It was able to process large amounts of data. Not much has changed in the last half century. We are fully entrenched in the information age, and data is more important now than ever. Developers must understand competing models for accessing and manipulating this data: relational, hierarchal, and file/directory-based (such as Microsoft Symbol Server) databases. In addition, there are Extensible Markup Language (XML) data stores and in-memory data collections. Working with these competing models creates unneeded complexity. LINQ abstracts the source and provides a single query language for these competing models. Of course, this also reduces errors and makes the application easier to maintain. The salient benefit is that instead of focusing on the intricacies of implementation, you can concentrate on creating robust and efficient solutions. From this perspective, LINQ provides a consistent data model for building data-driven applications.

Traditionally, the programming language and the query languages are separate artifacts. In the traditional model, learning a programming language is not sufficient for data management—particularly for persisted data. You also have to understand the query language and other nuances of your data provider, such as ADO.NET. This lack of integration causes several problems. Schema problems are uncovered at run time instead of compile time. Because the schema is not available at compile time, type safety is not guaranteed and IntelliSense is not provided. You are forced to treat information as data to be mined rather than as objects. LINQ is integrated into C# 3.0, a development that acknowledges the important role of data in modern-day programming. Data access is no longer an adjunct to the programming language.

In object-oriented languages, such as C#, objects and data are separated. Objects represent in-memory objects that are type-safe and support encapsulation. These attributes do not commonly extend to data. Data is neither type-safe nor extensible. For that reason, the preference is to work with objects rather than raw data. Data is fragile, while objects are not. LINQ removes the distinction between object-oriented and relational data models. This distinction is not easy to remove. Substantive differences exist: incompatible transaction models, varying type systems, and divergent optimization priorities are just a few of the problems in bridging objects and data. The traditional method, object mapping, is available. Instead of forcing relational data into the object-oriented box, LINQ abstracts the differences between the two paradigms. This is accomplished by promoting query expressions to the language level, creating a natural conduit between data and objects.

Query expressions, such as provided with LINQ, are declarative. A query expression declares *what* data is requested. Previously in C#, data has been accessed imperatively, for example through a *foreach* loop that iterates a collection. The term *imperative* describes *how* the data is retrieved. The declarative approach is preferred to the imperative. With the declarative approach, the method of retrieval remains largely with the query engine. The query engine can manage any optimization. Declarative code is easier to refactor in the future to accommodate changes. Refactoring an imperative algorithm, which is less specific, is undoubtedly more difficult.

There are several LINQ providers:

- **LINQ to Objects**   The most accessible data of an application are in-memory collections, such as the System.Array or List<T> collections. You can access collections with a declarative query instead of using the imperative approach. For example, you can enumerate the elements of an array with a query statement versus a foreach loop. This provides added flexibility while making coding actually simpler. LINQ to Objects also provides an important test case. You can validate the query expressions in the more transparent model provided by LINQ to Objects before using another provider, such as LINQ to ADO.NET. In this chapter, we use LINQ to Objects to explain the core concepts of LINQ.

- **LINQ to XML**   XML is ubiquitous in .NET. Configuration files, datasets, and Simple Object Access Protocol (SOAP) are a handful of the many implementations based on XML in .NET. Some of the ways to access XML include as a text file, through configuration settings, via the XmlReader type, and through the XmlDocument type. With LINQ to XML, you can access XML data sources in memory using stand query language syntax. LINQ to XML also provides the ability to navigate and manage XML trees.

- **LINQ to SQL**   Use LINQ to SQL to access relational databases. Importantly, LINQ to SQL allows data to be accessed as objects. This translation is done using data mapping, as described in Chapter 11, "LINQ Programming." The Visual Studio Integrated Development Environment (IDE) has support for LINQ to SQL beginning with LINQ to SQL classes and the Object Relational Designer (O/R Designer). With LINQ to SQL, you can browse, update, delete, and add records to a SQL database.

LINQ to Objects is the basis of this chapter. LINQ to XML and LINQ to SQL are discussed in detail in Chapter 11.

C# Extensions

As mentioned, C# 3.0 has been extended in support of LINQ. This includes support for type inference, anonymous types, and other elements. In addition, the .NET FCL 3.5 is extended to provide supporting types for LINQ. *Lookup*, *BinaryExpression*, *ChangeSet*, and *AssociationAttribute* represent a handful of new types added to the .NET FCL 3.5 for LINQ. The following sections are a review of the language extensions in C# related to LINQ.

Type Inference

You can declare a local variable without assigning a specific type. The actual type is inferred at compile time from the expression used to initialize the variable. This is called *type inference*. Because type inference is done at compile time, the variable is type-safe. As seen later in this chapter, there are occasions in LINQ where you might not be aware of the type of a variable. However, the compiler knows the appropriate type. Declare a local variable with the *var* keyword for type inference. The *var* keyword cannot be used with data members or properties. The following code declares a variable (*aVar*) with type inference. Because it is initialized as an integer variable, *aVar* becomes an integer type at compile time. This is confirmed with the *Console.WriteLine* statement, which will display System.Int32:

```
int iVar = 5;
var aVar = iVar;
Console.WriteLine(aVar.GetType().ToString());
```

Object Initializers

Object initializers allow you to initialize an object without a constructor. The public data members and properties can be initialized directly. Object initializers are a convenience. You do not have to create a constructor for every permutation of data members and properties that require initialization. In the initializer list, the members are named and assigned a value. You do not have to initialize every data member or property. The object initializer list, which is contained within curly braces, assigns a new instance to the reference. Within the list, each member is delimited with a comma. Here is an example of an object initializer list. In this example, an *Employee* object is initialized using the initializer list:

```
using System;

namespace CSharpBook {
    class Program {
        static void Main(string[] args) {
            Employee bob = new Employee
```

```
                    { Name = "Bob Kelly", Age = 25, Salary = 65000 };
        }
    }

    class Employee {
        public string Name { get; set; }
        public int Age{ get; set; }
        public decimal Salary { get; set; }
    }
}
```

Anonymous Types

Types typically have names. You use the *class* or *struct* keyword to declare and name a type formally. Anonymous types are declared inline and do not use the *class* or *struct* keyword. Because the *class* or *struct* keyword is not used, the type is unnamed and therefore anonymous. Declare an anonymous type using the *new* keyword and an object initializer list. The items in the initializer list can be named or unnamed. If a type is unnamed, its name is inferred from the name of the item. Because the resulting object type is anonymous, you must assign an instance of an anonymous type to an object using type inference (that is, using the *var* keyword). The following code defines an anonymous type with *Name*, *Age*, and *Salary* members. The name and type of the *Name* member is implied from the local variable in the initialize list:

```
using System;

namespace CSharpBook {
    class Program {
        static void Main(string[] args) {
            string Name = "Bob Kelly";
            var obj = new { Name, Age = 25, Salary = (decimal)65000 };
            Console.WriteLine("{0} {1} {2}",
                obj.Name, obj.Age, obj.Salary);
        }
    }
}
```

Extension Methods

Extension methods extend the interface of a class. Traditionally, you inherit a class and extend the base type in the derived class. However, this is not always possible. For example, the class might be sealed. The first parameter of an extension method must be prefixed with the *this* keyword. In addition, extension methods must be static and public. Extension methods are not defined in the target class but in another class. This class may hold one or more extension methods that are applicable to the target type. If the target type has a method that matches the extension method, the member method always has priority and is called. Look at the following code. *IsOdd* and *IsEven* are extension methods for integer (*int*) types. *IsOdd* returns *true* if the integer contains an odd value, such as 3, 5, or 7. *IsEven* returns *true* if the integer contains an even value:

```
static class IntegerExtensions {
    public static bool IsOdd(this int number) {
        return (number % 2) == 0 ? false : true;
    }
    public static bool IsEven(this int number) {
        return (number % 2) == 0 ? true : false;
    }
}
class Startup {
    public static void Main() {
        bool result = 6.IsOdd();
        if (result){
            Console.WriteLine("odd");
        }
        else {
            Console.WriteLine("even");
        }
    }
}
```

Lambda Expression

Lambda expressions encapsulate code without the keyword normal function signature or a formal function body. Define a lambda expression using the lambda operator (=>). The left-hand side of the lambda operator is the input. The right-hand side is the code. Similar to anonymous methods, lambda expressions are unnamed. However, lambda expressions are more flexible than anonymous methods. For example, lambda expressions can be delay-compiled. This is done with expression trees, which are explained in the next section. In the following example code, a lambda expression is defined that accepts a value and returns the square of that value. The lambda expression initializes a delegate, which is called on the subsequent line. The *func* method is called in the *Console.Writeline* statement, and the result (25) is displayed:

```
delegate int MyDel(int a);
static void Main(string[] args) {
    MyDel func = (a) => { return  a * a; };
    Console.WriteLine(func(5));
}
```

In the previous code, the verbose syntax is used for lambda expressions. There is also an abbreviated syntax. If the lamba expression has only a single statement, and that statement sets the return value, you can omit the curly braces and the *return* statement. In addition, when there is a single parameter, the parentheses can be dropped from the left-hand side. Here is an example of the abbreviated syntax:

```
    MyDel func = a => a * a;
```

The inputs for a lambda expression are normally the parameters. Within the body of the lambda expression, you also can refer to local variables, data members, and properties that are within scope at that time. The following code shows an example of a lambda expression that uses a local variable. (Do not attempt to use the lambda expression where elements of the lambda expressions are no longer within scope.)

```
int iVar = 5;
MyDel func = (int a) => {return  a * iVar; };
Console.WriteLine(func(5));
```

In LINQ, there are two special signatures for lambda expressions. A lambda expression that returns a Boolean value is called a *predicate*. *Projections* are lambda expressions that accept a single parameter of a specific type but that return a different type.

Expression Trees

In an expression tree, code is data. More accurately, code in an expression tree is populated using lambda expressions. As data, you can modify and even compile the code at run time. Expression trees are represented by the *Expression* type. *Expression* objects are initialized with lambda expressions. In LINQ, expression trees are used to parse, compile, and defer the execution of query expressions.

An expression tree can consist of multiple expressions, such as unary and binary expressions. The following code is an example of a binary expression. The lambda expression (*x * y*) is a binary expression. We initialize an *Expression* instance with the lambda expression. The generic argument for the *Expression* type is *Func<int, int, int>*. For a binary expression, *Func<T1, T2, TR>* is a delegate for a function that has two parameters and a return value. *T1* and *T2* are the parameters, and *TR* is the return type. *BinaryExpression* encapsulates a binary expression. The code then extracts the body, the left parameter, and the right parameter of the expression. Finally, the program compiles and executes the expression. Then the result is displayed:

```
using System;
using System.Linq.Expressions;

namespace CSharpBook {
    class Program {
        static void Main(string[] args) {
            Expression<Func<int, int, int>> product =
                (x, y) => x * y;
            BinaryExpression body = (BinaryExpression)product.Body;
            ParameterExpression left = (ParameterExpression)body.Left;
            ParameterExpression right = (ParameterExpression)body.Right;
            Console.WriteLine("{0}\nLeft: {1} Right: {2}", body, left, right);
            var lambda = product.Compile();
            Console.WriteLine(lambda(2, 3));
        }
    }
}
```

LINQ Essentials

Here is a regular LINQ query expression. It uses the C# extensions discussed in the previous section. This query returns the list of multithreaded processes that have more than five active threads. For each multithreaded process, the process identifier and process name are returned:

```
var processes =
    Process.GetProcesses()
    .Where(p  => p.Threads.Count > 5)
    .Select(p => new { p.Id, Name = p.ProcessName });
```

Figure 6-1 diagrams the preceding LINQ query expression. New features of C# 3.0 are mapped to various aspects of the query expression. The *processes* variable is an implicitly typed variable. The type is defined by the results of the query expression. The *Where* operator is an extension method. As with any extension method, the first parameter is a *this* argument. LINQ operators are reviewed in the section "LINQ Operators," later in this chapter. A lambda expression, as identified by the lambda (=>) operator, is used by the *Where* operator and the *Select* operator. Object initializers are used to initialize an anonymous type that has an *Id* and a *Name* field.

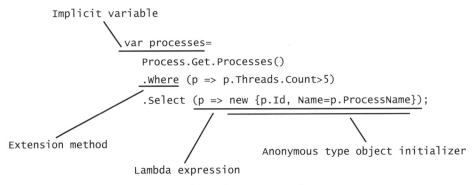

FIGURE 6-1 A query expression mapped to C# language extensions

Core Elements

The core elements of LINQ query expressions are implicitly typed variables, operators, and sequences. The result of a query expression typically is assigned to an implicitly typed variable. One reason is that query expressions sometimes return anonymous types. For the implicitly typed variable, the actual type is set from the result of the query expression.

Operators are extension methods and the building blocks of query expressions. There are many operators, which are grouped into categories for clarity. Filtering, Generation, Partitioning, and Sorting are some of the categories, and the entire list is presented in the section "LINQ Operators," later in this chapter. A *sequence* in a query expression is a series of dependent operators. The result of one operator is input to the next operator, the result of that operator is input to the following operator, and so on. Essentially, each operator, as an extension method, calls the next operator, and the result of each operator in the sequence is passed to the next. The following code contains a sequence, in which the *Where* operator calls the *OrderBy* operator, which in turn finally calls the *Select* operator. The result of the *Select* operator is stored in the *processes* variable.

```
var processes =
    Process.GetProcesses()
    .Where(p => p.Threads.Count > 5)
    .OrderBy(p => p.ProcessName)
    .Select(p => new { p.Id, Name = p.ProcessName });
```

The *Where, OrderBy,* and *Select* operators are extension methods and members of the *Enumerable* class. In the following code, the operators are called directly as extension methods. For example, the *Where* operator is called as the *Enumerable.Where* extension method. This is semantically equivalent and the results are identical to the previous code. The extension methods in this example actually execute inside-out.

```
var processes =
    Enumerable.Select(
        (Enumerable.OrderBy(
            (Enumerable.Where(Process.GetProcesses(),
                (p => p.Threads.Count > 5))),
            (p => p.ProcessName))),
        p => new { p.Id, Name = p.ProcessName });
```

To improve efficiency, LINQ supports lazy evaluation, meaning that query expressions do not execute and return results immediately. Instead, the results are iterated as needed. If a query expression returned a list of 10,000 people, would you want to enumerate that list all at once? Probably not: it would be a huge drain on performance and may have noticeable effects on your application. Less noticeable is the effect of distributing the cost of retrieval over the iteration of the collection. Another advantage to this approach is that it allows the querying and retrieval of a portion of the list if you want. This also helps performance. Otherwise, if your query returned 10,000 people, there would be no performance benefit to enumerating 10 names—the cost already has been paid. LINQ does provide the ability to force an immediate retrieval of the query results. For example, *IEnumerable.ToList* and *IEnumerable.ToArray* force the *entire* collection to be immediately returned in a query expression.

The following code demonstrates lazy evaluation. Actually, this code depends completely on lazy evaluation. Without it, this code would break. In the example, a series of factorials is being calculated. For example, a seed of 5 would return the factorial of every integral value from 1 to 5 (that is, 1, 2, 6, 24, and 120). However, the seed is specified *after* the query expression that returns the results. This is the line where the seed is set; note that it appears after the LINQ query:

```
end = 5;
```

In this example, the query could not have been performed without the seed. Without the seed, there is nothing to return, especially because the query expression is not enumerating a static list. Look closely at the code. There is no collection defined at compile time. Rather, the collection is generated at run time within the *Factorial* class inside the *GetEnumerator* method. The *GetEnumerator* method uses the seed, which is not set until after the query expression. (The use of *Cast<int>*is explained in the section "Conversion Operators," later in this chapter.)

```
using System;
using System.Collections;
using System.Collections.Generic;
using System.Linq;

namespace Donis.CSharpBook {
    public class Starter {

        public static int end = 0;

        private static void Main() {
            var result =
                new Factorial().Cast<int>()
                .Select(f => f);

            end = 5;
            foreach (uint item in result) {
                Console.WriteLine(item.ToString());
            }
        }
    }

    class Factorial : IEnumerable {

        private uint count = 1;
        public uint _factorial = 1;

        public IEnumerator GetEnumerator() {
            for (; 0 < Starter.end--; ) {
                _factorial = _factorial * (count++);
                yield return _factorial;
            }
        }
    }
}
```

As mentioned, the developer could force the immediate retrieval of query results with *ToList* or *ToArray.* The following code queries an array of names using lazy evaluation. In the *Person* class, there is a *Name* property. The *get* function traces to the console. Therefore, you will know any time the property is accessed. In addition, the remainder of the application is instrumented to document the sequence of events. For example, when the list is queried, is the *Name* property immediately accessed? Alternatively, is the *Name* property accessed in the *foreach* loop?

```csharp
using System;
using System.Diagnostics;
using System.Linq;

namespace CSharp {
    public class Starter {
        private static void Main() {
            Person[] names = { new Person{ Name = "Wilson" },
                               new Person{ Name = "Bob" },
                               new Person{ Name = "Lisa" },
                               new Person{ Name = "Sally" } };
            Console.WriteLine("***query expression***");
            var result =
                names
                .Where(n => n.Name.StartsWith("B"))
                .Select(n => n);
            Console.WriteLine("***after query expression***");
            Console.WriteLine("***foreach***");
            foreach (var item in result) {
                Console.WriteLine("{0}", item);
            }
            Console.WriteLine("***after foreach***");
        }
    }

    class Person {
        string _name = "";
        public string Name {
            get {
                Console.WriteLine("Retrieving " + _name);
                return _name;
            }
            set {
                _name = value;
            }
        }
        public override string ToString() {
            return _name;
        }
    }
}
```

Here is the output from the preceding program:

```
***query expression***
***after query expression***
***foreach***
Retrieving Wilson
Retrieving Bob
Bob
Retrieving Lisa
Retrieving Sally
***after foreach***
```

From examining the output of the program, you can see that the *Name* property is not accessed during the query. This is lazy evaluation. The *Name* property is accessed later only in the *foreach* loop, as each individual item is iterated. The following code is modified to request the names immediately with a call to *Enumerable.ToList*. The pivotal line is shown in bold:

```
private static void Main() {
    Person[] names = { new Person{ Name = "Wilson" },
                       new Person{ Name = "Bob" },
                       new Person{ Name = "Lisa" },
                       new Person{ Name = "Sally" } };
    Console.WriteLine("***query expression***");
    var result =
        names
        .Where(n => n.Name.StartsWith("B"))
        .Select(n => n);
    Console.WriteLine("***after query expression***");
    List<Person> immediate = result.ToList();
    Console.WriteLine("***foreach***");
    foreach(var item in immediate) {
        Console.WriteLine("{0}", item);
        Console.WriteLine("***after foreach***");
    }
}
```

Here are the results from the modified program:

```
***query expression***
***after query expression***
Retrieving Wilson
Retrieving Bob
Retrieving Lisa
Retrieving Sally
***foreach***
Bob
***after foreach***
```

The results show that the *Name* property is used after the query expression but before the *foreach* loop. It is used when the *ToList* method is invoked.

Conversion Operators

You may have noticed that in the Factorial example presented earlier in the chapter, the *Cast* operator was called. The reason is that the type that was queried was not LINQ-compliant. In LINQ to Objects, collections must implement the *IEnumerable<T>* interface. (Generic classes are discussed in Chapter 7, "Generics.") If not, the collection cannot be the source in a query expression. This is necessary, for example, when using nongeneric collection types with LINQ. The most common culprit is *ArrayList,* which was commonly used before .NET 2.0, when generic collections were introduced. The *Cast* operator converts a non-generic collection, such as *ArrayList,* into an IEnumerable<T> type. (Generic and non-generic collections were discussed in Chapter 5, "Arrays and Collections.")

Here is the *Cast* operator. It is an extension method that accepts a non-generic collection as input and returns a generic type:

```
public static IEnumerable<TResult> Enumerable.Cast<TResult>(this IEnumerable source)
```

Here is the relevant code from the Factorial example. The *Cast* operator converts an array of *int* to an *IEnumerable<T>* type:

```
var result =
    new Factorial().Cast<int>()
    .Select(f => f);
```

The *OfType* operator, another extension method, is an alternative to the *Cast* operator. It filters a non-generic collection into a generic collection of a specific type. Elements of the collection that are not of that type are removed. Here is the syntax of the *OfType* operator. The operator accepts a non-generic collection and returns a generic collection. The *TResult* generic parameter is the target type. Other element types are excluded and are not copied to the new generic collection:

```
public static IEnumerable<TResult> OfType<TResult>(this IEnumerable source)
```

Here is the modified query using the *OfType* operator:

```
var result =
    new Factorial().OfType<uint>()
    .Select(f => f);
```

LINQ Query Expression Syntax

In this chapter, the sample code has used the extension method syntax for LINQ query expressions. In the following code, *the Enumerable.Where* and *Enumerable.Select* extension methods are called:

```
var result =
    names
    .Where(n => n.Name.StartsWith("B"))
    .Select(n => n);
```

You have seen how to call the extension method directly. However, you also can use the query syntax intrinsic to C#. In C# 3.0, query expressions have been promoted to the language level, which provides a single interface for writing query expressions that transcends the domain of the data source. You don't have to learn a separate query syntax for SQL, ADO.NET, XML, and others. In addition, the language syntax for query expressions is more implicit than the extension method syntax. For example, you do not have to write lambda expressions explicitly into the query expression. The shortcoming of this approach is that the C# query expression does not support every LINQ operator. For example, the *SequenceEqual*, *Distinct*, and *Range* operators are not supported. In those circumstances, you have to use the extension method syntax for query expressions. In addition, you cannot mix and match the different syntaxes for query expressions. The query expression must use the expression method syntax or the C# language syntax exclusively. Here is the previous query using the C# language syntax:

```
var result =
    from item in names
    where item.Name.StartsWith("B")
    select item;
```

The *from* clause identifies the source collection (*names*) and the name (*item*) for each element of the collection. The *where* and *select* clauses are semantically equivalent to the *Where* and *Select* operators. This approach is less wordy and more transparent as to intent. Therefore, for the remainder of this book, the C# language query syntax is used whenever possible.

Where Is LINQ?

The core library where LINQ is implemented is the System.Core.Dll library. This library is an addition to the .NET Framework 3.5. System.Core.Dll is referenced automatically for any .NET Framework 3.5 application. System.Core.Dll contains most of the infrastructure of LINQ but also includes other classes, such as a *HashSet<T>* generic type. My favorite additions are the types for supporting anonymous and named pipes: the *AnonymousPipeServerStream* and *NamedPipeServerStream* types, respectively. Pipes are relatively common in Win32 applications, and it is nice to see them seamlessly integrated into the .NET Framework. Other dynamic-link libraries (DLLs) were added in support of different providers. System.XML.Linq.Dll supports LINQ to XML, while System.Data.Linq.Dll supports LINQ to DataSet.

Namespaces

Along with the new DLLs for LINQ, there are also new namespaces. Table 6-1 lists some of the namespaces related to LINQ.

TABLE 6-1 LINQ namespaces

Namespace	Description
System.Linq	The core namespace of LINQ, contains the essential ingredients, such as the extension methods for the query operators. The query operators are found in the *Enumerable* class. The *System.Linq* namespace supports LINQ to Objects types. This namespace is found in the System.Core.Dll library.
System.Linq.Expressions	Provides support for expression trees. The primary types in this namespace are *BinaryExpression, ConditionalExpression, ConstantExpression, LambdaExpression,* and *UnaryExpression.* The types represent binary, conditional, constant, lambda, and unary expressions, respectively. This namespace is found in the System.Core.Dll library.
System.XML.Linq	The core namespace for LINQ to XML. The primary types in this namespace are *XAttribute, XDocument,* and *XElement.* These types represent an XML attribute, a document, and an element, respectively. This namespace is found in the System.XML.Linq.Dll library.
System.Data.Linq	The core namespace for LINQ to SQL. The primary classes in this namespace are the *ChangeSet* and *Table<TEntity>* classes. The *ChangeSet* type is a collection of changes to the data. The generic *Table* class represents a database table. This namespace is found in the System.Data.Linq.Dll library.
System.Data.Linq.Mapping	This namespace is for database mapping from a hierarchal database to LINQ to SQL objects. The primary classes in this namespace are *ColumnAttribute, DatabaseAttribute, FunctionAttribute,* and *TableAttribute. ColumnAttribute* maps a database column to a class. *DatabaseAttribute* defines attributes for a class that maps to a database. *FunctionAttribute* maps a stored procedure to a class method. Finally, *TableAttribute* maps a database table onto a class. This namespace is found in the System.Data.Linq.Dll library.

LINQ to Objects

LINQ to Objects is used for accessing in-memory objects. LINQ to Objects is essentially the default LINQ implementation. It requires only the System.Core.Dll library, which is implicitly referenced in .NET Framework 3.5. Other providers, such as LINQ to SQL, require an additional interface and library. The source type for LINQ to Objects should implement the *IEnumerable<T>* interface. In addition, LINQ to Objects works with anything that can be described via an iterator. This provides considerable flexibility as to the range of data that is compatible with LINQ to Objects. The Factorial example presented earlier in this chapter is a perfect example. There are several advantages to using LINQ to Objects:

- You can access in-memory objects declaratively instead of imperatively.

- Declarative expressions typically are more concise than imperative code.

- Complicated queries are easier to design and are more transparent.

- Lazy evaluation generally is more efficient.

- It is easy to access information in a different data domain.

Accessing memory objects declaratively is more straightforward than doing so imperatively. The imperative approach has been the dominant access model for in-memory objects. Much of the complexity of imperative programming is hidden in the LINQ interface. As such, declarative expressions typically are shorter than code that provides similar results. This is particularly useful with complex queries. For example, sequences are much more complicated in imperative code. Maintaining parallel sequences is challenging to write and maintain in imperative code. Lazy evaluation has been discussed previously and is supported in LINQ to Objects through the iterator model. Most developers are familiar with some query language for accessing databases. Adopting a similar model makes the transition from query languages to the LINQ to Objects model easier.

IEnumerable<T> is the pivotal interface for LINQ to Objects. If the source type supports the non-generic *IEnumerable* interface, you need to cast the source to *IEnumerable<T>*. As shown previously, there are two options: the *Cast* method or the *OfType* operator. This was demonstrated previously using the extension method syntax for query expressions and is shown again here:

```
var result =
    new Factorial().Cast<int>()
    .Select(f => f);
```

The language syntax is even simpler. In the following code, you set the element type explicitly in the query expression:

```
var result =
    from int f in new Factorial()
    select f;
```

Interestingly, when disassembled, these two pieces of code are exactly the same. Here is the disassembled code for the query expression using C# language syntax, which does not explicitly use the *Cast* method. The compiler calls the same *Cast* operator, the only difference being that the compiler has done the work, which is preferable:

```
IL_0006:  call class [mscorlib]System.Collections.Generic.IEnumerable`1<!!0>
    [System.Core]System.Linq.Enumerable::Cast<int32>(class
        [mscorlib]System.Collections.IEnumerable)
```

Examples of LINQ to Objects

The following examples highlight the benefits of using LINQ to Objects. Each example highlights a different benefit of LINQ to Objects that was mentioned in the previous sections. Examples related to deferred execution (that is, lazy evaluation) were provided earlier in the chapter in the section "Core Elements."

Declarative versus Imperative

The following code iterates a string. A string is a collection of characters. In a *foreach* loop, the imperative code extracts uppercase characters from the string. Each uppercase character is then added to the result string:

```
string result = "";
string text = "Now Is The Time For All...";
foreach (char character in text) {
    if ((character > 64) && (character < 91)) {
        result += character;
    }
}
```

The following code accomplishes the same general task using LINQ to Objects (although this code returns a collection of characters versus a string). It is declarative, has fewer lines of code, and is more transparent:

```
var result = from character in "Now Is The Time For All..."
    where (character > 64) && (character < 91)
    select character;
```

LINQ to Objects Reduces Complexity

The following code iterates a list of stores and an inventory list. Items that are on sale are listed. The *store* type contains an inventory list. This code contains nested *foreach* loops and an *if* statement. This code is relatively complex, especially compared to code shown previously in this chapter:

```
foreach (Store store in stores) {
    foreach (Item i in store.inventory) {
        if (i.IsDiscounted) {
            Console.WriteLine("{0} {1}", store.Name, i.Name);
        }
    }
}
```

The following code performs the same task. However, its intention is clearer. LINQ to Objects is more self-documenting, and self-documenting code is easier to maintain and support. Another benefit to this code is that it is object-driven. The query expression returns an array of objects that combines data from the *Store* and *Item* classes. The preceding code is data-driven, which requires developer discipline for robustness. This query has two data sources, For that reason, there are two *from* statements—one for each data source:

```
var results = from store in stores
    from item in store.inventory
    where item.IsDiscounted == true
    select new { StoreName = store.Name, ItemName = item.Name};
foreach (var result in results) {
    Console.WriteLine(result.StoreName + " " + result.ItemName);
}
```

LINQ to Objects and Cross-Domain Access

One of the best features of LINQ is that it has a simple, straightforward method for cross-domain access using query expressions. This is particularly useful because it does not require converting the underlying types. A query expression can have several sources, where the sources can be from disparate data domains. You then can join the results from these different domains to create a cohesive result. For example, you can access a dataset and an XML data store simultaneously. The results can be combined in an anonymous class that consists of fields from both sources.

The following code has two sources: an in-memory collection and an XML store. The in-memory collection is *mystore.inventory* and contains a list of inventory items. The XML store is *products,* which contains a description of each inventory item. The query creates a collection of anonymous types that combine the products in inventory with the description of the product extracted from the XML store. The *join* operator used in the query expression is described in the section "LINQ Operators," later in this chapter:

```
var inventory = from item in mystore.inventory
    join product in products.Elements().Descendants("id")
    on item.ToString() equals product.Value.Trim(remove)
    select new { item, product.Parent };
```

This is the full listing of the program. At the start, a new store is created and items are added to the inventory. Then the *XElement.Load* function loads an XML file into memory, where *XElement.Elements* returns the collections of elements in the XML store. The *remove* array is used with the *String.Trim* method to remove extraneous characters from the value of XML elements:

```
using System;
using System.Collections.Generic;
using System.Linq;
using System.Xml.Linq;

namespace Donis.CSharpBook {
    class Program {
        static void Main(string[] args) {
            Store mystore = new Store();
            mystore.inventory.Add("101");
            mystore.inventory.Add("102");
            mystore.inventory.Add("101");
            mystore.inventory.Add("103");
            mystore.inventory.Add("101");

            char[] remove = { '\t', '\n', ' ' };

            XElement products = XElement.Load("inventory.xml");
```

```
        var inventory = from item in mystore.inventory
                        join product in products.Elements().Descendants("id")
                        on item.ToString() equals product.Value.Trim(remove)
                        select new { item, product.Parent };

        foreach (var stock in inventory) {
            Console.WriteLine("*******");
            Console.WriteLine(stock.item);
            Console.WriteLine(
                stock.Parent.Element("name").Value.Trim(remove));
            Console.WriteLine(
                stock.Parent.Element("price").Value.Trim(remove));
        }
    }
}

class Store {
    public string Name { get; set; }
    public List<string> inventory =
        new List<string>();
}
}
```

LINQ Operators

Operators are the essential ingredients of a LINQ query expression. Several operators, such as *Where, Join,* and *Select,* already have been featured in previous samples. The operators accept *IEnumerable<T>* and *IQueryable<T>* interfaces as input. The *IEnumerable<T>* interface supports iteration. *IQueryable<T>* is implemented by a LINQ provider to evaluate query expressions in that context. For example, the LINQ to XML provider implements the *IQuerable<T>* interface to provide XML-specific behavior. *IQueryable<T>* inherits the *IEnumerable<T>* interface. For that reason, *IQueryable<T>* objects are also enumerable.

There are several operators, which are grouped into categories. In this section, all the operators in LINQ are presented. The operators are available as extension methods and accept a collection as the *this* parameter. The core extension methods for LINQ are found in the *Enumerable<T>* class of the *System.Linq* namespace.

C# language syntax for query expressions supports relatively few LINQ operators. The expressions that are supported by C# syntax are documented in the following sections.

Aggregation Operators

Aggregation operators calculate a scalar value from a collection. Table 6-2 lists the aggregation operators.

TABLE 6-2 Aggregation operators

Extension method	C# syntax	Description
Aggregate	N/A	Performs aggregation using a custom accumulator function. The function is called for each element.
		The following extension method example is equivalent to the *Sum* operator, which is a predefined aggregation operator.
		`collection.Aggregate((accumulator,value) => accumulator += value);`
Average	N/A	Calculates the average of a collection.
		Example of extension method:
		`collection.Average();`
Count	N/A	Count of elements in a collection.
		Example of extension method:
		`collection.Count();`
LongCount	N/A	Count of elements in a large collection. Returns an Int64 value.
		Example of extension method:
		`collection.LongCount();`
Max	N/A	Maximum value in a collection.
		Example of extension method:
		`collection.Max();`
Min	N/A	Minimum value in a collection.
		Example of extension method:
		`collection.Min();`
Sum	N/A	Sum values in a collection.
		Example of extension method:
		`collection.Sum();`

Concatenation Operator

Concatenation operator concatenates two sequences into one sequence.

The sole concatenation operator is the *Concat* operator, which concatenates two collections or sequences.

Here is an example of the extension method:

```
collection1.Concat(collection2);
```

Data Type Conversion Operators

Data type conversion operators convert the source collection into another type. Some of these operators are not deferred, and the query expression immediately returns the results of the operator.

Table 6-3 lists the data type conversion operators.

TABLE 6-3 Data type conversion operators

Extension Method	C# Syntax	Description
AsEnumerable	N/A	For queryable objects, returns the separate *IEnumerable<T>* interface implementation, if any. Example of extension method: `collection.AsEnumerable();`
AsQueryable	N/A	For enumerable objects, returns the separate *IQueryable<T>* interface implementation, if any. Example of extension method: `collection.AsEnumerable();`

Cast	From *typevariable* in *nongeneric* select *variable*	Converts a non-generic enumerable collection into a generic enumerable collection of the specified type.
		
		Example of extension method:
		
		`nongeneric.Cast<Type>();`
		
		Example of C# language syntax:
		
		`from Type i in nongeneric select i;`

OfType	N/A	Returns only elements related to the specified type from the collection. Example of extension method: `collection.OfType<Type>();`
ToArray	N/A	Converts a collection to an array. The query expression is immediately evaluated. Example of extension method: `collection.ToArray<int>()`
ToDictionary	N/A	Converts a collection into a dictionary. In the following example, *collection* is an array of objects that have a field called *key*. The *key* field is a unique value. The query expression is immediately evaluated. Example of extension method: `collection.ToDictionary(d => d.key);`

TABLE 6-3 Data type conversion operators

Extension Method	C# Syntax	Description
ToList	N/A	Converts a collection to a list. The query expression is immediately evaluated. Example of extension method: `collection.ToList();`
ToLookup	N/A	Converts a collection to a lookup table. The query expression is immediately evaluated. Example of extension method: `collection.ToLookup(d => d.key);`

Element Operators

Element operators return a specific element of a collection. The elements of the collection comprise a zero-based list.

Table 6-4 lists the element operators.

TABLE 6-4 Element operators

Extension method	C# syntax	Description
ElementAt	N/A	Returns an element at a specific index. Example of extension method: `collection.ElementAt(1);`
ElementAtOrDefault	N/A	Returns an element at a specific index. If out of bounds, a default value (zero or *null*) is returned. Example of extension method: `collection.ElementAtOrDefault(20);`
First	N/A	Returns the first element of a collection. Example of extension method: `collection.First();`
FirstOrDefault	N/A	Returns the first element of a collection. If out of bounds, a default value (zero or *null*) is returned. Example of extension method: `collection.FirstOrDefault();`
Last	N/A	Returns the last element of a collection. Example of extension method: `collection.Last();`

TABLE 6-4 **Element operators**

Extension method	C# syntax	Description
LastOrDefault	N/A	Returns the last element of a collection. If out of bounds, a default value (zero or *null*) is returned.
		Example of extension method:
		`collection.LastOrDefault();`
Single	N/A	Confirms that a collection has a single element. An exception occurs if the collection does not have exactly one element. Otherwise, it returns that element.
		Example of extension method:
		`collection.Single();`
SingleOrDefault	N/A	Confirms that a collection has a single element. Returns a default value if the collection does not have exactly one element. Otherwise, it returns the single element of the collection.
		Example of extension method:
		`collection.SingleOrDefault();`

Equality Operator

Equality operator compares two sequences. If the sequences have the same number of elements and the values are equal, the sequences are equal.

The sole equality operator is the *SequenceEqual* operator, which compares two sequences and returns *true* if the sequences are equal. Otherwise, the operator returns *false*.

Here is an example of the extension method:

```
collection1.SequenceEqual(collection2);
```

Filtering Operator

Filtering operator filters a collection based on a function. The function is called on each element of the collection and returns a Boolean expression. If true, the element is included; otherwise, it is omitted.

The sole filtering operator is the *Where* operator, which returns a collection. The elements of the collection are chosen by evaluating for each element a function that returns a Boolean expression.

Here is an example of the extension method:

```
collection.Where(info => info > 3);
```

And here is an example of C# language syntax:

```
from info in data where info > 3 select info;
```

Generation Operators

Generation operators create a collection that contains a sequence of values.

Table 6-5 lists the generation operators.

TABLE 6-5 **Generation operators**

Extension method	C# syntax	Description
DefaultIfEmpty	N/A	Creates a singleton collection if the collection is empty. Otherwise, returns the collection. Example of extension method: `collection.DefaultIfEmpty();`
Empty	N/A	Creates an empty collection. This is a static method. Example of extension method: `Enumerable.Empty<Type>();`
Range	N/A	Creates a collection that contains a sequence of integers. This is a static method. The following *Range* operator will create a collection containing a sequence from 5 to 10, inclusive. Example of extension method: `Enumerable.Range(5,10);`
Repeat	N/A	Creates a collection that repeats a single value. This is a static method. The following example creates a collection with five elements. Each element has the value 2. Example of extension method: `Enumerable.Repeat(2,5);`

Grouping Operator

Grouping operator allows the grouping of elements by a field attribute.

The sole grouping operator is the *GroupBy* operator, which groups elements that share a common value.

Here is an example of the extension method:

```
collection.GroupBy(c => c.key);.
```

Join Operators

Join operators join two data sources based on a common field attribute. This allows the correlation of two data sources.

Table 6-6 lists the join operators.

TABLE 6-6 Join operators

Extension method	C# syntax	Description
GroupJoin	from *outer* join *inner* equals *Boolean* into *GroupCollection* select *resulttype*	Joins two data sources and groups the inner collection. If, for example, there are two lists (a list of car owners and a list of cars), a group join could return a collection of anonymous types. Each item in the collection would represent a car owner and the list of cars owned by that person.
		Example of extension method:

		`oCollection.GroupJoin(iData, outer => outer.key,`
		`    inner => inner.key, (outer, innerData) => new {`
		`    outer = outer,items = innerCollection.Select(inner.`
		`key) });`

		Example of C# language syntax:

		`from outer in oData join inner in iData`
		`    on outer equals inner.key into iGroup`
		`    select new { outer, items = iGroup };`

Join	from *outer* join *inner* equals *Boolean* select *result*	Joins two data sources based on a common field.
		Example of extension method:

		`oCollection.Join(iData, outer => outer.key, inner =>`
		`inner.key,`
		`    (outer, inner) => new { inner.name, outer.key });`

		Example of C# language syntax:

		`from outer in oData join inner in iData`
		`    on outer.key equals inner.key`
		`    select new { inner.name, outer.key };`

Partitioning Operators

Partitioning operators partition a collection and return the result.

Table 6-7 lists the partitioning operators.

TABLE 6-7 **Partitioning operators**

Extension method	C# syntax	Description
Skip	N/A	Skips the specified number of elements in a sequence. Example of extension method: `collection.Skip(3);`
SkipWhile	N/A	Skips while a condition is met. Example of extension method: `collection.SkipWhile(d => d < 45);`
Take	N/A	Takes elements up to the specified position. Example of extension method: `collection.Take(3);`
TakeWhile	N/A	Takes elements while a condition is met. Example of extension method: `collection.TakeWhile(d => d < 30);`

Quantifier Operators

Quantifier operators return a Boolean expression indicating whether all elements of a collection satisfy a particular condition.

Table 6-8 lists the quantifier operators.

TABLE 6-8 **Quantifier operators**

Extension method	C# syntax	Description
All	N/A	Returns *true* if all elements of a collection meet the specified condition. Example of extension method: `collection.All(d => d > 30);`
Any	N/A	Returns *true* if any element of a collection meets the specified condition. Example of extension method: `collection.Any(d => d > 30);`
Contains	N/A	Returns *true* if the collection contains the specified element. Example of extension method: `collection.Contains(45);`

Set Operators

Set operators extract a set of elements from the source collection and return the results in a new collection.

Table 6-9 lists the set operators.

TABLE 6-9 Set operators

Extension method	C# syntax	Description
Distinct	N/A	Deletes duplicate elements from a collection. Example of extension method: `collection.Distinct()`
Except	N/A	Compares two collections and returns the elements that appear in only one of the collections. Example of extension method: `collection1.Except(collection2);`
Intersect	N/A	Compares two collections and returns only those elements that appear in both. Example of extension method: `collection1.Intersect(collection2);`
Union	N/A	Combines two collections, while removing duplicates. Example of extension method: `collection1.Union(collection2);`

Sorting Operators

Sorting operators modify the sequence of elements in a collection.

Table 6-10 lists the sorting operators.

TABLE 6-10 **Sorting operators**

Extension method	C# syntax	Description
OrderBy	from *type* in *collection* orderby *key* select *result*	Sorts a collection in ascending order using a key. Example of extension method: `collection.OrderBy(item => item.key);` Example of C# language syntax: `from item in data orderby item.key select item;`
OrderByDescending	from *type* in *collection* orderby *key* descending select *result*	Sorts a collection in ascending order using a key. Example of extension method: `collection.OrderByDescending(item => item.key);` Example of C# language syntax: `from item in data orderby item.key descending select item;`
Reverse	N/A	Reverses the elements in a collection. Example of extension method: `collection.Reverse();`
ThenBy	from *type* in *collection* orderby *key1, key2, ... keyn* select *result*	Sorts a collection with a series of nested collections. Example of extension method: `collection.OrderBy(item => item.key).ThenBy(item => item);` Example of C# language syntax: `from item in data orderby item.key, item select item;`

ThenByDescending	from *type* in *collection* orderby *key1, key2, ... keyn* descending select *result*	Orders a collection first by the *Order* statement and then by the *ThenByDescending* statement. Example of extension method: `collection.OrderBy(item => item.key).`
		`    ThenByDescending(item => item);` Example of C# language Syntax: `from item in data orderby item.key, item descending`
		`    select item;`

Generics

Chapter 7 is about generics, which are templated collections. Generics improve upon non-generic collections. Generics improve performance mostly by eliminating boxing. They are bound to specific types at compile time. Non-generic collections rely on object types. When populating non-generic collections with values, boxing occurs because of casting from a value type to a reference type. Excessive boxing incurs both a performance and a memory penalty. Boxing also causes problems with type safety. You often cast elements that are object types to a specific type. The cast is not type-safe and can cause runtime errors when done incorrectly. Because generics are type-specific, the need for a cast is eliminated.

Generic types are classes with type parameters. The type parameter acts as a placeholder for a future type. When a generic type is declared, type arguments are substituted for the type parameters. At that time, the generic becomes type-specific, thus resolving many of the problems inherent in non-generic collection types. Generic methods, like generic types, have type parameters. However, the type argument can be inferred from the way the method is called.

Chapter 7
Generics

The definition of *generic*, as found in *Merriam-Webster's Collegiate Dictionary*, is "of a whole genus, kind, class, etc.; general; inclusive." Based on this definition, *a person* is generic, whereas *Donis Marshall* is quite specific. *City* is generic, whereas *Seattle* is specific. More specific to programming, a data algorithm is generic, whereas the implementation is specific. A stack is generic, whereas a stack of integers is specific. A spreadsheet is generic, whereas a spreadsheet of strings is specific.

In the Microsoft .NET Framework, an implementation of a class or structure is specific. A *StackInt* class is a specific type and a specialization of the stack pattern, which targets integers. A stack of strings or floats would require separate implementations of the same algorithm, such as *StackString* and *StackFloat*.

Here is an implementation of the *StackInt* class:

```
using System;

namespace Donis.CSharpBook {
    public class Starter {
        public static void Main() {
            StackInt stack = new StackInt(5);
            stack.Push(10);
            stack.Push(15);
            Console.WriteLine("Pushed 3 values");
            stack.ListItems();
            int iPop=stack.Pop();
            Console.WriteLine("Popped 1 value: {0}", iPop);
            Console.WriteLine("Remaining items:");
            stack.ListItems();
        }
    }

    public class StackInt {

        public StackInt(int firstItem) {
            list = new int[1] {firstItem};
            top++;
        }

        public int Pop() {
            if (top != (-1)) {
                return list[top--];
            }
            throw new Exception("Stack empty");
        }
```

```
        public void Push(int topitem) {
            ++top;
            if (top == list.Length) {
                int[] temp = new int[top+1];
                Array.Copy(list, temp, top);
                list = temp;
            }
            list[top] = topitem;
        }

        public void ListItems () {
            for (int item = 0; item <= top; ++item) {
                Console.WriteLine(list[item]);
            }
        }

        private int[] list;
        private int top = (-1);
    }
}
```

StackInt is not an extensible solution of the stack pattern. It applies only to integers. As the
application matures, there could be a need for additional implementations for other data
types. Writing separate implementations of the stack pattern is the antithesis of code reuse.
Inheritance is an alternative. *StackInt, StackFloat,* and *StackString* could be related through
inheritance, where *Stack* is the base class. This approach allows code reuse, which is one of
the strengths of an object-oriented language. But abstracting the stack algorithm based on
inheritance encourages bad design. Is a stack a kind of integer? Is an integer a kind of stack?
Neither statement is true. Inheritance in this scenario is a contrived solution at best.

A better solution is a general implementation, which allows a single implementation for
all types—a stack of anything, versus a stack of integers. This is how collections work.
Collections are part of the .NET Framework Class Library (FCL) and are general-purpose
containers. As general-purpose containers, they are collections of *any* type. *System.Object*
is the ubiquitous type in .NET and represents any specific type. Why? All types in .NET are
either directly or indirectly derived from *System.Object*. Collections are discussed in Chapter 5,
"Arrays and Collections."

In the following code, a stack of integers is implemented using the stack collection class from
the .NET FCL. The stack collection is also used for a stack of strings, which demonstrates the
amorphous nature of the stack collection class:

```
using System;
using System.Collections;

namespace Donis.CSharpBook {
    public class Starter {

        public static void Main() {
            Console.WriteLine("Integer stack");
```

```
            Integers();
            Console.WriteLine("String stack");
            Strings();
        }

        public static void Integers() {
            Stack list = new Stack();
            list.Push(5);
            list.Push(10);
            list.Push(15);
            foreach (int item in list) {
                Console.WriteLine(item);
            }
        }

        public static void Strings() {
            Stack list = new Stack();
            list.Push("a");
            list.Push("b");
            list.Push("c");
            foreach (string item in list) {
                Console.WriteLine(item);
            }
        }
    }
}
```

General-purpose collections (described in Chapter 5) are helpful, but there are some draw-backs. Performance is the first problem. These collections manage instances of *System.Object*. Casting is required to access items of a collection. For value types, boxing occurs as items are added to the collection. Conversely, unboxing happens when value-type items are retrieved from the collection. This is true for any collection of value types, such as integers. Frequent boxing can prompt earlier garbage collection, which is especially expensive. The performance penalty for boxing and unboxing can be substantial when iterating large collections of value types. For a collection of reference types, there is the penalty for down-casting, which is less expensive when compared to casting value types. However, there is still a cost. The second problem is type-safety. Although the *StackInt* type is type-safe, a *stack* collection of inte-gers is not. The *stack* collection stores elements as *System.Object*. As such, the items of the collection are cast to a specific type at run time. This assumes you are not intending the un-derlying type to be *System.Object*. Invalid casts at run time will cause an exception. The third problem is clarity. With collections, frequent casts often clutter the source code.

Generics are the solution. *Generics* are parameterized types and methods. Each type param-eter is a placeholder for an unspecified type. The polymorphic behavior of the generic type or method is conveyed through type parameters, which is called *parametric* polymorphism. There is a single implementation of the algorithm, which is generalized through type pa-rameters. Many developers were introduced to this concept as parameterized templates in C++. Other languages support a similar feature. However, generics in .NET avoid some of the problems found in parametric polymorphism in other languages.

Generics address some of the shortcomings of collections in the .NET FCL. For example, generics eliminate needless boxing and unboxing. At compile time, a generic expands into a specific type. A generic stack of integers becomes a type that represents an actual stack of integers. Because this is type-specific, generics are inherently type-safe. This also avoids the frequent need for casting and clarity is enhanced.

The entry point method cannot be a member of a generic type. The following is the full list of types and member functions that cannot be generic:

- Unmanaged types
- Constructors
- Operator member functions
- Properties
- Indexers
- Attributes

Generic Types

Classes, structures, and interfaces can be generic. Generic types have type parameters, which are placeholders to be completed later. Being generic does not change fundamental rules governing the type. A generic class, for example, remains a class—it is simply a class with type parameters.

Type Parameters

A *type parameter* is a placeholder for a specific type. You define the type parameter after the generic name at the type definition. The type parameters should be enclosed in angle brackets and comma-delimited. This is considered an open constructed type. Open and closed constructed types are explained in the section titled "Constructed Types," later in this chapter.

Type Arguments

When you declare an instance of a generic type, you must specify type arguments to replace type parameters. This is considered a closed constructed type. When creating an instance of a generic type, specify the type arguments after the name. Enclose the comma-delimited type arguments within angle brackets . A type argument is a specific type that replaces a type parameter (placeholder) of the generic definition.

The following code introduces the *Sheet* generic type. It abstracts an array of cells, rows, and columns:.

```
using System;

namespace Donis.CSharpBook {
    public class Starter {
        public static void Main() {
            int count = 1;
            Sheet<int> asheet = new Sheet<int>(2);
            for (byte row = 1; row < 3; ++row) {
                for (byte col = 1; col < 3; ++col) {
                    asheet[row,col] = count++;
                }
            }
            for (byte row = 1; row < 3; ++row) {
                for (byte col = 1; col < 3; ++col) {
                    Console.WriteLine("R {0} C{1}= {2}",
                        row, col, asheet[row,col]);
                }
            }

            Console.WriteLine("Current[{0},{1}] = {2}",
                asheet.R, asheet.C, asheet.Current);
            asheet.MoveDown();
            asheet.MoveRight();
            Console.WriteLine("Current[{0},{1}] = {2}",
                asheet.R, asheet.C, asheet.Current);
        }
    }

    class Sheet<T> {
        public Sheet(byte dimension) {
            if (dimension < 0) {
                throw new Exception("Invalid dimensions");
            }
            m_Dimension = dimension;
            m_Sheet = new T[dimension, dimension];
            for (byte row = 0; row < dimension; ++row) {
                for (byte col = 0; col < dimension; ++col) {
                    m_Sheet[row, col] = default(T);
                }
            }
        }

        public T this[byte row, byte col] {
            get {
                ValidateCell(row, col);
                return m_Sheet[row - 1, col - 1];
            }
            set {
                m_Sheet[row - 1, col - 1] = value;
            }
        }
```

```csharp
        public void ValidateCell(byte row, byte col) {
            if ((row < 0) || (row > m_Dimension)) {
                throw new Exception("Invalid Row");
            }
            if ((col < 0) || (col > m_Dimension)) {
                throw new Exception("Invalid Col");
            }
        }


        public T Current {
            get {
                return m_Sheet[curRow - 1, curCol - 1];
            }
            set {
                m_Sheet[curRow - 1, curCol - 1]=value;
            }
        }

        public void MoveLeft() {
            curCol=Math.Max((byte) (curCol - 1), (byte) 1);
        }

        public void MoveRight() {
            curCol=Math.Min((byte) (curCol + 1), (byte) m_Dimension);
        }

        public void MoveUp() {
            curRow=Math.Max((byte) (curRow - 1), (byte) 1);
        }

        public void MoveDown() {
            curRow=Math.Min((byte) (curRow + 1), (byte) m_Dimension);
        }

        private byte curRow = 1;
        public byte R {
            get {
                return curRow;
            }
        }

        private byte curCol = 1;
        public byte C {
            get {
                return curCol;
            }
        }

        private byte m_Dimension;
        private T[,] m_Sheet;
    }
}
```

Sheet is a generic type and collection with a single type parameter. For generics with a single parameter, by convention, *T* is the name of the parameter (*T* stands for type.) In the *Sheet* generic type, the type parameter is used as a function return and field type. You see *T* being used as a placeholder at those locations. When the sheet is instantiated, the specific type (type argument) is specified.

The following code defines a spreadsheet of strings that has two rows and columns:

```
Sheet<string> asheet = new Sheet<string>(2);
```

The following is the source code from the constructor of the *Sheet* generic type. Notice the use of the *default* keyword:

```
for (byte row = 0; row < dimension; ++row) {
    for (byte col = 0; col < dimension; ++col) {
        m_Sheet[row, col] = default(T);
    }
}
```

The preceding *for* loop initializes the state of the *Sheet* generic type. The type parameter (*T*) is used. There is a challenge to assigning default values to data of a generic type. The default value could vary based on type. For example, the default value could be different based on whether the type parameter is a reference or value type. The *default* expression returns null for a reference type and bitwise zero for a value type. This resolves the problem of initializing generic data correctly. This is the syntax of the default expression:

```
default(type_parameter)
```

The *Sheet* generic type has a single parameter. However, generics can have more than one type parameter. The *type_parameter* list is contained within angle brackets. Types in the *type_parameter* list are comma-delimited. If a generic has two type parameters, the parameters are often named *K* and *V*, for key and value. This is simply convention, though. You can name the parameters anything. Here is sample code of a generic type that has two parameters:

```
public class ZClass<K, V> {
    static void Method(K key, V data) {

    }
}
```

This code creates an instance of the generic *ZClass* with two type arguments:

```
ZClass<string, float> obj = new ZClass<string, float>();
```

As already demonstrated, generic types have type parameters. Those type parameters can themselves be generic types. In the following code, *XParameter* is a generic type. It is also used as a type parameter in the generic *ZClass*:

```
using System;

namespace Donis.CSharpBook {

    public class Starter {
        public static void Main() {
            ZClass<XParameter<string>, float> obj =
                new ZClass<XParameter<string>, float>();
        }
    }

    public class XParameter<P> {
        public static void MethodA(P data) {
        }
    }

    public class ZClass<K, V> {
        public static void MethodB(K key, V data) {
        }
    }
}
```

The syntax of nested type parameters can be interesting. What if the type parameter were extrapolated even further? You could have a type parameter that is a generic, which has a type parameter that is also generic, and so on—a structure that could become somewhat labyrinthine. Aliasing the declaration could make the use of nested parameters or arguments clearer. The following alias is used for this purpose:

```
using ZClass2=ZClass<XParameter<string>, int>;

public class Starter {
    public static void Main() {
        ZClass2 obj = new ZClass2();
    }
}


public class XParameter<P> {
    public static void MethodA(P data) {
    }
}

public class ZClass<K, V> {
    public static void MethodB(K key, V data) {
    }
}
```

Here is the syntax of a generic type:

```
attributes accessibility modifiers class classname : baselist

    <type_parameterlist> where type_parameter : constraintlist :

    { class body };
```

The constraint clause defined by the *where* keyword is explained in the section titled "Constraints," later in this chapter

Constructed Types

Generic types are also called *constructed types*. There are *open constructed* and *closed constructed* types. An open constructed type has at least one type parameter. The type parameter is a placeholder, which is unbound to a specific type. Here is an example of an open constructed type:

```
public class ZClass<K, V> {
    static void Method(K key, V data) {

    }
}
```

For a closed constructed type, all type parameters are bound. Bound parameters are called type arguments and are assigned a specific type. Closed constructed types are used in several circumstances, including to create an instance of a generic type and to inherit a generic type. In the following code, *ZClass<int, decimal>* is a closed constructed type. The first type parameter is bound to an integer, whereas the second is bound to a decimal. The type arguments are *int* and *decimal*.

```
ZClass<int, decimal> obj = new ZClass<int, decimal>();
```

Overloaded Methods

Methods with generic parameters or a return type can be overloaded, which creates an interesting dilemma. Can a method be overloaded based on type parameters alone? In the following code, *MethodA* is overloaded:

```
public void MethodA(T arg) {
}
public void MethodA(U arg) {
}
```

Both *MethodA* functions have a single type parameter. Each method has a differently named type parameter. However, when closed, each type could be the same. For example, *T* and *U* both could be integers. The overloaded *MethodA* functions are potentially ambiguous.

However, the C# compiler is concerned with actual ambiguity and does not highlight potential ambiguity related to overloading generic methods as an error or warning. A compiler error is manifested when *MethodA* is called in an ambiguous manner (if it ever is). This circumstance is a potential land mine for developers of libraries. You should test every permutation of type parameters in an overloaded method to uncover any potential ambiguity.

In the following code, *MethodA* is ambiguous. Both *T* and *U* are integers. As a result, both *MethodA* functions having a single parameter are identical. A compiler error occurs only if the method is actually called:

```
using System;

namespace Donis.CSharpBook {

    public class Starter {
        public static void Main() {
            ZClass<int, int> obj = new ZClass<int, int>();
            obj.MethodA(5); // ambiguous error
        }
    }

    public class ZClass<T, U> {
        public void MethodA(T arg) {
            Console.WriteLine("ZClass.MethodA(T arg)");
        }

        public void MethodA(U arg) {
            Console.WriteLine("ZClass.MethodA(U arg)");
        }

        public void MethodA() {
            Console.WriteLine("ZClass.MethodA()");
        }
    }
}
```

Overloaded methods can be a mix of generic and non-generic methods. If the combination of generic and non-generic method is ambiguous, the non-generic method is called. The compiler prefers non-generic methods over generic methods of the same signature.

The following code contains a generic and a non-generic version of *MethodA*. *MethodA* is overloaded. *MethodA* is called with an integer parameter, which seems to be ambiguous. However, the compiler simply calls the non-generic *MethodA*, because it always prefers non-generic methods over generic methods. When the type argument for *MethodA* is a double, there is no ambiguity. There is not an overloaded, non-generic version of *MethodA* with a single parameter of type double:

```
using System;

namespace Donis.CSharpBook {
```

```
public class Starter {
    public static void Main() {
        ZClass<int> obj1 = new ZClass<int>();
        obj1.MethodA(5);
        ZClass<double> obj2 = new ZClass<double>();
        obj2.MethodA(5.0);
    }
}

public class ZClass<T> {
    public void MethodA(T arg) {
        Console.WriteLine("ZClass.MethodA(T arg)");
    }

    public void MethodA(int arg) {
        Console.WriteLine("ZClass.MethodA(int arg)");
    }

    public void MethodA() {
        Console.WriteLine("ZClass.MethodA()");
    }
}
}
```

Generic Methods

Generic methods have type parameters. These parameters can be used in the method header or body. An open method has type parameters, which are nonspecific. A closed method has type arguments, where specific types are substituted for type parameters. For a generic method, the type parameters are listed after the function name. The type parameter list is enclosed in angle brackets. Each parameter is comma-delimited.

Here is a sample generic method:

```
using System;

namespace Donis.CSharpBook {

    public class Starter {
        public static void Main() {
            ZClass.MethodA<int>(20);
        }
    }

    public class ZClass{
        public static void MethodA<T>(T param) {
            Console.WriteLine(param.GetType().ToString());
        }
    }
}
```

When calling a generic method, insert the type arguments to replace type parameters. Inferring a type is an alternate syntax to calling a generic method, where the type
arguments are inferred from the actual method parameters. The type argument then can be
omitted with type inference. Basically, the generic method is called in the same manner as
a non-generic method. The benefit is ease of use. However, type inference can disguise the
true nature of the call, which could be relevant to someone maintaining or debugging an
application.

In the previous code, *ZClass.MethodA* is a generic method. The following statement calls
MethodA using type inference:

```
ZClass.MethodA(20);
```

Here is the syntax of a generic method, where both the parameters and return type can be
generic:

```
attributes accessibility modifiers returntype identifier<type_parameterlist>
    (parameterlist) where type_parameter : constraintlist
    { method body }
```

The *this* Reference for Generic Types

Like all types, generic types have a *this* reference, which is a reference to the current object.
The underlying type of the *this* reference is the same as the surrounding type. If the object is an *XClass* instance, the *this* reference is also of the *XClass* type. The *this* reference is
used implicitly and explicitly to refer to instance members. The underlying type of the *this*
reference to a generic type is the closed constructed type, which is defined at instantiation of
the generic type.

The following code displays the type of a *this* reference. It is a *this* reference of a generic
type, which is *Donis.CSharpBook.ZClass`1[System.Int32]*. From the output of the short
application, you know that the closed constructed type has a single type parameter that is a
32-bit integer:

```
using System;

namespace Donis.CSharpBook {

    public class Starter {
        public static void Main() {
            ZClass<int> obj = new ZClass<int>();
            obj.MethodA();
        }
    }

    class ZClass<T> {
        public T MethodA() {
            T var = default(T);
```

```
        Console.WriteLine(this.GetType().ToString());
        return var;
      }
    }
  }
```

Constraints

When a type parameter is defined, the eventual type argument is unknown. The type parameter could become *anything*. Only one thing is guaranteed. The type argument will inherit *System.Object,* which limits the functionality of the type argument to the *System. Object* interface.

In the following code, *ZClass* is generic and has a single type parameter, which is *T*. The code expects that *T* will be a collection. *ZClass.MethodA* will enumerate that collection and display each item. Collections should implement the *IEnumerable* interface. This is also necessary for the *foreach* loop. Unfortunately, the C# compiler spots a problem. Regardless of how the code expects to use *T*, *T* is an implied *System.Object*, which does not implement the *IEnumerable* interface. Therefore this code does not compile:

```
class ZClass<T> {

    public void Iterate(T data) {        // invalid
        foreach (object item in data) {
            Console.WriteLine(item);
        }
    }
}
```

This problem is resolved with a generic constraint. Constraints define the intent of a type parameter. The following program uses a constraint, defined in the *where* clause shown in bold type, to indicate the intention of the *T* parameter. It is intended that the *T* parameter will be related to the *IEnumerable* type. With this understanding, the program compiles and executes successfully:

```
using System;
using System.Collections;

namespace Donis.CSharpBook {

    public class Starter {
        public static void Main() {
            ZClass<int[]> obj = new ZClass<int[]>();
            obj.Iterate(new int[] {1,2,3,4});
        }
    }

    public class ZClass<T> where T : IEnumerable {
```

```
    public void Iterate(T data) {
        foreach (object item in data) {
            Console.WriteLine(item);
        }
    }
  }
}
```

There are five types of constraints:

- **Derivation constraints**   State the ascendancy of a type parameter
- **Interface constraints**   Specify Interfaces that must be implemented by the type parameter
- **Value type constraints**   Restrict a type parameter to a value type
- **Reference type constraints**   Restrict a type parameter to a reference type
- **Constructor constraints**   Stipulate that the type parameter must have a default or parameterless constructor

Constraints can be applied to both generic types and generic methods.

Derivation Constraints

A derivation constraint requires that the type argument be related to a specified type. The constraint is enforced by the C# compiler. By default, the derivation constraint is *System. Object,* from which everything is derived. Value types cannot be used as constraints. A derivation constraint makes a generic type more specific. Because C# supports single but not multiple inheritance, derivation constraints are restricted to a single constraint. However, each type parameter of a generic type can have a different constraint. A type parameter list is comma-delimited. A derivation constraint list is space-delimited. See the following example:

```
public class ZClass<K, V> where K : XClass where V : XClass {
    void MethodA() {
    }
}
```

The compiler requires that type arguments adhere to the constraint, which makes the type argument type-safe. This is different than in C++, where the compiler performs no such type-checking on type parameters. In C++, you can basically do anything with a type parameter. Errors are uncovered when the parameter template is expanded at compile time, deep in the bowels of the expansion code. This can lead to cryptic error messages that are hard to debug. Anyone that has used the Active Template Library (ATL) and had expansion errors can attest to this. The C# compiler also updates Microsoft IntelliSense such that it suggests only items that meet the derivation constraint.

In the following code, *ZClass* is a generic type. It has a *K* and *V* type parameter, each with a separate, space-delimited constraint. Per the constraints, the *K* parameter must be derived from *XClass* and the *V* parameter must be derived from *YClass*. *Main* instantiates three generic types. The first two are all right, but the third causes compiler errors. The problem is the first type argument. *WClass* is not derived from *XClass*, which is a requirement of the first type parameter per the constraint:

```
using System;

namespace Donis.CSharpBook {

    public class Starter {
        public static void Main() {

            // good
            ZClass<XClass, YClass> obj =
                new ZClass<XClass, YClass>();

            // good
            ZClass<XClass, WClass> obj2 =
                new ZClass<XClass, WClass>();

            // bad
            ZClass<WClass, YClass> obj3 =
                new ZClass<WClass, YClass>();

        }
    }

    public class ZClass<K, V> where K : XClass
                        where V : YClass {
    }

    public class XClass {

    }

    public class YClass {
    }

    public class WClass : YClass {
    }
}
```

Constraints also can be applied to generic methods. The following code shows a generic method with a derivation constraint:

```
class ZClass {
    public T MethodA<T>() where T : XClass {
        return default(T);
    }
}
```

A generic type can be used as a constraint. This includes both open and closed constructed types. This is demonstrated in the following code. *XClass* is a non-generic type, and *YClass* is a generic type with a single type parameter. *ZClass* is a generic type, also with a single type parameter, where *YClass<XClass>* is the constraint on that type parameter. *YClass<XClass>* is a closed constructed type. In *Main*, an instance of *YClass<XClass>* is created first. Next, an instance of *ZClass* is created, where the parameter type is *YClass<XClass>*, which is required by the aforementioned constraint. *ZClass. MethodA* is then called, where the *YClass* instance is passed as a parameter. As required by the constraint, this type argument is related to *YClass<XClass>*.

```
using System;

namespace Donis.CSharpBook {

    public class Starter {
        public static void Main() {
            YClass<XClass> param = new YClass<XClass>();
            ZClass <YClass<XClass>> obj = new ZClass <YClass<XClass>>();
            obj.MethodA(param);
        }
    }

    public class ZClass<T> where T : YClass<XClass> {
        public void MethodA(T obj) {
            Console.WriteLine("ZClass::MethodA");
            obj.MethodB();
        }
    }

    public class YClass<T> {
        public void MethodB() {
            Console.WriteLine("YClass::MethodB");
        }
    }

    public class XClass {
        public void MethodC() {
            Console.WriteLine("XClass::MethodA");
        }
    }
}
```

A type parameter can be used as a constraint. In this circumstance, one type of parameter is constraining another. You are stating that one parameter is derived from another parameter. In this code, the *T1* parameter must be derived from T2:

```
using System;
using System.Collections;

namespace Donis.CSharpBook {

    public class Starter {
```

```
        public static void Main() {
            XClass<YClass, ZClass> obj = new XClass<YClass, ZClass>();
        }
    }

    public class ZClass {
        public void MethodA() {
            Console.WriteLine("YClass::MethodA");
        }
    }

    public class YClass : ZClass {
    }

    public class XClass<T1, T2> where T1 : T2 {
        public void MethodB(T1 arg) {
        }
    }
}
```

An implementation of a linked list is ideal for a generic type. You can have nodes of integers, floats, employees, or even football teams. When creating a linked list, each node keeps a reference to the next and previous nodes. The nodes of the linked list consist of related types. For an employee linked list, the nodes must also be related to the *Employee* type, such as *HourlyEmployee, SalariedEmployee,* or *RetiredEmployee*. This relationship between nodes is enforced with a recursive constraint:

```
public class Node<T> where T : Node<T> {

    // partial implementation

    public T Previous {
        get {
            return default(T);
        }
        set {
        }
    }

    public T Next {
        get {
            return default(T);
        }
        set {
        }
    }
}
```

The type argument cannot exceed the visibility of the constraint. In the following code, *XClass* has internal accessibility and is visible in the current assembly alone. The *T* parameter is public and is visible outside the current assembly. The accessibility of the *T* parameter exceeds *XClass*. For this reason, it is an error to apply *XClass* as a constraint on the *T* type parameter.

```
public class ZClass<T> where T : XClass { // invalid
}

internal class XClass {
}
```

Look at the following code, which will not compile:

```
public class Arithmetic<T> {
    public T Cubed (T number) {
        return number * number * number;  // invalid
    }
}
```

Why doesn't it compile? As with any parameter, the *T* parameter is an inferred *System. Object* type. *System.Object* does not have an operator * symbol for multiplication. Therefore, *number * number * number* will not compile. An integer constraint should resolve this problem, which would force the type parameter to be an integer. Integers have a * operator. However, as previously stated, value types and primitives are not valid constraints. The following code also will not compile:

```
class Arithmetic<T> where T : System.Int32 { // invalid
    public T Cubed (T number) {
        return number * number * number;
    }
}
```

The inability to use standard operators with value types is a major limitation to generics. The workaround is implementing named operators, such as *Add*, *Multiply*, and *Divide*, as members of the generic type.

In addition to value types, the following types cannot be used as constraints:

- Sealed classes
- Open constructed types
- Primitive types
- *System.Array*
- *System.Delegate*
- *System.Enum*
- *System.ValueType*

Interface Constraints

Type constraints can also require that the type argument implement an interface. Although a type parameter can have a maximum of only one derivation constraint, it can have multiple interface constraints. This is expected because classes can inherit a single base class but can implement many interfaces. The syntax for an interface constraint is identical to a derivation constraint. Class and interface constraints can be combined in a list of constraints. Class constraints should precede any interface constraints in the type constraint list.

Interface and derivation constraints share many of the same rules and restrictions, for example the visibility of the interface constraint must equal or exceed that of the type parameter.

In the following code, the find capability has been added to the *Sheet* collection. The *Find* method returns an array of cells that contain a certain value. A comparison is made between the cell and value where both are the same type, as indicated in the type argument. Types that implement the *IComparable* interface support comparisons. If a comparison is equal, *IComparable.CompareTo* returns 0. *IComparable.CompareTo* is called to compare values in the sheet. To enforce this behavior, an interface constraint of *IComparable* is added to the type parameter. The following is a partial implementation of the *Sheet* collection that includes *Find* and related methods. (Some of the code already shown in this chapter is omitted.)

```
using System;

namespace Donis.CSharpBook {
    public class Starter {
        public static void Main() {
            Sheet<int> asheet = new Sheet<int>(5);
            for (byte row = 1; row < 6; ++row) {
                for (byte col = 1; col < 6; ++col) {
                    asheet[row,col] = row * col;
                }
            }

            Cell[] found = asheet.Find(6);
            foreach (Cell answer in found) {
                Console.WriteLine("R{0} C{1}",
                    answer.row, answer.col);
            }
        }
    }

    public struct Cell {
        public byte row;
        public byte col;
    }

    public class Sheet<T> where T : IComparable {
        ...

        public Cell[] Find(T searchValue) {
            int total = Count(searchValue);
            int counter = 0;
```

```
            Cell[] cells = new Cell[total];
            for (byte row = 1; row <= m_Dimension; ++row) {
                for (byte col = 1; col <= m_Dimension; ++col) {
                    if (m_Sheet[row - 1, col - 1].CompareTo(searchValue) == 0) {
                        cells[counter].row = row;
                        cells[counter].col = col;
                        ++counter;
                    }
                }
            }
            return cells;
        }

    public int Count(T searchValue) {
        int counter = 0;
        for (byte row = 1; row <= m_Dimension; ++row) {
            for (byte col = 1; col <= m_Dimension; ++col) {
                if (m_Sheet[row - 1, col - 1].CompareTo(searchValue) == 0) {
                    ++counter;
                }
            }
        }
        return counter;
    }
    ...
    }
}
```

This code works, but there is a subtle problem. The *IComparable* interface manipulates objects, which causes boxing and unboxing when working with value types. This could become expensive in a large collection of value types. In the preceding code, the type argument is an integer, which is a value type. This causes boxing with the *IComparable* interface. Generic interfaces would fix this problem. The .NET FCL includes several general-purpose generic interfaces for developers. This is the class header updated for the *IComparable* generic interface:

```
public class Sheet<T> where T : IComparable<T>
```

Value Type Constraints

A *value type constraint* restricts a type parameter to a value type. Value types are derived from the *System.ValueType* type. Primitives and structures are examples of value types. A value type constraint uses the *struct* keyword.

The following code demonstrates the value type constraint shown in bold type. The line of code that is commented out uses a reference type, which would cause compiler errors because of the value type constraint.

```
using System;
using System.Collections;

namespace Donis.CSharpBook {
```

```
    public class Starter {
        public static void Main() {
            ZClass<int> obj1 = new ZClass<int>();
            // ZClass<XClass> obj2 = new ZClass<XClass>();  // illegal
        }
    }

    public class ZClass<T> where T : struct {

        public void Iterate(T data) {
        }
    }

    public class XClass{
    }
}
```

Reference Type Constraints

A *reference type constraint* restricts a type parameter to a reference type. Reference types are generally user-defined types, including classes, interfaces, delegates, strings, and array types. A reference type constraint uses the *class* keyword.

The following code has a reference type constraint, shown in bold type. Although this code is similar to the code presented in the previous section, a reference type constraint is used instead of a value type constraint. For this reason, the illegal line has moved in this version of the previous code. You cannot use an integer type argument with a reference type constraint:

```
using System;
using System.Collections;

namespace Donis.CSharpBook {

    public class Starter {
        public static void Main() {
            // ZClass<int> obj1 = new ZClass<int>();      //illegal
            ZClass<XClass> obj2 = new ZClass<XClass>();
        }
    }

    public class ZClass<T> where T : class {

        public void Iterate(T data) {
        }
    }

    public class XClass{
    }
}
```

Default Constructor Constraints

Will this code compile? It looks fairly innocuous:

```
class ZClass<T> {
    public void MethodA() {
        T obj = new T();
    }
}
```

But the code does not compile. Why not? The problem is the default constructor. A default constructor, or a constructor with no arguments, sets the default state of an object. Not every type has a default constructor. The default constructor is called with a parameterless *new* operator. Because not every type has a default constructor, the parameterless *new* operator is not universally applicable. Therefore, unless explicitly allowed, the *new* operator is disallowed on type arguments.

The solution is the default constructor constraint. The derivation constraint does not help with constructors because a derived type does not inherit constructors from its base class. Constructor constraints mandate that a type parameter have a default constructor (which might be implicit rather than explicit). The constraint is confirmed at compile time. This allows the *new* operator to be used with the type argument. The constructor constraint is added to the *where* clause and is a *new* operator. When combined with other constraints, the default constructor constraint must be the last item in the constraint list and is separated by a comma. You still are prevented from using constructors with arguments.

Here is sample code showing the constructor constraint in bold type. The constructor constraint is used in the *ZClass:*

```
using System;

namespace Donis.CSharpBook {

    public class Starter {
        public static void Main() {
            ZClass obj = new ZClass();
            obj.MethodA<XClass>();
        }
    }

    public class ZClass {
        public void MethodA<T>()
                    where T : XClass, new() {
            Console.WriteLine("ZClass.MethodA");
            T obj = new T();
            obj.MethodB();
        }
    }
```

```
public class XClass{
    public void MethodB() {
        Console.WriteLine("XClass.MethodB");
    }
}
}
```

Casting

You might need to a cast an instance of a type argument. Because type arguments are implicitly *System.Object* types, the instance can always be cast to that type. In addition, the instance also can be cast to a derivation constraint because the type argument is related to the constraint, and therefore a safe cast is assured. Finally, an instance of a type argument can be cast to any interface even if the interface is not listed as an interface constraint. Because there is no restriction on casting to interfaces, it is not type-safe. For that reason, care should be taken to ensure that you appropriately cast to an implemented interface.

In the following code, *ZClass* is a generic type. It has a single type parameter (*T*) that has three constraints: *YClass* type derivation, *IA* interface derivation, and the default constructor constraint. An instance of the *T* parameter is created in the method called *Cast*. The instance is then cast in succession to the *YClass* class and then the *IA* and *IB* interfaces. The first two casts work as expected. The third cast fails only at run time. The type parameter is not related to *IB*. However, the compiler does not notice. Therefore, an exception is raised at run time, which is the worst possible scenario and underscores the type-unsafe nature of casting an instance of a type argument to an interface:

```
public class ZClass<T> where T : YClass, IA, new() {
    static public void Cast() {
        T obj = new T();
        ((YClass) obj).MethodA();
        ((IA) obj).MethodA();
        ((IB) obj).MethodB();      // runtime error
    }
}

public class YClass : IA {
    public void MethodA() {
        Console.WriteLine("YClass.MethodA");
    }
}
```

Inheritance

Generic types can be inherited, but some basic rules apply. For example, the derived class cannot be a closed constructed type. Table 7-1 lists all the possible permutations.

TABLE 7-1 Inheritance table for generic types

Base class	Derived class	Comments
Generic (open)	Generic (open)	Permitted when the derived class uses the type parameters of the base class
Generic (open)	Generic (closed)	Not permitted
Generic (open)	Non-generic	Permitted
Generic (closed)	Generic (open)	Permitted
Generic (closed)	Generic (closed)	Not permitted
Generic (closed)	Non-generic	Not permitted
Non-generic	Generic (closed)	Permitted
Non-generic	Generic (open)	Not permitted

This sample code shows some of the combinations that are permitted and not permitted:

```
public class ZClass<T> {
}

public class XClass<T> : ZClass<T> {
}

public class BClass<Y> {
}

public class AClass<Z> : BClass<int> {
}

public class YClass : ZClass<int> {
}

/*
public class AClass<Z> : BClass<Y> {    // illegal
}

public class YClass : ZClass<T> {       // illegal
}
*/
```

When inheriting an open constructed type, the constraints of the base class must be repeated in the derived type. The derived type also can add additional type parameters. This is not applicable to closed constructed types because closed constructed types do not have type parameters or constraints.

Here is sample code combining inheritance of generic types and constraints:

```
public class ZClass<T> where T : IComparable {
}

public class YClass<T> : ZClass<T> where T : IComparable {
}
```

```
public class XClass<T> : ZClass<T> where T : IComparable, IDisposable {
}

public class BClass<Y> where Y : IEnumerable<int> {
}

public class AClass<Z> : BClass<int[]> where Z :IDisposable {
}
```

Overriding Generic Methods

Methods that have type parameters can be overridden. Conversely, generic methods also can override other methods. Table 7-2 lists the various combinations of overriding generic and non-generic methods. If a base class is non-generic or closed, overriding methods cannot have type parameters. If the base class is open, the overriding method can have type parameters.

TABLE 7-2 Combination of overriding generic methods

Base method	Derived method	Comments
Non-generic	Generic (open)	Permitted
Non-generic	Generic (closed)	Permitted
Generic (open)	Non-generic	Not permitted
Generic (open)	Generic (open)	Permitted; must use the same type parameters
Generic (open)	Generic (closed)	Not permitted
Generic (closed)	Non-generic	Permitted
Generic (closed)	Generic (closed)	Permitted
Generic (closed)	Generic (open)	Not permitted

Here is example code of overriding a generic method:

```
using System;

namespace Donis.CSharpBook {

    public class Starter {
        public static void Main() {
        }
    }

    public class ZClass<T> {
        public virtual void MethodA(T arg) {
        }
    }

    public class YClass<T> : ZClass<T>{
        public override void MethodA(T arg) {
        }
```

```
//      public override void MethodA(int arg) { // illegal
//      }

    }

    public class XClass<X> : ZClass<int>{
        public override void MethodA(int arg) {
        }
//      public override void MethodA(X arg) {  // illegal
//      }

    }

    public class WClass : ZClass<int> {
        public override void MethodA(int arg) {
        }
    }
}
```

When a generic method overrides another generic method, it inherits the constraints of that method. The overriding method cannot change the constraints inherited from the base method.

The following code correctly overrides a generic method:

```
public class ZClass {
    public virtual void MethodA<T>(T arg)
        where T : new() {
    }
}

public class YClass : ZClass {
    public override void MethodA<T>(T arg) {
        T obj = new T();
    }
}
```

Nested Types

You can nest a generic type inside a non-generic type, and vice versa. This is straightforward. More intriguing is nesting generic types inside other generic types. The nested generic type can use the type parameters of the outer type. However, the type parameter of the outer type cannot be redefined as a new type parameter in the nested type. The nested generic type also can declare entirely new type parameters.

This is sample code of nested generic types:

```
using System;

namespace Donis.CSharpBook {
```

```
public class Starter {
    public static void Main() {
        ZClass<int>.Nested<double> obj =
            new ZClass<int>.Nested<double>();
        obj.MethodA(10, 12.34);
    }
}

public class ZClass<T> {
    public void MethodA(T arg) {

    }

    public class Nested<S> {
        public void MethodA(T arg1, S arg2) {
            Console.WriteLine("arg1: {0}",
                arg1.GetType().ToString());
            Console.WriteLine("arg2: {0}",
                arg2.GetType().ToString());
        }
    }
}
```

Static Members

Generic types can have static members. Static members cannot be bound to an open constructed type. Static members belong to the type where the member is defined. However, for a generic type, the type where the member is defined is an open constructed type, and static members of a generic type belong to the closed constructed type. There can be more than one closed constructed type for a generic type, each one having its own set of static members from the same generic type. Static members are accessible using the closed constructed type notation. Static constructors, which are called implicitly, initialize the static fields in the context of the current closed constructed type.

This is the constructed type notation for accessing a static member:

classname<type_argumentlist>.staticmember

In this syntax, *classname* is the name of the generic type, *type_argumentlist* is a comma-delimited list of type arguments, and *staticmember* is the name of the static member.

Static members are frequently used as counters. The following code counts the instances of a generic type. There are several generic type instantiations, each using a closed constructed type. The static count is specific to each closed constructed type. Running this code demonstrates that there are different sets of static members, one for each closed constructed type. There are separate counts for *ZClass<double>* and *ZClass<int>*:

```
using System;

namespace Donis.CSharpBook {
    public class Starter {
        public static void Main() {
            ZClass<int> obj1 = new ZClass<int>();
            ZClass<double> obj2 = new ZClass<double>();
            ZClass<double> obj3 = new ZClass<double>();
            ZClass<int>.DisplayCount(obj1);
            ZClass<double>.DisplayCount(obj2);
        }
    }

    public class ZClass<T> {

        public ZClass() {
            ++counter;
        }

        public static void DisplayCount(ZClass<T> _this) {
            Console.WriteLine("{0} : {1}",
                _this.GetType().ToString(),
                counter.ToString());
        }

        private static int counter = 0;
    }
}
```

Operator Functions

Generic types can contain operator member functions. As explained in Chapter 9, "Operator Overloading," operator member functions are static members. Operator member functions cannot be generic. However, operator member functions can use type parameters from the surrounding generic type.

In the following code, an *operator+* member function has been added to the *Sheet* generic type. It adds two *Sheet* collections. The results of the calculations are placed in a third sheet. Only integral sheets can be added. Because type parameters cannot be constrained by a value type, the compiler won't allow you to add variables of type *T*, and you aren't allowed to cast from a type parameter to an integer type. For these reasons, a helper function called *Add* is provided to add the values in two cells. (Error handling code could be added to ensure that the *Sheet* generic type is used only with addable types.)

```
public abstract class AddClass<T> {
    public abstract T Add(T op1, T op2);
}
```

```
public class Sheet<T> : AddClass<int> where T : IComparable {
    public Sheet(byte dimension) {
        if (dimension<0) {
            throw new Exception("Invalid dimensions");
        }
        m_Dimension = dimension;
        m_Sheet = new T[dimension, dimension];
        for (byte row = 1; row <= dimension; ++row) {
            for (byte col = 1; col <= dimension; ++col) {
                m_Sheet[row - 1, col - 1] = default(T);
            }
        }
    }

    public static Sheet<int> operator+(Sheet<int> sheet1,
        Sheet<T> sheet2)
        {
        byte dimension = Math.Max(sheet1.m_Dimension,
            sheet2.m_Dimension);
        Sheet<int> total = new Sheet<int>(dimension);

        for (byte row = 1; row <= dimension; ++row) {
            for (byte col = 1; col <= dimension; ++col) {
                total[(byte)row, (byte)col] =
                    sheet1.Add(sheet1[(byte)row, (byte)col],
                    (int) (object) (sheet2[(byte)row, (byte)col]));
            }
        }
        return total;
    }

    public override int Add(int op1, int op2) {
        return op1+op2;
    }
...
```

This is the signature of the *operator+* function in the *Sheet* generic type:

```
public static Sheet<int> operator+(Sheet<int> sheet1,
    Sheet<T> sheet2)
```

An *operator+* member function is a binary operator with two operands. Notice that one operand is a closed constructed type, whereas the other is an open constructed type. Why? The *operator+* requires that one of the operands be the containing class, which is the open constructed type. The second parameter is not similarly restricted and could be anything. For this reason, it is possible that the first and second parameters of the *operator+* member function are not compatible.

Serialization

Serialization persists the state of an object to a stream. Serializing an instance of a generic type is similar to serializing a regular type. This book does not present a detailed explanation of serialization. This section provides only essential information on serialization for generic types.

Serialization is performed mostly with the *SerializationInfo* object. *SerializationInfo.AddValue* and *SerializationInfo.GetValue* methods add data to and get data from the serialization data stream. For generic types, use the *SerializationInfo.AddValue(string, object, Type)* and *SerializationInfo.GetValue(string, Type)* overloaded methods.

SerializationInfo.GetValue returns an object type that should be cast to the target type.

Generic types must be adorned with the *Serializable* attribute to support serialization.

The *GetObjectData* method is where the serialization of an object is implemented. *GetObjectData* has a *SerializationInfo* and *StreamingContext* parameter. The *SerializationInfo. AddValue* method is called to serialize states, including any generic content:

```
public void GetObjectData(SerializationInfo info,
    StreamingContext ctx) {
    info.AddValue("fielda", fielda, typeof(T));
}
```

To deserialize, add a two-argument constructor to the generic type. The arguments are *SerializationInfo* and *StreamingContext* parameters. Call the *SerializationInfo.GetValue* method to rehydrate the instance, as shown in the following code. (The *StreamingContext* parameter provides user-defined information, which is not required in this sample code.)

```
private ZClass(SerializationInfo info,
    StreamingContext ctx) {
    fielda = (T) info.GetValue("fielda", typeof(T));
}
```

Objects can be serialized in different formats, such as binary or Simple Object Access Protocol (SOAP). This is done with formatters, such as the *BinaryFormatter* type. The *SoapFormatter* type cannot be used with generic types. Serialization also requires creating an appropriate stream for the formatter, such as a *FileStream*. The stream is where the instance is serialized or deserialized. For example, call *BinaryFormatter.Serialize* to serialize a generic type instance and *BinaryFormatter.Deserialize* to deserialize a generic type instance.

The following program accepts a command-line argument. Entering *set* from the command line instructs the program to serialize an instance of *ZClass* to a file. *ZClass* is a generic type. A *Get* command asks the program to deserialize the instance:

```
using System;
using System.Runtime.Serialization;
using System.Runtime.Serialization.Formatters.Binary;
using System.IO;
```

```
namespace Donis.CSharpBook {

    public class Starter {
        public static void Main(string[] args) {
            BinaryFormatter binary = new BinaryFormatter();
            FileStream file =
                new FileStream("data.bin", FileMode.OpenOrCreate);

            if (args[0].ToLower() == "set") {
                ZClass<int> obj = new ZClass<int>(5);
                binary.Serialize(file, obj);
                return;
            }

            if (args[0].ToLower() == "get") {
                ZClass<int> obj = (ZClass<int>)
                    binary.Deserialize(file);
                Console.WriteLine(obj.GetValue());
                return;
            }
        }
    }

    [Serializable] public class ZClass<T> {

        public ZClass(T init) {
            fielda = init;
        }

        private ZClass(SerializationInfo info,
            StreamingContext ctx) {
            fielda = (T) info.GetValue("fielda", typeof(T));
        }

        public void GetObjectData(SerializationInfo info,
            StreamingContext ctx) {
            info.AddValue("fielda", fielda, typeof(T));
        }

        public void SetValue(T data) {
            fielda = data;
        }

        public T GetValue() {
            return fielda;
        }

        private T fielda = default(T);
    }
}
```

Generics Internals

Generics are economical and expeditious, especially when compared with parametric polymorphism in other languages. The difference is found in the compile-time and run-time semantics of generics. This section focuses on improvements in these areas compared with parameterized types in C++, which is a widely recognized and well-documented implementation of parametric polymorphism.

Although an inspection of parameterized templates in C++ might unveil basic similarities with generics, there are considerable differences. These differences make generics more efficient and better-performing than parameterized templates. The exact implementation of templates is specific to each C++ compiler. Yet the concepts of parameterized templates are similar in all implementations.

The major difference between generics and parameterized templates is that the latter is purely compile-time-based. Instances of parameterized templates expand into separate classes at compile time. For example, the Standard Template Library (STL) of C++ offers a stack collection, which is a template. If ellipse, rectangle, triangle, and curve versions of the stack are defined, the stack template expands into separate classes—one for each type. The expansion occurs at compile time. What happens when two stacks of circles are defined separately? Is there a consolidation of the code? The answer is no, which can lead to significant code bloat.

In .NET, generic types expand at run time and are not language-specific. Therefore, generics are available to any managed language. The *Sheet* generic type presented in this chapter is written in C# but also can be used in Microsoft Visual Basic .NET. With C++, the particulars of the template, such as the parameterized types, are lost at compile time and are not available for later inspection. Managed code, including generics, undergoes two compilations. The first compilation, administered by the language compiler, emits metadata and Microsoft Intermediate Language (MSIL) code specific to generic types. Because the specifics of the generic type are preserved, it is available for later inspection, such as reflection. There are new metadata and MSIL instructions that target generic types. The second compilation, performed by the just-in-time compiler (jitter), performs the code expansion. The jitter is part of the Common Language Runtime (CLR).

Figure 7-1 shows the MSIL-specific code for a generic type.

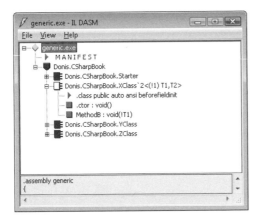

FIGURE 7-1 An MSIL view of a generic type

The CLR performs an intelligent expansion of generic types, unlike C++, which blindly expands parameterized types. Intelligent expansion is conducted differently for value type arguments and reference type arguments.

If a generic type has a value type argument, it is expanded into a class at run time. This new class has the type argument (value type) substituted for the type parameter throughout the class. The resulting class is cached in memory. Future instances of similar generic types reference the cached class. The code is shared across multiple instances of generic types with the same type arguments. This prevents additional class expansion as found in C++ to eliminate unnecessary code bloat.

If the type argument is a reference type, the CLR conducts intelligent expansion differently. The run time creates a specialized class for the reference type, where *System.Object* is substituted for the type parameter. The new class is cached in memory. Future instances of the generic type with *any* reference type argument will use this same class. Essentially, generic type instantiations that have a reference type argument all share the same code.

Look at the following code. How many specialized classes are created at run time?

```
Sheet<int> asheet = new Sheet<int>(2);
Sheet<double> bsheet = new Sheet<double>(5);
Sheet<XClass> csheet = new Sheet<XClass>(2);
Sheet<YClass> dsheet = new Sheet<YClass>(5);
Sheet<int> esheet = new Sheet<int>(3);
```

The preceding code results in three specialized classes. The *Sheet<int>* instantiations share a single class. *Sheet<double>* is a separate class. *Sheet<XClass>* and *Sheet<YClass>* share a class intended for type arguments that are references.

Generic Collections

As discussed in the previous chapter, the .NET FCL includes general-purpose collection classes for commonplace data algorithms, such as a stack, queue, dynamic array, and dictionary. These collections are object-based, a fact that affects performance, hinders type-safety, and potentially consumes the available memory. However, the .NET FCL also includes parameterized versions of most of the collections.

The parameterized collections are found in the *System.Collections.Generic* namespace. Generic interfaces are also included in that namespace. Table 7-3 lists some of the types and interfaces of this namespace.

TABLE 7-3 Generic types and interfaces

Description	Type
Dynamic array	*List<T>*
LIFO list	*Stack<T>*
FIFO list	*Queue<T>*
Collection of key/value pairs	*Dictionary<K,V>*
Compares a current and other object	*IComparable<T>*
Compares two objects	*IComparer<T>*
Returns an enumerator	*IEnumerable<T>*
Defines an enumerator	*IEnumerator<T>*

Enumerators

Chapter 8, "Enumerators," discusses enumerators, a topic that is a natural extension of this chapter. Enumerators typically are used to iterate collections. Enumerators are implemented and typically exposed by an enumerable object. Enumerable objects implement the *IEnumerable* interface, where the *IEnumerable.GetEnumerator* method returns an enumerator object.

The *foreach* statement is the best known expression of enumeration in C#. The target of the *foreach* statement is not any object—it has to be an enumerable object.

The next chapter documents the enumerator pattern, including how to implement an enumerator and enumerable object.

Chapter 8
Enumerators

Arrays and collections were introduced in Chapter 5, "Arrays and Collections"—both of these are collection types. Collections group related types, even if the types are related only through inheritance from *System.Object*. You could maintain a dynamic array of *Employee* types, which would include instances of *HourlyEmployee*, *ExemptEmployee*, and *CommissionedEmployee* types. You could have a queue of bank requests, such as *DepositTransaction*, *WithdrawalTransaction*, and *InterestTransaction* objects. The relationship of these classes is defined by inheritance at compile time, which allows polymorphism at run time. Enumerating such collections of related objects is a frequent and valuable behavior in many applications.

Enumeration is the process of iterating the items in a collection. A report that lists new employees would need to enumerate the employee collection. Generating a bank statement requires enumerating transactions of a bank account holder.

Because enumeration is a valuable tool to almost every developer and across a myriad of types, some standardization is helpful. Types that are enumerable implement the *IEnumerator* and *IEnumerable* interfaces. A generic implementation is available with the *IEnumerator<T>* and *IEnumerable<T>* interfaces. *IEnumerable* interfaces return an enumerator object. The enumerator object implements the *IEnumerator* interface, which is used to perform the iteration. Collections and arrays support enumeration and implement the enumeration interfaces.

Most types you would want to enumerate have some sort of interface that abstracts the details of enumeration. For example, the *ArrayList* type has indexes, the *BitArray* type has the *Get* method, and *Hashtables* have the *Keys* and *Values* properties. As enumerable types, collections also offer standard enumeration through the *IEnumerator* interface. Collections are iterated in loops. *Do* and *while* loops are prone to logic errors. The *foreach* statement helps alleviate some of these errors, where the enumeration is implicit. This reduces the code necessary to iterate a collection and makes the code more robust.

The following is a straightforward *foreach* loop. The *colors* array is an array of strings. Arrays are collections and are therefore enumerable. Instead of writing a *for* loop, with indexes and a counter to manage, the *foreach* loop keeps everything simple—no indexes, and no counters. The *foreach* loop automatically enumerates each element of the collection:

```
string[] colors = {"red", "green", "blue"};
foreach (string color in colors) {
    Console.WriteLine(color);
}
```

Here is another example of a *foreach* loop. This code manipulates a *Stack* collection—a more complex structure than a simple array. However, stacks are also collections, meaning that the *foreach* statement is applicable:

```
Stack<int> collection = new Stack<int>();
collection.Push(10);
collection.Push(15);
collection.Push(20);
foreach (int number in collection) {
    Console.WriteLine(number);
}
```

Enumerable Objects

Enumerable objects implement the *IEnumerable* interface. The *GetEnumerator* method is the only member of this interface. It returns an enumerator, which is used to enumerate the collections.

This is the *IEnumerable* interface:

```
public interface IEnumerable {
    IEnumerator GetEnumerator();
}
```

Each invocation of the *GetEnumerator* method returns a unique enumerator. The enumerator is a state machine that maintains a static view of the target collection and a cursor. The cursor points to the current item of the collection. What happens if a collection is modified while being enumerated? An exception should occur. You could lock the collection during enumeration, but that can cause substantial performance degradation. As a best practice, an enumerator should capture the collection as a snapshot. In addition, the snapshot collection is read-only. Depending on the size of the collection, creating a snapshot could stress memory resources. Finally, the *GetEnumerator* method should be thread-safe and guarantee the return of a unique enumerator, which references an isolated collection regardless of the thread context.

Enumerators

Enumerators are part of the enumeration pattern and normally are implemented as a nested class within the collection type. The primary benefit of nested classes is access to the private members of the outer class. This access allows you to avoid breaking the rules of encapsulation, while allowing the enumerator class to access the data store of the collection. The data store is likely a private member of the collection class and not an external entity.

Enumerators implement the *IEnumerator* interface, which has three members. This is the *IEnumerator* interface:

```
public interface IEnumerator {
    object Current { get; }
    bool MoveNext();
    void Reset();
}
```

The *Current* property returns the current element of the collection. *MoveNext* moves the current element to the next item in the collection. If the iteration has completed, *MoveNext* returns *false*. Otherwise, *MoveNext* returns *true*. Notice that there is no *MovePrevious* method; enumeration is forward-only. The *Reset* method returns the enumeration to the beginning, before the first element of the collection.

The enumerator is the state machine representing the enumeration. Part of the state machine is the cursor, which either directly or indirectly references the current element. The cursor is not necessarily an integral value, but normally it is. For example, the cursor within a linked list might be a node object. When the enumerator is created, the cursor initially points before the first element of the collection. Do not access the *Current* property while the cursor is in this initial state. Call *MoveNext* first, which positions the cursor at the first element of the collection.

The following is a typical constructor of an enumerator. In this example, the constructor makes a snapshot of the collection. For reasons of simplicity, the collection in this example is a basic array. The cursor is therefore set to –1, which is before the first element of the collection:

```
private int cursor;
private object[] elements = null;

public Enumerator(object[] items) {
    elements = new object[items.Length];
    Array.Copy(items, elements, items.Length);
    cursor = -1;
}
```

The *MoveNext* method moves the cursor to the next item. The *Current* property then can be used to return that element. If the list has been fully iterated, *MoveNext* returns *false*. Collections are not circular, where *MoveNext* can cycle through a collection. The *Current* property is not valid after the collection has been fully enumerated. For this reason, do not use the *Current* property after *MoveNext* returns *false*.

Here is one possible implementation of the *MoveNext* method:

```
public bool MoveNext() {
    ++cursor;
    if (cursor > (elements.Length - 1)) {
```

```
        return false;
    }
    return true;
}
```

The *Reset* method resets the enumeration. The cursor is updated to point to before the collection again.

Here is a *Reset* method:

```
public void Reset() {
    cursor = -1;
}
```

Current is a read-only property. Implement the *get* method of the property but not the *set* method. The implementation should check for fencepost errors. If the index is before or after the collection, the appropriate exception should be thrown.

Here is an implementation of the *Current* property:

```
public object Current {
    get {
        if (cursor > (elements.Length - 1)) {
            throw new InvalidOperationException(
                "Enumeration already finished");
        }
        if (cursor == -1) {
            throw new InvalidOperationException(
                "Enumeration not started");
        }
        return elements[cursor];
    }
}
```

Enumerator states   Enumerators can be in one of four possible states. Table 8-1 lists the enumerator states.

TABLE 8-1 Enumerator states

State	Description
Before	This is the state of the enumerator before enumeration has started or after it has been reset. The *Current* property is not available. The first call to *MoveNext* changes the state from *Before* to *Running*.
Running	This is the state when *MoveNext* is calculating the next element of the iteration. When *MoveNext* returns *true*, the next element has been enumerated, and the state changes to *Suspended*. If *MoveNext* returns *false*, the state changes to *After*.
Suspended	The state of the enumerator between enumerations. Calling *MoveNext* changes the state from *Suspended* to *Running*.
After	This is the state after enumeration has completed. The *Current* property is no longer available. Reset returns the enumeration to *Before*, and enumeration can be restarted.

An Enumerator Example

Here is sample code for an enumerator class and a consumer. This is also the complete listing for some of the partial code presented earlier in this chapter. The *SimpleCollection* is a thin wrapper for a static array. Actually, it is somewhat redundant because arrays are already fully functional collections, including exposing an enumerator. However, this simple example is ideal for demonstrating the enumerator pattern.

The enumerator pattern recommends isolation of the underlying collection. In this code, the enumerator is created as a nested class, in which a snapshot of the collection is made in the constructor. The isolated collection is a copy of the array. In addition, the *Current* property is read-only, which prevents changes to the collection data.

In *Main*, an instance of *SimpleCollection* is created. It is initialized with an integer array. The collection is then iterated using the *IEnumerator* interface:

```
using System;
using System.Collections;

namespace Donis.CSharpBook {

    public class Starter {

        public static void Main() {
            SimpleCollection simple = new SimpleCollection(
                new object[] {1,2,3,4,5,6,7});

            IEnumerator enumerator = simple.GetEnumerator();
            while (enumerator.MoveNext()) {
                Console.WriteLine(enumerator.Current);
            }
        }
    }

    public class SimpleCollection: IEnumerable {

        public SimpleCollection(object[] array) {
            items = array;
        }

        public IEnumerator GetEnumerator() {
            return new Enumerator(items);
        }

        private class Enumerator: IEnumerator {

            public Enumerator(object[] items) {
                elements = new object[items.Length];
                Array.Copy(items, elements, items.Length);
                cursor = -1;
            }
```

```
            public bool MoveNext() {
                ++cursor;
                if (cursor > (elements.Length - 1)) {
                    return false;
                }
                return true;
            }


            public void Reset() {
                cursor = -1;
            }

            public object Current {
                get {
                    if (cursor > (elements.Length - 1)) {
                        throw new InvalidOperationException(
                            "Enumeration already finished");
                    }
                    if (cursor == -1) {
                        throw new InvalidOperationException(
                            "Enumeration not started");
                    }
                    return elements[cursor];
                }
            }

            private int cursor;
            private object[] elements = null;
        }

        private object[] items = null;
    }
}
```

As shown, the *SimpleCollection* class makes a copy of the collection in the enumerator. This isolates the collection from changes in the target array. This is the recommended approach for collections that can be changed. If the collection is static, a copy might not be necessary. Isolation protects a collection against changes during iteration.

An Enumerator Example (Versioned Collection)

The following code offers another implementation of an enumerable class. In this example, a versioned collection is used. A private field called *version* has been added to the collection class. An indexer has been added to allow clients to modify the collection. The version is incremented whenever the collection is modified. A version number also has been added to the enumerator, which is the nested class. In the constructor, the version is initialized to the version of the outer collection. When the *Current* property is accessed, the version number inside the enumerator is compared to that of the collection. If unequal, the collection has been modified since the enumerator was created and an exception is raised. This is the implementation model of collections in the .NET Framework Class Library (FCL), such as the *ArrayList*, *Stack*, and *Queue* collections.

The *Main* method tests the versioning. The collection is modified in *Main* after the enumerator has been obtained. After the modification, the *Current* property is used, which triggers the expected exception:

```
using System;
using System.Collections;

namespace Donis.CSharpBook {

    public class Starter {

        public static void Main() {
            SimpleCollection simple = new SimpleCollection(
                new object[] {1,2,3,4,5,6,7});

            IEnumerator enumerator = simple.GetEnumerator();
            enumerator.MoveNext();
            Console.WriteLine(enumerator.Current);
            enumerator.MoveNext();
            simple[4] = 10;
            Console.WriteLine(enumerator.Current);  // Exception raised
            enumerator.MoveNext();
        }
    }

    public class SimpleCollection: IEnumerable {

        public SimpleCollection(object[] array) {
            items = array;
            version = 1;
        }

        public object this[int index] {
            get {
                return items[index];
            }
            set {
                ++version;
                items[index] = value;
            }
        }

        public IEnumerator GetEnumerator() {
            return new Enumerator(this);
        }

        private class Enumerator: IEnumerator {

            public Enumerator(SimpleCollection obj) {
                oThis = obj;
                cursor = -1;
```

```
            version = oThis.version;
    }

    public bool MoveNext() {
        ++cursor;
        if (cursor > (oThis.items.Length - 1)) {
            return false;
        }
        return true;
    }


    public void Reset() {
        cursor = -1;
    }

    public object Current {
        get {
            if (oThis.version != version) {
                throw new InvalidOperationException(
                    "Collection was modified");
            }

            if (cursor > (oThis.items.Length - 1)) {
                throw new InvalidOperationException(
                    "Enumeration already finished");
            }
            if (cursor == -1) {
                throw new InvalidOperationException(
                    "Enumeration not started");
            }
            return oThis.items[cursor];
        }
    }

    private int version;
    private int cursor;
    private SimpleCollection oThis;
    }

    private object[] items=null;
    private int version;
    }
}
```

IEnumerator Problem

Different techniques to implement the enumerator pattern have been shown. They share a common problem. Enumerators, which implement the *IEnumerator* interface, iterate *System. Object* types. The result is the following:

- There is a performance penalty from boxing and unboxing value types.

- There is a small performance cost for downcasting (casting from a parent type to a child type) to reference types.

- Frequent boxing can stress the managed heap.

- Boxing large collections of value types can also stress the managed heap.

- Casting to and from *System.Object* is required, which is not entirely type-safe.

These problems were identified in Chapter 7, "Generics." The solution was to use generic types. That is the solution here as well. The .NET Framework offers generic versions of the *IEnumerable* and *IEnumerator* interfaces.

Generic Enumerators

Nongeneric enumerable objects and enumerators lack type specialty, which leads to performance problems and other issues. You can implement enumerable objects and enumerators using generic interfaces, which avoid some of the problems mentioned at the end of the previous section. Implement the *IEnumerable<T>* interface for generic enumerable objects. For generic enumerators, implement the *IEnumerator<T>* interface. Both *IEnumerable<T>* and *IEnumerator<T>* are generic interfaces found in the *System.Collections.Generic* namespace. *IEnumerable<T>* and *IEnumerator<T>* inherit their nongeneric counterparts *IEnumerable* and *IEnumerator*, respectively. This means the nongeneric methods must be implemented as well.

IEnumerable<T> Interface

Generic enumerable objects implement the *IEnumerable<T>* interface. This is the *IEnumerable<T>* interface:

```
public interface IEnumerable<T> : IEnumerable {
    IEnumerator<T> GetEnumerator();
}
```

As shown, *IEnumerable<T>* inherits *IEnumerable*, which is the nongeneric version of the same interface. This includes a nongeneric version of the *GetEnumerator* method. Enumerators inheriting *IEnumerable<T>* therefore must implement both a generic and nongeneric *GetEnumerator* method. The two *GetEnumerator* methods differ in return type only. As you know, the return type alone is insufficient for overloading a method. To prevent ambiguity, one of the *GetEnumerator* methods must use explicit interface member implementation.

This is sample code of the *GetEnumerator* methods for a generic enumerable object. The nongeneric version of *GetEnumerator* is implemented explicitly:

```
public IEnumerator<T> GetEnumerator() {
    return new Enumerator<T>(this);
}

IEnumerator IEnumerable.GetEnumerator() {
    return new Enumerator<T>(this);
}
```

The generic version of *GetEnumerator* naturally returns a generic enumerator, which implements the *IEnumerator<T> interface.*

IEnumerator<T> Interface

Generic enumerators implement the *IEnumerator<T>* interface, shown here:

```
public interface IEnumerator<T>: IDisposable, IEnumerator {
    T Current { get; }
}
```

Current is a read-only property and the only member of the *IEnumerator<T>* generic interface. The remaining members are inherited from the *IDisposable* and *IEnumerator* interfaces. The *IDisposable* interface marks generic enumerators as disposable. This requires implementing the *IDisposable.Dispose* method. The *IEnumerator* interface adds the nongeneric enumerator interface. The *MoveNext* and *Reset* methods do not have an implementation specific to a generic type. Therefore the nongeneric versions are sufficient even for a generic implementation. A second *Current* property, a nongeneric version, is inherited from the *IEnumerable* interface. Therefore, *IEnumerator* has overloaded *Current* properties, both of which should be implemented in the enumerator.

The following is sample code of a generic and nongeneric implementation of the *Current* property. The nongeneric *Current* property simply calls the generic version:

```
public __T Current {
    get {
        if (oThis.version != version) {
            throw new InvalidOperationException(
                "Collection was modified");
        }

        if (cursor > (oThis.items.Length - 1)) {
            throw new InvalidOperationException(
                "Enumeration already finished");
        }
        if (cursor == -1) {
            throw new InvalidOperationException(
                "Enumeration not started");
        }
        return oThis.items[cursor];
    }
}

object IEnumerator.Current {
    get {
        return Current;
    }
}
```

The *Dispose* method supports deterministic garbage collection. This method is called explicitly to clean up for an object. In this circumstance, the method is called to clean up resources assigned to an enumerator. *Dispose* methods of enumerators are most frequently called in the iterators, which is the next topic of this chapter. In the *Dispose* method, set the state of the enumeration to *After* and perform any necessary cleanup. Some enumerators track the state using a flag (an enumeration type), where the flag is updated in the *Dispose* method and elsewhere in the enumerator. The code presented here does not employ a state flag. If the cursor is beyond the collection, the *After* state is assumed. Conversely, a cursor of –1 indicates the *Before* state. Based on these assumptions, this is the implementation of a *Dispose* method in our example for an enumerator:

```
public void Dispose() {
    cursor = oThis.items.Length + 1;
}
```

A Generic Enumerator Example (Versioned Collection)

Earlier in this chapter, source code was presented for enumerating a versioned collection. Here is the versioned collection example redone with generic interfaces. The following code also completes some of the partial code presented earlier in this section. In *Main*, the collection is enumerated in a generic and a nongeneric manner. The first *foreach* loop uses a generic enumerator. That is the default implementation of an enumerator provided by the *SimpleCollection* class. In the second *foreach* loop, the simple collection is cast to the nongeneric *IEnumerable* interface. This instructs the *foreach* statement to call the nongeneric *GetEnumerator* method, which returns a nongeneric enumerator. The nongeneric enumerator is then used to iterate the simple collection.

Here is the sample code:

```
using System;
using System.Collections;
using System.Collections.Generic;

namespace Donis.CSharpBook {

    public class Starter {

        public static void Main() {
            SimpleCollection<int> simple =
                new SimpleCollection<int>(
                    new int[] {1,2,3,4,5,6,7});

            foreach (int number in simple) {
                Console.WriteLine(number);
            }

            foreach (int number in
                (IEnumerable) simple) {
```

```
                    Console.WriteLine(number);
            }
        }
    }

    public class SimpleCollection<T>: IEnumerable<T> {

        public SimpleCollection(T[] array) {
            items = array;
            version = 1;
        }

        public T this[int index] {
            get {
                return items[index];
            }
            set {
                ++version;
                items[index] = value;
            }
        }

        public IEnumerator<T> GetEnumerator() {
            Console.WriteLine(
                "IEnumerator<T> GetEnumerator()");
            return new Enumerator<T>(this);
        }

        IEnumerator IEnumerable.GetEnumerator() {
            Console.WriteLine(
                "IEnumerator GetEnumerator()");
            return new Enumerator<T>(this);
        }

        private class Enumerator<__T>: IEnumerator<__T>

        {

            public Enumerator(SimpleCollection<__T> obj) {
                oThis = obj;
                cursor = -1;
                version = oThis.version;
            }

            public __T Current {
                get {
                    if (oThis.version != version) {
                        throw new InvalidOperationException(
                            "Collection was modified");
                    }

                    if (cursor > (oThis.items.Length - 1)) {
                        throw new InvalidOperationException(
                            "Enumeration already finished");
                    }
```

```
            if (cursor == -1) {
                throw new InvalidOperationException(
                    "Enumeration not started");
            }
            return oThis.items[cursor];
        }
    }

    public void Dispose() {
        cursor = oThis.items.Length + 1;
    }

    public bool MoveNext() {
        ++cursor;
        if (cursor > (oThis.items.Length - 1)) {
            return false;
        }
        return true;
    }

    public void Reset() {
        cursor = -1;
    }

    object IEnumerator.Current {
        get {
            return Current;
        }
    }

    private int version;
    private int cursor;
    private SimpleCollection<__T> oThis;
    }


    private T[] items = null;
    private int version;
    }
}
```

Iterators

Using iterators is an alternative to fully implementing *IEnumerator* or *IEnumerable* interfaces. Iterators also provide an easier way to implement complex enumerators, such as reverse enumerators. Previously in this chapter, different implementation strategies for enumerators have been shown. There are several options. The enumerator could be implemented as a nested class. A versioned collection could be used. The implementation could be generic or nongeneric. Why should all developers consider these options and implement their rendition of an enumerator? This would not appear to be a good use of their collective mental prowess. Almost assuredly, the various implementations of the enumerator pattern are within an acceptable delta in performance and memory requirements. It is also more robust if there is one tested solution. Anyway, some developers simply visit the MSDN Web site, from which they can copy and paste an enumerator implementation into their source code. Therefore, the various implementations are undoubtedly quite similar. Iterators augment the implementation of enumerators. Developers no longer have to write enumerators from scratch.

Implementing forward enumeration of a simple collection, as shown in this chapter, is not overly difficult. The real challenge is dealing with more complex enumerations such as reverse enumerations. Coding an enumerator to iterate a sparse collection, nodal list, or binary tree also can be more challenging. What about maintaining multiple enumerators, such as a forward and reverse enumerator? That does not sound fun either. In any of these circumstances, I would gladly pass the baton to the compiler.

.NET 2.0 introduced the iterator, which is a compiler-generated enumerator. When the enumerable object calls *GetEnumerator*, either directly or indirectly, the compiler generates and returns an appropriate iterator object. The iterator can implement either the enumerable or enumerator interface. You are not completely excluded from the process. Developers can affect the enumeration in an iterator block. The essential ingredient of an iterator block is the *yield* statement.

Yield Statement

The following code demonstrates brevity, one of the obvious benefits of an iterator block and the *yield* statement. Previous sample code of a generic enumerator required almost 100 lines of code. The following example implements a similar enumerator using the *yield* statement with just 3 lines of code:

```
public IEnumerator<T> GetEnumerator() {
    foreach (T item in items) {
        yield return item;
    }
}
```

In the preceding code, you explicitly implement the *IEnumerable* interface but the compiler implements the *IEnumerator* interface (i.e., the enumerator). The compiler can implement both the *IEnumerable* and *IEnumerator* interfaces for the iterator. If the iterator block returns *IEnumerable*, the compiler responds by creating an enumerable object and an enumerator object. This eliminates the need to implement the *GetEnumerator* method. The *yield* statement, as shown in the following sample code, is the key. (Iterator blocks are explained further in the next section of this chapter.)

```
public IEnumerable<T> MethodA() {
    foreach (T item in items) {
        yield return item;
    }
}
```

An *iterator* is a method that contains an iterator block. *Iterator* methods return either an enumerator or an enumerable object, as defined by the *IEnumerator* or *IEnumerable* interfaces. There is one major difference between the enumerator received from an iterator and a normal enumerator: enumerators from iterators do not implement the *Reset* method. Calling the *Reset* method on such an enumerator will cause an exception.

The pivotal statement of an iterator is *yield*. This is the syntax of the *yield* statement:

```
yield return expression;
```

```
yield break;
```

The *yield return* statement iterates the next element of a collection. The *expression* is assigned to the *Current* property. Enumerators start in the *Before* state. The initial *MoveNext* method calls the first *yield* statement. After the *Current* property is set, the enumerator is suspended. The next *MoveNext* calls the next *yield*. This pattern continues until the enumeration is finished. The iterator block is not called anew for each *MoveNext*. Between *yield* statements of the same iterator block, enumeration is suspended. While it is suspended, the state of the enumeration should not change. The iterator is a state machine that maintains the state of the enumeration between calls to the *MoveNext* method.

The *yield break* statement finishes an enumeration, which ultimately changes the enumerator state to *After*. The *Dispose* method is then called to clean up the enumerator. The following is sample code of the *yield break* statement. The *yield break* statement in this example stops the enumeration after the fourth element:

```
public IEnumerator<T> GetEnumerator() {
    int count = 0;
    foreach (T item in items) {
        ++count;
        yield return item;
        if (count == 4) {
            yield break;
        }
    }
}
```

Iterator Blocks

An iterator block contains the logic to enumerate a collection, contains a *yield* statement, and returns an enumerator or an enumerable object. Within the iterator block, there can be one or more *yield* statements. Iterator blocks are not executed continuously and are sometimes suspended. The function is suspended between successive *yield* statements, which are controlled by the *MoveNext* method. As mentioned, the iterator block maintains the state machine of the enumerator between iterations.

The following type of functions cannot be iterators:

- Event handlers

- Constructors

- Destructors

There are restrictions on iterator blocks. For example, iterator blocks cannot have a *return* statement. Only *yield return* statements are allowed:

```
public IEnumerator<T> GetEnumerator() {
    foreach (T item in items) {
        yield return item;
        return;  // not allowed
    }
}
```

There are several other restrictions on iterator blocks:

- Iterator blocks are not allowed in anonymous methods.

- Iterator blocks cannot be contained in a *try* with a *catch* handler.

- Iterator blocks cannot be placed in a *finally* block.

An iterator, which is a function, also has some restrictions:

- *Iterator* methods must return an *IEnumerable* or an *IEnumerator* interface.

- *Iterator* methods cannot have *ref* parameters.

- *Iterator* methods cannot have *out* parameters.

- *Iterator* methods cannot be unsafe.

When an iterator block is exited, the *Dispose* method of the enumerator is called. This provides an opportunity to clean up for the enumerator when the enumeration is completed.

Iterator Internals

Iterators are implemented as nested classes by the C# compiler. The nested class maintains the state of the current enumeration. It persists the enumeration state between *yield* statements. Iterators are created by the language compiler, not by the Common Language Runtime (CLR). Neither Microsoft Intermediate Language (MSIL) nor metadata has changed to accommodate iterators especially. The nested class for an enumerator is a normal class, which is created for each method that contains an iterator block. If three methods within a class have enumerator blocks, the compiler adds three nested classes to that class.

This is how the nested class is named:

[membername]uniqueid<T>

[membername]uniqueid

If the iterator method returns either the *IEnumerator<T>* or *IEnumerable<T>* interfaces, the name of the nested class has the *<T>* suffix.

In this code, *ZClass* has multiple iterator methods:

```
public class ZClass {

    public IEnumerator GetEnumerator() {
        int[] array = new int[] {1,2,3,4};
        int count = 0;
        for (count = 0; count < 4; ++count) {
            yield return array[count];
        }
    }
    public IEnumerator MethodA() {
        int[] array = new int[] {1,2,3,4};
        int count = 0;
        for (count = 0; count < 4; ++count) {
            yield return array[count];
        }
    }

    public IEnumerable<T> MethodB<T>() {
        T local=default(T);
        yield return local;
    }
}
```

The compiler adds three nested classes, one for each enumerator method, to the *ZClass* type. The various nested classes represent the state machine for different enumerators. Figure 8-1 shows *ZClass* and the nested classes.

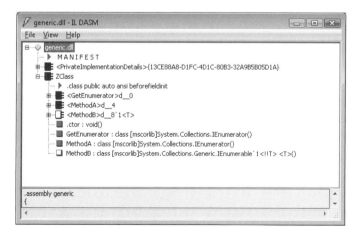

FIGURE 8-1 A view of the *ZClass* type, which includes the nested enumerator classes

The nested enumerator class has several private fields. The local variables of the iterator are lifted to fields of the nested class. The fields maintain the state of these local variables throughout the enumeration. The nested class also has three special purpose fields. The state of the enumeration, such as *Running* or *After*, is in the *<>1_state* field. The *<>2_current* field is the result of the last iteration. It is the current item. The *<>4_this* field is a back pointer to the outer class. If the iterator method is static, the back pointer is not initialized; it is initialized only for instance methods. Combined, the lifted and specialty fields represent the state of the enumeration.

Figure 8-2 shows the fields of a typical nested class for an enumerator.

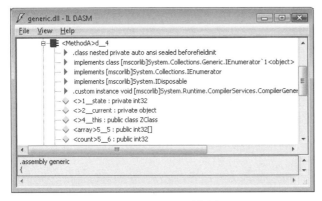

FIGURE 8-2 A view of a nested class and fields

Iterator Examples

This section presents several examples of iterators to demonstrate different implementation strategies and the flexibility of iterators.

Dual iteration   The first example iterates two collections simultaneously:

```
using System;
using System.Collections.Generic;

namespace Donis.CSharpBook {
    public class Starter {
        public static void Main() {
            ZClass obj = new ZClass();
            foreach (int item in obj) {
                Console.Write(item);
            }
        }
    }

    public class ZClass {

        private int[] list1 = new int[] {0,2,4,6,8};
        private int[] list2 = new int[] {1,3,5,7,9};
```

```
        public IEnumerator<int> GetEnumerator() {
            for (int index = 0; index < 5; ++index) {
                yield return list1[index];
                yield return list2[index];
            }
        }
    }
}
```

The preceding code alternates between yielding *list1* and *list2*. As the iteration moves between collections, the even and odd numbers are intermixed. The result is 0123456789. *ZClass* does not inherit the *IEnumerable* interface. However, it adheres to the enumerator pattern by implementing the *GetEnumerator* method. This is sufficient for an iterator.

Reverse iteration   The following example iterates a collection forward and in reverse. Two iterators are exposed for this reason. *GetEnumerator* exposes the standard forward iterator. The reverse iterator is implemented in the *Reverse* property. Because the property returns *IEnumerable*, the *Reverse* property is both an enumerable and an enumerator object. When an iterator method returns *IEnumerable*, the nested class generated by the compiler is implemented as both an enumerable and an enumerator object. In *Main*, there are two *foreach* loops: The first *foreach* loop uses the forward iterator, whereas the reverse iterator is requested in the second loop:

```
using System;
using System.Collections.Generic;

namespace Donis.CSharpBook {
    public class Starter {
        public static void Main() {
            Console.WriteLine("Forward List");
            ZClass obj = new ZClass();
            foreach (int item in obj) {
                Console.Write(item);
            }
            Console.WriteLine("\nReverse List");
            foreach (int item in obj.Reverse) {
                Console.Write(item);
            }
        }
    }

    public class ZClass {

        private int[] list1 = new int[] {0,2,4,6,8};

        public IEnumerator<int> GetEnumerator() {
            for (int index = 0; index < 5; ++index) {
                yield return list1[index];
            }
        }
```

```
        public IEnumerable<int> Reverse {
            get {
                for (int index = 4; index >= 0; --index) {
                    yield return list1[index];
                }
            }
        }
    }
}
```

Temporary collections   Temporary collections are calculated at run time and are useful in a variety of circumstances. The list of prime numbers, the records of a file, and fields in a dataset are examples of collections that can be calculated. Temporary collections can be populated lazily. You can read a flat file or dataset on demand at run time to hydrate a temporary collection.

The following code enumerates days from the current date until the end of the month, which is calculated using the *DateTime* structure. The method *ToEndOfMonth* is enumerable by virtue of the fact that it returns the *IEnumerable* interface and includes a *yield* statement. Each iteration of the *while* loop extrapolates the next day until the end of the month is reached. The *yield* statement iterates the days as they are calculated:

```
using System;
using System.Collections;

namespace Donis.CSharpBook {
    public class Starter {
        public static void Main() {
            foreach (string day in ToEndOfMonth()) {
                Console.WriteLine(day);
            }
        }

        public static IEnumerable ToEndOfMonth() {
            DateTime date = DateTime.Now;
            int currMonth = date.Month;
            while (currMonth == date.Month) {
                string temp = currMonth.ToString() +
                    "/" + date.Day.ToString();
                date = date.AddDays(1);
                yield return temp;
            }
        }
    }
}
```

Complex iteration   Iterators are particularly useful when iterating complex data structures, such as linked lists. Each item in the list is considered a node. Each node maintains a reference to the previous and the next node. From any node, you can walk the linked list either forward or backward. The iteration is more complex for several reasons. First, the linked list can be iterated forward and backward during the same iteration. Second, fenceposts are less obvious than in other data structures. Fenceposts in arrays, stacks, queues, and other sequenced containers are found easily, which helps avoid fencepost error exceptions. Finally, the iteration can start from any node in the linked list, not necessarily just at the beginning or end. For example, if the iteration starts in the middle of the linked list, how do you enumerate all the nodes?

The following code gives a partial listing of the *Node* class. The key portion of the code is in the *GetEnumerator* method. In the first *while* loop, the linked list is iterating in reverse—from the current node to the beginning of the list. This is accomplished by walking the *prevNode* member of the node class. The current node is enumerated next. Finally, the second *while* loop iterates the linked list going forward from the current note to the end of the list by walking the *nextNode* members:

```
public class Node<T> {

    public Node(Node<T> node, T data) {
        m_Info = data;
        if (node == null) {
            if (firstNode != null) {
                Node<T> temp = firstNode;
                this.nextNode = temp;
                this.prevNode = null;
                temp.prevNode = this;
                firstNode = this;
                return;
            }
            prevNode = null;
            nextNode = null;
            firstNode = this;
            lastNode = this;
            return;
        }

        this.prevNode = node;
        this.nextNode = node.nextNode;
        node.nextNode = this;
        if (this.nextNode == null) {
            lastNode = this;
        }
        else {
            this.nextNode.prevNode = this;
        }
    }

    public void AddNode(T data) {
        this.nextNode = new Node<T>(this, data);
    }

    public IEnumerator<T> GetEnumerator () {
        Node<T> temp = prevNode;
        while (temp != null) {
            yield return temp.m_Info;
```

```
        temp = temp.prevNode;
    }
    yield return m_Info;
    temp = nextNode;
    while (temp != null) {
        yield return temp.m_Info;
        temp = temp.nextNode;
    }
}

private T m_Info;
private static Node<T> lastNode = null;
private static Node<T> firstNode = null;
private Node<T> prevNode = null;
private Node<T> nextNode = null;
}
```

Operator Overloading

Operator overloading creates operator behavior for user-defined types. The best-known example of operator overloading is in C++. The >> and << operators, which are normally the bitwise shift operators, are overloaded to support input and output streams. The >>operator becomes the extraction operator, while the << operator becomes the insertion operator. You can overload operators for any user-defined types in C# to make those types functionally similar to standard or primitive types. However, when overloading operators you should adhere to the general meaning of the operator. For example, don't overload an *operator +* for a user-defined type to perform some type of subtraction or deletion. That would definitely confuse users.

Operator overloading has been referred to as syntactic sugar because it is never required. Member functions are an adequate substitute for any operator overloading. Member functions are explicit, which is helpful and adds clarity to code. For example, instead of overloading an *operator +*, you can provide an *Add* method in the user-defined type. Operator overloading is implicit and might lead to inadvertent problems or make the application more difficult to maintain. Despite this, operator overloading is common and is an important concept in C#. Operator overloading is the topic of the next chapter.

Part III
More C# Language

Chapter 9
Operator Overloading

Operator overloading is used to add implicit or explicit operator behavior to types. Primitive types, such as integers, floats, and doubles, implicitly support most operators, including mathematical and logical operators. Other commonly used types, such as strings, support a limited set of operators. This intrinsic integration of standard operators in primitive types makes using built-in types convenient. You might want to use a user-defined type just as conveniently. Unfortunately, the C# compiler does not know how to apply standard operators to user-defined classes. For example, what does *zclass+zclass* mean? *Operator overloading* teaches the compiler how to interpret standard operators in the context of a user-defined type. You can overload more than one operator in a user-defined type and create the same convenience as is available when manipulating a primitive type.

User-defined types that represent numerical constructs benefit the most from operator overloading. Fractions, complex numbers, summations, the hexadecimal numerical system, matrixes, and other similar types have behavior that might be expressed with operator over-loading. For example, if your application deals with matrixes, then an overloaded plus operator for adding two matrixes together would be beneficial.

Operator overloading also is useful for casting one type to another. Conversion operators are available to convert or cast a user-defined type to some other type. With few exceptions, you can cast between primitive types. For example, you can implicitly cast from a short value to a long one. You also can cast explicitly from a long value to a short one, and cast between related user-defined types, which is the basis of polymorphism. However, what does it mean to cast a *ZClass* instance to an *int* value? *ZClass* is not a primitive and is unrelated to an *int*. The compiler must be taught how to make this conversion. Developers create conversion operators to instruct the compiler in the conversions of user-defined types to unrelated types.

Operator overloading should be intuitive and is never required. Do not stray from the underlying intent of the operator. For example, the *plus* operator should perform some type of addition. *System.String* overloads *operator+* to concatenate strings. Concatenation and addition are similar concepts. If the implementation of *operator+* for a string type truncated characters instead, that would be nonintuitive and confusing. Operator overloading can be overused and is not appropriate in all circumstances. Overloading *operator+* is a reasonable addition to a string class. However, overloading *operator-*, although possible, would be nonsensical in a string class. Remember, the overloaded operator must be intuitive to everyone, not just to the developer. Confer with peers and validate your perception of intuitive behavior. An alternative to operator overloading, and sometimes a better solution, is simply imple-menting a named method, such as an *Add* method instead of an overloading *operator+* and a *Subtract* method instead of overloading an *operator-*. There is the added benefit that named methods are called explicitly, whereas operator functions are called implicitly. Because overloaded operators are called implicitly, their use sometimes hides what is occurring. Explicit method calls avert the type of surprises that drive maintenance programmers crazy.

Mathematical and Logical Operators

Mathematical and logical operators can be unary, binary, or ternary. Most binary and unary operators can be overloaded in a user-defined type. The sole ternary operator, which is the conditional operator, cannot be overloaded. This is the list of operators, including mathematical and logical operators, that *cannot* be overloaded in a user-defined type:

- Dot operator (*identifier.member*)
- Call operator (*methodname()*)
- Assignment and compound assignment operators (=, +=, /=, %=, and so on)
- Conditional operators (&&, ||, and the ternary *? : operator*)
- The *checked* and *unchecked* operators
- The *new* operator
- The *typeof* operator
- The *as* and *is* operators
- The array operator (*[]*)
- Pointer operators

The compound assignment operators, such as += and /=, are implicitly overloaded by overloading the derivative operator. For example, the += and /= operators are implicitly overloaded by overloading the + and / operators, respectively.

Operator overloading cannot define new operators. For example, you could not define a ^^ operator, which does not otherwise exist.

Many developers are familiar with operator overloading in C++. There are some notable differences between operator overloading in the C++ and C# languages. This may be an issue when porting code from C++ to C#. For example in C++, you can overload the *assignment*, *new*, and *array* operators. This is not allowed in C# for the following reasons:

- The Garbage Collector (GC) is responsible for managing dynamic memory. For that reason, the *new* operator cannot be overloaded in managed code.

- The *array* operator is commonly overloaded in C++ to create a secure array, where fencepost errors are usually checked. Fencepost errors are detected automatically by the CLR, which eliminates one of the primary reasons to overload the *array* operator.

- Instead of overloading the *assignment* operator as in C++, implement the *ICloneable* interface in C#.

For these reasons, porting the code for operator overloading from C++ to C# might not be trivial.

Operator overloading defines the behavior of an operator in the context of a type. The operator then can be used in an expression in the normal manner. You cannot change the syntax, precedence, or associativity of an operator through operator overloading. In other words, overloading an operator does not change the core principles of using the operator. For example, assume that the division operator is overloaded in a user-defined type. The syntax for employing the division operator remains *obj1 / obj2*. Precedence is also preserved. In *++obj1 + obj2 / obj3 - obj4*, the division operation is evaluated before a plus or minus operator, but after the increment operator. Multiple division operations, as in *obj1 / obj2 + obj3 / obj4* are evaluated from left to right, which maintains the normal associativity.

Implementation

Overloaded operators are implemented as static and public functions. Other modifiers, such as *virtual* and *sealed,* are not allowed. As an overloaded function, the unary operator has a single operand, whereas the binary operator has two operands. Parameters of an overloaded operator cannot be *ref* or *out*.

Here is the signature for overloading a unary or binary operator method:

```
public static type operator unaryoperator(type operand)
```

```
public static type operator binaryoperator(type lhsoperand, type rhsoperand)
```

When overloading a unary operator, the single operand must be of the same type as the containing class. When overloading a binary operator, at least one of the parameters should be the same type as the containing type. The first and second parameter in an overloaded binary operator represent the left-hand side (*lhs*) and right-hand side (*rhs*) of the related expression, respectively. In the expression *obj + 5*, the object instance *obj* is passed as *lhsoperand* to the *operator+* method, while the integer value *5* is passed as *rhsoperand*. Therefore an *operator+* overload must exist for the *obj* type with those parameter types. Operator overloading must return some type. The return type cannot be void.

The following is an example of the implementation and use of an overloaded operator. *ZClass* is a simple wrapper for two integer fields. The *operator+* method is overloaded to add two *ZClass* instances. Because the *operator+* method is part of the class, it has access to the private members of that class. This is convenient when accessing fields of that type in the overloaded operator method. In this code, *operator+* is called implicitly in the expression: *obj1 + obj2*. You cannot call an overloaded operator-method explicitly:

```csharp
using System;

namespace Donis.CSharpBook {
    public class Starter {
        public static void Main() {
            ZClass obj1 = new ZClass(5,10);
            ZClass obj2 = new ZClass(15,20);
            ZClass obj3 = obj1 + obj2;
            Console.WriteLine(obj3.Total);
        }
    }

    public class ZClass {

        public ZClass(int _fielda, int _fieldb) {
            fielda = _fielda;
            fieldb = _fieldb;
        }

        public static ZClass operator+(ZClass lhs, ZClass rhs) {
            return new ZClass(lhs.fielda + rhs.fielda,
                lhs.fieldb + rhs.fieldb);
        }

        public int Total {
            get {
                return fielda + fieldb;
            }
        }

        protected int fielda, fieldb;
    }
}
```

Operator methods are inherited in a derived class. Remember that the type of one of the parameters is the containing type. For an inherited overloaded operator method, the type of this parameter is the base type. A derived instance will be passed as the base type when the inherited operator method is called. The return type also might be the base type. Of course, you could simply implement operator overloading again in the derived class and override the inherited behavior. The implementation in the derived class would replace the base over-loaded operator method.

In the following code, *ZClass* implements the *operator+* method. *YClass* derives from *ZClass* and inherits *operator+*. It also inherits the *fielda* and *fieldb* fields. (*ZClass.operator+* was shown in the previous code.) *YClass* also implements an *operator-* method. In *Main*, both the *operator+* (inherited) and *operator-* methods are used. Calling the *operator+* method on *YClass* parameters returns an instance of *ZClass*, which is the base type:

```
namespace Donis.CSharpBook {
    public class Starter {
        public static void Main() {
            YClass obj1 = new YClass(5,10);
            YClass obj2 = new YClass(15,20);
            ZClass obj3 = obj1 + obj2;
            Console.WriteLine(obj3.Total);
            YClass obj4 = obj1 - obj2;
            Console.WriteLine(obj4.Total);
        }
    }

    // Partial listing

    public class YClass : ZClass {

        public YClass(int _fielda, int _fieldb) :
            base(_fielda, _fieldb) {
        }

        public static YClass operator-(YClass lhs, YClass rhs) {
            return new YClass(lhs.fielda - rhs.fielda,
                lhs.fieldb - rhs.fieldb);
        }
    }
}
```

You can overload an already overloaded operator method. The general rules of overloading a function apply. Each overloaded operator method must have a unique signature. Operators typically are overloaded to use the containing type as the *lhs* operand, as the *rhs* operand, or as both.

In the following code, *operator+* is overloaded three times:

```
public static ZClass operator+(ZClass lhs, ZClass rhs) {
    return new ZClass(lhs.fielda + rhs.fielda,
        lhs.fieldb + rhs.fieldb);
}

public static ZClass operator+(ZClass lhs, int rhs) {
    return new ZClass(lhs.fielda + rhs,
        lhs.fieldb + rhs);
}


public static ZClass operator+(int lhs, ZClass rhs) {
    return new ZClass(lhs + rhs.fielda,
        lhs + rhs.fieldb);
}
```

All three operator methods are used in the following code:

```
obj3 = obj1 + obj2;
obj1 = obj1 + 10;
obj2 = 20 + obj2;
```

Operator overloading is not included in the Common Language Specification (CLS) and therefore this feature is not automatically included in all managed languages. For this reason, it is good policy to implement a parallel named method for each operator method. This provides an explicit alternative to implicit operator overloading. The named method should call the corresponding operator method, as demonstrated in the following code:

```
public class ZClass {

    public ZClass(int _fielda, int _fieldb) {
        fielda = _fielda;
        fieldb = _fieldb;
    }

    public static ZClass operator+(ZClass lhs, ZClass rhs) {
        return new ZClass(lhs.fielda + rhs.fielda,
            lhs.fieldb + rhs.fieldb);
    }

    public ZClass Add(ZClass rhs) {
        return this + rhs;
    }

    public int Total {
        get {
            return fielda + fieldb;
        }
    }

    protected int fielda, fieldb;
}
```

The semantics of overloading some mathematical and logical operators are unique. For these operators, which are described later in this chapter, special rules must be followed when implementing operator overloading.

Increment and Decrement Operators

The *Increment* (++) and *Decrement* (--) operators have special semantics. These are unary operators, where the operand type and the return type must be the containing class or a derivative. The *Increment* and *Decrement* operators accept a single parameter, which represents the current object. You must update this parameter *and* return this object in both the *Increment* and *Decrement* operators. Remember that overloaded operators should preserve the underlying meaning of the operator. The *Increment* and *Decrement* operators normally alter the current object. Finally, overloading the *Increment* or *Decrement* operator revises both the prefix and postfix usage of the operator.

Here is sample code showing an overloading of both the *Increment* and *Decrement* operators:

```
public class ZClass {

    public ZClass(int _fielda, int _fieldb) {
        fielda = _fielda;
        fieldb = _fieldb;
    }

    public static ZClass operator++(ZClass curr) {
        ++curr.fielda;
        ++curr.fieldb;
        return curr;
    }


    public static ZClass operator--(ZClass curr) {
        --curr.fielda;
        --curr.fieldb;
        return curr;
    }

    public int Total {
        get {
            return fielda + fieldb;
        }
    }

    public int fielda, fieldb;
}
```

LeftShift and *RightShift* Operators

The *LeftShift* and *RightShift* operators normally perform a bitwise shift. Both are binary operators. When overloading these operators, the first operand must be the same type as the containing class. The second operand must be an *int*, which specifies the amount of the shift. The return type can be anything but not void. The *LeftShift* and *RightShift* operators are not paired operator methods. You can implement them independently of each other. However, I would recommend implementing both because the methods are logically related:

```
using System;

namespace Donis.CSharpBook {
    public class Starter {
        public static void Main() {
            ZClass obj1 = new ZClass(5,10);
            ZClass obj2 = obj1 << 2;
```

```
            Console.WriteLine(obj2.Total);
        }
    }

    public class ZClass {

        public ZClass(int _fielda, int _fieldb) {
            fielda = _fielda;
            fieldb = _fieldb;
        }


        public static ZClass operator<<(ZClass curr, int shift) {
            int newa = curr.fielda << shift;
            int newb = curr.fieldb << shift;
            return new ZClass(newa, newb);
        }


        public static ZClass operator>>(ZClass curr, int shift) {
            int newa = curr.fielda >> shift;
            int newb = curr.fieldb >> shift;
            return new ZClass(newa, newb);
        }

        public int Total {
            get {
                return fielda + fieldb;
            }
        }

        public int fielda, fieldb;
    }
}
```

Operator *True* and *Operator False*

True or false logical operators are used in conditional expressions and sometimes in assign-ments. They are paired operator methods, which require both functions of the pair to be implemented. If either the *operator true* or *operator false* method is overloaded, both must be implemented. The *operator* methods for true or false are unary operators, where the current object is passed as the operand. The return type of the function should be *bool*. Add *operator true* and *operator false* methods to classes that have a false or true representation that can be interpreted from the state of the object. When the target object is used within a Boolean expression, the *operator true* method is called. The *operator false* method is called in other circumstances, such as in an *AND (&&)* expression. Overloading the *&&* operator is discussed later in this chapter.

Here is sample code of an *operator true* and *operator false* method pair. The *operator true* method is used in the *Main* method within the *if* statement:

```
using System;

namespace Switch {
    class Program {
        static void Main(string[] args) {
            LightSwitch light = new LightSwitch();
            light.wattage = 60;
            light.on = true;
            if (light) {
                Console.Write("Light is on.");
            }
            else {
                Console.WriteLine("Light is off.");
            }
        }
    }

    class LightSwitch {

        public int wattage
        {
            set; get;
        }

        public bool on
        {
            set; get;
        }

        public static bool operator true(LightSwitch item)
        {
            return item.on;
        }

        public static bool operator false(LightSwitch item)
        {
            return !item.on;
        }
    }
}
```

Paired Operators

In addition to *operator true* and *operator false*, the relational operators are paired operators. Paired operators enforce a practical policy—two related operators both should be overloaded to maintain consistency. For example, because they are logically related, you should overload both the *operator==* and *operator!=* methods. Here is the complete list of paired relational operators:

- *operator==* and *operator!=*

- *operator|* and *operator&*

- *operator||* and *operator&&*

Operator== and Operator!=

The overloaded *operator==* method should call the *Equals* method, which ensures that the *operator==* and the *Equals* methods exhibit consistent behavior. If not, the definition of equality for an instance will vary based on circumstances, which could be confusing. The *operator==* and *operator!=* methods are paired methods. When overloading these operators, you also must implement the *Equals* method in the same class, as demonstrated in the following code:

```
using System;

namespace Wallet {
    class Program {
        static void Main(string[] args) {
            Wallet bob = new Wallet();
            bob.ten = 5;
            bob.five = 1;
            Wallet sally = new Wallet();
            sally.fifty = 1;
            sally.dollar = 5;
            Console.WriteLine("Bob {0}: Sally {1}\n",
                bob.Total(), sally.Total());
            if (bob == sally) {
                Console.WriteLine(
                    "They have the same amount of money.");
            }
            else {
                Console.WriteLine(
                    "They do not have the same amount of money.");
            }
        }
    }

    class Wallet {
        public uint dollar
        {
            set;
            get;
        }

        public uint five
        {
```

```
            set;
            get;
        }

        public uint ten
        {
            set;
            get;
        }

        public uint twenty
        {
            set;
            get;
        }

        public uint fifty
        {
            set;
            get;
        }

        public static bool operator ==(Wallet lhs, Wallet rhs) {
            return lhs.Equals(rhs);
        }

        public static bool operator !=(Wallet lhs, Wallet rhs) {
            return !lhs.Equals(rhs);
        }

        public override bool Equals(object o) {
            return this.GetHashCode() == o.GetHashCode();
        }

        public override int GetHashCode() {
            return (int) Total();
        }

        public uint Total() {
            return dollar +
                (five * 5) +
                (ten * 10) +
                (twenty * 20) +
                (fifty * 50);
        }
    }
}
```

Operator| and Operator&

You also can overload *operator |* and *operator&* in the context of a user-defined class. The *operator|* and *operator&* methods already are overloaded for integral or Boolean operands. These operators perform a bitwise operation on integral values; *operator|* performs a bitwise

OR, while *operator&* does a bitwise *AND*. These operators perform a logical comparison when used with Boolean values; *operator|* does a logical *OR*, while *operator&* conducts a logical *AND*. The Boolean overload of the *operator|* and *operator&* functions will not short-circuit. Both the left and right operands always will be evaluated.

The following code introduces the *Membership* class, which naturally maintains membership lists. The *operator|* method is overloaded to combine membership lists. The *operator&* method is overloaded in the same class to return the intersection of two lists. This usage adheres to the general concept of these operators, which is always important when over-loading operators.

Here is the code:

```
using System;
using System.Collections.Generic;
using System.Collections;
using System.Linq;
using System.Text;

namespace ConsoleApplication2 {
    class Program {
        static void Main(string[] args) {
            Membership store1 = new Membership();
            store1.Add("bob");
            store1.Add("sally");

            Membership store2 = new Membership();
            store2.Add("sally");
            store2.Add("fred");

            Membership store3 = store1 & store2;
            Membership store4 = store1 | store2;

            foreach (string name in store3.GetNames()) {
                Console.Write(name + " ");
            }
            Console.WriteLine("\nend of list 1\n");

            foreach (string name in store4.GetNames()) {
                Console.Write(name + " ");
            }
            Console.WriteLine("\nend of list 2.");
        }
    }

    class Membership
    {

        private List<string> members =
            new List<string>();
```

```
public void Add(string name) {
    members.Add(name);
}

public List<string> Detach() {
    return members.ToList();
}

public void Attach(List<string> newlist) {
    members = newlist;
}

public string[] GetNames() {
    return members.ToArray();
}

public static Membership operator |(Membership m1, Membership m2) {
    Membership obj = new Membership();
    obj.Attach(m1.Detach());

    string[] names = m1.GetNames();
    foreach (string name in m2.GetNames()) {
        if (!names.Contains(name)) {
            obj.Add(name);
        }
    }
    return obj;
}

public static Membership operator &(Membership m1, Membership m2) {
    Membership obj = new Membership();
    List<string> names = m1.Detach();
    foreach (string name in m2.Detach()) {
        if (names.Contains(name)) {
            obj.Add(name);
        }
    }
    return obj;
}
    }
}
```

Operator|| and Operator&&

Operator|| and operator&& cannot be overloaded directly. These are the logical AND and OR operators, respectively. The operator|, operator&, operator true, and operator false methods combine to overload operator|| and operator&& functionally.

The operator&& or operator|| methods can short-circuit and partially evaluate. If the lhs of an && expression is false, the entire expression is false. This means the rhs can be ignored. For || expressions, the entire expression is true if the lhs is true. When that occurs, the rhs of the || expression can be ignored. The possibility of short-circuiting complicates the understanding of how the compiler overloads the && and || operators.

Following are the steps the compiler follows for evaluating *operator &&* for the expression *lhs && rhs*. Let us assume that *lhs* and *rhs* are the same type as the containing class. This is also the case for *operator&* and *operator|*.

1. The *operator false(lhs)* method is called.

2. If *operator false* returns *true*, the expression evaluates to the *operator true(lhs)* method.

3. If *operator false* returns *false*, the overloaded *operator& (lhs, rhs)* is called, which returns *result*. The expression evaluates to *operator true(result)*.

The compiler executes the following steps for evaluating the *operator||*, where the expression is *lhs || rhs*. (The class for *lhs* and *rhs* must be the containing class.)

1. The *operator true(lhs)* method is called.

2. If *operator true* returns *true*, the expression evaluates to the *operator true(lhs)* method.

3. If *operator true* returns *false*, the overloaded *operator |(lhs, rhs)* is called, which returns *result*. The expression evaluates to *operator true(result)*.

The following code is stubbed to document the sequence of calls for *operator&&* and *operator||*. This code confirms the order of execution for a user-defined *operator&&* or *operator||*:

```
using System;
using System.Collections.Generic;
using System.Text;

namespace ConsoleApplication3
{
    class Program
    {
        static void Main(string[] args)
        {
            ZClass obj1 = new ZClass();
            obj1.tag = "lhs";

            // change obj1.state to test scenarios

            obj1.state = false;

            ZClass obj2 = new ZClass();
            obj2.tag = "rhs";

            obj2.state = false;
            if (obj1 || obj2) {
                Console.WriteLine("ojb1 || obj2 is true.");
            }
            else {
                Console.WriteLine("ojb1 || obj2 is false.");
            }
        }
    }
}
```

```
class ZClass {
    public static bool operator false(ZClass obj) {
        Console.WriteLine("operator false for " + obj.tag);
        return obj.state;
    }

    public static bool operator true(ZClass obj) {
        Console.WriteLine("operator true for " + obj.tag);
        return obj.state;
    }


    public static ZClass operator &(ZClass obj1, ZClass obj2) {
        Console.WriteLine("operator & : {0} {1} ",
            obj1.tag, obj2.tag);
        ZClass obj = new ZClass();
        obj.tag = "[obj from operator &]";
        return obj;
    }

    public static ZClass operator |(ZClass obj1, ZClass obj2) {
        Console.WriteLine("operator | : {0} {1} ",
            obj1.tag, obj2.tag);
        ZClass obj = new ZClass();
        obj.tag = "[obj from operator |]";
        return obj;
    }

    public string tag = "";
    public bool state = false;
    }
}
```

Conversion Operators

Conversion operators facilitate the implicit or explicit casting of user-defined types to built-in types or even other user-defined types. Developers implement a conversion operator so the compiler will know how to convert a user-defined type to another type. Like mathematical and logical operators, the primary reason for implementing conversion operators is convenience. It is never required. You could as easily expose *ToType* methods, such as *ToInt*, *ToFloat*, or *ToDecimal*. You are already familiar with *ToString*, which converts from any type to a string.

An implicit cast is available where truncation will not result (a safe cast), whereas explicit casting is required when truncation might occur. For primitive types, a safe cast is available when there is no potential loss of precision or accuracy. When there is potential loss of precision or accuracy, an explicit cast is required. For example, an *int* can be implicitly assigned to a *long*. A *long* value is eight bytes and an *int* value is four bytes. Therefore, no precision is lost. This makes the cast from *int* to *long* safe. The *int* value will be promoted to a *long* value. The promotion occurs silently—no warning or notice is given. The reverse, where a *long* is assigned to an *int*, requires an explicit cast. Why? There is a loss of precision. Implicit and explicit casting is shown in the following code:

```
int a = 5;
long b = 10;
b = a;          // implicit cast
a = (int) b;    // explicit cast
```

C# does not support conversion constructors. A conversion constructor is a one-argument constructor used to create an instance of a type from a different type. Conversion constructors are supported in C++ but not in C#. Conversion constructors were convenient—too convenient, in fact. Conversion constructors sometimes were called transparently when a compiler error for mismatched types was probably more appropriate.

Overload the cast behavior selectively with conversion operator methods. Here is the signature of a conversion operator:

```
public static implicit operator returntype(type obj)
```

```
public static explicit operator returntype(type obj)
```

The conversion operator syntax has many similarities with overloading mathematical and relational operators. Conversion operators must be public and static. Other modifiers, such as *virtual* and *sealed*, are not allowed. Conversion operators that are implicit do not require casting, whereas explicit conversion operators require casting for invocation. I recommend explicit casting in all circumstances. Implicit casting allows the conversion function to be called transparently and sometimes inadvertently, which might have unintended side effects. With explicit casting, developers affirmatively state their intentions through casting. That should be required. The sole parameter is an object of the type from which you are converting. Either the return type or the parameter type should be of the same type as the containing class. If the return type is the containing class, you are describing a conversion to that type. If the parameter is the containing class, the function describes a conversion from the containing type to another type.

Here is sample code of implicit and explicit conversion methods. The *ZClass* has two conversion operators. The first conversion operator converts *ZClass* to an *int*. The second conversion operator converts a *YClass* to a *ZClass*:

```
using System;

namespace Donis.CSharpBook {
    public class Starter {
        public static void Main() {
            ZClass obj1 = new ZClass(5,10);
            int ival = obj1;
```

```
            YClass obj2 = new YClass(5);
            ZClass obj3 = obj2;          // error
            ZClass obj3 = (ZClass) obj2;
        }
    }

    public class ZClass {

        public ZClass(int _fielda, int _fieldb) {
            fielda = _fielda;
            fieldb = _fieldb;
        }

        public static implicit operator int(ZClass curr) {
            return curr.fielda + curr.fieldb;
        }

        public static explicit operator ZClass(YClass curr) {
            return new ZClass(curr.field / 2, curr.field / 2);
        }

        public int fielda, fieldb;
    }

    public class YClass {

        public YClass(int _field) {
            propField = _field;
        }

        private int propField;
        public int field {
            get {
                return propField;
            }
            set {
                propField = value;
            }
        }
    }
}
```

Conversion operators often are overloaded to provide the level of flexibility and functionality
available with a primitive type, which can support a variety of casts. In the following code,
the conversion operator is overloaded several times to support the conversion of *ZClass*
instances to a variety of types:

```
using System;

namespace Donis.CSharpBook {

    public class ZClass {

        public ZClass(int _fielda, int _fieldb) {
            fielda = _fielda;
```

```
            fieldb = _fieldb;
        }

        public static explicit operator int(ZClass curr) {
            return curr.fielda + curr.fieldb;
        }

        public static explicit operator float(ZClass curr) {
            return (float) (curr.fielda + curr.fieldb);
        }

        public static explicit operator short(ZClass curr) {
            return (short) (curr.fielda + curr.fieldb);
        }

        // and so on

        public int fielda, fieldb;
    }
}
```

The *Operator String* Operator

The *operator string* operator is a special conversion operator that converts a user-defined type to a string. This appears to overlap with the *ToString* method, which is inherited from *System.Object*. Actually, every type is also provided an *operator string* method automatically, which simply calls the polymorphic *ToString* method. Look at the following code. If a class overrides both the *ToString* and *operator string* methods, which method is called by *Console.WriteLine*?

```
using System;

namespace Donis.CSharpBook {
    public class Starter {
        public static void Main() {
            ZClass obj = new ZClass();
            Console.WriteLine(obj);
        }
    }

    public class ZClass {

        public static implicit operator string(ZClass curr) {
            return "ZClass.operator string";
        }

        public override string ToString() {
            return "ZClass.ToString";
        }
    }
}
```

The preceding program displays *ZClass.operator string*. The *operator string* method is called to convert the *Console.WriteLine* operand. Unlike the default *operator string* method, the custom *operator string* method in this code does not call *ToString*. In most circumstances, calling *ToString* in the *operator string* method is the best practice eliminating the need to implement a separate *operator string* method. However, the default *operator string* method already implements this behavior. You simply override the *ToString* method with the proper string representation of the type. Inconsistencies and confusion can occur when the *operator string* method and *ToString* have separate and unrelated implementations.

A Practical Example

Until now, simple examples have been provided to demonstrate operator overloading and conversion operators. The following code contains a more practical example. Summation notation iterates and totals an expression in a specified range. Figure 9-1 provides three examples of summation notation.

$$\sum_{i=1}^{5} i \qquad \text{The answer is 15.}$$

$$\sum_{i=3}^{10} 2i \qquad \text{The answer is 104.}$$

$$\sum_{i=1}^{3} i^2 \qquad \text{The answer is 14.}$$

FIGURE 9-1 Examples of summation notation

Summation is not a predefined type in C#. The following class defines the *Summation* type. It contains several methods, and the objective is to make the *Summation* class as similar to a primitive type as possible:

- The *Summation* class has three constructors. The two- and three-argument constructors call the four-argument constructor.

- The *Calculate* method calculates the result of the summation, and updates the result whenever any of the parameters change.

- The class has two *operator+* methods, which allow instances of the class to be either the *lhs* operand or the *rhs* operand in a binary expression. The *operator+* methods of the *Summation* class extend the iteration by adding to the stop value of the summation. A new instance with an updated number of iterations is returned.

- The *operator++* method extends the number of iterations of the current object by one. The current object is then returned.

- The class has an operator *int* conversion constructor. This method converts a *Summation* object into an *int* value by returning the result of the summation.

- There are two string functions: *ToString* returns the result of the operation; *ToNotationString* displays in summation notation the object and the parameters of the summation.

Here is the code for the class:

```
public class Summation {

    public Summation(int _start, int _stop) :
            this(_start, _stop, 1, 1) {
    }

    public Summation(int _start, int _stop,
        int _product) :
            this(_start, _stop, _product, 1) {
    }

    public Summation(int _start, int _stop,
        int _product, int _power) {
        start=_start;
        stop=_stop;
        product=_product;
        power=_power;
        Calculate();
    }

    private void Calculate() {
        propResult=0;
        int temp;
        for (int count = start; count <= stop;
                ++count) {
            temp = (int)Math.Pow(count, power);
            temp = temp * product;
            propResult += temp;
        }
    }
```

```
    public static Summation operator+(Summation sum, int val) {
        return new Summation(sum.start, sum.stop + val,
            sum.product, sum.power);
    }

    public static Summation operator+(int val, Summation sum) {
        return new Summation(sum.start, sum.stop + val,
            sum.product, sum.power);
    }

    public static Summation operator++(Summation sum) {
        ++sum.stop;
        sum.Calculate();
        return sum;
    }

    public static explicit operator int(Summation sum) {
        return sum.propResult;
    }

    private int propResult;
    public int Result {
        get {
            return propResult;
        }
    }

    public override string ToString() {
        return propResult.ToString();
    }

    public string ToNotationString() {
        string line1 = "\n  " + stop.ToString();
        string line2 = "\n\neeeee";
        string line4 = "\nee     "+
            (product == 1 ? "" : product.ToString()) + "i";
        string line3 = "\ne" + new string(' ', line4.Length - 2);
        line3 += (power == 1 ? "" : power.ToString());
        string line5 = "\ne";
        string line6 = "\neeeee";
        string line7 = "\n\n i=" + start.ToString();
        return line1 + line2 + line3 + line4 + line5 + line6 + line7;
    }

    private int start;
    private int stop;
    private int product;
    private int power;
}
```

The following code tests the *Summation* type. In this example, the parameters of the summation are read from the command line in the following order: *start, stop, product,* and *power.* The number of iterations is from the start value to the stop value. In *Main* of the example code, the summation notation is displayed, followed by the result. The number of iterations then is increased using the *operator++*, and the new results are displayed:

```
public static void Main(string [] argv) {
    Summation sum =
        new Summation(int.Parse(argv[0]),
                      int.Parse(argv[1]),
                      int.Parse(argv[2]),
                      int.Parse(argv[3]));
    Console.WriteLine();
    Console.WriteLine(sum.ToNotationString());
    Console.WriteLine("\n[Result = {0}]",
        sum.Result);

    ++sum;
    int isum = (int)sum;
    Console.WriteLine();
    Console.WriteLine(sum.ToNotationString());
    Console.WriteLine("\n[Result = {0}]", isum);
}
```

Operator Overloading Internals

Internally, Microsoft Intermediate Language (MSIL) does not support operator methods. For that reason, the C# compiler converts operator methods into normal functions. Figure 9-2 presents a view of the *Summation* class discussed in the previous section. Instead of *operator* methods, there are functions such as *op_Addition* and *op_Explicit*.

FIGURE 9-2 A view of the Summation class

In Table 9-1, the functions that the C# compiler substitutes for mathematical and logical operators are listed.

TABLE 9-1 **Replacement methods for mathematical and logical operators**

Operator	Replacement method
operator+	op_Addition
operator-	op_Subtraction
operator*	op_Multiply
operator++	op_Increment
operator--	op_Decrement
operator/	op_Division
operator%	op_Modulus
operator&	op_BitwiseAnd
operator &&	op_LogicalAnd
operator|	op_BitwiseOr
operator ||	op_LogicalOr
operator^	op_ExclusiveOr
operator false	op_False
operator true	op_True
operator>>	op_RightShift
operator<<	op_LeftShift
operator!	op_LogicalNot
operator~	op_OnesComplement

Table 9-2 lists the conventional functions substituted for relational operators.

TABLE 9-2 **Replacement methods for relational operators**

Operator	Replacement method
operator>	op_GreaterThan
operator<	op_LessThan
operator>=	op_GreaterThanOrEqual
operator<=	op_LessThanOrEqual
operator==	op_Equality
operator!=	op_Inequality

Conversion operators are implemented as *op_Explicit* and *op_Implicit* methods. The methods are overloaded for every combination of the explicit or implicit conversion operator provided in the contained type. The following class has two explicit operators and one implicit conversion operator:

```
public class ZClass{

    public static explicit operator int(ZClass obj) {
        return 0;
    }
```

```
public static explicit operator float(ZClass obj) {
    return (float) 0;
}
public static implicit operator double(ZClass obj) {
    return 0;
}
}
```

Figure 9-3 is an internal view of the class. There are two overloaded *op_Explicit* methods and a single *op_Implicit* method.

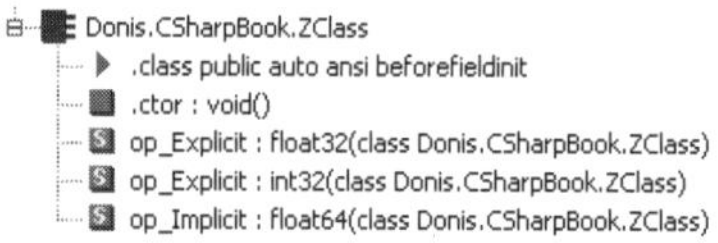

Donis.CSharpBook.ZClass
  ▶ .class public auto ansi beforefieldinit
  .ctor : void()
  op_Explicit : float32(class Donis.CSharpBook.ZClass)
  op_Explicit : int32(class Donis.CSharpBook.ZClass)
  op_Implicit : float64(class Donis.CSharpBook.ZClass)

FIGURE 9-3 A view of *ZClass*

Delegates and Events

The next chapter pertains to delegates and events, which are related topics. Function pointers are prevalent in unmanaged programming languages and helpful in streamlining algorithms and choosing functions at run time rather than statically at compile time. As function pointers, functions can be treated as local variables, function parameters, or even return values—which adds considerable flexibility in the way they are managed and called. Because pointers are simply pointers into raw memory, function pointers are not safe. .NET offers a type-safe version of function pointers called *delegates*. Delegates provide the same flexibility as function pointers but in a type-safe manner.

Delegates often are used as callbacks, where functions are called in response to an event or on demand. The *Event* model promotes an effective paradigm for callbacks, where there are publishers and subscribers. Publishers expose something that happens—better known as an *event*. One or more subscribers subscribe to that event with a delegate. The publisher then calls all the functions when the event occurs.

Chapter 10
Delegates and Events

A *delegate* is an abstraction of one or more function pointers. With a delegate, you can treat a function as data, which includes using a delegate as a variable or data member. Delegates allow functions to be passed as parameters, returned from a function as a value, and even stored in an array. Unlike function pointers in other languages, particularly C and C++, delegates are type-safe, object-oriented, and secure, which reduces common problems associated with using function pointers.

Delegates are derived from the *System.MulticastDelegate* class, which itself is derived from *System.Delegate*. *System.MulticastDelegate* is a reference type and is an interface for managing and executing delegates. An instance of a delegate encapsulates a function pointer and a target object. When a delegate is invoked, the delegate calls the function on that object.

Delegates have a signature and a return type. A function that is added to the delegate must be compatible with this signature, which helps make the delegate type-safe. The signature of the function is more important than the type. Regardless of the object or type that binds the function, it is assignable to any delegate with the same signature.

Functions called through a delegate have the security context of the caller, which prevents a delegate from performing a task not available to a lower-privilege client. Invoke only delegates from a known source. Executing code from an unknown source (including a delegate) is always dangerous. Use code access security to protect your code from misbehaving delegates.

In addition to general purposes, delegates can be used for callbacks, events, and threads. Callbacks are valuable in many scenarios, such as peer-to-peer relationships. In a peer-to-peer relationship between objects, peers can exchange delegates and send bilateral messages. Events support a publisher/subscriber model. A publisher exposes events. The underlying type of an event is a delegate. A subscriber registers functions (event handlers) to be called when the event occurs. Finally, the function reference in a delegate can be an entry point for a thread. This chapter focuses on general function pointers, callbacks, and events. Threads are mentioned but only as related to these other topics.

Delegates

There are several standard steps to define, create, and then invoke a delegate:

1. Define a delegate with the *delegate* keyword. The signature of functions referenced by the delegate must match the delegate signature. For example:

```
public delegate int DelegateClass(string info);
```

2. Create an instance of a delegate using the *new* keyword. You can pass a function reference to the constructor. Delegates also can be initialized implicitly without a constructor. Here are two different examples of initializing a delegate:

```
DelegateClass obj1 = new DelegateClass(MethodA);
DelegateClass obj2 = MethodA; // implicit
```

3. Invoke a delegate with the call operator *( )*. The call operator is convenient, but makes it harder to discern delegate invocation from a regular function call. Alternatively, invoke the delegate with the *Invoke* method, which clearly distinguishes delegate invocation from a normal function call:

```
obj1("1");
obj2.Invoke("2"); // Explicit delegate invocation alternative
```

4. As with any object, when the delegate is no longer needed, set the delegate instance to *null:*

```
obj = null;
```

The complete list of the example application is shown in the following code. There are two instances of delegates. The *MethodA* function is added to both delegates, and then they are both invoked. This calls *MethodA* twice—once for each delegate:

```
using System;

namespace Donis.CSharpBook {

    public delegate int DelegateClass(string info);

    public class Steps {

        public static void Main() {
            DelegateClass obj1 = new DelegateClass(MethodA);
            DelegateClass obj2 = MethodA; // implicit
            obj1("1");
            obj2.Invoke("2"); // Explicit delegate invocation alternative
            obj1 = null;
            obj2 = null;
        }

        public static int MethodA(string info) {
            Console.WriteLine("Steps.MethodA");
            return int.Parse(info);
        }
    }
}
```

Defining a Delegate

The *delegate* keyword defines a new delegate. A delegate definition looks like a function signature, but it defines a new delegate type. Function pointers matching the delegate signature and return type can be stored into the delegate. Therefore, only functions with similar signatures can be added and then called through the delegate. The following code defines a new delegate. Internally this generates a class named *DelegateClass*. Because defining a delegate creates a new class, delegates can be declared anywhere a class declaration is appropriate. A delegate can be defined in a namespace as a namespace member and within a class as a nested class. A delegate cannot be used as a data member of a class or as a local variable within a method.

```
public delegate int DelegateClass(string info);
```

This is the syntax for defining a new delegate class:

accessibility delegate *return delegatename(parameterslist)*

Accessibility of a delegate is limited to the valid accessibility of classes, such as public or private. The remainder of the syntax defines the signature and return type of the delegate. The delegate type is named *delegatename*.

Creating a Delegate

As a class, use the *new* keyword to create an instance of a delegate. As mentioned, delegates are derived from the *System.MulticastDelegate* type. Multicast delegates are repositories of zero or more function references. The list of functions referenced in a multicast delegate is called the *invocation list*. When multiple function references have been added to a delegate, the functions are called on a first-in, first-out (FIFO) basis.

The delegate constructor has a single parameter, which is the first method added to the delegate. For an instance method, use the *object.method* format. For a static method, use the *class.method* format. If the static method and delegate are in the same class, the class name is not required. You can simply use the function name as the parameter. The following code initializes a delegate in a variety of ways:

```
using System;

namespace Donis.CSharpBook {

    public delegate void DelegateClass();

    public class Constructors {

        public static void Main() {
            DelegateClass del1 = new
                DelegateClass(Constructors.MethodA);
```

```
            DelegateClass del2 = new DelegateClass(MethodA);

            ZClass obj = new ZClass();
            DelegateClass del3 = new DelegateClass(obj.MethodB);
        }

        public static void MethodA() {
        }
    }
    public class ZClass {

        public void MethodB() {
        }
    }
}
```

You can assign a function reference directly to a delegate and omit the new operator. This is called *delegate inference*. Delegate inference infers a delegate signature from the function reference. Assigning the function reference creates and initializes the delegate. Although delegate inference is more concise, the intent is not as obvious. Here is the previous code, changed to use delegate inference:

```
DelegateClass del1 = Constructors.MethodA;
DelegateClass del2 = MethodA;

ZClass obj = new ZClass();
DelegateClass del3 = obj.MethodB;
```

As previously mentioned, the signature of a function reference must match the signature of a target delegate. Through contravariance and covariance, this matching can be expanded.

Contravariance and Covariance

When is a function reference compatible with a delegate? Each parameter of the function reference must be the same type or a derivation type of the corresponding parameter type of the delegate—this is called *contravariance*. In this manner, the parameters of the delegate can refine that of the function reference. The return value of the delegate must be the same or a derivation of the return type of the function reference—this is called *covariance*. Contravariance and covariance expand the set of methods assignable to a delegate while maintaining type-safety. Here is an example of both contravariance and covariance:

```
using System;

namespace Donis.CSharpBook {
    delegate ZClass DelegateClass(BClass obj);
    public class Starter {
        public static void Main() {
            DelegateClass del = MethodA;
        }

        public static YClass MethodA(AClass obj) {
```

```
            return null;
        }
    }

    public class ZClass {
    }

    public class YClass : ZClass {
    }

    public class AClass {
    }

    public class BClass : AClass {
    }
}
```

In the preceding code, this is the signature of the delegate:

```
delegate ZClass DelegateClass(BClass obj);
```

And this is the signature of the function pointer:

```
public static YClass MethodA(AClass obj)
```

The signature of the delegate and function pointer are not exactly the same. This is all right because the parameter of the delegate (*BClass*) refines the parameter of the function (*AClass*), which is contravariance. In addition, the return type of the function (*YClass*) refines the return type of the delegate (*ZClass*), which is covariance.

Invoking a Delegate

Delegates are invoked through the call operator ( ) or through the *Invoke* method. The C# compiler translates the call operator into an *Invoke* method, which has the same signature as the delegate and calls the function references aggregated by the delegate. If the delegate contains four function references, invoking the delegate will call all four functions in the delegate. They are called in the same order as they are placed in the delegate. The parameters of the delegate are input arguments for the function calls. Delegates can have non-void returns, which means all functions contained in the delegate must return a value. The return from the last function becomes the return value of the delegate.

Arrays of Delegates

Creating an array of delegates is similar to declaring arrays of any type. Arrays of delegates can provide elegant solutions that would otherwise be unavailable. For example, a sample program presents the user with ten tasks. Users then can choose specific tasks at run time. A *switch* statement is one solution, where each case of the *switch* statement executes a chosen task. However, this approach is not extensible. Suppose three lines of code are required to call each task. Let us assume the next revision of the application goes from ten tasks to 20. The total amount of code doubles. This solution requires linear growth and is not particularly scalable. With an array of delegates, regardless of the number of tasks, the solution is simply a change to the single line of code that declares the delegate array—whether you are adding one task or a thousand. Even if additional tasks are added, the number of lines of code remains constant. This solution is more scalable than the *switch* statement approach. In the following code, an array of delegates facilitates invoking a task from a menu of choices. An array of delegates is created, one for each of the three tasks. When the user selects a task, an index into the delegate array is set. Executing the delegate takes two lines of code. You could add an additional 100 tasks and the number of lines of code would remain constant. It would take the same two lines of code to execute any of the 100 tasks:

```
using System;

namespace Donis.CSharpBook {

    public delegate void Task();

    public class Starter {

        public static void Main() {
            // array of delegates
            Task[] tasks = { MethodA, MethodB, MethodC };
            string resp;
            do {
                Console.WriteLine("TaskA - 1");
                Console.WriteLine("TaskB - 2");
                Console.WriteLine("TaskC - 3");
                Console.WriteLine("Exit - x");
                resp = Console.ReadLine();
                if (resp.ToUpper() == "X") {
                    break;
                }
                try {
                    int choice = int.Parse(resp) - 1;
                    // as promised, one line of code to invoke
                    // the correct method.
                    tasks[choice]();
                }
                catch {
                    Console.WriteLine("Invalid choice");
                }
            } while (true);
        }

        public static void MethodA() {
            Console.WriteLine("Doing TaskA");
        }

        public static void MethodB() {
            Console.WriteLine("Doing TaskB");
        }
```

```
        public static void MethodC() {
            Console.WriteLine("Doing TaskC");
        }
    }
}
```

System.MulticastDelegate Class

Delegates default to multicast delegates, which inherit from the *System.MulticastDelegate* class. A multicast delegate is similar to a basket. Multiple function references can be dropped into the basket. The list of functions is stored in an invocation list, which can even include multiple instances of the same function. When you invoke the delegate, the contents of the basket, which contains function references, is called in FIFO order. Multicast delegates are useful for invoking a chain of functions.

Combining delegates   Multiple delegates are combined using the *Combine* method, the plus operator (+), or the += compound assignment operator. *Combine* is a static method. The *Combine* method is called with either two delegate parameters or an array of delegates. The method returns the combined delegate. After combining, the function references of both delegates are in a single multicast delegate.

The following code combines two delegates that separately hold functions *MethodA* and *MethodB*. When the *Combine* delegate is invoked, *MethodA* is run first and *MethodB* second. This is the order in which the function pointers are added to the multicast delegate. Both the *Combine* method and the += operators are shown in this code, with the *Combine* statement commented out to avoid duplication:

```
using System;

namespace Donis.CSharpBook {
 public delegate void DelegateClass();
    public class Starter {
        public static void Main() {
            DelegateClass del = MethodA;
            del += MethodB;
            // del = (DelegateClass) DelegateClass.Combine(
            //     new DelegateClass[] { MethodA, MethodB });
            del();
        }
        public static void MethodA() {
            Console.WriteLine("MethodA...");
        }

        public static void MethodB() {
            Console.WriteLine("MethodB...");
        }
    }
}
```

Removing delegates To remove function references from a multicast delegate, use the *Remove* method, the minus operator (-), or the -= compound assignment operator. *Remove* is a static method that accepts the multicast delegate as the first parameter and a delegate as the second parameter. The second delegate contains the function reference to be removed. Be careful not to remove all delegates inadvertently from a multicast delegate, which will cause a runtime error when the delegate is invoked. The following code removes *MethodB* from a multicast delegate that contains *MethodA* and *MethodB*. When the delegate is invoked, *MethodA* is invoked, but not *MethodB*. The three ways to remove a delegate are shown, with the *Combine* statement and minus operator commented out to avoid duplication:

```csharp
using System;

namespace Donis.CSharpBook {

    public delegate void DelegateClass();

    public class Starter {
        public static void Main() {
            DelegateClass del = MethodA;
            del += MethodB;
            del += MethodC;
            del = del - MethodB;

            // del = (DelegateClass) DelegateClass.Remove(
            //     del, (DelegateClass) MethodB);
            // del -= MethodB;
            del();
        }
        public static void MethodA() {
            Console.WriteLine("MethodA...");
        }

        public static void MethodB() {
            Console.WriteLine("MethodB...");
        }

        public static void MethodC() {
            Console.WriteLine("MethodC...");
        }
    }
}
```

Invocation List

Multicast delegates maintain an invocation list, which has an entry for each function reference of the multicast delegate. Entries are added to the invocation list in the same order in which the functions are added. *GetInvocationList* returns the invocation list as an array of delegates, which contain each function in the multicast delegate.

Here is the syntax of the *GetInvocationList* method:

delegate[] *GetInvocationList*()

The following code gets the invocation list from a multicast delegate. The list is then iterated and the name of each function is displayed. The *Delegate.Method* property returns a *MethodInfo* object, which provides information on the function reference, including the name:

```
using System;

namespace Donis.CSharpBook {
    public delegate void DelegateClass();
    public class Starter {
        public static void Main() {
            DelegateClass del = (DelegateClass)
            DelegateClass.Combine(new DelegateClass[]
                { MethodA, MethodB, MethodA, MethodB } );
            del();
            foreach (DelegateClass item in del.GetInvocationList()) {
                Console.WriteLine(item.Method.Name +
                    " in invocation list.");
            }

        }
        public static void MethodA() {
            Console.WriteLine("MethodA...");
        }

        public static void MethodB() {
            Console.WriteLine("MethodB...");
        }
    }
}
```

A multicast delegate can have reference parameters in the delegate signature. When the delegate is invoked, the reference is passed in sequence to the called functions. In this manner, reference parameters are a way for functions on an invocation list to share state. Parameters that are value types are not shareable across the functions. Because the invocation list is called in order, beginning with the first function, each successive entry in the invocation list can view changes made to a reference parameter by previous functions. Furthermore, functions in invocation lists that have the same target object or class share the state of that object or class. If one reference modifies a field in the target object or class, any other functions that are bound to the same target can view the change. The following code uses the reference parameter of a multicast delegate as a counter. The delegate has a value and reference parameter—both are incremented. Changes to the count for the value parameter is lost between function calls in the invocation list. However, changes to the count for the reference parameter persists:

```
using System;

namespace Donis.CSharpBook {
```

```
        public delegate void DelegateClass(int valCount,
            ref int refCount);

        public class Counter {
            public static void Main() {
                DelegateClass del = (DelegateClass) AddOne +
                    (DelegateClass) AddThree + (DelegateClass) AddOne;
                int valCount = 0;
                int refCount = 0;
                del(valCount, ref refCount);
                Console.WriteLine("Value count = {0}",
                    valCount); // 0
                Console.WriteLine("Reference count = {0}",
                    refCount); // 5
            }

            public static void AddOne(int valCount, ref int refCount) {
                ++valCount;
                ++refCount;
            }

            public static void AddThree(int valCount, ref int refCount) {
                valCount += 3;
                refCount += 3;
            }
        }
    }
```

You can access the invocation list to execute individual functions of the multicast delegate directly. There are two reasons to directly invoke the functions from the invocation list. One reason is to invoke the delegates explicitly so you can obtain the return value of each. When the invocation list is invoked implicitly, the return value of only the last function is obtained. You might also want to invoke the invocation list directly to accommodate special circumstances (for example, to handle exceptions).

The following code uses the invocation list to calculate a factorial. The *Incrementer* method increments a number, which is a reference parameter. The incremented value is returned from the method. Five delegates are created and initialized with the *Increment* method and then combined into a multicast delegate. The *foreach* loop iterates the invocation list and invokes each method with the return value from the previous method. This is how the factorial is calculated:

```
using System;

namespace Donis.CSharpBook {

    public delegate int IncrementDelegate(
        ref short refCount);

    public class Factorial {
        public static void Main() {
```

```
        IncrementDelegate[] values =
            { Incrementer, Incrementer,
              Incrementer, Incrementer,
              Incrementer };
        IncrementDelegate del =
            (IncrementDelegate) IncrementDelegate.Combine(values);
        long result = 1;
        short count = 1;
        foreach (IncrementDelegate number in del.GetInvocationList()) {
            result = result * number(ref count);
        }
        Console.WriteLine("{0} factorial is {1}",
        del.GetInvocationList().Length, result);
    }

    public static int Incrementer(ref short refCount) {
        return refCount++;
    }
  }
}
```

Methods and properties   Several members of the delegate type, such as *GetInvocationList*, have already been introduced. Table 10-1 is a list of other public methods and properties of the *MulticastDelegate* type. Many of these members are inherited from *System.Delegate*.

TABLE 10-1   Additional *MulticastDelegate* members

Member	Description
BeginInvoke	Invokes a delegate asynchronously.
Combine	Combines delegates into a multicast delegate. This is a static method.
CreateDelegate	Creates a delegate at run time. This is a static method.
DynamicInvoke	Dynamically invokes a delegate that was created at run time.
EndInvoke	Requests the results from a delegate that was executed asynchronously.
Invoke	Executes a delegate, which calls all functions contained in the delegate.
Method	This property returns the *MethodInfo* type for the function reference.
Remove	Removes a delegate from a multicast delegate. This is a static method.
RemoveAll	Removes all function references of a delegate from the invocation list of another delegate. This is a static method.
Target	This is a property that returns the object that is bound to the function reference. If the function is static, *null* is returned.

Generics and Delegates

A delegate can contain closed generic methods, but open generic methods cannot be added to a delegate. Some existing permutation of the generic method must be compatible with the signature of the delegate. Otherwise, the generic cannot be added to the invocation list.

If the generic method contains actual parameters, the type is inferred. However, the return type cannot be inferred and must be specified.

In addition, the delegate itself can be generic and closed when the delegate is created. Functions added to a generic delegate need to match the signature of the closed generic delegate.

Here is an example of a normal delegate initialized with a generic method:

```
using System;

namespace Donis.CSharpBook {
    public delegate void DelegateClass(int data);
    public class Starter {
        public static void Main() {
            DelegateClass del1 = MethodA<int>;
            del1(5);
            DelegateClass del2 = MethodA;
            del2(10); // inferred
        }

        public static void MethodA<T>(T data) {
            Console.WriteLine("MethodA ({0})", data);
        }
    }
}
```

Here is an example of a generic delegate initialized with a normal method:

```
using System;

namespace Donis.CSharpBook {
    public delegate void DelegateClass<T>(T data);
    public class Starter {
        public static void Main() {
            DelegateClass<string> del = MethodA;
            del("text");
        }

        public static void MethodA(string data) {
            Console.WriteLine("MethodA ({0})", data);
        }
    }
}
```

Asynchronous Invocation

Delegate.Invoke and the delegate call operator ( ) invoke function references synchronously. Delegates also can be invoked asynchronously on a separate worker thread. Function references of a delegate that perform a time-consuming task might benefit by running on a separate thread. This is especially true for Microsoft Windows Forms applications, where the responsiveness of the user interface during a long task is a concern. The user interface could freeze during an extended task and inconvenience the user. Asynchronous delegates are also useful when monitoring hardware devices, communicating with network services waiting for timer routines, and more. Synchronous solutions are simpler. Developers should understand thread synchronization when invoking a delegate asynchronously, which undoubtedly adds complexity. Therefore, use synchronous solutions whenever possible.

Use *BeginInvoke* and *EndInvoke* methods for asynchronous invocation.

BeginInvoke Method

BeginInvoke can be called on delegates holding a single function reference. *BeginInvoke* adds the operation to a thread queue, where the function is invoked asynchronously on a thread from the Common Language Runtime (CLR) thread pool. The thread pool for asynchronous execution has a default maximum of 25 threads per processor.

Here is the syntax of the *BeginInvoke* method:

IAsyncResult BeginInvoke(*arguments*, AsyncCallback *callback*, object *asyncState*)

The parameters for *BeginInvoke* are the parameters of the function reference of the delegate followed by an *AsyncCallBack* parameter and an *object* parameter. If the function has four parameters, then *BeginInvoke* begins with those arguments. If the function has no parameters, *callback* is the first argument. The *callback* parameter is the callback that is invoked when the asynchronous function has completed. The callback is a delegate. The final parameter, *asyncState*, is a state object, which is passed into the callback function as a parameter, allowing the calling and called functions of the delegate to communicate and share data. The callback and state objects are optional and either can be set to *null*. The value returned from *BeginInvoke* is an *IAsyncResult* object. The return value allows you to query the status of the asynchronous operation. *IAsyncResult* has four properties, which are listed in Table 10-2.

TABLE 10-2 *IAsyncResult* **properties**

Property	Description
AsyncState	This is the same state object passed into the asynchronous invocation.
AsyncWaitHandle	Use *WaitHandle* to block the calling thread until the asynchronous operation is completed.
CompleteSynchronously	Indicates whether the asynchronous operation completed synchronously.
IsCompleted	Indicates whether the asynchronous operation has completed.

The following code is a generic template for invoking a delegate asynchronously. It highlights using the *IAsyncResult* return value and the state object:

```
using System;
using System.Threading;
```

```
namespace Donis.CSharpBook {
    public delegate void DelegateClass();

    public class Starter {

        public static void Main() {
            DelegateClass del = MethodA;
            DelegateStateBag state = new DelegateStateBag();
            IAsyncResult ar = del.BeginInvoke(Callback, state);
            if (ar.IsCompleted == true) {
                Console.WriteLine("MethodA completed");
            }
            else {
                Console.WriteLine("MethodA not completed");
            }
            ar.AsyncWaitHandle.WaitOne();

            // doing something else

            Thread.Sleep(100);
            lock (state) {
                Console.WriteLine("Back in Main");
                Console.WriteLine(state.message);
            }
        }

        public static void Callback(IAsyncResult ar) {
            DelegateStateBag state =
                (DelegateStateBag) ar.AsyncState;
            lock (state) {
                Console.WriteLine("Callback running");
                ((DelegateStateBag) ar.AsyncState).message =
                    "State object modified in callback.";
            }
        }

        public static void MethodA() {
            Console.WriteLine("MethodA running...");
            Thread.Sleep(200);
        }
    }

    class DelegateStateBag {
        public string message;
    }
}
```

Here is the output from running the application:

```
MethodA not completed
MethodA running...
Callback running
Back in Main
State object modified in callback.
```

Interestingly, the *not completed* message is received before *MethodA* has even started. *BeginInvoke* does not directly invoke the function in the delegate. Rather, it adds a request to the thread pool queue, which is eventually handled. There is a *Thread.Sleep* statement near the end of the *Main* method in the sample code. If that were removed, a race condition would exist between *Main* and the completion routine called *Callback*. What is the source of the race condition? Note the *WaitHandle.WaitOne* command in *Main*, which blocks *Main* until the asynchronous operation is completed. The callback function is called when the asynchronous operation finishes. When the asynchronous operation finishes, the *Main* and *Callback* routines are *both* started, and the race begins. *Callback* needs to update the state object before *Main* displays the contents of the same object. The *Thread.Sleep* statement is a primitive way of delaying *Main* and removing the race condition. This allows the callback function to lock the state object before *Main*.

EndInvoke Method

EndInvoke returns the result of an asynchronous operation. You can call *EndInvoke* in the callback routine or in the thread that asynchronously executed the delegate. *EndInvoke* has a similar signature as the delegate minus any value type parameters and an additional parameter for an *IAsyncResult* object. The *IAsyncResult* parameter is the same *IAsyncResult* object that is returned from *BeginInvoke* and described in the preceding section. The return type of *EndInvoke* is the same as the return type of the delegate.

Here is the syntax of the *EndInvoke* method:

returntype EndInvoke(*ref_out_arguments*, IAsyncResult ar)

Calling *EndInvoke* before the asynchronous function has finished will block the calling thread. Do not call *EndInvoke* more than once on the same thread for the asynchronous operation.

Here is generic sample code for the *EndInvoke* method:

```
using System;
using System.Threading;

namespace Donis.CSharpBook {
    public delegate int DelegateClass(out DateTime start,
        out DateTime stop);

    public class Starter {

        public static void Main() {
            DelegateClass del = MethodA;
            DateTime start;
            DateTime stop;
            IAsyncResult ar = del.BeginInvoke(out start, out stop,
                null, null);

            ar.AsyncWaitHandle.WaitOne();
```

```
        // doing something else

        int elapse = del.EndInvoke(out start, out stop, ar);
        Console.WriteLine("Start time: {0}",
        start.ToLongTimeString());
        Console.WriteLine("Stop time: {0}",
        stop.ToLongTimeString());
        Console.WriteLine("Elapsed time: {0} seconds",
            elapse);
    }


    public static int MethodA(out DateTime start,
            out DateTime stop) {
        start = DateTime.Now;
        Thread.Sleep(5000);
        stop = DateTime.Now;
        return (stop - start).Seconds;
    }
  }
}
```

Asynchronous Delegate Diagram

The preceding sections explained how to invoke a delegate asynchronously and to obtain the results. Figure 10-1 diagrams the relationship and sequence of the steps in this procedure, including the delegate, the *BeginInvoke* method, the *EndInvoke* method, and the function reference invocation.

Delegate Internals

Delegates may appear to developers to work by magic because so much is hidden. The real magician, though, is the C# compiler. This section explains the magic of the compiler. Why should you care about that? Understanding how delegates are implemented internally should help in knowing how, where, and when to use delegates. This knowledge also helps to debug problems if they occur.

The C# compiler builds a class for every delegate. The class has the same name as the delegate and four methods: a constructor, *Invoke*, *BeginInvoke*, and *EndInvoke*. Importantly, the delegate class is derived from *System.MulticastDelegate*. Here is a typical delegate:

```
public delegate int ADelegate(int arg1, ref int arg2);
```

Figure 10-2 shows the *ADelegate* class for this delegate viewed in the Intermediate Language Disassembler (ILDASM).

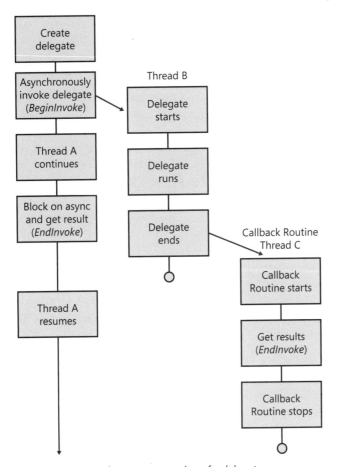

FIGURE 10-1 Asynchronous processing of a delegate

FIGURE 10-2 *ADelegate,* a class created for a delegate

Members of the delegate class, such as *Invoke* and *BeginInvoke*, were described earlier in this chapter. However, it is comforting to actually see them. It is not magic after all. There may be a slight surprise: The constructor of the delegate has two arguments. In C#, the constructor of the delegate has a single parameter, which is the function reference. The C# compiler interprets the single parameter as a target and a function pointer, which become the parameters of the two argument constructor.

Exceptions

What happens if an unhandled exception is raised in a function that is called through a delegate? If the delegate is invoked inside a protected block of code, the exception is trapped. In the case of a multicast delegate, the invocation list is called until an exception occurs. Functions after the failed function in the invocation list are not invoked. Let us assume that the invocation list has references to *MethodA*, *MethodB*, *MethodC*, and *MethodD* and that they were added to the delegate in that order. If an unhandled exception is raised in *MethodB*, *MethodC* and *MethodD* are not called.

When an exception is raised in an asynchronous function, the exception is routed to the thread that called the function reference through the delegate. The following code demonstrates this:

```
using System;
using System.Threading;

namespace Donis.CSharpBook {

    public delegate void DelegateClass();

    public class Starter {
        public static void Main() {
            Console.WriteLine("Main: Running on primary thread");
            try {
                DelegateClass del = MethodA;
                IAsyncResult ar = del.BeginInvoke(null, null);
                del.EndInvoke(ar);
            }
            catch(Exception except) {
                Console.WriteLine("Catch: Running on primary thread");
                Console.WriteLine("Exception caught: " +
                    except.Message);
            }
        }

        public static void MethodA() {
            if (Thread.CurrentThread.IsThreadPoolThread == true) {
                Console.WriteLine("MethodA: Running on a thread pool thread");
            }
```

```
        else {
            Console.WriteLine("MethodA: Running on primary thread");
        }
        throw new Exception("failure");
    }
  }
}
```

Anonymous Methods

An anonymous method is a nameless method. Sometimes a function is used exclusively with a delegate. It is never called directly as a stand-alone method. Without an anonymous method, you must define a separate function as a member of a class. The function then is assigned to the delegate. Using an anonymous method prevents creating a separate method unnecessarily, which is cleaner and more convenient than using a named method. Anonymous methods can be substituted for delegates in most circumstances. Lambda expressions might make anonymous methods irrelevant. However, anonymous methods remain an artifact of the C# language. Lambda expressions were introduced in Chapter 1.

Define an anonymous method with the *delegate* keyword and a nameless function body. This code assigns an anonymous method to a delegate:

```
using System;
using System.Threading;

namespace Donis.CSharpBook {

    public delegate void DelegateClass();

    public class Starter {
        public static void Main() {
            DelegateClass del = delegate { // anonymous method
                Console.WriteLine("Running anonymous method");
            };
            del();
        }
    }
}
```

As shown in the preceding example, the anonymous method need not have a signature. The signature of the anonymous method and the return type is inferred from the delegate, which is another example of delegate inference. If the delegate had two parameters and returned an integer, the anonymous method would have the same two parameters and return an integer. However, anonymous methods can be called without parameters, regardless of the delegate type. The advantage of an anonymous method without a signature is its compliance with almost any delegate. The disadvantage is that anonymous methods defined without a signature cannot access the parameters of the delegate. Therefore, the parameters cannot be used in the function body. For this reason, anonymous methods without a signature cannot be employed if the delegate has an *out* parameter. *Out* parameters must be initialized in the called method, which is impossible in an anonymous method without a signature. When an anonymous method is called through the delegate, the parameters still must be provided in the method invocation even though the anonymous methods cannot use them.

Here is the syntax of an anonymous method:

delegate *optional_signature {anonymous method expression}*

In support of an anonymous method, the C# compiler does several things:

- The compiler infers the signature of the anonymous method from the delegate.
- The compiler confirms there are no out parameters for anonymous methods without parameters.
- The compiler confirms that the return type of the delegate is compatible with the anonymous method.
- The compiler creates a new delegate that is initialized with a reference to the anonymous method.

If a signature is specified, the parameters for an anonymous method are appended to the *delegate* keyword. The parameters are initialized with the parameters from the delegate invocation. Here is an example of an anonymous method with a signature:

```
using System;
using System.Threading;

namespace Donis.CSharpBook {

    public delegate int DelegateClass(out int param);

    public class Starter {
        public static void Main() {
            int var;
            DelegateClass del = delegate(out int inner) {
                inner = 12;
                Console.WriteLine("Running anonymous method");
                return inner;
            };
            del(out var);
            Console.WriteLine("Var is {0}", var);
        }
    }
}
```

As demonstrated in the preceding code in this section, anonymous methods can be used similarly to the way delegates are used. The exception is the -= compound assignment operator, which removes function references of a delegate from a multicast delegate. Because anonymous methods are unnamed, you cannot remove the method from a multicast delegate.

Anonymous methods are not literally nameless. The C# compiler implements the anonymous method as a named method in the class where it is defined. This method is both static and private. The delegate is assigned this method in the class constructor. The following is the compiler's naming convention for anonymous methods:

<functionname>uniqueid

The method has the same signature as the target delegate.

A delegate initialized with the anonymous method also is added to the class as a static and private field. The following shows the format of the delegate name. The *id* and the # represent characters that are compiler generated to create a unique name.

<>id__CachedAnonymousMethodDelegate#

The following code has two delegates and two anonymous methods:

```
using System;

namespace Donis.CSharpBook {

    public delegate void ADelegate(int param);
    public delegate int BDelegate(int param1, int param2);

    public class Starter {
        public static void Main() {
            ADelegate del = delegate(int param) {
                param = 5;
            };
        }

        public int MethodA() {
            BDelegate del = delegate(int param1, int param2) {
                return 0;
            };
            return 0;
        }
    }
}
```

Figure 10-3 is an internal view of the preceding code using ILDASM. It shows the delegates that are created as fields and the named methods created in the class for the anonymous methods.

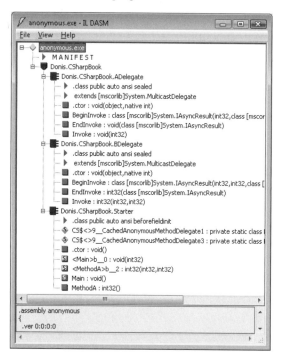

FIGURE 10-3 An internal view of delegates and the names created for the anonymous methods

Outer Variables

Anonymous methods can refer to local variables of the surrounding code. In the anonymous method, you can use anything available in the surrounding code. Local variables from the surrounding code that are used in an anonymous method are called *outer variables*.

The scope of a local variable is closely linked to the method where the variable is declared. A local variable is typically removed from memory when the function or block in which it is declared is exited. Outer variables used in an anonymous method are captured, which extends the lifetime of the variable. The lifetime of an outer variable is the same as that of the delegate. The outer variable is removed when the delegate is garbage-collected. Because the lifetime of an outer variable is aligned with the delegate, it can persist across invocations of the anonymous method.

In the following code, *MethodA* returns an anonymous function of type *DelegateClass*, which is added to the *del* delegate. The *increment* variable is local to *MethodA* and normally would be removed when *MethodA* returns. However, the *increment* variable is used in the anonymous method contained in *MethodA*. As such, the *increment* variable is an outer variable and persists beyond *MethodA*. The anonymous method returned by *MethodA* is called three times in *Main*, outside *MethodA* (that is, beyond the normal scope of the *increment* variable). Each time the anonymous method is called, the *increment* variable is available and is incremented:

```
using System;

namespace Donis.CSharpBook {

    public delegate void DelegateClass(out int var);

    public class Starter {

        public static void Main() {

            DelegateClass del = MethodA();
            int var1, var2, var3;
            del(out var1);
            del(out var2);
            del(out var3);
            Console.WriteLine(var3);
        }

        public static DelegateClass MethodA() {
            int increment = 0;
            return delegate(out int var) {
                var = ++increment;
            };
        }
    }
}
```

The C# compiler creates a private nested class for anonymous methods that have outer variables. This class is where outer variables are captured. Conversely, anonymous methods that have no outer variables are implemented as private static methods, as described previously. The nested class has a public field for each outer variable used in the anonymous method. The local variable is persisted to this public field. The nested class also has a named method for the anonymous method. The named method has the same signature as the related delegate. Figure 10-4 shows the nested class created for an anonymous method with outer variables.

Local variables usually are fixed in memory. They are not collected by the CLR during garbage collection. Local variables are located on the stack and removed from memory when the surrounding method ends. When a local variable is captured (the outer variable) in an anonymous method, it is placed on the managed heap and is movable. The outer variables are thus available for garbage collection. For this reason, outer variables must be pinned or otherwise fixed before using unsafe code.

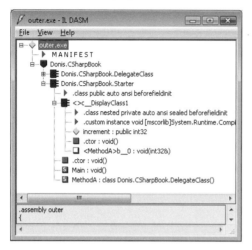

FIGURE 10-4 A view of the nested class created for an anonymous method with an outer variable

Generic Anonymous Methods

Anonymous methods can use generic parameters of the surrounding class or delegate. However, anonymous methods cannot define new generic parameters or constraints. Here are two examples of anonymous methods using generic parameters:

```
using System;

namespace Donis.CSharpBook {

    public delegate void ADelegate<T>(T tvalue);

    public class ZClass {
        public void MethodA() {
            ADelegate<int> del = delegate(int var) {
                Console.WriteLine("ZClass MethodA: {0}",var);
            };
            del(3);
        }
    }

    public class YClass<T> {
        public delegate void BDelegate(T tVal);
        public void MethodA(T tVal) {
            BDelegate del = delegate(T tValue) {
                Console.WriteLine("YClass MethodA: {0}",tValue);
            };
            del(tVal);
        }
    }
```

```
public class Starter {

    public static void Main() {
        ZClass z = new ZClass();
        z.MethodA();
        YClass<int> y = new YClass<int>();
        y.MethodA(55);
    }
}
}
```

Limitations of Anonymous Methods

Although anonymous methods are similar to other methods, they also have some limitations (some of which have already been mentioned):

- Do not attempt to jump out of an anonymous method.

- Do not define new generic parameters or constraints.

- Do not apply attributes to anonymous methods.

- Do not use anonymous method with the -= compound assignment operator.

- Cannot be an unsafe method.

Events

An *event* is a notification. By necessity, this definition is broad. Events encompass a wide range of occurrences and actions. Here is a description of some predefined events, which underscores the breadth of activities. A button-click event notifies a form that a button has been clicked. A timer event is a notification that a set period of time has elapsed. The unhandled exception event of the application domain is a notification of a fatal exception. The *Application_Start* event notifies a Web application that the application is loading. You also can create custom events for a variety of purposes. Typically an event is exposed as a member of a publisher class, such as a button class.

Anyone interested in an event can subscribe to that event. Subscribers register for an event by adding a delegate to the event. The delegate must contain a single function reference. The publisher notifies the subscriber by calling the function reference of the delegate. The subscriber's response to the event is coded in the function. When the event is raised, the publisher calls the function, affording the subscriber an opportunity to respond to or handle the event. For this reason, the function is called an *event handler*. Events can have multiple subscribers. For example, a building class could have a fire alarm event. Everyone in the building might want to subscribe to that event!

What happens when there are no subscribers to a particular event? In other words, *if a tree falls in the woods and no one hears it, does it make a sound?* If the tree is an event, no sound is made. If an event has no subscribers, no one is notified.

Publishing an Event

Both classes and objects can own events. Classes can publish events as static members, whereas objects publish events as instance members. Multicast delegates underlie events. Events are defined with the *event* keyword. Here is the syntax for defining an event:

accessibility event *delegatename eventname*

The accessibility of an event is typically *public* or *protected*, although private events are sometimes seen. Protected events restrict subscribers to children. A public event is available to any interested subscriber. The *delegate name* is the underlying delegate of the event. The delegate defines the signature of the event handler. Subscribers can subscribe only with delegates of a compatible signature. Here is some sample code:

```
public delegate void DelegateClass();
public event DelegateClass MyEvent;
```

As a best practice, event handlers should return *void* and have two arguments. The first parameter is the object that raised the event. The second parameter is an object derived from *EventArgs* having optional data that further explains the event. *EventHandler* is a predefined delegate that matches this signature. It is included in the .NET Framework Class Library (FCL) and frees you from having to declare a separate delegate for a standard event.

A field is added to the surrounding class in support of the event. The field has the same type as the underlying delegate. The C# compiler also adds methods to add and remove subscribers to the event. The names of the methods are *add_<EventName>* and *remove_<EventName>*, respectively. The event itself is also present in the class. Figure 10-5 shows an internal view of a class that contains an event.

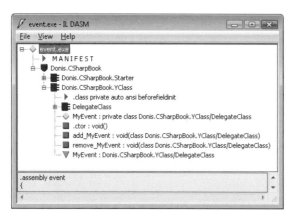

FIGURE 10-5 A class with an event and related members

Subscribers

The publisher/subscriber relationship supports a *one-to-many* or *many-to-many* relationship. For each publisher, there can be zero or more subscribers. Conversely, a subscriber can subscribe to multiple different events. For example, a form can subscribe to a button-click and a text-change event. Subscribers register for an event by adding a delegate to the event. The delegate includes a function reference to be called when the event is raised, which is how the subscriber is notified. Subscribe to an event using the *add* method or the += compound assignment operator (*eventname* += *delegatename*), as shown in the following sample code:

```
using System;

namespace Donis.CSharpBook {
    class Publisher {
        public event EventHandler MyEvent;
    }

    public class Subscriber {

        public static void Handler(object obj, EventArgs args) {
        }

        public static void Main() {
            Publisher pub = new Publisher();
            pub.MyEvent += Handler;
            // other processing
        }
    }
}
```

Subscribers can unregister for an event with the -= compound assignment operator (*eventname* -= *delegatename*).

Raising an Event

Publishers raise an event to notify subscribers that something has occurred, by calling an event handler in the subscriber. The publisher should not raise an event when there are no subscribers. Raising an event for no subscribers causes an exception. Events with no subscribers are *null*, which can be tested. Raise an event with the call operator *( )*. Just as with a delegate, you also can execute (or raise) an event with the *Invoke* method. The parameters of an event are passed as arguments to the event handlers. The return value of an event is set by the last event handler. Here is an example of the proper way to raise an event:

```
class Publisher {
    public event EventHandler MyEvent;

    public void SomeMethod() {
```

```
        if (MyEvent != null) {
            MyEvent(null, null);
        }
    }
}
```

EventArgs

Publishers sometimes provide subscribers additional information pertaining to an event. This valuable information is found in the *EventArgs*-derived class, which is typically the second parameter of the event. For example, the *MouseEventArgs* class provides the *x* and *y* coordinates of the mouse pointer for a mouse- click event. The *DataRowChangeEventArgs* class provides the row and action for database-related events, such as the *RowChanged* event. The *PaintEventArgs* class provides the clip rectangle and graphics object for a paint event. *MouseEventArgs*, *DataRowChangeEventArgs*, and *PaintEventArgs* are derived from the *EventArgs* class.

The following is code for a bank account. The *NSF* event is raised when the account is overdrawn. The *BankEventArgs* class provides the bank account balance and the amount of the transaction that would overdraw the account:

```
using System;

namespace Donis.CSharpBook {

    public class Starter {
        public static void Main() {
            Bank account = new Bank();
            account.NSF += NSFHandler;
            account.Deposit(500);
            account.Withdrawal(750);
        }

        public static void NSFHandler(object o, BankEventArgs e) {
            Console.WriteLine("NSF Transaction");
            Console.WriteLine("Balance: {0}", e.Balance);
            Console.WriteLine("Transaction: {0}",
                e.Transaction);
        }
    }

    public delegate void OverDrawn(object o, BankEventArgs e);
    public class Bank {
        public event OverDrawn NSF; // non-sufficient funds

        public decimal Deposit(decimal amountDeposit) {
```

```
            propBalance += amountDeposit;
            return propBalance;
        }

        public decimal Withdrawal(decimal amountWithdrawn) {
            decimal newBalance = propBalance - amountWithdrawn;
            if (newBalance < 0) {
                if (NSF != null) {
                    BankEventArgs args = new BankEventArgs(
                        Balance, amountWithdrawn);
                    NSF(this, args);
                }
            }
            return propBalance = newBalance;
        }

        private decimal propBalance = 0;
        public decimal Balance {
            get {
                return propBalance;
            }
        }
    }

    public class BankEventArgs: EventArgs {

        public BankEventArgs(decimal amountBalance, decimal amountTransaction) {
            propBalance=amountBalance;
            propTransaction=amountTransaction;
        }

        private decimal propBalance;
        public decimal Balance {
            get {
                return propBalance;
            }
        }

        private decimal propTransaction;
        public decimal Transaction {
            get {
                return propTransaction;
            }
        }
    }
}
```

LINQ Programming

LINQ programming was introduced in Chapter 6, "Introduction to LINQ." That chapter primarily focused on LINQ to Objects, which is the default provider. The next chapter introduces three additional providers: LINQ to XML, LINQ to SQL and LINQ to DataSet. These providers implement the *IQueryable* interface to implement their unique behavior and extend the *IEnumerable<T>* interface.

You can manage, query, and change an XML store using LINQ to XML. Discard the competing models (DOM, XmlTextReader, and so forth) for accessing XML. LINQ to XML provides a unified model for querying and managing XML documents and elements. LINQ to SQL is for managing and querying relational databases. LINQ to SQL also provides a straightforward method for making changes in a disconnected environment and later persisting those changes to the database. With LINQ to DataSet, you can query datasets. By the end of the next chapter, you will have a more complete view of LINQ.

Chapter 11
LINQ Programming

Chapter 6, "Introduction to LINQ," was a general introduction to Language Integrated Query (LINQ) and a review of LINQ to Objects. LINQ to Objects is the implicit LINQ provider, but other providers are available. Namely, LINQ to XML and LINQ to SQL are the more commonly used of these other providers. Because of the ubiquitous nature of Extensible Markup Language (XML) and SQL in .NET development, these two providers have particular importance. Both of them implement the *IQueryable* interface, which extends the *IEnumerable<T>* interface, to refine and implement the standard LINQ interface in the context of the provider. For example, LINQ to XML does more than query XML. You also can use LINQ to XML to browse an XML data store. LINQ to SQL also provides more than query functionality. You can perform SQL commands, such as insert, delete, and add operations.

This chapter demonstrates the extensible nature and strength of LINQ. In the future, the realm of LINQ will expand as additional providers are introduced. It will be the unifying model of data, in the most abstract of terms. LINQ probably will touch upon domains that have not even been envisioned in the hallways of Microsoft. There could be LINQ to Explorer, which could allow users to query files and directories with query expressions. LINQ to Internet could extend the concept of data mining to the Web. LINQ to Cloud could search for specific resources in your cloud. The possibilities are unlimited. Until then, we will focus on LINQ to XML and LINQ to SQL.

LINQ to XML

LINQ to XML manages XML data. *XElement* is the central component to LINQ to XML. *XElement* represents a collection of XML elements. You can load XML into an *XElement* component from memory using a string containing XML or another *XElement* object. *XElement* also can be loaded from a file using *TextReader* and *XmlTextReader* types. Conversely, you can persist XML to a string in memory, or you can persist XML to a file using the *TextWriter* or *XmlTextWriter* types.

As mentioned, LINQ to XML is about more than simply querying XML data. In addition to performing queries against XML stores, LINQ to XML presents a complete interface to validate, navigate, update, and otherwise manage XML data. Already, .NET supports competing application programming interfaces (APIs) for managing XML at various levels of sophistication and complexity: *XmlTextReader* and *XmlTextWriter* for reading and writing XML, *XmlDocument* for supporting the Document Object Model (DOM) for accessing XML, and finally *XPath*. Instead of supporting XML query capability only and deferring to another interface for other functionality, LINQ to XML provides a comprehensive interface to manage

XML. This is consistent with the overall objective of LINQ to provide a unified syntax over various domains. Instead of forcing you to understand two models (LINQ to XML and something else), you can learn a single syntax and methodology for accessing XML.

XML Schemas

Validation using schemas is an essential ingredient of XML management. The mantra of *garbage-in and garbage-out* is well founded. The concept of well-formed XML is also important. Both validation and well-formed XML are verifiable in LINQ to XML.

Validation

You can validate XML against a schema with either *XDocument.Validate* or *XElement.Validate*. The schema is normally found in an .xsd file. Here is a simple schema that defines the *book* element, which requires an *author* attribute. The *author* attribute is of the *string* type:

```
<xsd:schema xmlns:xsd='http://www.w3.org/2001/XMLSchema'>
    <xsd:element name="book">
        <xsd:complexType>
            <xsd:attribute name="author"
                type="xsd:string" use="required"/>
        </xsd:complexType>
    </xsd:element>
</xsd:schema>
```

The following code is a short XML file that includes a *book* element. Notice that the *author* attribute has been omitted. Therefore, based on the schema, this is not a valid XML file:

```
<?xml version="1.0"?>
<book xmlns:xsi="http://www.w3.org/2001/XMLSchema-instance"
    xsi:noNamespaceSchemaLocation="file:///c:/code/validate.xsd">
</book>
```

The following program uses LINQ to XML to validate the XML file with the schema. *XmlSchemaSet.Add* reads the schema file. The XML file is read with the *XDocument.Load* method and then is validated with the *XDocument.Validate* method. The first parameter of the *Validate* method identifies the schema. The next parameter is the callback function that is called to handle schema errors. In this example, the callback is *ReportSchemaError*, which displays the error message to the *Console* window. The application has several LINQ-related namespaces. *System.Linq* is the core namespace for LINQ, while *System.Xml.Linq* is the core namespace for LINQ to XML. The *System.Xml.Schema* namespace contains the *XmlSchemaSet* type. Here is the code:

```
using System;
using System.Linq;
using System.Xml.Linq;
using System.Xml.Schema;
```

```
namespace Validate {
    class Program {
        static void Main(string[] args) {

            XmlSchemaSet schemas = new XmlSchemaSet();
            schemas.Add("", @"validate.xsd");
            XDocument xml = XDocument.Load(@"c:\code\validate.xml");

            xml.Validate(schemas, new ValidationEventHandler(ReportSchemaError));
        }

        private static void ReportSchemaError(object sender, ValidationEventArgs e) {
            Console.WriteLine(e.Message);
        }
    }
}
```

Here is the message that is displayed:

```
The required attribute 'author' is missing.
```

Here is a modified XML file. This file will pass the validation:

```
<?xml version="1.0"?>
<book xmlns:xsi="http://www.w3.org/2001/XMLSchema-instance"
    xsi:noNamespaceSchemaLocation="file:///c:/code/validate.xsd"
    author="Donis Marshall">
</book>
```

In XML, quotes are required around string properties. For that reason, the following attribute would not be well-formed XML; the quotes are missing:

```
author=Donis Marshall
```

The quality of the XML formation is checked by LINQ to XML when loading the document into memory, using, for example, the *XDocument.Load function*. If the document is not well formed, an *XmlException* is thrown at that time.

Navigation

Navigation XML is another capability of LINQ to XML. Navigation allows you to browse XML nodes. Data is only as useful as it is accessible. Classes derived from *XNode* form the set of object types that can be navigated or browsed. For LINQ to XML, nodes encompass every aspect of the XML. These types include:

- Elements within a document (*XElement*)
- Parent and child elements (*XElement*)
- Element value (*XText*)
- Comments (*XComment*)
- Attributes of an element (*XAttribute*)

Table 11-1 lists the members of the *XNode* class related to navigation, which are common to the classes in the preceding list.

TABLE 11-1 *XNode* **members pertaining to navigation**

Member	Description

Ancestors	Returns the ancestors of the current element. The second overload restricts the result to elements of the specified name. Here are the signatures:
	
	`public IEnumerable<XElement> Ancestors()`
	
	`public IEnumerable<XElement> Ancestors(XName name)`

CreateNavigator	Creates a LINQ to XML cursor. (Cursors are discussed at the end of this section.) Here are the signatures:
	
	`public static XPathNavigator CreateNavigator(this XNode node)`
	
	`public static XPathNavigator CreateNavigator(this XNode node,`
	`    XmlNameTable nameTable)`

ElementsAfterSelf	Returns siblings after the current element. The second overload restricts the results to elements of the specified name. Here are the signatures:
	
	`public IEnumerable<XElement> ElementsAfterSelf()`
	
	`public IEnumerable<XElement> ElementsAfterSelf(XName name)`

ElementsBeforeSelf	Returns siblings before the current element. The second overload restricts the results to elements of the specified name. Here are the signatures:
	
	`public IEnumerable<XElement> ElementsBeforeSelf()`
	
	`public IEnumerable<XElement> ElementsBeforeSelf(XName name)`

IsAfter	Indicates whether the current node is after the specified node. Here is the signature: `public bool IsAfter(XNode node)`
IsBefore	Indicates whether the current node is before the specified node. Here is the signature: `public bool IsBefore(XNode node)`
NodesAfterSelf	Returns nodes after the current node. Here is the signature: `public IEnumerable<XNode> NodesAfterSelf()`
NodesBeforeSelf	Returns nodes before the current node. Here is the signature: `public IEnumerable<XNode> NodesBeforeSelf()`
NextNode	Returns the next node. Here is the definition: `public XNode NextNode {get;}`
Parent	Returns the parent of the current node. Here is the definition: `public XElement Parent {get;}`
PreviousNode	Returns the previous node. `public XNode PreviousNode{get;}`

In addition to being a valid XML node, *XElement* is an XML container class. Container classes inherit *XContainer,* which then inherits *XNode. XDocument* is another example of a container class and also inherits *XContainer.* Containers can manage nodes found in the container. Table 11-2 lists methods and properties of *XContainer* that help when navigating XML.

TABLE 11-2 *XContainer* members pertaining to navigation

Member	Description

DescendantNodes	Returns a collection of descendant nodes. The second overload restricts the results to elements of the specified name. Here are the signatures:
	
	`public IEnumerable<XElement> Descendants()`
	
	`public IEnumerable<XElement> Descendants(XName name)`

Descendants	Returns a collection of descendant elements. The second overload restricts the result to elements of the specified name. Here are the signatures:
	
	`public IEnumerable<XElement> Descendants()`
	
	`public IEnumerable<XElement> Descendants(XName name)`

FirstNode	Returns the first child node of the current element. Here is the definition: `public XNode FirstNode {get;}`
LastNode	Returns the last child node of the current element. Here is the definition: `public XNode LastNode {get;}`

XElement has additional members for navigation that are not inherited from *XNode* or *XContainer.* The list of these members is provided in Table 11-3.

TABLE 11-3 *XElement* navigation members

Member	Description

AncestorsAndSelf	Returns the current element and ancestors. The second overload restricts the result to elements of the specified name. Here are the signatures:
	
	`public IEnumerable<XElement> AncestorsAndSelf()`
	
	`public IEnumerable<XElement> AncestorsAndSelf(XName name)`

Attribute	Returns the specified attribute of the current element. The second overload restricts the results to nodes of the specified name. Here are the signatures:
	
	`public XAttribute Attribute(XName name)`
	
	`public IEnumerable<XElement> AncestorsAndSelf(XName name)`

Attributes	Returns the attributes of the current element. The second overload restricts the result to attributes of the specified name. Here are the signatures:
	
	`public IEnumerable<XAttribute> Attributes()`
	
	`public IEnumerable< XAttribute > Attributes(XName name)`

TABLE 11-3 *XElement* **navigation members**

Member	Description
DescendantNodeAndSelf	Returns a collection of descendant nodes. Here is the signature: `public IEnumerable<XNode> DescendantsNodesAndSelf()`
Element	Returns the specified child element. Here is the signature: `public XElement Element(XName name)`

Elements	Returns the child elements of the current element. The second overload restricts the result to elements of the specified name. Here are the signatures:
	
	`public IEnumerable<XElement> Elements()`
	
	`public IEnumerable<XElement> Elements(XName name)`

FirstAttribute	Returns the first attribute of the current element. Here is the definition: `public XAttribute FirstAttribute {get;}`
FirstNode	Returns the first child node of the current element. Here is the definition: `public XNode FirstNode {get;}`
LastAttribute	Returns the last attribute of the current element. Here is the definition: `public XAttribute LastAttribute {get;}`
LastNode	Returns the last child node of the current element. Here is the definition: `public XNode LastNode {get;}`

XML data is hierarchical. *XElement* reflects that hierarchical nature of XML onto LINQ to XML. In most XML models, *document* is the key component. However, in LINQ to XML, the focus is *XElement*. You can enumerate all the elements of the document from an *XElement* object that refers to the root element. From there, you can continue to drill down through child elements, values, and attributes until the XML document has been explored fully.

The following code is a console application that enumerates elements of an XML file. The filename is provided as a command-line parameter. In *Main,* the XML file is loaded and the root element is displayed. The *GetElements* method is called next. In this method, the child elements are requested using the *XElement.Descendants* method. Then the elements are enumerated. *GetElement* is called recursively until all the elements have been rendered. The attributes, if any, of every element also are displayed:

```
using System;
using System.Collections.Generic;
using System.Linq;
using System.Xml.Linq;
using System.Text;

namespace EnumerateXML
{
    class Program {
        static void Main(string[] args) {
```

```
        XElement xml = XElement.Load(args[0]);
        Console.WriteLine("Element: {0}", xml.Name);
        GetElements(xml);
    }

    static void GetElements(XElement xml) {
        foreach (XElement element in xml.Descendants()) {
            Console.WriteLine("Element: {0}", element.Name);
            foreach (XAttribute attribute in element.Attributes()) {
                Console.WriteLine("     " + attribute.Name);
            }
            GetElements(element);
        }
    }
  }
}
```

The *XPathNavigator* is an alternate model for browsing using LINQ to XML. It uses a cursor
to browse instead of requesting and then enumerating a collection of elements. The previous
code example used the latter model. The cursor model is simpler and probably more descriptive.
XNode.CreateNavigator returns an instance of an *XPathNavigator*. *XPathNavigator* has *Move*
methods that move the cursor, such as *MoveToAttribute, MoveToChild,* and *MoveToFollowing*.
The cursor can be moved forward and backward. *MoveToParent* and *MoveToRoot* are examples
of methods that jump the cursor backward in the LINQ to XML. More important than
navigation, the *XPathNavigator* type has methods that edit values and confirm relationships,
such as between parents and children. The objective of the following example is similar to
the previous example. This code browses an XML file using the *XPathNavigator*:

```
using System;
using System.Collections.Generic;
using System.Linq;
using System.Xml.Linq;
using System.Xml.XPath;
using System.Text;

namespace PathNavigator {
    class Program {
        static void Main(string[] args) {
            XElement xml = XElement.Load(args[0]);
            XPathNavigator nav = ((XNode) xml).CreateNavigator();

            Console.WriteLine("Element: {0}", nav.Name);
            GetElements(nav);

        }

        static void GetElements(XPathNavigator nav) {
            while (nav.MoveToFollowing(XPathNodeType.Element)) {
                Console.WriteLine("Element: {0}", nav.Name);
                if (nav.HasAttributes) {
                    nav.MoveToFirstAttribute();
                    Console.WriteLine("{0}", nav.Name);
```

```
                    while (nav.MoveToNextAttribute())
                    Console.WriteLine("{0}", nav.Name);
                }
            }
        }
    }
}
```

Explicit Casting

XML elements can contain values. These values are outside the control of the Common Language Runtime (CLR) and therefore are not type-safe. Nonetheless, you can cast these values to .NET primitives. The conversion occurs at run time. An invalid cast will raise an exception at that time. Here is a simple XML file:

```
<data>
    <item>
        bob
    </item>
</data>
```

The following code reads the simple XML file and selects the child node, which is the item element. That element is then cast to a string in the *Console.WriteLine* method. The cast is successful because the value (*bob*) is convertible to a string. The next line is commented out, where the element is cast to an integer. That is invalid for this element and would raise a *FormatException* exception at run time. Of course, you would prefer to raise an exception at compile time:

```
XElement xml = XElement.Load(@"..\..\simple.xml");
XElement child = (XElement)xml.FirstNode;
Console.WriteLine("Element: {0}", (string) child);
//Console.WriteLine("Element: {0}", (int) child);
```

Unlike *XElement*, the *XPathNavigator* type does not support explicit casting of element values. You have to use member properties to cast to the target type. The following simple XML file has been altered slightly. The item property now contains an integer value:

```
<data>
    <item>
        123
    </item>
</data>
```

The following code uses *XPathNavigator* to move to the child node and then to display the value. The *ValueAsInt* property is used to cast the value to an integer. Similar to explicit casting, this is not type-safe. Conversion problems occur at run time and cause a *FormatException* exception:

```
XElement xml = XElement.Load(@"..\..\simple.xml");
XPathNavigator nav = ((XNode)xml).CreateNavigator();
```

```
nav.MoveToChild(XPathNodeType.Element);
Console.WriteLine("Element: {0}", nav.ValueAsInt);
```

XML Modification

You can change the content of XML data using LINQ to XML. In the case of an XML file, you can read the XML into memory, modify the data, and then save the changes back to a file. The *XElement* element has several methods that support modifying XML. This includes adding and changing nodes. Table 11-4 lists members of *XElement* that are useful in modifying an XML data file.

TABLE 11-4 *XElement* **members pertaining to data modification**

Member	Description
Add	Adds content to the current element, which could be a child element. Here are the signatures: `public void Add(object content)` `public void Add(object[] content)`
AddAfterSelf	Adds content after the current element. Here are the signatures: `public void AddAfterSelf(object content)` `public void AddAfterSelf(object[] content)`
AddAnnotation	Adds an annotation (a comment) to the current element. Here is the signature: `public void Annotation (object content)`
AddBeforeSelf	Adds content before the current element. Here are the signatures: `public void AddBeforeSelf(object content)` `public void AddBeforeSelf(object[] content)`
AddFirst	Inserts content as the first child of the current element. Here are the signatures: `public void AddFirst(object content)` `public void AddFirst(object[] content)`
Remove	Removes the current element. Here is the signature: `public void Remove()`
RemoveAll	Removes child nodes of the current element. Here is the signature: `public void RemoveAll()`
RemoveAnnotations	Removes annotations of the type indicated from the current element. Here are the signatures: `public void RemoveAnnotations<T>() where T : class` `public void RemoveAnnotations(Type type)`

TABLE 11-4 *XElement* members pertaining to data modification

Member	Description
RemoveAttributes	Removes the attributes of the current element. Here is the signature: `public void RemoveAttributes()`
RemoveNodes	Removes the nodes of the current element. Here is the signature: `public void RemoveNodes()`

ReplaceAll	Replaces the children of the current element with the provided content. Here are the signatures:
	
	`public void ReplaceAll(object content)`
	
	`public void ReplaceAll(object[] content)`

ReplaceAttributes	Replaces the attributes of the current element with the provided content. Here are the signatures:
	
	`public void ReplaceAttributes(object content)`
	
	`public void ReplaceAttributes(object[] content)`

ReplaceNodes	Replaces the child nodes of the current element with the provided content. Here are the signatures:
	
	`public void ReplaceNodes(object content)`
	
	`public void ReplaceNodes(object[] content)`

Save	Saves XML data. *SaveOptions* enumeration has two values. *SaveOptions.None* indents the XML, while removing extraneous white space. *SaveOptions. DisableFormatting* persists the XML while preserving the formatting, including white space. Here are the signatures:
	
	`public void Save(string fileName)`
	
	`public void Save(TextWriter textWriter)`
	
	`public void Save(XmlWriter writer)`
	
	`public void Save(string fileName, SaveOptions options )`
	
	`public void Save(TextWriter textWriter, SaveOptions options)`

SetAttributeValue	Adds, modifies, or deletes an attribute. If the attribute does not exist, it is added. Otherwise, the attribute is changed. If *value* is *null,* the attribute is deleted. Here is the signature: `public void SetAttributeValue(XName name, object value)`
SetElementValue	Adds, modifies, or deletes a child element. If the element does not exist, it is added. If *value* is *null,* the element is deleted. Here is the signature: `public void SetElementValue(XName name, object value)`
SetValue	Sets the value of the current element. Here is the signature: `public void SetValue(object value)`

The following program demonstrates modifying XML data. It finds and replaces the value of an attribute or element. This is a console program where you specify the XML file, mode (attribute or element), find value, and replace value as command-line arguments—in that order. The mode is either *attribute* (or just *a*) or *element* (or just *e*). Results are saved back to the original file. In the application, the XML file is loaded with *XElement.Load*. In the *element* case, we enumerate the elements. Whenever a matching value is found, it is changed with the replace value. In the *attribute* case, the elements are enumerated. Within each element, the attributes are enumerated. If a matching value is found, it is changed with the replace value. After the *switch* statement, the XML file is updated using the *XElement.Save* method:

```
using System;
using System.Collections.Generic;
using System.Linq;
using System.Text;
using System.Xml.Linq;

namespace FindAndReplace {
    class Program {
        static void Main(string[] args) {
            XElement xml = XElement.Load(args[0]);
            char[] remove = { '\t', '\n', ' ' };
            switch (args[1].ToLower()) {
                case "element":
                case "e":
                    foreach (XElement element in xml.Elements()) {
                        if (args[2] == ((string)element).Trim(remove)) {
                            element.SetValue(args[3]);
                        }
                    }
                    break;
                case "attribute":
                case "a":
                    foreach (XElement element in xml.Elements()) {
                        foreach (XAttribute attribute in element.Attributes()) {
                            if (args[2] == ((string) (attribute)).Trim(remove)) {
                                attribute.SetValue(args[3]);
                            }
                        }
                    }
                    break;
            }
            xml.Save(args[0]);
        }
    }
}
```

XML Query Expressions

With LINQ to XML, you can apply LINQ query expressions to XML data. The query expression cannot be applied directly to an XML file. The file first must be read into memory as an

XElement or an *XDocument*. Chapter 6 explained the syntax of query expressions. The *XElement.Elements, XElement.Attributes,* and other members of *XDocument* and *XElement* return enumerable collections, which can be sources of LINQ query expressions. Here is an example of a query expression using LINQ to XML:

```
var saleitems = from item in xml.Elements()
                where item.FirstAttribute.Value == "sale"
                orderby item.Element("discount").Value
                select item;
```

LINQ to SQL

LINQ to SQL is used to access relational databases. A goal of LINQ to SQL is to offer a unified query expression language for relational databases regardless of the data source. You learn a single syntax that can be applied to a variety of native databases. The query expression is converted by the provider into a query string targeting a specific database, and the query string is submitted to the relevant database engine. You can retrieve the SQL-specific query string generated for a query expression with the *DataContext.GetCommand* method. To submit a SQL command directly to the database engine, use *DataContext.ExecuteQuery.* LINQ to SQL queries are not immediate and use deferred loading. This is accomplished via expression trees, which is a language extension of .NET 3.5. Expression trees were reviewed in Chapter 6.

In this book, *AdventureWorks_Data* is used as the sample database. *AdventureWorks_Data* is downloadable from this Microsoft Web site: *http://www.codeplex.com/MSFTDBProdSamples.* *Download the AdventureWorksDB.msi* installer. The following code uses the *AdventureWorks_ Data* database and displays the underlying native query string of a LINQ to SQL query expression. The *DataContext.GetComm*and method returns the native query string:

```
DataContext context = new DataContext(conn);

Table<Employee> employees = context.GetTable<Employee>();

var query = from e in employees
            where e.ManagerID == "21"
            select new { e.EmployeeID, e.ManagerID };
DbCommand command = context.GetCommand(query);
Console.WriteLine(command.CommandText);
```

Entity Classes

Entity classes map a native database table or view to a managed class. Intrinsically, this changes access from a data model to an object-oriented model. You can map database columns (fields) to data members and properties of a managed class. Mapping every column of the table is not required. You can map only needed columns to the class instead of the entire table. Columns not mapped are not accessible in LINQ to SQL. Entity classes also can define uniqueness and associations.

The *Table* attribute maps an entity class to a database table and cannot be applied to a structure. *Name* is the only property of the *Table* attribute and names the database table that the class is mapping. If the *Name* property is omitted, the class maps to the table that shares the name of the class. For example, by default, the class *XData* would map to a table in the database named *XData*.

A *Column* attribute maps a database column to a data member or property of the entity class. The *Name* property is optional and maps the member to a specific column in the database table. The default mapping is to the column with the same name as the member. The *Column* attribute has additional properties. Table 11-5 list all the properties of the *Column* attribute.

TABLE 11-5 Properties of the *Column* attribute

Property	Description	Type
AutoSync	Indicates how the CLR retrieves a value during an insert or update command.	*AutoSync*
CanBeNull	Indicates whether the table column can contain *null*.	*bool*
DbType	Maps a database type to the managed type of the class member.	*string*
Expression	This is the expression used in a computed column.	*string*
IsDbGenerated	Indicates that the column is auto-generated by the database.	*bool*
IsDiscriminator	Indicates whether a discriminator column is being used to filter derived classes.	*bool*
IsPrimaryKey	Indicates whether this column is the primary key. This can be assigned to multiple members to create a composite key.	*bool*
IsVersion	Indicates whether this column is used as a version number or timestamp.	*bool*
Name	Maps the data member or property to a specific column.	*string*
Storage	When a data column maps to a property, the *Storage* property identifies the underlying data member to bypass the property accessor method. This is used when setting the property.	*string*
UpdateCheck	Indicates how optimistic locking is handled.	*UpdateCheck*

An entity class is defined and used in the following example. *Employee* is the entity class. It is mapped to the *HumanResources.Employee* table in the SQL database. The *Id* data member is mapped explicitly to *EmployeeID* of the target entity. The other members are mapped implicitly to the correct member in the corresponding table. In *Main*, the connection string is set. The dots represent the path to the *AdventureWorks_Data* database. This is where the database is installed. You should substitute the correct path. Next, an instance of *DataContext* is created. *DataContext* is a bridge to the original data source. *DataContext.GetTable* binds the entity class to the database. The result is placed in the *Table<Employee>* type. The subsequent query returns employees that share a specific manager, where the manager ID is 21. The *foreach* loop displays the results. A reference to System.Data.Linq.dll is required to access the *System.Data.Linq* and *System.Data.Linq.Mapping* namespaces:

```
using System;
using System.Collections.Generic;
using System.Linq;
using System.Data.Linq;
using System.Data.Linq.Mapping;

namespace CSharpBook {
    class Program {
        static void Main(string[] args) {
            string conn = @"Data Source=DONISBOOK;AttachDbFilename=" +
                @"'...\AdventureWorks_Data.mdf';Integrated Security=True";
            DataContext context = new DataContext(conn);
            Table<Employee> employees = context.GetTable<Employee>();
            var query = from e in employees
                        where e.ManagerID == 21
                        select new { e.Id, e.Title};
            foreach (var item in query) {
                Console.WriteLine("{0} {1}",
                    item.Id, item.Title);
            }
        }

    }

    [Table(Name = "HumanResources.Employee")]
    public class Employee{
        [Column(Name="EmployeeID", IsPrimaryKey=true)] public int Id;
        [Column] public string Title;
        [Column] public int ManagerID;
    }
}
```

LINQ to SQL Query Expression

LINQ to SQL query expressions are applied to relational databases. The query expression is object-based, which might require mapping database tables and views to entities. Use the *DataContext* type to connect to the data source. Next, you apply a query expression to the resulting entity type. Here are the steps for applying a query expression to a table:

  1. Define entities for database tables to be used in the query.

  2. Define the connection string.

  3. Define a new *DataContext*.

  4. Call *DataContext.GetTable* to initialize each entity.

  5. Apply a query expression to the resulting entity objects.

The following sample code demonstrates these steps. This program displays the names of all salespeople. General salesperson information, sales information, and employee names are stored in separate tables. Entities are created for the *Employee, SalesOrderHeader,* and *Contact* tables. In *Main,* the connection string is defined. *DataContext.GetTable* then is called to create entity objects for the *Employee* and *Contact* tables. A query expression is performed on the table objects. A join is used to create a relationship between the two tables. The results then are enumerated and displayed:

```
using System;
using System.Collections.Generic;
using System.Linq;
using System.Data.Linq;
using System.Data.Linq.Mapping;

namespace SimpleQuery {
    class Program {
        static void Main(string[] args) {
            string conn = @"Data Source=DONISBOOK;AttachDbFilename=" +
                @"'...\AdventureWorks_Data.mdf';Integrated Security=True";
            DataContext context = new DataContext(conn);
            Table<Employee> employees = context.GetTable<Employee>();
            Table<Contact> contacts = context.GetTable<Contact>();
            var result = from employee in employees
                        join contact in contacts
                        on employee.ContactID equals contact.ContactID
                        where employee.Title == "Sales Representative"
                        select new { employee.ContactID, contact.FirstName, contact.
LastName };
            Console.WriteLine("Sales people are:");
            foreach (var item in result) {
                Console.WriteLine("{0} {1}", item.FirstName, item.LastName);
            }
        }
    }

    [Table(Name = "HumanResources.Employee")]
    public class Employee {
        [Column(IsPrimaryKey = true)] public int EmployeeID;
        [Column] public string Title;
        [Column] public int ContactID;
    }
    [Table(Name = "Person.Contact")]
    public class Contact {
        [Column(IsPrimaryKey = true)] public int ContactID;
        [Column] public string FirstName;
        [Column] public string LastName;
    }
}
```

LINQ to DataSet

You can query datasets using LINQ to DataSet. LINQ to DataSet query expressions accept datasets or derivative objects, such as data tables, as valid data sources. With LINQ to DataSet, you create datasets in the usual manner. Define a connection string, create an instance of a data adapter and dataset, and initialize the dataset using the *DataAdapter.Fill* method.

The *DataRowExtensions* class contains extensions to be used with LINQ to DataSet. The *Field* extension is a generic method and provides type-safe access to a database field (column), which is useful in a LINQ to DataSet query expression. The *SetField* extension is also a generic method and changes the value of a field.

The preceding example displays the names of salespeople. The following code does the same but uses a dataset. Two data adapters are defined that connect to the same database. The first data adapter selects the *Contact* table, while the second selects the *Employee* table. Next, both tables are added to the dataset using data adapters. References to the data tables are then extracted from the dataset. A LINQ to DataSet query expression is then performed to return a list of salespeople. The results are enumerated in a *foreach* loop, where the report is displayed:

```
using System;
using System.Collections.Generic;
using System.Linq;
using System.Text;
using System.Data;
using System.Data.SqlClient;
using System.Data.Linq;

namespace CSharpBook {
    class Program {
        static void Main(string[] args) {
            string conn =
                @"Data Source=DONISBOOK;AttachDbFilename=" +
                @"'...\AdventureWorks_Data.mdf';Integrated Security=True";
            string tablePerson= "select * from Person.Contact";
            string tableEmployee= "select * from HumanResources.Employee";

            SqlDataAdapter da1 = new SqlDataAdapter(tablePerson, conn);
            SqlDataAdapter da2 = new SqlDataAdapter(tableEmployee, conn);

            DataSet ds = new DataSet();
            da1.Fill(ds, "Contact");
            da2.Fill(ds, "Employee");
            DataTable employees=ds.Tables["Employee"];
            DataTable contacts=ds.Tables["Contact"];

            var results = from person in employees.AsEnumerable()
                        join contact in contacts.AsEnumerable()
                          on person.Field<int>("ContactID") equals contact.
Field<int>("ContactID")
                        where person.Field<string>("Title") == "Sales Representative"
```

```
            select new { ID = person.Field<int>("ContactID"),
                         First = contact.Field<string>("FirstName"),
                         Last = contact.Field<string>("LastName")};

        Console.WriteLine("Sales people are:");
        foreach (var item in results) {
            Console.WriteLine("{0} {1}", item.First, item.Last);
        }
      }
    }
}
```

Associations

Associations are integral to SQL programming. The most common associations are *one-to-many* and *one-to-one* associations. For example, an inventory database might consist of purchase order, product, and vendor tables. There would be a one-to-many relationship from the purchase order table to the product table. For any purchase order, there could be many products. A one-to-one relationship exists between the purchase order and vendor tables. This would match the vendor ID in the purchase order with the vendor name found in the vendor table. Associated tables must share a common field. The vendor ID field would be the common field between the purchase order and vendor tables. The common field provides the link between the associated tables.

In LINQ to SQL, tables are represented by entity classes. In an entity class, a relationship is defined with the *Association* attribute. The *ThisKey* and *OtherKey* properties describe the association between entities. *ThisKey* defines the common field (typically the primary key) in the current entity. *OtherKey* defines the common field in the other entity. In standard SQL terminology, *OtherKey* is equivalent to a foreign key.

Associations in LINQ to SQL are similar to joins in other query languages. A join defines the relationship between two tables. An association defines the relationship between objects. The *EntitySet* type defines a one-to-many relationship, while the *EntityRef* type defines a one-to-one relationship. Both are exposed as properties within the entity class. The *EntityRef* and *EntitySet* types also provide access to the related class or collection from within the current entity. For this reason, both typically are exposed as properties. Here is an example of the *Association* attribute, *EntityRef* type, and *EntitySet* type:

```
[Table(Name = "HumanResources.Employee")]
public class Employee {
    [Column(IsPrimaryKey = true)] public int EmployeeID;
    [Column] public string Title;
    [Column] public int ContactID;

    private EntitySet<SalesOrderHeader> propSales = null;
    [Association(Storage = "propSales", ThisKey = "EmployeeID",
        OtherKey = "SalesPersonID")]
    public EntitySet<SalesOrderHeader> Sales {
        get { return this.propSales; }
```

```
            set { this.propSales.Assign(value); }
        }

        private EntityRef<Contact> propName;
        [Association(Storage = "propName", ThisKey = "ContactID", OtherKey = "ContactID")]
        public Contact Name {
            get { return this.propName.Entity; }
            set { this.propName.Entity = value; }
        }
    }
```

Assuming that the employee is a salesperson, there is a one-to-many relationship between the *Employee* and *Sales* tables. For that reason, the relationship is defined with an *Association* attribute on an *EntitySet* type. The foreign key in the *Sales* table is defined by the *OtherKey* property, which is *SalesPersonID*. The local key is *EmployeeID* and is defined with the *ThisKey* property. In this example, the *ThisKey* property is self-documenting only. Without the property, the default is the primary key, which is *EmployeeID*. Properties in the class hide the details of the *EntityRef* and *EntitySet* types. You can access the related table (*Sales*) from this property.

There is a one-to-one relationship between the *Employee* and *Contact* tables. For that reason, the *EntityRef* type is used. The foreign key is *ContactID* of the *Contact* table, which is defined with the *ThisKey* property. The *EntityRef* is abstracted by a class property.

Here is the entire code. There are three entity classes: *Employee, Contact,* and *SalesOrderHeader.* The program generates a sales report, which is saved to a file. Notice that the query expression does not include an explicit join. The join is defined already via the *Association* attributes. The report is written to the file in the *foreach* loop. From each *Employee* entity, references to the other entity classes are available through the *EntityDef* and *EntityRef* properties. *Sales* is an *EntityDef* type, which represents the one-to-many relationship between the *Employee* and *Sales* tables. In this case, the "many" are sales records. Each sales record is retrieved in the nested *foreach* loop and is written to the sales report:

```
using System;
using System.Collections.Generic;
using System.Linq;
using System.Data.Linq;
using System.Data.Linq.Mapping;
using System.IO;

namespace SalesReport {
    class Program {
        static void Main(string[] args) {
            StreamWriter sw = new StreamWriter("report.txt");
            string conn = @"Data Source=DONISBOOK;AttachDbFilename=" +
                @"'...\AdventureWorks_Data.mdf';Integrated Security=True";
            DataContext context = new DataContext(conn);
            Table<Employee> employees = context.GetTable<Employee>();

            var sales = from person in employees
                        where person.Title == "Sales Representative"
```

```
                        select person;

        foreach (var item in sales) {
            sw.WriteLine(
                "\r\n{0} {1} {2}\r\n\r\nOrders:",
                item.EmployeeID,
                item.Name.FirstName,
                item.Name.LastName);

            foreach (var salesitem in item.Sales) {
                sw.WriteLine("{0}", salesitem.SalesOrderID);
            }
        }
    }
}

[Table(Name = "HumanResources.Employee")]
public class Employee {
    [Column(IsPrimaryKey = true)] public int EmployeeID;
    [Column] public string Title;
    [Column] public int ContactID;

    private EntitySet<SalesOrderHeader> propSales = null;
    [Association(Storage = "propSales", ThisKey = "EmployeeID",
        OtherKey = "SalesPersonID")]
    public EntitySet<SalesOrderHeader> Sales {
        get { return this.propSales; }
        set { this.propSales.Assign(value); }
    }

    private EntityRef<Contact> propName;
    [Association(Storage = "propName", ThisKey = "ContactID")]
    public Contact Name {
        get { return this.propName.Entity; }
        set { this.propName.Entity = value; }
    }

}

[Table(Name = "Sales.SalesOrderHeader")]
public class SalesOrderHeader {
    [Column(IsPrimaryKey=true)] public int SalesOrderID;
    [Column] public int CustomerID;
    [Column] public int SalesPersonID;

    private EntityRef<Employee> propSalesPerson;
    [Association(Storage = "propSalesPerson", ThisKey = "SalesPersonID")]
    public Employee SalesPerson {
        get { return this.propSalesPerson.Entity; }
        set { this.propSalesPerson.Entity = value; }
    }
}

[Table(Name = "Person.Contact")]
public class Contact {
    [Column(IsPrimaryKey = true)] public int ContactID;
```

```
        [Column] public string FirstName;
        [Column] public string LastName;
    }
}
```

LINQ to SQL Updates

As mentioned, the *DataContext* type is the bridge between LINQ to SQL and the relational database. *DataContext* creates an in-memory representation of a data table or view, which is cached in entity classes. This is the disconnected model with optimistic locking. This model is not ideal for highly contentious data sources, where there is likely to be a high number of conflicts in a short period of time. The *DataContext* is also responsible for updating changes back to the original data source and resolving possible conflicts. You can specify what action to take when a conflict occurs.

In LINQ to SQL, the Identity Management Service tracks changes to entities. The Identity Management Service keeps a single instance of a row in memory. For example, if separate queries return overlapping results, the common results reference the same entities. This keeps the in-memory representation synchronized. Entities must have a primary key defined to be tracked by the Identity Management Service. Entities without a primary key are read-only, and changes are discarded.

Changing an existing record is easy. Change a value of a mapped data member or property in the related entity. This will update the data in memory.

To add a new record, create a new instance or instances of the entity. Call *Table<TEntity>. InsertOnSubmit* to add a single entity (record). *Table<TEntity>.InsertOnAllSubmit* adds a collection of entities.

To delete a record, first find the record or records using a query expression. Then call *Table<TEntity>.DeleteOnSubmit* to delete a single entity (record). *Table<TEntity>. DeleteAllOnSubmit* deletes a collection of entities.

DataContext.SubmitChanges persists changes (updates, inserts, or deletions) to the data source. Prior to calling this method, only the in-memory representation is changed. You can obtain the pending changes with the *DataContext.GetChangeSet* method. The return value from this method is a *ChangeSet* type, which has a collection for each type of change: *Inserts, Updates,* and *Deletes.* The *ChangeSet.ToString* method returns a summary of changes. This is the signature of *DataContext.SubmitChanges:*

```
public void SubmitChanges()
```

```
public void SubmitChanges(ConflictMode failureMode)
```

ConflictMode is an enumeration, where *FailOnFirstConflict* and *ContinueOnConflict* are the values. *FailOnFirstConflict* means updates will stop on the first conflict. *ContinueOnConflict* means all updates are attempted even if a conflict occurs prior to completing.

ChangeTable is a console application that updates the *ContactType* table of the *AdventureWorks_Data* database. You enter individual commands from the command line. For example, the following commands add, delete, and modify a record in the *ContactType* table.

```
C:\>changetable -del 21

C:\>changetable -add "Senior Manager"

C:\>changetable -update 20 Director
```

The first command deletes the record that contains the specified *ContactID*. The second command adds a new record for *Senior Manager*. Finally, the last command updates the record with the specified *ContactID*. The name in that record is changed to *Director*. Running the program with no command-line arguments will list the *ContactType* records without making any updates.

In the sample code, the *switch* statement partitions and handles each command: *add, delete,* and *update*. After the *switch* statement, *DataContext.SubmitChanges* saves the changes to the actual database. The last action is to list the contents of the *ContactType* table, including any changes. Here is the code for the ChangeTable application. The entity class for the *ContactType* table is at the end of the sample code:

```
using System;
using System.Collections.Generic;
using System.Linq;
using System.Data.Linq;
using System.Data.Linq.Mapping;

namespace ChangeTable {
    class Program {
        static void Main(string[] args) {

                string conn = @"Data Source=DONISBOOK;AttachDbFilename=" +
                    @"'...\AdventureWorks_Data.mdf';Integrated Security=True";
                DataContext context = new DataContext(conn);
                Table<ContactType> contacts = context.GetTable<ContactType>();
                ContactType record = null;
                if (args.Length > 0) {
                    switch (args[0].ToLower()) {
                        case "add":
                        case "a":
                            record = new ContactType {
                                Name = args[1],
                                ModifiedDate = DateTime.Now
                            };
                            contacts.InsertOnSubmit(record);
                            break;
                        case "del":
                        case "d":
                            record = contacts.Where(c => c.ContactTypeID == int.Parse(args[1])).
First();

                            contacts.DeleteOnSubmit(record);
```

```
                            break;
                    case "update":
                    case "u":
                            record = contacts.Where(c => c.ContactTypeID == int.Parse(args[1])).
First();
                            record.Name = args[2];
                            break;
                }
                Console.WriteLine("{0}\n", context.GetChangeSet().ToString());
                context.SubmitChanges();
            }
            Console.WriteLine("Contact type list:\n");
            foreach (var contact in contacts) {
                Console.WriteLine("{0} {1} {2}",
                    contact.ContactTypeID,
                    contact.Name,
                    contact.ModifiedDate);
            }
        }
    }

    [Table(Name = "Person.ContactType")]
    public class ContactType {
        [Column(IsPrimaryKey=true, IsDbGenerated=true)] public int ContactTypeID;
        [Column] public string Name;
        [Column] public DateTime ModifiedDate;
    }
}
```

Exception Handling

Exception handling is an essential ingredient in software development and in creating a robust application. Chapter 12, "Exception Handling," discusses various aspects of exception handling, including protected bodies, exception handlers, and termination handlers. A protected body, also known as a *guarded body,* is a *try* block and encapsulates protected code. When an exception is raised in the protected code, execution is transferred to the exception filter. The exception filter is a *catch* statement that identifies which exceptions are handled at that location on the call stack. Termination handlers are *finally* blocks. Place cleanup code in a *finally* block, where code is executed whether an exception is raised or not.

There are system or hard exceptions such as access violations and software exceptions, which are thrown by the CLR. You can throw some system exceptions. However, you also can throw user-defined exceptions.

Unhandled exceptions can crash an application, causing a crash dialog box to be displayed. You can override this default behavior with the appropriate unhandled exception event handler. This and other topics related to exception handling are detailed in the next chapter.

Chapter 12
Exception Handling

Exception handling helps applications trap and respond in a predictable and robust manner to exceptional events. This enhances the correctness of an application, which naturally improves customer satisfaction. Exception handling is an important ingredient of a robust application, but it is often an afterthought. You should proactively consider exception handling as an integral part of the application design and include it in all aspects of application planning and development. Conversely, treating exception handling as an afterthought leads to poorly implemented solutions for exception handling and a less robust application.

What is an exception? *Exceptions* are events, often indicating an error, that alter the normal flow of execution within an application. Exceptions are categorized as system exceptions or application exceptions. System exceptions are raised by the Common Language Runtime (CLR) and include null-reference, out-of-memory, divide-by-zero, and stack overflow exceptions. Some exceptional events are detected by application logic, not by the run time. Application exceptions are useful in these circumstances. Application exceptions, considered user-defined exceptions, are thrown by the application, not by the CLR. As an example, constructors that fail are not always detectable by the CLR. In addition, constructors implicitly return *void*, which prevents returning an error code. For these reasons, throwing an application exception in the failed constructor is the best solution to notify the application and user.

It may sound silly to say it like this, but I'll say it anyway: Exceptions are for exceptions! Exception handling is not a substitute for transfer of control or a *goto* statement. Exceptions are expensive when compared with conventional methods of transferring control, which are relatively inexpensive. Whenever possible, applications should preempt an exception with error checking and avoid the elevated cost of exception handling. For example, you can perform data validation and return an error code, if incorrect values can cause exceptions. Data validation and, if necessary, returning an error code are undoubtedly cheaper performance-wise than raising an exception.

Overuse of exceptions makes code harder to read and maintain. Errors that frequently occur should not be handled with exception handling, but with error codes or returns. Remember that exceptions should be reserved for exceptional events.

An Exception Example

A common exception is caused by dividing by zero. Integer division, where the divisor is zero, triggers a divide-by-zero exception. (However, floating-point division by zero does not cause an exception; instead, infinity is returned.) The following code causes an unhandled divide-by-zero exception, which terminates the application:

```
using System;

namespace Donis.CSharpBook {
    public class Starter {
        public static void Main() {
            int var1 = 5, var2 = 0;
            var1 /= var2;    // exception occurs
        }
    }
}
```

Place code that you think is likely to raise an exception in a *try* block, where it is protected from exceptions. Exceptions raised in the *try* block are trapped. The stack then is walked by the CLR to locate an appropriate exception handler. Code not within the scope of a *try* block is unprotected from exceptions. In this circumstance, the exception eventually evolves into an unhandled exception. As demonstrated in the previous code, an unhandled exception is apt to abort an application.

In the following code, the divide-by-zero exception is caught in a *try* block. Trapping, catching, and handling an exception are separate tasks. The *catch* statement consists of a *catch* filter and a statement block. The *DivideByZeroException* filter catches the divide-by-zero exception. The *catch* statement block is where the exception is handled. In this example, the stack trace is displayed. The location of the infraction should be included in the stack trace, which is useful. After the exception is handled, the execution then continues at the first statement after the *catch* statement block:

```
using System;

namespace Donis.CSharpBook {
    public class Starter {
        public static void Main() {
            try {
                int var1 = 5, var2 = 0;
                var1 /= var2;    // exception occurs
            }
            catch(DivideByZeroException except) {
                Console.WriteLine("Exception " + except.StackTrace);
            }
        }
    }
}
```

A Standard Exception Model

.NET offers a standard exception model. Exception handling is implemented within the CLR and is not specific to a managed language. Each managed language exposes exception handling using language-specific syntax. The standard exception model contributes to language independence, which is an important tenet of .NET. In addition, exceptions raised in one managed language can be caught in a different managed language. Prior to .NET, there were competing models for error handling: Microsoft Visual Basic 6.0, Visual C++, the Win32 Software Development Kit (SDK), Microsoft Foundation Classes (MFC), and Component Object Model (COM) had different exception models. In a component-driven architecture, this diversity contributes to complexity and potential product instability. In .NET, exception handling between disparate components is consistent, simple, and stable.

In .NET, the standard exception model is structured exception handling, which is essentially the *try* and *catch* statements. C-based language developers and Java developers are probably familiar with structured exception handling. For Visual Basic developers, this is a seismic shift from unstructured exception handling. The unstructured model, such as *on error goto* and *on error resume*, is thankfully now obsolete.

Structured Exception Handling

At the advent of an exception, the CLR evaluates the stack to determine where an exception is trapped, if at all, and how it is handled. When an exception occurs, the stack is walked in search of an appropriate exception handler. When a *catch* filter that matches the exception is located, the exception is handled in the related exception handler, which is the *catch* statement block. This sets the scope of the exception on the stack. Before the exception is handled, the CLR unwinds the stack to that scope.

Try Statements

Try blocks are observers; they watch for exceptions in the code they protect. Place only code that is prone to an exception in a *try* block. Do not attempt to protect an entire application in a *try* block—there are more convenient and practical means of accomplishing the same feat, as described later in this chapter.

As mentioned, exceptions are stack-based. The following code contains a fencepost error that happens when the bounds of the array are exceeded. The result is an exception in the unprotected *MethodA* method. *Main* called *MethodA*, where the call site is protected in a *try* block. For this reason, the exception propagates from *MethodA* to *Main*, where the exception is caught and handled:

```
using System;

namespace Donis.CSharpBook {
    public class Starter {

        public static void Main() {
            try {
```

```
            MethodA();
        }
        catch(Exception except) {
            Console.WriteLine(except.Message);
        }
    }

    public static void MethodA() {
        int [] values = { 1,2,3,4 };
        for(int count = 0; count <= values.Length; ++count) {
            Console.WriteLine(values[count]);
        }
    }
    }
}
```

This is the syntax of the *try* statement:

```
try { protected } catch(filter1) { handler1 } ... catch(filtern) { handlern }

    finally { terminationhandler }
```

Try statements must be paired with either a *catch* statement or a *finally* statement. There can be zero or more *catch* statements attached to a *try* statement; there are zero or one *finally* statements. If both *catch* and *finally* are present, all *catch* statements should precede the *finally* statement. The following code demonstrates various combinations of *try*, *catch*, and *finally* statements:

```
// try..catch
try {
}
catch(Exception e) {
}

// try..finally
try {
}
finally {
}

// try..catch..finally
try {
}
catch(Exception e) {
}
finally {
}

// try..catches..finally
try {
}
catch(Exception e) {
}
```

```
catch {
}
finally {
}
```

Catch Statements

A *catch* statement filters exceptions and determines if the exception that was raised is handled in the *catch* statement block. It defines whether the exception is handled at that scope or earlier in the stack. If the filter matches the exception, the exception is suppressed, and control is transferred to the adjoining *catch* statement block to be handled. If not, the CLR continues to search the stack for an appropriate filter. If a matching filter is not found, the exception becomes an unhandled exception.

Exceptions are derived from *System.Exception*. The *catch* filter declares an *exception* object and catches that exception type and any descendant. The *exception* object contains details of the exception, such as a user-friendly message describing the exception. The *exception* object caught in the filter is accessible only in the *catch* statement block. *System.Exception* is the base class of .NET exceptions and can be used as a generic filter.

A *System.Exception* filter catches all exceptions. Derived classes of *System.Exception* catch more specific exceptions. In the previous code, the *DivideByZeroException* filter catches integer divide-by-zero exceptions and nothing else. A *try* block with multiple catch filters can catch distinct exceptions. The catches should be listed in the code from most specific first to most generic last. The following code has several exception filters, correctly ordered from specific to generic:

```
using System;

namespace Donis.CSharpBook {
    public class Starter {
        public static void Main() {
            try {
                int var1 = 5, var2 = 0;
                var1 /= var2;
            }
            catch(DivideByZeroException except) {
                Console.WriteLine("Exception " + except.Message);
            }
            catch(System.ArithmeticException except) {
                Console.WriteLine("Exception " + except.Message);
            }
            catch(Exception except) {
                Console.WriteLine("Exception " + except.Message);
            }
        }
    }
}
```

In the preceding code, *DivideByZeroException* is specific and catches only divide-by-zero exceptions. *ArithmeticException* is less specific and catches a variety of arithmetic exceptions, including the divide-by-zero exception. *Exception* catches all exceptions, which includes divide-by-zero and any other arithmetic exceptions. The exception in the sample code is caught by the *DivideByZeroException* catch filter and handled in that *catch* statement block.

The *catch* filter is optional. When omitted, the default filter is *catch all*—which is functionally similar to *System.Exception*:

```
using System;

namespace Donis.CSharpBook {
    public class Starter {
        public static void Main() {
            try {
                int var1 = 5, var2 = 0;
                var1 /= var2;
            }
            catch(DivideByZeroException except) {
                Console.WriteLine("Exception " + except.StackTrace);
            }
            catch {
                // catch remaining managed and unmanaged exceptions
            }
        }
    }
}
```

Propagating Exceptions

Exceptions are not always handled locally, where the exception is caught. It is sometimes beneficial to catch an exception and then propagate the exception. *Propagating* an exception involves catching and then rethrowing the exception. Rethrowing an exception continues the search along the call stack to find an appropriate handler. Here are some reasons to propagate an exception:

- Your application has a centralized handler for the exception. There are several reasons for implementing centralized handlers, including code reuse. Instead of handling the same exception in various locations in an application, concentrate code for certain exceptions in a centralized handler. Wherever the exception is raised, the proper response is to log the exception and then propagate it to the centralized handler.

- Resources required to handle the exception sometimes are not available locally. For example, assume an exception is raised because of an invalid database connection. However, the correct connection string is read from a file that is not available where the exception occurs. The solution is to propagate the exception to a handler that has access to the connection string.

- You might not want to handle the specific exception caught in a general exception filter. Propagate the unwanted exception. For example, this would be useful for catching all *DataException* types, with the exception of the *DuplicateNameException*. One solution would be to write 12 individual catches—one for each of the data exceptions except for the *DuplicateNameException* exception. A better solution is to catch the *DataException* type and propagate the *DuplicateNameException* when necessary. This involves a single *catch* statement versus 12 *catch* statements and eliminates redundant code.

- You want to catch an exception to gather information or to report on an exception and then propagate the exception to be further handled elsewhere. In this circumstance, you do not plan on handling the exception at that point in the call stack.

To propagate an exception, rethrow the same exception or a related exception in the *catch* statement block. An empty *throw* statement automatically propagates the caught exception.

Exceptions might propagate through several layers of an application. Ultimately, the exception could percolate to the user interface level. As an exception percolates, the exception should become less specific. Exceptions from the lower echelon of an application could contain detailed information that is appropriate to the application developer but probably not relevant to the user. Internal exceptions might contain security and other sensitive information not appropriate for a benign user (or a malicious one, for that matter). Exceptions that reach the user should present user-relevant information: a user-friendly message, steps to resolve the exception, or even a customer support link. If necessary, record the detailed information of the original exception in a log or some other convenient and retrievable location.

When an exception is rethrown, you can preserve the original exception in the *InnerException* field. Successive *InnerException* attributes form a chain of exceptions from the current exception back to the original exception. The *InnerException* field can be initialized in the constructor of the new exception. Here is sample code that propagates an exception and sets the inner exception:

```
using System;

namespace Donis.CSharpBook {
    public class Starter {
        public static void Main() {
            try {
                MethodA();
            }
            catch(Exception except) {
                Console.WriteLine(except.Message);
                Console.WriteLine(except.InnerException.Message);
            }
        }

        public static void MethodA() {
            try {
                MethodB();
```

```
            }
            catch(DivideByZeroException inner) {

                // record divide-by-zero exception in
                //     event log.

                // inner is the inner exception
                throw new Exception("Math exception",
                    inner);
            }
        }

        public static void MethodB() {
            int var1 = 5, var2 = 0;
            var1 /= var2;
        }
    }
}
```

Finally Statements

The *finally* block is the termination handler. When an exception occurs, protected code after the exceptional event is not executed. What if it includes cleanup code? If the cleanup code is not executed, resources are left dangling. Termination handlers are the solution. Code that must execute regardless of an exception occurring is placed in a termination handler. When an exception is raised, any *finally* blocks within scope are called as the stack is unwound. Note that the termination handler is executed even when there is no occurrence of an exception. Execution simply falls through the *try* block into the corresponding *finally* block. In the termination handler, you could close a file, release a database connection, or otherwise manage resources.

Here is a typical termination handler:

```
using System;
using System.IO;

namespace Donis.CSharpBook {
    public class FileWriter {
        public static void Main() {
            StreamWriter sw = null;
            try {
                sw = new StreamWriter("date.txt");
                sw.Write(DateTime.Now.ToLongTimeString());
                throw new ApplicationException("exception");
                // dangling code
            }
            finally {
                sw.Close();
```

```
                Console.WriteLine("file closed");
            }
        }
    }
}
```

Exception Information Table

The CLR uses the Exception Information Table to track protected code in an efficient manner. Because of the Exception Information Table, there is no overhead associated with an exception handler unless an exception occurs.

An Exception Information Table is constructed for every managed application. The table has an entry for each method in the program. Each entry is an array, where the array elements describe the filters and handlers of that method. Entries in the array represent a *catch* filter, *user-filtered* handler, *catch* handler, or *termination* handler. User-filtered handlers use the *when* clause and are available in Visual Basic .NET, but not in C#.

When an exception occurs, the CLR consults the Exception Information Table. The entry for the method hosting the exception is searched for a filter that matches the exception. If the array is empty or a matching filter is not found, the entry of the next method on the stack is examined. When the boundary of the application is reached, the exception is considered unhandled.

Nested *Try* Blocks

Try blocks can be nested. The order of evaluation is more complex with nested *try* blocks. *Try* blocks can be nested within a method call or call stack. Let us assume *FuncA* has a *try* block. Within that block, *FuncB* is called. *FuncB* also has a *try* block. The *try* block in *FuncB* is nested by the *try* block in *FuncA*. This is the order of execution when an exception occurs:

1. Find a *try* block. If an exception is raised outside a protected block, the exception is not trapped and is therefore unhandled.

2. From the *try* block, walk the stack until a matching *catch* filter is found. This defines the scope of the exception. If a matching *catch* filter is not found, the exception is unhandled.

3. As the stack is unwound, *finally* blocks within the scope of the exception are run. The innermost *finally* blocks are executed first.

4. The *catch* statement block of the matching *catch* filter is executed as the exception handler.

5. Execution continues at the first statement after the *catch* statement block.

6. *Finally* blocks at the scope of the exception handler are executed.

Figure 12-1 diagrams the sequence when an exception is raised in a nested *try* block.

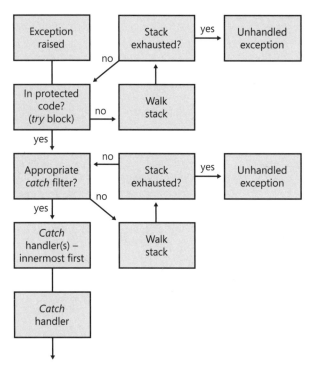

FIGURE 12-1 Execution sequence of exception handling

The following code has several nested *try* blocks:

```
using System;

namespace Donis.CSharpBook {
    public class Starter {

        public static void Main() {
            try {
                Console.WriteLine("outer - try");
                try {
                    Console.WriteLine("inner - try");
                    throw new ApplicationException("exception");
                }
                finally {
                    Console.WriteLine("inner - finally");
                }
            }
            catch(Exception except) {
                Console.WriteLine("outer - catch");
            }
            finally {
```

```
                   Console.WriteLine("outer - finally");
               }
           }
       }
   }
```

System.Exception

System.Exception is the base exception class. All exceptions in .NET are derived from *System. Exception*. *System.SystemException* is the base class for system exceptions raised by the CLR, such as *System.Data.DataException* or *System.FormatException*. *System.SystemException* is derived directly from *System.Exception*. *System.SystemException* does not refine *System. Exception*. However, it is an important marker that distinguishes between system and application exceptions, as demonstrated in the following code:

```
using System;

namespace Donis.CSharpBook {
    public class Starter {
        public static void Main() {
            try {
                int var1 = 5, var2 = 0;
                var1 /= var2;     // exception occurs
            }
            catch(Exception except) {
                if (except is SystemException) {
                    Console.WriteLine("Exception thrown by runtime");
                }
                else {
                    Console.WriteLine("Exception thrown by application");
                }
            }
        }
    }
}
```

System.Exception Functions

System.Exception has four constructors:

- *public Exception[1]()*
- *public Exception[2](string message)*
- *public Exception[3](string message, Exception innerException)*
- *protected Exception[4](Serialization info, StreamingContext context)*

Exception[1] is the default constructor. The *Exception*[2] constructor has a string parameter, which sets the user-friendly message of the exception. The *Exception*[3] constructor sets the user-friendly message and the inner exception, which is the originating exception. *Exception*[4] deserializes an exception raised remotely.

The *Exception* class has several other helpful methods. Table 12-1 lists the important methods of the class.

TABLE 12-1 Exception methods

Method	Result
GetBaseException	Returns the original exception in a chain of exception objects
GetObjectData	Serializes data of the *Exception* class
GetType	Returns the type of the exception
ToString	Returns a concatenation of the name of the *exception* object and the user-friendly message

The following code calls *GetBaseException* and outputs the error message of the initial exception. If the current exception is the first exception in a chain of exceptions, *GetBaseException* returns *null*. Alternatively, you can walk *InnerException* properties back to the first exception:

```
using System;

namespace Donis.CSharpBook {
    public class Starter {
        public static void Main() {
            try {
                MethodA();
            }
            catch(Exception except) {
                Exception original = except.GetBaseException();
                Console.WriteLine(original.Message);
            }
        }

        public static void MethodA() {
            try {
                MethodB();
            }
            catch(Exception except) {
                throw new ApplicationException("Inner Exception", except);
            }
        }

        public static void MethodB() {
            throw new ApplicationException("Innermost Exception");
        }
    }
}
```

System.Exception Properties

System.Exception has a full complement of properties providing information on the exception. Table 12-2 describes the properties of the *Exception* class.

TABLE 12-2 *Exception* **properties**

Property	Description	Type	Read/Write
Data	Returns a dictionary collection that provides additional information pertaining to the exception.	*IDictionary*	R
HelpLink	Link to a help file describing the exception.	*string*	R/W
HResult	The HRESULT, which is a 32-bit error code common to COM, assigned to the exception. This is a protected property and available to derived types.	*int*	R/W
InnerException	When exceptions are propagated, the inner exception represents the previous exception. When the outer exception is thrown, the *InnerException* can be set.	*Exception*	R
Message	User-friendly message describing the exception.	*string*	R
Source	Name of application or object where the exception occurred.	*string*	R/W
StackTrace	String representation of the call stack when the exception occurred.	*string*	R
TargetSite	Reference to the method where the exception was raised.	*MethodBase*	R

The *Message* and *InnerException* properties are settable in constructors of the *Exception* class.

The following code uses some of the properties of the *Exception* class. In *Main*, *MethodA* is called, and an exception is raised. The exception is then caught and handled in *Main*. In the *catch* statement block, leveraging the *TargetSite* property, *MethodA* is then called again successfully. The *TargetSite* property returns a reference to an object of *MethodBase* type, which can be used to invoke the method where the exception occurred. At that time, the method is invoked anew with a fresh state. *MethodBase.Invoke* is explained fully in Chapter 10, "Delegates and Events."

```
using System;
using System.Reflection;

namespace Donis.CSharpBook {
    public class Starter {
        public static bool bException = true;
        public static void Main() {
```

```
        try {
            MethodA();
        }
        catch(Exception except) {
            Console.WriteLine(except.Message);
            bException = false;
            except.TargetSite.Invoke(null, null);
        }
    }

    public static void MethodA() {
        if (bException) {
            throw new ApplicationException("exception message");
        }
    }
}
}
```

Application Exceptions

Application exceptions are custom exceptions and are thrown by the application, not by the CLR. Application exceptions are derived from *System.ApplicationException* or *System. Exception. System.ApplicationException* adds nothing to *System.Exception*. While *System. SystemException* is a marker for system exceptions, *System.ApplicationException* brands application exceptions. A custom exception derived from *System.Exception* can also be used to brand a group of custom exceptions; when several custom exceptions are planned, create a custom base exception class to categorize the exceptions. For convenience and maintainability, deploy application exceptions as a group in a separate assembly.

Do not accidentally create an application exception for an existing exception. Research the available system exceptions to avoid replicating an existing exception.

These are the steps for creating an application exception:

1. Name the application exception. As a best practice, the class name should have the *Exception* suffix, as in *DivideByZeroException*.

2. Derive the application exception from *System.Exception*.

3. Define constructors that initialize the state of the application exception. This includes initializing members inherited from the base class.

4. Within the application exception, refine *System.Exception* as desired, such as adding properties that further delineate this specific exception.

To raise an application exception, use the *throw* statement. You can also throw system exceptions. Thrown exceptions are considered software exceptions. The CLR reacts to software exceptions in the same way it does to standard exceptions. Here are some examples of *throw* syntax:

```
throw exceptioninstance;
```

```
throw;
```

The second syntax is specialized: It is available in a *catch* statement block but nowhere else. This version of the *throw* statement rethrows an exception caught in the *catch* statement block. However, the best policy is to add additional context to an exception before propagating the *exception* object. Propagating exceptions was reviewed earlier in this chapter.

Application exceptions are typically prompted by an exceptional event. What is an exceptional event? A strict definition for this term does not exist. Basically, you define the basis of an event. Remember that raising an exception simply for transfer of control or for a nonexceptional event is bad practice. In an application, the following could be considered exceptional events for which throwing an application exception is warranted:

- Constructor fails to initialize the state of an object.

- A property does not pass validation.

- Some parameters should refer to an object. If the parameter is *null*, throw an exception.

- An exceptional value is returned from a function.

- A function that returns *void* has an exceptional event. Since the function return type is *void*, it cannot return an error code on an exceptional event. In this circumstance, throwing an exception is appropriate.

ConstructorException is an application exception. In the following sample code, this exception is thrown when a constructor fails. It refines the *System.Exception* base class by adding a name and time property. In addition, the *Message* property is assigned an appropriate message. This is the code for the *ConstructorException* class:

```
using System;

namespace Donis.CSharpBook {

    public class ConstructorException: Exception {

        public ConstructorException(object origin)
                : this(origin, null) {
        }

        public ConstructorException(object origin, Exception innerException)
                : base("Exception in constructor", innerException) {
            prop_Typename = origin.GetType().Name;
            prop_Time = DateTime.Now.ToLongDateString() + " " +
```

```
                    DateTime.Now.ToShortTimeString();
        }

    protected string prop_Typename=null;
        public string Typename {
            get {
                return prop_Typename;
            }
        }

        protected string prop_Time = null;
        public string Time {
            get {
                return prop_Time;
            }
        }
    }
}
```

This code uses the *ConstructorException* class:

```
using System;

namespace Donis.CSharpBook {
    public class Starter {
        public static void Main() {
            try {
                ZClass obj = new ZClass();
            }
            catch(ConstructorException except) {
                Console.WriteLine(except.Message);
                Console.WriteLine("Typename: " + except.Typename);
                Console.WriteLine("Occurred: " + except.Time);
            }
        }
    }

    class ZClass {
        public ZClass() {
            // initialization fails
            throw new ConstructorException(this);
        }
    }
}
```

Exception Translation

In some circumstances, the CLR catches an exception and rethrows a different exception. The inner exception of the new exception contains the original exception. Check documentation in the Framework Class Library (FCL) to confirm when exception translation occurs. For example, invoking a method dynamically using reflection is one such circumstance. Exceptions raised in methods invoked by *MethodInfo.Invoke* are automatically trapped and converted to *Target InvocationException*. The following code produces an example of exception translation:

```
using System;
using System.Reflection;

namespace Donis.CSharpBook {

    public class ZClass {
        public static void MethodA() {
            Console.WriteLine("ZClass.MethodA");
            throw new Exception("MethodA exception");
        }
    }

    public class Starter {
        public static void Main() {
            try {
                Type zType = typeof(ZClass);
                MethodInfo method = zType.GetMethod("MethodA");
                method.Invoke(null, null);
            }
            catch(Exception except) {
                Console.WriteLine(except.Message);
                Console.WriteLine("original: " +
                    except.InnerException.Message);
            }
        }
    }
}
```

COM Interoperability Exceptions

.NET applications often host COM components or expose managed components to COM clients. These applications must be prepared to handle and possibly throw COM exceptions, respectively. The prevalence of COM components makes COM interoperability an important consideration for managed applications into the foreseeable future.

COM Exceptions

COM components should sandbox exceptions, which protects COM clients from potential language-specific or platform-specific exceptions. *COM* methods return an *HRESULT* structure, which is the result code of the method. An *HRESULT* is a 32-bit structure, where the severity bit is in the high-order bit. The severity bit is set if any exception is raised. The Win32 Software Development Kit (SDK) defines constants representing various *HRESULT* codes. *E_NOINTERFACE, E_INVALIDARG, E_OUTOFMEMORY, S_OK,* and *S_FALSE* are common *HRESULT* codes. *E_XXX* codes are error codes indicating that an exception was raised or some other exceptional event happened. *S_XXX* codes are success codes where no failure is reported.

When managed code calls methods on *COM* objects, the CLR consumes the resulting *HRESULT*. If the *HRESULT* represents a known *COM* error (an *E_XXX* code), the CLR maps the *HRESULT* to a managed exception. For example, *E_POINTER* maps to the *NullReferenceException*, which is a managed exception. An error code from an unknown *HRESULT* is mapped to a *COMException* object. No exception is thrown if the *HRESULT* is a success code (an *S_XXX* code). Table 12-3 shows the common translations of *HRESULT* to managed exceptions.

TABLE 12-3 *COM exception table*

COM Exception	Managed Exception
COR_E_OVERFLOW	*OverflowException*
COR_E_THREADSTOP	*ThreadStopException*
E_NOINTERFACE	*InvalidCastException*
E_NOTIMPL	*NotImplementedException*
E_OUTOFMEMORY	*OutOfMemoryException*
E_POINTER	*NullReferenceException*

The *COMException* is derived from *System.Runtime.InteropServices.ExternalException*, which indirectly derives from *System.Exception*. The *COMException* class has additional properties that hold the details of the unknown *COM* exception. For example, the *ErrorCode* property contains the *HRESULT* from the *COM* method.

COM components implement *Error* objects to provide extended error information to clients. An *Error* object implements the *IErrorInfo* interface. Members of the *IErrorInfo* interface correlate to members of the *COMException* class and are therefore accessible to the managed client. Table 12-4 maps members of the *Error* object to the *COMException* class.

TABLE 12-4 *IErrorInfo* to *COMException* mapping

IErrorInfo member	*COMException* member
IErrorInfo::GetDescription	*COMException.Message*
IErrorInfo::GetSource	*COMException.Source*
If *IErrorInfo::GetHelpFile* is non-zero, *IErrorInfo::GetHelpFile*+"#"+*IErrorInfo::GetHelpContext*	*COMException.HelpLink*

The following code is a partial listing from an Active Template Library (ATL) project that publishes a COM component. The COM component exposes the *CComponentZ::MethodA*. Using the *AtlReportError* API, *CComponentZ::MethodA* builds an *Error* object to return extended error information to the client. The method also returns a custom error code in *HRESULT*, which therefore will be unknown to the CLR:

```
// ComponentZ.cpp : Implementation of CComponentZ

#include "stdafx.h"
#include "ComponentZ.h"
#include ".\componentz.h"


// CComponentZ
```

```
STDMETHODIMP CComponentZ::MethodA(void) {
    // TODO: Add your implementation code here

    HRESULT hResult = MAKE_HRESULT( 1, FACILITY_NULL, 12 );

    MessageBox(NULL, "COM component", "Hello from", MB_OK);
    return AtlReportError (GetObjectCLSID(), "My error message", 5,
        "http://error.asp",GUID_NULL, hResult);
}
```

The following code is managed code, in which the ATL component is called from a managed COM client. Because the *HRESULT* is unknown, the error code appears as a *COMException* exception. The code uses *COMException* properties to report additional information about the custom exception:

```
using System;
using System.Runtime.InteropServices;

namespace COMClient {
    class Program {
        static void Main(string[] args) {
            try {
                COMLib.CComponentZClass com_object =
                    new COMLib.CComponentZClass();
                com_object.MethodA();
            }
            catch (COMException except) {
                Console.WriteLine(except.ErrorCode);
                Console.WriteLine(except.HelpLink);
                Console.WriteLine(except.Message);
            }
            catch (Exception) {

            }
        }
    }
}
```

Generating *COM* Exceptions

Managed exceptions have an *HRESULT* property that translates the exception to a *COM* error result. System exceptions are already assigned an appropriate *HRESULT*. For application exceptions, you should initialize the *HRESULT* property in the constructor. A managed component that expects COM clients must set the *HRESULT* for all exceptions.

The following code defines *TypeException* as an example of an application exception. *TypeException* should be thrown when an object is the wrong type. *TypeException* has two overloaded constructors. Both constructors set the *HResult* property of the exception to the *E_NOTIMPL* error code (0x80004001). The one-argument constructor accepts a type object, which indicates the required type that was not implemented. The name of the type is added to the error message of the exception:

```csharp
using System;

namespace Donis.CSharpBook {

    public class TypeException: Exception {

        public TypeException()
                : base("object type wrong") {
            HResult = unchecked((int) 0x80004001); // E_NOTIMPL
        }

        public TypeException(Type objectType)
                : base("Argument type wrong: " + objectType.Name +
                    " required") {
            prop_RequiredType=objectType.Name;
            HResult = unchecked((int) 0x80004001); // E_NOTIMPL
        }

        private string prop_RequiredType;
        public string RequiredType {
            get {
                return prop_RequiredType;
            }
        }
    }
}
```

In the following code, the *Delegator* class uses the *TypeException* class. *Delegator* delegates method calls of *Delegator.MethodA* to an external object. For the delegation to be successful, the external object must also implement the *MethodA* method, which is defined in *ZInterface*. Appropriately, the code in *Delegator.MethodA* checks for the implementation of *ZInterface*. If *ZInterface* is not implemented, *TypeException* is thrown. Otherwise, *Delegator.MethodA* proceeds with the delegation:

```csharp
using System;

namespace Donis.CSharpBook {
    interface ZInterface {
        void MethodA();
    }

    public class Delegator {
        public Delegator(object obj) {
            externalobject = obj;
        }

        public void MethodA() {
            if (externalobject is ZInterface) {
                ((ZInterface)externalobject).MethodA();
            }
```

```
        else {
            throw new TypeException(
                typeof(ZInterface));
        }
    }
}

        private object externalobject;
    }
}
```

The *YClass.UseDelegator* method shown in the following code creates an instance of the *Delegator* class. A *ZClass* object is passed into the *Delegator* constructor as the external object. *ZClass* does not implement *MethodA*. *Delegator.MethodA* is called in *YClass.UseDelegator*. A *TypeException* is thrown because *ZClass* does not implement the appropriate interface:

```
using System;
using System.Runtime.InteropServices;
using Donis.CSharpBook;

class ZClass {
}

[ClassInterface(ClassInterfaceType.AutoDual)]
public class YClass {
    public void UseDelegator() {
        ZClass obj = new ZClass();
        Delegator del = new Delegator(obj);
        del.MethodA();
    }
}
```

COM clients can access managed code through COM Callable Wrappers (CCWs). The following unmanaged code creates an instance of *YClass* and invokes *YClass.UseDelegator*. As expected, an exception occurs, which translates to *E_NOTIMPL* in unmanaged code. The COM client checks for this exception and displays the appropriate message:

```
#import "..\yclass.tlb" no_namespace, raw_interfaces_only, named_guids

#include "objbase.h"

void main() {
    CoInitialize(NULL);
    _YClassPtr obj(CLSID_YClass);
    HRESULT hResult = obj->UseDelegator();
    if (hResult == E_NOTIMPL) {
        MessageBox(NULL,"Required interface not implemented",
            "In Managed Component", MB_OK);
    }
    else {
        MessageBox(NULL, "Managed Component", "No error",
            MB_OK);
    }
}
```

Remote Exceptions

Exceptions sometime occur in remote code. An exception that is raised in a different application domain is a *remote exception*. Remote exceptions include exceptions thrown in a .NET Remoting application or a Web service application. Exceptions that cross application domains must be serialized to maintain their state. System exceptions are serializable. However, you need to make application exceptions serializable.

Follow these steps to serialize an application exception:

1. Adorn the application exception with the *serializable* attribute.

2. Implement a two-argument constructor with a *SerializationInfo* parameter and a *StreamingContext* parameter. In addition, call the two-argument constructor in the base class to allow the base class to deserialize its state. Deserialize the exception with the *SerializationInfo* parameter, which is a state bag. Retrieve the state information of the exception using the *Get* methods of the *SerializationInfo* object. The *StreamingContext* parameter provides additional data about the source or target of the serialization process.

3. Implement the *GetObjectData* method to serialize the exception. The method also has two parameters: *Serialization* and *StreamingContext*. Use the *Serialization.AddValue* method to serialize the state of the exception. Invoke *GetObjectData* on the base class to allow the base class to serialize itself.

4. For the exception to be available in the client assembly, share the assembly containing the exception in the global assembly cache or an application configuration file. If the assembly is not shared, the assembly must be copied into the private directory of the client application.

In the following code, *CustomException* is an application exception that supports remoting. There is one property, *prop_Time*, which is serialized in *GetObjectData* and deserialized in the two-argument constructor:

```
using System;
using System.Reflection;
using System.Runtime.Serialization;

[assembly:AssemblyVersion("1.1.0.0")]
[assembly:AssemblyCultureAttribute("")]

namespace Donis.CSharpBook {

    [Serializable]
    public class CustomException: Exception {

        public CustomException()
                : base("custom exception", null) {
            prop_Time=DateTime.Now.ToLongDateString() + " " +
```

```
                DateTime.Now.ToShortTimeString();
        }

        protected CustomException(SerializationInfo info,
                StreamingContext context) : base(info, context) {
            prop_Time = info.GetString("Time");
        }

        public override void GetObjectData(SerializationInfo info,
                StreamingContext context) {
            info.AddValue("Time", prop_Time, typeof(string));
            base.GetObjectData(info,context);
        }

        protected string prop_Time = null;
        public string Time {
            get {
                return prop_Time;
            }
        }
    }
}
```

In Microsoft Visual Studio, the assembly attributes, such as *AssemblyVersion*, are found in the *AssemblyInfo.cs* file. In the preceding example, the assembly level attributes are contained in the code listing rather than in a separate file for convenience.

Unhandled Exceptions

Unhandled exceptions are not handled directly in application code but deferred to a global handler. As the default behavior, the global handler reports the exception in an error box that presents a variety of choices. For applications running under the control of a debugger, the exception is usually trapped in the debugger.

What is the life cycle of an exception? Exceptions are initially categorized as first-chance exceptions. If the application is running under the auspices of a debugger, the debugger is first consulted about the exception. Debuggers typically ignore first-chance exceptions, and the exception is then forwarded to the application. When no debugger is present, the first-chance exception is immediately sent to the application. If the application does not handle the first-chance exception, the exception becomes a high-priority second-chance exception. If a debugger is attached, the second-chance exception typically is handled by the debugger. For example, upon finding a second-chance exception, the Visual Studio debugger transfers the user to the location in the source code where the exception occurred. This assumes that source code is available. If it is not, the user is shown a disassembly. If no debugger is present, execution is transferred to a global exception handler, which displays an error dialog box and then terminates the application. Figure 12-2 shows the life cycle of an exception.

Applications can trap unhandled exceptions. The mechanism is different between Microsoft Windows Forms and Console applications. For Windows Forms, add a handler to the *Application.ThreadException* event. For Console applications, the handler is added to the *AppDomain.UnhandledException* event. Methods added to the *Application.ThreadException* event chain catch and handle the exception. This is an advantage when compared with *AppDomain.UnhandledException*. Event handlers for the *AppDomain.UnhandledException* event can respond to an unhandled exception, but the exception is not caught. Therefore, the exception will resurface after the handlers have finished.

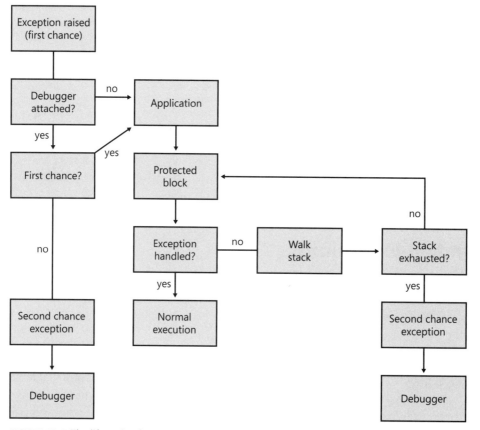

FIGURE 12-2 The life cycle of an exception, which begins when an exception is raised

Do not use the unhandled exception handler to catch all exceptions. Proper application design identifies specific exceptions that an application should anticipate. Those exceptions should be caught and handled within the boundaries of structured exception handling. Reserve the unhandled exception method for unanticipated exceptions.

Application.ThreadException

In a Windows Forms application, an *Application.ThreadException* event is raised upon an unhandled exception. Subscribe to the *ThreadException* event to handle the unhandled exception. The subscriber is an exception handler, which prevents the application from being terminated. Do not propagate the trapped exception in the *ThreadException* exception handler. The new exception would be unprotected and will likely terminate the application. After the unhandled exception handler completes, execution simply continues.

Subscribe to the *ThreadException* event with a *ThreadExceptionEventHandler* delegate, which has two parameters. The object parameter is the thread object of the thread that raised the exception. The *ThreadExceptionEventArg* parameter of the *System.Threading* namespace contains the exception that was unhandled. This is the signature of the *ThreadExceptionEventHandler*:

```
void ThreadExceptionEventHandler(object sender,
    ThreadExceptionEventArgs e)
```

In the following code, the *OnThreadException* handler is added to the *ThreadException* event. The *btnException_Click* method raises an unhandled divide-by-zero exception. The unhandled exception is then handled in the *OnThreadException* method, which displays an informative message. Run the application in release mode for the expected results. Otherwise, the Visual Studio debugger intercepts the exception:

```
private void btnException_Click(object sender, EventArgs e) {
    int vara = 5, varb = 0;
    vara /= varb;
}

private void Form1_Load(object sender, EventArgs e) {
    Application.ThreadException += new
        System.Threading.ThreadExceptionEventHandler(
            OnThreadException);
}

void OnThreadException(object sender, ThreadExceptionEventArgs e) {
    Thread t = (Thread) sender;
    Exception threadexception = e.Exception;
    string errormessage = "Thread ID: " +
        t.ManagedThreadId.ToString() +
            " [ " + threadexception.Message + " ]";
    MessageBox.Show(errormessage);
}
```

AppDomain.UnhandledException

When an unhandled exception occurs in a Console application, the *AppDomain. UnhandledException* event is raised. Subscribe to this event to clean up the resources of the application, with actions such as closing files and relinquishing data connections. You also might record the unhandled exception in the event log or other location. It is important to note that the exception is not caught in the *AppDomain.UnhandledException* handler. When the handler is completed, the unhandled exception will cause the application to be terminated. The *AppDomain.UnhandledException* event is triggered only in the starting application domain of the program.

Subscribe to the *AppDomain.UnhandledException* event with an *UnhandledExceptionEventHandler* delegate. The delegate has two parameters. The *object* parameter is the originating *AppDomain*. The *UnhandledExceptionEventArgs* parameter contains the specifics of the unhandled exception. This is the signature of the *UnhandledExceptionEventHandler*:

```
void UnhandledExceptionEventHandler(object sender, UnhandledExceptionEventArgs e)
```

UnhandledExceptionEventArgs offers the *IsTerminating* and *ExceptionObject* properties. *IsTerminating* is a Boolean property indicating the status of the application. If true, the application is terminating because of the exception. If false, the application can survive the exception. This property is always true. Unhandled exceptions on both managed and unmanaged threads terminate an application. This is cleaner than the previous unhandled exception model, where exceptions raised on managed threads were nonfatal. The *ExceptionObject* property is the exception object for the unhandled exception. Inexplicably, this property is an object type, not an exception type. Cast the property to the exception type to access the details of the exception.

In the following Console application, the *OnUnhandledException* method is added to the *AppDomain.UnhandledException* event. When the subsequent divide-by-zero exception occurs, the *OnUnhandledException* method is called:

```
using System;

namespace Donis.CSharpBook {
    public class Starter {
        public static void Main() {
            AppDomain.CurrentDomain.UnhandledException +=
                new UnhandledExceptionEventHandler(
                    OnUnhandledException);

            int vara = 5, varb = 0;
            vara /= varb;
        }

        public static void OnUnhandledException(
                object sender, UnhandledExceptionEventArgs e) {
            Exception except=(Exception) e.ExceptionObject;

            string errormessage = "Application has failed" +
                " [ Exception " + except.Message + " ]";
            Console.WriteLine(errormessage);
        }
    }
}
```

Managing Exceptions in Visual Studio

You can configure Visual Studio 2008 for exception handling in the Exception Assistant and Exceptions dialog boxes. The Exception Assistant dialog box provides helpful information to developers when an unhandled exception is raised. The Exceptions dialog box manages how the Visual Studio debugger handles exceptions.

The Exception Assistant

The Exception Assistant appears in Visual Studio when an unhandled exception occurs. It displays a translucent frame that partially obfuscates the application code. The source code that prompted the exception is highlighted and tethered to the Exception Assistant dialog box, which is shown in Figure 12-3.

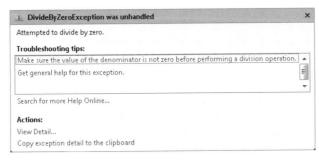

FIGURE 12-3 The Exception Assistant dialog box for a divide-by-zero exception

The Exception Assistant header identifies the unhandled exception and offers a brief explanation. The Troubleshooting Tips pane offers hints to diagnose the exception. Each hint is also a link to further information. The Actions pane specifies two actions:

- View Detail displays the properties of the exception object.

- Copy Exception Detail To The Clipboard copies basic information on the exception to the Clipboard.

The Exception Assistant can be disabled or otherwise configured by selecting Options from the Tools menu. Configure the Exception Assistant in the Debugging category of the Options dialog box.

The Exceptions Dialog Box

In the Exceptions dialog box, the Visual Studio debugger can be instructed to interrupt on first-chance exceptions. Open the Exceptions dialog box by selecting Exceptions from the Debug menu. Figure 12-4 shows the Exceptions dialog box.

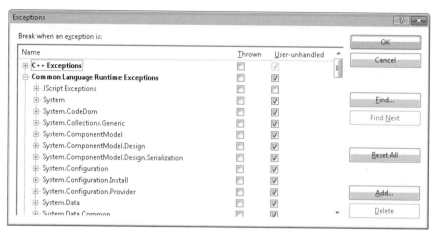

FIGURE 12-4 The Exceptions dialog box

The Thrown and User-unhandled columns contain a series of check boxes, which are organized via the Name column into categories and specific exceptions. Exceptions with the Thrown check box selected are interrupted as first-chance exceptions. For code in a *try* block, the debugger breaks at the origin of the exception, which is often useful. While developing an application, it can be instructive to be notified of an exception that otherwise would be consumed in an exception handler. The second column selects specific exceptions to interrupt in case of a second-chance exception. The Add button in the Exceptions dialog box adds application exceptions to the list of available exceptions. Of course, added exceptions can be deleted later.

Metadata and Reflection

.NET assemblies adhere to the Portable Executable Common Object File Format (PE COFF) specification. PE COFF files have headers and sections, such as a PE and CLR Header. .NET assemblies also consist of metadata and Microsoft Intermediate Language (MSIL) code. Metadata describes the types and other characteristics of the assembly. You can inspect the metadata of an assembly using reflection. Tools, such as the Intermediate Language Disassembler (ILDASM), can browse an assembly using reflection to provide helpful information. Reflection also provides support for late binding, which is often helpful to developers. The next chapter explores the topics of metadata and reflection.

Part IV
Debugging

Chapter 13
Metadata and Reflection

Metadata, which is often described as data about data, is a description of the data in an assembly. It represents the state of the assembly. Metadata is information pertaining to the assembly, including a detailed description of each type, the attributes of the assembly, and other particulars of the assembly itself. Metadata is similar to a type library in COM, except that metadata is persisted in the assembly that it describes. For this reason, assemblies are often referred to as self-describing. Because metadata is indigenous to the assembly, metadata cannot be lost and versioning problems are avoided. Metadata is emitted primarily by managed language compilers and consumed by metadata browsers, other .NET tools, and general managed applications. The Common Language Runtime (CLR) uses metadata extensively. Just-in-time compilation, code access security, garbage collection, and other services of the CLR rely heavily on metadata. Once emitted, metadata is read-only.

Metadata is important to anyone programming in the managed environment. Assembly inspection, late binding, and advanced concepts such as self-generating code require a nontrivial understanding of metadata. You also can interrogate metadata, which is called *reflection*. Reflection facilitates late binding and other uses of metadata. Most importantly, mastery of metadata promotes a better understanding of the managed world, which (one hopes) translates into better-written code.

This chapter introduces some advanced concepts. Further research may be required. However, it is important to introduce some of these concepts in the context of C# programming.

Metadata

Metadata about the overall assembly and modules (macro metadata) is called the *manifest*. Some of the macro information placed in the manifest includes the simple name, version number, external references, module name, and public key of the assembly. A portion of the manifest is created from the assembly attributes found in the AssemblyInfo. cs file of a Microsoft Visual Studio 2008 C#.NET project. Here is a partial listing of a typical AssemblyInfo.cs file:

```
using System.Reflection;
using System.Runtime.CompilerServices;
using System.Runtime.InteropServices;

// General Information about an assembly is controlled through the following
// set of attributes. Change these attribute values to modify the information
// associated with an assembly.
[assembly: AssemblyTitle("WindowsApplication4")]
```

```
[assembly: AssemblyDescription("")]
[assembly: AssemblyConfiguration("")]
[assembly: AssemblyCompany("")]
[assembly: AssemblyProduct("WindowsApplication4")]
[assembly: AssemblyCopyright("Copyright © 2008")]
[assembly: AssemblyTrademark("")]
[assembly: AssemblyCulture("")]
```

Metadata also chronicles the microdata of the assembly, such as types, methods, and attributes. Metadata paints a portrait of each type, including the type name, methods of the type, parameters of each method of the type, each field of the type, and further details related to the loading and executing of that type at run time. Types are probably the most important construct in a .NET application, and metadata about types is used throughout the life cycle of a managed application. Here are a couple of examples of this. At startup, metadata is used to identify the entry point method where the program starts executing. During program execution, when a class is first touched, an internal component is built from metadata to represent that type to the just-in-time compiler. This component is an important ingredient in the just-in-time compilation process. This is further discussed in detail in Chapter 16, "Advanced Debugging."

Use attributes to add additional metadata to the manifest or other metadata. *Attributes* are the adjectives of a managed application and extend the description of an assembly, class, method, field, or other target. Attributes are recorded as metadata and extend the axiomatic metadata of an assembly. In addition, the Microsoft .NET Framework Class Library (FCL) offers predefined custom and pseudo-custom attributes. *Obsolete* and *StructLayout* attributes are examples of predefined custom attributes. *Serializable* is an example of a pseudo-custom attribute. The *Obsolete* attribute marks an entity as deprecated, whereas the *StructLayout* attribute stipulates the memory layout of fields in native memory. Native memory is not on the managed heap and is beyond the scope of the CLR. The latter attribute is essential when passing a managed type to an unmanaged function or application programming interface (API). You can augment the predefined attributes with programmer-defined custom attributes, limited only by your imagination. Applying a version number to a class, assigning the name of the responsible developer or team to a class, and identifying design documents used to architect an application are potential ways to exploit custom attributes.

Metadata is organized as a nonhierarchical but relational database of cross-referencing tables. The metadata database has many tables that can—and often do—reference each other. However, no parent-child relationship between tables is ever implied. Each categorization of data is maintained in a separate table. Consider for example the TypeDef and MethodDef tables. Types alone are stored in the TypeDef table. Each record of the TypeDef table represents a type. If there were six types in the assembly, there would be six records or rows in the TypeDef table. Methods belonging to all types are stored in the MethodDef table, where each row describes a method. The TypeDef table references the MethodDef table to link a type to its member functions. The MethodList column of the TypeDef table has record indexes (RIDs) into the MethodDef table. Extending this model, the MethodDef table has a ParamList column, which has indexes to the method's parameters in the Param table.

Metadata tables are assigned unique table identifiers, which are one-byte unsigned integers. For example, the table identifier for the TypeDef table is 2, whereas 6 identifies the MethodDef table. Metadata tables reserved for the run time are not published and not assigned an external table identifier. Table 13-1 lists some of the popular metadata tables.

TABLE 13-1 Metadata tables

Table	Identifier	Description
Assembly	0x20	Data related to the overall assembly
Field	0x04	Fields (data members) of types
MethodDef	0x06	Methods (member functions) of types
NestedClass	0x29	Type definitions for nested types
Param	0x08	Method parameters of functions
Property	0x17	Properties of types
TypeDef	0x02	Type definitions of types in current assembly
TypeRef	0x01	Type definitions of types external to this module

Metadata Tokens

Metadata tables are collections of fixed-length records and columns. A metadata table contains a certain type of data, and each record is an instance of that type. Columns represent specific data on each instance, and each column contains either a constant or an index. An index in a metadata column references another table or heap and is also known as a *metadata token*. (Metadata heaps are explained in the next section.) Metadata tokens are used as metadata pointers, allowing tables to cross-reference each other. Metadata tables can be optimized (compressed) or not optimized. For the purpose of this book, it is assumed that metadata is optimized. Metadata that is not optimized requires intermediate tables for ordered access between tables.

Tokens are four-byte unsigned integers and a combination of the table identifier and RID. As shown in Figure 13-1, the first byte is the table identifier, and the last three bytes are the RID. A token referring to the Field table, for example, might be 0x04000002. This token refers to the second row of the Field table. RIDs start at one and are not zero-based. Because tokens are padded with zeros, the run time might optimize them. Metadata tokens are probably the most public manifestation of metadata. You will see metadata tokens often over the next few chapters of this book.

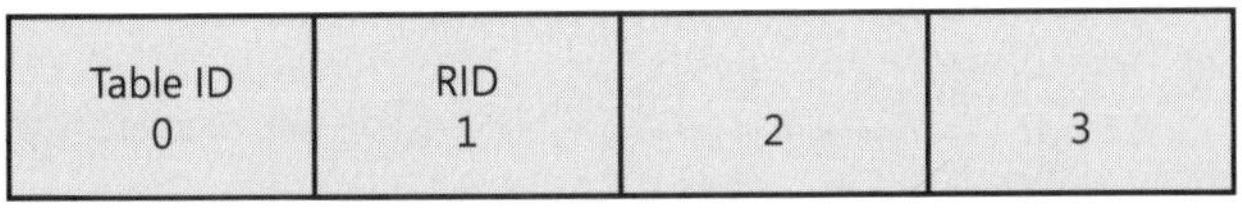

FIGURE 13-1 Layout of a metadata token

Metadata Heaps

Metadata tables reference metadata heaps and other tables. Records of metadata tables hold fixed-length metadata information. Variable-length data is stored in one of the metadata heaps. Method signatures are an example of data placed on a metadata heap. They are variable-length and stored on the *String* heap.

The four metadata heaps are as follows: *String, Userstring, Blob,* and *GUID*.

- The *String* heap is an array of null-terminated strings. Namespace, type, field, and method names, as well as other identifiers, are stored on the *String* heap.

- User-defined strings reside on the *Userstring* heap. The *Userstring* heap is an array of null-terminated strings.

- The *Blob* heap is a binary heap and a composite of length prefix data, such as default values, method signatures, and field signatures. Length prefix data precedes each binary blob with the length.

- The *GUID* heap is an array of globally unique identifiers (GUIDs). Yes, this is obvious. You might remember GUIDs from COM as 16-byte unique identifiers assigned to almost everything—most notably, class identifiers (CLSIDs) are assigned to class factories. There are also TYPEIDs, LIBIDs, IIDs, and much more. What kind of GUID is stored on the *GUID* heap? The GUID heap contains module version identifiers (MVIDs).

Streams

Physically, metadata tables and heaps are persisted in streams. Six possible streams, including streams for each metadata heap, are available in .NET. There are also two mutually exclusive streams, optimized and nonoptimized, which are reserved for metadata tables. Metadata tables are either completely optimized or not optimized—there's no such thing as partial optimization of metadata tables. If the metadata tables are optimized, the optimized stream is used. Otherwise, the nonoptimized stream is used. Therefore, any particular managed application has at most five streams. Table 13-2 provides a complete list of the metadata streams.

TABLE 13-2 Metadata streams

Name	Description
#~	Optimized or compressed metadata tables
#-	Nonoptimized metadata tables
#Blob	Physical repository of the *Blob* heap
#GUID	Physical repository of the *GUID* heap
#String	Physical repository of the *String* heap
#US	Physical repository of the *Userstring* heap

Metadata Validation

Successful execution of a managed application depends largely on metadata. Improperly formed metadata could cause a managed application to fail unceremoniously. An assembly with bad metadata is like a house built on quicksand. Loading a class, just-in-time compilation, code access security, and other run-time operations depend on robust metadata. Metadata validation tests the correctness of metadata and is performed preemptively, preventing applications with corrupt metadata from being executed. Preventing application crashes caused by improper metadata enforces code isolation.

Several tests are performed to validate metadata. Here is an abbreviated list of these tests:

- Cross-references between tables are validated.

- Offsets into metadata heaps are validated.

- Metadata tables must have a valid number of rows. For example, the Assembly table must have exactly one row.

- Metadata tables cannot have duplicate rows.

You can use the PEVerify and Intermediate Language Disassembler (ILDASM) tools to validate metadata. Both tools are included in the .NET Framework software development kit (SDK).

PEVerify submits an assembly for metadata validation and Microsoft Intermediate Language (MSIL) verification and then reports the results. (MSIL verification is discussed in Chapter 14, "MSIL Programming.") Run the PEVerify tool from a command prompt using the following basic syntax:

PEVerify assemblyname

PEVerify first validates the metadata of *assemblyname*. If metadata validation is successful, MSIL verification is conducted next. If metadata validation fails, the target assembly cannot be executed and MSIL verification is skipped. PEVerify offers a variety of optional arguments, including the option to perform MSIL verification even when the metadata validation fails.

Table 13-3 lists some of the PEVerify options.

TABLE 13-3 Selected PEVerify options

Argument	Description
/clock	Collects data and reports duration of verification and validation tests.
/HRESULT	Displays errors in hexadecimal format.
/ignore=errorcode1, errorcode2, ..., errorcoden	Ignores listed error codes.

TABLE 13-3 Selected PEVerify options

Argument	Description
/il	Conducts MSIL verification. With this option, if metadata validation is also desired, it must be requested explicitly.
/md	Explicitly conduct metadata validation. If MSIL verification is also required, MSIL verification must be requested explicitly.
/unique	Ignores repeating error codes.

The following is a simple "Hello World!" application, which is compiled to hello.exe. It is a minimal application, in which not much can go wrong. PEVerify will confirm this:

```
using System;

class Starter {
    static void Main() {
        Console.WriteLine("Hello, World!");
    }
}
```

The following output shows the result of running PEVerify on hello.exe with the /il and /clock options. Because the md command is omitted, metadata verification is skipped:

```
c:\>peverify /il /clock hello.exe

All Classes and Methods in hello.exe Verified.
Timing: Total run      125 msec
        IL Ver.cycle  125 msec
        IL Ver.pure    93 msec
```

The elapsed cycle and pure verification times are listed. Pure verification time is the duration of the test, whereas cycle verification time also encompasses the startup and shutdown processes.

ILDASM

ILDASM is a .NET tool that also can perform various validations. In addition, you can use this tool to browse and display the metadata of an assembly—including the manifest. ILDASM inspects an assembly using reflection and can present the results in a window, console, or file.

ILDASM, which is a .NET disassembler and metadata browser, is a popular tool for developers. It proffers an internal representation of an assembly, which includes the metadata and MSIL code of an assembly in a variety of formats. ILDASM uses reflection to inspect an assembly. The basic command-line syntax of ILDASM requires only an assembly name, which opens ILDASM and displays the metadata of the assembly:

ildasm *assemblyname*

The following simple application is a basic .NET application that references a library. The application has a *ZClass* and a *ZStruct* type:

```
using System;

namespace Donis.CSharpBook {

    interface IA {
    }

    struct ZStruct {
    }

    class Starter {

        public static void Main() {
            ZClass obj1 = new ZClass();
            obj1.DisplayCreateTime();
            ZClass obj2 = new ZClass();
            obj2.DisplayCreateTime();
        }
    }

    class ZClass : IA {

    public enum Flag {
        aflag,
        bflag
    }

    public event EventHandler AEvent = null;

        public void DisplayCreateTime() {
            Console.WriteLine("ZClass created at " + m_Time);
        }

        private string m_Time = DateTime.Now.ToLongTimeString();
        public string Time {
            get {
                return m_Time;
            }
        }
    }
}
```

Figure 13-2 is a view of simple.exe from ILDASM. ILDASM displays a hierarchal object graph with an icon for each element of the application.

Some icons are expandable or collapsible, as indicated by a + or – symbol, if you want to see more or less detail. The Assembly icon expands to show the details of the target assembly, the Namespace icon expands to show the members of the namespace, and so on. You can explore the object graph from the assembly down to the class members. Each icon depicts the category of item. Table 13-4 lists each icon and the action associated with double-clicking the icon.

FIGURE 13-2 The simple.exe assembly displayed in ILDASM

TABLE 13-4 Elements of ILDASM

Icon	Action
Assembly	Shows elements of the assembly
Class	Shows members of a class
Enum	Shows members of an *enum* type
Event	Shows metadata and MSIL code of an event
Field	Shows metadata of a field
Interface	Shows members of an interface
Manifest	Shows attributes of an assembly
Method	Shows metadata and MSIL code of a method
Namespace	Shows members of a namespace
Property	Shows metadata and MSIL code of a property
Static Field	Shows metadata of a static field
Static Method	Shows metadata and MSIL code of a static method
Value Type	Shows members of a value type

Some elements are displayed twice. For example, a property is presented as itself and separately as *accessor* and *mutator* methods.

ILDASM has a variety of command-line options. Table 13-5 lists these parameters.

TABLE 13-5 ILDASM options

ILDASM option	Description
/Out	Renders metadata and MSIL to a text file.
/Text	Renders metadata and related MSIL to a console.
/ HTML	Combines with the *Out* option to persist metadata and MSIL in Hypertext Markup Language (HTML) format.
/RTF	Renders metadata and MSIL in Rich Text Format (RTF).
/Bytes	Shows MSIL code with opcodes and related bytes.
/Raweh	Shows label form of *try* and *catch* directives in raw form.
/ Tokens	Shows metadata tokens.
/ Source	Shows MSIL interlaced with commented source code; for this option, the source code and debug file must be in the current path.
/ Linenum	Inserts line directives into an output stream that matches source code to MSIL. This option requires the debug file.
/Visibility	Disassembles only members with the stated visibility: *pub* (public), *pri* (private), *fam* (family), *asm* (assembly), *faa* (family and assembly), *foa* (family or assembly), and *psc* (private scope).
/Pubonly	Disassembles only public elements; short notation for *visibility=pub*.
/QuoteAllNames	Brackets all identifiers in single quotes.
/NOCA	Excludes custom attributes.
/CAVerbal	Displays blob information of custom attributes in symbolic form rather than binary.
/NOBAR	Suppresses progress bar display.
/ UTF8	Renders output file in UTF8 (8-bit UCS/Unicode Transformation Format). The default is American National Standards Institute (ANSI) format.
/UNICODE	Renders output file in UNICODE.
/NOIL	Prevents source code disassembly.
/TypeList	Displays list of types.
/Headers	Includes DOS, PE, COFF, CLR, and metadata header information.
/Item	Disassembles a particular class or method.
/Stats	Displays statistical information on the assembly file, which is a portable executable
/ClassList	Provides a list of classes in the target.
/All	Specifies combination of the *Header, Bytes, Stats, ClassList,* and *Tokens* commands.
/Metadata	Displays specific information related to metadata. This command has its own set of options.
/Objectfile	Shows metadata of a library file.

The user interface and command-line options for ILDASM are similar. The following command line is typical. It disassembles simple.exe and persists the resulting metadata, MSIL, metadata tokens, and source code to the simple.il file:

```
ildasm /out=simple.il /source /tokens simple.exe
```

The *source* option of the preceding command interlaces MSIL code with source code. The source code is commented. Associating MSIL to source code relates each source statement to the resulting MSIL code, which is invaluable when debugging. The tokens shown per the *Tokens* option are also commented.

The disassembly created by ILDASM is a valid MSIL program that can be recompiled For this reason the output text file should have an *il* extension, as in *client.il*. The assembly can be reassembled with the ILASM compiler, which compiles MSIL code. The newly assembled assembly is identical to the original assembly.

Some ILDASM options cause the assembly to be partially disassembled. When a partial disassembly occurs, you are presented with a warning. One limitation is that partial assemblies cannot be reassembled using ILASM. The following command creates a partial disassembly:

```
ildasm /out=simple.il /item=Donis.CSharpBook.ZClass simple.exe
```

The preceding command-line disassembles only the *ZClass* of the simple.exe assembly. Because other types are omitted from the disassembly, the result is a partial disassembly. For this reason, a warning is appended to the output. The following is a partial listing of the output file with the embedded warning:

```
//  Microsoft (R) .NET Framework IL Disassembler.  Version 3.5.21022.8
//  Copyright (c) Microsoft Corporation.  All rights reserved.

// warning : THIS IS A PARTIAL DISASSEMBLY, NOT SUITABLE FOR RE-ASSEMBLING

.class private auto ansi beforefieldinit Donis.CSharpBook.ZClass
       extends [mscorlib]System.Object
       implements Donis.CSharpBook.IA
{
  .class auto ansi sealed nested public Flag
         extends [mscorlib]System.Enum
  {
    .field public specialname rtspecialname int32 value__
    .field public static literal valuetype Donis.CSharpBook.ZClass/Flag
       aflag = int32(0x00000000)
    .field public static literal valuetype Donis.CSharpBook.ZClass/Flag
       bflag = int32(0x00000001)
  } // end of class Flag

  .field private class [mscorlib]System.EventHandler AEvent
  .field private string m_Time
  .method public hidebysig specialname instance void
```

Here is the final example of ILDASM and command-line options. The following command validates the metadata and persists the results to the simple.txt file:

```
ildasm /metadata=validate /out=simple.txt simple.exe
```

Reflection

An assembly is a piñata stuffed with goodies such as type information, MSIL code, and custom attributes. You use *reflection* to break open the assembly piñata to examine the contents. Reflection adds many important features to .NET, such as metadata inspection, run-time creation of types, late binding, MSIL extraction, and self-generating code. These features are crucial to solving complex real-world problems that developers face every day.

The *Reflection* namespace is the container of most things related to reflection. *Assembly, Module, LocalVariableInfo, MemberInfo, MethodInfo, FieldInfo,* and *Binder* are some of the important types and members of the *Reflection* namespace. There are also some reflection-related attributes in the *Reflection* namespace, such as *AssemblyVersionAttribute, AssemblyKeyFile Attribute,* and *AssemblyDelaySignAttribute.* The *Reflection* namespace contains other reflection-related namespaces, most notably the *Reflection.Emit* nested namespace. *Reflection.Emit* is a toolbox filled with tools for building assemblies, classes, and methods at run time, including the ability to emit metadata and MSIL code. *Reflection.Emit* is reviewed in Chapter 14.

The central component of reflection is the *Type* object. Its interface can be used to interrogate a reference or value type. This includes browsing the methods, fields, parameters, and custom attributes of the type. General information pertaining to the type is also available via reflection, including identifying the hosting assembly. Beyond browsing, *Type* objects support more execution-related operations. You can create instances of classes at run time and perform late binding of methods.

Obtaining a Type Object

There are several ways to obtain a *Type* object from an instance. The *Object.GetType* method, the *typeof* operator, and various methods of the *Assembly* object return a *Type* object. *GetType* is a member of the *Object* class, which is the ubiquitous base class. *GetType* is inherited by every .NET type. For that reason, you can call *GetType* on any managed object.

The *typeof* operator takes an object as a parameter and returns the related *Type* object.

Assemblies are natural boundaries for types. An *Assembly* object, which is a thin wrapper for an assembly, offers several member functions that return a *Type* object. For example, the *Assembly.GetTypes* method enumerates and returns all the *Types* of the current assembly.

GetType returns the *Type* object of the instance. Here is the signature of the *GetType* method:

```
Type GetType()
```

The following code creates a value and then a reference type, which are passed as parameters to successive calls to the *DisplayType* method. The parameter accepts an object type, which homogenizes the parameter. The function first obtains the *Type* object from the parameter. The type name is then displayed. Next, run-time type information (RTTI) is used. If the *Type* object is a *ZClass*, the *ZClass.Display* method is called on the parameter object. One of the advantages of reflection is making decisions at run time:

```
using System;

namespace Donis.CSharpBook {
    class Starter {

        static void Main() {
            int localvalue = 5;
            ZClass objZ = new ZClass();
            DisplayType(localvalue);
            DisplayType(objZ);
        }

        static void DisplayType(object parameterObject) {
            Type parameterType = parameterObject.GetType();
            string name = parameterType.Name;
            Console.WriteLine("Type is " + name);
            if (name == "ZClass") {
                ((ZClass) parameterObject).Display();
            }
        }
    }

    class ZClass {
        public void Display() {
            Console.WriteLine("ZClass::Display");
        }
    }
}
```

The *typeof* operator returns a *Type* object from a type. The *typeof* operator is evaluated at compile time, whereas the *GetType* method is invoked at run time. For this reason, the *typeof* operator is more efficient but less flexible than the *GetType* method. Here is the syntax for the *typeof* operator:

```
typeof(type)
```

An assembly typically contains multiple types. The *Assembly.GetTypes* method enumerates the types contained in an assembly. Use another method, *Assembly.GetType*, to return a *Type* object of a specific instance. *Assembly.GetType* is overloaded four times. The zero-argument version of *GetType* returns the *Type* of the current instance. The one-argument version has a string parameter. That parameter is the fully qualified name of the type to be returned. The final two versions of *GetType* are an extension of the one-argument version of the method. The two-argument method also has a Boolean parameter. When true, the method throws an exception if the type, which is defined in the string parameter, is not located. The three-argument version has a second Boolean parameter that stipulates case sensitivity. If this parameter is false, the case of the type name in the string parameter is significant.

Here are the signatures for the methods:

```
Type[] GetTypes()

Type GetType()
Type GetType(string typename)
Type GetType(string typename, bool throwError)
Type GetType(string typename, bool throwError, bool ignoreCase)
```

An assembly can be diagrammed through reflection. The result is called the *reflection tree* of that assembly. Figure 13-3 shows the reflection tree starting with an application domain (AppDomain). Each level of reflection, such as an assembly, a type, and a method, represents a different branch on the tree. *AppDomain* is the root of the tree; *AppDomain.GetAssemblies* expands the tree from the root. The reflection tree is a logical, not a physical representation. You can realize the reflection tree using reflection to enumerate the metadata of the application. For example, *Assembly.GetCurrentAssembly* returns the current assembly. With the assembly instance, *Assembly.GetTypes* enumerates the types defined in the assembly. For each type, *Type.GetMethods* will enumerate the methods of that type. This process continues until the application is fully reflected and the logical reflection tree is constructed.

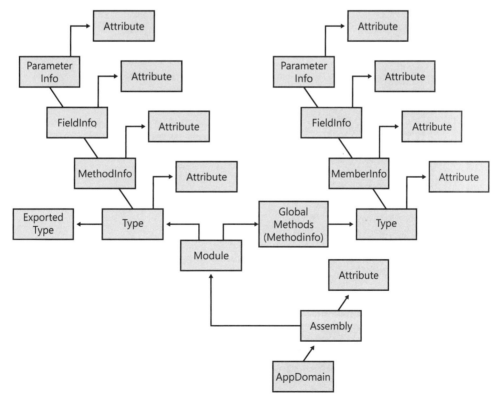

FIGURE 13-3 Diagram of the reflection tree

Loading Assemblies

Assemblies reside near the root of the reflection tree and are loaded at run time using *Assembly.Load* and *Assembly.LoadFrom*. *Assembly.Load* uses the assembly loader to locate and bind an assembly. *Assembly.LoadFrom* consults the assembly resolver to locate and load the correct assembly. This method uses a combination of the strong name identifier and probing to bind and then load an assembly. The *strong name* includes the simple name, version, culture, and public key token of the assembly. *Probing* is the algorithm for locating an assembly. For example, when loading an assembly, the current directory typically is probed first. Both *Assembly.Load* and *Assembly.LoadFrom* are static methods that are overloaded several times. Here is the signature of a couple of the overloaded methods:

```
static Assembly Load(string AssemblyName)
```

```
static Assembly LoadFrom(string AssemblyFile)
```

Assembly.Load and *Assembly.LoadFrom* fail when the target assembly is not found. When these functions fail, the Assembly Binding Log Viewer tool is helpful in diagnosing the problem. The Assembly Binding Log Viewer tool (fuslogvw.exe), included in the .NET Framework SDK, is a useful tool for diagnosing any probing failure.

The following sample code demonstrates the difference between *Assembly.Load* and *Assembly.LoadFrom*:

```
using System;
using System.Reflection;

namespace Donis.CSharpBook {
    class Starter {
        static void Main() {
            Assembly library = Assembly.Load("library, Version=2.0.0.0, " +
                "Culture=Neutral, PublicKeyToken=9b184fc90fb9648d");
            Console.WriteLine("Assembly.Load:  {0}", library.FullName);
            library=Assembly.LoadFrom("library.dll");
            Console.WriteLine("Assembly.LoadFrom {0}", library.FullName);
        }
    }
}
```

Assembly.Load and *Assembly.LoadFrom* reference other assemblies. How about referencing the currently executing assembly? *Assembly.GetExecutingAssembly* is a static method and returns a reference to the currently executing assembly. This is valuable for interrogating the metadata, manifest, or MSIL of the running assembly. Here is the signature of the *GetExecutingAssembly* method:

```
static Assembly Assembly.GetExecutingAssembly()
```

Both *Assembly.Load* and *Assembly.LoadFrom* return a reference to an assembly. That assembly then can be reflected. The code for the assembly also can be loaded and then executed. *Assembly.ReflectionOnlyLoad* and *Assembly.ReflectionOnlyLoadFrom* load an assembly for reflection but not for execution. This means the code cannot be executed for the newly loaded assembly. In this circumstance, you can reflect a type and iterate all the methods. Yet the methods cannot be invoked. To confirm the way an *Assembly* is loaded, use the *ReflectionOnly* property. *ReflectionOnly* is a Boolean attribute of an *Assembly* and is true if an *Assembly* is loaded for reflection only. *Assembly.ReflectionOnlyLoad* and *Assembly. ReflectionOnlyLoadFrom* are equivalent to *Assembly.Load* and *Assembly.LoadFrom*, respectively, without the execute capability. *ReflectionOnly* yields performance benefits assuming the code of the assembly does not need to be executed.

The following program provides performance benchmarks of *Assembly.Load* versus *Assembly .ReflectionOnlyLoad*. The *DateTime* function has poor resolution and is inferior for most testing scenarios. Instead, a high-performance timer is required to obtain the needed resolution. The *QueryPerformanceCounter* API returns a high-performance counter accurate to a nanosecond. Prior to .NET Framework 2.0, *QueryPerformanceCounter* was available only through platform invoke interoperability (a managed-to-native call using *PInvoke*). The *Stopwatch* class, which is a thin wrapper for the *QueryPerformanceCounter* and related APIs, was introduced in .NET Framework 2.0 and is found in the *System.Diagnostics* namespace:

```
using System;
using System.Reflection;
using System.Diagnostics;

namespace Donis.CSharpBook {
    class OnlyLoad {
        static void Main() {
            Stopwatch duration = new Stopwatch();
            duration.Reset();
            duration.Start();
            Assembly a = Assembly.Load("library");
            duration.Stop();
            Console.WriteLine(duration.ElapsedTicks.ToString());
            duration.Reset();
            duration.Start();
            a = Assembly.ReflectionOnlyLoad("library");
            duration.Stop();
            Console.WriteLine(duration.ElapsedTicks.ToString());
        }
    }
}
```

Execution time of *Assembly.Load* versus *Assembly.ReflectionOnlyLoad* might vary between different implementations of the Common Language Infrastructure (CLI) and other factors. The program compares ticks, which is an abstraction of time. Running the program several times indicates that *Assembly.ReflectionOnlyLoad* is about 29 percent faster than *Assembly. Load*. This data is only anecdotal, though.

Type.ReflectionOnlyGetType is a static method and combines the functionality of *Assembly. ReflectionOnlyLoad* and the *typeof* operator. The named assembly is loaded for inspection only, and a *Type* object is returned for the specified type that is found in that assembly. Because the assembly is opened only for inspection, you cannot create an instance of the type or invoke a method on that type. Here is the signature of the *Type.ReflectionOnlyGetType* method:

```
static Type ReflectionOnlyType(string typeName, bool notFoundException,
    bool ignoreCase)
```

The *typeName* parameter is a combination of the *Assembly* and the *Type* name. The *Assembly* and the *Type* name are comma-delimited. *Null* is returned if the assembly or the type is not located. To raise an exception if the assembly or type is not found, set the *notFoundException* parameter to *true*. Setting the *ignoreCase* parameter to *false* indicates that the *Type* name is case-sensitive:

```
using System;
using System.Reflection;

namespace Donis.CSharpBook {
    class ReflectOnlyType {
        static void Main() {
            Type zType=Type.ReflectionOnlyGetType(
                "Donis.CSharpBook.ClassA, Library", false, false);
            Console.WriteLine(zType.Name);
        }
    }
}
```

Browsing Type Information

Inspecting a type begins with obtaining a *Type* object. *Reflection* has a straightforward interface for examining the metadata of a *Type* object. The *Type* object public interface exposes several methods and properties related to reflection. Inspecting the metadata of a type essentially consists of spanning a series of collections.

Type.GetMembers returns a collection that includes all members of the current type. Every member, whether it is a method, field, event, or property, is included in the collection. *GetMembers* returns a *MemberInfo* array that contains an element for each member. Another method, *GetMember*, returns a single *MemberInfo* object for the named member. *MemberInfo.MemberType* is a property of the *MemberInfo.MemberTypes* type, which is a bitwise enumeration identifying a member as a method, field, property, event, constructor, or something else. (See Table 13-6 for a list of the *MemberTypes*.) *MemberInfo* has relatively few properties and methods. Here are some of the more useful. The *MemberInfo.Name* method returns the name of the type member. The *MemberInfo.MetadataToken* property returns the metadata token of the member. *MemberInfo.ReflectedType* provides the *Type* object of which the *MemberInfo* object is an instance.

TABLE 13-6 MemberTypes enumeration

MemberType	Value
MemberTypes.Constructor	0x01
MemberTypes.Custom	0x40
MemberTypes.Event	0x02
MemberTypes.Field	0x04
MemberTypes.Method	0x08
MemberTypes.NestedType	0x80
MemberTypes.Property	0x10
MemberTypes.TypeInfo	0x20
MemberTypes.All	0xBF

As mentioned, *Type.GetMembers* returns a collection that contains all the members of the reflected type. You can be somewhat more specific. *Type.GetMethods* or *Type.GetMethod* returns a collection of methods or a specific method. *Type.GetFields* or *Type.GetField* similarly returns a collection of fields or a specific field. Table 13-7 lists the methods that return specific collections (the nonplural version of the method returns a single item).

TABLE 13-7 *Type* methods that return metadata collections

Method	Returns	Type of returned item(s)
GetConstructors	ConstructorInfo[]	Constructor
GetCustomAttributes	Object[]	Custom attribute
GetDefaultMembers	MemberInfo[]	Default member
GetEvents	EventInfo[]	Event
GetFields	FieldInfo[]	Field
GetInterfaces	Type[]	Implemented interface
GetMembers	MemberInfo[]	All members
GetMethods	MethodInfo[]	Method
GetNestedTypes	Type[]	Nested type
GetProperties	PropertyInfo[]	Property

The *Type.GetMethods* method returns a collection of *MethodInfo* elements and is overloaded to be called with no parameters or with a single parameter, which is *BindingFlags*:

```
MethodInfo[] GetMethods();
MethodInfo[] GetMethods(BindingFlags binding)
```

BindingFlags is a bitwise enumeration that expands or filters the results of a collection. For example, to include private members in a collection, specify the *BindingFlags.NonPublic* flag. Some *BindingFlags*, such as *InvokeMember*, are not applicable in all contexts. When stipulating *BindingFlags*, there are no default flags. You must specify the flag for every item desired in the collection.

The zero-argument version of *GetMethods* obviously does not have a parameter for *BindingFlags*. Instead, this version of the method has default bindings, which includes public methods. Notably, the *BindingFlags.Static* flag is not included and static methods are excluded from the method collection by default. The following code iterates private instance (nonpublic) members of a class first. Second, the static public members are iterated:

```
using System;
using System.Reflection;

namespace Donis.CSharpBook {
    class DumpType {
        public static void Main() {
            ZClass zObj = new ZClass();
            Type tObj = zObj.GetType();
            MemberInfo[] members = tObj.GetMembers(
                BindingFlags.Instance |
                BindingFlags.NonPublic);
            foreach (MemberInfo member in members) {
                Console.WriteLine(member.Name);
            }
            members = tObj.GetMembers(
                BindingFlags.Public |
                BindingFlags.Static);
            Console.WriteLine(" ");
            foreach (MemberInfo member in members) {
                Console.WriteLine(member.Name);
            }
        }
    }

    class ZClass {
        private int vara = 5;
        public int PropA {
            get {
                return vara;
            }
        }
        static public void MethodA() {
            Console.WriteLine("ZClass::MethodA called.");
        }
    }
}
```

The following application calls *DumpMethods* to dump the public methods of a class. This code demonstrates various aspects of *Reflection*:

```
using System;
using System.Reflection;

namespace Donis.CSharpBook {
    class DumpType {
        static void Main(string[] argv) {
            targetType=LoadAssembly(argv[0], argv[1]);
```

```
        DumpReportHeader();
        DumpMethods();
    }

    static public Type LoadAssembly(string t, string a) {
        return Type.ReflectionOnlyGetType(t + "," + a, false, true);
    }

    static void DumpReportHeader() {
        Console.WriteLine("\n{0} type of {1} assembly",
            targetType.Name, targetType.Assembly.GetName().Name);
        Console.WriteLine("\n{0,22}\n", "[ METHODS ]");
    }

    static void DumpMethods() {
        string dashes = new string('-', 50);
        foreach (MethodInfo method in targetType.GetMethods()) {
            Console.WriteLine("{0,12}{1,-12}", " ", method.Name + " " +
                "<" + method.ReturnParameter.ParameterType.Name + ">");
            int count = 1;
            foreach (ParameterInfo parameter in method.GetParameters()) {
                Console.WriteLine("{0, 35}{1, -12}",
                    " ", (count++).ToString() + " " + parameter.Name +
                    " (" + parameter.ParameterType.Name + ")");
            }
            Console.WriteLine("{0,12}{1}", " ", dashes);
        }
    }

    private static Type targetType;
    }
}
```

In the preceding code, a type name and an assembly name are read from the command line. The type to be dumped is *argv[0]*, while the assembly hosting the type is *argv[1]*. With this information, the *LoadAssembly* method calls *Type.ReflectionOnlyGetType* to load the type for inspection only. The *DumpMethods* function iterates the methods of this type, and then iterates the parameters of each method. The name of each method and parameter is displayed. The following command dumps the members of the *Console* class:

```
dumpmethods System.Console mscorlib.dll
```

Dynamic Invocation

Methods can be dynamically invoked at run time using reflection. The benefits and perils of early binding versus late binding with delegates are discussed in Chapter 10, "Delegates and Events."

In dynamic binding, you build a method signature at run time and then invoke the method. This is somewhat later than late binding with delegates. When compared with delegates, dynamic binding is more flexible, but marginally slower. With delegates, the method signature of the function call must match the delegate. This is determined at compile time. Dynamic binding removes this limitation, and any method can be invoked at the call site, regardless of the signature. This is more flexible and extensible but less safe.

In reflection, there are two approaches to invoking a method dynamically: *MethodInfo.Invoke* and *Type.InvokeMember*. Using *MethodInfo.Invoke* is the simpler approach. However, *Type. InvokeMember* is more malleable. The basic syntax of *MethodInfo.Invoke* requires only two parameters: an instance of a type and an array of parameters. The method is bound to the instance provided. If the method is static, the instance parameter should be *null*. To avoid an exception at run time, which is never desirable, care must be taken to ensure that the instance and parameters given to *MethodInfo.Invoke* match the signature of the function.

Here are the *MethodInfo.Invoke* overloaded signatures:

```
object Invoke(object obj, object[] arguments)
object Invoke(object obj, BindingFlags flags, Binder binderObj,
    object[] arguments, CultureInfo culture)
```

The second *Invoke* method has several additional parameters. The *obj* parameter is the instance to which the method is bound. The method is invoked on this object. If invoking a static method, the *obj* parameter should be *null*. *BindingFlags* is the next parameter and further describes the *Invoke* operation, such as *Binding.InvokeMethod*. This binding flag indicates that a method must be invoked. The default is *BindingFlags.Default*. *BindingFlags. Default* is not binding. *Binderobj* is used to select the appropriate candidate among overloaded methods. (Binders are discussed in the next section.) *Arguments* is the array of method arguments as defined by the method signature. The *culture* argument sets the culture, which defaults to the culture of the system. *Invoke* returns the return value of the invoked method.

Alternatively, you can invoke a method dynamically at run time using *Type.InvokeMember*, which is overloaded several times.

Here are the *Type.InvokeMember* overloaded signatures:

```
object InvokeMember¹(string methodName, BindingFlags flags,
    Binder binderObj, object typeInstance, object[] arguments)
object InvokeMember²(string methodName, BindingFlags flags,
    Binder binderObj, object typeInstance, object[] arguments,
    CultureInfo culture)
object InvokeMember³(string methodName, BindingFlags flags,
    Binder binderObj, object typeInstance, object[] arguments,
    ParameterModifier[] modifiers, CultureInfo culture,
    string[] namedParameters)
```

InvokeMember¹ is one of the overloaded methods, and it has five parameters. The *method-Name* parameter is the name of the method to invoke. The next parameter is *BindingFlags*. *Binderobj* is the binder used to discriminate between overloaded methods. (Binders are discussed in the next section.) The method binds to the *typeInstance* object. Next, *arguments* is the array of method parameters. *InvokeMember*[2] adds another parameter, which is the culture parameter for setting the culture. *InvokeMember*[3] is the final overload. The *ParameterModifier* parameter is an array of attributes for the method arguments. The *namedParameters* parameter is used to specify named parameters.

In the following code, dynamic invocation is demonstrated with both the *MethodInfo.Invoke* and *Type.InvokeMember* methods:

```csharp
using System;
using System.Reflection;

namespace Donis.CSharpBook {

    class Starter {

        static void Main() {
            ZClass obj = new ZClass();
            Type tObj = obj.GetType();
            MethodInfo method = tObj.GetMethod("MethodA");

            method.Invoke(obj, null);
            tObj.InvokeMember("MethodA", BindingFlags.InvokeMethod,
                null, obj, null);
        }
    }
    class ZClass {

        public void MethodA() {
            Console.WriteLine("ZClass.Method invoked");
        }
    }
}
```

Binders

Members such as methods can be overloaded. In reflection, binders identify the specific method from a list of possible candidates. The default binder selects the best match based on the number and type of arguments. You can provide a custom binder and explicitly choose a specific overloaded member. Both *MethodInfo.Invoke* and *Type.InvokeMember* offer a binder argument for this reason.

The *Binder* class is an abstract class; as such, it is implemented through a derived concrete class. *Binder* has abstracted methods to select a field, property, and method from available overloaded candidates. *Binder* is a member of the *Reflection* namespace. Table 13-8 lists the public members of the *Binder* class. Each method included in the table is abstract and must be overridden in any derivation.

TABLE 13-8 Abstract methods of the *Binder* class

Binder method	Description
BindToField	Selects a field from a set of overloaded fields
BindToMethod	Selects a method from a set of overloaded methods
ChangeType	Coerces the type of an object
ReorderArgumentArray	Resets the argument array; associated with the state parameter of *BindToMethod* member
SelectMethod	Selects a method from candidate methods
SelectProperty	Selects a property from candidate properties

If a binder is provided, *Binder.BindToMethod* is called when a method is invoked dynamically. To override the default selection criteria for an overloaded method, first create a custom *Binder* class that inherits the *Binder* class. Override and implement or stub (partially implement) each abstract method of the base class. How the binder is used determines which methods of the base class (*Binder*) you should fully implement. To select a specific overloaded method, *BindToMethod* should be completely implemented.

The *Binder.BindToMethod* syntax is as follows:

```
public abstract BindToMethod(BindingFlags flags, MethodBase[] match,
    ref object[] args, ParameterModifier[] modifiers, CultureInfo culture,
    string[] names, out object state)
```

The first parameter of *BindToMethod* is *BindingFlags*, which is the usual assortment of binding flags. Next, *match* is a *MethodBase* array with an element for each possible overloaded function candidate. If a method is overloaded three times, the *match* array should have three elements. The *args* array holds the values of the method parameters. The *modifiers* parameter is an array of *ParameterModifier,* which are the modifiers that apply to the parameters. The *culture* parameter sets the culture. The *names* parameter is an array of identifiers of methods included as candidates. The *modifiers*, *culture*, and *names* parameters can be *null*. The final parameter, *state*, is used with parameter reordering. If this parameter is not *null, Binder. ReorderArgumentArray* is called after *BindToMethod* and returns the parameters to the original order.

There are no rules for selecting a method from a set of candidates. You are free to be creative and employ whatever logic seems reasonable. Here is a partially implemented but workable custom *Binder* class. *BindToMethod* is implemented but the other methods are essentially stubbed. This code is not written for general-purpose usage. It is a limited example for this book:

```
using System;
using System.Reflection;
using System.Globalization;
```

```
class CustomBinder:Binder {
    public override FieldInfo BindToField(BindingFlags bindingAttr,
            FieldInfo[] match, object value, CultureInfo culture) {
        return null;
    }

    public override MethodBase BindToMethod(BindingFlags bindingAttr,
            MethodBase[] match, ref object[] args,
            ParameterModifier[] modifiers, CultureInfo culture,
            string[] names, out object state) {
        Console.WriteLine("Overloaded Method:");
        foreach (MethodInfo method in match) {
            Console.Write("\n {0} (", method.Name);
            foreach (ParameterInfo parameter in
                    method.GetParameters()) {
                Console.Write(" " + parameter.ParameterType.ToString());
            }
            Console.WriteLine(" )");
        }
        Console.WriteLine();
        state = null;
        if (long.Parse(args[0].ToString()) > int.MaxValue) {
            return match[0];
        }
        else {
            return match[1];
        }
    }

    public override object ChangeType(object value, Type type,
            CultureInfo culture) {
        return null;
    }

    public override void ReorderArgumentArray(ref object[] args,
            object state) {
    }

    public override MethodBase SelectMethod(BindingFlags bindingAttr,
            MethodBase[] match, Type[] types,
            ParameterModifier[] modifiers) {
        return null;
    }

    public override PropertyInfo SelectProperty(BindingFlags bindingAttr,
            PropertyInfo[] match, Type returnType, Type[] indexes,
            ParameterModifier[] modifiers) {
        return null;
    }
}

class ZClass {
    public void MethodA(long argument) {
        Console.WriteLine("Long version: " + argument.ToString());
    }
```

```
    public void MethodA(int argument) {
        Console.WriteLine("Int version: " + argument.ToString());
    }

    public void MethodA(int argument, int argument2) {
        Console.WriteLine("ZClass::two-argument Method " +
            argument.ToString() + ", " + argument2.ToString());
    }
}

class Starter {
    public static void Main() {
    ZClass obj = new ZClass();
    Type tObj = obj.GetType();
        CustomBinder theBinder = new CustomBinder();
        tObj.InvokeMember("MethodA", BindingFlags.InvokeMethod,
            theBinder, obj, new Object[] {int.MinValue});
        Console.WriteLine();
        tObj.InvokeMember("MethodA", BindingFlags.InvokeMethod, theBinder,
            obj, new Object[] {long.MaxValue});
    }
}
```

In the preceding code, *CustomBinder* inherits from the *Binder* class. *BindToMethod* is the only method fully implemented in the example. The implementation lists the signatures of each candidate. The appropriate method to invoke then is chosen in the method. More specifically, the first *foreach* loop iterates the candidates, listing the method names. The inner *foreach* loop iterates and lists the parameters of each *MethodInfo* object. This version of *BindToMethod* is written specifically for the one-argument methods of the *ZClass BindToMethod*. The argument value is tested. If the value is long, the first method is returned. This method has a long parameter. Otherwise, the second candidate, which has an integer parameter, is returned.

In *Main*, an instance of the *ZClass* and custom binder is created. *ZClass* is a simple class with an overloaded method. *ZClass.MethodA* is overloaded three times. The type object then is obtained from the *ZClass* instance, and *Type.InvokeMember* is called twice with the custom binder. *InvokeMember* is called to invoke "MethodA" dynamically, first with an integer parameter and then with a long parameter. Here is the output from the application:

```
Overloaded Method:

 MethodA ( System.Int64 )

 MethodA ( System.Int32 )

Int version: -2147483648

Overloaded Method:

 MethodA ( System.Int64 )

 MethodA ( System.Int32 )

Long version: 9223372036854775807
```

Type Creation

Until now, the emphasis of this chapter has been on reflecting existing objects. Object instances also can be created dynamically at run time. You can reflect, bind methods, and otherwise treat the dynamic object as a static object. As often is the case with *Reflection*, the primary benefit is added flexibility. What if the type or number of instances is not known at compile time? With *Reflection*, that decision can be delayed until run time, when the particular class can be chosen by the user, stipulated in a configuration file, or otherwise selected dynamically.

The *Activator* class can create instances at run time and is a member of the *Reflection* namespace. *Activator* consists of four static member methods: *CreateInstance* creates an instance of a type; *CreateInstanceFrom* leverages *Assembly.LoadFrom* to reference an assembly and then create an instance of a type found in the assembly; and *CreateComInstanceFrom* and *GetObject* instantiate a COM object and a proxy to a *Remote* object, respectively. To simply create an instance of a .NET type, call *CreateInstance* or *CreateInstanceFrom*. Both *CreateInstance* and *CreateInstanceFrom* are overloaded several times. Here is the list of the overloaded *CreateInstance* methods:

```
static public T CreateInstance<T>()
static public ObjectHandle CreateInstance<T, U> (T, U)
static public ObjectHandle CreateInstance(ActivationContext context)
static public ObjectHandle CreateInstance(ActivationContext context, string[] customData)
static public ObjectHandle CreateInstance(string assemblyName, string typeName)
static public ObjectHandle CreateInstance(string assemblyName, string typeName,
    object[] activationAttributes)
static public ObjectHandle CreateInstance(string assemblyName, string typeName,
    bool ignoreCase, BindingFlags bindingAttr, Binder Binder,
    object[] args, CultureInfo culture, object[] activationAttributes,
    Evidence securityInfo)
static public object CreateInstance(Type type)
static public object CreateInstance(string assemblyName, string TypeName,
    object[] activationAttributes)
static public object CreateInstance(Type type, bool ctorPublic)
static public object CreateInstance(Type type, object[] ctorArgs)
static public object CreateInstance(Type type, BindingFlags bindingAttr,
    Binder binder, object[] args, CultureInfo culture)
static public object CreateInstance(Type type, object[] args, object[] activationAttributes)
static public object CreateInstance(Type type, BindingFlags bindingAttr, Binder binder,
    object[] args, CultureInfo culture, object[] activationAttributes)
```

Some *CreateInstance* methods—and all *CreateInstanceFrom* methods—return an *ObjectHandle* when creating an instance of a type foreign to the current assembly. *ObjectHandle* is found in the *System.Runtime.Remoting* namespace. *ObjectHandle.Unwrap* unwraps the *ObjectHandle* to uncover a proxy to the remote object. Alternatively, the *AppDomain.CreateInstanceFromAndUnwrap* method creates an instance of the type and returns the proxy in one less step.

The following code creates three instances of a type that has been copied into different locations. A local and two remote proxies to object instances are constructed:

```
using System;
using System.Reflection;
using System.Runtime.Remoting;

namespace Donis.CSharpBook {

    class ZClass {
        public void MethodA(DateTime dt) {
            Console.WriteLine("MethodA invoked at " +
            dt.ToLongTimeString());
        }
    }

    class Starter {

        static void Main() {
            CreateLocal();
            CreateRemote1();
            CreateRemote2();
        }

        static void CreateLocal() {
            object obj = Activator.CreateInstance(typeof(ZClass));
            ((ZClass) obj).MethodA(DateTime.Now);
        }

        static void CreateRemote1() {
            ObjectHandle hObj = Activator.CreateInstance("library",
                "Donis.CSharpBook.ZClass");
            object obj = hObj.Unwrap();
            MethodInfo method = obj.GetType().GetMethod("MethodA");
            method.Invoke(obj, new object[1] {DateTime.Now});
        }

        static void CreateRemote2() {
            AppDomain domain = AppDomain.CurrentDomain;
            object obj = domain.CreateInstanceFromAndUnwrap("library.dll",
                "Donis.CSharpBook.ZClass");
            MethodInfo method = obj.GetType().GetMethod("MethodA");
            method.Invoke(obj, new object[1] {DateTime.Now});
        }
    }
}
```

The preceding code presents three approaches to creating an instance of a type, and two approaches to binding a method to the type and invoking that method dynamically.

Dynamically invoking a method through casting is a mechanism not previously demonstrated. The code for calling a method through casting is shown again here:

```
((ZClass) obj).MethodA(DateTime.Now);
```

Calling a method dynamically through casting has substantial performance gains when compared with *MethodInfo.Invoke* or *Type.InvokeMember*. (*MethodInfo.Invoke* and *Type. InvokeMember* were reviewed earlier in this chapter.)

Either directly or indirectly, the *CreateInstance* and *CreateInstanceFrom* methods return an object. As the preceding code demonstrates, you can cast the generic object to a specific type and invoke the chosen method. This combines late and early binding, which has favorable performance benefits when compared with entirely late binding the type and method.

Late Binding Delegates

A delegate is a repository that contains type-safe function pointers. A *single-cast delegate* holds one function pointer, whereas a *multicast delegate* is a basket of one or more delegates. Delegates are type-safe because the signatures of the delegate and function pointer must match. A compiler error occurs if there is a mismatch. Unlike *MethodInfo*, a function pointer is discriminatory and bound to a specific object or static class. *MethodInfo* is nondiscriminatory and can be associated with *any* object with a member that shares that method identity. This is the reason why *MethodInfo.Invoke* and *Type.InvokeMember* methods have an object parameter to associate an instance with the target method. This section assumes a fundamental understanding of delegates. If you would like a review of this topic, read Chapter 10. The following code is typical of delegates:

```
using System;
using System.Reflection;

namespace Donis.CSharpBook {
    delegate void XDelegate(int arga, int argb);

    class ZClass {
        public void MethodA(int arga, int argb) {
            Console.WriteLine("ZClass.MethodA called: {0} {1}", arga, argb);
        }
    }

    class Starter {
        static void Main() {
            ZClass obj = new ZClass();
            XDelegate delObj = new XDelegate(obj.MethodA);
            delObj.Invoke(1,2);
            delObj(3,4);
        }
    }
}
```

In this code, *XDelegate* is the delegate type. *MethodA* then is added to the delegate and invoked. First, the methods in the delegate are invoked using the *Delegate.Invoke* method. Second, the function is invoked through the delegate using the normal C# method-calling syntax—*Invoke* is called implicitly. At compile time, *XDelegate* expands into a class derived from a *Delegate* type. The signature of *Invoke* matches the signature of the delegate. Therefore, *XDelegate.Invoke* has two integer parameters, which enforces type safety on related function pointers.

The preceding code assumes that the delegate signature is known at compile time. If it is not, you could not define the delegate type. What if the signature of the delegate is not known at compile time? Ultimately, a delegate becomes a class. Like any other class, an instance of the delegate can be created at run time. You can then bind a method to the delegate and later invoke the method through the delegate. The *Delegate.CreateDelegate* and *Delegate. DynamicInvoke* methods allow this approach. As already mentioned, late binding of function pointers is not as type-safe as compile-time type checking. This also pertains to late binding of delegates. Care must be taken to avoid run-time exceptions. As always, the seminal benefit of late binding is additional flexibility, but performance might suffer.

The *Delegate.CreateDelegate* method creates a new delegate at run time and then adds the function pointer to the delegate. *CreateDelegate* is an overloaded method where the essential parameters are the delegate type, target (for non-static methods), and method identity. The delegate type is the type of delegate being created. The *target* parameter is the object to bind the method to. If *target* is *null* or missing, the method must be static. The *method* parameter is the initial function pointer being assigned to the delegate. The signature of the specified method should match that of the delegate type. These are the overloaded *CreateDelegate* methods:

```
static Delegate CreateDelegate(Type type, MethodInfo method)
static Delegate CreateDelegate(Type type, MethodInfo method, bool thrownOnBindFailure)
static Delegate CreateDelegate(Type type, object firstArgument, MethodInfo method)
static Delegate CreateDelegate(Type type, object firstArgument, MethodInfo method,
    bool throwOnBindFailure)
static Delegate CreateDelegate(Type type, object firstArgument, Type target, string method)
static Delegate CreateDelegate(Type type, object firstArgument, Type target, string method,
    bool ignoreCase)
static Delegate CreateDelegate(Type type, object target, string method)
static Delegate CreateDelegate(Type type, object target, string method, bool ignoreCase)
static Delegate CreateDelegate(Type type, object target, string method, bool ignoreCase,
    bool throwOnBindFailure)
static Delegate CreateDelegate(Type type, Type target, string method)
static Delegate CreateDelegate(Type type, Type target, string method, bool ignoreCase)
static Delegate CreateDelegate(Type type, Type target, string method, bool ignoreCase,
    bool throwOnBindFailure)
static Delegate CreateDelegate(Type type, object firstArgument, Type target, string method,
    bool ignoreCase, bool throwOnBindFailure)
```

After creating a delegate at run time, call *DynamicInvoke* to invoke function pointers added to the delegate. You cannot call *Invoke* on a delegate returned from *CreateDelegate*. This is a major difference between compile-time and run-time instances of delegates. An array of function arguments is the only parameter of *DynamicInvoke*.

Here is the *DynamicInvoke* signature:

```
object DynamicInvoke(object[] args)
```

CreateDelegate and *DynamicInvoke* are demonstrated in the following code:

```
using System;
using System.Reflection;

namespace Donis.CSharpBook {
    delegate void theDelegate(int arga, int argb);

    class ZClass {
        public void MethodA(int arga, int argb) {
            Console.WriteLine("ZClass.MethodA called: {0} {1}", arga, argb);
        }
    }

    class Starter {
        static void Main() {
            Type tObj=typeof(System.MulticastDelegate);
            ZClass obj = new ZClass();
            Delegate del = Delegate.CreateDelegate(typeof(theDelegate), obj,
                "MethodA");
            del.DynamicInvoke(new object[] {1,2});
        }
    }
}
```

Function Call Performance

Several ways to invoke a method have been presented in this chapter—from a simple method call to the more complex dynamic invocation. Performance is an important criterion when evaluating competing approaches. For example, a simple call bound at compile time should be quicker than a method bound at run time. Depending on the application and usage patterns of the method, the difference might be material. Losing a few nanoseconds might be trivial for a user interface–driven application. However, a loss of a few nanoseconds in a server application multiplied by thousands of users, each with multiple transactions, can pose a real problem.

Reflection and Generics

In .NET Framework 2.0, *Reflection* was extended to accommodate open and closed generic types and methods. The *Type* class is the focal point of changes that extend reflection to accommodate generic types, while *MethodInfo* has been enhanced to reflect generic methods.

(Generics were introduced in Chapter 7, "Generics.") Open constructed types are generic types with unbound type parameters, whereas closed constructed types have bound type arguments. With *Reflection*, you can browse bound and unbound parameters, create instances of generic types, and invoke generic methods at run time.

IsGeneric and *IsGenericTypeDefinition*

With reflection, you can query the status of a type or method. Is a type or method generic? If generic, is the type or method open or closed?

Type.IsGeneric is a Boolean property that confirms whether a type is generic; *Type. IsGenericTypeDefinition*, another Boolean property, indicates whether the generic type is open or closed. For methods, the *MethodInfo.IsGenericMethod* property confirms whether a method is a generic method. The *MethodInfo.IsGenericTypeDefinition* property indicates whether the generic method is open or closed. The following program demonstrates the four properties:

```
using System;
using System.Reflection;

public class ZClass<T, V> {
    public T membera;
}

public class XClass {
    public void MethodA<T>() {
    }
}

namespace Donis.CSharpBook {

    class Starter {

        static void Main() {
            Type[] types = { typeof(ZClass<,>), typeof(ZClass<int,int>) };
            bool[,] bresp = { { types[0].IsGenericType,
                                types[0].IsGenericTypeDefinition },
                              { types[1].IsGenericType,
                                types[1].IsGenericTypeDefinition } };
            Console.WriteLine("Is ZClass<,> a generic type? " + bresp[0,0]);
            Console.WriteLine("Is ZClass<,> open? " + bresp[0,1]);
            Console.WriteLine("Is ZClass<int,int> a generic type? " + bresp[1,0]);
            Console.WriteLine("Is ZClass<int,int> open? " + bresp[1,1]);

            Type tObj = typeof(XClass);
            MethodInfo method = tObj.GetMethod("MethodA");
            bool[] bMethod = { method.IsGenericMethod,
                               method.IsGenericMethodDefinition };
            Console.WriteLine("Is XClass.MethodA<T> a generic method? " + bMethod[0]);
            Console.WriteLine("Is XClass.MethodA<T> open? " + bMethod[1]);
        }
    }
}
```

typeof

The *typeof* operator, demonstrated several times already in this chapter, also can be used with generic types. The *Type* object has a single parameter, which identifies the type. For a generic type, connote an open constructed type using empty type parameters. For example, *ZClass<T>* would be indicated as *ZClass<>*. Multiple generic type parameters (*n* parameters) are indicated with *n-1* commas. For the *typeof* operator, *ZClass<,>* connotes the open constructed type for *ZClass<K,V>*. Indicate a closed constructed type by including the actual argument types, such as *ZClass<int, int>*. In addition to the *typeof* operator, *Type.GetType* and *Type.GetGenericTypeDefinition* methods can return *Type* objects for generic types.

GetType

Type.GetType is available in two flavors: an instance and a static method. *Type.GetType,* as an instance method, returns the type from an object, which can be an instance of a generic type. The method has no parameters. The *Type.GetType* static method is overloaded to return a *Type* object of a type. The pivotal parameter of the static *GetType* method is a string naming the type. This parameter can be used to indicate a generic type. To specify an open constructed type, the string is the name of the generic with the number of parameters affixed. The suffix is preceded with a grave accent character (`). For example, the string *"NamespaceA.XClass`2"* would represent *XClass<K,V>*. *XClass* has two type parameters. For a closed constructed type, you need to add the bound type arguments. After specifying the number of type arguments, list the bound type arguments. The bound type arguments are contained in square brackets. For example, the string *"NamespaceB.ZClass`3[System.Int32, System.Int32, System.Decimal]"* identifies *ZClass<int, int, decimal>*. Here is the general format for an open constructed type:

```
GenericType`NumberOfParameters
```

Here is the general format for a closed constructed type:

```
GenericType`NumberOfParameters[parameterList]
```

The following sample code demonstrates both the instance and static *GetType* methods:

```
using System;

namespace Donis.CSharpBook {

    class ZClass<K,V> {
        public void FunctionA(K argk, V argv) {
        }
    }

    class XClass<T> {
```

```
        public void FunctionB(T argt) {
        }
    }

    class Starter {

        public static void Main() {
            ZClass<int, decimal> obj = new ZClass<int, decimal>();
            Type typeClosed = obj.GetType();
            Console.WriteLine(typeClosed.ToString());

            Type typeOpen = Type.GetType("Donis.CSharpBook.XClass`1");
            Console.WriteLine(typeOpen.ToString());
            Type typeClosed2 = Type.GetType(
                "Donis.CSharpBook.ZClass`2[System.Int32, System.Decimal]");
            Console.WriteLine(typeClosed2.ToString());
        }
    }
}
```

GetGenericTypeDefinition

Closed constructed types are created from open constructed types. *Type.GetGenericTypeDefinition* returns the *Type* object for the underlying type (the open constructed type) used to build a closed constructed type.

Here is the *Type.GetGenericTypeDefinition* signature:

```
Type GetGenericTypeDefinition()
```

The following code highlights the *GetGenericTypeDefinition* method:

```
using System;

namespace Donis.CSharpBook {

    class ZClass<K,V> {
        public void FunctionA(K argk, V argv) {
        }
    }

    class Starter {

        public static void Main() {
            ZClass<int, decimal> obj = new ZClass<int, decimal>();
            ZClass<string, float> obj2 = new ZClass<string, float>();

            Type closedType = obj.GetType();
            Type openType = closedType.GetGenericTypeDefinition();

            Type closedType2 = obj2.GetType();
            Type openType2 = closedType2.GetGenericTypeDefinition();

            Console.WriteLine(openType.ToString());
```

```
        Console.WriteLine(openType2.ToString());
      }
    }
  }
```

The preceding code displays identical strings in the console window. Why? The underlying open constructed type of *ZClass<int, decimal>* and *ZClass<string, float>* is the same, namely *ZClass<K, V>*.

MethodInfo.GetGenericMethodDefinition is comparable to *Type.GetGenericTypeDefinition*, but pertains to methods rather than types. Similarly, the *Type.GetMethod* method is comparable to *Type.GetType* but pertains to methods.

GetGenericArguments

You can now extract a *Type* object for a generic type and a *MethodInfo* object for a generic method. Determining the number of unbound or bound parameters is a natural next step. For example, if bound, looking at the type of each parameter is an appropriate error-checking step. *GetGenericArguments* is the universal method for enumerating parameters of a generic type or method. *GetGenericArguments* enumerates unbound and bound parameters.

Here is the *Type.GetGenericArguments* signature:

```
Type[] GetGenericArguments()
```

The MethodInfo.GetGenericArguments signature is identical:

```
Type[] GetGenericArguments()
```

The following code demonstrates both *Type.GetGenericArguments* and *MethodInfo. GetGenericArguments*:

```
using System;

namespace Donis.CSharpBook {

    class ZClass<K, V>{
        public void FunctionA(K argk, V argv) {
        }
    }

    class Starter {
        public static void Main() {
            int count=0;
            ZClass<int, decimal> obj = new ZClass<int, decimal>();
            Type zObj = obj.GetType();
            object[] arguments = zObj.GetGenericArguments();
            foreach (object argument in arguments) {
                Console.WriteLine("zObj argument {0}: {1}",
```

```
                     (++count).ToString(), argument.ToString());
            }
            count = 0;
            Type zType = typeof(ZClass<,>);
            object[] parameters = zType.GetGenericArguments();
            foreach (object parameter in parameters) {
                Console.WriteLine("ZClass parameters {0}: {1}",
                    (++count).ToString(), parameter.ToString());
            }
        }
    }
}
```

Creating Generic Types

Generic types can be created at run time using reflection. First, determine the open constructed type of the generic. This chapter has already shown several ways to accomplish this, including using *GetType* and *GetGenericTypeDefinition*. Next, bind the type arguments of the open constructed type. The result will be a closed constructed type. Finally, create an instance of the closed constructed type in the customary manner. (*Activator.CreateInstance* works well.)

The *Type.MakeGenericType* method binds type arguments to a generic open constructed type. *MakeGenericType* has a single parameter, which is an array of *Type* objects. Each element of the array is a type argument. If the generic has three parameters, the array passed to *MakeGenericType* will have three elements, each representing a type argument.

Here is the signature of the *MakeGenericType* method:

```
Type.MakeGenericType syntax:
void MakeGenericType(Type[] genericArguments)
```

Generic methods, like non-generic methods, can be invoked dynamically at run time. *MethodInfo.MakeGenericMethod* binds type arguments to generic methods, similar to *Type. MakeGenericType*. The benefits and pitfalls of dynamic invocation are similar to non-generic methods. After binding parameters to a generic method, the method can be invoked using reflection. The following code creates a generic type and then invokes a generic method at run time:

```
using System;
using System.Reflection;


namespace Donis.CSharpBook {

    public class GenericZ <K, V, Z>
        where K: new()
        where V: new() {
```

```
    public void MethodA<A>(A argument1, Z argument2) {
        Console.WriteLine("MethodA invoked");
    }

    private K field1 = new K();
    private V field2 = new V();
}

class Starter {

    static void Main() {
        Type genericType = typeof(GenericZ<,,>);
        Type[] typeArguments = {typeof(int),typeof(float),
            typeof(int)};
        Type closedType = genericType.MakeGenericType(typeArguments);
        MethodInfo openMethod = closedType.GetMethod("MethodA");
        object newObject = Activator.CreateInstance(closedType);
        typeArguments = new Type[] {typeof(int)};
        MethodInfo closedMethod =
            openMethod.MakeGenericMethod(typeArguments);
        object[] methodargs = {2, 10};
        closedMethod.Invoke(newObject, methodargs);
    }
}
}
```

Reflection Security

Some reflection operations, such as accessing protected and private members, require
the *ReflectionPermission* security permission. *ReflectionPermission* is typically granted
to local and intranet applications, but not to Internet applications. Set the appropriate
ReflectionPermission flag to grant or deny specific reflection operations. Table 13-9 lists the
ReflectionPermission flags.

TABLE 13-9 *ReflectionPermission* **flags**

Flag	Description
MemberAccess	Reflection of visible members granted.
NoFlags	Reflection and enumeration allowed for types and members. However, invocation only allowed on visible members.
ReflectionEmit	*System.Reflection.Emit* operations granted. Not required after .NET Framework 2.0 Service Pack 1.
TypeInformation	This flag is now deprecated.
AllFlags	Combines *TypeInformation*, *MemberAccess*, and *ReflectionEmit* flags.

Attributes

Attributes extend the description of a member of an assembly. Attributes fulfill the role of adjectives in .NET and can annotate assemblies, classes, methods, parameters, and other items. Attributes are commonplace in .NET and fulfill many roles, including delineating serialization, stipulating import linkage, setting class layout, indicating conditional compilation, and marking a method as deprecated.

Attributes extend the metadata of the target member. An instance of the attribute is stored alongside the metadata and sometimes alongside the MSIL code of the constituent. The attributes in the following code are shown in Figure 13-4. The *Conditional* attribute marks a method for conditional compilation. With this attribute, the target method and call sites are included in the compiled application if the *LOG* symbol is defined. If it is not defined, the method and any invocation are omitted from the compilation:

```
#define LOG

using System;
using System.IO;
using System.Diagnostics;

namespace Donis.CSharpBook {

    class Starter {
        static void Main() {
            LogInfo(new StreamWriter(@"c:\logfile.txt"));
        }

        [Conditional("LOG")]
        private static void LogInfo(StreamWriter sr) {
            // write information to log file
        }
    }
}
```

Figure 13-4 shows the MSIL code of the *LogInfo* method as displayed in ILDASM. Notice the custom directive that defines the *Conditional* attribute. It is integrated into the MSIL code of the method.

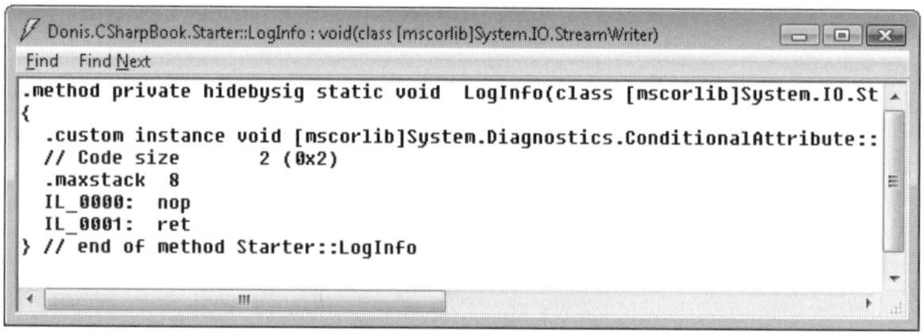

FIGURE 13-4 The *Conditional* attribute in MSIL code

Attributes are available in different flavors: predefined custom attributes, programmer-defined custom attributes, and pseudo-custom attributes. All three are explained next.

Predefined Custom Attributes

Predefined custom attributes, which are defined in the FCL, are the most prevalent custom attributes. Predefined custom attributes include *AssemblyVersion*, *Debuggable*, *FileIOPermission*, *Flags*, and *Obsolete*. Many responsibilities in .NET are fulfilled by predefined custom attributes. The following code uses the *Obsolete* attribute to flag a method as deprecated:

```
[Obsolete("Deprecated Method", false)]
public static void MethodA() {
    Console.WriteLine("Starter.MethodA");
}
```

Pseudo-custom Attributes

Pseudo-custom attributes are interpreted by the run time and modify the metadata of the assembly. Unlike predefined custom attributes, pseudo-custom attributes do not extend metadata. Examples of pseudo-custom attributes include *DllImport*, *MarshalAs*, and *Serializable*.

Combining Attributes

A member can be assigned more than one attribute. In certain circumstances, the same attribute can even be applied multiple times. There are two ways to combine attributes. They can be listed separately or combined. Here, the attributes are applied separately:

```
[Obsolete("Deprecated Method", false)]
[FileIOPermission(SecurityAction.Demand,
    Unrestricted = true)]
public static void MethodA() {
    Console.WriteLine("Starter.MethodA");
}
```

In the following code, two attributes are combined and applied to a method:

```
[Obsolete("Deprecated Method", false),
 FileIOPermission(SecurityAction.Demand,
    Unrestricted = true)]
public static void MethodA() {
    Console.WriteLine("Starter.MethodA");
}
```

Anatomy of an Attribute

Attributes are types derived from the *System.Attribute* class, which is the common base class of all attributes. *System.Attribute* is an abstract class defining the required services of any attribute. Managed compilers and the run time sometimes act differently based on an attribute. For example, the *ObsoleteAttribute* causes the compiler to generate error or warning messages when a deprecated member is used.

Here is the syntax of an attribute:

```
[type: attributeName(positionalParameter1, ..., positionalParametern,

    namedParameter1 = value, ..., namedParametern = value)] target
```

The attribute name is the class name of the attribute. By convention, attribute names have an *Attribute* suffix. *OneWayAttribute* is representative of an attribute name. You also can use the alias of an attribute, which omits the *Attribute* suffix. The alias for *OneWayAttribute* would be *OneWay*.

Attributes accept zero or more positional parameters. Positional parameters are ordered and must be used in a specific sequence. In addition, an attribute might have any number of named parameters, which must follow positional parameters. Named parameters are optional. Named parameters are not ordered and can be presented in any sequence.

The following code applies the *UIPermissionAttribute* to the *Starter* class:

```
[type: UIPermissionAttribute(SecurityAction.Demand,
    Clipboard = UIPermissionClipboard.OwnClipboard)]
class Starter {
    static void Main() {

    }
}
```

Here is the same attribute expressed somewhat more succinctly:

```
[type: UIPermissionAttribute(SecurityAction.Demand,
    Clipboard = UIPermissionClipboard.OwnClipboard)]
class Starter {
    static void Main() {

    }
}
```

Programmer-Defined Custom Attributes

You can create custom attributes for private consumption or to be published in a library for others. There are definitive procedures to creating a programmer-defined custom attribute. Here are the steps to follow:

1. Select an appropriate name for the custom attribute. Attribute names should conclude with the *Attribute* suffix.

2. Derive the attribute class from *System.Attribute*.

3. Set potential targets with the *AttributeUsage* attribute.

4. Implement class constructors, which determine the positional parameters.

5. Implement write-accessible properties, which define the named parameters.

6. Implement other members of the class as needed based on the role of the attribute.

I will use *ClassVersionAttribute* to demonstrate these steps. This attribute is a programmer-defined custom attribute that can apply a version number to types. By default, you can assign version numbers only to assemblies. The attribute assigns two version numbers to a type: a target version and a current version. The target version is the version number of the present type. The current version number is the version number of the most recent version of that type. When the type is the most recent version, the target and current version numbers are the same. In addition, the *ClassVersionAttribute* can request that the most recent version of the type should always be used.

The first and most important task of creating a programmer-defined attribute is selecting a name. Alas, *ClassVersionAttribute* is a mundane but descriptive name. As an attribute, *ClassVersionAttribute* must inherit *System.Attribute*. *AttributeUsageAttribute* sets the potential target of the attributes. *AttributeTargets* is the only positional parameter of the *AttributeUsageAttribute* and is a bitwise enumeration. *AttributeUsageAttribute* has three named parameters: *AllowMultiple*, *Inherited*, and *ValidOn*. *AllowMultiple* is a Boolean flag. When *true*, the attribute can be applied multiple times to the same target. The default is *false*. *Inherited* is another Boolean flag. If *true*, which is the default, the attribute is inheritable from a base class. *ValidOn* is an *AttributeTargets* enumeration. This is an alternate method of setting the potential target of the attribute.

Here is a list of the available *AttributeTargets* flags:

- *All*
- *Assembly*
- *Class*
- *Constructor*
- *Delegate*
- *Enum*
- *Event*
- *Field*
- *GenericParameter*
- *Interface*

- *Method*

- *Module*

- *Parameter*

- *Property*

- *ReturnValue*

- *Struct*

Here is the start of the *ClassVersionAttribute* class:

```
[AttributeUsage(AttributeTargets.Class | AttributeTargets.Struct,
    Inherited = false)]
public class ClassVersionAttribute : System.Attribute {
}
```

Instance constructors of an attribute provide the positional parameters for the attribute. When an attribute is used, the constructor runs. The positional arguments should match the signature of a constructor in the attribute class. Overloading the constructor allows different sets of positional parameters. Positional and named parameters are restricted to certain types. For example, a positional or named parameter cannot be a decimal. The following is a list of available attribute parameter types:

- *bool*

- *byte*

- *char*

- *double*

- *float*

- *int*

- *long*

- *sbyte*

- *short*

- *string*

- *uint*

- *ulong*

- *ushort*

ClassVersionAttribute has two overloaded constructors. The first constructor sets the target version and the current version to a single specified value; the second constructor sets the target and current version number to different specified values:

```
public ClassVersionAttribute(string target)
    : this(target, target) {
}

public ClassVersionAttribute(string target,
        string current) {
    m_TargetVersion = target;
    m_CurrentVersion = current;
}
```

Define named parameters as write-only or read-write instance properties of the attribute class. You can duplicate positional parameters as named parameters for additional flexibility. *ClassVersionAttributes* offers a *UseCurrentVersion* and *CurrentName* named parameter. *UseCurrentVersion* is a Boolean value. If *true,* the most current type should be used in all circumstances. *CurrentName* assigns a string name to this version, which is optional. This is how the named parameters are implemented in the *ClassVersionAttribute* class:

```
private bool m_UseCurrentVersion = false;
public bool UseCurrentVersion {
    set {
        if (m_TargetVersion != m_CurrentVersion) {
            m_UseCurrentVersion = value;
        }
    }
    get {
        return m_UseCurrentVersion;
    }
}

private string m_CurrentName;
public string CurrentName {
    set {
        m_CurrentName = value;
    }
    get {
        return m_CurrentName;
    }
}
```

For completeness, read-only properties are added to the *ClassVersionAttribute* class for the target and current version. Here is the completed *ClassVersionAttribute* class:

```
using System;

namespace Donis.CSharpBook {
    [AttributeUsage(AttributeTargets.Class | AttributeTargets.Struct,
        Inherited = false)]
    public class ClassVersionAttribute : System.Attribute {

        public ClassVersionAttribute(string target)
            : this(target, target) {
        }
```

```
            public ClassVersionAttribute(string target,
                    string current) {
                m_TargetVersion = target;
                m_CurrentVersion = current;
            }

            private bool m_UseCurrentVersion = false;
            public bool UseCurrentVersion {
                set {
                    if (m_TargetVersion != m_CurrentVersion) {
                        m_UseCurrentVersion = value;
                    }
                }
                get {
                    return m_UseCurrentVersion;
                }
            }

            private string m_CurrentName;
            public string CurrentName {
                set {
                    m_CurrentName = value;
                }
                get {
                    return m_CurrentName;
                }
            }

            private string m_TargetVersion;
            public string TargetVersion {
                get {
                    return m_TargetVersion;
                }
            }

            private string m_CurrentVersion;
            public string CurrentVersion {
                get {
                    return m_CurrentVersion;
                }
            }
        }
    }
}
```

The *ClassVersionAttribute* class is compiled and published in a DLL. The following application nominally uses the *ClassVersionAttribute*:

```
using System;

namespace Donis.CSharpBook {
    class Starter {
        static void Main() {

        }
    }
```

```
    [ClassVersion("1.1.2.1", UseCurrentVersion = false)]
    class ZClass {
    }
}
```

Attributes and Reflection

Programmer-defined custom attributes are sometimes valuable simply as information. However, the real fun and power lies in associating a behavior with an attribute. You can read custom attributes with reflection using the *Attribute.GetCustomAttribute* and *Type. GetCustomAttributes* methods. Both methods return an instance or instances of an attribute. You can downcast the attribute instance to a specific attribute type and use the public inter-face to invoke the appropriate behavior at run time.

Type.GetCustomAttributes returns attributes applied to a type. *GetCustomAttributes* also is available with other members to extract their attributes, including *Assembly MemberInfo*, and *ParameterInfo. GetCustomAttributes* has a single Boolean parameter. If *true,* the inheritance hierarchy of the type is evaluated for additional attributes.

Here is the *Type.GetCustomAttributes* method:

```
object[] GetCustomAttributes(bool inherit)
object[] GetCustomAttribute(type AttributeType, bool inherit)
```

Attribute.GetCustomAttribute, which is a static method, returns an instance of a spe-cific attribute. When a specific attribute is desired, *GetCustomAttribute* is more efficient. *GetCustomAttribute* is overloaded for two and three arguments. The two-argument versions have the target and attribute type as parameters. The three-argument version has an additional parameter, which is the *inherit* parameter. If the *inherit* parameter is *true,* the ascendants of the target class also are searched for the attribute.

Here is a sampling of the two-argument overloaded *Attribute.GetCustomAttribute* method:

```
static Attribute GetCustomAttribute(Assembly targetAssembly, type attributeType)
static Attribute GetCustomAttribute(MemberInfo targetMember, type attributeType)
static Attribute GetCustomAttribute(Module targetModule, type attributeType)
static Attribute GetCustomAttribute(ParameterInfo targetParameter, type attributeType)
```

The following sample code uses *GetCustomAttribute*:

```
using System;
using System.Reflection;

namespace Donis.CSharpBook {

    class Starter {

        static void Main() {
            Type tObj = typeof(Starter);
```

```
            MethodInfo method = tObj.GetMethod("AMethod");
            Attribute attrib = Attribute.GetCustomAttribute(
                method, typeof(ObsoleteAttribute));
            ObsoleteAttribute obsolete = (ObsoleteAttribute) attrib;
            Console.WriteLine("Obsolete Message: " + obsolete.Message);
        }

        [Obsolete("Deprecated function.", false)]
        public void AMethod() {
        }
    }
}
```

The following sample code uses *GetCustomAttributes*. The application inspects the
ClassVersionAttribute attribute with the *GetCustomAttributes* method and acts upon
the results. The application contains two versions of *ZClass* and both are applied to the
ClassVersionAttribute. Each version of *ZClass* shares a common interface: *IZClass*. The
ClassVersionAttribute of *Donis.CSharpBook.ZClass* lists *ANamespace.ZClass* as the current version or most recent version. Also, *UseCurrentVersion* is assigned *true* to indicate that the newer
version should replace instances of *Donis.CSharpBook.ZClass*. The function *CreateZClass* is
a helper method for the *ClassVersionAttribute*. It accepts a *ZClass* as defined by the *IZClass*
interface. Within the *foreach* loop, *GetCustomAttributes* enumerates the attributes of the
ZClass. If the attribute is a *ClassVersionAttribute*, the attribute is saved and the *foreach* loop
is exited. Next, the properties of the attribute are examined. If *UseCurrentVersion* is true and
a current version is named, an instance of the new version is created and returned from the
method. Otherwise, the target version is returned:

```
using System;
using System.Reflection;

interface IZClass {
    void AMethod();
}

namespace Donis.CSharpBook {
    class Starter {
        static void Main() {
            IZClass obj = CreateZClass(typeof(ZClass));
            obj.AMethod();
        }

        private static IZClass CreateZClass(Type tObj) {
            ClassVersionAttribute classversion = null;
            foreach (Attribute attrib in tObj.GetCustomAttributes(false)) {
                if (attrib.ToString() ==
                    typeof(ClassVersionAttribute).ToString()) {
                    classversion = (ClassVersionAttribute) attrib;
                }
                else {
                    return null;
                }
            }
```

```
        if (classversion.UseCurrentVersion &&
            (classversion.CurrentName != null)) {
            AppDomain currDomain = AppDomain.CurrentDomain;
            return (IZClass) currDomain.CreateInstanceFromAndUnwrap(
                "client.exe", classversion.CurrentName);
        }
        else {
            return (IZClass) Activator.CreateInstance(tObj);
        }
    }
}

[ClassVersion("1.1.2.1", "2.0.0.0", UseCurrentVersion = true,
    CurrentName = "Donis.CSharpBook.ANamespace.ZClass")]
public class ZClass: IZClass {
    public void AMethod() {
        Console.WriteLine("AMethod: old version");
    }
}

namespace ANamespace {
    [ClassVersion("2.0.0.0", UseCurrentVersion = false)]
    public class ZClass: IZClass {
        public void AMethod() {
            Console.WriteLine("AMethod: new version");
        }
    }
}
```

MSIL

Metadata and the ability to inspect metadata using reflection were the topics of this chapter. .NET assemblies consist of metadata and MSIL. MSIL is the topic of Chapter 14. Understanding MSIL is important for writing, maintaining, and debugging a C# application. Reflection can be used with MSIL code. You can inspect MSIL code at run time, create self-generating code, and otherwise manipulate MSIL using reflection.

Chapter 14
MSIL Programming

Microsoft Intermediate Language (MSIL) is the programming language of the Common Language Runtime (CLR) and the Common Instruction Language (CIL) for managed code. A managed application undergoes two compilations. The first compilation is from source code to MSIL and is performed by the language compiler. The second compilation occurs at run time, when the MSIL code is compiled to native code. The CLR performs the second compilation as part of process execution. From the perspective of the CLR, managed applications are simply MSIL code and metadata. The original source code language is unimportant to the CLR. For this reason, .NET is considered language-agnostic, or language-independent. One of the goals of the CLR is that process execution of a managed application is identical regardless of the source language, whether C# or Microsoft Visual Basic .NET.

MSIL promotes the concept of compile-once-and-run-anywhere in the .NET environment. Just-in-time (JIT) compilers, otherwise known as *jitters,* compile assemblies into native binary code that targets a specific platform. You can write an application or component once and then deploy the application to Microsoft Windows, Linux, and other environments that support a compliant .NET run time. A benefit to compile-once-and-run-anywhere is the ability to assemble applications from components deployed on disparate hardware and platforms. This was one of the objectives of component technologies such as Component Object Model (COM) and Common Object Request Broker Architecture (CORBA), but the objective was never truly realized. .NET makes this a reality. If platform-agnostic code is a design goal for an application, best practices must be adopted to insulate the managed application from platform-specific code. This includes avoiding or isolating interoperability and calls to native application programming interfaces (APIs).

Your application also can be pre-jitted. The jitter distributes the cost of compiling your program, whenever a method is first used, across the execution of the application. Pre-jitting provides an alternative to this methodology. You can compile the entire application up front and cache the resulting native binary in the global assembly cache. When pre-jitted, the cost of compiling an application is incurred prior to execution. The cached binary is used whenever the application is run versus incremental compilation. A tool called Ngen is provided with the .NET Framework for pre-jitting .NET applications. Pre-jitting is sometimes preferred, such as with a large application where most of the features are touched in common usage scenarios, or when optimal runtime performance is critical

MSIL is a full-featured, object-oriented programming (OOP) language. A C# program compiles to MSIL. However, there are differences when compared with C# programming. For example, global functions are allowed in MSIL but not supported in the C# language. Despite being a lower-level language, MSIL has expanded language elements. It encompasses the constituents common to most object-oriented languages: classes, structures, inheritance, transfer-of-control statements, an assortment of arithmetic operators, and much more. Indeed, you can write .NET applications directly in MSIL.

This is a book on C# programming. In that context, why is understanding MSIL important? An understanding of MSIL code advances a deeper appreciation and comprehension of C# programming and .NET. Managed code isn't just magic. Understanding MSIL removes much of the mystery and helps C# developers better maintain, debug, and write smart, efficient, and robust code.

Applications, particularly production applications purchased from third-party vendors, are sometimes available without the original source code. How is an application maintained or debugged without the source code? A native application would require not only the ability to disassemble the code but also solid knowledge of assembly language, which is a challenge for many developers. For a managed application, as part of the assembly, the MSIL code is usually available. MSIL is much easier to understand and interpret when compared to assembly language. The exception is when the assembly is obfuscated. Several tools, including Intermediate Language Disassembler (ILDASM), can disassemble an assembly to provide access to the MSIL code. With the MSIL code, a developer can essentially read the application. You can even modify the code as MSIL and reassemble the application. This is called *roundtripping*. Of course, this assumes that the developer is competent in MSIL programming.

In a native application, debugging without a debug file (.pdb) is a challenge (which is an understatement). Debugging a native application without symbol files invariably means interpreting assembly code. As previously mentioned, that is a challenge. More than a general understanding of assembly programming is needed to debug without symbol files. MSIL can be viewed as the assembly code of the CLR. Debugging a managed application without the germane symbol files requires more than a superficial understanding of MSIL. However, when compared to the tedious task of reading assembly, working with MSIL is a leisure cruise.

MSIL is instructive in managed programming. Learning MSIL programming is learning C# programming. What algorithms are truly efficient? When has boxing occurred? Which source code routines expand the footprint of the application? These secrets can be found in understanding MSIL code.

The ability to code inline MSIL in a C# application is suggested in numerous blogs on programming, but it is not currently available. I am an advocate of inline MSIL for C#. MSIL is more than an abstraction of higher-level source code. There are unique features in MSIL code that are not exposed in C#. In addition, C# is a code generator that emits MSIL code. In rare circumstances, compiler-generated MSIL might not be optimal for your specific application.

For these reasons, I favor inline MSIL. However, the problem with inline MSIL is maintaining safe code. Inline MSIL is inherently unsafe and could lead to abuse. If a safe implementation of inline MSIL is not possible, it should not be added to the language.

As mentioned, managed applications undergo two compilations. First the language compiler and then the run time (jitter) compiles the application. You can compile MSIL code directly into an assembly with the MSIL compiler, which is the Intermediate Language Assembler (ILASM). Conversely, you can disassemble an assembly with ILDASM.

This chapter is an overview of MSIL programming, not a comprehensive narrative on MSIL. The intention is to convey enough information on the language to aid in the interpretation, maintenance, and debugging of C# applications. For an authoritative explanation of MSIL, I recommend *Inside Microsoft .NET IL Assembler*, written by Serge Lidin (Microsoft Press, 2002). Serge Lidin is one of the original architects of the ILASM compiler, the ILDASM disassembler, and other tools included in the .NET Framework. Alternatively, consult the European Computer Manufacturers Association (ECMA) documents pertaining to CIL, which are available online at *http://www.ecma-international.org/publications/standards/Ecma-335.htm*.

"Hello World" Application

An example is a great place to begin the exploration of MSIL code programming. The following is a variation of the universally known "Hello World!" application. It displays "Hello *Name!*". (*Name* is a local variable.)

```
// Hello World Application

.assembly extern mscorlib {}
.assembly hello {}

/* Starter class with entry point method */

.namespace Donis.CSharpBook {
    .class Starter {
        .method static public void Main() cil managed {
            .maxstack 2
            .entrypoint
            .locals init (string name)
            ldstr "Donis"
            stloc.0
            ldstr "Hello, {0}!"
            ldloc name
            call void [mscorlib] System.Console::WriteLine(
                string, object)
            ret
        }
    }
}
```

Here is the command line that compiles the MSIL code to create a *hello* executable:

```
ilasm /exe /debug hello.il
```

The *exe* option indicates that the target is a console application, which is also the default. The *dll* option specifies a library target. The *debug* option asks the compiler to generate a debug file (.pdb) for the application. A debug file is useful for a variety of reasons, including viewing source code in a debugger or disassembler.

The elements of the application are explained in more detail throughout this chapter. A brief explanation is given here. The application begins with comments and three declaratives:

```
// Hello World Application
.assembly extern mscorlib {}
.assembly hello {}
/* Starter class with entry point method */
.namespace Donis.CSharpBook {
```

MSIL supports C# style comments—both single and multiline comments. The first declarative is an external reference to the Mscorlib library. Mscorlib.dll contains the core of the .NET Framework Class Library (FCL), which includes the *System.Console* class. The second assembly directive is the simple name of the assembly, which is *hello*. Notice that the simple name does not include the extension. The third directive defines a new namespace.

The next two lines define a class and a method within that class. The class directive introduces a public class named *Starter*, which implicitly inherits the *System.Object* class. The method directive, which is the next directive, defines *Main* as a member method. *Main* is a managed, public, and static function. The *cil* keyword indicates that the method contains Intermediate Language (IL) code:

```
.class Starter {
    .method static public void Main() cil managed {
```

The *Main* method begins with three directives. The *.maxstack* directive sets the size of the evaluation stack to two slots. The *.entrypoint* directive designates *Main* as the entry point of the application. By convention, *Main* is always the entry point of a C# executable. In MSIL, the entry point method is whatever method contains the *.entrypoint* directive, which could be a method other than *Main*. Finally, the *.locals* directive declares a local string variable called *name*. The *init* option of the *.locals* directive initializes a local variable to a default value before the method executes:

```
.maxstack 2
.entrypoint
.locals init (string name)
```

Table 14-1 explains the MSIL code of the *Main* method.

TABLE 14-1 **Hello World MSIL code**

Instruction	Description
ldstr "Donis"	Loads the string "Donis" onto the evaluation stack.
stloc.0	Stores "Donis" from the evaluation stack into the first local variable, which is called *name*.
ldstr "Hello, {0}!"	Loads the string "Hello, {0}!" onto the evaluation stack.
ldloc name	Loads the local variable onto the evaluation stack. (Local variables can be referenced by index or by name.)
call void [mscorlib] System.Console::WriteLine(string, object)	Calls the *Console::WriteLine* method, which consumes the two items on the evaluation stack as parameters from right to left. "Hello *xxx!*" is displayed, where *xxx* is replaced by the topmost item on the evaluation stack.
ret	Returns from the method.

Evaluation Stack

The evaluation stack, which is mentioned often in the preceding description of the "Hello World!" application, is the pivotal structure of MSIL applications. It is the bridge between your application and memory locations. It is similar to the conventional stack frame, but there are salient differences. The evaluation stack holds function parameters, local variables, temporary objects, and much more. In .NET, function parameters and local variables are stored in separate repositories, where memory is reserved for them. You cannot access the function parameter or local variable repositories directly. Accessing them requires moving data from memory to slots on the evaluation stack using a *load* command. Conversely, you update a local variable or parameter with content from the evaluation stack using a *store* command. Slots on the evaluation stack are either 4 or 8 bytes.

Figure 14-1 shows the relationship between the evaluation stack and the repositories for function parameters and local variables.

The evaluation stack is a *stack* and thereby a last in/first out (LIFO) instrument. When a function starts, the evaluation stack related to that method is empty. As the function runs, items are pushed on and popped from the evaluation stack. Before the function exits, except for a return value, the evaluation stack must be empty once again. The *jmp* and *tail* instructions, explained in the section "Branching," later in this chapter, are exceptions to this rule. If the evaluation stack is improper at exit, the run time raises an *InvalidProgramException* exception.

The *.maxstack* directive limits the number of items permitted simultaneously on the stack. The directive is optional. If the directive is not present, eight slots are reserved on the evaluation stack. The *.maxstack* directive is a check confirming that an application is performing as expected. Extra items on the evaluation stack are an indication of potential logic problems in an application or a security violation. In either circumstance, this is a violation worthy of a notification.

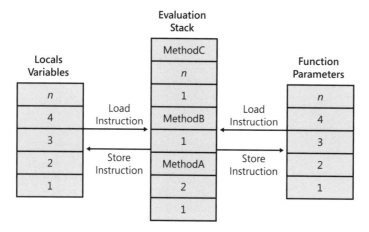

FIGURE 14-1 A depiction of the evaluation stack, function parameters, and local variables

MSIL in Depth

Here are some basic facts about MSIL programming. The content of an MSIL program is case-sensitive. MSIL is also a free-form language. Statements can span multiple lines of code, with lines broken at the white space. Statements are not terminated with a semicolon. Comments are the same as in the C# language. Double slashes (//) are used for single-line comments, and "/* comment */" is used for multiline comments. Code labels are colon-terminated and reference the next instruction. Code labels must be unique within the scope of the label in question.

In addition to the evaluation stack, the other important elements of an MSIL application are directives and the actual MSIL source code. Directives are dot-prefixed and are the declarations of the MSIL program. Source code is the executable content and flow control of the application.

Directives

There are several categories of directives. Assembly, class, and method directives are the most prominent. Assembly directives contain information that the compiler emits to the manifest, which is metadata pertaining to the overall assembly. Class directives define classes and the members of the class. This information is emitted as standard metadata, which is data about types. Method directives define the particulars of a method, such as any local variables and the size of the evaluation stack.

Assembly Directives

This section lists common assembly directives.

.assembly   The *.assembly* directive defines the simple name of the assembly. The simple name does not include the extension. Assembly probing will discover the correct extension. Adding the extension will cause normal probing to fail. A binding exception will occur when the assembly is referenced.

Here is the syntax of the *.assembly* directive:

```
.assembly name { block }
```

The *assembly* block contains additional directives that further describe the assembly. These directives are optional. You need to provide only enough directives to identify the assembly uniquely. Here is an *assembly* block with additional details:

```
.assembly Hello {
    .ver 1:0:0:0
    .locale "en.US"
}
```

These are some of the directives available in the *assembly* block:

- *.ver*   The four-part version number of the assembly
- *.publickey*   The 8-byte public key token of the public/private key pair used to encrypt the hash of the assembly
- *.locale*   The language and culture of the assembly
- *.custom*   Custom attributes of the assembly

.assembly extern   The *.assembly extern* directive references an external assembly. The public types and methods of the referenced assembly are available to the current assembly.

Here is the syntax of the *.assembly extern* directive:

```
.assembly extern name as aliasname {block}
```

The *as* clause is optional. Use this clause to reference an assembly with the same name that has a different version, public key, or culture.

Add the *.ver*, *.publickey*, *.locale,* and *.custom* directives to the *assembly extern* block to refine the identification of that assembly.

Because of the importance of mscorlib.dll, the ILASM compiler automatically includes an external reference to that library. Therefore, adding an *.assembly extern mscorlib* directive is purely informative.

.file   The *.file* directive adds a file to the manifest of the assembly. This is useful for associating documents, such as a readme file, with an assembly.

Here is the syntax of the *.file* directive:

```
.file nometadata filename .hash = (bytes) .entrypoint
```

The file name is the sole required element of the declaration. *Nometadata* is the primary option and stipulates that the file is unmanaged. Here is an example:

```
.file nometadata documentation.txt
```

.subsystem   The *.subsystem* directive indicates the subsystem used by the application, such as the graphical user interface (GUI) or console subsystem. This is distinct from the target type of the application, which is an executable, library, module, or other type. The ILASM compiler inserts this directive based on options specified when the application is compiled. You also can add this directive explicitly.

Here is the syntax of the *.subsystem* directive:

```
.subsystem number
```

Number is a 32-bit integer in which 2 is a GUI application and 3 is a console application.

.corflags   The *.corflags* directive sets the runtime flag in the Common Language Infrastructure (CLI) header. This defaults to 1, which stipulates an IL-only assembly. The *corflags* tool, introduced in .NET 2.0, allows the configuration of this flag.

Here is the syntax of the *.corflags* directive:

```
.corflags flag
```

where *flag* is a 32-bit integer.

.stackreserve   The *.stackreserve* directive sets the stack size. The default size is 0x00100000. The following code calls *MethodA* recursively. Without the *.stackreserve* directive, which defaults to 0x00100000, the *MethodA* method is called recursively more than 110,000 times before exhausting the stack. If you set the stack size to 0x0001000 using the *.stackreserve*

directive, *MethodA* is called only about 21,000 times before quitting. Although the results may vary on your actual computer, the relative values are consistent:

```
.assembly recursive {}
.imagebase 0x00800000
.stackreserve 0x00001000

.namespace Donis.CSharpBook {
    .class Starter {
        .method static public void Main() il managed {
            .entrypoint
            ldc.i4.0
            call void Donis.CSharpBook.Starter::MethodA(int32)
            ret
        }

        .method static public void MethodA(int32) il managed {
            ldarg.0
            ldc.i4.1
            add
            dup
            call void [mscorlib] System.Console::WriteLine(int32)
            call void Donis.CSharpBook.Starter::MethodA(int32)
            ret
        }
    }
}
```

.imagebase   The *.imagebase* directive sets the base address where the application is loaded. The default is 0x00400000. The load address of the application image and the stack size are confirmable using the *dumpbin* tool. For example, see the following code:

```
dumpbin /headers recursive.exe >recursive.txt
```

Class Directives

This section describes the important class directives.

.class header *{members}*   The *.class* directive defines a new reference, value, or interface type.

Here is the syntax of the *header* portion of the *.class* directive:

attributes classname extends *basetype* implements *interfaces*

There are a variety of attributes. Here is a short list of the most common of these:

- *abstract*   The type is abstract, and instances cannot be created.

- *ansi* and *Unicode*   Strings can be marshaled in American National Standards Institute (ANSI) format or in UNICODE format.

- *auto*   The memory layout of fields is controlled by the CLR.

- *beforefieldinit*   The type should be initialized before a static field is accessed.

- *private* **and** *public*   Sets the visibility of the class outside of the assembly.

- *sealed*   The class cannot be inherited.

- *serializable*   The contents of the class can be serialized.

The *extends* option is used if the type inherits from another type. .NET supports only single class inheritance. The *extends* option is optional. If that option is not present, the type inherits implicitly from *System.Object*.

The *implements* option lists the interfaces implemented by the type. The *implements* clause is optional, and there are no default interfaces. The list of interfaces is comma-delimited.

In the *members* block, members are declared with the appropriate directive: *.method*, *.field*, *.property*, and so on.

.custom constructorsignature   The *.custom* directive adds a custom attribute to the type.

.method   The *.method* directive defines a method. C# does not support global methods. Therefore, in MSIL that is derived from C# source code, the *.method* directive always is included within a type.

Here is the syntax of the *.method* directive:

```
.method attributes callingconv return methodname arguments implattributes { methodbody }
```

The *method* attributes are varied, including the accessibility attributes: *public, private, family*, and others. The default is *private*. Static methods have the *static* attribute, whereas instance methods have the *instance* attribute. The default is an *instance* method.

Here are additional attributes:

- *final*   The method cannot be overridden (it is sealed).

- *virtual*   The method is virtual.

- *hidebysig*   Hides the base class interface of this method. This flag is used only by the source language compiler.

- *newslot*   Creates a new entry in the vtable for this method. This method does not override the same method in the base class. For example, this option is used with the *add_Event* and *remove_Event* methods of an event.

- *abstract*   The method has no implementation and is assumed to be implemented in a descendant.

- **specialname**   The method is special, such as *get_Property* and *set_Property* methods. These methods are treated in a special way by tools.

- **rtspecialname**   The method has a special name, such as a constructor. These methods are treated in a special way by the CLR.

The calling convention pertains mostly to native code, in which a variety of calling conventions are supported: *fastcall*, *cdecl*, and others.

The implementation attributes include (but are not limited to) the following:

- **cil or il**   The method contains MSIL code.

- **native**   The method contains platform-specific code.

- **runtime**   The implementation of the method is provided by the CLR. For example, when defining delegates, the delegate class and methods are generated by the run time.

- **managed**   The implementation is managed.

Here is the declaration of a C# method:

```
virtual public int MethodA(int param1, int param2)
```

Here is the MSIL code for that same method:

```
.method public hidebysig newslot virtual instance int32 MethodA(
    int32 param1, int32 param2) cil managed
```

.field   The *.field* directive defines a new field, which is state information for a class. Instance fields are data for an object. Static fields are data for a class.

The syntax of the *.field* directive is as follows:

```
.field attributes type fieldname fieldinit at datalabel
```

The accessibility attributes are the same as described with methods. Static fields must be assigned the *static* attribute. The default is an *instance* field. The *initonly* attribute defines a read-only field.

Here is a field defined in a C# class:

```
private readonly int fielda = 10;
```

Here is the same field translated to MSIL code. The compiler also adds a no-argument constructor, where *fielda* is initialized to 10 (not shown here).

```
.field private initonly int32 fielda
```

.property   The *.property* directive adds a property member to a class. It also declares the *get* and *set* methods for the property.

Here is the syntax of the *.property* directive:

```
.property attributes return propertyname parameters default { propertyblock }
```

The *attributes* of a property are similar to those of a class and method. *Return* is the return type of the property. *Propertyname* and *parameters* are the signature of the property. The *default* option sets the default value of the property.

Within *propertyblock*, the *.get* directive declares the signature of the *get* method, whereas the *.set* directive declares the *set* method. The *propertybody* block includes only the method declarations. The *get* and *set* methods actually are implemented at the class level, not within the property.

Here is a property defined and implemented in a C# application:

```
public int propa {
    get {
        return 0;
    }
}
```

Here is the declaration of the property in the MSIL code (the implementation of the *get. propa* method is not shown):

```
.property instance int32 propa()
{
    .get instance int32 Donis.CSharpBook.Starter::get_propa()
}
```

.event   The *.event* directive adds an event in a class.

Here is the syntax of the *.event* directive:

```
.event classref eventname { eventbody }
```

Classref is the underlying type of the event, such as *EventHandler*.

The *eventbody* block encapsulates the *.addon* and *.removeon* directives. The *.addon* directive declares the method used to add subscribers. The *.removeon* directive declares the method for removing subscribers. The *add* and *remove* methods are implemented in the class and not within the event.

Here is the C# code that declares an event:

```
public event EventHandler EventA;
```

Here is the MSIL code for the event:

```
.event [mscorlib]System.EventHandler EventA {
    .addon instance void Donis.CSharpBook.Starter::add_EventA(
        class [mscorlib]System.EventHandler)
    .removeon instance void Donis.CSharpBook.Starter::remove_EventA(
        class [mscorlib]System.EventHandler)
}
```

Method Directives

The *.method* directive adds a method to a class. MSIL allows for global methods. Global methods break the rules of encapsulation and other tenets of OOP. For this reason, C# does not support global methods. The *method* block can contain both directives and the implementation code (MSIL).

This section lists the directives that frequently are included in the *method* block.

.locals   The *.locals* directive declares local variables that are available by name or index. Local variables form a zero-based array.

Here is the syntax of the *.locals* directive:

```
.locals¹ ([index]local1, [index] local2, [index] localn)

.locals² init ([index]local1, [index] local2, [index] localn)
```

The *.locals¹* directive defines one or more local variables. Explicit indexes can be set for each local variable. By default, the local variables are indexed sequentially starting at zero.

The *.locals²* directive adds the *init* keyword, which requests that local variables be initialized to either *null* or zero . The *init* keyword is required for the assembly to pass code verification. Therefore, the C# compiler emits only the *.locals²* directive.

Local variables do not have to be declared at the beginning of a method.

.maxstack   The *.maxstack* directive sets the number of slots available on the evaluation stack, which is the number of items that can exist on the evaluation stack simultaneously. Without this directive, the default is eight slots.

Here is the syntax of the .*maxstack* directive:

```
.maxstack slots
```

.entrypoint   The .*entrypoint* directive designates a method as the entry point method of the application. This directive can appear anywhere in the method, but best practice is to put the .*entrypoint* directive at the start of the method.

In C#, the entry point method is *Main*. In MSIL, any static method can be given this status.

Method Directive Example

The following program defines *MSILFunc* as the entry point method. The .*entrypoint* directive is found at the end of this method. This demonstrates that the .*entrypoint* declarative can be placed anywhere within the static method. The .*locals* directive defines two local variables and assigns explicit indexes. Our program simply reverses the default indexes. The instruction *stloc.0* will update the second local variable. In the *MSILFunc* method, local variables are referenced using both the name and index. At the end, the method displays the values of 10 and then 5. The *MSILFunc* method returns *void*. In MSIL code, the *ret* instruction is required even when a function returns nothing. In C#, the *return* statement is optional for methods returning *void*.

```
.assembly extern mscorlib {}
.assembly application {}

.namespace Donis.CSharpBook {

    .class Starter {

        .method static public void MSILFunc() il managed {
            .locals init ([1] int32 locala, [0] int32 localb)
            ldc.i4.5
            stloc.0
            ldc.i4 10
            stloc.1
            ldloc locala
            call void [mscorlib] System.Console::WriteLine(int32)
            ldloc localb
            call void [mscorlib] System.Console::WriteLine(int32)
            .entrypoint
            ret
        }
    }
}
```

MSIL Instructions

MSIL includes a full complement of instructions, many of which are demonstrated in previous examples. Each instruction is also assigned an opcode, which is commonly 1 or 2 bytes. The 2-byte opcodes are always padded with a 0xFE byte in the high-order byte. Opcodes often are followed with operands. Opcodes, which provide an alternate means of identifying MSIL instructions, are used primarily when emitting code dynamically at run time. The *ILGenerator. Emit* method emits instructions based on opcodes. This method is found in the *System. Reflection.Emit* name space.

The byte option of ILDASM adds opcodes to a disassembly. The following is a partial listing of the hello.exe disassembly that includes just the *Main* method. As seen from the disassembly, the opcode for *ldstr* is 0x72, the opcode for *stloc* is 0x0A, and the opcode for *call* is 0x28.

```
.method public static void Main() cil managed
{
    .entrypoint
    .maxstack 2
    .locals init ([0] string name)
    IL_0000: /* 72   | (70)000001 */ ldstr     "Donis"
    IL_0005: /* 0A   |            */ stloc.0
    IL_0006: /* 72   | (70)00000D */ ldstr     "Hello, {0}!"
    IL_000b: /* FE0C | 0000       */ ldloc     name
    IL_000f: /* 28   | (0A)000001 */ call      void [mscorlib]System.Console::WriteLine(
                                               string, object)

    IL_0014: /* 2A   |            */ ret
}
```

Short Form   Some MSIL instructions have a normal and a short-form syntax. The short form of the instruction has an .s suffix. The short form of the *ldloc* instruction is *ldloc.s*. The short form of the *br* instruction is *br.s*. Normal instructions have 4-byte operands, and short-form instructions are limited to 1-byte operands.

When used injudiciously, the short-form syntax can cause unexpected results. Consider the following example:

```
.assembly extern mscorlib {}
.assembly application {}

.namespace Donis.CSharpBook {

    .class Starter {
        .method static public void Main() il managed {
            .entrypoint
            ldc.i4.s 50000
```

```
        call void [mscorlib] System.Console::WriteLine(int32)
        ret
      }
    }
  }
```

In the preceding application, a constant of 50000 is placed on the evaluation stack. However, the *ldc* instruction is in the short form. You cannot fit 50000 into a single byte, so the constant overflows the byte. For this reason, the application incorrectly displays *80*.

There are categories of MSIL instructions. The next section reviews these categories, such as branch, arithmetic, call, and array groups of instructions. Because of the prevalence of the evaluation stack, *load* and *store* instructions are the most frequently used of all MSIL instructions. That is a good place to start.

Load and Store Methods

Load and store instructions transfer data between the evaluation stack and memory. Load commands push memory, such as a local variable, onto the evaluation stack. Store commands move data from the evaluation stack to memory. Information placed on the evaluation stack is consumed by method parameters, arithmetic operations, and other MSIL instructions. The return value from a method also is placed on the evaluation stack after the invocation. Data not otherwise consumed should be removed from the evaluation stack before the current method returns. The *pop* instruction is the best command to remove extraneous data from the evaluation stack. Information needed for an instruction should be placed on the evaluation stack immediately prior to the execution of that instruction. If not, an *InvalidProgramException* is triggered.

Table 14-2 lists the basic load instructions.

TABLE 14-2 Load instructions

Instruction	Description
ldc	The *ldc* instruction pushes a constant on the evaluation stack. The constant can be an integral or a floating-point value.
	Here is the syntax of the *ldc* instruction:
	ldc[1].type *value*
	ldc[2].i4.*number*
	ldc[3].i4.s *number*
	The *ldc[1]* instruction places a constant of the specified type onto the evaluation stack.
	The *ldc[2]* instruction is more efficient if you need to transfer an integral value of –1 or an integral value between 0 and 8 to the evaluation stack. The special format for –1 is *ldc.i4.m1*.

TABLE 14-2 Load instructions

Instruction	Description
ldloc	The *ldloc* instruction copies the value of a local variable to the evaluation stack.
	Here is the syntax of the *ldloc* instruction:
	ldloc[1] *index*
	ldloc[2].s *index*
	ldloc[3] *name*
	ldloc[4].s *name*
	ldloc[5].n
	The *ldloc[1]* and *ldloc[2]* instructions use an index to identify a local variable, which is then placed on the evaluation stack. The *ldloc[3]* and *ldloc[4]* instructions identify the local variable with the symbolic name. The *ldloc[5]* instruction is optimized to place local variables from index 0 to index 3. The short form, *ldloc[2]*, efficiently loads local variables from index 4 to index 255.
ldarg	The *ldarg* instruction places a method argument on the evaluation stack. The value then can be used in the program, such as in an arithmetic expression, or it can be stored in a local variable.
	Here is the syntax of the *ldarg* instruction, which is identical to the *ldloc* instruction:
	ldarg *index*
	ldarg.s *index*
	ldarg *name*
	ldarg.s *name*
	ldarg.n
ldnull	The *ldnull* instruction places a *null* on the evaluation stack. This instruction has no operands.

Table 14-3 lists the basic store instructions.

TABLE 14-3 Store instructions

Instruction	Description
stloc	The *stloc* instruction removes a value from the evaluation stack and places it in a local variable.
	Here is the syntax of the *stloc* instruction, which is the same as the syntax of the *ldloc* and *ldarg* instructions:
	stloc *index*
	stloc.s *index*
	stloc *name*
	stloc.s *name*
	stloc.n
starg	The *starg* instruction moves a value from the evaluation stack to a method argument. The value also is removed from the evaluation stack.
	Here is the syntax of the *starg* instruction:
	starg *num*
	starg.s *num*
	The short form of the *starg* instruction is efficient for index 0 to index 255.

Complex Tasks

Until now, the focus has been on individual instructions. Most programs consist of complex tasks, such as creating a new class, creating an array, or executing a *for* loop. Complex tasks typically comprise multiple instructions.

Managing Types

Classes contain static and instance members. The static members are accessible through the class name, whereas instance members are bound to an object. The *WriteLine* method is a static method. As demonstrated in previous sample code, *WriteLine* is called directly on the *Console* class (for example, *System.Console::WriteLine*).

Instance members require an object. The *newobj* instruction creates an object (an instance of a class) and then invokes the constructor to initialize the members of the object. It also deposits a reference to the object onto the evaluation stack. The reference then can be used to call a member method or to access a member field. Such an action consumes the reference and removes it from the evaluation stack. Several actions might require several references. The *dup* instruction is useful for duplicating a reference or whatever happens to be on the top of the evaluation stack.

The following shows two versions of the syntax for the *newobj* instruction:

```
newobj instance ctorsignature :
```

```
newobj ctorsignature
```

The *instance* signature in the preceding syntax calls an instance constructor.

Constructors are specially named methods. The name of a constructor is *ctor*, and a constructor is declared with the *.ctor* directive. By convention in C#, constructors return *void*, which is enforced by the C# compiler. In MSIL code, a constructor can return a value. Static constructors are named *cctor* and are declared with the identically named directive. The static constructor is called by the CLR when the class or instance is first accessed.

The *.field* directive adds a field to the class. The *ldfld* and *ldsfld* instructions load an instance and static field onto the evaluation stack, respectively. Conversely, the *stfld* and *stsfld* instructions store data from the evaluation stack into a field. The *stfld* and *stsfld* instructions consume a reference to the related object. These instructions have a single operand, which is the field type of the related object on the evaluation stack.

The following program creates a class that contains an instance field and a static field and in which the instance and static constructors initialize the fields. The *AddField* and *SubtractField* methods return the total and difference of the fields. An instance of the object is created in the *Main* method. The resulting reference is duplicated with the *dup* instruction. Why? Both the *AddFields* and *SubtractFields* methods are called, each of which requires a reference. The *box* instruction is explained in the section "Boxing," later in this chapter.

```
.assembly extern mscorlib {}
.assembly application {}

.namespace Donis.CSharpBook {

    .class Starter {

        .method static public void Main() il managed {
            .entrypoint
            .locals (int32 temp)
            newobj instance void Donis.CSharpBook.ZClass::.ctor()
            dup
            call instance int32 Donis.CSharpBook.ZClass::AddFields()
            stloc.0
            ldstr "The total is {0}"
            ldloc.0
            box int32
            call void [mscorlib] System.Console::WriteLine(string, object)
            call instance int32 Donis.CSharpBook.ZClass::SubtractFields()
            stloc.0
            ldstr "The difference is {0}"
            ldloc.0
            box int32
            call void [mscorlib] System.Console::WriteLine(string, object)
            ret
        }
    }

    .class ZClass {

        .method private hidebysig specialname rtspecialname
                static void .cctor() cil managed {
            ldstr "In static constructor"
            call void [mscorlib] System.Console::WriteLine(string)
            ldc.i4.s 10
            stsfld int32 Donis.CSharpBook.ZClass::fielda
            ret
        }

        .method public hidebysig specialname rtspecialname
                instance void .ctor() cil managed {
            ldstr "In constructor"
            call void [mscorlib] System.Console::WriteLine(string)
            ldarg.0
            ldc.i4.s 5
            stfld int32 Donis.CSharpBook.ZClass::fieldb
            ret
        }

        .method public int32 AddFields() cil managed {
```

```
          ldsfld int32 Donis.CSharpBook.ZClass::fielda
          ldarg.0
          ldfld int32 Donis.CSharpBook.ZClass::fieldb
          add
          ret
      }

      .method public int32 SubtractFields() cil managed {
          ldsfld int32 Donis.CSharpBook.ZClass::fielda
          ldarg.0
          ldfld int32 Donis.CSharpBook.ZClass::fieldb
          sub
          ret
      }

      .field static private int32 fielda
      .field private int32 fieldb
  }
}
```

In the preceding code, the *ldarg.0* instruction appears near the beginning of each method. This instruction places the *this* reference to the current object on the evaluation stack.

Boxing

The previous sample code included the *box* instruction. Here is the code snippet:

```
ldstr "The total is {0}"
ldloc.0
box int32
call void [mscorlib] System.Console::WriteLine(string, object)
```

The *box* instruction prepares a value type argument for the *Console::WriteLine* method. The *Console::WriteLine* method has two parameters, which are both reference types. However, the top of the evaluation stack has a value type and a reference type. The assignment of a value to a reference type is the problem. The memory models are inconsistent. The *box* instruction removes the value type from the evaluation stack, creates an object on the managed heap that boxes the value type, and places a reference to the newly created object back on the evaluation stack. Now that the value type has been replaced with a reference type, *Console:: WriteLine* can be called successfully.

The *unbox* instruction works in reverse. It unboxes a reference that is on the evaluation stack to the specified value type. The reference is replaced on the evaluation stack with the un-boxed value.

Here is the syntax of the *box* and *unbox* instructions:

```
box valuetype
```

```
unbox valuetype
```

Inheritance

In previous examples in this chapter, no class inherited directly from another class. The classes implicitly inherited *System.Object*. Most classes can be inherited explicitly, including *System.Object*, by using the *extends* keyword. The child class will inherit most members of the base class, except constructors. In the base class, methods that are expected to be overridden in the child should be prefixed with the keyword *virtual*. The *callvirt* instruction calls the overridden function in a child. A child instance should be on the evaluation stack before using *callvirt*.

The following sample code demonstrates inheritance in MSIL code. Two classes are defined in the example. *ZClass* is an abstract class. *XClass* is a concrete class that inherits *ZClass*. *MethodA* and *MethodB* are implemented in both classes. In *ZClass*, *MethodA* is not virtual, but *MethodB* is virtual. The four methods are stubbed with console messages. In *Main*, an instance of *XClass* is created. Then both *MethodA* and *MethodB* are called through *ZClass* to demonstrate polymorphism. Although both *MethodA* and the virtual *MethodB* are called using the same calling syntax, the *ZClass* implementation of *MethodA* is executed but the *XClass* implementation of *MethodB* is executed:

```
.assembly extern mscorlib {}
.assembly application {}

.namespace Donis.CSharpBook {

    .class Starter {

        .method static public void Main() il managed {
            .entrypoint
            newobj instance void Donis.CSharpBook.XClass::.ctor()
            dup
            callvirt instance void Donis.CSharpBook.ZClass::MethodA()
            callvirt instance void Donis.CSharpBook.ZClass::MethodB()
            ret
        }
    }

    .class abstract ZClass {

        .method public instance void MethodA() il managed {
            ldstr "ZClass::MethodA"
            call void [mscorlib] System.Console::WriteLine(string)
            ret
        }

        .method public virtual instance void MethodB() il managed {
            ldstr "ZClass::MethodB"
            call void [mscorlib] System.Console::WriteLine(string)
            ret
        }
    }
```

```
.class XClass extends Donis.CSharpBook.ZClass {

    .method public specialname rtspecialname
        instance void .ctor() cil managed {
        ret
    }

    .method public instance void MethodA() il managed {
        ldstr "XClass::MethodA"
        call void [mscorlib] System.Console::WriteLine(string)
        ret
    }

    .method public virtual instance void MethodB() il managed {
        ldstr "XClass::MethodB"
        call void [mscorlib] System.Console::WriteLine(string)
        ret
    }
  }
 }
}
```

Interfaces

MSIL can define an interface. There is no interface directive; instead, add the *interface* keyword to the specifics of the class directive. The *interface* keyword enforces the semantics of an interface type on the class. Member methods of the interface must be public, abstract, and virtual. Fields are not allowed in an interface class. In addition, constructors and destructors are not permitted. The ILASM compiler enforces these and other rules for interfaces.

A class uses the *implements* keyword to list interfaces that must be implemented. If there are multiple interfaces, the interface list is comma-delimited. A derived class must implement all members of those interfaces. This code demonstrates creating an interface and an implementation of the interface:

```
.assembly extern mscorlib {}
.assembly application {}

.namespace Donis.CSharpBook {

    .class interface public abstract IA {
        .method public abstract virtual instance void MethodA() il managed {
        }
    }

    .class Starter {
        .method static public void Main() il managed {
            .entrypoint
            newobj instance void Donis.CSharpBook.ZClass::.ctor()
            callvirt instance void Donis.CSharpBook.ZClass::MethodA()
            ret
        }
    }
```

```
.class ZClass implements Donis.CSharpBook.IA {
    .method public specialname rtspecialname instance void .ctor() cil managed {
        ret
    }

    .method public virtual instance void MethodA() il managed {
        ldstr "ZClass:MethodA"
        call void [mscorlib] System.Console::WriteLine(string)
        ret
    }
}
}
```

MethodA is defined as part of interface *IA* and is an abstract function. In C#, abstract functions do not have a function body. In MSIL code, however, abstract methods have a body, but the body cannot contain an implementation. Essentially, an abstract method has a body but no code.

Structures   To define a structure, declare a type with the class directive and add the *value* keyword to the class detail. The semantics of a structure then are enforced by the MSIL compiler. For example, a structure cannot have an explicit default constructor or destructor, a structure is sealed, and so on. The *value* keyword is implemented by the ILASM compiler as an implicit inheritance of *System.ValueType*. You could drop the *value* keyword and inherit *System.ValueType* directly. The compiler also adds keywords required for a structure, such as the *sealed* keyword.

As a value type, structures are defined as local variables with the *.locals* directive. Value types are stored on the stack, not on the managed heap. Accessing a member, such as calling a member method, requires binding to the address of the structure. You must load the address of the structure onto the evaluation stack before accessing a member. To do so, you need the address of the structure. To load the address of a local variable, use the *ldloca* instruction instead of *ldloc*. (The "a" variation of an MSIL instruction refers to an address.)

Call the constructor of a structure explicitly with the *call* instruction, not the *newobj* instruction. Structures are not created on the heap. When the constructor is called directly, the structure is simply initialized but not placed on the managed heap.

This code creates and initializes a structure:

```
.assembly extern mscorlib {}
.assembly application {}

.namespace Donis.CSharpBook {

    .class Starter {

        .method static public void Main() il managed {
```

```
        .entrypoint
        .locals init (valuetype Donis.CSharpBook.ZStruct obj)
        ldloca.s obj
        ldc.i4.s 10
        call instance void Donis.CSharpBook.ZStruct::.ctor(int32)
        ldloca.s obj
        ldfld int32 Donis.CSharpBook.ZStruct::fielda
        call void [mscorlib]System.Console::WriteLine(int32)
        ret
    }
}

.class value ZStruct {
    .method public specialname rtspecialname
            instance void .ctor(int32) cil managed {
        ldarg.0
        ldarg.1
        stfld int32 Donis.CSharpBook.ZStruct::fielda
        ret
    }

    .field public int32 fielda
    }
}
```

Branching

The branch instruction is available in various permutations, but in all circumstances it is essentially a goto. The target of a branch instruction is a label. Most branch instructions are conditional and based on a Boolean condition. For an unconditional goto, use the *br* instruction. Loop and other transfer-of-control statements in C# are implemented with some combination of branch instructions.

A conditional branch can be made with the *brtrue* and *brfalse* statements. The *brtrue* instruction branches on a true condition, whereas the *brfalse* branches on a false condition. These instructions consume a Boolean value, which must be placed on the evaluation stack prior to the statements.

Comparison instructions perform a comparison of the top two values of the evaluation stack. The two values are replaced on the evaluation stack with the result of the comparison, which is either *true* or *false*. The comparison should be between related types.

Table 14-4 lists the comparison instructions. In the table, assume that *t2* is the top value on the evaluation stack, *t1* is the next value (*t2* is the last item placed on the evaluation stack and the next to be removed).

TABLE 14-4 Comparison instructions

Instruction	Comparison
ceq	*t1* equal to *t2*
cgt	*t1* greater than *t2*
clt	*t1* less than *t2*
cgt.un and *clt.un*	Unsigned or unordered version of the comparison operations

This sample code shows unconditional and conditional branching. It also contains an example of a comparison instruction:

```
.assembly extern mscorlib {}
.assembly application {}

.namespace Donis.CSharpBook {

    .class Starter {

        .method static public void Main() il managed {
            .entrypoint
            ldc.i4.3
            ldc.i4.1
            cgt
            brtrue greater
            ldstr "{0} is less than or equal to {1}"
            br end
greater:    ldstr "{0} is greater than {1}"
end:        ldc.i4.3
            box int32
            ldc.i4.1
            box int32
            call void [mscorlib] System.Console::WriteLine(
                string, object, object)
            ret
        }
    }
}
```

As a convenience, branch and comparison instructions are combinable. The combined instruction compares the top two values of the evaluation stack and branches on the result. These are called *comparative branching instructions*. Instead of requiring two instructions to perform the test, only one instruction is needed.

Table 14-5 lists comparative branching instructions.

TABLE 14-5 Comparative branching instructions

Instruction	Description
beq	Branch on *equal*
bne	Branch on *not equal*

TABLE 14-5 **Comparative branching instructions**

Instruction	Description
bge	Branch on *greater than* or *equal*
bgt	Branch on *greater than*
ble	Branch on *less than* or *equal*
blt	Branch on *less than*
bgt.un, blt.un, and *bne.un*	The unsigned version of these instructions

Here is an example of a *for* loop in MSIL code. The loop increments the count from zero to five. The current count is displayed to the console in iterations of the loop. The sample code uses the short form of the branch instruction. As with all short-form instructions, the operand is limited to a single byte. The short form of branch instructions cannot jump to a label that is more than a one-byte offset from the beginning of the next instruction. If the branch offset is greater than one byte, ILASM generates a compiler error:

```
.assembly extern mscorlib {}
.assembly application {}

.namespace Donis.CSharpBook {

    .class Starter {

        .method static public void Main() il managed {
            .entrypoint
            .locals (int32 count)
            ldc.i4.0
            stloc.0
            br.s loop
for:        ldloc count
            ldc.i4.1
            add
            dup
            stloc count
            call void [mscorlib] System.Console::WriteLine(int32)
loop:       ldloc count
            ldc.i4.5
            clt
            brtrue.s for
            ret
        }
    }
}
```

Calling Methods

There are many ways to call methods. So far in this chapter, only the *call* and *callvirt* instructions have been shown in the sample code. Some instructions or actions, such as *newobj*, call a method implicitly. The *newobj* instruction calls a constructor, whereas the *static* constructor is called implicitly on the first access to the class or object.

The call instructions have the same general syntax:

```
callsuffix returntype [assembly] signature
```

The value of the *returntype* is placed on the evaluation stack by the method; *assembly* is the location of the method. If the method is in the current assembly, the *assembly* element can be omitted. The complete signature of the method is represented by *signature*.

This section lists the call instructions in MSIL.

call   The *call* instruction is intended for calling nonvirtual methods. The *call* instruction can be used with a virtual method. In this circumstance, the virtual method is called as a normal method, which is based on the class in which the method is declared rather than on the derived instance.

callvirt   The *callvirt* instruction calls a virtual method. For nonvirtual methods, a nonvirtual call is conducted.

calli   The *calli* instruction calls a function indirectly through a function pointer. Place each function parameter and then the function pointer on the evaluation stack. The *calli* syntax is slightly different from other call instructions. It does not include the target assembly or method name in the syntax, but it does include the return type and the signature other than the name. Use the *ldftn* instruction to place a function pointer for a particular method on the stack.

This sample code shows both the *calli* and *ldftn* instructions:

```
.assembly extern mscorlib {}
.assembly application {}

.namespace Donis.CSharpBook {

    .class Starter {

        .method static public void Main() il managed {
            .entrypoint
            ldstr "Donis"
            ldftn void   Donis.CSharpBook.Starter::Name(string)
            calli void(string)
            ret
        }
```

```
        .method static public void Name(string)
                il managed {
            ldstr "Hello, {0}!"
            ldarg.0
            call void [mscorlib] System.Console::WriteLine(string, object)
            ret
        }
    }
}
```

jmp   The *jmp* instruction jumps from the current method to the target method and transfers the arguments. The caller and callee must have matching signatures, and the evaluation stack for the current method must be empty. The code after the *jmp* site in the calling function is abandoned.

Here is sample code of the *jmp* instruction:

```
.assembly extern mscorlib {}
.assembly application {}
.namespace Donis.CSharpBook {
    .class Starter {
        .method static public void Main() il managed {
            .entrypoint
            ldstr "Aloha!"
            call void Donis.CSharpBook.Starter::MethodA(string)
            ret
        }
        .method static public void MethodA(string) il managed {
            ldstr "Before jump"
            call void [mscorlib] System.Console::WriteLine(string)
            ldstr "In MethodA: {0}"
            ldarg.0
            call void [mscorlib] System.Console::WriteLine(string, object)
            jmp void Donis.CSharpBook.Starter::MethodB(string)
            ldstr "After jump"
            call void [mscorlib] System.Console::WriteLine(string)
            ret
        }
        .method static public void  MethodB(string) il managed {
            ldstr "In MethodB: {0}"
            ldarg.0
            call void [mscorlib] System.Console::WriteLine(string, object)
            ret
        }
    }
}
```

This program jumps from *MethodA* to *MethodB*. In *MethodA*, the instructions after the *jmp* instruction are orphaned. Therefore, the message "After jump" is not displayed. *MethodB* returns directly to *Main*, not *MethodA*.

tail   The *tail* instruction is a prefix instruction and similar to the *jmp* instruction. However, the arguments must be loaded explicitly on the evaluation stack and the method signatures can be different. Otherwise, the functions are operationally equivalent.

Here is the syntax of the *tail* instruction:

```
tail callsuffix returntype [assembly] signature
```

Arrays

An array is a collection of related types, and there are several ways to declare an array in MSIL. The underlying type of any array is always *System.Array*. With an array reference, you can call the methods and access the properties of *System.Array*.

Table 14-6 lists different syntax for defining an array.

TABLE 14-6 Syntax for defining arrays

Syntax	Description
type [] *arrayname*	Declares a one-dimensional array of an undetermined size.
type [,] *arrayname*	Declares a two-dimensional array of an undetermined size. You can expand the array beyond two dimensions by extending the comma-delimited list. For example, "type [,,,] *arrayname*" defines a four-dimensional array.
type [*n*] *arrayname*	Declares an array of *n* size.
type [*m,n*] *arrayname*	Declares an array in which the size is *m* columns and *n* rows.
type [][] *arrayname*	Declares a jagged array of an undetermined size.
type [*m*][] *arrayname*	Declares a jagged array of *m* arrays.

The *newarr* instruction initializes a one-dimensional array. In addition, the instruction pushes a reference to the array onto the evaluation stack. You might want to use the array for some time. Move the array reference from the evaluation stack to memory, such as to a local variable, to maintain access to the array. Alternatively, use the *dup* instruction to push additional references to the array on the evaluation stack, as needed. The *newarr* instruction takes as an argument the number of elements, which must be placed on the evaluation stack prior to the instruction call.

The syntax is as follows:

```
newarr type
```

Elements of an array can be accessed with the *ldelem* or *stelem* instructions. The *ldelem* instruction loads an element of an array onto the evaluation stack; the *stelem* instruction stores a value from the evaluation stack into an element of an array. Both instructions have variations that depend on the type of data being manipulated. The variations of *ldelem* and *stelem* are shown in Table 14-7.

TABLE 14-7 *Ldelem* **and** *stelem* **variations**

Load element instructions	Store element instructions
ldelem	*stelem*
ldelem.i1	*stelem.i1*
ldelem.i2	*stelem.i2*
ldelem.i4	*stelem.i4*
ldelem.i8	*stelem.i8*
ldelem.u1	
ldelem.u2	
ldelem.u4	
ldelem.u8	
ldelem.r4	*stelem.r4*
ldelem.r8	*stelem.r8*
ldelem.i	*stelem.i*
ldelem.ref	*stelem.ref*

The *ldelem* instruction requires the array reference and the element index on the evaluation stack, in that order. The *stelem* instruction requires the array reference, element index, and the new value, again in that order.

In the following code, an array of three strings is created. Each element is initialized to a different color name. The array elements then are displayed in a loop:

```
.assembly extern mscorlib {}
.assembly application {}

.namespace Donis.CSharpBook {

    .class starter {

        .method static public void Main() il managed {
            .locals init (string [] names, int32 count)
            .entrypoint
            ldc.i4.3
            newarr string
            stloc names
            ldloc names
            ldc.i4.0
            ldstr "Aqua"
            stelem.ref
            ldloc names
            ldc.i4.1
            ldstr "Violet"
            stelem.ref
            ldloc names
```

```
            ldc.i4.2
            ldstr "Orange"
            stelem.ref
            ldc.i4.0
            stloc count
loop:       ldloc names
            ldloc count
            ldelem.ref
            call void [mscorlib] System.Console::WriteLine(string)
            ldloc count
            ldc.i4.1
            add
            dup
            stloc count
            ldc.i4.3
            blt loop
            ret
        }
    }
}
```

Arithmetic Instructions

MSIL supports the standard arithmetic instructions. The operands of the arithmetic operation are retrieved from the evaluation stack and replaced with the result. For example, the *add* instruction has two addends, which are removed from the evaluation stack and replaced with their sum.

Table 14-8 lists the common arithmetic instructions. The third column is the number of operands consumed from the evaluation stack during the instruction.

TABLE 14-8 Arithmetic instructions

Instruction	Description	Number of Operands
add	Addition	2
sub	Subtraction	2
mul	Multiplication	2
div	Division	2
rem	Remainder	2
neg	Negate	1

Conversion Operations

It is often necessary to convert between types. The *conv* instruction casts between primitive types. The instruction has a single operand, which is the destination type of the cast. A conversion can cause an overflow when the memory size of the source is larger than the target. For example, this could happen when casting from a 64-bit integer to a 32-bit integer.

The high-order bits are trimmed when an overflow occurs, which naturally changes the normal results. It's important to note that when overflows are ignored, subtle bugs are possible. The *conv.ovf* instruction prevents an overflow from going undetected. When an overflow occurs, an overflow exception is raised.

The following code contains an overflow condition, where the cast conversion raises the overflow exception. This code is not protected from exceptions, and the exception will terminate the application:

```
.assembly extern mscorlib {}
.assembly application {}

.namespace Donis.CSharpBook {

    .class Starter {

        .method static public void Main() il managed {
            .entrypoint
            ldc.i8 4000000000
            conv.ovf.i4
            pop
            ret
        }
    }
}
```

Exception Handling

Exception handling is implemented in the CLR. Each managed language exposes exception handling in a language-specific manner. In C#, there are the *try*, *catch*, *throw*, and *finally* keywords. The language compiler, such as *csc*, compiles code for exception handling into language-agnostic MSIL code. For the details of exception handling in C#, read Chapter 12, "Exception Handling."

There are two strategies for implementing exception handling in MSIL code: as an exception clause or as scoped exceptions.

Exception clauses are found after the core MSIL code of a method in the exception-handling section. An exception clause identifies the protected block, the exception filter, and the exception handler. Execution must fall into a protected block naturally. To exit the protected block or handler, use the *leave* instruction. Of course, when an exception is raised, execution is transferred away from the protected block. You should fall out of a protected block or exception handler. Do not attempt to exit a protected block or exception handler with a branch statement.

Here is the syntax of the try clause:

```
.try label¹ to label² exceptiontype handler label³ to label⁴
```

label[1] and *label*[2] define the protected code, whereas *label*[3] and *label*[4] define the range of the handler. The *exceptiontype* element specifies the type of handler as *catch*, *filter*, *finally*, or *fault* handler. Fault handlers are not directly available in C#.

In the previous example, an overflow exception is thrown and not caught. The following code catches the overflow exception:

```
.assembly extern mscorlib {}
.assembly application {}

.namespace Donis.CSharpBook {

    .class Starter {

        .method static public void Main() il managed {
            .entrypoint
start:      ldc.i8 4000000000
            conv.ovf.i4
            pop
            leave done
stop:       callvirt instance string [mscorlib] System.Exception::get_Message()
            call void [mscorlib] System.Console::WriteLine(string)
            leave done
done:       ret
            .try start to stop catch [mscorlib] System.Exception
                handler stop to done
        }
    }
}
```

Scoped exceptions are similar to exception handling in C#, in which there is a *try* block and a *catch* block. Scoped exceptions do not employ exception clauses at the end of the method.

In the following sample code, the conversion exception code is handled with a scoped exception handler:

```
.assembly extern mscorlib {}
.assembly application {}

.namespace Donis.CSharpBook {

    .class Starter {

        .method static public void Main() il managed {
            .entrypoint
            .try {
                ldc.i8 4000000000
                conv.ovf.i4
                pop
                leave done
            }
            catch [mscorlib] System.Exception {
                callvirt instance string [mscorlib] System.Exception::get_Message()
                call void [mscorlib] System.Console::WriteLine(string)
```

```
                leave done
            }
done:       ret
        }
    }
}
```

Miscellaneous Operations

This chapter already has included several sections and tables that explain various MSIL instructions—but not all of them have been covered. In particular, some MSIL instructions that appear in the sample code of this chapter have not been reviewed. Table 14-9 details some of these miscellaneous MSIL instructions.

TABLE 14-9 Miscellaneous MSIL instructions

Instruction	Description
and	Performs a bitwise AND
break	Inserts a debugger break point
castclass	Casts an instance to a different type
nop	Nonoperational instruction (a blank instruction)
or	Performs a bitwise OR
pop	Removes the top element of the evaluation stack
rethrow	Propagates an exception
throw	Throws an application exception

Process Execution

How and when is MSIL code compiled to native binary? The MSIL code is compiled into binary at run time. Only managed methods that are called are compiled into binary. This is part of a larger procedure called process execution. Most of the information in this section is obtained from the Shared Source CLI, which is an open-source implementation of the CLI. The Shared Source CLI is often referred to as *Rotor*. For more information on Rotor, visit this Web site: *http://msdn.microsoft.com/net/sscli*. This section explains method compilation and how the entry point method is identified and executed. What is important is not the specific details, which may change with time, but the concepts.

Process execution begins when a managed application is launched. At that time, the CLR is bootstrapped into the application. The CLR is bootstrapped from the mscoree.dll library. This library starts the process of loading the CLR into the memory of the application. *_CorExeMain* is the starting point in mscoree.dll. Every managed application includes a reference to mscoree.dll and _CorExeMain. You can confirm this with the dumpbin.exe tool. Execute the following command at a command prompt on any managed application for confirmation:

```
dumpbin /imports application.exe
```

Figure 14-2 shows the result of the *dumpbin* command.

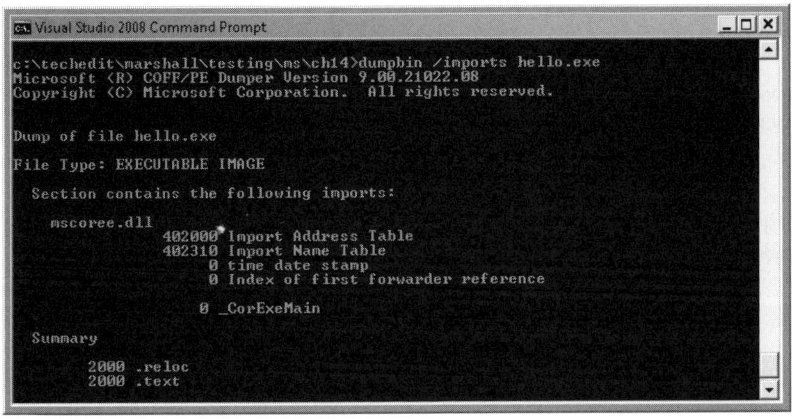

FIGURE 14-2 The *dumpbin* command with the *imports* option

Managed applications have an embedded stub. The stub fools the Windows environment into loading a managed application and temporarily masks the managed application as a native Windows application. The stub calls _CorExeMain in moscoree.dll. _CorExeMain then delegates to _CorExeMain2 in mscorwks.

_CorExeMain2 eventually calls *SystemDomain::ExecuteMainMethod*. As the name implies, *ExecuteMainMethod* is responsible for locating and executing the entry point method. The entry point method is a member of a class. The first step in executing the entry point method is locating that class.

During process execution, classes are represented by *EEClass* structures internally. *ExecuteMainMethod* calls *ClassLoader::LoadTypeHandleFromToken* to obtain an instance of *EEClass* for the class that contains the entry point method. *LoadTypeHandleFromToken* is provided the metadata token for the class and returns an instance of an *EEClass* as an *out* parameter. In a managed application, only classes that are touched have a representative *EEClass* structure. The important components of *EEClass* are a pointer to the parent class, a list of fields, and a pointer to a method table.

The method table contains an entry for each function in the class. The entries are called *method descriptors*. The method descriptor is subdivided into parts. The first part is *m_CodeOrIL*. Before a method is jitted, *m_CodeOrIL* contains the relative virtual address (RVA) to the MSIL code of the method. The second part is a stub containing a thunk to the JIT compiler. The first time the method is called, the jitter is invoked through the stub. The jitter uses the

IL RVA part to locate and then compile the implementation of the method into a binary. The resulting native binary is cached in memory. In addition, the stub and *m_CodeOrIL* parts are updated to reference the virtual address of the native binary. This is an optimization and prevents additional jitting of the same method. Future calls to the function simply invoke the cached native binary.

Roundtripping

Roundtripping refers to disassembling an application, modifying the resulting code, and then reassembling the application. This provides a mechanism for maintaining or otherwise updating an application without the original source code.

The following C# application simply totals two numbers. The program is called "Add," and the results are displayed in the console window:

```
using System;

namespace Donis.CSharpBook {
    public class Starter {
        public static void Main(string[] args) {
            if (args.Length < 2) {
                Console.WriteLine("Not enough parameters.");
                Console.WriteLine("Program exiting...");
                return;
            }
            try {
                byte value1 = byte.Parse(args[0]);
                byte value2 = byte.Parse(args[1]);
                byte total = (byte) (value1 + value2);
                Console.WriteLine("{0} + {1} = {2}",
                    value1, value2, total);
            }
            catch(Exception e) {
                Console.WriteLine(e.Message);
            }
        }
    }
}
```

Let's assume that the above program was purchased from a third-party vendor for a quintillion dollars. Of course, the source code was not included with the application—even for a quintillion dollars. Almost immediately, the purchaser discovers a bug in the application, such that when the program is executed, the total is sometimes incorrect. Look at the following example:

```
C:\ >add 200 150

200 + 150 = 94
```

The result of this equation should equal 350, not 94. How can the purchaser fix this problem without the source code? Roundtripping is the answer. This begins by disassembling the application. For convenience, the ILDASM disassembler is used:

```
ildasm /out=newadd.il add.exe
```

Open *newadd.il* in a text editor. In examining the MSIL code, we can find the culprit easily. The *add* instruction adds two byte variables. The result is cached in another byte variable. This is an unsafe action that occasionally causes an overflow in the total. Instead of notifying the application of the overflow event, an incorrect value is stored. This is the reason for the errant results. Add the *ovf* suffix to the *conv* instruction to correct the problem. An exception is now raised when the overflow occurs.

You can use roundtripping to add features that are not otherwise available in C#. For example, C# supports general exception handling but doesn't support exception filters directly. You can implement an exception filter directly in MSIL. In MSIL, when an exception is raised, the exception filter determines whether the exception handler executes. If the exception filter evaluates to one, the handler runs. If the result is zero, the handler is skipped.

Here is a partial listing of the disassembled program. It is modified to throw an exception when the addition overflows the total. An exception filter also has been added to the exception handling. Changes in the code are highlighted:

```
.try

{

    IL_0029:  nop

    IL_002a:  ldarg.0

    IL_002b:  ldc.i4.0

    IL_0035: ldelem.ref
    IL_0036: call uint8 [mscorlib]System.Byte::Parse(string)
    IL_003b: stloc.1
    IL_003c: ldloc.0
    IL_003d: ldloc.1
    IL_003e: add
    IL_003f: conv.ovf.u1
    IL_0040: stloc.2
    IL_0041: ldstr "{0} + {1} = {2}"
    IL_0046: ldloc.0
    IL_0047: box [mscorlib]System.Byte
    IL_004c: ldloc.1
    IL_004d: box [mscorlib]System.Byte
    IL_0052: ldloc.2
    IL_0053: box [mscorlib]System.Byte
```

```
    IL_0058: call void [mscorlib]System.Console::WriteLine(string,
        object,
        object,
        object)
    IL_005d: nop
    IL_005e: nop
    IL_005f: leave.s IL_0072
} // end .try
filter
{
pop
ldc.i4.1
endfilter
}
// catch [mscorlib]System.Exception
{
IL_0061: stloc.3
IL_0062: nop
IL_0063: ldloc.3
```

Because the filter returns one, the exception is always handled. Use the ILASM compiler to reassemble the application, which completes the round trip. Here is the command:

```
ilasm newadd.il
```

Run and test the *newadd* application. The changed program is more robust. Roundtripping has succeeded!

Debugging with Visual Studio 2008

We have reviewed metadata and MSIL programming in Chapter 13, "Metadata and Reflection," and in this chapter, respectively. This information is helpful when debugging a managed application. The next two chapters continue that trend and pertain to specific debuggers. There is actually a variety of debuggers available for managed code. Chapter 15, "Debugging with Visual Studio 2008," reviews the Microsoft Visual Studio 2008 debugger.

The Visual Studio 2008 debugger has two primary advantages. First, Visual Studio uses a familiar graphic user interface. Second, the debugger is integrated with other aspects of the programming environment. You can develop, test, debug, and return to developing an application within a single integrated development environment. This is very convenient.

The debugger in Visual Studio 2008 has a plethora of rapid application development (RAD) tools for debugging, including various debug windows, a specialized toolbar, the ability to open dumps, and much more. Chapter 15 explores these tools and how to debug an application within Visual Studio 2008.

Chapter 15
Debugging with Visual Studio 2008

The Microsoft Visual Studio 2008 Integrated Development Environment (IDE) includes a full-feature debugger that provides an assortment of windows, tools, and behavior to help you identify and resolve bugs quickly. Use the Visual Studio debugger to inspect the values of variables, view the call stack, monitor threads, examine memory, set breakpoints, and much more. One of the primary benefits of the Visual Studio debugger is the familiar user interface. Professionals who are experienced with the Visual Studio environment will be comfortable with the look and feel of the debugger's user interface and windows.

Visual Studio debugging is extensible. Developers can customize many aspects of the debugger, including extending many of the types related to debugging. For example, developers can create user-defined visualizers and trace listeners. Therefore, Visual Studio debugging is adaptable to specific problems, objectives, and goals.

In a debugging session, you control how an application executes. You can start, interrupt, or stop a debugging session. Table 15-1 details debugging session control

TABLE 15-1 Control of a debugging session

Control	Description
Start Execution	From the Debug menu, there are various commands to start a debugging session. If you choose the Start Debugging, Step Into, or Step Over menu command, the application starts within a debugging session. Alternatively, the Start Without Debugging menu command starts an application outside a debugging session—the Visual Studio debugger is not attached. You also can start a debugging session with the Run To Cursor command. In the source editor, right-click the target line of source code or disassembly and select the Run To Cursor command. The application will start in a debugging session and stop at the next breakpoint or at the cursor location, whichever is encountered first. If neither is encountered, the application runs without interruption.
Break Execution	You can break a debugging session of an application, which is most commonly accomplished by setting breakpoints. Forcibly break into an application using the Break All command from the Debug menu. This command interrupts all applications being debugged in the current Visual Studio debugging session. After breaking into the application, the source code or instruction is highlighted. When no source code is available, you are always transferred to disassembly. When execution is interrupted, the application is in break mode. A debugging session can be interrupted and restarted again. On the Debug menu, the Restart command restarts a debugging session.
Stop Execution	Select Stop Debugging from the Debug menu to end a debugging session. You also can stop debugging from the Processes window. In that window, right-click the executing process and select the Detach Process command or the Terminate Process command.

Applications in a debugging session are in either running mode or break mode. In running mode, an application is executing. In break mode, an application is interrupted. Many features, especially debug windows and the Thread and Call Stack windows, are available only in break mode. For this reason, break mode is where most of the work is done to debug an application. While debugging, an application can transition from running to break mode. The following actions can transfer an application from running to break mode:

- A breakpoint is hit.

- A trace point is hit.

- The cursor is hit after starting a debugging session with the Run To Cursor command.

- The Break All command is selected.

- An unhandled exception is raised.

- Stepping through an application.

You can transition from break mode to running mode by starting execution again. The procedures for resuming or starting an application are detailed in Table 15-1.

Debugging Overview

Debugging techniques vary between project types. For example, the strategy for debugging a Windows Forms application is different from the strategy for debugging a Dynamic Link Library (DLL). This section provides an overview of debugging strategies for basic project types.

Debugging Windows Forms Projects

Of the various project types, managing a debugging session for a Windows Forms project is probably the easiest. Begin debugging a Windows Forms project by starting a debugging session with a start execution action, such as the Start Debugging menu command. When the execution starts, the Visual Studio debugger will attach to the Windows Forms application.

Set breakpoints before or during the debugging session. When the breakpoint is hit, the debugging session switches to break mode. At that time, use the debug windows and other debugging tools to debug the application. To step between breakpoints, use the Start Debugging menu command.

Attaching to a Running Process

You can attach the debugger to processes running outside Visual Studio. At that time, the target process is inserted into a debugging session. There are several reasons to attach to a process:

- The application you want to debug is already running.

- When a problem occurs in an application, you can attach and debug it immediately.

- You can debug a production application. If you attach to an application that is not a debug build, a warning is displayed. You then can proceed into a debugging session. However, source code, symbols, and other instruments helpful when debugging might not be available. Care must be taken when debugging a production application. Debugging activities can interfere with the normal execution of a program. For example, breakpoints can interrupt execution of the application and potentially strand users.

Open the Attach To Process window to attach to a process. (From the Debug menu, choose the Attach To Process command.) Figure 15-1 shows the Attach To Process window. The Debug menu is not available when no solution is open in Visual Studio. In that circumstance, choose the Attach To Process command from the Tools menu.

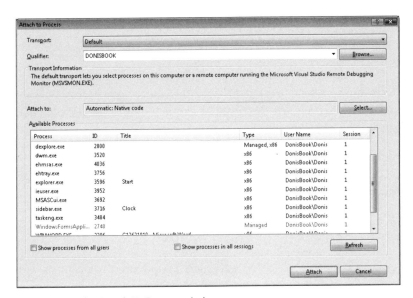

FIGURE 15-1 The Attach To Process window

A list of processes is presented in the Attach To Process window. To attach to a specific process, select a process from the Available Processes list and then click Attach. As mentioned, a warning is displayed if the process is not a debug version. You can select and then debug multiple processes by clicking the mouse button while holding down the Ctrl key. All processes currently being debugged by Visual Studio or another debugger are unavailable in the process list. Even if attached to multiple processes, you can actively debug only a single process, which defaults to the last process attached. Open the Debug Location toolbar for the list of processes being debugged in the debugging session. You then can change the current process from the Process drop-down list, which is shown in Figure 15-2. You can select the Debug Location toolbar from the Toolbars submenu on the View menu or by right-clicking any visible toolbar.

FIGURE 15-2 The Debug Location toolbar

The Attach To Process window has several options. The Transport drop-down list specifies the transport used to connect to a target device or remote machine. The Default entry connects to a local or remote machine using the Microsoft Visual Studio Remote Debugging Monitor (msvsmon.exe). The Qualifier drop-down list is the name of the target machine. Click Select to select the target type as managed, native, script, or T-SQL. The default is based on the type of application. Normally, Visual Studio selects the appropriate type by default. The Show Processes For All Users option lists processes from all users of the current logon session. For example, with this option selected, the process list would include system processes not otherwise shown. For Terminal Service clients remotely connected to a machine, Show Processes In All Sessions displays the processes of the remote machine session. The process list is not static. As new processes start up and existing processes finish, the list of running processes changes. Click Refresh to update the list box on demand.

After attaching to an application, you can begin debugging it using various debugging windows and techniques. To set a breakpoint, open the source code of the application and insert a breakpoint. Alternatively, use the Break All command from the Debug menu to interrupt the application where it is executing.

Terminate the debugging session to detach the debugger from the running process. For example, the Stop Debugging command on the Debug menu terminates a debugging session and detaches from a running process. The running process will continue to execute.

Debugging Console Application Projects

Debugging a Console project is similar to debugging a Windows Forms project, with some notable differences:

- Console applications typically output to the console, while debug messages are displayed in the Output window. Displaying messages in separate windows has both advantages and disadvantages. The separation of debug messages is the primary advantage and can provide clarity. Conversely, the advantage of a single window for all output is convenience. You need not switch between the Console and Output windows. With the *TraceSource* class, you have the option of displaying trace (debug) messages in several locations, including the console, the Output window, or both places simultaneously.

- Console applications sometimes use command-line arguments. To start debugging a console application with command-line arguments, select the *<project>* Properties command from the Project menu. Select the Debug tab in the *<project>* Properties window and enter the command-line arguments in the Start Options frame. Be sure to update the command-line arguments as needed.

- In a debugging session, the results of a console application are removed when the application finishes. This can make the results difficult to view. Freeze the window by inserting a *Console.ReadLine* statement before program exit. Alternatively, after debugging the application, execute in release mode to persist the text shown in the console.

Debugging Class Library Projects

A class library project creates a DLL, which does not execute directly. This makes debugging the DLL more challenging. The DLL must run within the context of another application, which loads the DLL as needed.

You can specify the host application in the debug settings for the project. On the Debug tab of the *<project>* Properties window, select the Start External Program option within the Start Action frame and enter the name of the hosting application. When a debugging session is started, the specified application allows debugging into the DLL. You can then set break-points or otherwise debug the library.

If the host application and class library projects are in the same solution, setting the external program is not necessary. Simply set the host application as the startup project. You then can start a debugging session and debug both the host application and the library.

When the host application is already running, open the project for the library and then attach to the host process in the Attach To Process window. A debug session will start through which the DLL can then be debugged.

Debug Setup

The Visual Studio debugger is fully configurable. Debugging sessions can be tailored to specific requirements of an application. For convenience, debug settings are saved in a configuration. There are two initial predefined configurations, Debug and Release, which represent the most commonly used settings. The Debug configuration contains the default project settings for creating debug builds, whereas the Release configuration has common options for release builds.

Prior to changing project settings, it is good policy to confirm the active configuration. This prevents inadvertent changes to the wrong configuration.

Debug and Release Configurations

As mentioned, the default configurations are Debug and Release. There are literally dozens of project options set in the predefined Debug and Release configurations. You can view these options on the Build tab of the *<project>* Properties window.

The important settings of the Debug configuration are as follows:

- The *DEBUG* and *TRACE* constants—which control the behavior of the *TraceSource*, *Debug*, and *Trace* classes—are defined.

- The Debug Info option is set to *full*. This option requests the creation of a symbol (*.pdb*) file whenever a project is built.

- The output path is *bin\debug*.

- The Optimize Code option is set to *false*, which disables code optimization.

The key debug settings of the Release configuration are as follows:

- The *DEBUG* constant is not defined; however, the *TRACE* constant remains defined.

- The Debug Info option is set to *pdb-only*.

- The output path is *bin\release*.

- The Optimize Code option is set to *true*, which enables code optimization.

Configuration Manager

Use the Configuration Manager to view, edit, and create new configurations. To open the Configuration Manager, choose the Configuration Manager command from the Build menu. Figure 15-3 shows the Configuration Manager. The Configuration Manager lists the current configuration of each project in the solution. Initially, there should be the Debug and Release configurations.

Display the available configurations in the Active solution configuration drop-down list. You can set the current configuration from the drop-down list. You also can create a new configuration. Finally, you can rename or remove an existing configuration. The Active Solution Platform drop-down list assigns a platform to the current configuration.

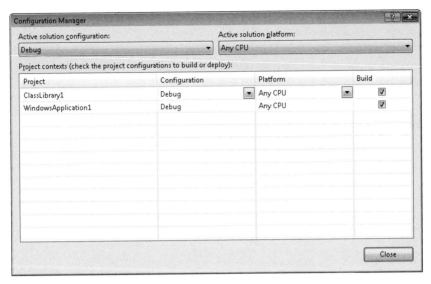

FIGURE 15-3 The Configuration Manager

Each row of the Configuration Manager window is a project. The project list has several columns of information:

- **Project** This column shows the name of each project.

- **Configuration** This column sets the current configuration of the project.

- **Platform** This column sets the target platform of the project.

- **Build** This column is an option box, which includes or excludes a project in the build when building the solution.

Debug Settings

The Visual Studio environment, solution, and project have separate debug settings:

- Debug settings of the Visual Studio environment are set in the Options window. (From the Tools menu, choose the Options command, and select the Debugging entry in the left-hand pane.)

- Debug settings of a project are set in the *<project>* Properties window, which is opened by using the *<project>* Properties command on the Project menu.

- Debug settings of a solution are set in the Solution Property Pages dialog box, which is opened by right-clicking the solution in Solution Explorer and choosing Properties from the context menu.

Visual Studio Environment Debug Settings

The debugging settings for Visual Studio apply to all projects. You can configure Edit And Continue, just-in-time (JIT) debugging, native debugging options, symbol servers, and general debugging options for the environment.

General Options

The general debugging options are an assortment of miscellaneous options. Each option can be enabled or disabled. Figure 15-4 shows the General settings in the Debugging category of the Options window.

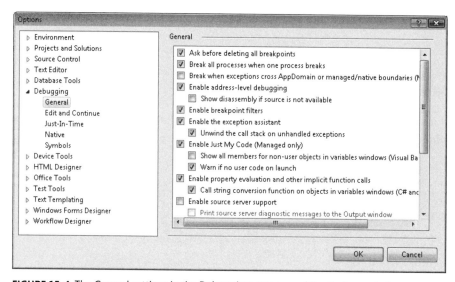

FIGURE 15-4 The General settings in the Debugging category of the Options window

Each option for C# is described in Table 15-2.

TABLE 15-2 General debugging options

Option	Description	Default
Ask Before Deleting All Breakpoints	Requires confirmation when using the Delete All Breakpoints command.	Enabled
Break All Processes When One Process Breaks	Breaks all processes being debugged by Visual Studio in the current debugging session when any process is interrupted.	Enabled
Break When Exceptions Cross Appdomain Or Managed/Native Boundaries (Managed Only)	Asks the Common Language Runtime (CLR) to catch exceptions that cross an application domain or that cross between managed and native code.	Disabled
Enable Address-Level Debugging	Enables some operations at the address level, such as setting breakpoints on instruction addresses.	Enabled

TABLE 15-2 General debugging options

Option	Description	Default
Show Disassembly If Source Is Not Available	Requests that the disassembly window be displayed when user source code is not available.	Disabled
Enable Breakpoint Filters	Lets developers set filters on breakpoints, where filters can be based on the thread, process, and machine context.	Enabled
Enable The Exception Assistant	Automatically displays the Exception Assistant for managed exceptions.	Enabled
Unwind The Call Stack On Unhandled Exceptions	Asks Visual Studio to unwind the call stack when an exception occurs.	Enabled
Enable Just My Code (Managed Only)	Has the debugger step into only user code. System code, optimized code, and code without symbols are not stepped into.	Enabled
Warn If No User Code On Launch	Displays a warning when debugging is initiated if no user code is available.	Enabled
Enable Property Evaluation And Other Implicit Function Calls	Allows properties and other implicit functions to be evaluated in the QuickWatch and variables windows.	Enabled
Call String Conversion Function On Objects In Variables Windows (C# And JavaScript Only)	Converts objects to strings when displayed in variables windows.	Enabled
Enable Source Server Support	Requests that Visual Studio get source from the source server (srcsrv.dll).	Disabled
Print Source Server Diagnostics Messages To The Output Window	Displays messages from the source server in the Output window.	Disabled
Highlight Entire Source Line For Break Points And Current Statement	Highlights an entire line of source code to emphasize the current breakpoint or statement.	Disabled
Require Source Files To Exactly Match The Original Version	Asks the Visual Studio debugger to verify that the current source file matches the version used to build the application.	Enabled
Redirect All Output Window Text To The Immediate Window	Redirects debugger messages from the Output window to the Immediate window.	Disabled
Show Raw Structure Of Objects In Variables Windows	Disables debugger display customizations, such as the *DebuggerDisplay* attribute.	Disabled
Suppress JIT Optimizations On Module Load (Managed Only)	Disables JIT optimizations while debugging. These optimizations make debugging more difficult.	Enabled
Warn If No Symbols On Launch (Native Only)	Displays a warning when debugging is initiated if no symbol information is available.	Enabled
Warn If Script Debugging Is Disabled On Launch	Displays a dialog box when debugging is started if script debugging is disabled.	Enabled

Edit And Continue Options

Edit And Continue supports changes to the source code while debugging. The changes are applied immediately without having to rebuild and restart the application. Edit And Continue is enabled automatically when breaking and then stepping through an application.

Some changes within a method are supported, such as deleting a line of code. Changes are more limited outside a method. For example, deleting class members is not allowed. The following changes are not supported in Edit And Continue:

- Modifying an active statement
- Surrounding an active statement with a *foreach*, *using*, or *lock* block
- Surrounding the active statement in the current function with a *catch* or *finally* block
- Adding a nested exception handler beyond six levels
- Changing code in the *try* block that contains the active statement
- Adding a new member
- Adding a global symbol
- Changing the signature of a member
- Editing an anonymous method or a function containing an anonymous method
- Changing, adding, or deleting an attribute
- Changing or deleting a local variable
- Modifying a method that contains a *yield return* or *yield break* statement
- Changing, adding, or deleting a *using* directive
- Modifying a constructor that contains a local variable that is initialized in an anonymous method (an outer variable)

Furthermore, Edit And Continue is not available in the following situations:

- Mixed-mode debugging
- SQL debugging
- After an unhandled exception, unless the Unwind The Call Stack On Unhandled Exceptions general debugging option is enabled
- After attaching to an application for debugging
- In a 64-bit managed application

In the Edit And Continue settings in the Debugging category of the Options window, the Edit And Continue feature can be enabled or disabled. Figure 15-5 shows the Edit And Continue settings in the Debugging category of the Options window. The settings in the Native-Only Options frame pertain to native code.

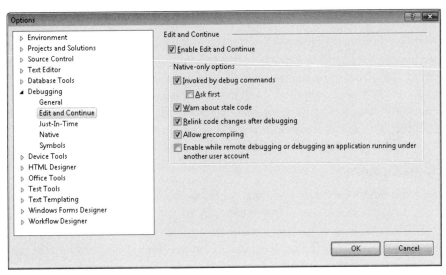

FIGURE 15-5 The Edit And Continue settings in the Debugging category of the Options window

Just-In-Time Options

The JIT debugger is attached to a running application when the program crashes. Register Visual Studio as the JIT debugger in the Just-In-Time Debugging window (shown in Figure 15-6). Visual Studio can be the JIT debugger for managed code, native code, and scripting. JIT debugging is discussed in Chapter 16, "Advanced Debugging." When Visual Studio is installed on your machine, it registers itself as the JIT debugger for native and managed code.

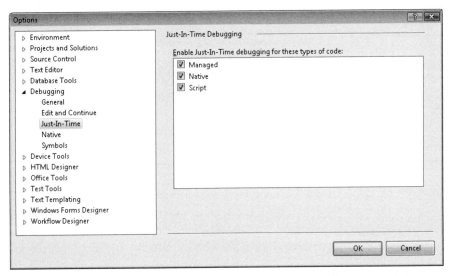

FIGURE 15-6 The Just-In-Time settings in the Debugging category of the Options window

Native Options

The Native settings in the Debugging category of the Options window have two debugging options. Enable the Load DLL Exports option to load the export tables for DLLs. This is beneficial when the debug symbols are not available for the DLL. For example, you can set breakpoints on function names exported from the library even though symbols are not available. The Enable RPC Debugging option enables stepping into Component Object Model (COM) remote procedure calls. Both options are disabled by default.

Symbols Options

Visual Studio can be configured to use a symbol server to download the correct debugging symbols in a local symbol cache. Developers can use the Microsoft public symbol server or a custom symbol server. Identify symbol servers and downstream paths (caches) in the Symbols window, which is shown in Figure 15-7. In the Symbol File Locations list box, enter the Uniform Resource Locator (URL) for symbol servers. They are searched for in the textual order of the list. Enter downstream servers in the Cache Symbols From Symbol Servers To This Directory text box. Missing symbols are downloaded from symbol servers into downstream servers, where the symbol can be obtained in the future.

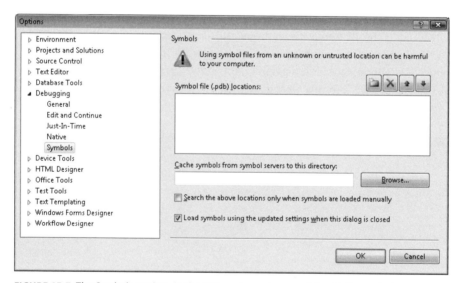

FIGURE 15-7 The Symbols settings in the Debugging category of the Options window

Symbols can be loaded manually in the Modules window, which is shown in Figure 15-8. Open the Modules window from the Debug menu and the Windows submenu. The Modules window lists the modules loaded in the current application. Each row represents a module and has the name of the module, path to the module, whether the module is optimized, source code availability, symbol status, and fully qualified path to the symbol file. The Symbol Status column indicates whether the symbols are loaded or skipped. Symbols are skipped automatically for optimized code. The Symbol File column displays the path to the loaded symbol file. For skipped symbols, you can load the symbols for a specific module manually by right-clicking the module and choosing the Load Symbols command from the context menu. After loading the symbols for a module, the Symbol Status and Symbol File columns are updated. If the symbol file cannot be found for the specified module, you are prompted with the Find Symbols dialog box, as shown in Figure 15-9. From there, you can browse to the relevant symbol file.

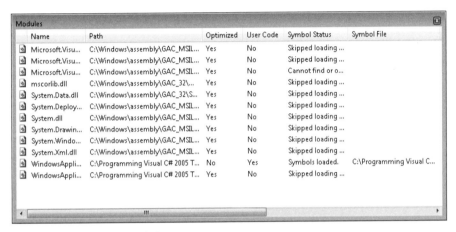

FIGURE 15-8 The Modules window

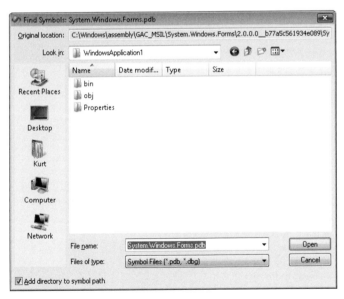

FIGURE 15-9 The Find Symbols dialog box

For more commands on symbols, right-click an item in the Modules window to display the context menu. From the context menu, the Symbol Load Information menu command displays information about the symbol file of the module. There is also a Symbol Settings menu command, which opens the Symbols settings in Debugging category of the Options window. You can configure symbols for the overall application in this window.

Debug Settings for a Solution

Debug settings for a solution are set in the Solution Property Pages window. The only available debug setting is the Debug Source Files setting. (The Debug Source Files settings of the Solution Property Pages window are shown in Figure 15-10.) In this window, you can set directories to include or exclude source files.

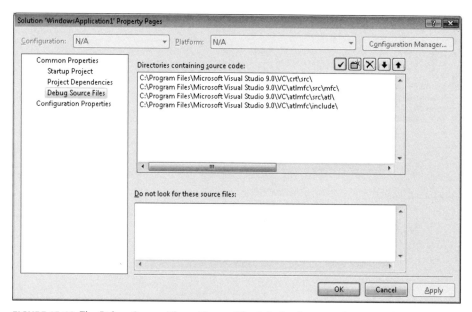

FIGURE 15-10 The Debug Source Files settings of the Solution Property Pages window

Debug Settings for a Project

Debug settings for a project set the startup action, command-line arguments, and other debug options. Figure 15-11 shows the Debug tab of the *<project>* Properties window.

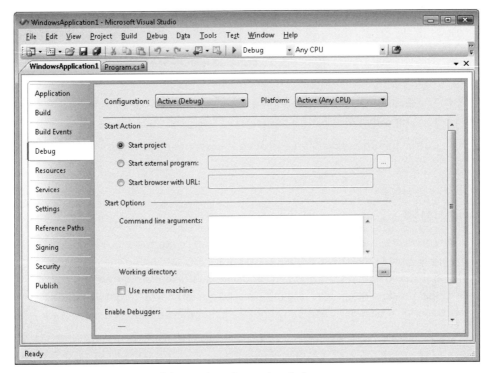

FIGURE 15-11 The Debug tab of the *<project>* Properties window

Settings in the Start Action frame indicate the startup action for debugging, which determines the application to launch when starting a debugging session. Here are the options:

- The Start Project option, which is the default, starts the application from the startup project specified in the Application tab of the Options window.

- The Start External Program option typically is selected when debugging class library projects. Specify the hosting application that loads the related DLL. You then can debug into the class library project.

- The Start Browser With URL option is useful for debugging Web applications. Browse to a URL that is controlled by the Web application. The Web application then is loaded via the Web server. You then can debug the Web application in Visual Studio.

The Start Options frame contains the following miscellaneous settings:

- Enter command-line arguments for the application in the Command Line Arguments text box.

- The Working Directory text box sets the working directory of the application. This is the path for directory- and file-related tasks.

- The Use Remote Machine option identifies a remote machine. The application is started at that location.

Settings in the Enable Debuggers frame indicate the kind of code that can be debugged, as follows:

- The Enable Unmanaged Code Debugging option enables mixed-mode debugging. Developers can debug between managed and unmanaged code.

- The Enable SQL Server Debugging option allows developers to debug CLR assemblies running within Microsoft SQL Server.

- The Enable The Visual Studio Hosting Process option activates Visual Studio hosting, which is a .vshost.exe process.

Breakpoints

Breakpoints are stop signs in code where execution is interrupted. When a breakpoint is hit, the application enters break mode. At that time, you can debug the application with a variety of Visual Studio debugger commands and windows. There are different kinds of breakpoints. A normal breakpoint appears as a red circle to the left of the target line of disassembly or source code. Breakpoints also can appear in other places, such as the call stack window.

In the code editor window, pressing F9 sets a simple breakpoint on the current disassembly or source code line. F9 is a toggle, setting or clearing a breakpoint. In addition, clicking in the leftmost (shaded) column sets or clears a breakpoint. When debugging, an application runs until a breakpoint is hit, the application is otherwise interrupted, or the debug session ends. You can continue the application by pressing F5, which functions the same as the Continue Debugging menu command. You also can choose Continue from the Debug menu. Other commands, such as Run To Cursor, also resume execution.

You can also add new breakpoints from the New Breakpoint submenu of the Debug menu. Break At Function adds a function breakpoint. New Data Breakpoint is not available for managed code.

Function Breakpoints

Function breakpoints break immediately prior to the first line of a function and can be set at compile time or run time.

Set a function breakpoint by choosing the New Breakpoint submenu of the Debug menu, then selecting Break At Function. In the example illustrated in the following figures, a breakpoint is set on the first line of the *WClass.MethodA* function. As a shortcut, select the name of the target function first and then open the New Breakpoint dialog box. The function name appears automatically in the New Breakpoint dialog box, as shown in Figure 15-12. If breaking on an ambiguous or overloaded name, the Choose Breakpoints dialog box opens.

In the sample code, *MethodA* is ambiguous because there are several instances of *MethodA* in the application, as shown in Figure 15-13. To avoid ambiguity, you can enter the class and method name (*Classname.Methodname*) or the complete method signature.

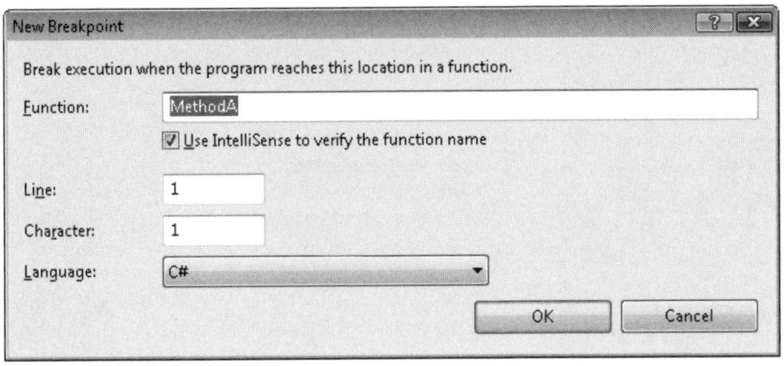

FIGURE 15-12 The New Breakpoint dialog box

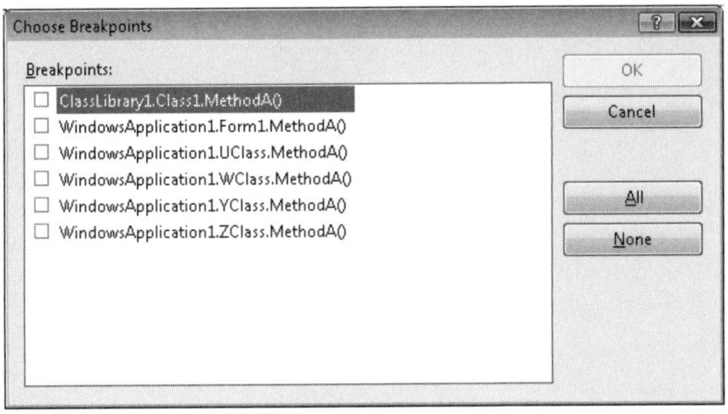

FIGURE 15-13 The Choose Breakpoints dialog box

The Use IntelliSense To Verify The Function Name option of the New Breakpoint dialog box displays the Choose Breakpoint dialog box whenever a user enters an ambiguous or over-loaded function name. With this option, users also are notified of invalid function names. With the option disabled, an ambiguous function name sets a breakpoint on all functions in the set. In addition, there is no notification of an invalid function name, and the New Breakpoint dialog box simply closes without setting the breakpoint.

You also can set breakpoints in the Call Stack window, which is available on the Debug menu within the Windows submenu. A function breakpoint on the call stack breaks upon re-entering that method as the stack unwinds. For example, *MethodA* calls *MethodB*. *MethodB* then calls *MethodC*. A breakpoint then is set on *MethodA* in the Call Stack window. When *MethodB* returns and the related stack frame is removed, the application is interrupted on re-entering *MethodA*. The Call Stack window is available in break mode. Set a breakpoint for a specific method in the Call Stack window using the context menu or the F9 keyboard shortcut. A breakpoint set on *MethodA* in the call stack is shown in Figure 15-14.

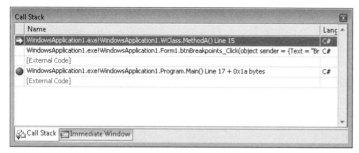

FIGURE 15-14 A break point in the Call Stack window

Breakpoints Window

You can manage breakpoints in the Breakpoints window (opened from the Debug menu and the Windows submenu). Figure 15-15 shows the Breakpoints window.

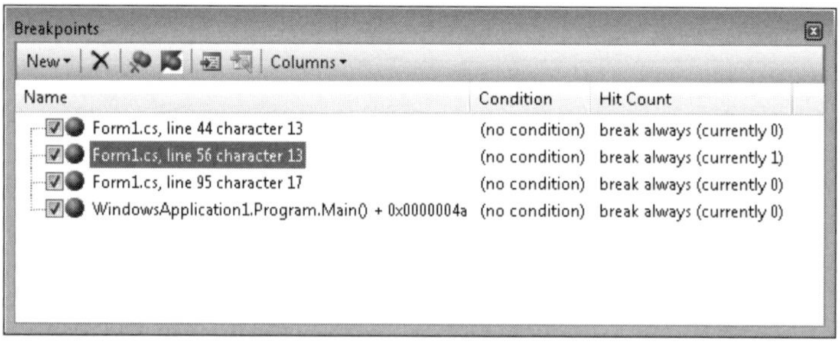

FIGURE 15-15 The Breakpoints window

In the Breakpoints window, breakpoints are shown on separate rows. The first column of each row is the enabled/disabled options box. If a breakpoint is enabled, the option box is checked. Clear the option box to disable the breakpoint. The next column is the description and location of the breakpoint. The Condition column shows any conditions set on the breakpoint. The final column shows the hit count. In that column, Break Always indicates that every time the breakpoint is hit, the application is interrupted.

The context menu for an individual breakpoint has several valuable options that affect the selected breakpoint. The Delete command removes the breakpoint. The Go To Source Code command opens the source code where the breakpoint is set. The Go To Disassembly menu command opens the disassembly at the breakpoint. The remaining commands customize the selected breakpoint and are explained in the following sections.

Location

This command changes the location of a breakpoint. You are presented with the Address Breakpoint, File Breakpoint, or Function Breakpoint dialog box, depending on the type of breakpoint. For example, the Function Breakpoint dialog box is displayed when a function breakpoint is selected in the Breakpoints window. The File Breakpoint dialog box, shown in Figure 15-16, is displayed for line breakpoints in source code. A Function Breakpoint dialog box was shown earlier in the chapter (in Figure 15-12).

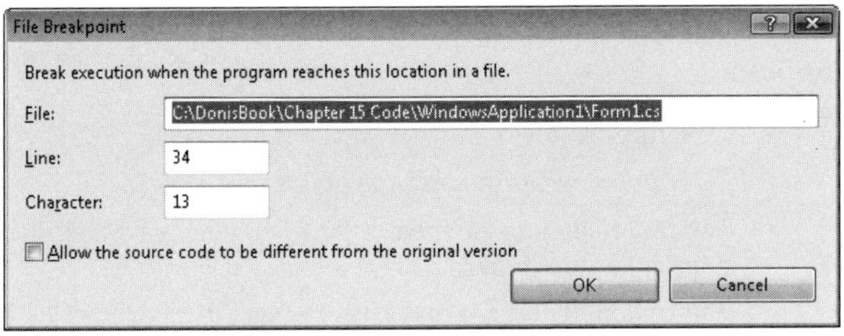

FIGURE 15-16 The File Breakpoint dialog box

Condition

This command sets additional criteria for a breakpoint. There are two ways to set a conditional breakpoint. First, the condition can be a Boolean expression. If the expression is true, the breakpoint is honored. Otherwise, the breakpoint is ignored. Second, the condition can be based on changes to a value. If the value is changed, the breakpoint becomes active.

Look at the following sample code. A breakpoint is set on the single statement in the *foreach* block. You would like the breakpoint to interrupt only when *ivalue* contains an even value:

```
int[] numbers = { 1,2,3,4,5,6,7,8,9,10,
    11,12,13,14,15,165,17,18,18,20 };
int total = 0;
foreach (int ivalue in numbers)
{
    total += ivalue;
}
```

The Breakpoint Condition dialog box, shown in Figure 15-17, sets the condition to break on even values.

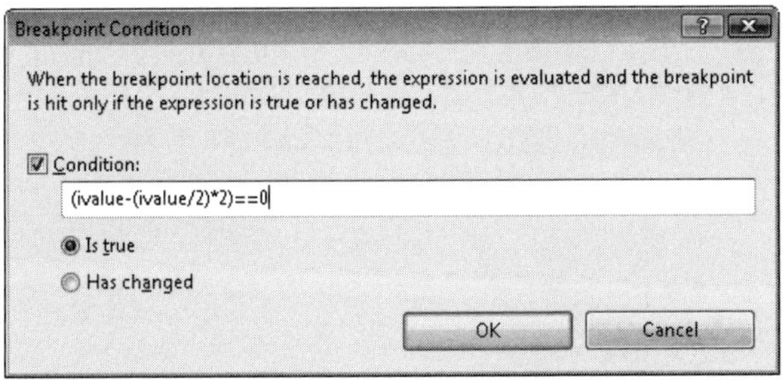

FIGURE 15-17 The Breakpoint Condition dialog box

Hit Count

This command sets a breakpoint based on the hit count. Table 15-3 lists the hit count options. The breakpoint count is the number of times the breakpoint has passed, whether honored or not.

TABLE 15-3 Hit count options

Option	Description
Break Always	This option means the breakpoint is always active.
Break When The Hit Count Is Equal To	This option honors the breakpoint when the breakpoint hit count equals the stated value.
Break When The Hit Count Is A Multiple Of	This option honors the breakpoint when the breakpoint hit count is a multiple of the stated value. For example, a count of four interrupts on every four occasions of the breakpoint: the 4th, 8th, 12th, and so on.
Break When The Hit Count Is Greater Than Or Equal To	This option honors the breakpoint when the breakpoint count is equal to or greater than the stated value; for example, it honors the breakpoint at counts greater than three.

The Breakpoint Hit Count dialog box, shown in Figure 15-18, honors the breakpoint at increments of four.

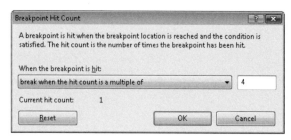

FIGURE 15-18 The Breakpoint Hit Count dialog box

Filter

This command sets the affinity of a breakpoint to a machine, thread, or process. The break-point interrupts only in the context of the stated filter. Table 15-4 lists the available contexts.

TABLE 15-4 Filter contexts

Context	Description
MachineName	The named machine. The break point is honored if the process is running on that machine.
ProcessId	The process identified by the process identifier. The break point is honored if code is executing in the specified process.
ProcessName	Any instance of the process name.
ThreadId	A thread as identified by a thread identifier. The break point is honored if code is executing on the specified thread.
ThreadName	Any thread with the specified thread name.

The following code creates two threads that asynchronously execute the same method (*MethodA*). The threads are named *FirstThread* and *SecondThread*. A breakpoint is set on the *Thread.Sleep* statement in *MethodA*. As an unfiltered breakpoint, both threads are interrupted—probably alternating between the threads:

```
private void btnFilter_Click(object sender, EventArgs e)
{
    Thread t1 = new Thread(new
        ThreadStart(MethodA));
    t1.Name = "FirstThread";
    t1.IsBackground = false;
    Thread t2 = new Thread(new
        ThreadStart(MethodA));
    t2.Name = "SecondThread";
    t2.IsBackground = false;
    t1.Start();
    t2.Start();
}

public void MethodA()
{
    while (true)
    {
        Thread.Sleep(3000);
    }
}
```

To break on the first thread alone, open the Breakpoint Filter dialog box, shown in Figure 15-19. Specify **FirstThread** as the thread name. Continue the application. Future instances of the breakpoint interrupt on the first thread, but not the second thread.

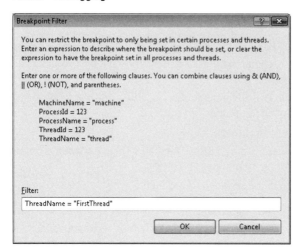

FIGURE 15-19 The Breakpoint Filter dialog box

When Hit Command

This command creates a trace point (discussed in the next section).

The Breakpoints window toolbar, shown in Figure 15-20, offers several shortcuts. The buttons on the toolbar are New, Delete, Delete All Breakpoints, Disable All Breakpoints, Go To Source Code, Go To Disassembly, and Columns. The New drop-down list inserts a new function or data breakpoint. As mentioned, data breakpoints are not available in managed code. The Columns button customizes the Breakpoints window, where the developer can choose which columns to display in the window. The rest of the buttons are self-explanatory.

FIGURE 15-20 The Breakpoints window toolbar

Trace Points

Trace points can print a message (a trace), assign a macro to a breakpoint, or both. There are two methods for setting a trace point. You can set a trace point on an individual line in a code editor window or a disassembly window. Right-click the line of code, select the Breakpoint submenu, and then select the When Hit command. Or right-click the target breakpoint in the Breakpoints window and choose the When Hit command. Either approach opens the When Breakpoint Is Hit dialog box (shown in Figure 15-21), where a trace point is described.

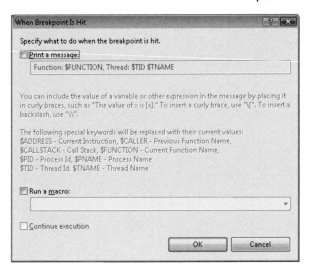

FIGURE 15-21 The When Breakpoint Is Hit dialog box

In the Print A Message text box, enter a display string, which is converted and displayed in the Output window. Expressions can be entered within curly braces: {*expression*}. Special keywords can be used, such as *$ADDRESS*, *$TID*, and *$FUNCTION*, which display the current address, thread identifier, and function name, respectively. There are other options, too. In the Run A Macro edit box, enter the name of a macro. IntelliSense works for macro names. There are predefined macros for most Visual Studio commands. The macro runs when the breakpoint is hit. The Continue Execution option sets a soft breakpoint. When the breakpoint is hit, soft breakpoints do not interrupt the application. However, the message is displayed and the specified macro is run. With the Continue Execution option enabled, the breakpoint appears as a diamond rather than as a red circle.

The statement in the When Breakpoint Is Hit dialog box shown in Figure 15-22 adds two local variables and displays the results in the Output window.

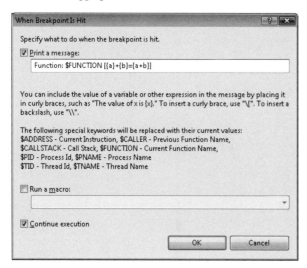

FIGURE 15-22 The Print A Message text box in the When Breakpoint Is Hit dialog box

From the trace point shown in Figure 15-22, the following code is displayed in the Output window:

```
Function: WindowsApplication1.WClass.MethodA() [5 + 10 = 15]
```

Table 15-5 lists the special keywords that can be used in the Print A Message text box.

TABLE 15-5 Trace point keywords

Keyword	Description
$ADDRESS	Returns the address of the current instruction
$CALLER	Returns the name of the previous function on the call stack, which is the caller
$CALLSTACK	Returns the call stack
$FUNCTION	Returns the name of the current function
$PID	Returns the process identifier of the current process
$PNAME	Returns the name of the current process
$TID	Returns the thread identifier of the current thread
$TNAME	Returns the name of the current thread

Breakpoint Symbols

Breakpoints are annotated with icons. The shape of the icon indicates the state of the breakpoint, as described in Table 15-6.

TABLE 15-6 Breakpoint symbols

Symbol	Description
Filled circle	Signifies an enabled breakpoint, such as a function or location breakpoint.
Diamond	Signifies a trace point that has the *Continue execution* option enabled.
Filled circle with a plus sign (+)	Signifies a filter breakpoint. Filter breakpoints include the Condition, Hit Count, and Filter breakpoints.
Hollow circle	Signifies a disabled breakpoint.

Code Stepping

Stepping through source code is the most common action in a debugging session. Step commands step an application in source line or instruction increments, depending on the open window. With each step, execution continues incrementally. Between steps, expressions can be evaluated, variables updated, functions called, and scopes changed. Debug windows are updated between steps to reflect changes that occurred during the incremental execution. Excessive tracing, watches, and expressions in debug windows can precipitously hurt performance when stepping through an application.

Step Commands

There are several step commands, described as follows:

- **Step Into**   Steps to the next source line or instruction. If that line includes a function call, the debugger steps into the function. You then can step through that function. For nested function calls, the Step Into command steps into the innermost functions first.

- **Step Over**   Steps to the next source line or instruction. However, it will not step into a function call.

- **Step Out**   Executes the remainder of the current function. Execution is then interrupted at the first source line or instruction after the call site.

- **Set The Next Statement**   Lets developers move the next source line or instruction to execute, which is useful for skipping one or more lines of code. This also allows you to repeat instructions or blocks of code. In the source editor, the current line (the next statement to execute) is highlighted in yellow and a yellow arrow appears in the left-most (shaded) column. When the cursor hovers over the yellow arrow, the cursor changes into an arrow itself. You then can drag the yellow arrow up or down. The statement you choose must be within the scope of the current source or instruction. For example, dragging the yellow arrow to another function is illegal. This command is not available when debugging a *StackOverflowException* exception or a *ThreadAbortException* exception.

Example of Setting The Next Statement

This example demonstrates the Set Next Statement command. In the sample application, variables *locala* and *localb* are initialized in *MethodA,* and then they are incremented. The *SwitchValues* method is called to swap the values of the local variables. The parameters are passed by reference. After the method call, *locala* is 11 and *localb* is 6. Here is the code:

```
public void MethodA()
{
    int locala = 5, localb = 10;
    ++locala;
    ++localb;
    SwitchValues(ref locala, ref localb);
    MessageBox.Show(locala.ToString());
    MessageBox.Show(localb.ToString());
}

public void SwitchValues(ref int param1,
    ref int param2)
{
    int temp = param1;
    param1 = param2;
    param2 = temp;
}
```

The following procedure uses the preceding code:

1. Set a breakpoint on the source line where *locala* is incremented. When the breakpoint is hit, the current line (the next statement to execute) is marked with a yellow arrow. The breakpoint and the current line are initially at the same location, as shown in Figure 15-23.

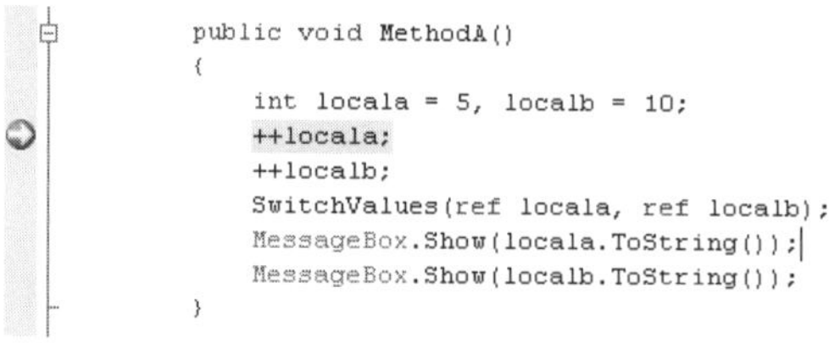

FIGURE 15-23 A break point and current line

2. Drag the yellow highlight for the current line down to the first *MessageBox.Show* statement, which jumps past the statements that increment the local variables and past the *SwitchValues* method call. Therefore, the values are neither incremented nor swapped. Figure 15-24 shows the repositioned current line.

```
public void MethodA()
{
    int locala = 5, localb = 10;
    ++locala;
    ++localb;
    SwitchValues(ref locala, ref localb);
    MessageBox.Show(locala.ToString());
    MessageBox.Show(localb.ToString());
}
```

FIGURE 15-24 A repositioned current line

3. Continue execution, and the values for *locala* and *localb* are displayed. The *locala* variable is 5, whereas *localb* is 10. If the current line had not been changed, the values would have been 11 and 6, respectively.

Debug Toolbar

The Debug toolbar (shown in Figure 15-25) contains shortcuts to several debugging commands, including the step commands. Some of the buttons and commands are enabled only in break mode.

FIGURE 15-25 The Debug toolbar

The first set of buttons on the toolbar is the Start Debugging, Break All, Stop Debugging, and Restart buttons. The next set of buttons is the Show Next Statement, Step Into, Step Over, and Step Out buttons. The Show Next Statement button repositions the window (if necessary) to display the next statement to be executed. This statement is highlighted in yellow and marked with a yellow arrow in the left-most (shaded) column. Next is the Hexadecimal button, which toggles the values in the debug windows between decimal format and hexadecimal format. The Show Threads In Source button follows, which adds an icon to the left margin that highlights each thread that is running. The final button is a drop-down list that displays a menu of debug commands.

Data Tips

While you are debugging, a data tip is displayed when the cursor is paused over a variable. Data tips are used with both simple and complex data types. A complex data type is collapsed in the data tip, and you can expand it to view members.

Visualizers

Visualizers display data tips in an alternate format, when the default format is not convenient or is unrelated to the underlying data type. For example, there is a DataSet visualizer and an Extensible Markup Language (XML) visualizer. A dataset object is more than the composition of all its members, which is normally presented in a data tip. Datasets are an abstraction of a hierarchal data source. Viewing the dataset in that format could be helpful. Another example is reading and processing data from an XML data source. Let's assume that you are getting incorrect results when handling an XML file. Is the problem the data source or the program logic? Seeing the data in XML format, the underlying format, versus an incomprehensible string could help isolate the problem.

Depending on the variable type, data tips have an optional menu that displays available visualizers. Visualizers are presented based on the type being inspected. Different types support different visualizers, if any. When a data tip detects compatible visualizers, the Visualizer menu is displayed automatically with the data tip, which is the magnifying glass. If a magnifying glass is not presented, no visualizers are available for the target type. Available visualizers are listed in the Visualizer menu.

In the following code, *myxml* is a field that contains XML defining an array of books. This code is found in the *btnVisualizer_Click* method. Set a breakpoint at the beginning of the method:

```
private string myxml = "<books><book><title>" +
    "The Gourmet Microwave</title>" +
    "<price>19.95</price>" +
    "</book><book><title>Sushi, Anyone?</title>" +
    "<price>49.99</price></book></books>";
```

The following code attempts to change the content of the *myxml* field. A string that contains XML describing another book is added to the *myxml* string:

```
string newbook = "<book><title>" +
    "Donis's Great Adventure</title>" +
    "<price>9.95</price>" +
    "</book>";

myxml = myxml.Insert(5, newbook);
```

A data tip can display the resulting *myxml* string easily. Viewing *myxml* as XML, and not as a raw string, provides clarity. Move the cursor over the *myxml* variable, and a data tip appears. The raw string is displayed. From the data tip's Visualizer menu, select XML Visualizer. The XML Visualizer opens, as shown in Figure 15-26. The visualizer uncovers a problem, which is that the underlying XML is not well formed. Why is that? The reason is that the additional book was inserted at the wrong location in the *myxml* string. This error is not easily detected from examining a raw string manually. However, the problem is caught quickly by the XML Visualizer.

FIGURE 15-26 The XML Visualizer showing a problem

The following code is modified to insert the book at the correct location in the *myxml* string. Now the XML Visualizer correctly displays the XML of the string, as shown in Figure 15-27. You have just found and successfully resolved a bug!

```
myxml = myxml.Insert(7, newbook);
```

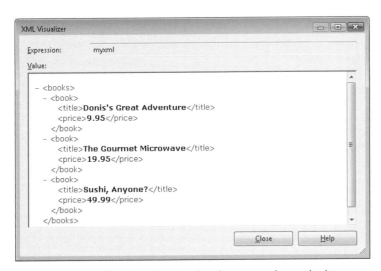

FIGURE 15-27 The XML Visualizer showing the corrected *myxml* string

The DataSet Visualizer is another example of a useful visualizer. The following code displays rows of a dataset. A breakpoint is placed on the source line that declares the *DataRowCollection* variable called *rows*, shown in bold here:

```
DataSet ds = new DataSet();
ds.ReadXml(@"C:\Xml\titles.xml");
```

```
DataRowCollection rows = ds.Tables[0].Rows;
foreach (DataRow row in rows)
{
    lblData.Items.Add(row[0].ToString());
}
```

When the breakpoint is hit, place the cursor over the *ds* variable, which is an instance of a dataset. A data tip appears. From the data tip's Visualize menu, choose DataSet Visualizer. The dataset is displayed in the DataSet Visualizer, as shown in Figure 15-28. You can choose the data table to view using the Table drop-down list in this window. In the data table, you can sort the data and make basic changes to the fields in memory.

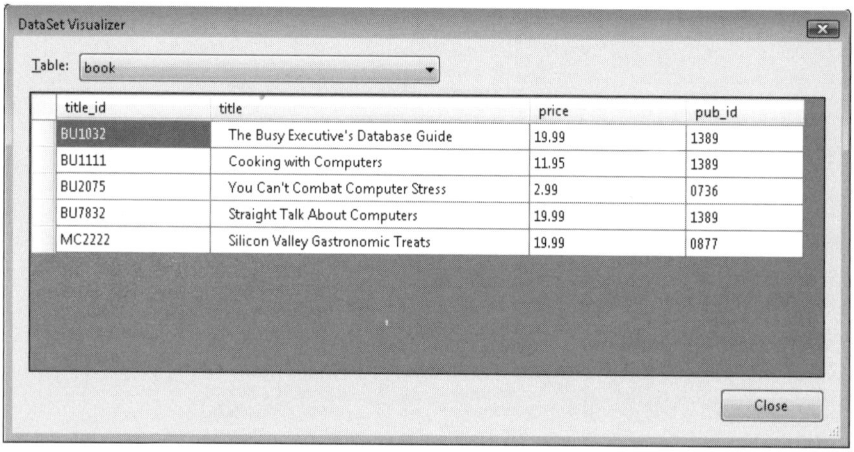

FIGURE 15-28 The DataSet Visualizer

Debug Windows

To assist in debugging, Visual Studio offers a variety of debug windows, described in the following sections.

Breakpoints Window

Manage breakpoints in the Breakpoints window. In this window, you can insert, delete, and disable breakpoints. (The Breakpoints window was shown and discussed in detail earlier in this chapter.)

Output Window

The Output window (shown in Figure 15-29) contains messages from various sources from Visual Studio. The Output window is available on the View menu.

FIGURE 15-29 The Output window

The Output window has a toolbar with a drop-down list and several buttons. The Show Output From drop-down list filters the sources of messages such as Build and Debug messages. The first three buttons locate build errors in the code editor: Find Message In Code, Go To Previous Message, and Go To Next Message. The next button, Clear All, erases the content of the Output window. The Toggle Word Wrap button toggles word wrap in the Output window.

Watch Window and Other Variables Windows

You can watch variables and expressions in a variables window. The Watch, Locals, Auto, and QuickWatch windows are considered variables windows—they have the same general user interface and functionality. The variables windows are disabled in running mode; you must be in break mode to use them. A Watch window, like other variables windows, has three columns. The Name column displays the variable name or expression to evaluate. The Value column displays the variable value or result of the expression. The Type column is the data type of the variable or expression. There are four Watch windows for grouping related values.

Variable values can be modified directly in a variables window. Changed values are highlighted in red. This is an excellent way to test applications with values that stress the program. You also can use this technique to test how the application handles error conditions.

You can add variables and expressions in a variables window directly. The QuickWatch dialog box is a convenient means of inspecting a variable or expression and optionally adding that item to a permanent variables window. The QuickWatch dialog box has an Add Watch button. If desired, you can enter new expressions in the Expression text box. The QuickWatch window is available on the Debug menu. Shortcuts for QuickWatch are either pressing Shift+F9 or Ctrl+D followed by Ctrl+Q . Before opening the QuickWatch window, select the target variable or expression in the source editor. For convenience, you also can select a variable or expression in the source editor and drag it into an open Watch window.

Expressions

Debugger expressions are expressions entered in the Watch, QuickWatch, Breakpoints, or Immediate window. These expressions are evaluated by the Managed Expression Evaluator of the Visual Studio debugger. Use debugger expressions to calculate values or to call methods. IntelliSense is available when entering debugger expressions in a debug window or visualizer.

Debugger expressions are evaluated similarly to regular expressions. However, there are some unique idiosyncrasies of the Managed Expression Evaluator:

- It ignores access modifiers.

- All members of the current object, regardless of accessibility, are available.

- Checked blocks are ignored and evaluated as unchecked.

- Anonymous methods are not supported in debugger expressions.

Expressions can contain constants, function calls, and identifiers within scope, such as locals, parameters, and fields. Most operators, such as +, -, ==, !=, ++, --, and /, are available. You can even use the *typeof* and *sizeof* operators. The *this* reference is supported. In addition, simple casts are allowed.

Expressions are evaluated between every step command. Beware of side effects, which can alter the state or execution of the program unexpectedly. For example, calling in a Watch expression a function that changes the state of the current object might change the outcome of the application and cause adverse side effects.

Expression example

The following procedure demonstrates using variables windows. Set a breakpoint in the *Form_Load* function in the Expressions application. Run the application until the breakpoint is hit.

1. Open a Watch window from the Debug menu. The *Form_Load* method has a *sender* parameter and an *e* parameter. Drag the sender and the *e* parameter to the Watch window. Now you can view their values in the Watch window. The Watch window, containing the two parameters, is shown in Figure 15-30. Continue the application and click the Test button on the form that appears.

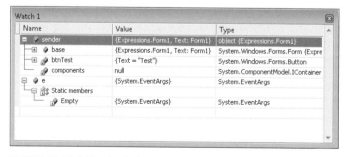

FIGURE 15-30 A Watch window with two parameters

2. The Expressions sample application has a *ZClass* type, which is relatively simple. Open
   the related source file:

```
class ZClass
{
    private int fielda = 5;
    private int fieldb = 10;

    public int MethodA()
    {
        int locala = 5;
        locala = 12;
        return fielda + fieldb;
    }
}
```

3. You should set a breakpoint on the declaration of *locala* in *MethodA*. When the breakpoint is hit, add *fielda*, *fieldb*, *locala*, and *localb* to the Watch window manually by typing the variables names into the Watch window. The *localb* variable is not declared in
   the function. For that reason, it is displayed with an exclamation symbol. In the Watch
   window, add the *++fielda* expression, which has the side effect of changing the value
   of *fielda*. Because the *fielda* watch expression references the same value, the value displayed for that expression also changes. Figure 15-31 shows the new Watch window.

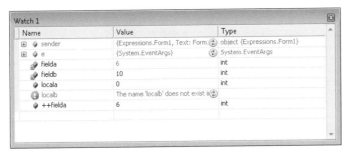

FIGURE 15-31 The Watch window with *locala, localb, fielda,* and *fieldb* values

4. Step through two individual statements by pressing F10 twice. Click the Refresh button
   (the green swirling button to the right of the field) to update the value controlled by
   the *++fielda* expression.

5. The application also has a *DumpType* class. It has a static method, which dumps the
   methods and parameters of a type. The *DumpType.GetReflection* method returns
   a string that lists the methods of a type. This function is not called explicitly in the
   program. It exists purely for debugging purposes. Call the *DumpType.GetReflection*
   function from the Watch window as an expression, as shown in Figure 15-32. Pass
   the type of the current object (*typeof(ZClass)*) as the sole parameter.

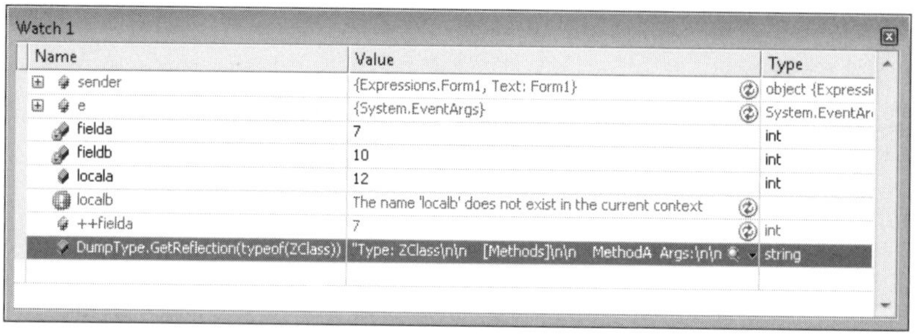

FIGURE 15-32 The *DumpType.GetReflection* expression in the Watch window

Autos Window

The Autos window lists variables and data members used in the current and preceding lines of code. The items of the Autos window are displayed automatically by the Visual Studio debugger, not the developer. You can change the values in the window, which are then highlighted in red. Figure 15-33 shows the Autos window.

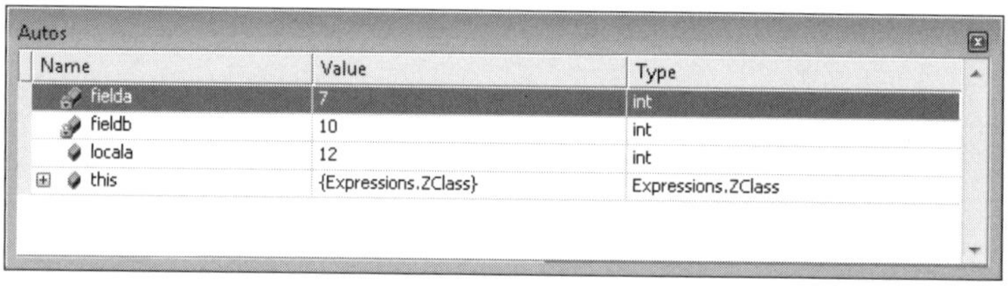

FIGURE 15-33 The Autos window

Locals Window

The Locals window lists the local variables that are currently in scope. Otherwise, the window is similar to the Autos window.

Immediate Window

The Immediate window is the command-line version of the Visual Studio debugger. You can display values in the Immediate window, evaluate expressions, perform menu commands, execute statements, and perform other actions. Command and Immediate windows are in either Command or Immediate mode. The Command window is in Command mode, while the Immediate window is in Immediate mode. Command mode is preferred for executing one or more Visual Studio commands. These are menu commands and other kinds of commands. For evaluating expressions, inspecting values, and otherwise debugging an application, Immediate mode is preferred. The default is Command mode. When in

Immediate mode, switch to Command mode temporarily by prefixing commands with a greater than (>) symbol.

From the Immediate window, entering the >*cmd* command switches to Command mode and the Command window. Switch back to Immediate mode and the Immediate window with the *immed* command.

You can navigate through commands already entered in the Immediate window with the arrow keys. Table 15-7 shows the various ways to navigate the window.

TABLE 15-7 Navigating in the Immediate or Command window

Keystroke	Description
Up arrow on the command line	Previous command
Down arrow on the command line	Next command
Ctrl+Up arrow or Up arrow in the Command window	Move up in the window
Ctrl+Down arrow or Down arrow in the Command window	Move down in the window
Esc	Transfer focus to a blank line if not on a blank line, or to the code editor if already on a blank line

There are limitations to the tasks that can be performed in the Immediate window. For example, you cannot declare new variables, define a label, or create an instance of an object. Special commands such as the *k* command (see Table 15-8) are not available in managed-only code. In addition, the Immediate window does not allow *goto*, *return*, and *loop* statements, or any statement requiring transfer of control.

Some commands can have arguments or options. For example, the *Edit.FindinFiles* command has both. IntelliSense will present the options, which are preceded with a forward slash (/). You must type the forward slash to prompt IntelliSense to display the available options. The following statement is an example of the *Edit.FindinFiles* command:

```
>Edit.FindinFiles /case /lookin:"c:\*" donis
```

If a command displays a window, consult that window to understand the options and arguments. (Of course, you also could check the documentation.) Edit text boxes in the window become arguments for the command, and everything else is represented by an option in the command. Figure 15-34 shows the Find In Files dialog box, which has one text box and several options. The settings shown in the figure correspond to the arguments and options in the preceding example. The text box is the single argument of the *Edit.FindinFiles* command. Several options are available. Arguments are required, while options (not surprisingly) are optional. In the preceding example, the *Edit.FindinFiles* command is used with two options: The first option requests a case-sensitive search, and the second option directs the command to search all files in the root directory. The command has a single argument, which is the search text.

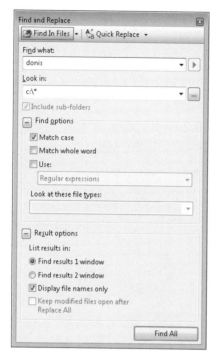

FIGURE 15-34 The Find In Files dialog box

Aliases are short forms of debugging commands. They are convenient, but they are never required. Table 15-8 lists some useful aliases.

TABLE 15-8 Command aliases

Alias	Command
?	Debug.Print
bl	Debug.Breakpoints
callstack	Debug.CallStack
cls	Debug.ClearAll
cmd	View.CommandWindow
du	Dump Unicode
g	Debug.Start
immed	Tools.ImmediateMode
k	Debug.ListCallStack
locals	Debug.Locals
memory1	Debug.Memory1
memory2	Debug.Memory2
p	Debug.StepOver
pr	Debug.StepOut
print	File.Print

TABLE 15-8 Command aliases

Alias	Command
q	*Debug.StopDebugging*
rtc	*Debug.RunToCursor*
saveall	*File.SaveAll*
t	*Step.Into*
threads	*Debug.Threads*
~	*Debug.ListThreads*
~*k	*Debug.ListCallStack /AllThreads*

You might want to create user-defined aliases for frequently performed tasks. The Alias command defines a new alias. The following command defines two new aliases. The *pripro* alias replaces all instances of the *private* keyword with the *protected* keyword in the current source file. The *propri* alias performs the reverse operation. These aliases then can be used in the command window.

```
>alias pripro edit.replace /all private protected
>alias propri edit.replace /all protected private
```

Call Stack Window

The Call Stack window shows functions that are presently on the stack. The current function is highlighted with a yellow arrow. By default, the window has two columns: the name of the function and the source language. The Name column combines several items: module name, function name, parameter information, line number, and byte offset. Parameter information includes parameter type, parameter name, and parameter value. Right-click to customize the display. Except for the function name, every column is optional. Figure 15-35 shows the Call Stack window, which is available only in break mode.

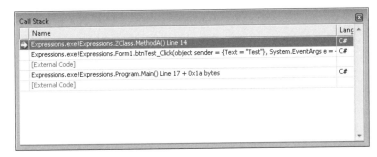

FIGURE 15-35 The Call Stack window

The call stack does not include external code. In some circumstances, information from external functions can be helpful. To view external code, disable the Enable Just My Code (Managed Only) option in the General settings in the Debugging category of the Options window (which you access by choosing Options from the Tools menu). Figure 15-36 shows the Call Stack window with this option disabled. The call stack now includes *System* functions, which can be helpful.

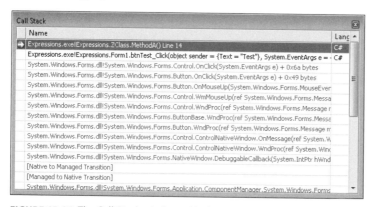

FIGURE 15-36 The Call Stack window with the Enable Just My Code (Managed Only) option disabled

Each row of the call stack represents the stack frame of a function. A stack frame has information related to the function, such as local variables and parameters. The current function is highlighted with a yellow arrow. By default, this also marks the current stack frame. You can switch stack frames. Right-click a row and choose the Switch To Frame menu command from the Context menu. A curved green arrow will appear and mark the current stack frame, which may be different from the current function. Some variables windows are based on the current stack frame. For example, the Autos and Locals windows present information based on the current stack frame. If you change the current stack frame, the content in these windows also changes.

Another option from the Call Stack context menu is the Include Calls To/From Other Threads command. This command shows calls from other threads in the Call Stack. For example, this is helpful when tracing the call stack from an XML Web Service into an ASP.NET application.

Function breakpoints and trace points can be set in the Call Stack window. You can use shortcut keys, such as F9, to do this, or you can right-click a row and use the Context menu.

Threads Window

The Threads window lists the active threads of the current process. This window is available only in break mode. A thread is a single path of execution in a process. Threads also own assets, such as local variables, thread context, and thread local storage. Threads can be assigned a priority. Naming threads is particularly useful when debugging an application that is experiencing synchronization problems.

The Thread application creates threads. In the sample application, each new thread executes the *MethodA* function. Run the Thread application, select the BreakAll command from the Debug menu, and then open the Threads window, which is shown in Figure 15-37, by choosing Threads from the Windows submenu of the Debug menu.

FIGURE 15-37 The Threads window

The columns of the Threads window are thread identifier, category, thread name, method location, thread priority, and suspend count. Right-click a thread and choose Freeze from the context menu to suspend the thread. Suspended threads are shown with a pause (double-bar) icon. Right-click the thread and choose Thaw to resume a suspended thread. Forcibly suspending a thread can affect the normal operation of an application.

The Switch To Thread command of the context menu changes the current thread. The new thread will immediately receive CPU time. You also can double-click the target thread to switch the current thread. The content presented in some windows, such as the Call Stack window, is based on the current thread. The information in these windows will update as the current thread is changed.

Modules Window

The Modules window lists the modules, executables, and DLLs that are loaded into the application. There is considerable information presented on each module, as described in Table 15-9.

TABLE 15-9 Modules window columns

Column	Description
Name	Gives the name of the module.
Path	Presents the fully qualified path to the module.
Optimized	Indicates whether the module is optimized during JIT compilation. Debug versions of modules usually are not optimized.
User Code	Indicates whether user code is available for the module.
Symbol Status	Indicates whether symbols are loaded for the module.
Symbol File	When loaded, displays the fully qualified path and name of the symbol file.
Order	Lists the load order of modules.
Version	Provides the version number of the module.
Timestamp	Displays the timestamp of when the module was created.
Address	Displays the start and end load address of the module.
Process	Displays the process identifier of the application that hosts the module.

Processes Window

The Processes window enumerates processes being debugged in the current debugging session. Table 15-10 describes each column of the window.

TABLE 15-10 Processes window columns

Column	Description
Name	The name of the process.
ID	The process identifier of the process.
Path	The path to the executable.
Title	The title of the application. For a Windows Forms application, this is the content of the title bar.
State	The state of the application, such as the break or running state.
Debugging	The type of debugging, such as managed or native debugging.
Transport	The transport to the application. An entry of Default indicates the Native With No Authentication transport.
Transport Qualifier	The machine name where the application resides.

Memory Window

The Memory window (shown in Figure 15-38) displays the memory of the current process. Unlike other windows, the Memory window provides an unfiltered and raw presentation of process memory. The different Memory windows provide four distinct views into the memory of the application. Memory windows are available in break mode and only if the Enable Address-Level Debugging Option is enabled. Find this option in the General settings in the Debugging category of the Options window (which you access by choosing Options from the Tools menu).

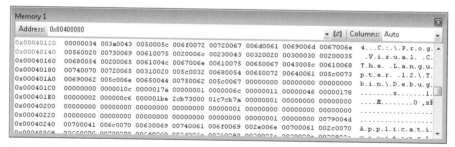

FIGURE 15-38 The Memory window

To view specific memory, enter a memory address in the Address edit box. You can enter a memory address directly or you can drag symbols, such as local variables, into the Address edit box. The Memory window will display rows of data beginning at the specified memory address. Multiple columns of data are shown. The first column shows the memory address. The final column is the text translation. The memory dump is in the intervening columns.

The Memory window can be formatted by right-clicking it. You can change the size of the data columns to 1-, 2-, 4-, or 8-byte columns. The display can also be changed to 32- or 64-bit data presentation. The text translation in the final column can be formatted as ANSI or Unicode, or it can be hidden.

Disassembly Window

The Disassembly window (shown in Figure 15-39) shows the native assembly of the application as generated by the JIT compiler. By default, if available, the source code also is displayed. Each assembly instruction is displayed with several columns: the instruction address, mnemonic, and parameters. Right-click the Disassembly window to change its format.

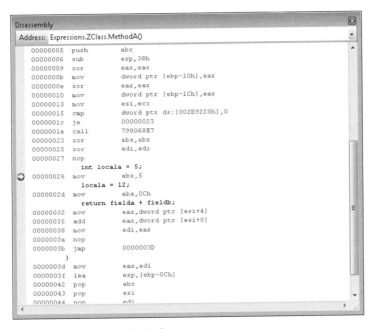

FIGURE 15-39 Disassembly window

Registers Window

The Registers window (shown in Figure 15-40) displays the state of the registers. Assembly-level programming typically relies heavily on registers. For this reason, the Disassembly and Registers windows often are used together. Right-click the window to change the format of the display. The Registers window displays the contents of registers in the context of the current thread.

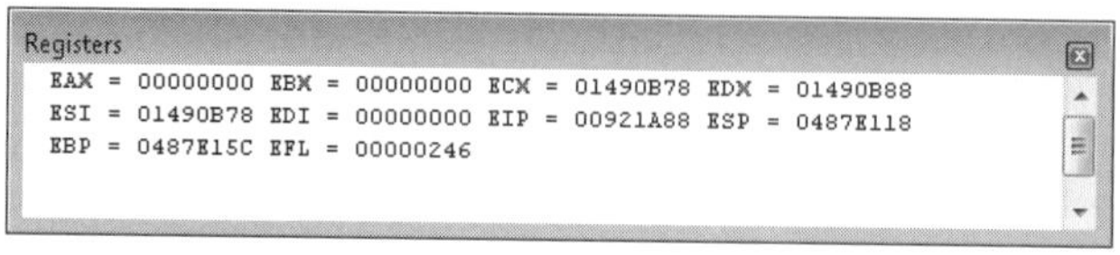

FIGURE 15-40 The Registers window

Table 15-11 describes the common registers.

TABLE 15-11 Registers

Register	Description
EAX	This register is general-purpose. It is used commonly as the destination of a math operation.
EBX	This register is general-purpose.
ECX	This register is general-purpose and is used commonly for counting.
EDX	This register is general-purpose.
EIP	This register contains the address of the next instruction.
ESP	This register contains the pointer to the top of the stack.
ESI	This register is the source index. The ESI and EDI registers are used frequently in string operations.
EDI	This register is the destination index. The ESI and EDI registers are used frequently in string operations.
EBP	This register contains the base pointer to the current stack frame.

Tracing

To instrument an application, developers commonly use trace messages. By default, trace messages are displayed in the Output window. Trace messages are used for a variety of reasons but primarily for diagnostic purposes. Traces can validate program flow (often the cause of bugs). Trace messages can display the state of the application at different stages. You can display the values of objects, local variables, or other data throughout the lifetime of an application. Finally, trace messages are useful for tracking events, such as start, stop, and user-defined events.

Various classes in the Framework Class Library (FCL) support tracing. *TraceSource* is the primary tracing type. The *TraceSource* class is found in the *System.Diagnostics* namespace.

To enable tracing, the *TRACE* symbol must be defined in the application. In the source code, this is accomplished with the *#define* statement. Alternatively, define the symbol as a compiler option. The */d* compiler option defines a symbol:

```
csc /d:TRACE test.cs
```

In Visual Studio, both the Debug and Release configurations define the *TRACE* symbol by default.

Table 15-12 explains the important methods of the *TraceSource* class.

TABLE 15-12 *TraceSource* **methods**

Level	Description
Constructors Both constructors assign a name to the *TraceSource* object. The two-argument constructor also sets a default severity level for all trace messages sent from this trace source.	*TraceSource(string name)* *TraceSource(string name, SourceLevels defaultLevel)*
Close This method closes all the trace listeners assigned to this trace source.	*void Close()*
Flush This method flushes the trace listeners assigned to this trace source, ensuring that cached trace messages are sent to listeners.	*void Flush()*

TraceData
 	
This method creates a trace message consisting of the event type, a trace identifier, and any trace data. The event type is the severity level.
	[ConditionalAttribute("TRACE")]
	public void TraceData(
	    TraceEventType eventType,
	    int id,
	    Object data)
	
	[ConditionalAttribute("TRACE")]
	public void TraceData(
	    TraceEventType eventType,
	    int id,
	    Object[] data)

TraceEvent
 	
This method creates a trace message consisting of an event type and message, which is written to the *Listeners* collection. The first overload—the method without a *message* or *data* parameter—writes an empty trace message. This is sufficient for simply acknowledging an event.
	[ConditionalAttribute("TRACE")]
	public void TraceEvent(
	    TraceEventType eventType,
	    int id)
	
	[ConditionalAttribute("TRACE")]
	public void TraceEvent(
	    TraceEventType eventType,
	    int id,
	    string message)
	
	[ConditionalAttribute("TRACE")]
	public void TraceEvent(
	    TraceEventType eventType,
	    int id,
	    object [] data)

TABLE 15-12 *TraceSource* **methods**

Level	Description

TraceInformation
 	
This method creates an informational message, which is written to the *Listeners* collection.
	[ConditionalAttribute("TRACE")]
	public void TraceInformation(
	    string message)
	
	[ConditionalAttribute("TRACE")]
	public void TraceInformation(
	    string format,
	    params Object[] args)

TraceTransfer
 	
This method creates a transfer message, which is written to the listeners of this trace source.
	[ConditionalAttribute("TRACE")]
	public void TraceTransfer(
	    int id,
	    string message,
	    Guid relatedActivityID)

The *TraceSource* type also has several properties. Table 15-13 lists these properties.

TABLE 15-13 *TraceSource* **properties**

Property	Type
Attributes This property gets the custom attributes that are defined in an application configuration file.	*StringDictionary*
Listeners This property returns an array of listeners. Listeners are the targets of trace messages.	*TraceListenerCollection*
Name This property returns the name of the *TraceSource* object. The name can be used with the *SourceFilter* property of a listener.	*string*
Switch This property gets or sets the trace switch associated with the *TraceSource* object. Trace switches filter trace messages sent to listeners.	*SourceSwitch*

Tracing can be simple or complex. Severity levels, switches, listeners, and listener filters determine when, where, and how trace messages are reported. Severity levels are assigned to trace messages, which establish the priority of the message. Switches filter trace messages based on their severity levels. Trace messages are sent to listeners, where listener filters control the final messages reported to the user. Tracing is configurable either programmatically or using an application configuration file. The application configuration file is recommended over programmatic control. With the application configuration file, tracing is controlled, enabled, or disabled without needing to recompile the program. For a production application, this is essential.

Trace messages are assigned severity levels. Trace levels set the category or importance of a message. Some trace messages, such as the start and stop time of an application, are activity related. Informational trace messages are used to stub methods and to check program flow. The *TraceEventType* enumeration defines the trace levels, which are listed in Table 15-14. The levels are listed in descending order of priority.

TABLE 15-14 Trace levels

Level	Description
TraceEventType.Critical	Conditions that destabilize an application and are fatal
TraceEventType.Error	Conditions that destabilize an application but are recoverable
TraceEventType.Warning	Noncritical conditions
TraceEventType.Information	General information that might aid in the diagnosing of an error condition
TraceEventType.Verbose	General information not necessarily associated with an error condition
TraceEventType activities	See Table 15-15

Some trace levels are related to activities, which are linked to events. The activity traces are grouped at the same trace level, which is the lowest trace level, beneath the Verbose level. Table 15-15 shows the list of activity traces.

TABLE 15-15 Activity traces

Activity	Description
TraceEventType.Start	Indicates that an operation is starting
TraceEventType.Stop	Indicates that an operation is stopping
TraceEventType.Suspend	Indicates that an operation is suspended
TraceEventType.Resume	Indicates that an operation has resumed
TraceEventType.Transfer	Indicates a change of correlation identity

Switches filter trace messages based on trace levels. This determines the messages sent from a *TraceSource* object to listeners. With switches, you can enable or disable groups of trace messages selectively. If an application is crashing, you might decide to send only critical and error trace messages that could indicate the application is failing. When algorithms are performing incorrectly, you might want to enable general and activity traces to show program flow.

Tracing can be helpful but excessive tracing can harm performance. Unrestricted tracing can generate copious amounts of information. Filters reduce trace messages and conserve resources. Switch filters are defined by the *SourceSwitch* class. The *SourceSwitch* class has the *Level* property, which is a *SourceLevels* type. *SourceLevels* is an enumeration and defines the level of the filter. This is a bitwise flag, and the various *SourceLevels* can be combined. The source levels are detailed in Table 15-16.

TABLE 15-16 Source levels

Filter	Description
SourceLevels.ActivityTracing	Allows activity trace messages. Other messages are filtered.
SourceLevels.All	Allows all trace messages.
SourceLevels.Critical	Allows only critical trace messages.
SourceLevels.Error	Allows error and critical trace messages. Other trace levels are filtered.
SourceLevels.Information	Filters verbose and activity trace messages. Other trace messages are sent.
SourceLevels.Off	Excludes all trace messages.
SourceLevels.Verbose	Filters activity trace messages. All other messages are sent.
SourceLevels.Warning	Filters all trace messages except for Critical, Error, and Warning events.

To establish a filter, assign an instance of *SourceSwitch* to the *TraceSource.Switch* property. The *SourceSwitch* has two constructors:

```
public SourceSwitch(string name)
```

```
public SourceSwitch(string name, string defaultLevel)
```

SourceSwitch also has several useful properties, which are listed in Table 15-17.

TABLE 15-17 *SourceSwitch* properties

Property	Type
Attributes This property gets custom attributes that are defined in the application configuration file.	StringDictionary
Description This property returns a general description of the switch. It defaults to an empty string.	string
DisplayName This property returns the name of the switch.	string
Level This property gets or sets the level of the switch.	SourceLevels

The following code creates an instance of *TraceSource* and *TraceSwitch*. The switch then is assigned to the *TraceSource:*

```
TraceSource ts = new TraceSource("sample");
SourceSwitch sw = new SourceSwitch("switch");
sw.Level = SourceLevels.All;
ts.Switch = sw;
```

The event type of trace messages and the switch source level combine to determine which messages are sent. The following code sends trace messages of each event type: critical, error, information, and so on. The switch level, which is case-sensitive, is read from the command line and determines which messages are sent rather than filtered. A console listener is used in the application, which displays the unfiltered trace messages in the console. This is an excellent program for understanding the combination of trace event types and switch levels:

```csharp
#define TRACE
using System;
using System.Diagnostics;

namespace Donis.CSharpBook {
    public class Starter {
        public static void Main(string[] argv) {
            TraceSource ts = new TraceSource("sample");
            SourceSwitch sw = new SourceSwitch("switch");

            sw.Level = (SourceLevels)Enum.Parse(
                typeof(SourceLevels), argv[0]);
            ts.Switch = sw;
            ConsoleTraceListener console =
                new ConsoleTraceListener();
            ts.Listeners.Add(console);
            ts.TraceEvent(TraceEventType.Start, 0,
                "Activity trace messages on");
            ts.TraceEvent(TraceEventType.Verbose, 0,
                "Verbose trace messages on");
            ts.TraceEvent(TraceEventType.Information, 0,
                "Information trace messages on");
            ts.TraceEvent(TraceEventType.Warning, 0,
                "Warning trace messages on");
            ts.TraceEvent(TraceEventType.Error, 0,
                "Error trace messages on");
            ts.TraceEvent(TraceEventType.Critical, 0,
                "Critical trace messages on");

            ts.Flush();
            ts.Close();

        }
    }
}
```

Trace messages can be sent to a variety of targets, including the console, a text file, and an XML file. Trace targets are called *listeners*. An array of listeners called the *Listeners* collection can be associated with a trace source. By default, the *Listeners* collection has a single item, the *DefaultTraceListener*, which displays trace messages in the Output window of Visual Studio. When the *Listeners* collection contains more than one listener, trace messages are sent to multiple targets. If the collection contains a *ConsoleTraceListener* and the *XMLWriterTraceListener*, trace messages are displayed in the console and are saved in an XML file. Trace listeners receive trace messages sent from a trace source. Only messages not filtered at the trace source are sent to the listeners.

Table 15-18 reviews the available predefined listeners.

TABLE 15-18 Trace listeners

Listeners	Description
TextWriterTraceListener	Sends trace messages to a stream-related destination, such as a TextWriter class.
EventLogTraceListener	Sends trace messages to the event log.
DefaultTraceListener	Sends trace messages to the Output window. This is the default listener and is initially the only member of the Listeners collection.
ConsoleTraceListener	Sends trace messages to a standard output or error stream.
DelimitedListTraceListener	Similar to the TextWriterTraceListener class, sends messages to an instance of a stream-related class. However, the messages are separated with user-defined delimiters.
XmlWriterTraceListener	Saves traces messages as XML-encoded text.

Trace listeners inherit the *TraceListener* base class, which provides the core functionality of a listener. All listeners have a default constructor. Some listeners have multi-argument constructors that assign the listener a name or that define a destination. For example, the following code creates a new *TextWriterTraceListener*. It is named *samplelistener* and writes to the test.txt file.

```
TextWriterTraceListener file = new
    TextWriterTraceListener("samplelistener", "test.txt");
```

Table 15-19 details the properties of the *TraceListener* class.

TABLE 15-19 *TraceListener* properties

Property	Type
Attributes Gets custom attributes that are defined in the application configuration file.	StringDictionary
Filter Gets and sets the filter of the listener.	TraceFilter
IndentLevel Gets and sets the level of indentation in the target.	int
IndentSize Gets and sets the amount of indentation per indentation level in the target.	int
IsThreadSafe Indicates whether the listener is thread-safe.	bool

TABLE 15-19 *TraceListener* **properties**

Property	Type
Name	*string*
Gets and sets the name of the listener.	
NeedIndent	*bool*
Enables or disables indentation. This is a protected property.	
TraceOutputOptions	*TraceOptions*
Gets and sets an enumeration that controls additional data sent to the listener.	

The values of the *TraceOptions* enumeration are listed in Table 15-20. These values are bitwise, which allows multiple options to be combined.

TABLE 15-20 *TraceOptions* **values**

Value	Description
TraceOptions.CallStack	Adds the call stack to tracing. The *Environment.StackTrace* property provides the call stack.
TraceOptions.DateTime	Adds the date and time in each trace message.
TraceOptions.LogicalOperationStack	Adds the logical operation stack to tracing. This information is provided by the *orrelationManager.LogicalOperationStack* property.
TraceOptions.None	Excludes any additional data.
TraceOptions.ProcessId	Adds the current process identifier in each trace message. This information is found at the *Process.Id* property.
TraceOptions.ThreadId	Adds the current thread identifier in each trace message. This information is found at the *Thread.ManagedThreadId* property.
TraceOptions.TimeStamp	Adds a timestamp in each trace message. This information is returned from the *Stopwatch.GetTimeStamp* method.

The listeners of a *TraceSource* type are set at the *TraceSource.Listeners* property. The *Listeners* property is a *TraceListenerCollection* type, which implements the standard interfaces of a collection. You can add a listener with the *Add* method. The *TraceListenerCollection* type also implements the *AddRange* method. Call this method to add multiple listeners to the *Listeners* collection in a single call. The *AddRange* method is overloaded to accept an array of listeners or a *TraceListenerCollection* parameter. The following code adds a *ConsoleTraceListener* to a *Listeners* collection:

```
ConsoleTraceListener console =
    new ConsoleTraceListener();
ts.Listeners.Add(console);
```

Trace messages can be filtered at the *Listeners* collection. Listener filters are perfect for identifying important messages when sent a flood of messages from the trace source. Both listener filters and trace switches are filters. A trace switch filters messages from the *TraceSource* object before being sent to a listener. The listener can filter the trace messages further. There are two types of listener filters: *SourceFilter* and *EventTypeFilter*. *SourceFilter* constrains the listener to a specific source. For example, when tracing messages from several classes, you use *SourceFilter* to limit trace messages to those generated by a specific type. *EventTypeFilter* filters trace messages based on priority. You can use *SourceFilter* and *EventTypeFilter* together or independently.

Here is the constructor of the *SourceFilter* type:

```
public SourceFilter(string source)
```

The only parameter is the name of the source. The listener will output only messages from the specific source. If the name is invalid, the filter is ignored.

Here is the constructor of the *EventTypeFilter* type:

```
public EventTypeFilter(SourceLevels level)
```

The *SourceLevels* parameter states the priority of trace messages that the listener will output. Other trace messages are ignored.

The following code demonstrates the *SourceFilter* type. The *EventTypeFilter* is demonstrated in an example later in this chapter. Three *TraceSource* instances are defined in the code. A *ConsoleTraceListener* is also defined, which displays trace messages in the console. *ConsoleTraceListener.Filter* then is updated to display trace messages from only the second trace source. Later, the *SourceFilter* is changed to limit trace messages to the first trace source:

```
#define TRACE

using System;
using System.Diagnostics;

namespace Donis.CSharpBook {
    public class Starter {

        public static void Main() {
            TraceSource ts1 = new TraceSource("ts1");
            TraceSource ts2 = new TraceSource("ts2");
            TraceSource ts3 = new TraceSource("ts3");
            SourceSwitch sw = new SourceSwitch("sw",
                "Information");
            ts1.Switch = sw;
            ts2.Switch = sw;
            ts3.Switch = sw;
            ConsoleTraceListener cs = new ConsoleTraceListener();
            ts1.Listeners.Add(cs);
            ts2.Listeners.Add(cs);
            ts3.Listeners.Add(cs);
```

```
        // Include only the ts2 source

        Console.WriteLine("Filters t1 and t3 messages");
        ts1.Listeners[1].Filter = new SourceFilter("ts2");
        ts1.TraceInformation("ts1:trace");
        ts2.TraceInformation("ts2:trace");
        ts3.TraceInformation("ts3:trace");

        // Include only the ts1 source

        Console.WriteLine("\nFilters t2 and t3 messages");
        ts1.Listeners[1].Filter = new SourceFilter("ts1");
        ts1.TraceInformation("ts1:trace");
        ts2.TraceInformation("ts2:trace");
        ts3.TraceInformation("ts3:trace");

        ts1.Flush();
        ts2.Flush();
        ts3.Flush();

        ts1.Close();
        ts2.Close();
        ts3.Close();
    }
  }
}
```

Tracing Example

The following example code declares a *ZClass* and a *YClass*; both classes contain a *TraceSource* instance. It is a best practice to maintain separate *TraceSource* instances for different classes, which affords individualized management of tracing at the class level. For example, you could filter or expose trace messages from specific classes. Expose *TraceSource* as a static member of the class. Class methods use the static *TraceSource* member to send trace messages. If using the disposable pattern, clean up the *TraceSource* object in the *Dispose* method:

```
public class ZClass : IDisposable {
    static ZClass() {
        ts = new TraceSource("ZTrace");
        ts.Switch = new SourceSwitch("sw1", "All");
        ts.Listeners.Add(new ConsoleTraceListener());
        TextWriterTraceListener file = new
            TextWriterTraceListener("samplelistener", "test.txt");
        file.Filter = new EventTypeFilter(SourceLevels.Critical);
        file.TraceOutputOptions = TraceOptions.DateTime;
        ts.Listeners.Add(file);
    }
    static private TraceSource ts;
    public void MethodA() {
        ts.TraceEvent(TraceEventType.Error,
            GetHashCode(), "ZClass.MethodA");
```

```
    }

    public void MethodB(int parama, int paramb,
            int paramc) {
        ts.TraceData(TraceEventType.Critical,
            GetHashCode(), "ZClass.MethodB", parama,
            paramb, paramc);
    }
    public void Dispose() {
        ts.Flush();
        ts.Close();
    }
}
public class YClass : IDisposable {
    static YClass() {
        ts = new TraceSource("YTrace");
        ts.Switch = new SourceSwitch("sw2", "Information");
        ts.Listeners.Add(new ConsoleTraceListener());
        ts.Listeners[1].IndentSize = 4;
        ts.Listeners[1].IndentLevel = 2;
    }
    static private TraceSource ts;
    public void MethodC() {
        ts.TraceEvent(TraceEventType.Error,
            GetHashCode(), "YClass.MethodC");
    }
    public void Dispose() {
        ts.Flush();
        ts.Close();
    }
}
```

The following code is a complete listing of the sample code used in this section. *Main* also has a trace source, which sends trace messages to listeners for the Output window and the console. Both *ZClass* and *YClass* have separate trace sources. The methods of *ZClass* and *YClass* use their respective *TraceSource* instances to send trace messages. To demonstrate different methods for tracing, the *TraceEvent* and *TraceData* methods are called. The hash codes of the objects are used as the trace identifier, which identifies trace messages by class type and instance. It is sometimes useful to associate a trace message with a specific object. The trace source of *ZClass* sends trace messages to listeners for the Output window, for the console, and for a text file. The trace switch of the trace source does not filter trace messages—all messages are sent. However, the filter for the text file limits tracing to critical messages. The *YClass* trace source sends informational trace messages to listeners for the Output window and the console:

```
#define TRACE

using System;
using System.Diagnostics;

namespace Donis.CSharpBook {
    public class Starter {
```

```
public static void Main() {

    TraceSource ts =
        new TraceSource("StarterTrace");
    ts.Switch = new SourceSwitch("sw3");
    ts.Switch.Level = SourceLevels.ActivityTracing;
    ts.Listeners.Add(new ConsoleTraceListener());
    ts.TraceEvent(TraceEventType.Start,
        0, "Starting");

    ZClass obj1 = new ZClass();
    obj1.MethodA();
    obj1.MethodB(1,2,3);

    YClass obj2 = new YClass();
    obj2.MethodC();

    ZClass obj3 = new ZClass();
    obj1.MethodA();
    obj1.MethodB(4,5,6);

    ts.TraceEvent(TraceEventType.Stop,
        0, "Stopping");

    obj1.Dispose();
    obj2.Dispose();

    }
}

public class ZClass: IDisposable {

    static ZClass() {
        ts = new TraceSource("ZTrace");
        ts.Switch = new SourceSwitch("sw1", "All");
        ts.Listeners.Add(new ConsoleTraceListener());
        TextWriterTraceListener file = new
            TextWriterTraceListener("samplelistener", "test.txt");
        file.Filter = new EventTypeFilter(SourceLevels.Critical);
        file.TraceOutputOptions = TraceOptions.DateTime;
        ts.Listeners.Add(file);
    }

    static private TraceSource ts;


    public void MethodA() {
        ts.TraceEvent(TraceEventType.Error,
            GetHashCode(), "ZClass.MethodA");
    }

    public void MethodB(int parama, int paramb,
            int paramc) {
        ts.TraceData(TraceEventType.Critical,
            GetHashCode(), "ZClass.MethodB",
```

```
                  parama,  paramb, paramc);
        }

        public void Dispose() {
            ts.Flush();
            ts.Close();
        }
    }

    public class YClass: IDisposable {

        static YClass() {
            ts = new TraceSource("YTrace");
            ts.Switch = new SourceSwitch("sw2", "Information");
            ts.Listeners.Add(new ConsoleTraceListener());
            ts.Listeners[1].IndentSize = 4;
            ts.Listeners[1].IndentLevel = 2;
        }

        static private TraceSource ts;

        public void MethodC() {
            ts.TraceEvent(TraceEventType.Error,
                GetHashCode(), "YClass.MethodC");
        }

        public void Dispose() {
            ts.Flush();
            ts.Close();
        }
    }
}
```

Configuration File

Trace switches, listeners, and listener filters are configurable in an application configuration file. Using an application configuration file is the best practice and is preferable to programmatic configuration. That way, tracing is configurable without recompiling the application. Where there is a conflict between programmatic configuration and a configuration file, programmatic settings take precedence.

The application configuration file has the same name as the target assembly plus a *.config* extension. For example, the application configuration file for hello.exe is hello.exe.config. The application configuration file should be in the same directory as the assembly. For a software system, you can configure multiple applications within the system with a single publisher policy file, which is deployed in the global assembly cache. Visit this link for a primer on publisher policy files: *http://msdn2.microsoft.com/en-us/library/dz32563a*.

In the configuration file, the tracing configuration settings are placed within the *system.diagnostics* element. For the complete explanation of the *system.diagnostics* element, visit this link: *http://msdn2.microsoft.com/en-us/library/1txedc80*. Here is an example:

```
<?xml version="1.0" encoding="utf-8" ?>
<configuration>
    <system.diagnostics>
    </system.diagnostics>
</configuration>
```

The *sources* Element

Define the trace sources within the *sources* element. A specific trace source is declared in a *sources* element. The important attributes of the *sources* element are *name* and *switchName*. The *name* attribute is the name of the trace source, and *switchName* names the switch assigned to the trace source. Here is an example:

```
<sources>
    <source name="ZTrace" switchName="sw1">
    </source>
</sources>
```

The *listeners* Element

The listeners of a particular source are listed within the *sources* elements. The *listeners* element encapsulates the listeners of a trace source. Individual listeners are added to the *Listeners* collection with the *add* element. The key attributes of the *add* element are *type*, *name*, *traceOutputOptions*, and *initializeData*. The *type* attribute is the kind of listener, which is the target. The *name* attribute is the name assigned to the listener. The *initializeData* attribute is additional data used to create the listener, such as the target file name. The *traceOutputOtions* attribute adds optional data to trace messages sent to the listener, such as a timestamp. Here are example elements:

```
<sources>
    <source name="ZTrace" switchName="sw1">
        <listeners>
            <add name="tListener"
                type="System.Diagnostics.TextWriterTraceListener"
                initializeData="data.txt" />
            <add name="cListener"
                type="System.Diagnostics.ConsoleTraceListener"/>
        </listeners>
    </source>
</sources>
```

The *sharedListeners* Element

As shown in the previous code, the *listeners* element assigns a listener to a specific trace source. You also can share listeners. Listeners can be shared between multiple trace sources. Use the *sharedListeners* element to define shared listeners. A shared listener is added with an *add* element. Shared listeners are added to a specific trace source the same way as a regular listener, as demonstrated in the preceding example. For a shared listener, the *add* element need only have the *name* attribute, which identifies the shared listener:

```
<system.diagnostics>
    <sharedListeners>
        <add type="System.Diagnostics.ConsoleTraceListener"
            name="cListener"
            traceOutputOptions="None" />
    </sharedListeners>
</ system.diagnostics >
```

The *switches* Element

Switches are defined within the *switches* element. An individual switch is added with an *add* element. The basic attributes are *name* and *value*. The *name* attribute is the name of the switch, and the *value* attribute is the filter level. Here is an example:

```
<system.diagnostics>
    <switches>
        <add name="sw1" value="Critical" />
        <add name="sw2" value="Information" />
    </switches>
</system.diagnostics>
```

Tracing Example with a Configuration File

The previous example of configuring tracing programmatically has been rewritten to leverage an application configuration file. The following code is the new source code for the application. The switch and collection code is removed from the source code and placed in a configuration file:

```
#define TRACE

using System;
using System.Diagnostics;

namespace Donis.CSharpBook {
    public class Starter {
        public static void Main() {

            TraceSource ts =
                new TraceSource("StarterTrace");
```

```
                ts.TraceEvent(TraceEventType.Start,
                    0, "Starting");

                ZClass obj1 = new ZClass();
                obj1.MethodA();
                obj1.MethodB(1,2,3);

                YClass obj2 = new YClass();
                obj2.MethodC();

                ZClass obj3 = new ZClass();
                obj1.MethodA();
                obj1.MethodB(4,5,6);


                ts.TraceEvent(TraceEventType.Stop,
                    0, "Stopping");

                obj1.Dispose();
                obj2.Dispose();

            }
        }

        public class ZClass: IDisposable {

            static ZClass() {
                ts = new TraceSource("ZTrace");
            }

            static private TraceSource ts;


            public void MethodA() {
                ts.TraceEvent(TraceEventType.Error,
                    GetHashCode(), "ZClass.MethodA");
            }

            public void MethodB(int parama, int paramb, int paramc) {
                ts.TraceData(TraceEventType.Critical,
                    GetHashCode(), "ZClass.MethodB",
                    parama, paramb, paramc);
            }

            public void Dispose() {
                ts.Flush();
                ts.Close();
            }
        }

        public class YClass: IDisposable {

            static YClass() {
                ts = new TraceSource("YTrace");
            }
```

```
    static private TraceSource ts;

    public void MethodC() {
        ts.TraceEvent(TraceEventType.Error,
            GetHashCode(), "YClass.MethodC");
    }

    public void Dispose() {
        ts.Flush();
        ts.Close();
    }
  }
}
```

The following configuration file sets up tracing for the application. The three trace sources share the same *Console* listener. The *YTrace* trace source also has an *XML* listener. The *XML* and *Console* listeners also record a date/time stamp with each trace. Otherwise, the results are essentially the same as the previous example using programmatic tracing:

```xml
<?xml version="1.0" encoding="utf-8" ?>
<configuration>
    <system.diagnostics>
        <sources>
            <source name="StarterTrace" switchName="sw3">
                <listeners>
                    <add name="cListener" />
                </listeners>
            </source>
            <source name="ZTrace" switchName="sw1">
                <listeners>
                    <add initializeData="data.txt"
                        type="System.Diagnostics.TextWriterTraceListener"
                        name="tListener" />
                    <add name="cListener" />
                </listeners>
            </source>
            <source name="YTrace" switchName="sw2">
                <listeners>
                    <add name="cListener" />
                    <add name="xListener" />
                </listeners>
            </source>
        </sources>
        <sharedListeners>
            <add initializeData="data.xml"
                type="System.Diagnostics.XmlWriterTraceListener"
                name="xListener" traceOutputOptions="DateTime" />
            <add type="System.Diagnostics.ConsoleTraceListener" name="cListener"
                traceOutputOptions="DateTime" />
        </sharedListeners>
        <switches>
            <add name="sw1" value="Information" />
            <add name="sw2" value="All" />
```

```
                <add name="sw3" value="ActivityTracing" />
        </switches>
    </system.diagnostics>
</configuration>
```

DebuggerDisplayAttribute

The *DebuggerDisplayAttribute* type is an attribute that controls how values are displayed in a debugger window. This attribute is valid for assembly, class, struct, enum, indexer, property, field, and delegate entities. You cannot use *DebuggerDisplayAttribute* on methods. When this attribute is used as an assembly-level attribute, the *Target* property must be assigned the name of the target type. The *DebuggerDisplayAttribute* type is found in the *System. Diagnostics* namespace.

The *DebuggerDisplayAttribute* type has a one-argument constructor. The single argument, which is a string, is the display value of the type in the Debug window. The value can contain an expression, which must be enclosed in curly braces: {*expression*}. Constants, static members, and instance members are valid in the expression. Prefix static members with the class name. The expression cannot contain pointers, aliases, or local variables.

The *DebuggerDisplayAttribute* type is inheritable. A derived class inherits the attribute from the base class. However, the derived class can redefine the *DebuggerDisplayAttribute* as required.

Figure 15-41 shows the values in a debug window for the *ZClass* and *YClass* instances without *DebuggerDisplayAttribute*.

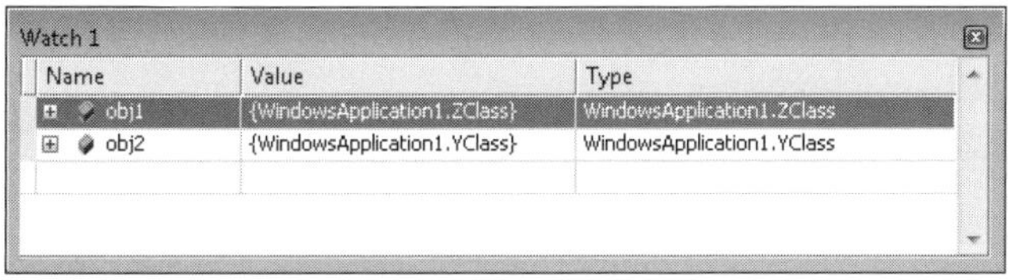

FIGURE 15-41 A view of the *ZClass* and *YClass* instances without *DebuggerDisplayAttribute* applied

The following code decorates the *ZClass* and *YClass* with the *DebuggerDisplayAttribute* type, shown in bold. *ZClass* is assigned the value *NewName*, which is overridden in the derived class. In addition, *ZClass.fielda* is adorned with a *DebuggerDisplayAttribute* attribute that contains an expression:

```
[DebuggerDisplay("NewName")]
class ZClass
{
    public static int test = 1;
    public virtual void MethodA()
    {
```

```
        int vara = 5, varb = 10;
        Console.WriteLine("{0} {1}", vara, varb);
    }

    public void MethodB()
    {
        Console.WriteLine("ZClass.MethodB");
        Console.WriteLine("ZClass.fielda {0}", fielda);
    }

    [DebuggerDisplay("fielda = {fielda}")]
    private int fielda = 5;
}

[DebuggerDisplay("DerivedName")]
class YClass : ZClass
{
    public override void MethodA()
    {
        Console.WriteLine("YClass.MethodA");
        Console.WriteLine("Fieldb: {0}", fieldb);
    }

    private int fieldb = 10;
}
```

Figure 15-42 shows the results of using the *DebuggerDisplayAttribute* type with *ZClass* and *YClass*.

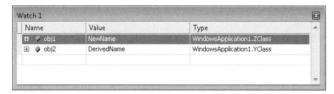

FIGURE 15-42 A view of *ZClass* and *YClass* instances with *DebuggerDisplayAttribute* applied

DebuggerBrowsableAttribute

Another debugger attribute is the *DebuggerBrowsableAttribute* type, which determines how a member is displayed in a debug window. This attribute is valid for properties, indexers, and fields.

DebuggerBrowsableAttribute has a one-argument constructor only. The parameter is the *DebuggableBrowsableState* enumeration. Table 15-21 lists the elements of the enumeration.

TABLE 15-21 *DebuggableBrowserState* **values**

Value	Description
Never	Hides the member in the Debug window.
Collapsed	Displays the member as collapsed.
RootHidden	Hides the root member but displays the child elements if the element is an array or a collection. For example, when applied to a property that is an integer array, the integer elements are displayed instead of the array itself.

Figure 15-43 shows the values for the *ZClass* and *YClass* types without the *DebuggerBrowsable Attribute* type.

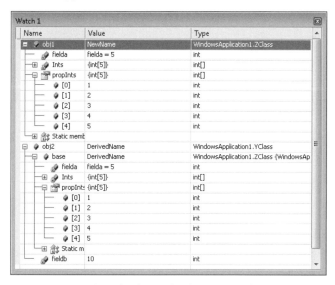

FIGURE 15-43 A view of *ZClass* and *YClass* types without *DebuggerBrowsableAttribute* applied

The following code shows the *ZClass* and *YClass* types decorated with *DebuggerBrowsable Attribute*, shown in bold. In *ZClass*, the array members related to the *propInts* property is displayed. In *YClass*, *fieldb* is hidden:

```
[DebuggerDisplay("NewName")]
class ZClass
{
    public static int test = 1;
    public virtual void MethodA()
    {
        int vara = 5, varb = 10;
        Console.WriteLine("{0} {1}", vara, varb);
    }

    public void MethodB()
    {
        Console.WriteLine("ZClass.MethodB");
```

```
            Console.WriteLine("ZClass.fielda {0}",
                fielda);
        }

    private int[] Ints = { 1, 2, 3, 4, 5 };
    [DebuggerBrowsable(DebuggerBrowsableState.RootHidden)]
    public int[] propInts
    {
        get
        {
            return Ints;
        }
    }

    private int fielda = 5;
}

[DebuggerDisplay("DerivedName")]
class YClass : ZClass
{
    public override void MethodA()
    {
        Console.WriteLine("YClass.MethodA");
        Console.WriteLine("Fieldb: {0}", fieldb);
    }

    [DebuggerBrowsable(DebuggerBrowsableState.Never)]
    private int fieldb = 10;
}
```

Figure 15-44 shows the results of using the *DebuggerBrowsableAttribute* type on *ZClass* and *YClass*. Elements of the *propInts* array are displayed directly and *fieldb* is no longer displayed.

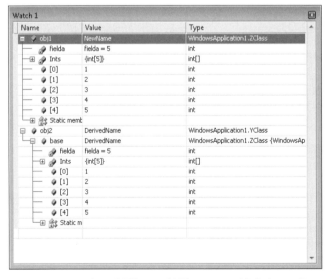

FIGURE 15-44 A view of *ZClass* and *YClass* types with *DebuggerBrowsableAttribute* applied

DebuggerTypeProxyAttribute

The *DebuggerTypeProxyAttribute* type assigns a display proxy for another type. The type proxy is displayed instead of the actual type in debug windows. The *DebuggerType ProxyAttribute* is an attribute that is valid for assembly, class, and struct constructs. When used at the assembly level, the target name property identifies the target type.

The proxy type must have a one-argument constructor that accepts an instance of the underlying type. For this reason, it is recommended that the proxy type be nested within the target type. This provides the proxy type constructor easy access to the instance of the surrounding object. Only public members of the proxy are visible in the debug window.

The *DebuggerTypeProxyAttribute* type is useful for hiding sensitive data from users. In the following code, *XClass* has a password field. This field should not be exposed during debugging because passwords are sensitive data. The *DebuggerTypeProxyAttribute* type in the sample code names *XClassDebug* as the proxy. *XClassDebug* hides the password field and displays an appropriate alternative value of *"Not Available"*.

Here is the code for *XClass* and the nested *XClassDebug* class, which is the proxy class:

```
[DebuggerTypeProxy(typeof(XClassDebug))]
public class XClass
{
    public XClass(string _password)
    {
        password = _password;
    }
    private string password;
    internal class XClassDebug
    {
        public XClassDebug(XClass obj)
        {
        }

        public string password = "Not Available";
    }
}
```

Dump Files

Visual Studio can open dump files created from managed, native, or mixed-mode applications. A *dump* is a snapshot of an application's memory that lets a developer debug an application postmortem. Dumps are particularly beneficial for debugging production applications. You can create a dump on a production machine and debug elsewhere without interfering with the production application. Several tools are available for creating a dump, including Windbg, Dr. Watson, Autodump+ (ADPlus), and Visual Studio. Visual Studio creates dumps for native applications, such as Microsoft Visual C++ applications, but not for managed applications. Dump files and other advanced debugging topics are discussed in Chapter 16.

In Visual Studio, dump files are opened as projects. Choose Solution/Project from the Open submenu of the File menu. Dump files usually have the *.dmp* extension. After opening the file, start a debugging session to examine the dump file. Remember that the Debug Start command on the Debug menu (which also can be invoked by pressing the F5 key) starts a debug session. You then can debug and diagnose the dump using the various debug windows. Figures 15-45 and 15-46 show the Call Stack and Modules debug windows, which provide different views of the dump.

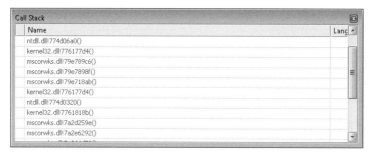

FIGURE 15-45 The Call Stack window for a dump

Modules						
Name	Path	Optimized	User Code	Symbol Status	Symbol File	
Store.exe	C:\Programming Visual C# 2005 T...	N/A	N/A	No native symb...		
ntdll.dll	C:\Windows\System32\ntdll.dll	N/A	N/A	Symbols not loade...		
mscoree.dll	C:\Windows\System32\mscoree.dll	N/A	N/A	Symbols not loade...		
kernel32.dll	C:\Windows\System32\kernel32.dll	N/A	N/A	Symbols not loade...		
advapi32.dll	C:\Windows\System32\advapi32.dll	N/A	N/A	Symbols not loade...		
rpcrt4.dll	C:\Windows\System32\rpcrt4.dll	N/A	N/A	Symbols not loade...		
shlwapi.dll	C:\Windows\System32\shlwapi.dll	N/A	N/A	Symbols not loade...		
gdi32.dll	C:\Windows\System32\gdi32.dll	N/A	N/A	Symbols not loade...		
user32.dll	C:\Windows\System32\user32.dll	N/A	N/A	Symbols not loade...		
msvcrt.dll	C:\Windows\System32\msvcrt.dll	N/A	N/A	Symbols not loade...		
imm32.dll	C:\Windows\System32\imm32.dll	N/A	N/A	Symbols not loade...		
msctf.dll	C:\Windows\System32\msctf.dll	N/A	N/A	Symbols not loade...		
lpk.dll	C:\Windows\System32\lpk.dll	N/A	N/A	Symbols not loade...		
usp10.dll	C:\Windows\System32\usp10.dll	N/A	N/A	Symbols not loade...		
comctl32.dll	C:\Windows\winsxs\x86_microsof...	N/A	N/A	Symbols not loade...		
mscorwks.dll	C:\Windows\Microsoft.NET\Fram...	N/A	N/A	Symbols not loade...		

FIGURE 15-46 The Modules window for a dump

Load the Son of Strike debugger extension (*SOS.DLL*) for a managed perspective of a dump. Load Son of Strike with the *.load sos* command in the Immediate window. You can then issue various Son of Strike commands, which are prefixed with an exclamation point (*!*). In Figure 15-47, Son of Strike is loaded. The DumpHeap command is invoked and the output is shown in the Immediate window.

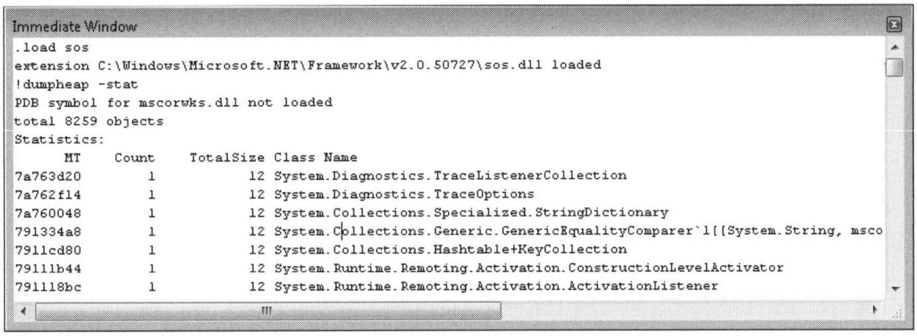

FIGURE 15-47 Son of Strike in the Immediate window

Advanced Debugging

The next chapter is about advanced debugging with tools other than Visual Studio. Most of these tools are available at the Debugging Tools for Windows Web site, which is located at *http://www.microsoft.com/whdc/DevTools/Debugging/default.mspx*. Windbg, the latest version of Son of Strike (*SOS.DLL*), and Auto-Dump Plus are three of the most valuable tools available at the Web site.

Windbg is a native and kernel debugger, which is used commonly by software support engineers to diagnose problems and by developers for advanced debugging. It supports live and postmortem debugging. Live debugging is performed by attaching the debugger to a running process. Postmortem analysis is done by examining dumps. With Windbg, you can examine memory, evaluate call stacks, set breakpoints, view thread states, and much more. SOS.DLL is a debugger extension that provides an interface for managed debugging. Son of Strike can be used in Windbg and Visual Studio 2008, as discussed earlier in this chapter.

Mdbg is the new managed debugger. As the dedicated managed debugger, it has capabilities that are not found in either Visual Studio or the Windbg debugger. Mdbg is also introduced in the next chapter.

Chapter 16
Advanced Debugging

Successful debugging is about asking the correct questions. Many (but not all) of those questions can be answered with the Microsoft Visual Studio Debugger. Some questions require the use of advanced debugging tools to find the answer. If an application deadlocks, what are the outstanding synchronization objects? When there is a memory leak, how much native memory has been allocated, compared to managed memory? Is a memory leak associated with a particular generation or with the large object heap? These and other questions cannot be answered by the Visual Studio Debugger, but they might be essential to resolving a problem quickly.

Effective debugging often is about having the correct tools. The .NET Framework includes a variety of debugging tools, such as the Son of Strike (SOS) debugging extension (SOS.dll), DbgClr, and CorDbg. Installing Visual Studio provides Spy++, Dependency Walker, OLE Viewer, and many other basic tools. Finally, a host of debugging tools can be downloaded from the Debugging Tools for Windows Web site (*http://www.microsoft.com/whdc/devtools/debugging*). WinDbg, Adplus, and GFlags are probably the most commonly used debugging tools available from this site. The tools at this site are updated periodically, and new versions should be downloaded on occasion. Finally, the Reliability and Performance Monitor and Windows Task Manager are distributed with the Microsoft Windows environment.

These tools are not intended to replace the Visual Studio Debugger. The first rule of debugging is to employ lightweight debugging before resorting to the heavy arsenal. The Visual Studio Debugger is ideal for initial debugging. As part of the Visual Studio Integrated Development Environment (IDE), the Visual Studio debugger is more convenient than WinDbg, offers a familiar user interface, and has superior documentation. Lightweight debugging consists of checking for uninitialized variables or parameters, errant loop counters, logic errors, and other basic problems. These items are most often the cause of simple bugs versus more dramatic circumstances.

The goal of debugging is to resolve abnormal error conditions. Program hangs, crashes, memory leaks, and unhandled exceptions are possible error conditions. Some abnormal conditions, primarily logic errors, do not generate exceptional events. For example, a program that reports incorrect results has a bug. It might not be as intrusive as an exception, but it is a bug nonetheless.

Debugging is conducted in three phases: discovery, analysis, and testing. The *discovery phase* is when data on the problem is gathered. During this stage, you can capture the state of the application in a dump or perform live debugging. The *analysis phase* is when the abnormal condition is diagnosed using the results of the discovery phase. The *testing phase* validates the analysis phase and later validates the solution. Debugging is an iterative process. Based on the results of the testing phase, further discovery, analysis, and testing could be required.

Debugging can be invasive or noninvasive. For applications that should not be interrupted, noninvasive debugging, such as debugging production applications, is preferred. The advantage of noninvasive debugging is that the debuggee is not affected by the debugging process. Invasive debugging provides additional data and flexibility, but invasive debugging should be limited to the development environment.

You can debug running applications (live debugging) or perform postmortem analysis using a dump. With live debugging, breakpoints are essential. When a breakpoint is hit, you then can step through the application to verify program logic, monitor local variables, inspect the heap, watch the call stack, and perform other tasks. The opposite of live debugging is postmortem analysis. Postmortem analysis has some advantages over live debugging. You can create a dump and then debug at your convenience. Because a dump is a static snap-shot, it preserves the history of a problem. But it also has some disadvantages. It is harder to pose future-tense questions with postmortem analysis. For example, what is the call stack after a future operation is performed? What is the effect of future iterations of a *for* loop? What is the impact of changing the value of a local variable? How is native memory trending versus managed memory? Finding these kinds of answers from a single dump is difficult.

Debugging a production application is different from debugging the debug build of an application. First, the constraints are not the same. The priority for debugging a production application is often to minimize downtime. For example, with a high-traffic retail Web site, the primary concern of the company might be lost revenue. Second, the production machine might lack debugging resources, such as symbols, source code, and debugging tools. This could make it difficult to debug the production application locally. Third, re-creating the abnormal condition could be problematic. Load factors, memory stress, and other conditions common to the production server could be hard to replicate in a developer environment. This could make it difficult to reproduce the problem consistently. Fourth, accessibility might be an issue. The production application might be offsite, in a locked server closet, or in some otherwise inconvenient location. This might necessitate remote debugging, which could entail setup and possible trust issues between machines. Finally, production applications are typically release builds with optimizations, which can make debugging less transparent. Conversely, debug builds normally are not optimized, but they are easier to debug.

This chapter presents different versions of the Store application. Each version demonstrates a different aspect of debugging. The Store application is included with the companion content for the book posted on the Web.

DebuggableAttribute Attribute

Just-in-time (JIT) optimizations are controlled by the *DebuggableAttribute* attribute. The *DebuggableAttribute* type contains the *IsJITOptimizerDisabled* and *IsJITTrackingEnabled* properties, which control JIT optimizations. If *IsJITOptimizerDisabled* is true, code is not optimized for release. If *IsJITTrackingEnabled* is true, the Common Language Runtime (CLR) tracks information that is helpful for debugging.

Configuring JIT optimizations, as discussed next, can aid in debugging a production (release version) application that is optimized for execution. Create an initialization file for the release application that sets optimization for debugging. The initialization file must be in the same directory as the application and named *application*.ini, where *application* is the name of the executable file. The initialization file has two entries in the .NET Framework Debugging Control section for optimizations. The *GenerateTrackingInfo* entry enables or disables tracking information. The *AllowOptimize* entry controls code optimization. In the initialization file, 1 is true and 0 is false. The following is an initialization file that disables both JIT optimizations:

```
[.NET Framework Debugging Control]
GenerateTrackingInfo=1
AllowOptimize=0
```

Problems that occur in a release version of a product sometimes might disappear in a debug build and vice versa. Optimizations can alter the resulting application subtly. These differences can cause the debug and the release versions to behave differently. An abnormal condition in a production application might disappear mysteriously in a debug version. This is a frustrating but not uncommon circumstance. For this reason, test extensively both the debug and the release versions of the product.

Debuggers

As mentioned, there are several useful tools for debugging managed applications. The following list is a compilation of some of these tools. (This list does not include third-party tools.)

- **Visual Studio Debugger**   The Visual Studio Debugger is part of the Visual Studio 2008 IDE. Most Windows developers have some experience with this tool from product development. Lightweight debugging usually starts with the Visual Studio Debugger.

- **Managed Debugger (MDbg)**   This tool is a console debugger dedicated to managed debugging. It has a variety of commands and options that are specific to managed code. You can download the MDbg project from the Microsoft download Web site (*http://www.microsoft.com/downloads*). There is a graphic user interface (GUI) extension available for MDbg that also can be downloaded. It provides a user-friendly veneer to MDbg.

- **CLR Debugger (DbgClr)**   DbgClr is another dedicated managed debugger and an abbreviated version of the Visual Studio Debugger. It has the familiar Visual Studio interface, but it supports only the debugging features. This tool is distributed with the .NET Framework. DbgClr is particularly useful on production machines where Visual Studio might not be installed but the .NET Framework is present. DbgClr is limited in some ways and does not support remote or mixed-mode debugging.

- **Performance Monitor**   The Performance Monitor portion of the Reliability and Performance Monitor instruments a live application. It can plot a host of data points onto a variety of graphs and reports. Results also can be stored in log files for later examination. The complete tool is distributed with the Windows Vista and Windows Server 2008 operating systems.

- **Windows Console Debugger (CDB)**   CDB is both a kernel- and user-mode debugger. Download CDB from the Debugging Tools for Windows Web site. For managed debugging capabilities, load the SOS debugger extension (SOS.dll) into CDB.

- **Windows Debugger (WinDbg)**   Like CDB, WinDbg is a kernel-mode and user-mode debugger. This tool provides a user interface to CDB. For this reason, the commands of CDB and WinDbg are the same. WinDbg is a native debugger. To debug managed applications, load Son of Strike (SOS.dll) into WinDbg. You can download WinDbg from the Debugging Tools for Windows Web site.

- **ADPlus (ADPlus.vbs)**   This text file is a Visual Basic script that automates common CDB tasks, such as creating dumps. This is another tool that can be downloaded at the Debugging Tools for Windows Web site.

- **Son of Strike (SOS.dll)**   SOS.dll is a debugging extension that has commands for debugging managed applications. This tool is distributed with the .NET Framework and is downloadable from the Debugging Tools for Windows Web site. Installing Visual Studio or the .NET Framework also installs SOS.dll. Therefore, there might be multiple SOS.dll files on your machine. Download the most recent version from the Debugging Tool for Windows Web site.

Managed Debugger (MDbg)

MDbg is a user-mode debugger for managed applications. It does not support native or mixed-mode debugging. Because MDbg focuses on managed code, it offers a unique repertoire of debugging commands that are specific to managed code. It is also a console debugger, which supersedes the Runtime Debugger (CorDbg), the previous console debugger for managed applications.

MDbg and CorDbg share many of the same commands. This makes the transition from CorDbg to MDbg easier. However, MDbg commands are different from those of WinDbg and

SOS. For developers who switch among these three tools frequently, leveraging the benefits of each, the nonstandardization of the public interface of these tools can be frustrating. For example, those three tools have three distinct commands to display a call stack. In WinDbg, you have the *k* commands, such as *k*, *kb*, and *kp*. SOS offers the *!clrstack* command. Of the three, MDbg has the least intuitive name for a stack trace command, which is the *w* (for *where*) command.

The following example demonstrates many of the unique features of MDbg. As mentioned, store.exe is the demonstration application used for examples throughout this chapter. In this application, you enter sales transactions. To add a transaction, enter the number of transactions in the # of Transactions text box and then click Add Transactions. The default number of transactions is 1. The Transaction dialog box, where you enter information about the transaction, appears next. When you accept the transaction, the transaction is added to the list of existing transactions. The Store application is shown in Figure 16-1. This example assumes that you have downloaded and built the MDbg project from the Microsoft download Web site.

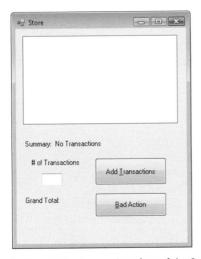

FIGURE 16-1 The user interface of the Store application

MDbg Example

MDbg has the normal assortment of commands common to any debugger: show threads, display the call stack, list local variables, and so on. However, it also has unique commands that target managed code. For example, you can create instances of managed objects and invoke managed functions. You can seed an application with classes and functions that are used exclusively during a debugging session. Otherwise, they are not called during normal execution. The Store application has a *MyDebug* class that exists solely for debugging. *MyDebug.Reset* is a static method and is the sole member of the *MyDebug* class. The *Reset* method resets the Store application and deletes the current transactions. The *MyDebug* class and *Reset* method are a normal class and method. There are no hooks in them that are especially designed for the debugger. This is the *MyDebug* class:

```
public class MyDebug
{
    public static void Reset()
    {
        Form1.formItems.Clear();
        Form1.formListBox.Items.Clear();
        Form1.formMessage.Text = "Grand Total:";
        Form1.formSummary.Text = "Summary: No Transactions";
        Console.WriteLine("Application reset.");
    }
}
```

Follow these steps to experiment with using the *MyDebug* class:

1. Start the demonstration by running the Store application in the Mdbg subfolder and adding two or more transactions.

2. Start MDbg.

3. Display the active processes with the *pro(cessnum)* command. The command lists the process identifier, executable, and domain of each process. The Store application is included in the list:

    ```
    mdbg> proc
    Active processes on current machine:
    (PID: 1232) C:\mdbg\bin\Debug\Store.exe
            (ID: 1) Store.exe
    (PID: 2084) C:\mdbg\bin\Debug\Store.vshost.exe
            (ID: 1) Store.vshost.exe
    (PID: 3788) C:\Program Files\Microsoft Visual Studio 9.0\Common7\IDE\devenv.exe
            (ID: 1) DefaultDomain
    ```

4. The *a(ttach)* command attaches MDbg to a running application. The prompt will change to indicate that you have started a debugging session. After attaching to the Store application, the debugger immediately interrupts the program:

    ```
    mdbg> a 2812
    [p#:0, t#:0] mdbg>
    ```

5. How is the *Reset* method seen in the debugger? Knowing that answer would help in calling that method. The *x* command can display functions in a module. The basic *x* command lists all the modules in an application. List the modules:

    ```
    mdbg> a 1232
    [p#:1, t#:0] mdbg> x
    Please specify module.
    Loaded Modules:
     :0      mscorlib.dll#0  (no symbols loaded)
     :1      Store.exe#0
    ```

```
:2      System.Windows.Forms.dll#0  (no symbols loaded)
:3      System.dll#0  (no symbols loaded)
:4      System.Drawing.dll#0  (no symbols loaded)
:5      System.Configuration.dll#0  (no symbols loaded)
:6      System.Xml.dll#0  (no symbols loaded)
```

6. Module ":1" is store.exe. With that knowledge, the functions in that module can be listed using the *x* command again, this time with the ":1" parameter. This should show the *Reset* method:

```
[p#:1, t#:0] mdbg> x :1
~0. Store.Item..ctor()
~1. Store.Item.get_Products()
~2. Store.Item.set_Products(value)
~3. Store.Item.get_ItemId()
~4. Store.Item.Dispose()
~5. Store.Item..cctor()
~6. Store.Transaction.Dispose(disposing)
~7. Store.Transaction.InitializeComponent()
~8. Store.Transaction..ctor()
~9. Store.Transaction.btnAdd_Click(sender,e)
~10. Store.Transaction.chkComputer_CheckedChanged(sender,e)
~11. Store.Transaction.chkLaptop_CheckedChanged(sender,e)
~12. Store.Transaction.chkPrinter_CheckedChanged(sender,e)
~13. Store.Transaction.chkSoftware_CheckedChanged(sender,e)
~14. Store.Transaction.get_newItem()
~15. Store.Transaction.btnCancel_Click(sender,e)
~16. Store.Program.Main()
~17. Store.Form1..ctor()
~18. Store.Form1.get_formItems()
~19. Store.Form1.get_formMessage()
~20. Store.Form1.get_formSummary()
~21. Store.Form1.get_formListBox()
~22. Store.Form1.btnTransaction_Click(sender,e)
~23. Store.Form1.btnBad_Click(sender,e)
~24. Store.Form1.Dispose(disposing)
~25. Store.Form1.InitializeComponent()
~26. Store.Form1..cctor()
~27. Store.Properties.Resources..ctor()
~28. Store.Properties.Resources.get_ResourceManager()
~29. Store.Properties.Resources.get_Culture()
~30. Store.Properties.Resources.set_Culture(value)
~31. Store.MyDebug.Reset()
~32. Store.MyDebug..ctor()
~33. Store.Properties.Settings.get_Default()
~34. Store.Properties.Settings..ctor()
~35. Store.Properties.Settings..cctor()
[p#:1, t#:0] mdbg>
```

7. The *Store.MyDebug.Reset* method is found towards the bottom of the list. *Store* is the namespace, *MyDebug* is the class, and *Reset* is the method. The next time a transaction is added, we want to call this method to reset the application, which deletes existing transactions. The button-click handler for adding transactions is *Store.Form1.btnTransaction_Click*, which also is found in the preceding list. Set a breakpoint on this method

and resume the Store application. The *b(reakpoint)* command sets breakpoints, and the *g(o)* command resumes an interrupted application:

```
[p#:0, t#:0] mdbg> b Store.Form1.btnTransaction_Click
Breakpoint #1 bound (Store.Form1::btnTransaction_Click(+0))
[p#:0, t#:0] mdbg> g
```

8. Click Add Transaction in the Store application. The breakpoint is hit, and the MDbg debugger interrupts the application. The source line where the program is interrupted is displayed. We no longer need this breakpoint. The *b* command without parameters lists all breakpoints. Using information displayed by the *b* command, you can delete a breakpoint with the *del(ete)* command:

```
STOP: Breakpoint 1 Hit
64:         {
[p#:0, t#:0] mdbg> b
Current breakpoints:
Breakpoint #1 bound (Store.Form1::btnTransaction_Click(+0))
[p#:0, t#:0] mdbg> del 1
```

9. We could use the *newo(bj)* command to create a new instance of a class. However, *Reset* is a static method and does not require an instance. The method is called directly on the class. Invoke the method with the *f(unceval)* command:

```
[p#:0, t#:0] mdbg> f Store.MyDebug.Reset
STOP EvalComplete
```

10. Resume the Store application with the *g* command and the application should have no transactions. Enter a new transaction in the dialog box.

Here is a second demonstration of the MDbg debugger. This example highlights exception management. When a second-chance exception is raised in a debuggee, MDbg does not intercede and the application will crash. This is contrary to the behavior of most debuggers, which would trap the second-chance exception. At your discretion, you can request that MDbg catch second-chance exceptions.

1. Restart the Store application.

2. Attach MDbg to the application and resume the program.

3. Click Bad Action. As advertised, a bad action occurs, which is an unhandled exception. An error dialog box will appear for the second-chance exception. From this dialog box, terminate the application. The Bad Action button handler, shown here, is not particularly creative in generating an exception:

```
private void btnBad_Click(object sender, EventArgs e)
{
    int a = 5, b = 0;
    ++a;
    a /= 2;
    a /= b;
}
```

4. Restart the Store application.

5. Attach the MDbg debugger.

6. Ask the MDbg debugger to catch all second-chance exceptions with the *ca(tch)*
   ex(ception) command:

   ```
   [p#:0, t#:0] mdbg> ca ex
   ```

7. Resume the application and then click Bad Action. This time, the exception is trapped in
   MDbg. In the debugger, the exception type and the properties of the current exception
   object are displayed, providing important information on the exception. The source
   code line where the exception occurred also is displayed. You now have plenty of
   information to debug the problem:

   ```
   [p#:0, t#:0] mdbg> g
   STOP: Exception thrown
   Exception=System.DivideByZeroException
           _className=<null>
           _exceptionMethod=<null>
           _exceptionMethodString=<null>
           _message="Attempted to divide by zero."
           _data=<null>
           _innerException=<null>
           _helpURL=<null>
           _stackTrace=array [24]
           _stackTraceString=<null>
           _remoteStackTraceString=<null>
           _remoteStackIndex=0
           _dynamicMethods=<null>
           _HResult=-2147352558
           _source=<null>
           _xptrs=1240048
           _xcode=-1073741676
   134:          a /= b;
   ```

MDbg Commands

MDbg has a full complement of commands for debugging managed applications. Some
of the commands were demonstrated in the previous examples. Table 16-1 lists the MDbg
commands.

TABLE 16-1 MDbg commands

Command	Description
? or h(elp)	Displays MDbg commands with brief descriptions.
ap(rocess)	Changes the context to another managed process, which also is being debugged. MDbg can debug multiple applications simultaneously. Without parameters, the command displays all processes in the current debugging session.
a(ttach)	Attaches the MDbg debugger to a managed process. Without parameters, the command lists the available managed processes.

TABLE 16-1 MDbg commands

Command	Description
b(reak)	Sets a specific breakpoint or displays all the breakpoints.
ca(tch)	Stipulates which events to catch, such as an exception. It also can display events.
conf(ig)	Sets a particular configuration or displays the configuration options.
del(ete)	Deletes a breakpoint.
de(tach)	Detaches the debugger from the current application.
d(own)	Moves the current stack frame down.
echo	Echoes text to the console.
ex(it) or q(uit)	Exits the debugger.
fo(reach)	Executes an action on all threads.
f(unceval)	Calls a method.
g(o)	Resumes execution of an interrupted application.
ig(nore)	Displays events or sets events to ignore. Complements the ca(tch) command.
int(ercept)	Intercepts exceptions at the specified stack frame.
k(ill)	Kills a process.
l(ist)	Lists loaded modules, application domains, or assemblies.
lo(ad)	Loads a debugging extension.
mo(de)	Sets a specific MDbg option or displays all the options.
newo(bj)	Creates an instance of a type.
n(ext)	Steps over the next instruction.
o(ut)	Steps out of a function.
pa(th)	Sets or displays the source path.
p(rint)	Displays the values of the local variables.
pro(cessenum)	Lists active managed processes.
re(sume)	Resumes a suspended thread.
r(un)	Runs a program and immediately attaches MDbg.
set	Sets a local variable to a new value.
setip	Moves the instruction pointer. (The move must be within the current function.)
sh(ow)	Shows the source code at the current instruction.
s(tep)	Steps into a function.
su(spend)	Suspends a running thread.
sy(mbol)	Sets or displays the symbol path.
t(hread)	Switches to a specified thread or displays all threads.
u(p)	Moves the current stack frame up.
uwgc(handle)	Displays the object referenced by the GCHandle.
when	Executes a command when a debugger event occurs.

TABLE 16-1 MDbg commands

Command	Description
w(here)	Displays the call stack.
x	Displays the symbols in a module or lists all the modules.
Ctrl+C	This keystroke interrupts the running application to which MDbg is attached.
Ctrl+Break	This keystroke terminates the running application and exits the debugger.

WinDbg

WinDbg is both a kernel-mode and user-mode debugger. It is pronounced *Wind-bag, Win-d-b-g,* or, more descriptively, *Win-Debug.* For many developers and support engineers, WinDbg is the center of the advanced debugging universe. It has been available for some time and has evolved to encompass an impressive assortment of commands. Learning WinDbg requires a small commitment of time, but it can help you solve even the most complex debugging problems.

The focus of this book is C# and managed code. For this reason, this book is not the ideal place to explore the depths of WinDbg. However, knowing some basic WinDbg commands is helpful even when debugging managed applications.

Basic WinDbg Commands

When WinDbg is started, you can attach the debugger to an existing application with command-line arguments. Doing this requires the process identifier (PID) of the target application. Tlist is a utility installed with Debugging Tools for Windows. This tool lists the process identifier of active processes.

The following is sample output from the Tlist utility. Applications are listed in execution sequence. The first column is the process identifier, the second column is the program, and the final column contains the title bar information or description, if available:

```
C:\store>tlist
   0 System Process
   4 System
 784 smss.exe
 844 csrss.exe
 872 winlogon.exe
 916 services.exe
 928 lsass.exe
 936 KHALMNPR.exe         KHALHPP_MainWindow
1052 gcasDtServ.exe       GIANT AntiSpyware Data Service
1444 DVDRAMSV.exe
1488 inetinfo.exe
1524 mdm.exe
```

```
1748 sqlservr.exe
1828 nvsvc32.exe        NVSVCPMMWindowClass
1440 wscntfy.exe
2380 iPodService.exe
2620 alg.exe
3384 iTunes.exe         iTunes
3648 WINWORD.EXE        MarshallChap14_0830 - Microsoft Word
2892 cmd.exe            Visual Studio 2008 Command Prompt - tlist
2572 Store.exe          Store
2696 tlist.exe
```

Use the PID from the Tlist command to attach to a process. WinDbg uses the *–p* command-line option to attach an application with identifier given PID:

```
windbg -p 2572
```

You also can attach to a running process simply with the application name. If more than one instance of the process is running, an error is reported and the attach fails:

```
windbg -pn store.exe
```

You can start WinDbg and then attach to an application. From the File menu, select the Attach To A Process command. Choose the target application from the list of available and active processes. Alternatively, you can start and debug an application. The Open Executable command on the File menu starts an application and immediately attaches the debugger. This is convenient if the application is not running already.

When using WinDbg, some essential commands are helpful. Most of the WinDbg commands are not case-sensitive—check the documentation for confirmation. Table 16-2 lists the basic commands in WinDbg.

TABLE 16-2 Basic WinDbg commands

Command	Description
g(o)	If in break mode, resumes execution of a debugged application.
Ctrl+Break	Interrupts the running application. The application changes from running to break mode.
q(uit)	Quits the WinDbg debugger.
?	Displays help documentation.

Now that the basic commands have been presented, we can discuss the more interesting commands.

Displaying the active threads and changing thread context is commonly useful. In WinDbg, the tilde (_) command is for thread management.

■ The command without parameters lists all the threads. The thread identifier, status, and address of the thread environment block are some of the information presented for each thread. The current thread is prefixed with a dot (.). The pound sign (#) prefixes the thread that raised an exception (if any) that interrupted the attached application.

- The _*n* command, where *n* is the thread number, displays information on the specified thread instead of all the threads.

- The _*ns* command changes the current thread and context. The WinDbg prompt is updated to reflect the current thread. Some commands, such as the stack trace command, display information based on the current thread. After selecting a different thread, the register values of that thread are displayed.

The following demonstration lists all the threads, displays information pertaining to Thread 2, and then sets Thread 3 as the current thread:

```
0:001> ~
   0  Id: a1c.9c0 Suspend: 1 Teb: 7ffde000 Unfrozen
.  1  Id: a1c.804 Suspend: 1 Teb: 7ffdd000 Unfrozen
   2  Id: a1c.ea0 Suspend: 1 Teb: 7ffdc000 Unfrozen
   3  Id: a1c.de0 Suspend: 1 Teb: 7ffdb000 Unfrozen
#  4  Id: a1c.c04 Suspend: 1 Teb: 7ffda000 Unfrozen
0:001> ~2
   2  Id: a1c.ea0 Suspend: 1 Teb: 7ffdc000 Unfrozen
      Start: mscorwks!Thread::intermediateThreadProc (79ee80cf)
      Priority: 2  Priority class: 32
0:001> ~3s
eax=4ec62ef0 ebx=0103fe7c ecx=0000d9c7 edx=7c90eb94 esi=00000000 edi=7ffdf000
eip=7c90eb94 esp=0103fe54 ebp=0103fef0 iopl=0         nv up ei pl zr na po nc
cs=001b  ss=0023  ds=0023  es=0023  fs=003b  gs=0000              efl=00000246
ntdll!KiFastSystemCallRet:
7c90eb94 c3              ret
```

Stack Trace Commands

The stack trace commands present views of the native call stack, which is invaluable when debugging. Even with managed code, viewing the unmanaged call stack can be informative. In WinDbg, variations of the *k* command display the call stack with different information or a different level of detail. A stack trace listing can be quite long. To minimize this problem, you can follow a stack trace command with a number, which limits the depth of the call stack.

Table 16-3 details the common stack trace commands.

TABLE 16-3 Stack trace commands

Command	Description
k	Lists the methods on the call stack. In addition, the pointer to the child frame and function return address of the calling method is listed. No parameters are displayed.
kb	Lists the call stack with the first three arguments of each method.

TABLE 16-3 **Stack trace commands**

Command	Description
kP	Lists the call stack and all the parameters of each method. This command is case-sensitive.
kn	Lists the call stack and the frame number for each method. You can use the frame information to move between frames on the call stack using the .frame directive. This is sometimes useful for such actions as viewing local variables that would be out of scope otherwise.

The following command lists the call stack from a thread in the Store application. The *kb* command lists the first three arguments of each method:

```
0:003> kb
ChildEBP RetAddr  Args to Child
0103fe50 7c90e9ab 7c8094f2 00000002 0103fe7c ntdll!KiFastSystemCallRet
0103fe54 7c8094f2 00000002 0103fe7c 00000001 ntdll!ZwWaitForMultipleObjects+0xc
0103fef0 77d495f9 00000002 0103ff18 00000000 KERNEL32!WaitForMultipleObjectsEx+0x12c
0103ff4c 77d496a8 00000001 0103ffac ffffffff USER32!RealMsgWaitForMultipleObjectsEx+0x13e
0103ff68 4ec95846 00000001 0103ffac 00000000 USER32!MsgWaitForMultipleObjects+0x1f
0103ffb4 7c80b50b 00000000 00000000 0012e0d0 gdiplus!BackgroundThreadProc+0x59
0103ffec 00000000 4ec957ed 00000000 00000000 KERNEL32!BaseThreadStart+0x37
```

What if you want the stack trace of every thread? Each thread could be selected individually and then the *k* command issued for each one. However, that approach becomes tedious if there are more than a few threads. The solution is to use "~*". Commands prefixed with "~*" are applied to all threads of the application. This command lists the call stack for every thread:

```
~* k
```

Display Memory Commands

Displaying raw memory is often useful when debugging. The *d* command is the basic display memory command. There are variants on the *d* command that format memory differently. Memory commands display rows and columns of data. Rows begin with a memory address. This is the starting address for the contiguous memory displayed on that row. The memory is organized in row order. By default, bytes are shown in two-byte columns. As an option, the final column is the text translation of the current row.

This is a typical display of memory:

```
0:003> d 0103fe50
0103fe50  cc 33 66 00 ab e9 90 7c-f2 94 80 7c 02 00 00 00  .3f....|...|....
0103fe60  7c fe 03 01 01 00 00 00-00 00 00 00 00 00 00 00  |..............
0103fe70  00 00 00 00 02 00 00 00-00 00 00 00 94 06 00 00  ..............
0103fe80  8c 06 00 00 cc 99 99 00-cc 99 cc 00 cc 99 ff 00  ..............
0103fe90  cc cc 00 00 cc cc 33 00-cc cc 66 00 14 00 00 00  ......3...f.....
```

```
0103fea0  01 00 00 00 00 00 00 00-00 00 00 00 10 00 00 00   ................
0103feb0  cc ff 66 00 cc ff 99 00-cc ff cc 00 00 b0 fd 7f   ..f.............
0103fec0  00 c0 fd 7f ff 00 33 00-00 00 00 00 7c fe 03 01   ......3.....|...
```

Here is the general syntax of the display memory commands:

dL address1 address2

The second letter (*L*) of the display memory command indicates the specific command, such as *dc*, *dd*, and *du*, which is case-sensitive. The *address1* parameter is the beginning address and *address2* is the ending address. Memory is displayed from *address1* to *address2*. Omit the ending address, and a default number of bytes are displayed. The default is set from the previous command. If neither the beginning nor the ending memory address is provided, memory is displayed from the current address.

Table 16-4 lists some of the commands that display memory.

TABLE 16-4 Common display memory commands

Command	Description
d	Repeats the previous display command. It defaults to the *db* command.
da	Displays memory with ASCII text translation.
db	Displays memory within a stated range.
dc	Displays memory in four-byte columns.
dd	Same as *dc*, but with no text translation.
du	Displays memory with Unicode text translation.

The following command displays memory in three columns of four-byte data. The */c* option sets the number of columns:

```
0:003> dd /c 3 0103fe50
0103fe50  006633cc 7c90e9ab 7c8094f2
0103fe5c  00000002 0103fe7c 00000001
0103fe68  00000000 00000000 00000000
0103fe74  00000002 00000000 00000694
0103fe80  0000068c 009999cc 00cc99cc
0103fe8c  00ff99cc 0000cccc 0033cccc
0103fe98  0066cccc 00000014 00000001
0103fea4  00000000 00000000 00000010
0103feb0  0066ffcc 0099ffcc 00ccffcc
0103febc  7ffdb000 7ffdc000 003300ff
0103fec8  00000000 0103fe7c
```

Breakpoint Memory Commands

In WinDbg, you can set a variety of breakpoints, such as memory address, source location, data, and event. The breakpoint commands are detailed in Table 16-5.

TABLE 16-5 Breakpoint commands

Command	Description
bp	This is the basic breakpoint command, where the program is interrupted when execution reaches the specified location.
	Here is the syntax for the *bp* command:
	`bp location options`
	There are several options. For example, the */1* option is useful for defining one-time breakpoints. This type of breakpoint is removed automatically after being hit. This is similar to the Run To Cursor command in Visual Studio.
ba	This command breaks on access to a memory address.
	Here is the basic syntax for the *ba* command:
	`ba options size address`
	Options include which action to break on:
	■ *e* – execute
	■ *r* – read/write
	■ *w* – write
	■ *i* – input/output
	The *size* element gives the width of the memory address.
bc	This command clears a breakpoint. You can clear multiple breakpoints in a space-delimited or comma-delimited list. Alternatively, specify a range with a hyphen.
bl	This command lists the set breakpoints.

The following is a demonstration of the breakpoint command (bp). The *sxe* command is the set exception command. This command requests that the debugger interrupt on an exception or other event, which is similar to a breakpoint. In this example, the *sxe* command instructs the debugger to interrupt when the *mscorwks* module is loaded, which is where the CLR is found. For a compound statement in WinDbg, use a semicolon. In the following command, the *sxe* and *g* commands are combined into a compound statement.

The following command asks the debugger to break on a *mscorwks* module load event (the application then resumes):

```
0:000> sxe ld mscorwks;g
ModLoad: 77dd0000 77e6b000   C:\WINDOWS\system32\ADVAPI32.dll
ModLoad: 77e70000 77f01000   C:\WINDOWS\system32\RPCRT4.dll
ModLoad: 77f60000 77fd6000   C:\WINDOWS\system32\SHLWAPI.dll
ModLoad: 77f10000 77f56000   C:\WINDOWS\system32\GDI32.dll
ModLoad: 77d40000 77dd0000   C:\WINDOWS\system32\USER32.dll
ModLoad: 77c10000 77c68000   C:\WINDOWS\system32\msvcrt.dll
ModLoad: 76390000 763ad000   C:\WINDOWS\system32\IMM32.DLL
ModLoad: 629c0000 629c9000   C:\WINDOWS\system32\LPK.DLL
ModLoad: 74d90000 74dfb000   C:\WINDOWS\system32\USP10.dll
ModLoad: 79e70000 7a3cf000   C:\WINDOWS\Microsoft.NET\Framework\v2.0.50727\mscorwks.dll
```

```
eax=00000000 ebx=00000000 ecx=009f0000 edx=7c90eb94 esi=00000000 edi=00000000
eip=7c90eb94 esp=0012f1c0 ebp=0012f2b4 iopl=0         nv up ei ng nz ac po nc
cs=001b  ss=0023  ds=0023  es=0023  fs=003b  gs=0000             efl=00000296
ntdll!KiFastSystemCallRet:
7c90eb94 c3              ret
```

The following compound command sets a breakpoint on the *ExecuteMainMethod* method and then continues execution. You must have properly configured symbols for this command to work. (See the section "Symbols," later in this chapter, for more information.)

```
0:000> bp mscorwks!SystemDomain::ExecuteMainMethod;g
ModLoad: 78130000 781ca000   C:\WINDOWS\Microsoft.NET\Framework\v2.0.50727\MSVCR80.dll
ModLoad: 7c9c0000 7d1d4000   C:\WINDOWS\system32\shell32.dll
ModLoad: 773d0000 774d2000   C:\WINDOWS\WinSxS\x86_Microsoft.Windows.Common-Controls_
6595b64144ccf1df_6.0.2600.2180_x-ww_a84f1ff9\comctl32.dll
ModLoad: 5d090000 5d127000   C:\WINDOWS\system32\comctl32.dll
ModLoad: 60340000 60348000   C:\WINDOWS\Microsoft.NET\Framework\v2.0.50727\culture.dll
ModLoad: 790c0000 79baa000   C:\WINDOWS\assembly\NativeImages_v2.0.50727_32\mscorlib\
cee6ddb471db1c489d9b4c39549861b5\mscorlib.ni.dll
Breakpoint 0 hit
eax=0012ff38 ebx=00000002 ecx=00000000 edx=ffffffff esi=00000000 edi=00000000
eip=79efb428 esp=0012ff1c ebp=0012ff68 iopl=0         nv up ei pl nz na pe nc
cs=001b  ss=0023  ds=0023  es=0023  fs=003b  gs=0000             efl=00000202
mscorwks!SystemDomain::ExecuteMainMethod:
79efb428 55              push    ebp
```

After the breakpoint is hit, the *kb* command performs a stack trace, as shown here. You see *ExecuteMainMethod* is at the top of the call stack:

```
0:000> kb
ChildEBP RetAddr  Args to Child
0012ff18 79efb3cb 00400000 00000000 b4ebfe93 mscorwks!SystemDomain::ExecuteMainMethod
0012ff68 79ef8bc8 00400000 b4ebfe4b 00080000 mscorwks!ExecuteEXE+0x59
0012ffb0 790122f6 00d9fa9c 79e70000 0012fff0 mscorwks!_CorExeMain+0x11b
0012ffc0 7c816d4f 00080000 00d9fa9c 7ffd8000 mscoree!_CorExeMain+0x2c
0012fff0 00000000 790122c2 00000000 78746341 KERNEL32!BaseProcessStart+0x23
```

Step Commands

After reaching a breakpoint, you can step through the application and watch variables, evaluate memory, inspect register values, or view the call stack. The WinDbg toolbar is the most convenient way to step through an application. If it is not visible, open the View menu and choose the Toolbar command to display the toolbar.

Figure 16-2 shows the Step buttons on the Debugging toolbar: from left to right, these are the Step In, Step Over, Step Out, and Run To Cursor buttons.

FIGURE 16-2 Step buttons on the WinDbg toolbar

WinDbg Directives   Standard commands in WinDbg affect or control the application being debugged. Commands such as *kb* (call stack), ~ (list threads), and *da* (display memory—ASCII) are standard commands and apply to the application being debugged. Conversely, WinDbg directives affect the debugger and not the debuggee. For example, the *.load* directive loads a debugging extension dynamic-link library (DLL). The *.logopen* directive opens a log file and records future commands and results to that log file.

There are several WinDbg directives. Table 16-6 lists some of the more common ones. Directives are prefixed with a dot (.).

TABLE 16-6 WinDbg directives

Command	Description
.load dllname	Loads a debugger extension DLL. Extension commands are exposed as exported functions from the DLL. Developers of managed code routinely load the SOS (SOS.dll) debugger extension. Commands from debugger extensions are prefixed with an exclamation point (!).
.unload dllname	Unloads a debugger extension.
.chain	Lists the debugger extensions that are presently loaded and available.
.reload	Reloads symbols and usually is requested after the symbol path has been updated. Typically, symbols are retrieved as needed by the debugger. The */f* option forces the immediate load of all symbols for a specific module or all modules.
.logopen filename	Opens a log file. Future commands and results are written into the log file.
.logclose	Closes the log file.
.kill	Terminates the current debuggee and ends the debugging session.
.frame n	Changes the current stack frame. Some information, such as local variables and register values, are affected by changing the current stack frame.
.srcpath	Sets or displays the source code path.
.dump options filename	Creates a dump, which is used for postmortem analysis. For managed dumps, this is the appropriate command. The following options—"m" and "a" are separate options—create a dump appropriate for SOS: .dump /ma filename.

Son of Strike (SOS)

SOS is a debugger extension used to debug managed code. As a debugging extension, it must be loaded into a Win32-compliant debugger, such as WinDbg. SOS can provide information about the inner workings of a managed application. This might require that the user have a better understanding of the internal workings and structures of the CLR. SOS abstracts as much of the details as possible, allowing you to concentrate on the problem—debugging the application. When using a debugging extension, the debugger and debugging extension collaborate. Without a doubt, you will rely on both to resolve any application bugs.

Any of the following statements loads the SOS.dll debugging extension. To load a particular version of SOS, provide the fully qualified directory path. Here are some examples of loading SOS:

.load sos

.load sos.dll

.load c:\path\sos.dll

You might have multiple versions of the .NET Framework installed on your computer. There also will be comparable versions of SOS.dll—one for each version of the .NET Framework. The following command loads the correct version of SOS.dll for the appropriate version of the CLR:

.loadby sos mscorwks

SOS Example, Part I

This example provides an introduction to SOS. Some of the output from the example has been shortened for clarity.

1. Start the Store application in the sos subfolder outside a debugger. Only one debugger can be attached to an application at any time. Open the Transaction dialog box, as shown in Figure 16-3. Do not complete or close this dialog box.

FIGURE 16-3 The Store application's Transaction dialog box

2. Start the WinDbg debugger and attach to the Store application. Load SOS.

3. Enter the *!threads* command, which lists the managed threads and related information. Here is the abbreviated result:

```
0:004> !threads
ThreadCount: 2
UnstartedThread: 0
BackgroundThread: 1
PendingThread: 0
DeadThread: 0
Hosted Runtime: no
                                    PreEmptive   GC Alloc             Lock
        ID OSID ThreadOBJ   State     GC       Context      Domain   Count
   0     1  424 001501f8     6020 Enabled  013da5dc:013dadb8 001483a8    0
   2     2  c24 00153e40     b220 Enabled  00000000:00000000 001483a8    0
```

4. Change to Thread 0, which is a managed thread. This is a native WinDbg command:

```
0:004> ~0s
eax=790ff90c ebx=01392b50 ecx=013a7704 edx=0000ce7d esi=00000000 edi=013da5b8
eip=7c90eb94 esp=0012edb4 ebp=0012ee4c iopl=0         nv up ei pl zr na po nc
cs=001b  ss=0023  ds=0023  es=0023  fs=003b  gs=0000              efl=00000246
ntdll!KiFastSystemCallRet:
7c90eb94 c3              ret
```

5. Enter the *!clrstack* command to display the stack trace for thread 0. The *-p* option shows the parameters for each method:

```
0:000> !clrstack -p
OS Thread Id: 0x424 (0)
ESP       EIP
0012edc0 7c90eb94 [InlinedCallFrame: 0012edc0] System.Windows.Forms.
UnsafeNativeMethods.WaitMessage()
0012edbc 7b094838 System.Windows.Forms.Application+ComponentManager.System.Windows.
Forms.UnsafeNativeMethods.IMsoComponentManager.FPushMessageLoop(Int32, Int32, Int32)
    PARAMETERS:
        this = 0x013a76ac
        dwComponentID = <no data>
        reason = 0x00000004
        pvLoopData = 0x00000000

0012eef8 7b22e03e System.Windows.Forms.Form.ShowDialog(System.Windows.Forms.IWin32Window)
    PARAMETERS:
        this = 0x013b4494
        owner = <no data>
```

6. The *ShowDialog* method and its parameters appear in the stack trace. The *this* reference is the first parameter of the method. The address of the *this* reference is provided. Use the *dumpobj* command to dump the *this* reference with this address. The output shows the identity of the *this* object as a *Store.Transaction* type. From the fields of *Store. Transaction*, it appears that *Store.Transaction* is a form:

```
0:000> !dumpobj 0x013b4494
Name: Store.Transaction
MethodTable: 00d453a4
EEClass: 00db3034
```

```
Size: 372(0x174) bytes
(C:\store\Store.exe)
Fields:
      MT    Field   Offset          Type VT    Attr   Value Name
790fa098  4000184        4   System.Object  0 instance 00000000 __identity
7a765ca4  40008bc        8  ...ponentModel.ISite  0 instance 00000000 site
7a762e84  40008bd        c  ....EventHandlerList  0 instance 013b6964 events
790fa098  40008bb      108   System.Object  0   static 00000000 EventDisposed
7b4777e4  40010fa       10  ...ntrolNativeWindow  0 instance 013b55c4 window
7b4754b4  40010fb       14  ...ows.Forms.Control  0 instance 00000000 parent
7b4754b4  40010fc       18  ...ows.Forms.Control  0 instance 00000000 reflectParent
7b478924  40010fd       1c  ...orms.CreateParams  0 instance 013b560c createParams
790fe920  40010fe       34   System.Int32  0 instance      346 x
790fe920  40010ff       38   System.Int32  0 instance       22 y
790fe920  4001100       3c   System.Int32  0 instance      266 width
```

SOS Commands

Table 16-7 gives an overview of some of the SOS commands. For a complete listing, use the *!help* command.

TABLE 16-7 **SOS commands**

Command	Description
!ClrStack option	Displays the call stack of the current thread. Here are some of the options: ■ The *-l* option lists the local variables. ■ The *-p* option lists the function parameters. ■ The *-a* option combines both the *-l* and *-p* options.
!DumpHeap option startaddress endaddress	Displays objects that are on the managed heap and then displays statistics about the type of objects on the managed heap. Here are some of the options: ■ The *–stat* option displays the type of objects alone. ■ The *–min* option excludes objects beneath the specified memory address from the list. ■ The *–max* option excludes objects located above the specified memory address from the list. ■ The *–mt* option lists objects with the specified method table. ■ The *startaddress* parameter is the starting address; for example: 　　　!DumpHeap 7b471e40. ■ The *endaddress* parameter is the end address for the command: 　　　!DumpHeap 7b471e40 7b471e88.
!DumpIL mdaddress	Displays the Microsoft Intermediate Language (MSIL) of a method, based on the method descriptor.
!DumpMT mtaddress	Displays information about the method table. The *–md* option lists the methods of the method table.
!DumpObj objaddress	Displays information on the specific object.

TABLE 16-7 SOS commands

Command	Description
!DumpStackObjects option	Lists objects that are referenced from the current stack.
!EEHeap options	Displays information on generations 0, 1, 2, and the large object heap. (The large object heap is explained in the section "Generations," later in this chapter.) The *gc* option limits the display to information pertaining to the generations and the large object heap.
!EEVersion	Displays information about the runtime environment, such as the version number.
!FinalizeQueue option	Lists objects currently on the finalization queue.
!GCroot option objaddress	Shows how references are rooted, which is the path from the object to the root. In C#, root objects include static and local references. These objects represent the base of a branch in the object graph. The *–nostacks* option excludes references held on the stack.
!IP2MD jitaddress	Displays the method descriptor of a jitted method.
!Name2EE programtarget	If the target is a type, provides information on that type. If the target is a method name, displays information on the method descriptor.
!Syncblk	Lists the entries of the *sync block* table.
!Threads	Lists the managed threads.
!Token2EE token	For this command, the token must reference the *typedef* or *methoddef* table. If it is a *typedef* token, the command displays information on the referenced type. If it is a *methoddef* token, the command displays information on the referenced methods.
!u	This command displays the disassembly for a jitted method.
!Help command	Displays help for SOS commands. Without the *command* option, the command provides an overview of all the commands.

SOS Example, Part II

Now that a few more commands have been introduced, an additional example is helpful. This example lists the source, MSIL, and assembly code of the *btnTransaction_Click* button handler, which is informative.

1. Start the Store application in the sos subfolder and then attach WinDbg to the application. Load SOS.

2. Dump information about the *btnTransaction_Click* method with the *!name2ee* command. Notice that the method has not been jitted yet, which means that the method has not been invoked. A method is jitted the first time it is invoked. Here is the code:

```
0:004> !name2ee store.exe Store.Form1.btnTransaction_Click
Module: 00d40c14 (Store.exe)
Token: 0x06000004
MethodDesc: 00d43968
Name: Store.Form1.btnTransaction_Click(System.Object, System.EventArgs)
```

```
Not JITTED yet. Use !bpmd -md 00d43968 to break on run.
0:004> !u 00d43968
Not jitted yet
```

3. Restart the Store application from break mode using the *g(o)* command. Click Add Transactions. In WinDbg, press Ctrl+Break to interrupt the application. Dump information on the *Store.Form1.btnTransaction_Click* method again. This time, the method is shown as jitted, and the virtual address of the cached native binary is displayed:

```
0:004> !name2ee store.exe Store.Form1.btnTransaction_Click
Module: 00d40c14 (Store.exe)
Token: 0x06000004
MethodDesc: 00d43968
Name: Store.Form1.btnTransaction_Click(System.Object, System.EventArgs)
JITTED Code Address: 00de07c0
```

4. The *!u* command displays the assembly code of a jitted method. Execute the *!u* command on the *btnTransaction_Click* method using the address shown for the method descriptor (Method Desc) by the *!name2ee* command:

```
0:004> !u 00d43968
Normal JIT generated code
Store.Form1.btnTransaction_Click(System.Object, System.EventArgs)
Begin 00de07c0, size 3e9
00de07c0 55                 push    ebp
00de07c1 8bec               mov     ebp,esp
00de07c3 57                 push    edi
00de07c4 56                 push    esi
00de07c5 53                 push    ebx
00de07c6 83ec50             sub     esp,0x50
00de07c9 33c0               xor     eax,eax
00de07cb 8945d0             mov     [ebp-0x30],eax
00de07ce 8945c4             mov     [ebp-0x3c],eax
00de07d1 33c0               xor     eax,eax
00de07d3 8945e8             mov     [ebp-0x18],eax
00de07d6 894dc0             mov     [ebp-0x40],ecx
00de07d9 8955dc             mov     [ebp-0x24],edx
00de07dc 833dc80dd40000     cmp     dword ptr [00d40dc8],0x0
```

5. The next challenge is to list the MSIL code for the *btnTransaction_Click* method. The *dumpil* command shows the MSIL code of the method. *Method descriptor* is the only parameter, which also is provided by the *!name2ee* command:

```
0:004> !dumpil 00d43968
ilAddr = 0040247c
IL_0000: nop
.try
{
  IL_0001: nop
  IL_0002: ldarg.0
  IL_0003: ldfld Store.Form1::txtNumber
  IL_0008: callvirt System.Windows.Forms.Control::get_Text
  IL_000d: call System.Int32::Parse
  IL_0012: stloc.0
  IL_0013: nop
```

```
    IL_0014: leave.s IL_001d
} // end .try
.catch
{
  IL_0016: pop
  IL_0017: nop
  IL_0018: ldc.i4.1
  IL_0019: stloc.0
  IL_001a: nop
  IL_001b: leave.s IL_001d
} // end .catch
```

6. The final task is to display the source code. Set the source code path in WinDbg. From the File menu, choose the Source File Path command and then enter the source code path. This should be the path for the store.exe source code in the sos subfolder. Next, enter the *lsf* command to set *form1.cs* as the current source code file. List the source with the *ls* command. For this example, 40 lines are displayed, beginning with line 10. You now have displayed the source, intermediate language, and assembly code for a function:

```
0:004> lsf form1.cs
0:004> ls 10, 40
    22:
    23:            private void btnTransaction_Click(object sender, EventArgs e)
    24:            {
    25:                int numofTransactions;
    26:                try
    27:                {
    28:                    numofTransactions= int.Parse(txtNumber.Text);
    29:                }
    30:                catch
    31:                {
    32:                    numofTransactions = 1;
    33:                }
    34:                for (int count = 0; count < numofTransactions; ++count)
    35:                {
    36:                    int itemTotal=0;
```

Dumps

Dumps are used for postmortem analysis, which is sometimes the most effective means of debugging an application. When a program intermittently crashes, postmortem analysis might be the sole way to resolve the problem. With tools such as ADPlus, you can specify that a dump be created whenever a crash occurs, even if the application is unattended. Then the dump can be used to diagnose the problem. Production applications are not ideal for live debugging. How do you perform live debugging on an active Web server? Convenience is another advantage to postmortem analysis. You can move the dump to a developer machine, where there are a host of debugging tools and resources. In this environment, diagnosing the problem is much easier.

There are full dumps and minidumps. A *minidump* is a partial snapshot of the application memory, which consists of the primary module. Full dumps also include other modules in the memory snapshot—even system modules. The benefit of a full dump is convenience, and symbols are aligned more easily. The disadvantage is that full dumps tend to be large. Not all minidumps are equivalent—some contain more information than others. Check the documentation for the command or tool that creates the minidump to see what options are available.

Remember that memory dumps are static. The debugging paradigm is different from performing live debugging. For example, you cannot step through the application, set breakpoints, or change the state of the application.

As documented earlier, the *.dump /ma* directive in WinDbg creates dump files that can be used with SOS. Dump files also can be created with ADPlus and other tools.

ADPlus

The ADPlus tool can be downloaded from the Debugging Tools for Windows Web site. It is a Microsoft VBScript file that automates the CDB debugger. Use ADPlus to automate the creation of dumps for applications. ADPlus operates in either crash or hang mode, and it creates other files, such as log files, to aid in postmortem analysis. Unique names are assigned to the dump and other files to avoid overriding previously generated files.

In crash mode, ADPlus attaches CDB to the target processes. You will see that CDB is minimized on your desktop. It is attached invasively to the target application. Run ADPlus before the application crashes. When a crash occurs, a minidump and a log file are created. ADPlus also will generate an entry in the Event Log. A crash is interpreted as the application ending from an unhandled exception. To detach prematurely before a crash, open the minimized CDB console and press Ctrl+C. ADPlus can attach CDB to multiple processes simultaneously. The debugger attaches all instances of the named processes. Here is the syntax for running ADPlus in crash mode:

adplus –crash –pn *processname1* –pn *processname2* ... –pn *processnamen*

Alternatively, the process identifier can be used to identify a specific instance:

adplus –crash –p *pid* –p *pid* ... –p *pidn*

In hang mode, run ADPlus after the hang occurs, which attaches CDB to the target application noninvasively. You must decide when the application is hung (a somewhat subjective call) and then apply ADPlus. The debuggee is resumed after the dump is created. Here is the syntax to start ADPlus in hang mode, where *pn* is the process name and *pid* is the process id:

adplus –hang –pn *processname1* –pn *processname2* ... –pn *processnamen*

adplus –hang –p *pid1* –p *pid2* –p ... *pidn*

These are other important options:

- **O(utput) option**   This option sets the output directory for dump and log files.

- **Q(uiet) option**   This option suppresses alerts from ADPlus.

- **N(otify) option**   This option notifies a user when an application has crashed.

- **C(onfiguration) option**   This option associates a configuration file, which describes the behavior of ADPlus.

- **iis option**   This option is for debugging Web servers. It is applicable with Microsoft Internet Information Server (IIS) 4.0 and later.

An ADPlus Example

In this example, the Store application has an error and unexpectedly crashes. ADPlus is used to create a dump when the application crashes. The dump then is opened in WinDbg, and the problem is isolated.

1. Start the Store application in the Adplus subfolder.

2. Click Hang. As expected, this action hangs the application.

3. Run ADPlus in Hang mode to attach the CDB debugger to the Store application and create a dump. (Get the correct process identifier for the Store application using the Tlist utility.)

```
C:\store>adplus -hang -p 3520 -o c:\dumps
Attaching the debugger to: STORE.EXE
                        (Process ID: 3520)
```

4. Start WinDbg and open the dump. From the File menu, select the Open Crash Dump command. From the dialog box, find and open the dump.

5. Load the SOS debugging extension. Change to Thread 0 and show the call stack. The following is a partial listing of the call stack. It shows correctly that the *btnHang_Click* handler was the last method entered. This provides a starting point in uncovering the problem that caused the hang:

```
0:000> .load sos
0:000> !clrstack
OS Thread Id: 0xae8 (0)
ESP        EIP
0012f030 00de0906 Store.Form1.btnHang_Click(System.Object, System.EventArgs)
0012f044 7b070a8b System.Windows.Forms.Control.OnClick(System.EventArgs)
0012f054 7b114cd9 System.Windows.Forms.Button.OnClick(System.EventArgs)
0012f060 7b114ddf System.Windows.Forms.Button.OnMouseUp(System.Windows.Forms.MouseEventA
0012f084 7b0dfeea System.Windows.Forms.Control.WmMouseUp(System.Windows.Forms.Messa
0012f0d0 7b082bbf System.Windows.Forms.Control.WndProc(System.Windows.Forms.Message By
0012f0d4 7b09149e [InlinedCallFrame: 0012f0d4]
0012f170 7b0913bb System.Windows.Forms.Button.WndProc(System.Windows.Forms.Message ByRe
0012f178 7b08a70d System.Windows.Forms.Control+ControlNativeWindow.OnMessage(System
```

```
0012f17c 7b08a6e6 System.Windows.Forms.Control+ControlNativeWindow.WndProc(System.
0012f190 7b08a535 System.Windows.Forms.NativeWindow.Callback(IntPtr, Int32, IntPtr, IntP
0012f324 003420d4 [NDirectMethodFrameStandalone: 0012f324] System.Windows.Forms.Uns
0012f334 7b094682 System.Windows.Forms.Application+ComponentManager.System.Windows.
Forms.UnsafeNativeMethods.IMsoComponentManager.FPushMessageLoop(Int32, Int32, Int32
0012f3d4 7b094249 System.Windows.Forms.Application+ThreadContext.RunMessageLoopInne
0012f440 7b094087 System.Windows.Forms.Application+ThreadContext.RunMessageLoop(Int
0012f470 7b0d66ea System.Windows.Forms.Application.Run(System.Windows.Forms.Form)
0012f480 00de00a8 Store.Program.Main()
0012f69c 79e80b8b [GCFrame: 0012f69c]
```

Memory Management

Historically, memory-related issues are the origin of many bugs. Win32 processes, including managed applications, own resources. Of those resources, virtual memory is one of the most important. Win32 processes normally own 4 gigabytes (GB) of virtual memory, where the operating system resides in the upper 2 GB. The upper 2 GB are shared and protected from user mode access. The lower 2 GB are private memory, where the application code, heaps, static data area, stack, and other sections of the individual application are loaded. This memory is protected from access by other processes. The Virtual Memory Manager (VMM), which is the kernel-level component of the NT Executive, guards private memory from incidental or deliberate changes from other applications.

The managed heap is created in the private memory of a managed application. There are several families of native application programming interfaces (APIs) that allocate memory from the available virtual memory, including the Heap APIs such as *HeapCreate*, *HeapAlloc*, and *HeapFree*. The Memory Mapped family of APIs, *CreateFileMapping*, *MapViewOfFile*, *UnmapViewOfFile*, and related functions, also allocate memory. Finally, the Virtual APIs, including *VirtualAlloc* and *VirtualFree*, allocate memory dynamically at run time. Internally, all memory allocations, including Heap and Memory Mapped APIs, decompose to Virtual APIs.

VirtualAlloc is used to allocate memory in contiguous memory. Here is the syntax of *VirtualAlloc*:

```
LPVOID VirtualAlloc(LPVOID lpAddress, SIZE_T dwSize,
    DWORD flAllocationType, DWORD flProtect)
```

The following stack trace shows *VirtualAlloc* being called in a managed program. The first argument (0x00b54000) is the address of the allocation. This is where the memory is being allocated:

```
0:000> kb
ChildEBP RetAddr  Args to Child
0012e674 79e74391 00b54000 00001000 00001000 KERNEL32!VirtualAlloc
0012e6b4 79e74360 00b54000 00001000 00001000 mscorwks!EEVirtualAlloc+0x104
0012e6c8 79e74348 7a38b1b0 00b54000 00001000 mscorwks!CExecutionEngine::ClrVirtualAlloc+
0012e6e0 79e8b7a4 00b54000 00001000 00001000 mscorwks!ClrVirtualAlloc+0x1b
0012e718 79e9f940 000000a8 00000001 00010000 mscorwks!UnlockedLoaderHeap::GetMoreCommitt
```

```
0012e750 79e7f89f 000000a4 00000004 0012e794 mscorwks!UnlockedLoaderHeap::UnlockedAllocA
0012e764 79e7f853 000000a4 00000004 0012e794 mscorwks!UnlockedLoaderHeap::UnlockedAllocA
0012e7a4 79e85010 0012e7d0 000000a4 00000004 mscorwks!LoaderHeap::RealAllocAlignedMem+0x
0012e7f0 79e84eca 7a389bec 00000094 00000000 mscorwks!Stub::NewStub+0xc1
0012e834 79e8733c 7a389bec 00000000 00000000 mscorwks!StubLinker::Link+0x59
```

Object graph

The Garbage Collector (GC) does not perform reference counting. Some memory models maintain a reference count on components. When the count drops to zero, the object is removed from memory immediately. Overhead from reference counting, especially for objects that are never reclaimed, is considerable. There are two benefits to the reference counting model. First, the cost of garbage collection is distributed across the lifetime of the application. Second, it is proactive. Memory is reclaimed prior to being needed.

In managed code, an object graph is built when garbage collection is initiated, which avoids expensive reference counting. Objects without references in a tree are assumed to be collectable, and the memory for those objects is reclaimed. Memory then is consolidated and outstanding references are updated. This phase of memory management prevents future fragmentation of the managed heap. (We are ignoring finalization for the moment—we will cover this topic in the section "Finalization," later in this chapter.) The object graph is not cached between garbage collection cycles. Rebuilding the trees at each garbage collection cycle is one reason why garbage collection is expensive. However, garbage collection is performed only when needed, which is a considerable efficiency.

An object is *rooted* when another rooted object holds a direct or indirect reference to it. Rooted objects are not referenced by another object and reside at the base of an object graph. Rooted objects include static, global, and local objects. C# does not support global objects.

Memory Example

In this example, the Store application is explored again. Three transactions are added and the root reference of each transaction is displayed.

1. Start the Store application in the memory subfolder and add three transactions.

2. Attach to the Store application with WinDbg. Load SOS.

3. Transactions are instances of the *Item* class. Display information on the *Item* class using the *!name2ee* command:

```
0:004> !name2ee store.exe Store.Item
Module: 00d40c14 (Store.exe)
Token: 0x02000002
MethodTable: 00d442dc
EEClass: 00db21c4
Name: Store.Item
```

4. Use the *dumpheap* command and the *MethodTable* address to list the address of each transaction item:

```
0:004> !dumpheap -mt 00d442dc
 Address       MT      Size
013a03b8 00d442dc       20
013b409c 00d442dc       20
013bca10 00d442dc       20
total 3 objects
Statistics:
      MT    Count TotalSize Class Name
00d442dc      3          60 Store.Item
Total 3 objects
```

5. Confirm the root of each object using the *!gcroot* command. This shows how the object is rooted. Here is a partial listing from the first *Item* object. For this object, the root is the *Application* object:

```
0:004> !gcroot 013a03b8
Note: Roots found on stacks may be false positives. Run "!help gcroot" for
more info.
ebx:Root:01392b60(System.Windows.Forms.Application+ThreadContext)->
01392214(Store.Form1)->
01392454(System.Collections.Generic.List`1[[Store.Item, Store]])->
013d5f2c(System.Object[])->
013a03b8(Store.Item)
Scan Thread 0 OSTHread ee4
Scan Thread 2 OSTHread c48
DOMAIN(001483A8):HANDLE(WeakLn):9f1088:Root:013a074c(System.Windows.Forms.
    NativeMethods+WndProc)->
0139ec94(System.Windows.Forms.Control+ControlNativeWindow)->
0139ebc4(System.Windows.Forms.CheckBox)->
0139d6f8(Store.Transaction)->
013a03b8(Store.Item)
```

6. As shown with the *dumpheap* command, transaction objects are 20 bytes. You might be curious about what those 20 bytes contain. To answer that question, look at the source code for the *Item* class:

```
public class Item: IDisposable {
    public Item() {
        ++nextPropId;
        propItemId = nextPropId;
    }

    public enum eProducts {
        Computer = 1,
        Laptop = 2,
        Printer = 4,
        Software = 8
    };

    private eProducts propProducts = 0;
    public eProducts Products {
```

```
        get {
            return propProducts;
        }
        set {
            propProducts = value;
        }
    }

    static private int nextPropId=0;
    private int propItemId;
    public int ItemId {
        get {
            return propItemId;
        }
    }

    public void Dispose() {
        --nextPropId;
    }

    private float[] buffer = new float[100];
}
```

Listing the source code is easy if the source code is available. But what if the source code is not available (which would not be unusual for a production application)? The *!dumpclass* command displays a class, including members. It uses the *EEClass* address, which is provided with the *!name2ee* command. The *!dumpclass* command provides not only type information but also the state of static members. Static members belong to the class. In the following listing, the class is listed. It also shows that the static *nextPropId* property is 3 at the moment:

```
0:004> !dumpclass 00db21c4
Class Name: Store.Item
mdToken: 02000002 (C:\store\Store.exe)
Parent Class: 790fa034
Module: 00d40c14
Method Table: 00d442dc
Vtable Slots: 5
Total Method Slots: 9
Class Attributes: 100001
NumInstanceFields: 3
NumStaticFields: 1
      MT    Field   Offset                 Type  VT     Attr    Value Name
00d44224  4000001        8  System.Int32     0 instance           propProducts
790fe920  4000003        c  System.Int32     0 instance           propItemId
79129180  4000004        4  System.Single[]  0 instance           buffer
790fe920  4000002       24  System.Int32     0   static        3  nextPropId
```

Generations

The managed heap is organized into three generations and a large object heap. Generations are numbered 0, 1, and 2. New objects are placed in a generation or a large object heap. Younger and smaller objects are found in the earlier generations, whereas older and larger objects are found in the later generations and the large object heap. This is efficiency by proximity. Objects that are apt to communicate with other objects are kept close together in memory. This decreases page faults, which are costly, and decreases the amount of physical memory required at any time. Reducing page faults makes your application perform faster.

Garbage collection in .NET often is described as nondeterministic, which means that garbage collection is not called on demand. Garbage collection occurs automatically when memory allocation exceeds the memory reserved for a particular generation. When an application starts, Generation 0 is available for allocation. Eventually, the memory available to Generation 0 is exceeded, which triggers garbage collection on Generation 0 alone. This is more efficient because only a portion of the managed heap is experiencing garbage collection. If enough memory is reclaimed during garbage collection, the pending allocation is performed on Generation 0. If enough memory cannot be reclaimed, Generation 0 objects are promoted to Generation 1. This continues until Generations 0 and 1 are replete with objects. This time, garbage collection is performed on Generations 0 and 1. At that time, Generation 0 and Generation 1 objects are promoted to Generation 1 and Generation 2, respectively. By design, the older and larger objects tend to migrate toward the higher generations, whereas younger and smaller objects are found in lower generations.

Memory on the managed heap is allocated top-down. In Win32 applications, zero is at the bottom of the memory. Higher addresses are at the top of the memory space. New objects in managed code are allocated at higher addresses on the managed heap. The lower generations are at higher memory addresses. 256 kilobytes (KB), 2 megabytes (MB), and 10 MB are reserved for Generation 0, Generation 1, and Generation 2, respectively. These thresholds can be adjusted. The GC changes these thresholds based on the pattern of allocations in the managed application.

As the name implies, the large object heap hosts large objects (that is, objects greater than 85 KB). Instead of promoting these objects from one generation to another, which is costly, large objects are placed on the large object heap immediately at allocation.

Generations Example

This time, the Store application has both an Add Transactions button and an Add Large Transactions button. The Add Large Transactions button adds large transactions (not surprisingly), which are instances of the *LargeItem* class. The *LargeItem* class inherits from the *Item* class and adds additional fields, such as the *largeStuff* field. The *largeStuff* field is greater than 85 KB and therefore qualifies as a large object. The objective of this example is to determine the generation of each *Item*, *LargeItem*, and *largeStuff* instance.

1. Start the Store application in the Generations subfolder. Add three regular transactions and four large transactions.

2. Start WinDbg and attach to the Store application. Load SOS.

3. There should be three instances of the *Item* class in memory. Retrieve the method table address of the *Item* class with the *!name2ee* command. Then dump the *Item* instances using the *!dumpheap —mt* command:

```
0:004> !name2ee Store.exe Store.Item
Module: 00d40c14 (Store.exe)
Token: 0x02000005
MethodTable: 00d4431c
EEClass: 00db22f4
Name: Store.Item
0:004> !dumpheap -mt 00d4431c
Address       MT     Size
013a8bd0 00d4431c      20
013aabb0 00d4431c      20
013aadd8 00d4431c      20
013adffc 00d4431c      20
013b513c 00d4431c      20
013c1a4c 00d4431c      20
total 6 objects
Statistics:
      MT    Count TotalSize Class Name
00d4431c        6       120 Store.Item
Total 6 objects
```

4. Unexpectedly, there are six instances, not three. Has a bug been uncovered? The answer to this question will be provided shortly.

5. Use the *!name2ee* command to obtain the method table address of the *LargeItem*. Dump the *LargeItem* objects. As expected, there are four objects:

```
0:004> !dumpheap -mt 00d460a8
Address       MT     Size
013ab03c 00d460a8    5016
013ae5a4 00d460a8    5016
013be020 00d460a8    5016
013ca900 00d460a8    5016
total 4 objects
Statistics:
      MT    Count TotalSize Class Name
00d460a8        4     20064 Store.LargeItem
Total 4 objects
```

6. There should be four *largeStuff* fields—one for each *LargeItem* object. One way to locate them is to use the *!dumpheap —stat* command. The objects are sorted by size, with the larger objects at the bottom of the list:

```
0:004> !dumpheap -stat
total 16356 objects
Statistics:
      MT    Count TotalSize Class Name
7b481adc        1        12 System.Windows.Forms.OSFeature
7b47fd04        1        12 System.Windows.Forms.FormCollection
7b47efec        1        12 System.Windows.Forms.Layout.DefaultLayout
7ae86e80      134      5896 System.Drawing.BufferedGraphics
790f8230      374      5984 System.WeakReference
```

```
79124ec4        41        8136 System.Collections.Hashtable+bucket[]
790fd688       341        8184 System.Version
79116738       250        9000 System.Collections.Hashtable+HashtableEnumerator
79124d8c         5       10596 System.Byte[]
79110f78       523       12552 System.Collections.Stack
7ae868e8      1049       12588 System.Drawing.KnownColor
00d460a8         4       20064 Store.LargeItem
7b47e850       522       33408 System.Windows.Forms.Internal.DeviceContext
7910acbc      2104       42080 System.SafeGCHandle
79124ba8       642       57496 System.Object[]
00152760        14       77744       Free
790fa860      7067      407316 System.String
00e80838         4    16000128 System.Single[,]
```

7. The last item in the report is a two-dimensional array of *Single* types. This is the *largeStuff* field. Four instances are shown. The first column of the command is the method table address. Dump the *largeStuff* instances using that address with the *!dumpheap –mt* command:

```
0:004> !dumpheap -mt 00e80838
Address       MT     Size
02396da8 00e80838   4000032
027676c8 00e80838   4000032
02b37fe8 00e80838   4000032
02f08918 00e80838   4000032
total 4 objects
Statistics:
      MT     Count TotalSize Class Name
00e80838         4  16000128 System.Single[,]
Total 4 objects
```

8. Finally, list the memory ranges for Generations 0, 1, and 2, and the large object heap. This is accomplished with the *!eeheap –gc* command:

```
0:004> !eeheap -gc
Number of GC Heaps: 1
generation 0 starts at 0x013d2488
generation 1 starts at 0x013af93c
generation 2 starts at 0x01391000
ephemeral segment allocation context: none
 segment    begin allocated      size
0016bf58 7a74179c  7a76248c 0x00020cf0(134384)
001687e0 7b45baa0  7b471f0c 0x0001646c(91244)
00154b20 790d6314  790f575c 0x0001f448(128072)
01390000 01391000  013ff3ac 0x0006e3ac(451500)
Large object heap starts at 0x02391000
 segment    begin allocated      size
02390000 02391000  032d9248 0x00f48248(16024136)
Total Size   0x100cb98(16829336)
-----------------------------
GC Heap Size  0x100cb98(16829336)
```

Based on the addresses of the *Item*, *LargeItem*, and *largeStuff* instances, Table 16-8 shows where each object is allocated on the managed heap. None of the instances resides in Generation 0.

TABLE 16-8 Location on managed heap of *Item, LargeItem,* and *largeStuff* instances

Item	Address
No objects in Generation 0	N/A
Generation 0 starts	0x013d2488
LargeItem[4]	0x013ca900
Item[6]	0x013c1a4c
LargeItem[3]	0x013be020
Item[5]	0x013b513c
Generation 1 starts	0x013af93c
LargeItem[2]	0x013ae5a4
LargeItem[1]	0x013ab03c
LargeItem[2]	0x013ae5a4
Item[3]	0x013aadd8
Item[2]	0x013aabb0
Item[1]	0x013a8bd0
Generation 2 starts	0x01391000
largeStuff[4]	0x02f08918
largeStuff[3]	0x02b37fe8
largeStuff[2]	0x027676c8
largeStuff[1]	0x02396da8
largeStuff[2]	0x027676c8
Large object heap	0x02391000

It is time to resolve the earlier question. Remember that there were six instances of the *Item* type. However, three regular transactions were created. Actually, this result is correct because of nondeterministic collection. In the Store application, every transaction starts as an *Item* object. *LargeItem* objects are created within the transaction. At that point, the *Item* object is no longer required, but the memory is not reclaimed. Therefore, there is a shadow item in memory for every *LargeItem*, which is the reason for the extra *Item* instances. At the next garbage collection, those unneeded items will be removed from memory. For demonstration purposes, there is a version of the Store application included that can force garbage collection. It has a Collect Memory button that calls *GC.Collect* and removes the extra *Item* instances and other unused objects. This version of the application is found in the gccollect subfolder. When using this Store application, display the *Item* instances (with the *dumpheap* command) both before and after clicking Collect Memory to confirm that *GC.Collect* is reclaiming the extra items. In general, however, calling *GC.Collect* is not recommended because it is costly.

Finalization

Up to now we have ignored the finalization process. But it must be considered because it plays a vital role in garbage collection. Finalization affects the performance and effectiveness of garbage collection. In C#, finalization is linked to class destructors. For C++ programmers, .NET presents a different model for destructors.

Object.Finalize is the universal destructor in .NET. In C#, *Finalize* calls the class destructor. Destructors are called deterministically in C++. However, in C# the CLR calls destructors nondeterministically during garbage collection. You cannot invoke destructors directly. Destructors are called as part of the garbage collection process and are not called in a guaranteed sequence. In addition, you should clean up for only unmanaged resources in the destructor. Other managed objects might have been removed from memory already during garbage collection.

For deterministic garbage collection, implement the *IDisposable* interface and the *Dispose* method. You then can call the *Dispose* method directly.

Destructors add processing overhead to an object. The overhead is incurred even before the object is collected. The GC adds references for objects with destructors to the Finalization queue when the object is created. (This does not occur for objects without destructors.) Thus, the extra overhead starts at the beginning of the object's lifetime.

Objects that have destructors but no outstanding references require at least two garbage collections to be reclaimed. During the first garbage collection cycle, references to collectable objects with destructors are transferred from the *Finalization* queue to the *FReachable* queue, which is serviced by a dedicated thread. These objects are added to the list of objects already waiting on the *FReachable* queue to have their destructors called. The *Finalization* thread is responsible for invoking destructors on objects and then removing that object from the *FReachable* queue. When that happens, the object can be reclaimed and deleted from memory at the next garbage collection.

The *!finalizequeue* command reports on objects, which are waiting to have their destructors called on the *FReachable* queue.

Reliability and Performance Monitor

In Windows Vista, the Reliability and Performance Monitor is located in the Administrative Tools folder on the Control Panel. The Performance Monitor has several counters that are helpful when debugging managed applications. Table 16-9 itemizes some of the more useful memory-related counters. These counters are found in the .NET CLR Memory category.

TABLE 16-9 Performance Monitor counters

Name	Description
# GC Handles	The number of GC handles to external resources, such as windows and files.
# Bytes In All Heaps	The total bytes allocated for Generation 0, 1, 2, and the large object heap.

TABLE 16-9 **Performance Monitor counters**

Name	Description
# Induced GC	The peak number of times that garbage collection was induced because of *GC.Collect*.
# Of Pinned Objects	The number of pinned objects discovered during the last garbage collection.
# Of Sync Blocks In Use	A count of syncblock entries. (Syncblock entries are discussed in the section "Threads," later in this chapter.)
# Gen 0 Collections	The number of times that Generation 0 has been garbage-collected.
# Gen 1 Collections	The number of times that Generation 1 has been garbage-collected.
# Gen 2 Collections	The number of times that Generation 2 has been garbage-collected.
# Total Committed Bytes	The total bytes of virtual memory committed by the GC.
# Total Reserved Bytes	The total bytes of virtual memory reserved by the GC.
Gen 0 Heap Size	The total bytes allocated for Generation 0.
Gen 1 Heap Size	The total bytes allocated for Generation 1.
Gen 2 Heap Size	The total bytes allocated for Generation 2.
Large Object Heap Size	The total bytes allocated for the large object heap.
% Time In GC	The percentage of application execution time spent in garbage collection, which is updated at each garbage collection cycle.
Allocated Bytes/Sec	The number of bytes allocated per second, which is updated at each garbage collection cycle.
Finalization Survivors	The number of objects that survived garbage collection and are waiting for destructors to be called.
Gen 0 Promoted Bytes/Sec	The number of bytes per second promoted from Generation 0 to 1.
Gen 1 Promoted Bytes/Sec	The number of bytes per second promoted from Generation 1 to 2.
Promoted Finalization-Memory from Gen 0	The number of bytes promoted to Generation 1 because of pending finalizers.
Promoted Finalization-Memory from Gen 1	The number of bytes promoted to Generation 2 because of pending finalizers.

Threads

Applications are sometimes multithreaded. Multithreaded applications are much more susceptible to bugs, including synchronization problems. Each thread represents a separate path of execution and owns resources, such as stack, thread local storage, local variables, and thread environment blocks. Proper use of threads can enhance the performance of an application, whereas poor implementation can hinder performance.

Creating threads is not difficult. Managing threads is the real challenge—at times, it can be like herding cats. Thread synchronization, which is the management of threads, can be complicated, including preventing race conditions and controlling access to shared resources.

Improperly implemented threads can lead to a high-utilization or low-utilization condition. High utilization is characterized by one or more threads consuming at or near 100-percent CPU cycles. Other threads are starved for time, which makes the application appear to hang or behave incorrectly. Low utilization is the reverse; a process and threads are receiving minimal or no CPU cycles.

There are two primary reasons for high utilization:

- Threads are in tight loops that usurp all CPU resources.
- Active high-priority threads prevent lower-priority threads from receiving attention from the CPU.

There are several reasons for low utilization:

- Threads are waiting for resources that never become available. Threads in that state are suspended indefinitely and receive little CPU time.
- Threads are mutually blocked on each other. This deadlock suspends both threads indefinitely, and both receive little CPU time. This often is caused by nested synchronization.
- A low-priority thread in a sea of high-priority threads has little opportunity to sail. It is given little CPU time.
- Threads with erroneously high suspend counts are not resumed when planned. For this reason, the thread continues to receive no CPU time.

High and low utilization are not the only issues with multithread applications. The list of potential transgressions from multithreading is almost endless. Threading is fertile ground for debugging.

For brevity, this section focuses on synchronization problems related to monitors and mutexes. Synchronization problems from semaphores, events, and reader-writer locks are not discussed. Monitors synchronize access to a single resource. The resource could be an object, data structure, or even an algorithm—anything that requires exclusive access. Monitors provide synchronization within a process. Like a monitor, a *mutex* synchronizes access to a single resource. However, mutexes can synchronize across processes.

Monitors are the most frequently used synchronization device. For that reason, the CLR tracks monitors for efficient access and synchronization. Instances of managed objects have an additional field called the *syncblock index*. This is an index into the syncblock table where monitors are tracked. The syncblock index of an object defaults to zero. When an object is used with a monitor, the syncblock index is updated to point to an entry in the syncblock table. Another thread attempting to claim the same resource with a monitor would notice the entry in the *syncblock* table and be blocked. The command *!syncblk –all* lists the outstanding syncblocks. Thin locks are used when possible, where locking information is cached in the object header. However, the header is of a limited size and the lock might need to be inflated, which is moving the lock information from the header into the syncblock table.

Markers of thread synchronization, both monitors and mutexes, can be found on the call stack. Finding *AwareLock.Enter*, *WaitHandle.WaitAll*, and *WaitForMultipleObjects* in the call stack are indications of thread synchronization activity, as explained in the following list:

- **AwareLock.Enter**   This method is called when an object is bound to a monitor. Set a breakpoint on this symbol, as shown here:

  ```
  bp mscorwks!AwareLock::Enter
  ```

  If hit, the current thread is entering a monitor.

- **WaitHandle.WaitAll**   Except for monitors, most synchronization objects in .NET are derived from the *WaitHandle* class. Look for method calls from this class on the managed call stack, including *WaitOne* and *WaitAll*, as a sign of pending synchronization.

- **WaitForMultipleObjects**   Most waits on synchronization objects, managed or unmanaged, devolve to the *WaitForMultipleObjects* API, which is the workhorse of thread synchronization. This is another marker that can be found on the call stack. Here is the syntax of the *WaitForMultipleObjects* API:

  ```
  DWORD WaitForMultipleObjects(DWORD nCount, const HANDLE* lphandles,
      BOOL bWaitAll, DWORD dwMilliseconds)
  ```

Threads Commands

The first step to debugging threads in WinDbg and SOS is using a thread command. In WinDbg, the tilde (~) is the thread command; in SOS, the thread command is *!threads*. However, the ~ command lists only managed threads.

Here is sample output from the WinDbg thread command:

```
0:000> ~
. 0  Id: f7c.f80 Suspend: 1 Teb: 7ffdd000 Unfrozen
   1  Id: f7c.f9c Suspend: 1 Teb: 7ffdc000 Unfrozen
   2  Id: f7c.fa0 Suspend: 1 Teb: 7ffdb000 Unfrozen
   3  Id: f7c.fa4 Suspend: 1 Teb: 7ffda000 Unfrozen
   4  Id: f7c.de0 Suspend: 1 Teb: 7ffd9000 Unfrozen
```

Listed in order, the columns represent the thread number, process identifier, thread identifier, suspend count, address of thread environment block, and status of the thread.

Here is output from the SOS thread command:

```
0:000> !threads
ThreadCount: 4
```

```
UnstartedThread: 1
BackgroundThread: 1
PendingThread: 0
DeadThread: 0
Hosted Runtime: no
                              PreEmptive   GC Alloc           Lock
      ID OSID ThreadOBJ  State    GC       Context      Domain   Count APT Exception
   0   1  f80 001501f8   6020 Disabled 013c2cf0:013c32bc 001483a8     0 STA
   2   2  fa0 00153e40   b220 Enabled  00000000:00000000 001483a8     0 MTA (Finalizer)
   4   3  de0 0018b898   b020 Disabled 013b4cdc:013b52bc 001483a8     2 MTA
XXXX   4    0 0018e750   9400 Enabled  00000000:00000000 001483a8     0 Ukn
```

The first column, which is untitled, is the thread identifier assigned by the debugger. Unknown threads are marked as "xxxx". The remaining columns are as follows:

- **ID**   Unmanaged thread number

- **OSID**   Managed thread number

- **ThreadObj**   Address of the related thread object

- **State**   State of the thread

- **Preemptive GC**   Whether a thread can be preempted for garbage collection

- **Domain**   Address of the *AppDomain* that hosts the thread

- **Lock Count**   Lock count

- **APT**   Apartment model

Threads Example

Multithread capabilities have been added to the Store application in the Threading subfolder. There are two additional buttons. The Enumerate button writes the current transactions to the forward.txt file. The Reverse Enumerate button writes the transactions, in reverse order, to the reverse.txt file. Each button handler starts a thread to accomplish the task.

1. Close all instances of the Store application.

2. Start the Store program in the Threading subfolder and add three transactions. Click Enumerate to write the transactions to the forward.txt file. Close the Store program and open the forward.txt file, which is empty. It should contain three transactions—so that's a problem!

3. Try again. Reopen the Store application and add three transactions. However, when you click Enumerate, an unhandled exception occurs. What is the problem? You need to investigate.

4. Start the Store application yet again. Get the process identifier using the Tlist command. You should notice that there are two Store applications running. Apparently a previous version is still running in the background. This kind of problem is typical of a hung thread, which keeps an application alive even after the user closes the main window.

5. Use ADPlus to obtain a dump from the first Store application in the list. Here is the command:

   ```
   adplus -hang -o c:\dumps -p 2696
   ```

6. Open the dump file in WinDbg.

7. Load the SOS debugging extension and list the managed threads. For readability, some of the columns have been removed from this listing:

   ```
   0:000> .load sos
   0:000> !threads
   ThreadCount: 3
   UnstartedThread: 0
   BackgroundThread: 2
   PendingThread: 0
   DeadThread: 0
   Hosted Runtime: no
   ```

	ID	OSID	ThreadOBJ	State	PreEmptive GC	GC Alloc Context	Domain	Lock Count
0	1	a90	001501f8	2016220	Enabled	013dbe2c:013dc990	001483a8	0
2	2	9c8	00153e40	b220	Enabled	00000000:00000000	001483a8	0
4	3	3e0	00190718	b020	Disabled	013d63b0:013d6990	001483a8	2

8. Thread 4 is the only thread with a positive lock count, so it appears to be the culprit. What is the thread waiting for? This question is answered with the *!dumpheap –thinlock* command:

   ```
   0:000> !dumpheap -thinlock
    Address        MT     Size
   01392440 00d443e8       24          ThinLock owner 3 (00199a78) Recursive 0
   01392468 790fa098       12          ThinLock owner 3 (00199a78) Recursive 0
   ```

9. From the preceding listing, both thin locks are owned by Thread 4. This is why the lock count for that thread is 2. The address of the Thread 4 object is 0x00199a78, as the thread list shows. The MT column is the method table of the object that is being waited on. Dump both method tables to find what Thread 4 is waiting for:

   ```
   0:000> !dumpmt 00d443e8
   EEClass: 79126bb0
   Module: 790c2000
   Name: System.Collections.Generic.List`1[[Store.Item, Store]]
   mdToken: 02000287   (C:\WINDOWS\assembly\GAC_32\mscorlib\2.0.0.0__b77a5c561934e089\msco
       rlib.dll)
   BaseSize: 0x18
   ComponentSize: 0x0
   Number of IFaces in IFaceMap: 6
   Slots in VTable: 30
   0:000> !dumpmt 790fa098
   EEClass: 790fa034
   Module: 790c2000
   Name: System.Object
   mdToken: 02000002   (C:\WINDOWS\assembly\GAC_32\mscorlib\2.0.0.0__b77a5c561934e089\msco
       rlib.dll)
   BaseSize: 0xc
   ```

```
ComponentSize: 0x0
Number of IFaces in IFaceMap: 0
Slots in VTable: 14
```

10. What is known? When the program hung, Thread 4 had outstanding locks on a *Store. Item* instance and an *Object* instance. No other thread is holding a lock, which narrows the problem to Thread 4. Here is the source code for Thread 4:

```
private void Forward() {
    lock (items) {
        lock (syncObj) {
            StreamWriter sw = new StreamWriter("forward.txt");
            IEnumerator<Item> enumerator = items.GetEnumerator();
            while (true) {


            }

            while (true)  {
                if (enumerator.MoveNext()) {
                    Item current = enumerator.Current;
                    string message = current.ItemId + " Product Mask: " +
                        ((int)current.Products).ToString();
                    sw.WriteLine(message);
                }
                else {
                    break;
                }
            }
            sw.Close();
        }
    }
}
```

11. Review the code—I hope that the problem is obvious. The lock statement is a shortcut to calling the *Monitor.Enter* method. After acquiring the locks, the program enters an infinite loop. For this reason, the locks are never released. Remove the extraneous *while(true)* loop and rebuild the application (after killing any hung instances of the process that remain in memory). Run the new application and create a few transactions. The program should operate correctly. The forward.txt file is created and contains transactions.

Threads Example #2

The Store application appears to be working, but not in all circumstances. Delete any forward.txt or reverse.txt files that have been created. Then step through the following procedure:

1. Close all instances of the Store application that are running. Now run the Store application in the Threading subfolder and add a couple of transactions. Click Reverse Enumerate, and then click Enumerate. Close the application and check for the forward. txt and reverse.txt files. Neither file has been created. Why not?

2. Restart the Store application. Add two new transactions. Again click Reverse Enumerate, and then click Enumerate.

3. Start WinDbg and attach to the Store application.

4. List the available threads with the *!threads* command. Threads 4 and 5 have a positive lock count, so both are waiting for something:

```
0:006> !threads
ThreadCount: 4
UnstartedThread: 0
BackgroundThread: 1
PendingThread: 0
DeadThread: 0
Hosted Runtime: no
                                       PreEmptive    GC Alloc               Lock
        ID OSID ThreadOBJ    State      GC      Context        Domain     Count
   0     1 e54 001501f8       6020 Enabled  013e7afc:013e7b68 001483a8       0
   2     2 d84 00153e40       b220 Enabled  00000000:00000000 001483a8       0
   4     3 2e0 00191f60   200b020 Enabled  013d9bec:013dbb68 001483a8       1
   5     4 ccc 00190b98   200b020 Enabled  013dfb9c:013e1b68 001483a8       1
```

5. The *!syncblk* command reports on syncblock entries. In the Store application, Thread 5 is waiting for a *Store.Item* instance, while Thread 4 is waiting for an *Object* instance. The fact that no other threads are listed with the *!syncblk* command reaffirms that the problem is probably in Threads 4 and 5:

```
0:006> !syncblk
Index SyncBlock MonitorHeld Recursion Owning Thread Info   SyncBlock Owner
    2 00174854            3          1 00190b98   ccc    5   01392440 System.
            Collections.Generic.List`1[[Store.Item, Store]]
   21 001747f4            3          1 00191f60   2e0    4   01392468 System.Object
-----------------------------
Total             44
CCW                0
RCW                0
ComClassFactory 0
Free               0
```

6. Perform a stack trace on Thread 4. Before displaying the call stack, confirm that the active thread is Thread 4. If not, switch to that thread (~4s). Notice that the *AwareLock:: Enter* method is found on the call stack, which is a marker of thread synchronization. The *WaitForMultipleObjects* method is near the top of the call stack. This means the threads likely are being blocked by something:

```
0:004> kb
ChildEBP RetAddr  Args to Child
0358f4a0 7c90e9ab 7c8094f2 00000001 0358f4cc ntdll!KiFastSystemCallRet
0358f4a4 7c8094f2 00000001 0358f4cc 00000001 ntdll!ZwWaitForMultipleObjects+0xc
0358f540 79f4aa60 00000001 00174868 00000000 KERNEL32!WaitForMultipleObjectsEx+0x12c
0358f5a8 79f16d92 00000001 00174868 00000000 mscorwks!WaitForMultipleObjectsEx_SO_TOL
     ERANT+0x6f
0358f5c8 79f16d03 00000001 00174868 00000000 mscorwks!Thread::DoAppropriateAptStateWa
     it+0x3c
```

```
0358f64c 79f16b9e 00000001 00174868 00000000 mscorwks!Thread::DoAppropriateWaitWorker
    +0x144
0358f69c 79f4a9d9 00000001 00174868 00000000 mscorwks!Thread::DoAppropriateWait+0x40
0358f6f8 79ebc06e ffffffff 00000001 00000000 mscorwks!CLREvent::WaitEx+0xf7
0358f708 7a0fd093 ffffffff 00000001 00000000 mscorwks!CLREvent::Wait+0x17
0358f794 7a0fd28f 00191f60 ffffffff 00191f60 mscorwks!AwareLock::EnterEpilog+0x94
0358f7b0 79f0fe6a 8a20e59b 0358f888 01392214 mscorwks!AwareLock::Enter+0x61
```

7. Look at the parameters for *WaitForMultiple* objects. The first parameter is 1 and indicates that Thread 4 is waiting for a single synchronization object. The second parameter is a pointer to an array of handles. Each handle represents a synchronization object. Because Thread 4 is waiting for one object, there should be only one handle in the array. Display the memory at the address to view that handle:

```
0:004> dd 00174868
00174868  00000658 0000000d 00000000 00000000
00174878  00000000 00000000 00000000 00000000
00174888  00000000 00000000 00000000 80000023
```

8. The handle to the synchronization object is 0x00000658. Use the *!handle* command to obtain more information on that handle. It is an event handle. We have now discovered that Thread 4 is waiting for an event object:

```
0:004> !handle 00000658
Handle 658
    Type          Event
```

9. Repeat steps 6 and 7 for Thread 5. The result should be similar.

10. The problem has been isolated to Threads 4 and 5. Threads 4 and 5 are run as the *Forward* and *Reverse* methods, respectively. Here is the source code for these methods. Both methods have nested locks. However, the locks in the *Forward* and *Reverse* methods are in the opposite order, which is causing a deadlock:

```csharp
private void Forward() {
    lock (items) {
        lock (syncObj) {
            StreamWriter sw = new StreamWriter("forward.txt");
            IEnumerator<Item> enumerator = items.GetEnumerator();

            while (true) {
                // other code
            }
            sw.Close();
        }
    }
}

Object syncObj = new Object();

private void Reverse() {
    lock (syncObj) {
        Thread.Sleep(5000);
```

```
            lock (items) {
                StreamWriter sw = new StreamWriter("reverse.txt");
                items.Reverse();
                IEnumerator<Item> enumerator = items.GetEnumerator();
                while (true) {
                    // other code
                }
                items.Reverse();
                sw.Close();
            }
        }
    }
```

11. Swap the order of the locks in the *Reverse* method and the problem is solved. Restart the Store application and test this.

Exceptions

Have you ever experienced an exception? (See Figure 16-4 for an example.) Of course, I am sure that any exception occurred while you were using an application that *someone else* wrote. As a kind gesture, you volunteered to help diagnose the problem and correct their unstable application.

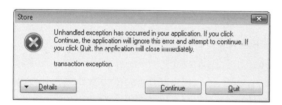

FIGURE 16-4 A typical dialog box reporting an exception

Managed exceptions start life as native exceptions. To raise an exception, the CLR calls *mscorwks!RaiseTheException*. *RaiseTheException* then calls *RaiseException*, which is a system-level API. *RaiseException* assigns all managed exceptions the exception code of *E0434F4D*. Because all managed exceptions are raised with this same exception code, they are indistinguishable as native exceptions. Fortunately, the first parameter of the *RaiseTheException* function call is a managed exception object. You can inspect that object for the specifics of the managed exception.

Exception Example

The Store application in the Exceptions folder has been modified to raise an exception when the Add Transactions button is clicked. The objective of this example is to determine the type of exception.

1. Start the Store application in the Exceptions subfolder. Open WinDbg and attach to the Store program.

2. Set a breakpoint on the *RaiseException* API and resume the application:

```
0:004> bp Kernel32!RaiseException;g
```

3. Click Add Transaction. The exception is raised and the breakpoint is hit in WinDbg. Display the call stack. You should see both *RaiseException* and *RaiseTheExceptionInternalOnly* methods on the call stack.

4. Use the *!dumpobj* command to dump the first parameter of *RaiseTheExceptionInternalOnly*, which is the managed exception object. You now have the details of the exception, including the exception type.

The following two commands are helpful in debugging managed exceptions:

- **sxe clr**   This command has WinDbg break on all unhandled managed exceptions. You then can display the call stack for the details of the exception. This is an alternative to setting a breakpoint on the *RaiseException* API.

- **!soe exceptiontype**   The *Stop On Exception (soe)* command is an SOS command. When the specified managed exception occurs, the application is interrupted. Here is an example:

```
!soe System.DivideByZeroException
```

Symbols

Having the correct symbols for the operating system and your application makes debugging easier. Symbols provide symbolic information on function names, parameter names, and local variables. They also provide line number information for the source code and data to fix frame pointer omissions (FPOs). Without symbol files, little of this valuable information is available and debugging is less transparent. Symbols are contained in a symbol file, which has a *.pdb* extension.

Separate packages of symbol files are available for the different Windows operating systems. Windows 98, Windows 2000, Windows XP, Windows NT Server 2003, and Windows Vista require different symbols. In addition, individual service packs and builds might have some additional symbols. For these reasons, obtaining the correct symbols is sometimes a trial-and-error process. This is further complicated with dumps. You might open a dump on a machine that did not create the dump, and the machine that created the dump might have had a different operating system. Therefore, the local machine must have the symbols for the operating system where the dump was created, as well as symbols for its own operating system. All this makes having the correct symbols for debugging complicated at times. It would be nice if the required symbols could be downloaded to your local machine automatically. Well, they can. That is the purpose of a symbol server.

A *symbol server* is a database of symbol files. It can download to a local cache the correct symbols needed for debugging. For example, Microsoft offers a public symbol store that can download the operating system symbols that you need. It can download the correct symbols from all the Microsoft operating systems. You no longer have to invest a lot of time investigating this. The Web address for the Microsoft Public Symbol Store is *http://msdl. microsoft.com/download/symbols.*

Before using the Microsoft Public Symbol Store, install the correct symbol package for your operating system. You then can use the Microsoft symbol store to fine-tune the remaining symbols. Symbol packages for different Windows environments are downloadable from this location: *http://www.microsoft.com/whdc/devtools/debugging/symbolpkg.mspx.*

Symsrv Symbol Server

The file symsrv.dll is the symbol server engine distributed with Debugging Tools for Windows, and it must be installed in the same directory as the debugger. Symsrv manages downloading symbols from a symbol server to a local cache, which also is called a *downstream store*. Files can be transferred over *http* and *https*.

Here is the generic syntax to download symbol files from a symbol server to a downstream store. It will download only the necessary symbols:

Symsrv*ServerDLL*DownstreamStore*SymbolStore*

In this syntax, *ServerDLL* identifies the symbol server engine. The following command uses the symsrv.dll symbol server engine. It will contact the Microsoft Public Symbol Store to download required symbol files. The symbols are transferred to c:\ symbols, which is specified as the downstream store in this example:

Symsrv*Symsrv*c:\symbols*http://msdl.microsoft.com/download/symbols

Because symsrv.dll is the most prevalent symbol server, an abbreviated syntax is available:

srv*DownstreamStore*SymbolStore*

The following command uses the abbreviated syntax and is identical to the previous expanded command that referenced the symsrv.dll symbol server explicitly and downloaded symbols from the Microsoft Public Symbol Store:

srv*c:\symbols*http://msdl.microsoft.com/download/symbols

As shown in the following syntax, symbol servers can have multiple downstream servers. If the symbol file is not in *DownstreamStore[1]*, it is downloaded from *DownstreamStore[2]*. Furthermore, if the file is not in *DownstreamStore[2]*, *DownstreamStore[3]* is contacted. If the file is found there, it is downloaded from *DownstreamStore[3]* into *DownstreamStore[2]* and then from *DownstreamStore[2]* into *DownstreamStore[1]*. This pattern continues until the debug symbol is found or the symbol stores are exhausted. It is a best practice to list the downstream store in order of proximity. The nearest, such as a local cache, should be listed first:

srv*$DownstreamStore^1$*$DownstreamStore^2$*$DownstreamStore^n$*SymbolStore

In most debuggers, you can set the symbol path, including symbol server and downstream stores. However, to avoid configuring the symbol path separately in each debugger, you can use the _NT_SYMBOL_PATH environment variable. Most debuggers automatically read the _NT_SYMBOL_PATH environment variable to set the default symbol path.

Application Symbols

The Microsoft Public Symbol Store downloads the symbols for the environment. The symbols for your application also are required. You should build symbols for both the release and debug versions of your product. Building symbols for a release version of a product does not affect the performance of that application. Symbols also should be checked into source control to keep correct symbol packages with different versions of the product. Preserve symbols for all public versions of your product, so that when you are debugging a client problem, you are assured of having the correct symbols available.

Visual Studio .NET automatically creates a symbol file (PDB) for both debug and release versions of the product.

WinDbg

In WinDbg, the symbol path can be set via the user interface or via the command line. From the user interface, select the Symbol File Path command from the File menu. Alternatively, at the command line, use the .sympath directive to set or display the symbol path. The .sympath command without options will display the symbol path. Otherwise, the .sympath command will set the symbol path to the path provided. Whenever you change the symbol path, reload the symbols with the .reload command. In the Symbol File Path dialog box, there is a Reload check box.

For symbol problems, the !sym noisy command is helpful. It displays additional information when symbols are loaded to diagnose possible problems. The !sym quiet command, which is the default, suppresses the additional data.

Memory Management

Memory management was introduced in this chapter. Concepts such as root objects, reference trees, generations, and finalization queues were reviewed. The next chapter expands the conversation to include the disposable pattern, weak references, unsafe pointers, and other topics related to memory management.

Understanding the managed paradigm to memory management is particularly important to C-based and C++-based programmers. C programmers are accustomed to managing their own memory with minimal assistance from the environment. For them, memory management in .NET represents a different mindset, which includes adopting different best practices for allocating, managing, and releasing memory. Some C developers perceive the managed memory model as confining, when actually it is liberating. You are liberated from the internal intricacies of memory management.

Although the CLR provides memory management, developers can influence the process, which includes pinned pointer, memory stress, forcing garbage collection, and allocation patterns. These topics are introduced in the next chapter.

Part V
Advanced Features

Chapter 17
Memory Management

Memory management is an essential ingredient of every program except the most trivial applications. There are different classifications of memory. Registers, static data area (SDA), stacks, thread local storage (TLS), heaps, virtual memory, and file storage are types of memory. Registers hold data that require quick and efficient memory access. Critical system information, such as the instruction pointer and the stack pointer, are stored in dedicated registers. Static and global values are stored automatically in the SDA. Stacks are thread-specific and hold function-related information. Local variables, parameters, return values, the instruction pointer of the calling function, and other function-related information is placed on the stack. There is a stack frame on the call stack for each outstanding function. TLS is also thread-specific storage. The TLS table is 64 slots of 32-bit values that contain thread-specific data. TLS slots frequently hold pointers to dynamically allocated memory that belongs to the thread. Heaps contain memory allocated at run time, from the virtual memory of an application, and are controlled by the heap manager. An application can have more than one heap. Large objects are commonly placed on the heap, whereas small objects are typically placed on the stack. Virtual memory is memory that developers directly manipulate at run time with transparent assistance from the environment. Virtual memory is ideal for collections of disparate-sized data stored in noncontiguous memory, such as a link list.

Managed applications can directly manipulate the stack, managed heap, and TLS. Other forms of memory, such as registers and virtual memory, are largely unavailable except through interoperability. Instances of value types and references (not the referenced objects) reside on the stack. These are generically called the *locals*. Referenced objects are found on the managed heap.

The lifetime of a local is defined by scope. When a local loses scope, it is removed from the stack. For example, the parameters of a function are removed from the stack when the function is exited. The lifetime of an object on the managed heap is controlled by the Garbage Collector (GC), which is a part of the Common Language Runtime (CLR). The GC periodically performs garbage collection to remove unused objects.

The policies and best practices of the GC and garbage collection are the primary focus of this chapter. The tradition of C-based developers, as related to memory management, is somewhat different from other developers—particularly Microsoft Visual Basic and Java developers. The memory model employed in Visual Basic and Java is cosmetically similar to the managed environment. However, the memory model of most C-based languages is dissimilar to this environment. These differences make this chapter especially important to developers with a C background.

Developers in C-based languages are accustomed to deterministic garbage collection, where developers explicitly set the lifetime of an object. The *malloc/free* and *new/delete* statement combinations create and destroy objects and values that reside on a heap. Managing the memory of a heap with these tools requires programmer discipline, which proves to be inconsistent with robust code. Memory leaks and other problems are common in C and C++. These leaks can eventually destabilize an application or cause complete application failure. Instead of each developer individually struggling with these issues, the managed environment has the GC, which is omnipresent and controls the lifetime of objects located on the managed heap.

The GC offers nondeterministic garbage collection. Developers explicitly allocate memory for objects. However, the GC determines when garbage collection is performed to clean up unused objects from the managed heap. There is no *delete* operator.

When memory for an object is allocated at run time, the GC returns a reference for that object. As mentioned, the reference is placed on the stack. The *new* operator requests that an instance of a type (an object) be placed on the managed heap. A reference is an indirect pointer to that object. This indirection helps the GC transparently manage the managed heap, including the relocation of objects when necessary.

In .NET, the GC removes unused objects from the heap. When is an object unused? Reference counting is not normally performed in the managed environment. Reference counting was common to Component Object Model (COM) components. When the reference count became zero, the related COM component was considered no longer relevant and was removed from memory. This model had many problems. First, it required careful synchronization of the *AddRef* and *Release* methods. Breakdown of synchronization could sometimes cause memory leakage and exceptions. Second, reference counting was expensive. Reference counting was applied to both collectable and noncollectable components, and it was unnecessarily expensive to perform reference counting on objects that were never collected. Finally, programs incurred the overhead of reference counting, even when there was no memory stress on the application. For this reason, reference counting was deservedly abandoned for a more efficient model that addresses the memory concerns of modern applications. When there is memory stress in the managed environment, garbage collection occurs, and an object graph is built. Objects not on the graph become candidates for collection and are removed from memory sometime in the future.

Unmanaged Resources

Unmanaged resources and memory can cause problems.

Some managed types are wrappers from unmanaged resources. A wrapper can have a managed and unmanaged memory footprint, which affects memory management and garbage collection. The underlying unmanaged resource of a managed object might consume copious amount of unmanaged memory, which cannot be ignored. This sometimes leads to a disparity between the amount of memory used in managed memory versus the amount used in native memory. Developers can compensate for this disparity and avoid unpleasant surprises. You can no longer hide an unmanaged elephant inside a managed closet.

A managed wrapper class for a bitmap is one example. The wrapper class is relatively small (a thimble), and the memory associated with the managed object is trivial. However, the bitmap is the elephant. A bitmap requires large amounts of memory, which cannot be ignored. If ignored, creating several managed bitmaps could cause your application to be trampled unexpectedly by a stampede of elephants.

The relationship between an unmanaged resource and the related managed wrapper can be latent. This can delay the release of sensitive resources, which in turn can result in resource contention, poor responsiveness, or application failure. For example, the *FileStream* class is a wrapper for a native resource: a physical file. The *FileStream* instance, which is a managed component, is collected nondeterministically. Therefore, the duration between when the file is no longer needed and when the managed component is collected could be substantial. This could prevent access to the file from within and outside your application, even though the file is not being used. When the file is no longer needed, the ability to release the file deterministically is imperative. You need the ability to say "Close the file *now*." The *Disposable* pattern provides this ability and helps developers manage memory resources.

Some unmanaged resources are discrete. When consumed in a managed application, discrete resources must be tracked to prevent overconsumption. The overconsumption of unmanaged resources can have an adverse affect on the managed application, including the potential of resource contention or raising an exception. For example, suppose that a device can support three simultaneous connections. What happens when a fourth connection is requested? In the managed environment, you should be able to handle this scenario gracefully.

The topics in this section highlight unmanaged resources management, which potentially has an impact on proper memory management. For this reason, these topics are discussed throughout this chapter.

Garbage Collection Overview

This section is an overview of garbage collection. A detailed explanation of the mechanics of garbage collection is presented in Chapter 16, "Advanced Debugging." Two assumptions guide the implementation of garbage collection in the managed environment. The first assumption is that objects are more likely to communicate with other objects of a similar size. The second assumption is that smaller objects are short-lived objects, whereas larger objects are long-lived objects. For these reasons, the GC attempts to organize objects based on size and age.

In the managed environment, garbage collection is nondeterministic. With the exception of the *GC.Collect* method, whose use is discouraged, developers cannot explicitly initiate garbage collection. The managed heap is segmented into Generations 0, 1, and 2. The initial sizes of the generations are about 256 kilobytes (KB), 2 megabytes (MB), and 10 MB, respectively. As the application executes, the GC fine-tunes the thresholds based on the pattern of memory allocations. Garbage collection is prompted when the threshold for Generation 0 is exceeded. At that time, objects that can be discarded are removed from memory. Objects that survive garbage collection are promoted from Generation 0 to 1. The generations then are compacted and references are updated. If Generation 0 and Generation 1 exceed their thresholds during garbage collection, both generations are collected. Surviving objects are promoted from Generation 1 to Generation 2 and from Generation 0 to Generation 1. In fewer instances, all three generations will exceed thresholds and require collection. The later generations typically contain larger objects, which live longer. Because the short-lived objects reside primarily on Generation 0, most garbage collection is focused in this generation. Generations allow garbage collection to implement a partial cleanup of the managed heap at a substantial performance benefit.

Objects larger than 85 KB are considered large, and they are treated differently from other objects. Large objects are placed on the large object heap, not in a generation. Large objects are generally long-lived components. Placing large objects on the large object heap eliminates the need to promote these objects between generations, thereby conserving resources and reducing the number of overall collection cycles. The large object heap is collected with Generation 2, so large objects are collected only during a full garbage-collection cycle.

When garbage collection is performed, the GC builds a graph of live objects, called an *object graph,* to determine which objects are not rooted and can be discarded. First the GC populates the object graph with root references. The root references of an application are global, static, and local references. Local references include references that are function variables and parameters. The GC then adds to the graph those objects reachable from a root reference. An embedded object of a local is an example of an object reachable from a root reference. Of course, the embedded object could contain other objects. The GC extrapolates all the reachable objects to compose the branches of the object graph. Objects can appear only once in the object graph, which avoids circular references and related problems. Objects not in the graph are not rooted and are considered candidates for garbage collection.

Objects that are not rooted can hold outstanding references to other objects. In this circumstance, the object and the objects that it references potentially can be collected. (See Figure 17-1.)

The Rooted application demonstrates how non-rooted objects are collected. In the application, the *Branch* class contains the *Leaf* class, which contains the *Leaf2* class. In the *Form1* class, an instance of the *Branch* class is defined as a field. When an instance of the *Branch* class is created, it is rooted through the *Form1* instance. *Leaf* and *Leaf2* instances are rooted through the *Branch* field. (See Figure 17-2.)

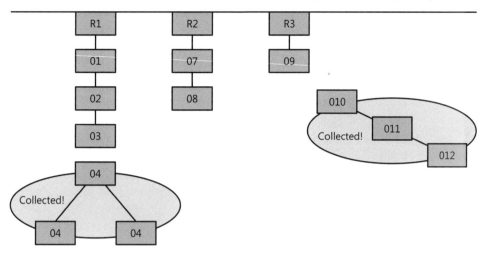

FIGURE 17-1 Rooted and nonrooted objects

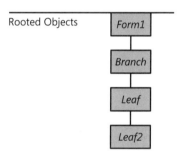

FIGURE 17-2 An object graph of the Rooted application

In the following code, a modal message box is displayed in the finalizer. This is done here for demonstration purposes only—it generally is considered bad practice:

```
public class Branch {
    ~Branch() {
        MessageBox.Show("Branch destructor");
    }
    public Leaf e = new Leaf();
}


public class Leaf {
    ~Leaf() {
        MessageBox.Show("Leaf destructor");
    }
    public Leaf2 e2 = new Leaf2();
}


public class Leaf2 {
    ~Leaf2() {
```

```
            MessageBox.Show("Leaf2 destructor");
        }
    }
}
```

The user interface of the Rooted application allows users to create the *Branch*, which includes *Leaf* instances. (See Figure 17-3.) You then can set the *Branch* or any specific *Leaf* to *null*, which interrupts the path to the root object. That nullified object is collectable. Objects that are rooted through the nullified object are also now collectable in this application. For example, if the *Leaf* instance is set to *null*, the *Branch* instance is not collectable; it is before the *Leaf* reference in the object graph. However, any *Leaf2* object belonging to the *Leaf* is immediately a candidate for collection. After setting the *Branch* or *Leaf* objects to *null*, garbage collection can occur. If it doesn't occur, click the Collect Memory button in the application to force garbage collection.

FIGURE 17-3 The Rooted application

As mentioned, garbage collection occurs when the memory threshold of Generation 0 is exceeded. Other events, which are described in the following list, can prompt garbage collection:

- Frequent allocations can accelerate garbage collection cycles by stressing the memory generations.

- Garbage collection is conducted when the memory available to any generation is exceeded. The *GC.AddMemoryPressure* method artificially applies pressure to the managed heap to account for the memory footprint of an unmanaged resource.

- The limit of handles for an unmanaged resource is reached. The *HandleCollector* class sets limits for handles.

- Garbage collection can be forced with the *GC.Collect* method. This behavior is not recommended because forcing garbage collection is expensive. Nonetheless, this is sometimes necessary.

- Garbage collection also occurs when overall system memory is low.

Certain suppositions are made for garbage collection in the managed environment. For example, small objects are generally short-lived. Coding contrary to these assumptions can be costly. Although it makes for an interesting theoretical experiment, this is not recommended for production applications. Defining a basket of short-lived but larger objects is an example of coding against assumptions of managed garbage collection, which would force frequent and full collections. Full collections are particularly expensive. Defining a collection of near-large objects—objects that are slightly less than 85 KB—is another example. These objects would apply immediate and significant memory pressure. Because they are probably long-lived, you have the overhead of eventually promoting the near-large objects to Generation 2. It would be more efficient to pad the near-large objects with a buffer, forcing them into large object status, in which the objects are directly placed onto the large object heap. You must remain cognizant of the underlying principle of garbage collection: Implement policies that enhance, rather than exacerbate, garbage collection in the managed environment.

One such policy is to limit boxing. Constant boxing of value types can trigger more frequent garbage collection. Boxing creates a copy of the value type on the managed heap. Most value types are small, and the resulting object placed on the managed heap is larger than the original value. This is yet another reason that boxing is inefficient and should be avoided when possible. This is particularly a problem with collection types. The best solution is to use generic types as described in Chapter 7, "Generics."

Finalization is discussed in complete detail in the section titled "Finalizers" later in this chapter.

GC Flavors

There are two flavors of garbage collection: Workstation GC is optimized for a workstation or single-processor system, whereas Server GC is fine-tuned for a server machine that has multiple processors. Workstation GC is the default; Server GC is never the default—even with a multiprocessor system. Server GC can be enabled in the application configuration file. If your application is hosted by a server application, that application might be preconfigured for Server GC. Your application then will execute with Server GC.

Workstation GC can have concurrent garbage collection enabled or disabled. *Concurrent* is a single thread concurrently servicing the user interface and garbage collection. The thread simultaneously responds to events of the user interface while also handling garbage collection responsibilities. The alternative is non-concurrent. When garbage collection is performed, other responsibilities, such as servicing the user interface, are deferred.

Workstation GC with Concurrent Garbage Collection

Workstation GC with concurrent garbage collection is the default. It is ideal for desktop applications, where the user interface must remain responsive. When garbage collection occurs, it will not subjugate the user interface. Concurrency applies only to full garbage collection, which involves the collection of Generation 2. When Generation 2 is collected, Generation 0 and Generation 1 also are collected. Partial garbage collection of Generation 0 or Generation 1 is a quick action. The potential impact on the user interface is minimal, and concurrent garbage collection is not merited.

The following are the garbage collection steps for Workstation GC with concurrent processing:

1. A GC thread performs an allocation.

2. Garbage collection is triggered.

3. All managed threads are paused.

4. Garbage collection occurs. If garbage collection is completed, proceed to step 5.

5. Interrupt garbage collection. Resume threads for a short time to respond to user interface requests. Return to step 3.

6. Resume threads.

In step 2, threads are suspended at a secure point. The CLR maintains a table of secure points for use during garbage collection. If a thread is not at a secure point, it is hijacked until a secure point is reached or the current function returns. Then the thread is suspended.

Workstation GC Without Concurrent Garbage Collection

Workstation GC without concurrent garbage collection is selected when Server GC is chosen on a single-processor machine. With this option, priority is placed on garbage collection rather than on the user interface.

Here are the garbage collection steps for Workstation GC without concurrent processing:

1. A GC thread performs an allocation.

2. Garbage collection is triggered.

3. All managed threads are paused.

4. Garbage collection is conducted.

5. Managed threads resume.

Server GC

Server GC is designed for multiprocessor machines that are commonly deployed as servers, such as Web, application, and database servers. In the server environment, emphasis is on throughput and not the user interfaces. The Server GC is fine-tuned for scalability. For optimum scalability, garbage collection is not handled on a single thread. The Server GC allocates a separate managed heap and garbage collection thread for every processor.

Here are the garbage collection steps with Server GC:

1. A GC thread performs an allocation.

2. Garbage collection is triggered.

3. Managed threads are suspended.

4. Garbage collection is performed.

5. Managed threads are resumed.

Configuring GC Flavor

Workstation GC with concurrent garbage collection can be enabled or disabled in an application configuration file. Because concurrent is the default, the configuration file is used primarily to disable concurrent garbage collection. This is set in the *gcConcurrent* tag, as shown in the following code:

```
<configuration>
    <runtime>
        <gcConcurrent enabled="false"/>
    </runtime>
</configuration>
```

When needed, Server GC is also stipulated in the application configuration file. Remember that Server GC is never the default—even in a multiprocessor environment. Select the Server GC using the *gcServer* tag, as demonstrated in the following code:

```
<configuration>
    <runtime>
        <gcServer enabled="true"/>
    </runtime>
</configuration>
```

Finalizers

Resources of an object are cleaned up in a *Finalize* method. Before an object is removed from memory, the *Finalize* method is called to allow for cleanup that is related to the object. *Finalize* methods are called *finalizers*. Every object inherits the *Finalize* method from the *System.Object* type. Here is the signature of the *Finalize* method:

protected virtual void Finalize()

Finalizers are not called programmatically; they are called automatically during the garbage collection cycle. Garbage collection is nondeterministic, which means that the finalizer may not be called immediately after the object no longer is needed. Unmanaged resources that might be released in a finalizer, such as files, database connections, and devices, might not be released in a timely manner. This delay in relinquishing resources can have adverse side effects on the current application and possibly other applications as well.

Instead of a *Finalize* method, C# has a destructor. Calling a *Finalize* method explicitly is not allowed and would cause a compiler error. Destructor methods are preceded with a tilde (~) and share the name of the class.

Here is the Destructor syntax:

~Classname()

The Destructor syntax has the following limitations:

- Destructors do not have modifiers.

- Destructors are protected and virtual by default.

- Destructors have no parameters.

- Destructors cannot be overloaded.

- Destructors do not have a return type. The implied return type of a destructor is *void*.

The C# compiler converts destructors to *Finalize* methods, which override the inherited method. Here is a simple destructor:

```
~ZClass() {
    --propCount;
}
```

The C# compiler will emit a *Finalize* method for the *ZClass*. The *Finalize* method replaces the destructor in Microsoft Intermediate Language (MSIL) code. Figure 17-4 shows the *ZClass* class. Notice the *Finalize* method and the absence of the *Destructor* method.

FIGURE 17-4   A view of the *ZClass* class

The C# compiler generates the following MSIL code for the *ZClass* destructor (for clarity, extraneous code has been removed from the listing):

```
.method family hidebysig virtual instance void Finalize() cil managed
{
    .maxstack  2
    .try
    {
        IL_0001:  ldsfld     uint8 Donis.CSharpBook.ZClass::propCount
        IL_0006:  ldc.i4.1
        IL_0007:  sub
        IL_0008:  conv.u1
        IL_0009:  stsfld     uint8 Donis.CSharpBook.ZClass::propCount
        IL_000f:  leave.s    IL_0019

    }
```

```
    finally
    {
        IL_0011:  ldarg.0
        IL_0012:  call        instance void[mscorlib]System.Object::Finalize()
        IL_0018:  endfinally
    }
    IL_0019:  nop
    IL_001a:  ret
}
```

The *Finalize* method provided by the C# compiler contains a termination handler, which is the *finally* block. The *try* block contains the code from the original C# *ZClass* destructor. The termination handler calls the *Finalize* method of the base class. Because the call is in a termination handler, the finalizer of the base class is called even if an unhandled exception is raised in the destructor of the current class. This means that calls to the *Finalize* method propagate through the class hierarchy even when an exception is raised. This also means that developers should never attempt to call the destructor of the base class directly. The compiler-generated *Finalize* method assumes this responsibility.

Many developers have lamented the decision to associate finalizers with destructors. C++ developers are familiar with destructors. They are an integral part of the C++ language. This familiarity creates a level of expectation, which is honored only partially in C#. There are tangible differences between C++ and C# destructors, including the following:

- C++ destructors can be called deterministically, whereas C# destructors are called nondeterministically.

- C++ destructors can be virtual or nonvirtual, whereas C# destructors are implicitly virtual.

- C++ destructors execute on the same thread that created the object, whereas C# destructors execute on a dedicated finalizer thread.

- C++ destructors cannot be suppressed at run time, whereas C# destructors can be suppressed.

> **Note** For the remainder of this chapter, the terms *destructor* and *finalizer* are used synonymously.

As mentioned already, finalizers are called nondeterministically. In code, you cannot call them directly. When are finalizers called?

- During the garbage collection process

- When the *AppDomain* of an object is unloaded

- When the *GC.Collect* method is called

- When the CLR is shutting down

Knowing the specific reason for finalization can be helpful. You can confirm that finalization is initiated by an application unload or by a CLR shutdown. The *AppDomain.IsFinalizingForUnload* method, which is an instance method, returns *true* if the application domain is unloading and finalization has begun on objects in that domain. Otherwise, the method returns *false*. The *Environment.HasShutdownStarted* property is a static property that returns *true* if the CLR is shutting down or the application domain is unloading. Otherwise, the property returns *false*.

The Recycle application resurrects an instance of the *ZClass* type. When the object is being finalized, the *Environment.HasShutdownStarted* property is checked. If *false*, the reference to the object is re-established, which ends finalization. This resurrects the object. (We'll discuss more about resurrection in the section titled "Resurrection" later in this chapter.) If the property is *true*, the object is not recycled. There is no reason to recycle an object if the current application domain is unloading or the CLR is shutting down. Here is the *ZClass* type from the Recycle application:

```
public class ZClass {
    public ZClass() {
        ++propCount;
        _count = propCount;
    }

    ~ZClass() {
        AppDomain current = AppDomain.CurrentDomain;
        if (!Environment.HasShutdownStarted) {
            Form1.obj = this;
            GC.ReRegisterForFinalize(this);
        }
    }

    private static int propCount = 0;
    private int _count;
    public int Count {
        get {
            return _count;
        }
    }
}
```

At application shutdown, finalizers have a limited amount of time to complete their tasks. This prevents an indefinite shutdown. Each *Finalize* method has 2 seconds to complete. If the time allotment is exceeded, that finalizer terminates, and the remaining finalizers then can execute. As a group, the *Finalize* methods have 40 seconds to complete all finalization chores. When this time limit is exceeded, the remaining finalizers are skipped. In terms of processing time, 40 seconds is nearly an eternity and should be sufficient to complete even the most elaborate housecleaning of an application.

In the following application, you can adjust the duration of the finalizer and view the results. Entering a number between 1 and 10 provides the best comparative results. Entering 1 from the command line causes the shortest destructor from a *ZClass* object. Larger numbers make the destructor run longer. Specify the value as a command-line argument:

```csharp
using System;
using System.Threading;

namespace Donis.CSharpBook {
    public class Starter {
        private static void Main(string[] args) {
            Shutdown.ZTime = int.Parse(args[0]);
            ZClass[] obj = new ZClass[500];
            for(int count = 0; count < 500; ++count) {
                obj[count] = new ZClass();
            }
        }
    }

    public class Shutdown {
        static public int ZTime = 0;
    }

    public class ZClass {

        public ZClass() {
            ++globalcount;
            localcount = globalcount;
        }

        private int localcount = 0;
        private static int globalcount = 0;

        ~ZClass() {
            for(int i = 0; i < Shutdown.ZTime; ++i) {
                Thread.Sleep(50);
            }
            Console.WriteLine(localcount + " " +
                "ZClass destructor");
        }
    }
}
```

Finalizer Thread

The finalizer thread calls finalizers on objects waiting in the *FReachable* queue. After the finalizer is called, the object is removed from the *FReachable* queue and deleted from memory during the next garbage collection cycle. The finalizer thread executes the finalizer asynchronously. Finalizer threads service all finalizers of the application, which creates a potential bottleneck. For this reason, finalizers should be short and simple. A long finalizer can delay the finalization of the remaining objects on the *FReachable* queue. This extends the lifetime of those objects pending finalization and increases memory pressure on the managed heap. This in turn causes more garbage collection, which is costly.

Finalizer Considerations

When implementing finalizers, developers should consider several factors. Some of these considerations emphasize that finalizers should be avoided whenever possible. For example, you should never implement an empty finalizer. In the C++ language, an empty destructor is harmless. In C#, an empty destructor (finalizer) is costly, as explained in this section. These are the factors:

- The high expense of finalizers
- Lack of guarantee
- Multithreading
- One finalizer thread
- Finalizers and virtual functions
- Unpredictable order of finalization
- Resurrection
- Finalizers and reentrancy
- Deep object graphs
- Finalizer race conditions
- Constructors
- The *Console* class and finalization

High expense of finalizers   As demonstrated several times already in this chapter, finalizers are expensive. At least two garbage collection cycles are required to collect a finalizable object that is not rooted. During the first garbage collection, the finalizable object is moved from the *Finalizable* queue to the *FReachable* queue. After the finalizer has been called, the memory of the object is reclaimed in a future garbage collection. The lifetime of objects referenced by the finalizable object are equally extended. They must wait for the finalizable object to be reclaimed before being released themselves. This extra object retention increases memory pressure, which causes additional garbage collection. The finalizable objects are promoted to later generations, which make a full garbage collection more likely, and full garbage collection is even more expensive.

The extra expense of defining a finalizable object actually starts at its allocation. When a finalizable object is created, a reference to the object must be added to the *Finalizable* queue. Objects without finalizers avoid this additional expense at allocation.

Lack of guarantee   Finalizers are not always called. Some of the reasons why a finalizer might not be called have already been mentioned. One such reason is the shutdown of the CLR by a host application. Another cause is if the finalizers exceed the remaining available time. In addition, you can programmatically suppress a finalizer with the *GC.SuppressFinalize* method. An asynchronous exception, such as a thread abort exception, can cause a finalizer not to run.

Multithreading Finalizable objects are multithreaded. Object code and the finalizer execute on different threads. For this reason, certain activities should be avoided in the finalizer. Most notably, never access TLS associated with the object in the finalizer. Because the thread context has changed, using TLS in the finalizer is inappropriate.

The TLS sample application contains the following code, which uses TLS. This is a Windows Forms application. It contains a *TMonitor* class that logs messages to a file. The *TMonitor* class maintains a reference to several *StreamWriter* objects, which are stored in the TLS table of each thread. For this reason, threads accessing the same *TMonitor* object will use different *StreamWriter* objects that are retrieved from each thread's individual TLS table. Therefore, each thread will write status messages to a different file. In the sample application, two threads are accessing a *TMonitor* instance. In the destructor of the *TMonitor* type, a *StreamWriter* is retrieved from TLS and closed. Which *StreamWriter* is closed? Is this the *StreamWriter* of the first or second thread? The answer is *neither*. The destructor is running on the finalizer thread, which is unrelated to the other threads. This thread has no *StreamWriter* reference, and an error is reported using the *Console.WriteLine* method. In Microsoft Visual Studio, *Console.WriteLine* in a Windows Forms application displays text in the Output window. The following application is for demonstration purposes only. In a finalizer, you should not reference other managed objects. A corrected version of this code is presented in the section titled "TLS Example" later in this chapter.

```
class TMonitor {
    public void WriteFile() {
        StreamWriter sw = Thread.GetData(Form1.Slot) as StreamWriter;
        if (sw == null) {
            sw = new StreamWriter(string.Format(
                @"C:\{0}File.txt",
                Thread.CurrentThread.Name),
                true);
            Thread.SetData(Form1.Slot, sw);
        }
        sw.WriteLine(DateTime.Now.ToLongTimeString());
    }

    ~TMonitor() {
        StreamWriter sw = Thread.GetData(Form1.Slot) as StreamWriter;
        if (sw != null) {
            sw.Close();
        }
        else {
            Console.WriteLine("Error in destructor");
        }
    }
}
```

One finalizer thread   There is a single finalizer thread that services the *FReachable* queue. It calls pending finalizers of finalizable objects. The finalizer thread is different from other threads that might be accessing the object methods. Do not change the context of the finalization thread. *This is not your thread.* Changing the context of the finalization thread can have adverse effects on the finalization process.

Finalizers and virtual functions   Do not call virtual functions from finalizers. This can cause unexpected behavior such as inadvertent leaks and resources not being cleaned up. If overridden, there is no assurance that the derived class will provide the appropriate implementation related to the destructor. This is especially true for classes published in a class library, in which the developer of the derived class might have limited knowledge of the base class, including the destructor.

Look at the following sample code:

```csharp
using System;

namespace Donis.CSharpBook {
    public class Starter {
        private static void Main() {
            YClass obj = new YClass();
        }
    }

    public class ZClass {

        protected virtual void CloseResource() {
            Console.WriteLine("Closing ZClass resource.");
        }

        ~ZClass() {
            CloseResource();
        }
    }


    public class YClass : ZClass {

        protected override void CloseResource() {
            Console.WriteLine("Closing YClass resource.");
        }

        ~YClass() {
            CloseResource();
        }

    }
}
```

In the preceding code, the finalizer in the *ZClass* calls the *CloseResource* method, which is a virtual method. *YClass* is derived from *ZClass* and overrides the *CloseResource* method.

An instance of the derived class is created in the *Main* method. At garbage collection, the following messages are displayed:

```
Closing YClass resource.
Closing YClass resource.
```

Yes, *CloseResource* of the derived class is called twice—from the *ZClass* and the *YClass* destructors. Because *CloseResource* is virtual in the base class, the *ZClass* destructor calls *CloseResource* on the derived type. Calling *CloseResource* incorrectly twice creates a couple of problems. First, an exception could be raised on the second attempt to close the resource. Second, the *CloseResource* method is not called in the *ZClass*. The *ZClass* resource is leaked and not removed.

Unpredictable order of finalization   Garbage collection on objects is not performed in a guaranteed sequence. For this reason, you do not want to access another managed object in the finalizer. There is no assurance that the other managed object has not been collected and removed from memory.

In the following code, the *ZClass* has a *StreamWriter* field. In the finalizer, the *StreamWriter* is closed. Normally, this is perfectly acceptable behavior, but not in a finalizer. In the application, an exception is raised in the finalizer during garbage collection. The *StreamWriter* object was collected before the finalizer of the *ZClass* is called. Therefore, an exception is raised in the finalizer:

```
public class ZClass {
    public ZClass() {
        sw = new StreamWriter("test.txt");
    }

    ~ZClass() {
        sw.Close();
    }

    private StreamWriter sw;
}
```

Resurrection   You can intentionally (or, more likely, inadvertently) resurrect an object permanently during the finalization process. At that time, the object is resurrected without the finalizer attached. Therefore, the resurrected object is not completely returned to live status and becomes a zombie. Zombies pose a distinct problem because of their dangling finalizers. Because a finalizer is not called on the resurrected object, proper cleanup is not performed when the zombie is collected later. The result could be a memory leak, a resource not being released, or other related problems. You can reconnect the finalizer manually with the *GC.ReRegisterForFinalize* method. Afterward, the object is normal and is no longer a zombie.

Conversely, another problem with resurrection is that the original finalizer might have executed. This could render the object unusable because needed resources might have been relinquished.

During finalization, a common cause of accidental resurrection is the creation of a new reference to the current object. At that moment, the object is resurrected. Objects with a reference cannot be collected. Despite being resurrected, the finalizer of the object runs to completion. In the following code, the current object is directly referenced in the finalizer. For most applications, indirect references are more likely the culprit. Developers are unlikely to place a direct reference to the current object in a destructor. Referencing another managed object in a finalizer can have a domino effect, which could cause an indirect reference and should be avoided. That object might access another managed object, which might reference another object and so on until something references the current object. *Voilà*—resurrection has occurred:

```
using System;
using System.IO;

namespace Donis.CSharpBook {

    public class Starter {

        private static void Main() {
            obj = new ZClass();
            obj.TimeStamp();
            obj = null;
            GC.Collect();
            GC.WaitForPendingFinalizers();
            obj.TimeStamp(); // exception raised
        }

        public static ZClass obj;
    }

    public class ZClass {

        public ZClass() {
            sw = new StreamWriter("test.txt");
        }

        public void TimeStamp() {
            sw.WriteLine(DateTime.Now.ToLongTimeString());
        }

        ~ZClass() {
            Starter.obj = this;
            sw.Close();
            sw = null;
        }
```

```
        static private StreamWriter sw;
    }
}
```

In the preceding code, the first statement in the *ZClass* destructor resurrects the object. That statement assigns the object reference to a static field of the *Starter* class. Because this creates another reference, the object will be resurrected. Next in the destructor, the underlying file of the *StreamWriter* instance is then closed. In *Main*, where the program starts, an instance of the *ZClass* is created. The instance is assigned to a static field of the *Starter* class. Afterward, the reference is assigned *null*, and garbage collection is forced with *GC.Collect*. This kills and then resurrects the object. The next call on the object (*obj.TimeStamp*) raises an exception because the underlying file has been closed in the previous finalization. The *TimeStamp* method refers to the file, which is now closed.

The following destructor is a modification of the previous code that reconnects the finalizer upon resurrection. The first statement confirms whether the CLR is shutting down. If true, the managed application is exiting. In that circumstance, it would be nonsensical to resurrect the object. In the *if* block, the object is resurrected and the finalizer is reattached:

```
~ZClass() {
    if (Environment.HasShutdownStarted == false) {
        Starter.obj = this;
        sw.Close();
        sw = null;
        GC.ReRegisterForFinalize(this);
    }
}
```

The *TimeStamp* method must also be updated. The *StreamWriter* instance might be *null*. This is checked in the revised *TimeStamp* method. If *null*, the *sw* reference is reinitialized. The file resource is then available again for writing:

```
public void TimeStamp() {
    if (sw == null) {
        sw = new StreamWriter("test.txt", true);
    }
    sw.WriteLine(DateTime.Now.ToLongTimeString());
    sw.Flush();
}
```

Here is the revised application:

```
using System;
using System.IO;

namespace Donis.CSharpBook {

    public class Starter {
```

```
        private static void Main() {
            obj = new ZClass();
            obj.TimeStamp();
            obj = null;
            GC.Collect();
            GC.WaitForPendingFinalizers();
            obj.TimeStamp();  // exception not raised
        }

        public static ZClass obj;
    }

    public class ZClass {

        public ZClass() {
            sw = new StreamWriter("test.txt", true);
        }

        public void TimeStamp() {
            if (sw == null) {
                sw = new StreamWriter("test.txt", true);
            }
            sw.WriteLine(DateTime.Now.ToLongTimeString());
            sw.Flush();
        }

        ~ZClass() {
            if (Environment.HasShutdownStarted == false) {
                Starter.obj = this;
                sw.Close();
                sw = null;
                GC.ReRegisterForFinalize(this);
            }
        }

        static private StreamWriter sw;
    }
}
```

Finalizers and reentrancy   A finalizer is reentrant. The best example of this is complete resurrection, in which the finalizer is reattached. In that circumstance, the finalizer is called at least twice. When a finalizer is called more than once, resurrection is the likely culprit. Redundant calls on a finalizer should not cause a logic error or an exception.

Deep object graphs   A deep object graph can make garbage collection more expensive. Roots and branches of the object graph can be anchored with a finalizable object. As mentioned, the lifetime of a finalizable object is extended to encompass at least two garbage collections. All objects on the finalizable object branch, even nonfinalizable objects, have their lives similarly extended. Therefore, one finalizable object can keep several other objects from being garbage-collected. Deeper object graphs by definition have longer branches and can extend the problem to more objects.

Finalizer race conditions   The finalizer can execute at the same time as other functions of the same object. Because the finalizer executes on a dedicated thread, other functions of the finalizable object could be running when finalization starts. This can cause a race condition to occur between that behavior and finalization. Standard thread-synchronization techniques can protect against a finalization race condition.

In the following code, *MethodA* is called on a *ZClass* instance. *MethodA* has a built-in delay. Shortly thereafter, the related object is set to *null* and collected. Because *MethodA* is stalled, the finalizer then runs concurrently with *MethodA*. The race has begun! The results are unpredictable:

```
public class Starter {

    private static void Main() {
        Thread t = new Thread(
            new ThreadStart(MethodA));
        obj = new ZClass();
        t.Start();
        obj = null;
        GC.Collect();
    }

    private static void MethodA() {
        obj.MethodB();
    }

    private static ZClass obj;
}

public class ZClass {

    public void MethodB() {
        Console.WriteLine("ZClass.MethodB Started");
        Thread.Sleep(1500);
        Console.WriteLine("ZClass.MethodB Finished");
    }

    ~ZClass() {
        Console.WriteLine("ZClass.~ZClass Started");
        // Destructor operation
        Console.WriteLine("ZClass.~ZClass Finished");
    }
}
```

Constructors   An exception in a constructor does not prevent an object from being finalized. The finalizer is called regardless of the success of the constructor, which can create an interesting dilemma in which an object that is unsuccessfully constructed is still finalized. Cleanup of a partially constructed object can pose risks.

The following code demonstrates the problems that can occur when an exception is raised in a constructor. The exception is caught by the exception handler in *Main*. At that time, the object exists but is not correctly initialized. Despite this, the finalizer is called as the application exits and attempts to clean up fully for the object. In actual code (not stubbed, as it is in the following sample), this could cause an exception or other fault:

```
using System;

namespace Donis.CSharpBook {
    public class Starter {
        private static void Main() {
            try {
                ZClass obj = new ZClass();
            }
            catch {
            }
        }
    }

    public class ZClass {

        public ZClass() {
            Console.WriteLine("ZClass constructor");
            throw new Exception("Error");
        }

        ~ZClass() {
            Console.WriteLine("ZClass destructor");
        }
    }
}
```

The following code resolves the problem of a finalizable object with a failed constructor. If the constructor does not complete successfully, *GC.SuppressFinalize* prevents the finalizer from being called later. In addition, a flag is maintained that indicates the state of the object. The *bPartial* flag is set to *true* if the constructor fails. The flag is checked in instance methods. If the flag is *true*, the methods raise an exception because the object might not be stable:

```
using System;

namespace Donis.CSharpBook {
    public class Starter {
        public static void Main() {
            try {
                ZClass obj = null;
                obj = new ZClass();
                if (obj != null) {
                    obj.MethodA();
                }
            }
            catch(Exception ex) {
                Console.WriteLine(ex.Message);
            }
```

```
        }
    }

    public class ZClass {

        public ZClass() {
            try {
                Console.WriteLine("ZClass constructor");
                throw new Exception("Error");
            }
            catch {
                GC.SuppressFinalize(this);
                bPartial = true;
            }
        }

        public void MethodA() {
            if (bPartial) {
                throw new Exception("Partial construction error");
            }
            Console.WriteLine("ZClass.MethodA");
        }

        ~ZClass() {
            Console.WriteLine("ZClass destructor");
        }

        private bool bPartial = false;
    }
}
```

The *Console* class and finalization   You can safely use the *Console* class in a finalizer. It is exempted from the rule not to use other managed classes in a finalizer. The *Console* class is specially written for use during finalization.

IDisposable.Dispose

Dispose methods complement finalizers. Contrary to finalizers, *Dispose* methods are deterministic and can access managed types. *Dispose* methods are sometimes referred to as *explicit garbage collection*. You can call *Dispose* for immediate cleanup of resources associated with an object, such as closing a file handle. Remember that accessing a managed object in a finalizer is inadvisable. This requirement greatly limits the flexibility and functionality of a finalizer. The *Dispose* method does not have this limitation because garbage collection is not occurring simultaneously.

The *Dispose* method is defined in the *IDisposable* interface, which is found in the *System* namespace. Disposable objects should inherit and implement the *IDisposable* interface, where the *Dispose* method is the only member. You then call the *Dispose* method as a normal method to start deterministic garbage collection. Although possible, you should not implement the *Dispose* method apart from the *IDisposable* interface. The *IDisposable* interface is an important marker that confirms the presence of a disposable object. There are statements and behaviors, such as the *using* statement, that rely on this marker.

The following code demonstrates a simple implementation of the *Dispose* method:

```
public class Starter {
    private static void Main() {
        ZClass disposableobject = new ZClass();
        disposableobject.Dispose();
        disposableobject = null;
    }
}

public class ZClass : IDisposable {
    public ZClass() {
        // Allocate resources
    }

    public void Dispose() {
        // Release resources
    }
}
```

In the preceding code, the *Dispose* method is not guaranteed to run. Raising an exception prior to the *Dispose* method call could cause the cleanup to be skipped and result in resource leakage. To protect against this possibility, place the *Dispose* method call in a *finally* block. This ensures that the *Dispose* method is called whether or not an exception is raised in the *try* block. In this updated version of the code, the *Dispose* method is placed in a *finally* block:

```
public static void Main() {
    ZClass disposableobject = null;
    try {
        disposableobject = new ZClass();
    }
    finally {
        disposableobject.Dispose();
        disposableobject = null;
    }
}
```

The *using* block is the short form of the preceding code. The *using* block is an abbreviated *try* and *finally* block. The *Dispose* method of the referenced object is called automatically in an implicit *finally* block. The referenced object is defined in the *using* statement. Here is the equivalent code written with a *using* statement:

```
public static void Main() {
    using(ZClass disposableobject = new ZClass()) {
        // use object
    }
}
```

The C# compiler substitutes a *try* and a *finally* block for the *using* block. This is some of the MSIL code emitted for a *using* block from the C# compiler:

```
IL_0006:  stloc.0
.try
{
    IL_0007:  nop
    IL_0008:  nop
    IL_0009:  leave.s    IL_001b
}  // end .try
finally
{
    // partial listing…

    IL_0014:  callvirt   instance void[mscorlib]System.IDisposable::Dispose()
    IL_0019:  nop
    IL_001a:  endfinally
}  // end handler
```

Multiple objects of the same type can be declared in one *using* statement. Delimit the objects with commas. All objects declared in the statement are accessible within the *using* block. When the *using* block exits, the *Dispose* method is called on each of the objects declared in the *using* statement. In the following code, two objects of the same type are declared in the *using* statement:

```
using System;

namespace Donis.CSharpBook {

    public class Starter {
        public static void Main() {
            using(ZClass obj1 = new ZClass(),
                       obj2 = new ZClass()) {
            }
        }
    }

    public class ZClass : IDisposable {
        public void Dispose() {
            Console.WriteLine("ZClass.Dispose");
        }
    }
}
```

You also can declare objects of different types by providing multiple *using* statements. In the following code, three objects are declared for the *using* block. There are two *ZClass* objects and an *XClass* object. All three are disposed at the end of the *using* block:

```
using System;

namespace Donis.CSharpBook {
    public class Starter {
        private static void Main() {
```

```
                using(XClass obj3 = new XClass())
                using(ZClass obj1 = new ZClass(),
                            obj2 = new ZClass()) {
                }
            }
        }

    public class ZClass: IDisposable {
        public void Dispose() {
            Console.WriteLine("ZClass.Dispose");
        }
    }

    public class XClass: IDisposable {
        public void Dispose() {
            Console.WriteLine("XClass.Dispose");
        }
    }
}
```

Classes can have both a *Dispose* method and a destructor. You can relinquish both managed and unmanaged resources in the *Dispose* method, whereas the destructor can clean up only unmanaged resources. Because finalizers are called, they are effective safety nets. However, finalization should not be performed on an already-disposed object. A second iteration of cleanup could have unexpected results. For this reason, developers typically suppress the finalizer in the *Dispose* method. The *GC.SuppressFinalize* method is called in the *Dispose* method to suppress the finalizer. Performance is improved because future finalization of the object is eliminated.

In the following code, the *ZClass* has both a *Dispose* and finalizer method. Note that *GC.SuppressFinalize* is invoked in the *Dispose* method to suppress future finalization:

```
using System;

namespace Donis.CSharpBook {
    public class Starter {
        private static void Main() {
            using(ZClass obj1 = new ZClass()) {
            }
        }
    }

    public class ZClass: IDisposable {
        public void Dispose() {
            Console.WriteLine("Disposing resources");
            GC.SuppressFinalize(this);
        }

        ~ZClass() {
            Console.WriteLine("ZClass.constructor");
            // Cleanup unmanaged resources
        }
    }
}
```

This section reviewed the simple implementation of the *Dispose* method, which is sufficient for sealed classes. However, inheritable classes require the more complex *Disposable* pattern, which is discussed in the section titled "*Disposable* Pattern" later in this chapter.

TLS Example

In the section titled "Multithreading" earlier in this chapter, an improper version of a TLS application with the *TMonitor* class was presented. The following code shows the corrected version that uses the *Dispose* method. The *Dispose* method runs on the same thread as the *WriteFile* method of the object. For the *TMonitor* class, the *Dispose* method (instead of a destructor) is called from each thread that is using the class, which correctly releases the relevant resources of each thread:

```
class TMonitor: IDisposable {
    public void WriteFile() {
        StreamWriter sw = Thread.GetData(Form1.Slot) as StreamWriter;
        if (sw == null) {
            sw = new StreamWriter(string.Format(
                @"C:\{0}File.txt",
                Thread.CurrentThread.Name),
                true);
            Thread.SetData(Form1.Slot, sw);
        }
        sw.WriteLine(DateTime.Now.ToLongTimeString());
    }

    public void Dispose() {
        StreamWriter sw = Thread.GetData(Form1.Slot) as StreamWriter;
        Thread.SetData(Form1.Slot, null);
        if (sw != null) {
            sw.Close();
            MessageBox.Show("sw closed");
        }
    }
}
```

Disposable Pattern

The *Disposable* pattern provides a template for implementing the *Dispose* method and the destructor in a base class and a derived class. The *Disposable* pattern, shown in the following code, should be implemented where there is a base class and a derived class that require some form of cleanup:

```
using System;
using System.Threading;

namespace Donis.CSharpBook {

    public class Base: IDisposable {
```

```
        public void Dispose() {
            Dispose(true);
            GC.SuppressFinalize(this);
        }

        protected virtual void Dispose(bool disposing) {
            if (disposing) {
                // Release managed resources
            }
            // Release unmanaged resources
        }

        ~Base() {
            Dispose (false);
        }
    }

    public class Derived: Base {
        protected override void Dispose(bool disposing) {
            if (disposing) {
                // Release managed resources.
            }
            // Release unmanaged resources
            base.Dispose(disposing);
        }
    }
}
```

Let us focus first on the base class, which implements the *IDisposable* interface and contains two *Dispose* methods.

The one-argument *Dispose* method has a Boolean *disposing* argument. This argument indicates whether the method is being called during deterministic or nondeterministic garbage collection. If called during nondeterministic garbage collection, the *disposing* argument is *false*. Otherwise, the argument is *true*. When the argument is *false*, only unmanaged resources should be released in the method. When *true*, both managed and unmanaged resources can be released.

There is also a no-argument *Dispose* method. Both the no-argument *Dispose* method and the destructor delegate to the one-argument *Dispose* method. The no-argument *Dispose* method is public and is called explicitly for deterministic garbage collection. This *Dispose* method delegates to the one-argument destructor with the disposing flag set to *true*, which indicates deterministic garbage collection. It then calls *GC.SuppressFinalize* to suppress finalization and avoid further garbage collection.

The destructor delegates to the one-argument *Dispose* method with the disposing flag set to *false*, which indicates nondeterministic garbage collection.

In the base class, the no-argument *Dispose* method is not a virtual method and should not be overridden in the derived class. This method should always delegate to the most derived one-argument *Dispose* method to access the correct behavior. Any other behavior would seriously break the *Disposable* pattern.

In the derived class, override the one-argument *Dispose* method to clean up managed and unmanaged resources of the derived class. The one-argument *Dispose* method in the derived class should call the same method of the base class, affording the base class the opportunity to release its resources.

In the derived class, you should not implement a destructor. The base class implementation of the destructor method will correctly call the most derived *Dispose* method. Disposal then propagates from the most derived class to all ascendants. Therefore, resource cleanup is performed in the correct order.

Disposable Pattern Considerations

There are several factors to consider when implementing a simple *Dispose* or the more complex *Disposable* pattern. This section describes many of the factors that should be considered when implementing a *Dispose* method. Here are the factors:

- Redundant *Dispose* method
- *Close* method
- Thread-safe *Dispose* method
- Reusable objects
- Disposing inner objects

Redundant *Dispose* Method

In the following code, the *Dispose* method is called twice (once explicitly and once implicitly, as a result of the *using* statement). You should be able to call the *Dispose* method multiple times safely. Set a flag the first time *Dispose* is called, and check the flag to confirm whether the object is disposed already. If the object is disposed, do not dispose it again. Alternatively, you might be able to confirm the disposability of an object from the state of the object. It is a good practice to confirm the disposed status at the beginning of other member methods. If the object is disposed, you have two options. Either revive the object and execute the method, or throw the *ObjectDisposedException:*

```
private static void Main() {
    using(ZClass disposableobject =
            new ZClass()) {
        disposableobject.Dispose();
    }
}
```

The following code demonstrates a resilient *Dispose* method, which can be called multiple times. The *ReverseReader* type is a thin wrapper for a *StreamReader*. It inverts information read from a file source. *ReverseReader* contains a *StreamReader* field. It is initialized in the class constructor and closed in the *Dispose* method. If the *StreamReader* is null, the object is presumed disposed. This is checked in the *Dispose* method. If the object is already disposed, the *Dispose* method simply returns. In addition, the *ReverseReader.ReadLine* method throws the *ObjectDisposedException* exception if the object has been disposed. You cannot call this method successfully if the object has been disposed. To test this implementation, there is a *using* block in *Main*. The *Dispose* method is called explicitly within the *using* block. After the *using* block, the *Dispose* method is called implicitly again, which proves to be harmless. A second call to the *ReadLine* method is commented out, because the object now has been disposed. If the second call to *ReadLine* were uncommented, an exception would be raised, as expected:

```
using System;
using System.IO;

namespace Donis.CSharpBook {
    public class Starter {

        private static void Main() {
            using(ReverseReader input = new ReverseReader("text.txt")) {
                string result = input.ReadLine();
                while (result != null) {
                    Console.WriteLine(result);
                    result = input.ReadLine();
                }
                input.Dispose();
                // input.ReadLine();
            }
        }
    }

    public class ReverseReader:IDisposable {

        public ReverseReader(string filename) {
            file = new StreamReader(filename);
        }

        public string ReadLine() {
            if (file == null) {
                throw new ObjectDisposedException(
                    "ReadLine object");
            }
            if (file.Peek() < 0) {
                return null;
            }
            string temp = file.ReadLine();
            char[] tempArray = temp.ToCharArray();
            Array.Reverse(tempArray);
```

```
            return new string(tempArray);
    }

    public void Dispose() {
        if (file == null) {
            return;
        }
        else {
            file.Close();
            file = null;
        }
    }

    private StreamReader file = null;
    }
}
```

Close Method

Instead of the *Dispose* method, some classes expose another method for deterministic cleanup. Although this should not be done as a general practice, the exception is when a differently named method would be more intuitive than the *Dispose* method. For example, the *FileStream* class exposes the *Close* method. (*Close* is the traditional term for releasing a file.) The alternate method should delegate to the proper *Dispose* method. Do not implement the disposable routine more than once. Both the *Dispose* and the alternative methods are available to the clients for deterministic garbage collection. The correct implementation is demonstrated with the *StreamWriter.Close* method, as shown in the following code. *StreamWriter.Close* delegates to *TextWriter.Dispose* for deterministic garbage collection. *TextWriter.Dispose* is inherited by the *StreamWriter* class. The *Close* method suppresses the finalizer, which is standard behavior of a deterministic method. Both the *Close* and *Dispose* methods are available on the *StreamWriter* class. You should clearly document any alternate method for deterministic garbage collection:

```
.method public hidebysig virtual instance void Close() cil managed
{
    // Code size       14 (0xe)
    .maxstack  8
    IL_0000:  ldarg.0
    IL_0001:  ldc.i4.1
    IL_0002:  callvirt    instance void System.IO.TextWriter::Dispose(bool)
    IL_0007:  ldarg.0
    IL_0008:  call        void System.GC::SuppressFinalize(object)
    IL_000d:  ret
} // end of method StreamWriter::Close
```

Thread-Safe *Dispose* Method

The *Dispose* method is not implicitly thread-safe. As a public method, *Dispose* is callable from multiple threads simultaneously. Thread synchronization is required for thread-safety. The *lock* statement, as demonstrated in the following code, is a convenient means of providing thread-safe access to the *Dispose* method:

```
public class ZClass : IDisposable {

    public void Dispose() {
        lock(this) {
        }
    }
}
```

Reusable Objects

The *Disposable* pattern accommodates reusable objects. Unless the object is nondisposed, it can be recycled. You should not recycle an object implicitly where recycling can occur inadvertently or without detection. Expose a method that explicitly recycles the object. There is no convention for naming this method. However, an *Open* method is usually a good choice. If disposed, this method should recycle the object using the object constructor. Recyclable objects should also expose a property that confirms the status of the object as alive or disposed.

The following code is a revision of the *ReverseReader* class, which was presented earlier in this chapter. This version is recyclable. It has both a default and a one-argument constructor. The one-argument constructor delegates to the *Open* method. You can call the *Open* method directly to recycle a *ReverseReader* instance. The *Active* property returns the status of the object. If *true*, the object is active and is not disposed:

```
public class ReverseReader :IDisposable {

    public ReverseReader() {
    }

    public ReverseReader(string filename) {
        Open(filename);
    }

    public bool Open(string filename) {
        if (file != null) {
            return false;
        }
        file = new StreamReader(filename);
        return true;
    }

    public string ReadLine() {
        if (file == null) {
            throw new ObjectDisposedException(
                "ReadLine object");
        }
        if (file.Peek() < 0) {
```

```
            return null;
        }
        string temp = file.ReadLine();
        char[] tempArray = temp.ToCharArray();
        Array.Reverse(tempArray);
        return new string(tempArray);
    }

    public void Dispose() {
        if (file == null) {
            return;
        }
        else {
            file.Close();
            file = null;
        }
    }

    public void Close() {
        Dispose();
    }

    private StreamReader file = null;

    public bool Active {
        get {
            return !(file == null);
        }
    }
}
```

Disposing Inner Objects

When disposing, a class should call the *Dispose* method on disposable member fields. Call the *Dispose* method of those inner objects in the *Dispose* method of the containing class. After disposing, set the disposable fields to *null*. Of course, the inner objects dispose the disposable objects they contain, and so on. In this way, the *Dispose* method could be considered transitive.

The proper disposal of inner objects is shown in the following code:

```
public class ZClass : IDisposable{

    public ZClass() {
        inner = new YClass();
    }

    public void Dispose() {
        Console.WriteLine("ZClass.Dispose");
        inner.Dispose();
        inner = null;
    }
```

```
        private YClass inner = null;

}

public class YClass : IDisposable{
    public void Dispose() {
        Console.WriteLine("YClass.Dispose");
    }
}
```

An object should not dispose any object not within its full control, as doing so can cause unwanted side effects. In the following code, *ZClass* has a property called *inner,* which is backed by the *_inner* field. The *_inner* field is of the *YClass* type, which is disposable. In *Main,* two instances of *ZClass* are created. Through the *inner* property, the *_inner* fields of both are set to the same object. Therefore, neither object has full control of their respective *_inner* object. When the *using* block is exited, the *_inner* field of the second object is disposed. However, the other object, which shares the *_inner* field, remains active. When the remaining active object attempts to access the *inner* property, and subsequently the shared *_inner* field, an exception is raised:

```
using System;

namespace Donis.CSharpBook {
    public class Starter {
        private static void Main() {
            ZClass obj1 = new ZClass();
            obj1.Inner = new YClass();
            using(ZClass obj2 = new ZClass()) {
                obj2.Inner = obj1.Inner;
            }
            obj1.MethodA();  // exception
            obj1.Dispose();
            obj1 = null;
        }
    }

    public class ZClass: IDisposable{

        public ZClass() {
        }

        public void Dispose() {
            Console.WriteLine("ZClass.Dispose");
            _inner.Dispose();
        }

        public void MethodA() {
            Console.WriteLine("ZClass.MethodA");
            _inner.MethodA();
        }
```

```
        public YClass Inner {
            set {
                _inner = value;
            }
            get {
                return _inner;
            }
        }

        private YClass _inner = null;
    }

    public class YClass: IDisposable{
        public void Dispose() {
            Console.WriteLine("YClass.Dispose");
            disposed = true;
        }

        public void MethodA() {
            if (disposed) {
                throw new ObjectDisposedException(
                    "YClass disposed");
            }
            Console.WriteLine("YClass.MethodA");
        }

        private bool disposed = false;
    }
}
```

Weak Reference

Weak references are one of my favorite features of the .NET Framework. As you might guess
from the name, a weak reference has less persistence than a strong reference, which is a
conventional reference created with the *new* operator. So long as there is a strong reference
for the object, the object persists in memory and cannot be collected. If there is no outstanding
reference, the object becomes a candidate for removal in a future garbage collection.
Conversely, a weak reference to an object is insufficient to retain that object in memory. A
weak reference can be collected as memory is needed. For this reason, you must confirm that
weakly referenced objects have not been collected before you use the object.

Weak references are not ideal for objects that contain information that is expensive to
rehydrate. Information read from a persistent source such as a file or data store is preferred.
You can simply reread the file or request the dataset again. Rehydrating a dataset can be
light or heavy based on several factors, including the location of the data, such as local,
network share, or remote.

Use the *WeakReference* type to create a weak reference object. These are the steps for creating and using a weak reference:

1. A weak reference usually begins as a strong reference, so create a strong reference:

```
XNames objTemp = new XNames();
```

2. Create a *WeakReference* type. In the constructor, initialize the weak reference with the strong reference. Afterward, set the strong reference to *null*. An outstanding strong reference prevents the weak reference from controlling the lifetime of the object. Therefore, it is imperative to set the strong reference to *null:*

```
XNames objTemp = new XNames();
weaknames = new WeakReference(objTemp);
objTemp = null;
```

3. Before using the object, request a strong reference to the weakly referenced object. *WeakReference.Target* returns a strong reference to the weak object. If *WeakReference.Target* is *null*, the object has been garbage-collected and no longer is in memory. The object must be rehydrated. If *WeakReference.Target* is not *null* then the object has not been garbage-collected and is available for immediate use. Here is code that tests the *Target* property:

```
if (weaknames.Target == null)
{
    // rehydrate
}
```

The following class is used in the sample code for weak references to read a list of names from a file (shown later in this section):

```
class XNames
{
    public XNames()
    {
        StreamReader sr = new StreamReader("names.txt");
        string temp = sr.ReadToEnd();
        _Names = temp.Split('\n');
    }
    private string[] _Names;

    public IEnumerator<string> GetEnumerator()
    {
        foreach (string name in _Names)
        {
            yield return name;
        }
    }
}
```

The preceding code is from the Weak application. It uses the *XNames* class to display the names from a file in a list box. The Weak application is shown in Figure 17-5.

In the Weak application, a weak reference is created and initiated with an instance of the *XNames* class. The code for the Fill List button (the *btnFill_Click* method) enumerates the names of the *XNames* instance to populate the list box. Before using the instance, the status of the instance, which is a weak reference, must be confirmed. Has it been garbage-collected or not? If it has been garbage-collected, the user is prompted whether to rehydrate or not. The Apply Pressure button applies memory pressure to the application. Clicking the button repeatedly will cause garbage collection eventually and might force the weakly referenced object to be garbage-collected. You can test the application by updating the list box using the Fill List button.

FIGURE 17-5 The Weak application

Here is some of the code from the Weak application that pertains to weak references:

```
public partial class Form1 : Form {
    public Form1() {
        InitializeComponent();
    }
    private void btnFill_Click(object sender, EventArgs e) {
        if (weaknames.Target == null) {
            DialogResult result = MessageBox.Show(
                "Rehydrate?",
                "Names removed from memory.",
                MessageBoxButtons.YesNo);
            if (result == DialogResult.No) {
                return;
            }
            else {
                weaknames.Target = new XNames();
            }
        }
        foreach (string name in (XNames)weaknames.Target) {
            lblNames.Items.Add(name);
        }
    }
}
```

```
    private WeakReference weaknames;

    private void Form1_Load(object sender, EventArgs e) {
        XNames objTemp = new XNames();
        weaknames = new WeakReference(objTemp);
        objTemp = null;
    }

    private void btnApply_Click(object sender, EventArgs e) {
        objs.Add(new ZClass());
        if (weaknames.Target == null) {
            lblNames.Items.Clear();
        }
    }

    List<ZClass> objs = new List<ZClass>();
}

internal class ZClass {
    public long[] array = new long[7500];
}
```

Weak Reference Internals

Weak references are tracked in short weak reference tables and long weak reference tables. Both tables are initially empty.

Each entry in the short weak reference table is a reference to a managed object on the heap. When garbage collection occurs, objects referenced in the short weak reference table that are not strongly rooted are collectable. The related slot in the table is set to *null*.

Entries in the long weak reference table are evaluated next. Long weak references are weak references that track an object through finalization. Objects referenced in the long weak reference table that are not strongly rooted are collectable.

WeakReference Class

Table 17-1 lists the important members of the *WeakReference* class.

TABLE 17-1 *WeakReference* class members

Member name	Description
WeakReference(object target)	The one-argument constructor initializes the weak reference with the target object.
WeakReference(object target, bool trackResurrection)	The two-argument constructor initializes the weak reference with the target object. If *trackResurrection* is true, the object is also tracked through finalization.

TABLE 17-1 *WeakReference* **class members**

Member name	Description
IsAlive	This is a property and returns whether or not the target object has been garbage-collected.
Target	This is an object property and gets or sets the object being referenced.

Reliable Code

Reliable code helps prevent and handle memory leaks. It is particularly useful in interoperability, where a handle might be shared between managed and native environments. These are the primary reasons to use reliable code:

- Asynchronous events can cause memory leaks when a catch or a termination handler (a *finally* block) is interrupted. This is most likely when managed code is deployed in a hosted environment, such as ASP.NET or Microsoft SQL Server. When interrupted, cleanup is not completed and a leak of memory or resources can occur. You can place a *catch* or *finally* block in a constrained execution region (CER), which is a region of reliable code, to prevent any such interruption.

- Destructors are not guaranteed to be called. When this occurs, memory or resources can be leaked. The solution is to derive the class from the *CriticalFinalizerObject* class. This places the destructor in a CER, where the CLR guarantees that the destructor will be called.

- There are several problems with handles and interoperability. For example, a managed function calls into native code using interoperability. While the native code is executing, the managed object is cleaned up and the handle is released. This corrupts the handle. At that time, the outcome of the still-running native code is undetermined. Safe handles protect a native handle by incrementing the handle count while the native method is executing. This prevents an early release and possible handle corruption. Safe handles are derived from the *CriticalFinalizerObject*, which uses a CER.

Constrained Execution Region

The CER is a region of reliable managed code that is guaranteed to run to completion without interruption. Even an asynchronous exception will not prevent the region from executing to completion. Within the CER, developers are constrained to certain actions. These are actions that will not cause an asynchronous exception, such as a memory exception or thread abort. The CLR performs a variety of checks and does some preparation to ensure that code in the CER runs without interruption. This is a short list of some of the actions that should be avoided in a CER:

- Boxing
- Unsafe code

- Locks

- Serialization

- Calling unreliable code

- Allocating new objects

In a CER, the CLR delays an asynchronous exception event, such as a thread abort, until the region is exited.

You can create CER regions using the *RuntimeHelpers.PrepareConstrainedRegions* method. Call the *PrepareConstrainedRegions* static method immediately prior to a *try* statement. This places the subsequent *catch* or *finally* block in a CER. The *RuntimeHelpers* class is in the *System.Runtime.CompilerServices* namespace. The code in the *try* block is not reliable and can be interrupted. However, the related *catch* or *finally* block is within a CER and is uninter-ruptible. From the *catch* or *finally* block in a CER, you can call only methods with a strong reliability contract.

Code in a CER can call only reliable methods. Reliable methods have a reliability contract as defined within the *ReliabilityContractAttribute,* which is an attribute. This class is found in the *System.Runtime.ConstrainedExecution* namespace. Reliability contracts can be applied to an individual method, methods of a class, or an entire assembly. The *ReliabilityContractAttribute* constructor has two parameters. The first parameter is the *ConsistencyGuarantee* property, which indicates the potential scope of corruption if an asynchronous exception occurs during execution. For example, *Consistency.MayCorruptAppDomain* means that an asynchronous exception can leave the application domain in an unreliable state. The second parameter is the *Cer* property, which is a completion guarantee. *Cer.Success* is the highest guarantee and promises that the code will successfully complete, assuming valid input. With the reliability contract, developers make reliability assurances. The CLR does not strictly enforce the reliability constraints. Instead, the CLR relies on developer commitment.

Here is an example of a CER region:

```
[ReliabilityContract(Consistency.WillNotCorruptState,
        Cer.Success)]
class ZClass {

    void MethodA() {
        RuntimeHelpers.PrepareConstrainedRegions();
        try {
        }
        finally {
            // CER Region
        }
    }
}
```

Stephen Toub has written a detailed and informative article on CERs called "Keep Your Code Running with the Reliability Features of the .NET Framework." It can be found at the following link: *http://msdn.microsoft.com/msdnmag/issues/05/10/reliability/default.aspx.*

A CER is used in a variety of places: with annotated *try* statements, as described in this section, methods executed using the *RuntimeHelpers.ExecuteCodeWithGuaranteedCleanup* method, and classes derived from the *CriticalFinalizerObject* class. *CriticalFinalizerObject* class is introduced in the next section; but the *ExecuteCodeWithGuaranteedCleanup* method is outside the scope of this book.

Critical Finalizer Class

Asynchronous exceptions can prevent a finalizer from running, and critical cleanup code might not execute. Resource leakage and other problems can occur when critical finalization code is abandoned. Objects derived from the *CriticalFinalizerObject* class, which is located in the *System.Runtime* namespace, have critical finalizers. The finalizer runs uninterrupted in a CER. As such, any method called from the finalizer must have a strong reliability contract. The CLR assures that critical finalizables of critical finalizer objects are executed. Conditions that can prevent a normal finalizer from running, such as a forcible thread abort or an unload of the application domain, do not affect a critical finalizer. This is especially an issue in environments that host managed applications, such as SQL Server. A CLR host can asynchronously interrupt a managed application, which can strand important finalizers. Critical finalizer objects solve this potential problem. During normal garbage collection, regular finalizers always run before critical finalizers.

Safe Handles

When passing handles during interoperability, handles can be mishandled, which can cause leaks or other problems. There are two primary causes:

- Managed code can call native code through platform invocation. If the native function is passed in a handle, that handle must be managed carefully. While in native code, the managed object could be released. When this occurs, the handle might be improperly released. If that happens, the handle is corrupted, which may cause an exception or other error.

- As mentioned previously, asynchronous code might prevent finalization. This could prevent a handle from being released, which would cause a handle leak.

The solution is to use safe handles, which are classes derived from *SafeHandle*. The *SafeHandle* class itself derives and implements the *CriticalFinalizerObject* type. *SafeHandle* is an abstract class and must be inherited in another class. Specifically implemented safe handles include *SafeHandle, SafeFileHandle, SafeWaitHandle, SafeHandleMinusOneIsInvalid, and SafeHandleZeroOrMinusOneIsInvalid. SafeHandle* is in the *System.Runtime.InteropServices* namespace. The remaining *SafeHandle* classes mentioned in this paragraph are found in the

Microsoft.Win32.SafeHandles namespace. Safe handles support reference counting. Review the documentation of the *SafeHandle* class for information on the specific implementation of reference counting.

When passed as a parameter in platform invocation, safe handles increment the reference count. After the call is completed, the reference count is decremented automatically, which prevents the handle from being inadvertently released in managed code during a native call.

In the following code, the *PipeHandle* class is a safe wrapper for a pipe handle. The class exposes the *CreatePipe* and the *CloseHandle* application programming interfaces (APIs) through interoperability. Because the *CloseHandle* method will be called in a CER, a reliability contract is placed on that method. *PipeHandle* derives from the *SafeHandleMinusOneIsInvalid* class for the proper behavior, which is derived from *SafeHandle*. The finalizer of the base class automatically calls the *ReleaseHandle* method. The overridden *ReleaseHandle* method should implement the proper behavior to release the pertinent handle.

In the *AnonymousPipe* constructor, two *PipeHandle* instances are initialized, which are a read and write handle. Because these are safe handles, the underlying handle is safer from leaks and corruption. In the following sample code, the *DllImport* attribute imports a native function:

```
public sealed class PipeHandle :
    SafeHandleMinusOneIsInvalid {

    private PipeHandle()
        : base(true) {

    }

    [ReliabilityContract(Consistency.WillNotCorruptState,
            Cer.Success)]
    protected override bool ReleaseHandle() {
        return CloseHandle(handle);
    }

    [DllImport("kernel32.dll")]
     extern public static bool CreatePipe(
        out PipeHandle hReadPipe,
        out PipeHandle hWritePipe,
        IntPtr securityAttributes,
        int nSize);

    [ReliabilityContract(Consistency.WillNotCorruptState,
            Cer.Success)]
    [DllImport("kernel32.dll")]
     public static extern bool CloseHandle(IntPtr handle);

}

public class AnonymousPipe {
```

```
    public AnonymousPipe() {

        PipeHandle.CreatePipe(out readHandle, out writeHandle,
            IntPtr.Zero, 10);
        MessageBox.Show((readHandle.DangerousGetHandle())
            .ToInt32().ToString());
        MessageBox.Show((writeHandle.DangerousGetHandle())
            .ToInt32().ToString());
    }

    private PipeHandle readHandle = null;
    private PipeHandle writeHandle = null;
}
```

Managing Unmanaged Resources

Managed code often relies on unmanaged resources. The unmanaged resource is typically accessible through a managed wrapper. The MyDevice program is an unmanaged application that emulates a hardware device. *DeviceWrapper* is a managed wrapper for the *MyDevice* unmanaged resource. This is the code for the *DeviceWrapper* class:

```
public sealed class DeviceWrapper {
    static private int count = 0;

    public DeviceWrapper () {
        obj = new MyDeviceLib.DeviceClass();
        ++count;
    }

    private MyDeviceLib.DeviceClass obj;

    public void Open() {
        obj.OpenDevice();
    }

    public void Close() {
        obj.CloseDevice();
    }

    public void Start() {
        obj.StartCommunicating();
    }

    public void Stop() {
        obj.StopCommunicating();
    }

    ~DeviceWrapper() {
        // resource released
        --count;
    }
}
```

Memory Pressure

The wrapper for an unhandled resource can hide the true memory cost of an object. Incorrect accounting of unhandled memory in the managed environment can cause unexpected out-of-memory exceptions.

To solve this problem, you can add memory pressure, which accounts for unmanaged memory in the managed environment. This prevents a wrapper to an unmanaged resource from hiding an elephant in the closet. Memory pressure forces garbage collection sooner, which collects unused instances of the wrapper class. The wrapper releases the unmanaged resource to reduce the memory pressure on both managed and unmanaged memory.

The *GC.AddMemoryPressure* method adds artificial memory pressure on the managed heap for an unmanaged resource, whereas the *GC.RemoveMemoryPressure* method removes memory pressure. Both methods should be integrated into the wrapper class of the unmanaged resource. Call *AddMemoryPressure* and *RemoveMemoryPressure* in the setup and cleanup for the class, respectively. Each instance of the *MyDevice* unmanaged resource uses 40 KB of memory on the unmanaged heap. In the following code, the constructor and destructor for the *MyDevice* wrapper now account for the unmanaged memory:

```
public MyDevice() {
    GC.AddMemoryPressure(40000);
    obj = new MyDeviceLib.DeviceClass();
    ++count;
}

~MyDevice() {
    GC.RemoveMemoryPressure(40000);
    // resource released
    --count;
}
```

Handles

Some native resources are available in limited quantities. Exhausting the resource can hang the application, crash the environment, or cause other adverse reactions. The availability of a limited resource should be tracked. When the resource is exhausted, corrective action should occur. Some limited kernel resources, such as a window, are assigned handles. The *HandleCollector* class manages handles to limited kernel resources. Despite the name, the *HandleCollector* class is not limited to tracking kernel handles. You can use the *HandleCollector* class to manage any resource that has limited availability. The *HandleCollector* class is found in the *System.Runtime.InteropServices* namespace.

The *HandleCollector* class has a three-argument constructor that configures the important properties of the type. The arguments are the name, initial threshold, and maximum threshold. Names allows you to name the collector. The initial threshold sets the minimal level for possible garbage collection. The maximum threshold sets the level where garbage collection is forced. Hopefully, this will garbage-collect managed resources that are holding unmanaged resources. In the cleanup, these objects will release these resources and lower the handle count.

In the managed classes, define a static instance of the *HandleCollector*. In the constructor, call *HandleCollector.Add*. In the cleanup code, call *HandleCollector.Remove*.

The following code shows the *MyDevice* class revised for the *HandleCollector* class. The *MyDevice* unmanaged resource supports an initial threshold of three simultaneous connections and a maximum of five. You can test the effectiveness of the wrapper in the UseResource application by clicking the Connect button, which applies pressure, and monitoring the message boxes:

```
public sealed class MyDevice {
    static private HandleCollector track =
        new HandleCollector("devices", 3, 5);

    static private int count = 0;

    public MyDevice() {
        GC.AddMemoryPressure(40000);
        track.Add();
        obj = new MyDeviceLib.DeviceClass();
        ++count;
        MessageBox.Show("Device count: " + count.ToString());
    }

    private MyDeviceLib.DeviceClass obj;
    public void Open() {
        obj.OpenDevice();
    }

    public void Close() {
        obj.CloseDevice();
    }

    public void Start() {
        obj.StartCommunicating();
    }

    public void Stop() {
        obj.StopCommunicating();
    }

    ~MyDevice() {
        GC.RemoveMemoryPressure(40000);
        track.Remove();
        // resource released
        --count;
    }
}
```

The *GC* Class

The *GC* class publishes services to interface with the garbage collector. You can manipulate and monitor garbage collection with the *GC* class. While some of the commands provide status information, other GC commands affect the default behavior of garbage collection. Table 17-2 lists the static members of the *GC* class.

TABLE 17-2 *GC* class static members

Member name	Description
MaxGeneration	This property is an integer property and returns the maximum number of generations.
AddMemoryPressure	This method recognizes memory allocations for unmanaged resources.
Collect	This method forces garbage collection on a specific generation. There are two overloads of the method. The no-argument *Collect* does garbage collection on all generations. The one-argument *Collect* specifies the oldest generation to be collected.
CollectionCount	This method returns the number of garbage collection cycles for the specified generation.
GetGeneration	This method returns the generation of the specified object.
GetTotalMemory	This method returns the total number of bytes allocated for the managed heap. You can wait on garbage collection and finalization by setting the Boolean parameter to *true*.
KeepAlive	This method keeps alive the specified object from the beginning of the current routine to where the *KeepAlive* method is called.
RemoveMemoryPressure	This method removes some of the memory pressure set aside for unmanaged resources.
ReRegisterForFinalize	This method reattaches a finalizer to a resurrected object.
SuppressFinalize	This method suppresses future finalization of the specified object.
WaitForPendingFinalizers	This method suspends the current thread until the Finalization queue is empty.

Unsafe Code

Unsafe code is an ominous name. What developer wants to purposely write unsafe code? In .NET, unsafe code really means *potentially* unsafe code, which is code or memory that exists outside the normal boundaries of the CLR. For this reason, developers should approach the use of unsafe code with caution.

In unsafe code, developers can access raw pointers. You can use pointer operators, such as * and &, with these pointers. Pointers should be avoided because they interrupt the normal operation of the GC. However, using unsafe pointers is sometimes necessary. For example, porting algorithms from C++ that rely heavily on pointers is one situation in which unsafe pointers might be beneficial.

Managed developers must call unmanaged routines sometimes. Although the breadth of the .NET Framework Class Library (FCL) is expanding, there is system behavior that still resides outside its realm. In addition, many third-party routines are not managed—particularly legacy applications. Finally, some code will never be managed for performance or other considerations. Interoperability allows managed developers to build bridges back to unmanaged code. You can call unmanaged code from a managed routine. Conversely, you can call managed code from unmanaged routines.

Unsafe code is discussed in more detail in the next chapter.

Chapter 18
Unsafe Code

Unsafe code can access unmanaged memory, which is outside the realm of the Common Language Runtime (CLR). Conversely, safe code is limited to accessing the managed heap. The managed heap is managed by the Garbage Collector, which is a component of the CLR. Code restricted to the managed heap is intrinsically safer than code that accesses unmanaged memory. The CLR automatically releases unused objects, performs type verification, and conducts other checks on managed memory. This is not done automatically for unmanaged memory; rather, the developer is responsible for these tasks. With managed code, developers can focus on core application development instead of administrative tasks such as memory management. For this reason, safe code improves programmer productivity and customer satisfaction.

You can access unmanaged memory with raw pointers, which are only available to unsafe code. Pointers point to a fixed location in unmanaged memory, whereas reference types point to a movable location in managed memory. The CLR manages reference types, which includes controlling the lifetime of objects and calling cleanup code. Developers do not delete memory allocated for reference types. In C and C++ programs, where pointers are used extensively, developers are preoccupied with memory management. Despite this, improper pointer management causes many common problems, including memory leaks, accessing invalid memory, deleting bad pointers, and fencepost errors. Abstracting the nuances of pointer management and manipulation with reference types has made managed code safer than unmanaged code. However, when needed, you can write unsafe code and access pointers directly.

When is unsafe code appropriate? Unsafe code should be used as an exception, not the rule. There are specific circumstances in which unsafe code is recommended:

- Unmanaged code often relies heavily on pointers. When porting this code to C#, incorporating some unsafe code in the managed application might make the conversion more straightforward. Most nontrivial C and C++ programmers heavily leverage pointers.

- Implementing a software algorithm where pointers are integral to the design might necessitate unsafe code.

- Calling an unmanaged function that requires a function pointer as a parameter.

- Pointers might be easier and more convenient when working with binary and memory-resident data structures.

- Unmanaged pointers might improve performance and efficiencies in certain circumstances.

Code in an unmanaged section is considered unsafe and not accessible to the CLR. Therefore, no code verification, stack tracing, or other checking is performed on the unmanaged code, which makes the code less safe.

Developers sometimes need to call unmanaged code from managed applications. Although the Microsoft .NET Framework Class Library (FCL) contains most of the code needed for .NET application development, the FCL umbrella does not encompass everything. You might need to call application programming interfaces (APIs) in operating system libraries for behavior defined outside the FCL. In addition, third-party software might be available only as unmanaged code.

Alternatively, you might need to call managed code from an unmanaged module, such as during a callback. In addition, managed components might be exposed as COM objects to COM clients, which are unmanaged.

Platform invoke (P/Invoke) is the bridge between managed and unmanaged execution. The bridge is bidirectional. Marshaling is the primary concern of cross-platform calls and is the responsibility of the Interop marshaler. *Marshaling* converts parameters and return values between unmanaged and managed formats. Fortunately, marshaling is not always required, which can avoid unnecessary overhead. Certain types, known as blittable types, do not require transformation and are the same in managed and unmanaged memory.

You also can build bridges between managed code and COM components, which contain unmanaged code. The Runtime Callable Wrapper (RCW) helps managed code call COM components. The COM Callable Wrapper (CCW) wraps a managed component as a COM component. This makes the managed component accessible to unmanaged COM clients. COM components also are available directly via P/Invoke. However, the CCW and RCW are more convenient and are the recommended solutions in most circumstances. COM interoperability is not a topic for this book. *COM Programming with Microsoft .NET*, by John Paul Mueller and Julian Templeman (Microsoft Press, 2003), is an excellent resource for additional information on COM interoperability and .NET.

Because code access security does not extend to unsafe code, unsafe code is not trusted. Type verification, which helps prevent buffer overrun attacks, is not performed, nor is code verification. Therefore, the reliability of the unsafe code is undetermined. Because it is not trusted, elevated permissions are required to call unsafe code from managed code. For this reason, applications that rely on unsafe code might not execute successfully in every deployment situation and should be thoroughly tested in all potential scenarios. Managed code requires the *SecurityPermission.UnmanagedCode* permission to call unsafe code. The *SuppressUnmanagedCodeSecurityAttribute* attribute disables the stack walk that confirms the *SecurityPermission.UnmanagedCode* permission in callers. This attribute is a free pass for other managed code to call unsafe code. This option is convenient but potentially dangerous.

Managed applications that include unsafe code must be compiled with the *unsafe* option. The C# compiler option is simply */unsafe*. In Microsoft Visual Studio 2008, this option is found in the project properties. In Solution Explorer, right-click the project name and choose

Properties from the context menu. Alternatively select *<project>* Properties from the Project menu. In the Build window, choose the Allow Unsafe Code option, as shown in Figure 18-1.

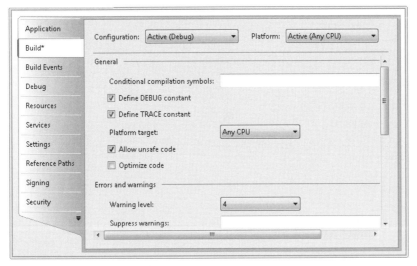

FIGURE 18-1 The Build tab of the *<project>* Properties window, with the Allow Unsafe Code option selected

Unsafe Keyword

The *unsafe* keyword specifies the location of unsafe code. Code inside the target can be unsafe. When the keyword is applied to a type, all the members of that type are considered unsafe as well. You also can apply the *unsafe* keyword to specific members of a type. If applied to a function member, the entire function operates in the unsafe context.

In the following code, the *ZStruct* contains two fields that are pointers. Each is annotated with the *unsafe* keyword:

```
public struct ZStruct {
    public unsafe int* fielda;
    public unsafe double* fieldb;
}
```

In the following example, *ZStruct* is marked as unsafe. The unsafe context extends to the entire structure, which includes the two fields. Both fields are therefore considered unsafe.

```
public unsafe struct ZStruct {
    public int* fielda;
    public double* fieldb;
}
```

In addition, You can create an unsafe block using the *unsafe* statement. All code encapsulated by the block is in the unsafe context. The following code has an unsafe block and an unsafe method. Within the unsafe block in the *Main* method, *MethodA* is called and passed an *int* pointer as a parameter. *MethodA* is an unsafe method. It assigns the *int* pointer to a byte pointer, which now points to the lower byte of the *int* value. The value at that lower byte is returned from *MethodA*. For an *int* value of 296, *MethodA* returns 40.

```
public static void Main() {
    int number = 296;
    byte b;
    unsafe {
        b = MethodA(&number);
    }
    Console.WriteLine(b);
}

public unsafe static byte MethodA(int* pI) {
    byte* temp = (byte*) pI;

    return *temp;
}
```

The unsafe status of a base class is not inherited by a derived class. Unless explicitly designated as unsafe, a derived class is safe. The derived class can use unsafe members of the base class that are visible.

In the following code, a compiler error occurs in the derived type. The *fieldb* member of *YClass* requires an unsafe context, which is not inherited from the *ZClass* base class. Add the *unsafe* keyword explicitly to *fieldb*, and the code will compile successfully:

```
public unsafe class ZClass {
    protected int* fielda;
}

public class YClass: ZClass {
    protected int* fieldb;  // compiler error
}
```

Pointers

Unsafe code is often about direct access to pointers, which point to a fixed location in memory. Because the location is fixed, the pointer is reliable and can be used for dereferencing, pointer math, and other traditional pointer-type manipulation. Pointers are outside the control of the Garbage Collector. The developer (not the Garbage Collector) is responsible for managing the lifetime of the pointer, if necessary.

C# does not expose pointers automatically. Exposing a pointer requires an unsafe context. In C#, pointers normally are abstracted using references. The reference abstracts a pointer to memory on the managed heap. The reference and related memory are managed by the Garbage Collector and the related memory is subject to relocation. A movable pointer underlies a reference, which is why references are not available for direct pointer manipulation. Pointer manipulation on a movable address would yield unreliable results.

Here is the syntax for declaring a pointer:

unmanagedtype* identifier;

unmanagedtype* identifier = initializer;

You can declare multiple pointers in a single statement using comma delimiters. Notice that the syntax is slightly different from C or C++ languages:

```
int* pA, pB, pC;  // C++:  int *pA, *pB, *pC;
```

The unmanaged types (a subset of managed types) that can be used with pointers are *sbyte, byte, short, ushort, int, uint, long, ulong, char, float, double, decimal, bool,* and *enum.* Some managed types, such as *string,* are not included in this list. You can create pointers to user-defined structures, assuming that they contain only unmanaged types as fields. Pointer types do not inherit from *System.Object,* so they cannot be cast to or from *System.Object.*

Void pointers are allowed, but they are dangerous. This is a typeless pointer that can emulate any other pointer type. All pointer types can be cast implicitly to a void pointer. This unpredictability makes void pointers particularly unsafe. You cannot cast implicitly between unrelated pointer types. Explicit casting between most pointer types is allowed. As expected, the following code would cause a compiler error because of the pointer mismatch. This assignment could be forced with an explicit cast to another pointer type. In that circumstance, the developer assumes responsibility for the safety of the pointer assignment.

```
int val = 5;
float* pA = &val; // compiler error
```

You can initialize a pointer with the address of a value or with another pointer. In the following code, both methods of initializing a pointer are shown:

```
public unsafe static void Main() {
    int ival = 5;
    int* p1 = &ival;  // dereference
    int* p2 = p1;      // pointer initialized to another pointer
}
```

In the preceding code, the asterisk (*) is used to declare a pointer. The ampersand (&) is used to dereference a value pointed to by a pointer. Table 18-1 describes the various symbols that are used with pointers.

TABLE 18-1 **Pointer symbols**

Symbol	Description
Pointer declaration (*)	For pointers, the asterisk symbol has two purposes. The first is to declare new pointer variables: `int* pA;`

TABLE 18-1 **Pointer symbols**

Symbol	Description

Pointer dereference (*)	The second purpose of the asterisk is to dereference a pointer. Pointers point to an address in memory. Dereferencing a pointer returns the value at that address in memory:
	
	```int val = 5;```
	```int* pA = &val;```
	```Console.WriteLine(*pA); // displays 5```
	
	You cannot dereference a void pointer.

Address of (&)	The ampersand symbol returns the memory location of a variable, which is a fixed value. The following code initializes the pointer *pA* to the memory address of an *int* named *val*. It is used to initialize an *int* pointer: ```int* pA = &val;```

Member access (->)	Arrow notation dereferences members of a pointer type found at a memory location. For example, you can access members of a structure using arrow notation and a pointer. In the following code, *ZStruct* is a structure, and *fielda* is an integer member of that type:
	
	```ZStruct obj = new ZStruct(5);```
	```ZStruct* pObj = &obj;```
	```int val1 = pObj->fielda;```
	
	Alternatively, you can deference the pointer and access a member using dot syntax (.):
	
	```int val2 = (*pObj).fielda; // dot syntax```

Pointer element ([])	A pointer element is an offset from the memory address of a pointer. For example, *p[2]* is an offset of two. Offsets are incremented by the size of the pointer type. If *p* is an *int* pointer, *p[2]* is an increment of eight bytes. In the following code, assume that *ZStruct* has two *int* fields in contiguous memory: *fielda* and *fieldb*:
	
	```ZStruct obj = new ZStruct(5);```
	```int* pA = &obj.fielda;```
	```Console.WriteLine(pA[1]); // fieldb```

Pointer to a pointer (**)	A pointer to a pointer contains a location in memory that lists the address of another pointer. Although rarely useful, you can extend the chain of pointers even further (***, ****, and so on). You can dereference a pointer to a pointer with a double asterisk (**). Alternatively, you can dereference a pointer to a pointer using individual asterisks in separate steps:
	
	```int val = 5;```
	```int* pA = &val;```
	```int** ppA = &pA;```
	```// Address stored in ppA, which is pA.```
	```Console.WriteLine((int)ppA);```
	```// Address stored in pA.```
	```Console.WriteLine((int)*ppA);```
	```// value at address stored in pA (5).```
	```Console.WriteLine((int)**ppA);```

TABLE 18-1 **Pointer symbols**

Symbol	Description
Pointer addition (+)	Pointer addition adds the size of the pointer type to the memory location. This changes a pointer so that it points to a different location:
| | ```
ZStruct obj = new ZStruct(5);
int* pA = &obj.fielda;
pA = pA + 2; // Add eight to pointer
``` |
| Pointer subtraction (-) | Pointer subtraction subtracts from the pointer the size of the pointer type. This changes a pointer so that it points to a different location: |
| | ```
ZStruct obj = new ZStruct(5);
int* pA = &obj.fieldd;
pA = pA - 3; // Subtract twelve from pointer
``` |
| Pointer increment (++) | Pointer increment increments the pointer address by the size of the pointer type: |
| | ```
ZStruct obj = new ZStruct(5);
int* pA = &obj.fielda;
++pA; // increment pointer by four
``` |
| Pointer decrement (--) | Pointer decrement decrements the pointer address by the size of the pointer type: |
| | ```
ZStruct obj = new ZStruct(5);
int* pA = &obj.fieldb;
--pA; // decrement pointer by four
``` |
| Relational symbols | The relational operators, such as < > >= <= != ==, can be used to compare pointers. The comparison is based on memory location rather than on pointer type: |
| | ```
ZStruct obj = new ZStruct(5);
int* pA = &obj.fielda;
int val = 5;
int* pB = &val;
if (pA == pB) {

  Console.WriteLine("Pointers point to the same object.");
}
``` |

Pointer Parameters and Pointer Return Values

A pointer is a legitimate variable. As such, a pointer can be used as a variable in most circumstances, including as a parameter or return type. When used as a return type, you should ensure that the lifetime of the pointer target is the same as or greater than that of the function caller. For example, do not return a pointer to a local variable from a function—the local variable loses scope outside the function and the pointer then becomes invalid.

In the following code, a pointer is used as both a parameter and return type. *MethodA* accepts a pointer as a parameter. It then returns the same pointer. After the method call, both *pB* and
```

pA point to the same location in memory. They are aliases. Therefore, *Console.WriteLine* displays the same number when the values at the pointers are displayed:

```
using System;

namespace Donis.CSharpBook {
    public class Starter {
        public unsafe static void Main() {
            int val = 5;
            int* pA = &val;
            int* pB;
            pB = MethodA(pA);
            Console.WriteLine("*pA = {0} | *pB = {0}",
                *pA, *pB);
        }

        public unsafe static int* MethodA(int* pArg) {
            *pArg += 15;
            return pArg;
        }
    }
}
```

The *ref* or *out* modifier can be applied to pointer parameters. Without the modifier, the memory location is *passed by pointer*. The pointer itself is *passed by value* on the stack. In the function, you can dereference the pointer and change values at the memory location. These changes will persist even after the function exits. However, changes to the pointer itself are discarded when the function exits. With the *ref* or *out* modifier, a pointer parameter is *passed by reference*. In the function, the pointer can be changed directly. Those changes continue to persist even after the function exits.

In the following code, both *MethodA* and *MethodB* have a pointer as a parameter. *MethodA* passes the pointer by value, whereas *MethodB* passes the pointer by reference. In both methods, the actual pointer is changed. The change is discarded when *MethodA* exists. When *MethodB* exits, the change persists:

```
using System;

namespace Donis.CSharpBook {
    public class Starter {

        public unsafe static void Main() {
            int val = 5;
            int* pA = &val;
            Console.WriteLine("Original: {0}", (int) pA);
            MethodA(pA);
            Console.WriteLine("MethodA:  {0}", (int) pA);
            MethodB(ref pA);
            Console.WriteLine("MethodB:  {0}", (int) pA);
        }
```

```
    public unsafe static void MethodA(int* pArg) {
        ++pArg;
    }

    public unsafe static void MethodB(ref int* pArg) {
        ++pArg;
    }
  }
}
```

Fixed Statements

What is wrong with the following code?

```
int[] numbers = { 1,2,3,4,5,6 };
int* pI = numbers; // compiler error
```

The problem is that the *numbers* variable is an array, which is a reference type. The code will not compile because the array is assigned to a pointer. References are movable types and cannot be implicitly converted to pointers. However, structures are value types and are placed on the stack and outside of the control of the Garbage Collector. *Struct* values have a fixed address and are easily converted into pointers. In the preceding code, if the type were changed from an array to a structure, it would compile successfully. With the *fixed* statement, you pin the location of a movable type—at least temporarily. Be careful, though. Pinning memory for an extended period of time can interfere with efficient garbage collection.

Here is the code revised with the *fixed* statement. This code compiles successfully:

```
int[] numbers = { 1,2,3,4,5,6 };
fixed (int* pI = numbers) {
    // do something
}
```

The *fixed* statement pins memory for the span of a fixed block. In the block, the memory is unmovable and is exempt from garbage collection. You can access the pinned memory using the pointer from the *fixed* statement, which is a read-only pointer. When the fixed block exits, the memory is unpinned. Multiple pointers can be declared in the *fixed* statement. The pointers are delimited with commas, and only the first pointer is prefixed with the asterisk (*):

```
int[] n1 = { 1,2,3,4 };
int[] n2 = { 5,6,7,8 };
int[] n3 = { 9,10,11,12 };
fixed (int* p1 = n1, p2 = n2, p3 = n3) {
}
```

Here is a more complete example of using the *fixed* statement:

```
using System;
```

```
namespace Donis.CSharpBook {
    public class Starter {

        private static int[] numbers = { 5,10,15,20,25,30 };

        public unsafe static void Main() {
            int count = 0;
            Console.WriteLine(" Pointer    Value\n");
            fixed (int* pI = numbers) {
                foreach (int a in numbers) {
                    Console.WriteLine("{0} : {1}",
                        (int)(pI+count), *((int*)pI + count));
                    ++count;
                }
            }
        }
    }
}
```

In the following code, *ZClass* is a class and a movable type. The *fixed* statement makes the *ZClass* object fixed in memory. A pointer to the integer member then is obtained:

```
public class Starter {
    public unsafe static void Main() {
        ZClass obj = new ZClass();
        fixed (int* pA = &obj.fielda) {
        }
    }
}

public class ZClass {
    public int fielda = 5;
}
```

The *stackalloc* Command

The *stackalloc* command allocates memory dynamically on the stack instead of the heap, which provides another option for allocating memory at run time. The lifetime of the allocation is the duration of the current function. The *stackalloc* command must be used within an unsafe context. It can be used to initialize only local pointers. The CLR will detect buffer overruns caused by the *stackalloc* command.

Here is the syntax for *stackalloc*:

```
type* stackalloc type[expression]
```

These are the particulars of the *stackalloc* command. It returns an unmanaged type. The expression should evaluate to an integral value, which is the number of elements to be allocated. The resulting pointer points to the base of the memory allocation. This memory is fixed and not available for garbage collection. It is automatically released at the end of the function.

The following code allocates 26 characters on the stack. The subsequent *for* loop assigns alphabetic characters to each element. The final loop displays each character:

```
using System;

namespace Donis.CSharpBook {
    public unsafe class Starter {
        public static void Main() {
            char* pChar = stackalloc char[26];
            char* _pChar = pChar;
            for (int count = 0; count < 26; ++count) {
                (*_pChar) = (char)(((int)('A')) + count);
                ++_pChar;
            }
            for (int count = 0; count < 26; ++count) {
                Console.Write(pChar[count]);
            }
        }
    }
}
```

P/Invoke

You can call unmanaged functions from managed code using P/Invoke. Managed and unmanaged memory might be laid out differently, which could require marshaling of parameters or the return type. In .NET, marshaling is the responsibility of the Interop marshaler.

Interop Marshaler

The Interop marshaler is responsible for transferring data between managed and unmanaged memory. It automatically transfers data that is similarly represented in managed and unmanaged environments. For example, integers are identically formatted in both environments and automatically marshaled between managed and unmanaged environments. Types that are the same in both environments are called *blittable* types. *Nonblittable* types, such as strings, are managed types without an equivalent unmanaged type and must be marshaled. The Interop marshaler assigns a default unmanaged type for many nonblittable types. Developers can also explicitly marshal nonblittable types to specific unmanaged types with the *MarshalAsAttribute* type.

DllImport

DllImportAttribute imports a function exported from an unmanaged library, where the library must export the function. *DllImportAttribute* is in the *System.Runtime.InteropServices* name space. *DllImportAttribute* has several options that configure the managed environment for importing the named function. The library is dynamically loaded with the *LoadLibrary* native API, and the underlying function pointer is initialized at run time. Because the attribute is evaluated at run time, most configuration errors are not found at compile time; they are found later. Because many errors related to *DllImportAttribute* do not occur at compile time, you should be careful when using this attribute.

Here is the syntax of *DllImportAttribute*:

```
[DllImport(options)] accessibility static extern returntype functionname(parameters)
```

Options are used to configure the import of the external function. The name of the library is the only required option. If it is not found in a directory within the environment path variable, the name of the library should include the fully qualified path. Accessibility is the visibility of the function, such as *public* or *protected*. Imported functions must be *static* and *extern*. The remainder of the statement is the managed signature of the function.

The following code imports three functions to display the vertical and horizontal size of the screen. *GetDC*, *GetDeviceCaps*, and *ReleaseHandle* are Microsoft Win32 APIs. The imported functions are configured and exposed in the *API* class, which is a static class. The functions then are called from managed code. In the code, the *IntPtr* type is used. *IntPtr* is an abstraction of an integer pointer, where *IntPtr.Zero* is a null integer pointer:

```
using System;
using System.Runtime.InteropServices;

namespace Donis.CSharpBook {
    public class Starter {
        public static void Main() {
            IntPtr hDC = API.GetDC(IntPtr.Zero);
            int v = API.GetDeviceCaps(hDC, API.VERTRES);
            Console.WriteLine("Vertical size of window {0}mm.", v);
            int h = API.GetDeviceCaps(hDC, API.HORZRES);
            Console.WriteLine("Horizontal size of window {0}mm.", h);
            int resp = API.ReleaseDC(IntPtr.Zero, hDC);
            if (resp != 1) {
                Console.WriteLine("Error releasing hdc");
            }
        }
    }

    public static class API {
        [DllImport("user32.dll")] public static extern
          IntPtr GetDC(IntPtr hWnd);

        [DllImport("user32.dll")] public static extern
          int ReleaseDC(IntPtr hWnd, IntPtr hDC);

        [DllImport("gdi32.dll")]public static extern
          int GetDeviceCaps(IntPtr hDC, int nIndex);

        public const int HORZSIZE = 4;   // horizontal size in pixels
        public const int VERTSIZE = 6;   // vertical size in pixels
        public const int HORZRES = 8;    // horizontal size in millimeters
        public const int VERTRES = 10;   // vertical size in millimeters
    }
}
```

In the preceding code, the only option used with *DllImportAttribute* is the library name. There are several other options, which are described in the following sections.

EntryPoint   This option explicitly names the imported function. Without this option, the name is implied from the managed function signature, as demonstrated in the preceding code example. When the imported name is ambiguous, the *EntryPoint* option is helpful. You can specify a unique name for the related managed function to remove ambiguity.

In the following code, *MessageBox* is being imported. Instead of using that name, which is the default, the assigned managed name is *ShowMessage:*

```
using System;
using System.Runtime.InteropServices;

namespace Donis.CSharpBook {
    public class Starter {
        public static void Main() {
            string caption = "Visual C# 2008";
            string text = "Hello, world!";
            API.ShowMessage(0, text, caption, 0);
        }
    }

    public class API {
        [DllImport("user32.dll", EntryPoint="MessageBox")]
        public static extern int ShowMessage(int hWnd,
            string text, string caption, uint type);
    }
}
```

CallingConvention   This option sets the calling convention of the function. The default calling convention is *Winapi,* which maps to the standard calling convention in the Win32 environment as well as to the standard calling convention in the CE .NET environment. The calling convention is set with the *CallingConvention* enumeration. Table 18-2 lists the members of this enumeration.

TABLE 18-2 *CallingConvention* **enumeration members**

Member	Description
Cdecl	The caller removes the parameters from the stack, which is the calling convention for functions that have a variable-length argument list.
FastCall	This calling convention is not supported.
StdCall	The called method removes the parameters from the stack. This calling convention is commonly used for APIs and is the default for calling unmanaged functions with P/Invoke.
ThisCall	The first parameter of the function is the *this* pointer followed by the conventional parameters. In the function, the *this* pointer is cached in the ECX register and used to access instance members of an unmanaged class.
Winapi	Default calling convention of the current platform. For a Win32 environment, this is the *StdCall* calling convention. For Windows CE .NET, *Cdecl* is the default.

The following code imports the *printf* function, which is found in the C Runtime Library. The *printf* function accepts a variable number of parameters and supports the *Cdecl* calling convention:

```
using System;
using System.Runtime.InteropServices;

namespace Donis.CSharpBook {
    public class Starter {
        public static void Main() {
            int val1 = 5, val2 = 10;
            API.printf("%d+%d=%d", val1, val2, val1 + val2);
        }
    }

    public class API {
        [DllImport("msvcrt.dll", CharSet=CharSet.Ansi,
            CallingConvention=CallingConvention.Cdecl)]
        public static extern int printf(string formatspecifier,
            int lhs, int rhs, int total);
    }

}
```

ExactSpelling   This option stipulates that the exact spelling of the function name is used to resolve the symbol. Names are not always what they seem. For example, the function names of many Win32 APIs are actually macros that map to the *real* API, which is an A-suffixed or W-suffixed method. The A version is the American National Standards Institute (ANSI) version, whereas the W (wide) version is the Unicode version of the function. The ANSI versus Unicode extrapolation pertains mostly to Win32 APIs that have string parameters. For example, the supposed *CreateWindow* API is a macro that maps to either the *CreateWindowW* or *CreateWindowA* API. For the *DllImportAttribute*, the version selected is determined in the *CharSet* option. If *ExactSpelling* is *true,* the function name is treated as the actual name and not translated regardless of the *CharSet* option. The default is *false,* which allows the function name to be translated to either the A or W version of the method.

The following code imports the *GetModuleHandleW* function specifically. *ExactSpelling* is *true* to use the name "as is":

```
using System;
using System.Runtime.InteropServices;

namespace Donis.CSharpBook {
    public class Starter {
        public static void Main() {
            int hProcess = API.GetModuleHandleW(null);
        }
    }
```

```
    public class API {
        [DllImport("kernel32.dll", ExactSpelling=true)]
        public static extern int GetModuleHandleW(string filename);
    }
}
```

PreserveSig   This option preserves the signature of a method. COM functions usually return an *HRESULT*, which is the error status of the call. The real return is the parameter decorated with the *[out, retval]* Interface Definition Language (IDL) attribute. In managed code, the *HRESULT* is consumed for error handling and the *[out, retval]* parameter is returned as the actual return. To resolve a COM function, the original signature cannot be preserved; it should be mapped to a COM signature. Conversely, the signature of non-COM functions should be preserved. *PreserveSig* defaults to *true*.

The following code demonstrates the *PreserveSig* option with a fictitious COM function:

```
public class API {
    [DllImport("ole32.dll", PreserveSig=false)]
    public static extern int SomeFunction();
}
```

Here is the original signature in COM:

```
HRESULT SomeFunction([out, retval] int param)
```

SetLastError   This option asks the CLR to preserve the error code of the imported function. Most Win32 APIs return *false* if the function fails. *False* is minimally descriptive, so developers can call *GetLastError* for an integer error code that provides additional detail. *GetLastError* must be called immediately after the failed API; if not, the next API might reset the error code. In managed code, call *Marshal.GetLastWin32Error* to retrieve the error code. The *Marshal* type is in the *System.Runtime.InteropServices* namespace. *SetLastError* defaults to false.

In the following code, *CreateDirectory* and *FormatMessage* are imported in the *API* class. *CreateDirectory* creates a file directory; *FormatMessage* converts a Win32 error code into a user-friendly message. For *CreateDirectory*, the *SetLastError* option is set to *true*. In *Main*, *CreateDirectory* is called with an invalid path. The "c*" drive is probably an incorrect drive on most computers. The resulting error code is stored in the *resp* variable, which is then converted into a message using the *FormatMessage* API. *FormatMessage* returns the user-friendly message as an *out* parameter:

```
using System;
using System.Text;
using System.Runtime.InteropServices;

namespace Donis.CSharpBook {
    public class Starter {
        public static void Main() {
            bool resp = API.CreateDirectory(@"c*:\file.txt",
```

```
                IntPtr.Zero);
        if (resp == false) {
            StringBuilder message;
            int errorcode = Marshal.GetLastWin32Error();
            API.FormatMessage(
                API.FORMAT_MESSAGE_ALLOCATE_BUFFER |
                API.FORMAT_MESSAGE_FROM_SYSTEM |
                API.FORMAT_MESSAGE_IGNORE_INSERTS,
                IntPtr.Zero, errorcode,
                0, out message, 0, IntPtr.Zero);
            Console.WriteLine(message);
        }
    }
}

public class API {
    [DllImport("kernel32.dll", SetLastError=true)]
    public static extern bool CreateDirectory(
        string lpPathName, IntPtr lpSecurityAttributes);

    [DllImport("kernel32.dll", SetLastError=false)]
    public static extern System.Int32 FormatMessage(
        System.Int32 dwFlags,
        IntPtr lpSource,
        System.Int32 dwMessageId,
        System.Int32 dwLanguageId,
        out StringBuilder lpBuffer,
        System.Int32 nSize,
        IntPtr va_list);

    public const int FORMAT_MESSAGE_ALLOCATE_BUFFER = 256;
    public const int FORMAT_MESSAGE_IGNORE_INSERTS = 512;
    public const int FORMAT_MESSAGE_FROM_STRING = 1024;
    public const int FORMAT_MESSAGE_FROM_HMODULE = 2048;
    public const int FORMAT_MESSAGE_FROM_SYSTEM = 4096;
    public const int FORMAT_MESSAGE_ARGUMENT_ARRAY = 8192;
    public const int FORMAT_MESSAGE_MAX_WIDTH_MASK = 255;
    }
}
```

CharSet   This option indicates the proper interpretation of strings in unmanaged memory, which can affect the *ExactSpelling* option. *CharSet* is also an enumeration with three members. The default is *CharSet.Ansi*. Table 18-3 lists the members of the *CharSet* enumeration.

TABLE 18-3 *CharSet* **enumeration members**

Value	Description
CharSet.Ansi	Strings should be marshaled as ANSI.
CharSet.Unicode	Strings should be marshaled as Unicode.
CharSet.Auto	The appropriate conversion is decided at run time depending on the current platform.

The following code marshals a string for unmanaged memory as ANSI. The *ExactSpelling* option defaults to *false,* and the *GetModuleHandleA* API is called. *GetModuleHandleA* has ANSI parameters:

```
using System;
using System.Runtime.InteropServices;

namespace Donis.CSharpBook {
    public class Starter {
        public static void Main() {
            int hProcess = API.GetModuleHandle(null);
        }
    }

    public class API {
        [DllImport("kernel32.dll", CharSet=CharSet.Ansi)]
        public static extern int GetModuleHandle(string filename);
    }
}
```

BestFitMapping   This option affects the Unicode-to-ANSI mapping of text characters passed from managed to unmanaged functions running in the Microsoft Windows 98 or Microsoft Windows Millennium Edition (Windows Me) environment. If true, best-fit mapping is enabled. When there is not a direct character match, the Unicode character is mapped to the closest match in the ANSI code page. If no match is available, the Unicode character is mapped to a "?" character. The default is *true.*

ThrowOnUnmappableChar   This option can request an exception when an unmappable character is found in the Unicode-to-ANSI translation for Windows 98 and Windows Me. If *true,* an exception is raised when a Unicode character cannot be mapped to ANSI, and the character is converted to a *?* character. If *false,* no exception is raised. See the *BestFitMapping* option for additional details on Unicode-to-ANSI mapping.

Blittable Types

Blittable types are represented similarly in managed and unmanaged memory. Therefore, no conversion is necessary from the Interop marshaler when marshaling between managed and unmanaged environments. Because conversion can be expensive, blittable types are more efficient than nonblittable types. For this reason, when possible, parameters and return types should be blittable types, which include *System.Byte, System.SByte, System.Int16, System. UInt16, System.Int32, System.UInt32, System.Int64, System.IntPtr, System.UIntPtr, System. Single,* and *System.Double.* Arrays of blittable types and formatted value types that contain only blittable types also are considered blittable. (Formatted types are explained in the next section.)

Nonblittable types have different representations in managed and unmanaged memory. Some nonblittable types are converted automatically by the Interop marshaler, whereas others require explicit marshaling. Strings and user-defined classes are examples of nonblittable types. A managed string can be marshaled as a variety of unmanaged string types: *LPSTR, LPTSTR, LPWSTR,* and so on. Classes are nonblittable unless they are formatted. In addition, a formatted class marshaled as a formatted value type is blittable.

Formatted Type

A formatted type is a user-defined type in which the memory layout of the members is explicitly specified. Formatted types are prefixed with the *StructLayoutAttribute,* which sets the layout of the members as described in the *LayoutKind* enumeration. Table 18-4 lists the members of the *LayoutKind* enumeration.

TABLE 18-4 *LayoutKind* **enumeration members**

Value	Description
LayoutKind.Auto	The CLR sets the location of members in unmanaged memory. The type cannot be exposed to unmanaged code.
LayoutKind.Sequential	Members are stored in contiguous (sequential) unmanaged memory. The members are stored in textual order. If desired, set packing with the *StructLayoutAttribute.Pack* option.
LayoutKind.Explicit	This flag allows the developer to stipulate the order of the fields in memory using *FieldOffsetAttribute*. This is useful for representing a managed type as a C or C++ union type in unmanaged code.

In the following code, the *API* class imports the *GetWindowRect* unmanaged API. This function returns the location of the client area in the screen. The parameters of *GetWindowRect* are a window handle and a pointer to a *Rect* structure, which also is defined in the *API* class. The *Rect* structure, which is initialized inside the function, is a formatted value type and is blittable. By default, value types are passed by value. To pass a value type by reference, the *out* modifier is assigned to the *Rect* parameter:

```
public class API
{
    [DllImport("user32.dll")]
    public static extern bool GetWindowRect(
        IntPtr hWnd,
        out Rect windowRect);

    [StructLayout(LayoutKind.Sequential)]
    public struct Rect
    {
        public int left;
        public int top;
        public int right;
        public int bottom;
    }
}
```

Here is the code that uses the *GetWindowRect* API and the *Rect* structure:

```
API.Rect client = new API.Rect();
API.GetWindowRect(this.Handle, out client);
string temp = string.Format("Left {0} : Top {1} : "+
    "Right {2} : Bottom {3}", client.left,
    client.top, client.right, client.bottom);
MessageBox.Show(temp);
```

The following code is a version of the *API* class that defines a *Rect* class instead of a structure. Because the *Rect* class has the *StructLayout* attribute, it is a formatted type. Classes are passed by reference or by pointer by default, depending on the signature of the native API. The *out* modifier required for a structure (shown in the previous example code) is not necessary for a class:

```
class API2
{
    [DllImport("user32.dll")]
    public static extern bool GetWindowRect(
        IntPtr hWnd,
        Rect windowRect);

    [StructLayout(LayoutKind.Sequential)]
    public class Rect
    {
        public int left;
        public int top;
        public int right;
        public int bottom;
    }
}
```

Here is the code to call the *GetWindowRect* API using the *Rect* class:

```
API2.Rect client = new API2.Rect();
API2.GetWindowRect(this.Handle, client);
string temp = string.Format("Left {0} : Top {1} : " +
    "Right {2} : Bottom {3}", client.left,
    client.top, client.right, client.bottom);
MessageBox.Show(temp);
```

Unions are fairly common in C and C++ code. A *union* is a type in which the members share the same memory location. This conserves memory by overlaying mutually exclusive data in shared memory. C# does not offer a union type. In managed code, emulate a union in unmanaged memory with the *LayoutKind.Explicit* option of *StructLayoutAttribute*. Set each field of the union to the same offset, as shown in the following code:

```
[StructLayout(LayoutKind.Explicit)]
struct ZStruct {
    [FieldOffset(0)] int fielda;
    [FieldOffset(0)] short fieldb;
    [FieldOffset(0)] bool fieldc;
}
```

Directional Attributes

Directional attributes explicitly control the direction of marshaling. Parameters can be assigned *InAttribute*, *OutAttribute*, or both attributes to affect marshaling. This is equivalent to *[in]*, *[out]*, and *[in, out]* of the IDL. *InAttribute* and *OutAttribute* are also represented by keywords in C#. Table 18-5 lists the attributes and related keywords.

TABLE 18-5 **Directional attributes and C# keywords**

Keyword	Attribute	IDL
No keyword available explicitly. (This is the underlying default.)	*InAttribute*	*[in]*
Ref	*InAttribute* and *OutAttribute*	*[in, out]*
Out	*OutAttribute*	*[out]*

The default directional attribute depends on the type of parameter and any modifiers.

StringBuilder

Strings are immutable and dynamically sized. An unmanaged API might require a fixed-length and modifiable string. In addition, some unmanaged APIs initialize the string with memory allocated at run time. The string type should not be used in these circumstances. Instead, use the *StringBuilder* class, which is found in the *System.Text* name space. *StringBuilders* are fixed-length and not immutable. Furthermore, you can initialize the *StringBuilder* with memory created in the unmanaged API.

In the following code, the *GetWindowText* unmanaged API is imported twice. *GetWindowText* retrieves the text from the specified window. For an overlapped window, this is text from the title bar. The second parameter of *GetWindowText* is a string, which is initialized with the window text during the function call. The first version of *GetWindowText* in the *API* class has a string parameter, whereas the version in the *API2* class has a *StringBuilder* parameter. The *GetWindowText* application is a Windows Forms application that has two buttons. The first button calls *API.GetWindowText* and the second button calls *API2.GetWindowText*. Click the first button. Because of the string parameter in *API.GetWindowText*, an exception is raised because the API attempts to change that parameter. The second button invokes *API2. GetWindowText*, which uses the *StringBuilder* type, and the function runs successfully:

```
public class API
{
    [DllImport("user32.dll")]
    public static extern int GetWindowText(
        IntPtr hWnd, ref string lpString, int nMaxCount);
}

public class API2
{
    [DllImport("user32.dll")]
    public static extern int GetWindowText(
```

```
        IntPtr hWnd, StringBuilder lpString, int nMaxCount);
}
```

Here is the code from the button-click handlers of the form:

```
private void btnGetText_Click(object sender, EventArgs e)
{
    string windowtext=null;
    API.GetWindowText(this.Handle, ref windowtext, 25);
    MessageBox.Show(windowtext);
}

private void btnGetText2_Click(object sender, EventArgs e)
{
    StringBuilder windowtext = new StringBuilder();
    API2.GetWindowText(this.Handle, windowtext, 25);
    MessageBox.Show(windowtext.ToString());
}
```

Unmanaged Callbacks

Some unmanaged functions accept a callback as a parameter, which is a function pointer. The unmanaged function then invokes the function pointer to call a function in the managed caller. Callbacks typically are used for iteration. For example, the *EnumWindows* unmanaged API uses a callback to iterate handles of top-level windows.

.NET abstracts function pointers with delegates, which are type-safe and have a specific signature. In the managed signature, substitute a delegate for the callback parameter of the unmanaged signature.

These are the steps to implement a callback for an unmanaged function:

1. Determine the unmanaged signature of the callback function.

2. Define a matching managed signature as a delegate for the callback function.

3. Implement a function to be used as the callback. The implementation of the function is essentially the response to the callback.

4. Create a delegate and initialize it to the callback function.

5. Invoke the unmanaged API and provide the delegate as the callback parameter.

The following code imports the *EnumWindows* unmanaged API. The first parameter of *EnumWindows* is a callback. *EnumWindows* enumerates top-level windows. The callback function is called at each iteration and is given the current window handle as a parameter. In this code, *APICallback* is a delegate and is compatible with the unmanaged signature of the callback:

```
class API
{
    [DllImport("user32.dll")]
```

```
public static extern bool EnumWindows(
    APICallback lpEnumFunc,
    System.Int32 lParam);


public delegate bool APICallback(int hWnd, int lParam);
}
```

EnumWindows is called in the click handler of a Windows Forms application. *GetWindowHandle* is passed as the callback function in the second parameter via an *APICallback* delegate. *GetWindowHandle* is called for each handle that is enumerated. During the enumeration, the managed function adds each handle to a list box:

```
private void btnHandle_Click(object sender, EventArgs e)
{
    API.EnumWindows(new API.APICallback(GetWindowHandle), 0);
}


bool GetWindowHandle(int hWnd, int lParam)
{
    string temp = string.Format("{0:0000000}", hWnd);
    listBox1.Items.Add(temp);
    return true;
}
```

Explicit Marshaling

Explicit marshaling sometimes is required to convert nonblittable parameters, fields, or return types to proper unmanaged types. Marshaling is invaluable for strings, which have several possible representations in unmanaged memory. Strings default to *LPSTR*. Use *MarshalAsAttribute* to marshal a managed type explicitly as a specific unmanaged type. The *UnmanagedType* enumeration defines the unmanaged types available for marshaling. Table 18-6 lists the members of the *UnmanagedType* enumeration.

TABLE 18-6 *UnmanagedType* **enumeration members**

Member	Description
AnsiBStr	Length-prefixed ANSI string
AsAny	Dynamic type where the type is set at run time
Bool	Four-byte Boolean value
BStr	Length-prefixed Unicode string
ByValArray	Marshals an array by value; *SizeConst* sets the number of elements
ByValTStr	Inline fixed-length character array that is a member of a structure
Currency	COM currency type
CustomMarshaler	To be used with *MarshalAsAttribute.MarshalType* or *MarshalAsAttribute. MarshalTypeRef*
Error	HRESULT

TABLE 18-6 *UnmanagedType* enumeration members

Member	Description
FunctionPtr	C-style function pointer
I1	One-byte integer
I2	Two-byte integer
I4	Four-byte integer
I8	Eight-byte integer
IDispatch	*IDispatch* pointer for COM
Interface	COM interface pointer
IUnknown	*IUnknown* interface pointer
LPArray	Pointer to the first element of an unmanaged array
LPStr	Null-terminated ANSI string
LPStruct	Pointer to an unmanaged structure
LPTStr	Platform-dependent string
LPWStr	Null-terminated Unicode string
R4	Four-byte floating point number
R8	Eight-byte floating point number
SafeArray	Safe array in which the type, rank, and bounds are defined
Struct	Formatted value and reference types
SysInt	Platform-dependent integer (32 bits in Win32 environment)
SysUInt	Platform-dependent unsigned integer (32 bits in Win32 environment)
TBStr	Length-prefixed, platform-dependent string
U1	One-byte unsigned integer
U2	Two-byte unsigned integer
U4	Four-byte unsigned integer
U8	Eight-byte unsigned integer
VariantBool	Two-byte VARIANT_BOOL type
VBByRefStr	Microsoft Visual Basic–specific

GetVersionEx is imported in the following code. The function is called in *Main* to obtain information on the current operating system. *GetVersionEx* has a single parameter, which is a pointer to an *OSVERSIONINFO* structure. The last field in the structure is *szCSDVersion*, which is a universally unique identifier (UUID). A UUID is a 128-byte array. In the sample code, the *MarshalAs* attribute marshals the field as a 128-character array. Each character is one byte long:

```
using System;
using System.Runtime.InteropServices;

namespace Donis.CSharpBook {
```

```
public class Starter {
    public static void Main() {
        API.OSVERSIONINFO info = new API.OSVERSIONINFO();
        info.dwOSVersionInfoSize = Marshal.SizeOf(info);
        bool resp = API.GetVersionEx(ref info);
        if (resp == false) {
            Console.WriteLine("GetVersion failed");
        }
        Console.WriteLine("{0}.{1}.{2}",
            info.dwMajorVersion,
            info.dwMinorVersion,
            info.dwBuildNumber);
    }
}


public class API {

    [DllImport("kernel32.dll")] public static extern
    bool GetVersionEx(ref OSVERSIONINFO lpVersionInfo);

  [StructLayout(LayoutKind.Sequential)]
    public struct OSVERSIONINFO {
        public System.Int32 dwOSVersionInfoSize;
        public System.Int32 dwMajorVersion;
        public System.Int32 dwMinorVersion;
        public System.Int32 dwBuildNumber;
        public System.Int32 dwPlatformId;
        [MarshalAs( UnmanagedType.ByValTStr, SizeConst=128 )]
            public String szCSDVersion;

    }
  }
}
```

Fixed-Size Buffers

In the previous code, the *MarshalAs* attribute defined a fixed-size field of 128 characters or bytes. As an alternative to the *MarshalAs* attribute, C# provides fixed-size buffers using the *fixed* keyword. The primary purpose of this keyword is to embed aggregate types, such as an array, in a structure. Fixed-size buffers are allowed in structures but not in classes.

There are several rules for using fixed-size buffers:

- Fixed-size buffers are available only in unsafe contexts.

- Fixed-size buffers can represent only one-dimensional arrays (vectors).

- The array must have a specific length.

- Fixed-size buffers are allowed only in *struct* types.

- Fixed-sized buffers are limited to *bool, byte, char, short, int, long, sbyte, ushort, uint, ulong, float,* and *double* types.

Here is the syntax of the fixed-sized buffer:

attributes accessibility modifier fixed *type identifier[expression]*

The following code is another version of the *OSVERSIONINFO* structure. This version uses the *MarshalAs* attribute and uses the fixed keyword for the *szCSDVersion* field:

```
public class API {
[StructLayout(LayoutKind.Sequential)]
    unsafe public struct OSVERSIONINFO {
        public System.Int32 dwOSVersionInfoSize;
        public System.Int32 dwMajorVersion;
        public System.Int32 dwMinorVersion;
        public System.Int32 dwBuildNumber;
        public System.Int32 dwPlatformId;
        public fixed char szCSDVersion[128];
    }
}
```

Summary

Although pointers are not normally available in C#, developers can choose to use them at their discretion. Pointers are available in the context of unsafe code, which requires the *unsafe* keyword. You can create pointers to unmanaged types, such as the *int*, *float*, and *char* types. In addition, unsafe code must be compiled with the *unsafe* compiler option.

You cannot create pointers to managed memory. Managed memory is movable and managed by the Garbage Collector. The *fixed* statement pins managed memory within a block. Pinned memory is fixed. While pinned, that memory is not accessible to the Garbage Collector.

DllImportAttribute, which describes an unmanaged function that is exported from a library, has various options to configure a function for importing. The Interop marshaler marshals parameters and returns values between managed and unmanaged memory. Blittable types do not require conversion, but nonblittable types require conversion to unmanaged memory. Developers can marshal nonblittable types explicitly using the *MarshalAs* attribute.

Index

Symbols

About the Author

Donis Marshall began programming nearly 25 years ago. Over that length of time, he has written thousands of lines of code for several companies. In the last 15 years, he has written many books on computer programming. His books, which include *Programming Microsoft Visual C# 2005: The Language, Programming Directory Services for Windows 2000, .NET Security Programming,* and *ActiveX/OLE Programming: Building Stable Components with Microsoft Foundation Class,* encompass a variety of topics. They represent the collective knowledge that he has learned through his years of programming, consulting, and training experience.

Presently, Donis Marshall is the president and chief technology officer of DebugLive (*www.debuglive.com*). DebugLive offers an assortment of innovative tools to support engineers and developers in debugging and monitoring Win32 and .NET applications. DebugLive is a virtual room where professionals can collaborate and debug remotely.

Donis Marshall also teaches computer programming and consults at software companies, including Microsoft Corporation. He teaches C#, VB.NET, C++, debugging, Microsoft .NET Framework, best practices and policies, and other topics. In this role, Mr. Marshall has traveled the world, giving dozens of classes to Microsoft developers and engineers in the United States, Europe, and Asia. He also has written more than 30 courses on Win32 programming and .NET programming.

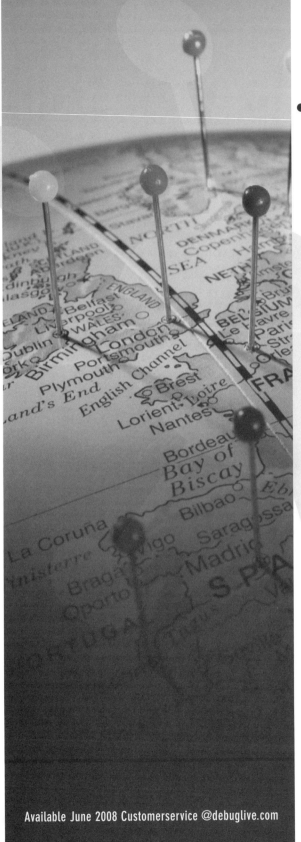

powerful

easy

remote

collaborative

debugging

debuglive
remote collaborative solutions

The most powerful

and easy to use tool

for remote, collaborative,

and production debugging

for software development

and application support.

Available June 2008 Customerservice @debuglive.com

www.debuglive.com

What do you think of this book?

We want to hear from you!

Do you have a few minutes to participate in a brief online survey?

Microsoft is interested in hearing your feedback so we can continually improve our books and learning resources for you.

To participate in our survey, please visit:

www.microsoft.com/learning/booksurvey/

...and enter this book's ISBN-10 or ISBN-13 number (located above barcode on back cover*). As a thank-you to survey participants in the United States and Canada, each month we'll randomly select five respondents to win one of five $100 gift certificates from a leading online merchant. At the conclusion of the survey, you can enter the drawing by providing your e-mail address, which will be used for prize notification only.

Thanks in advance for your input. Your opinion counts!

* Where to find the ISBN on back cover

ISBN-13: 000-0-0000-0000-0
ISBN-10: 0-0000-0000-0

Example only. Each book has unique ISBN.

Microsoft®
Press